Social Work
with Groups

THE NELSON-HALL SERIES IN SOCIAL WORK

Consulting Editor: Charles Zastrow
University of Wisconsin—Whitewater

FOURTH EDITION

SOCIAL WORK WITH GROUPS

*Using the Class as a
Group Leadership Laboratory*

CHARLES ZASTROW

University of Wisconsin—Whitewater

NELSON-HALL PUBLISHERS
Chicago

Senior Editor: Libby Rubenstein
Production/Design Manager: Tamra Phelps
Photo Researcher: Charlotte Goldman
Cover Painting: Jim Zwadlo, *Pedestrians 66*
Typesetter: E. T. Lowe
Printer: The Maple-Vail Book Manufacturing Group

Library of Congress Cataloging-in-Publication Data

Zastrow, Charles.
    Social work with groups: using the class as a group
leadership laboratory/Charles Zastrow.—4th ed.
      p.   cm.
    Includes bibliographical references and index.
    ISBN 0-8304-1443-6
    1. Social group work—Study and teaching—
United States. 2. Group relations training—United
States. I. Title.
HV45.Z37 1996
361.4—dc20   96-11196
                                    CIP

Manufactured in the United States of America

10 9 8 7 6 5 4 3

Material in chapters 1 and 3 adapted from chapter 21, "Social Work Practice with Groups," in C. Zastrow, *Introduction to Social Welfare Institutions*, 2d ed. (Homewood, Ill.: Dorsey Press, 1982), pp. 506–29, and from chapter 12, "Group Work and Group Therapy," by Grafton H. Hull, Jr., and Charles Zastrow, in C. Zastrow, *The Practice of Social Work* (Homewood, Ill.: Dorsey Press, 1981), pp. 339–77. Used by permission of Dorsey Press. Material in chapters 17, 22, and 29 on counseling, assertiveness training, and identity formation is adapted from Charles Zastrow and Dae H. Chang, eds., *The Personal Problem Solver* (Englewood Cliffs, N.J.: Spectrum Books, A Division of Simon & Schuster, 1977), pp. 236–43; 267–74; and 365–70). Adapted by permission of the publisher. The excerpt on near-death experiences in chapter 25 is reprinted from Raymond A. Moody, Jr., *Life After Life* (New York: Bantam Books, 1975), pp. 21–23. Reprinted by permission of Mockingbird Books. Material in chapters 18, 20, and 22 adapted from chapters 15, 18, and 20 in C. Zastrow, *The Practice of Social Work*, 3d ed. (Homewood, IL: Dorsey Press, 1989), pp. 356–65; 398–410; and 430–54. Used by permission of Wadsworth Publishing Co. Material in chapter 17 adapted from "Starting and Leading Therapy Groups: A Beginner's Guide" by Charles Zastrow in *Journal of Independent Social Work*, Vol. 4(4), 1990, pp. 7–26. Adapted by permission of The Haworth Press, Inc.

CONTENTS

PART ONE
INTRODUCTION TO SOCIAL GROUP WORK

CONTENTS

PART TWO
LEADING GROUPS

PART THREE
COMMUNICATION IN GROUPS

PART FOUR
PROBLEM-SOLVING AND
DECISION-MAKING GROUPS

PART FIVE
ORGANIZATIONS AND COMMUNITIES

PART SIX
SELF-HELP AND EDUCATIONAL GROUPS

PART SEVEN
THERAPEUTIC GROUPS

PART EIGHT
SENSITIVITY GROUPS

PART NINE
TERMINATION AND EVALUATION

APPENDICES

CONTRIBUTING AUTHORS

Virginia Dotson, Ph.D.
Psychotherapist and Licensed Psychologist
Milwaukee, Wisconsin

Grafton H. Hull, Jr., MSW, Ed.D.
Professor and Director
School of Social Work
Southwest Missouri State University

Karen K. Kirst-Ashman, MSW, Ph.D.
Professor
Department of Social Work
University of Wisconsin—Whitewater

Michael O. Koch, Ph.D., BC, CSW
Psychotherapist and Licensed Psychologist
Milwaukee, Wisconsin

LaVonne J. Cornell-Swanson, MSW, ACSW
Instructor
Department of Social Work
University of Wisconsin—Whitewater

Carey Tradewell, BSW, CADC III
Executive Director
The Milwaukee Women's Center
Milwaukee, Wisconsin

Thomas P. Troast, MA
Psychotherapist
Milwaukee, Wisconsin

Daniel Paul Vega, MSW
Clinical Social Worker
Billings, Montana

PREFACE

The basic assumption of this text is that the best way for students to learn how to run groups is by leading groups in class. The classroom thus becomes a laboratory for students to practice and develop their group leadership skills. This text is designed to facilitate this laboratory approach to undergraduate and graduate group-work courses.

PLAN OF THE BOOK

Each chapter is designed according to the following format:

1. The goal or goals of the chapter are stated.
2. Theoretical material is presented on how the goals can be achieved. If the goal is to learn how to handle disruptive members of a group, for example, the chapter describes appropriate strategies.
3. One or more group exercises illustrating key concepts are then explained. The exercises give students practice in acquiring the skills described in the chapter.

USING THE BOOK

After the instructor covers the introductory material contained in the first chapter, it is suggested that students (either individually or in small groups) prepare and conduct future class sessions by summarizing the theoretical material in a chapter and leading the class in related exercises. (Students may also be given the opportunity to select a topic not covered in the text.)

Students not presenting material should read the chapter and group exercises *after* the chapter is covered in class. With this format, the class presentations introduce the material, and the subsequent reading reinforces and expands it. Students should make their presentations stimulating, interesting, and educational by speaking extemporaneously rather than reading, and by adapting chapter topics, using personal observations or research. Students should also prepare and distribute handouts that summarize the key points of their presentations and move around the classroom to maintain and increase the interest of the class.

ACKNOWLEDGMENTS
....

Sincere thanks are extended to the following contributing authors: Grafton H. Hull, Jr., Karen Kirst-Ashman, LaVonne Cornell-Swanson, Virginia Dotson, Michael O. Koch, Thomas P. Troast, Carey Tradewell, and Daniel Paul Vega for contributing chapters. Vicki Vogel is recognized for helping to conceptualize various chapters and for assisting with the writing.

I also want to thank the reviewers of the third edition whose valuable suggestions have helped to shape this volume: Susan T. Dennison, University of North Carolina at Greensboro; James A. Marley, University of Illinois at Urbana; and Christine M. Tappan, University of New Hamsphire

PART ONE

INTRODUCTION TO SOCIAL GROUP WORK

CHAPTER ONE

TYPES OF GROUPS: THEIR NATURE AND DEVELOPMENT

Goal: Each group develops a unique character or personality because of the principles of group dynamics. This chapter presents a brief history of social group work and introduces the primary types of groups in social work. Factors in the initial development and establishment of a group are summarized. Differences between reference and membership groups are described, and several ice-breaker exercises are presented. Guidelines on how to conduct classroom exercises are summarized.

Every social service agency uses groups, and every practicing social worker is involved in a variety of groups. Social work with groups is practiced in adoption agencies, correctional settings, halfway houses, substance abuse treatment centers, physical rehabilitation centers, family service agencies, private psychotherapy clinics, mental hospitals, nursing homes, community centers, public schools, and many other social service settings. To effectively serve clients in human service systems today, social workers in generalist practice positions must be trained in group methods. Often, social workers serve as leaders and participants in myriad groups requiring skills ranging from the simple to the complex. The beginning social worker is likely to be surprised at the diverse groups in existence and excited by the challenge of practicing social work in such settings.

HISTORICAL DEVELOPMENT OF GROUP WORK

The roots of group social work are in the settlement houses, the YMCAs and YWCAs, Boy Scouts and Girl Scouts, and Jewish centers of the 1800s.[1] These agencies focused on providing group programs for people considered "normal." Recipients of early group services came for recreation, informal education, friendship, and social action. Gerald Euster notes that these recipients "learned to cooperate and get along with others socially; they enriched themselves through new knowledge, skills, and interests, and the overall state of society was bettered through responsible involvement in community problems."[2] The early use of groups is highlighted in the following descriptions of settlement houses and YMCAs.

Settlement Houses

The first settlement house, Toynbee Hall, was established in London in 1884; many others were soon formed in large U.S. cities.[3] Many of the early settlement house workers were daughters of ministers. Usually from the middle and upper classes, they would live in a poor neighborhood so they could experience the harsh realities of poverty. Simultaneously, they sought to cooperate with neighborhood residents to improve living conditions. Using the missionary approach of teaching residents how to live moral lives and improve their circumstances, early settlement workers sought to improve housing, health, and living conditions; find jobs for workers; teach English, hygiene, and occupational skills; and change environmental surroundings through cooperative efforts. The techniques settlement houses used to effect change are now called social group work, social action, and community organization.

Settlement houses emphasized "environmental reform," but they also "continued to struggle to teach the poor the prevailing middle-class values of work, thrift, and abstinence as the keys to success."[4] In addition to dealing with local problems through local action, settlement houses played important roles in drafting legislation and organizing to influence social policy and legislation. The most noted leader in the settlement-house movement was Jane Addams of Hull House in Chicago.

Jane Addams was born in 1860 in Cedarville, Illinois, the daughter of parents who owned a successful flour mill and a wood mill.[5] After graduating from Rockford Seminary in Rockford, Illinois, she attended medical school briefly but was forced to leave due to

4

illness. She then traveled for a few years in Europe, perplexed as to what her life work should be. At the age of twenty-five, she joined the Presbyterian church, which helped her find a focus for her life: religion, humanitarianism, and serving the poor. (She later joined the Congregational church, now known as the United Church of Christ.) Addams heard about the establishment of Toynbee Hall in England and returned to Europe to study the approach. The staff of college students and graduates, mainly from Oxford, lived in the slums of London to learn conditions firsthand and to improve life there with their own personal resources, including financial ones.

Jane Addams returned to the United States and rented a two-story house in Chicago. Later named Hull House, it was located in an impoverished neighborhood. With a few friends, Addams initiated a variety of group and individual activities for the community. Group activities included a literature reading group for young women, a kindergarten, and groups with the following focuses: social relationships, sports, music, painting, art, and discussion of current affairs. Hull House also provided services to individuals who needed immediate help, such as food, shelter, and information on and referral for other services. A Hull House Social Science Club studied social problems in a scientific manner and then became involved in social action efforts to improve living conditions. This group worked successfully for passage of Illinois legislation to prevent the employment of children in sweatshops. Addams also became interested in the various ethnic groups in the neighborhood around Hull House. She was fairly successful in bringing the various nationalities together at Hull House where they could interact and exchange cultural values.

The success of Hull House served as a model for the establishment of settlement houses in other areas of Chicago and in many other large cities in the United States. Settlement-house leaders believed that by changing neighborhoods, they would improve communities, and by altering communities, they would develop a better society. For her extraordinary contributions, Jane Addams received the Nobel Prize for Peace in 1931.

Young Men's Christian Association (YMCA)

The founder of the Young Men's Christian Association was George Williams,[6] who was born and reared on a small farm in England. He stopped attending school at the age of thirteen to work on his father's farm, but at fourteen, he became an apprentice to a draper (a manufacturer of and dealer in cloth and woolen materials) and learned the trade. He grew up in a religious environment and joined the Congregational church at the age of sixteen. At twenty, he moved to London and worked for another drapery firm. Like Williams, the owner, George Hitchcock, was deeply religious and allowed his new employee to organize prayer meetings at work. The "prayer circle" Williams formed with twelve fellow employees marked the beginning of YMCAs.

The size of the prayer circle gradually grew, and the meetings featured Bible reading as well as prayers. The success of this group inspired Williams and his associates to organize similar groups at other drapers' establishments. In 1844 the resulting prayer circles at fourteen businesses formed an association called the Young Men's Christian Association. Each group conducted weekly religious services that included prayer, Bible readings, and discussions of spiritual topics.

The YMCA soon began to expand its activities. Prominent speakers from various fields of public and scholarly life addressed its members. An office was selected, and

Protestant clergy in France, Holland, and other countries were persuaded to form YMCAs. Gradually, the programs were expanded to meet the unique needs of the communities in which the YMCAs were located.

In 1851, Thomas V. Sullivan, a retired mariner, picked up a religious weekly in Boston and read about the YMCA movement in London.[7] Sullivan gathered a few friends and established the first YMCA in the United States. Similar to the London association, the American movement spread quickly to other communities. In only seven years, YMCAs were serving communities throughout the United States.

The American Y had many "firsts." It was the first organization to aid troops during wartime in the field and in prison camps. It pioneered community sports and athletics, invented volleyball and basketball, and taught water safety and swimming. It devised an international program of social service similar to that of the Peace Corps today. It originated group recreational camping, developed night schools and adult education, initiated widespread nondenominational Christian work for college students, and reached out to assist foreign students. From an origin that involved a narrowly focused religious objective, YMCAs have expanded their objectives in a variety of directions. The success of YMCAs helped spur the formation of the Young Women's Christian Association, which was formed in Boston in 1866.[8]

TYPES OF GROUPS

There are a variety of groups in social work: social conversation, recreation-skill building, educational, task, problem-solving and decision-making, focus, self-help, socialization, therapeutic, and sensitivity and encounter. According to Johnson and Johnson, a group may be defined as: . . . two or more individuals in face-to-face interaction, each aware of his or her membership in the group, each aware of the others who belong to the group, and each aware of their positive interdependence as they strive to achieve mutual goals.[9]

Social Conversation

Social conversation is often employed to determine what kind of relationship might develop with people we do not know very well. Since talk is often loose and tends to drift aimlessly, there is usually no formal agenda for such conversations. If the topic of conversation is dull, the subject can simply be changed. Although individuals may have a goal (perhaps only to establish an acquaintanceship) such goals need not become the agenda for the entire group. In social work, social conversation with other professionals is frequent, but groups involving clients generally have objectives other than conversation, such as resolving personal problems.

Recreation/Skill Building

Recreational groups may be categorized as *informal recreational groups* or *skill-building recreational groups*.

A recreational group service agency (such as the YMCA, YWCA, or neighborhood center) may offer little more than physical space and the use of some equipment to provide activities for enjoyment and exercise. Often activities such as playground games and informal athletics are spontaneous, and the groups are practically leaderless. Some agencies claim that recreation and interaction with others help to build character and prevent delinquency among youths by providing an alternative to street life.

In contrast to informal recreational groups, a skill-building recreational group usually has an increased focus on tasks and is generally guided by an adviser, coach, or instructor. The objective is to improve a set of skills in an enjoyable way. Examples of activities include arts and crafts, as well as golf, basketball, and swimming, which may develop into competitive team sports with leagues. These groups are frequently led by professionals with recreational training rather than social work training, and the agencies involved include the YMCA, YWCA, Boy Scouts, Girl Scouts, neighborhood centers, and school recreational departments.

Education

While the topics covered vary widely, all educational groups teach specialized skills and knowledge. Classes on child-rearing, stress management, parenting, English as a foreign language, and assertiveness training are examples. Orientations offered by social service organizations to train volunteers fall into this category as well. Educational groups usually have a classroom atmosphere, involving considerable group interaction and discussion; a professional person with expertise in the area, often a social worker, assumes the role of teacher.

Task

Task groups are formed to achieve a specific set of tasks or objectives. The following examples are types of task groups that social workers are apt to interact with or become involved in. A *board of directors* is an administrative group charged with responsibility for setting the policy governing agency programs. A *task force* is a group established for a special purpose and is usually disbanded after the task is completed. A *committee* of an agency or organization is a group that is formed to deal with specific tasks or matters. An *ad hoc committee*, like a task force, is set up for one purpose and usually ceases functioning after completion of its task.

Problem Solving and Decision Making

Both providers and consumers of social services may become involved in groups concerned with problem solving and decision making. (There is considerable overlap between task groups and these groups; in fact, problem-solving and decision-making groups can be considered a subcategory of task groups.)

Providers of services use group meetings for such objectives as developing a treatment plan for a client or a group of clients, or deciding how best to allocate scarce resources. Potential consumers of services may form a group to meet a current community need. Data on the need may be gathered, and the group may be used as a vehicle either to develop a program or to influence existing agencies to provide services. Social workers may function as stimulators and organizers of these group efforts.

In problem-solving and decision-making groups, each participant normally has some interest or stake in the process and stands to gain or lose personally by the outcome. Usually, there is a formal leader, and other leaders sometimes emerge during the process.

Focus

Focus groups are closely related to task groups and problem-solving and decision-making groups. They may be formed for a variety of purposes, including (1) to identify needs or issues; (2) to generate proposals that resolve an identified issue; and (3) to test reactions to alternative approaches to an issue. A focus group is a specially assembled collection of people who respond through a semistructured or structured discussion to the concerns and interests of the person, group, or organization that invited the participants. Members of the group are encouraged to express their own ideas and views. A *representative group* is a version of the focus group. Its strength is that its members have been selected specifically to represent different perspectives and points of view in a community. At its best, the representative group is a focus group that reflects the cleavages in the community and seeks to bring diverse views to the table; at its worst, it is a front group for people who seek to make the community *think* it has been involved.

Self-Help

Self-help groups are increasingly popular and are often successful in helping individuals with social or personal problems. Katz and Bender provide a comprehensive definition:

> Self-help groups are voluntary, small group structures . . . usually formed by peers who have come together for mutual assistance in satisfying a common need, overcoming a common handicap or life-disrupting problem, and bringing about desired social and/or personal change. The initiators and members of such groups perceive that their needs are not, or cannot be, met by or through existing social institutions. . . . They often provide material assistance as well as emotional support, they are frequently "cause"-oriented, and promulgate an ideology or [set of] values through which members may attain an enhanced sense of personal identity.[10]

Alcoholics Anonymous, developed by two former alcoholics, was the first self-help group to demonstrate substantial success. In a text entitled *Self-Help Organizations and Professional Practice*, Thomas J. Powell describes a number of self-help groups that are now active.[11]

Many self-help groups use individual confession and testimony techniques. Each member explains his or her problem and recounts related experiences and plans for handling the problem. When a member encounters a crisis (for example, an abusive parent

A SELF-HELP GROUP: PARENTS ANONYMOUS[1]

Parents Anonymous (PA), a national self-help organization for parents who have abused or neglected their children, was established in 1970 by Jolly K. in California. For four years before forming the group, Jolly had struggled with an uncontrollable urge to severely punish her daughter. One afternoon she attempted to strangle the child. Desperate, she sought help from a local child-guidance clinic and was placed in therapy. When asked by her therapist what she could do about her problem, Jolly developed an idea. As she explained, "If alcoholics could stop drinking by getting together, and gamblers could stop gambling, maybe the same principle would work for [child] abusers, too." With her therapist's encouragement she formed "Mothers Anonymous" in 1970 and organized a few chapters in California. Nearly every major city in the United States and Canada now has a chapter, and the name has been changed to Parents Anonymous because fathers who abuse their children are also eligible to join.

PA is a crisis intervention program that offers two main forms of help: a weekly group meeting and personal and telephone contact. Members share experiences and feelings during weekly meetings and learn to better control their emotions. During periods of crisis, personal and telephone contact is especially important, particularly when a member feels a nearly uncontrollable desire to take anger or frustration out on a child. Parents may be referred to PA by a social agency (including protective services), or be self-referred as parents who recognize that they need help.

Cassie Starkweather and S. Michael Turner describe why abusive parents would rather participate in a self-help group than receive professional counseling.

It has been our experience that most [abusive] parents judge themselves more harshly than other, more objective people tend to judge them. The fear of losing their children frequently diminishes with reassurance from other members that they are not the monsters they think they are.

Generally speaking, PA members are so afraid they are going to be judged by others as harshly as they judge themselves that they are afraid to go out and seek help. Frequently our members express fears of dealing with a professional person, seeing differences in education, sex, or social status as basic differences that would prevent easy communication or mutual understanding.

Members express feelings of gratification at finding that other parents are "in the same boat." They contrast this with their feelings about professionals who, they often assume, have not taken out the time from their training and current job responsibilities to raise families of their own.[2]

PA emphasizes honesty and directness, since parents who are prone to abuse their children have learned to hide this problem because society finds it difficult to acknowledge. In contrast to society's tendency to deny the problem, the goal of PA is to help parents admit that they are abusive. The term *abuse* is used liberally at meetings, and this insistence on frankness has a healthy effect on members. Abusive parents are relieved because they've finally found a group of people able to accept them as they are. Furthermore, only when they are able to admit they are abusive can they begin to find ways to heal themselves.

During meetings parents are expected to actually admit to beating their child or engaging in other forms of abuse, and the members challenge each other to find ways to curb these activities. Members share constructive approaches to anger and other abuse-precipitating emotions and help each other develop specific plans for dealing with situations that have resulted in abusive episodes. Members learn to recognize danger signs and to take action to avoid abuse.

Leadership is provided by a group member selected by other members. The leader, called a chairperson, is normally assisted by a professional sponsor who serves as resource and back-up person to the chair and the

(continued next page)

9

A SELF-HELP GROUP: PARENTS ANONYMOUS (con't.)

group. The social worker who assumes the role of sponsor must be prepared to perform a variety of functions, including teacher-trainer, broker of community services needed by parents, advocate, consultant, and counselor.

1. Adapted from Charles Zastrow, "Parents Anonymous," in *Introduction to Social Welfare Institutions*, 2d ed.

(Homewood, Ill.: Dorsey Press, 1982), pp. 159–61. Used with permission.

2. Cassie L. Starkweather and S. Michael Turner, "Parents Anonymous: Reflections on the Development of a Self-Help Group," in *Child Abuse: Intervention and Treatment*, eds. Nancy C. Ebeling and Deborah A. Hill (Acton, Mass.: Publishing Sciences Group, 1975), p. 151.

having an urge to abuse a child), he or she is encouraged to call another group member who helps the person cope. Having experienced the misery and consequences of the problem, group members are highly dedicated to helping themselves and their fellow sufferers. The participants also benefit from the "helper therapy" principle; that is, the helper gains psychological rewards.[12] Helping others makes a person feel worthwhile, enabling the person to put his or her own problems into perspective.

Most self-help groups are "direct service" in that they help members with individual problems. Other self-help groups work on community-wide issues and tend to be more social-action oriented. Some direct service self-help groups attempt to change legislation and policy in public and private institutions. Others (parents of children with a cognitive disability, for example) also raise funds and operate community programs. However, many people with personal problems use self-help groups in the same way others use social agencies. An additional advantage of self-help groups is that they generally operate with a minimal budget. (For further discussion, see chapter 14.)

Socialization

The primary objective of most socialization groups is to develop attitudes and behaviors in group members that are more socially acceptable.[13] Developing social skills, increasing self-confidence, and planning for the future are other focuses. Leadership roles in socialization groups are frequently filled by social workers who work with such groups as the following: predelinquent youths to curb delinquency; youths of diverse racial backgrounds to reduce racial tensions; and pregnant, unmarried young females to help them make plans for the future. Elderly residents in nursing homes are often remotivated by socialization groups and become involved in various activities. Teenagers at correctional schools are helped to make plans for returning to their home community. Leadership of all the groups

10

mentioned in this section requires considerable skills and knowledge in using the group to foster individual growth and change.

Therapy

Therapy groups are generally composed of members with severe emotional, behavioral, and personal problems. Leaders of such groups must have superb counseling and group leadership skills, including the ability to accurately perceive the core of each member's response to what is being communicated. Group leaders must also have the personal capacities to develop and maintain a constructive atmosphere within a group. As in one-on-one counseling, the goal of therapy groups is to have members explore their problems in depth and then develop strategies for resolving them. One or more global therapy approaches, such as reality therapy, learning theory, rational therapy, transactional analysis, and client-centered therapy may be used as guides for changing attitudes and behaviors.

In summary, to be a competent group therapist the professional should have (*a*) superb interviewing and counseling skills, (*b*) a working knowledge of the principles of group dynamics (described in parts 1, 2, 3, and 4 of this text), and (*c*) a working knowledge of contemporary therapy approaches (many of which are described in part 7).

Group therapy has several advantages over one-on-one therapy. The "helper" therapy principle generally is operative. Members at times interchange roles and become the helper for someone else, receiving psychological rewards and putting their own problems into perspective in the process. Group therapy also allows members with interaction problems to test new approaches. In addition, research has shown it is generally easier to change the attitudes of an individual in a group than one-on-one.[14] Group therapy permits a social worker to treat more than one person at a time and represents a substantial savings of professional time. An illustration of a therapeutic group is presented in chapter 20.

Sensitivity and Encounter Training

Encounter groups, sensitivity training groups, and T (training)-groups (these terms are used somewhat synonymously) refer to a group experience in which people relate to each other in a close interpersonal manner and self-disclosure is required. The goal is to improve interpersonal awareness. Jane Howard offers a typical description of an encounter group:

> Their destination is intimacy, trust, and awareness of why they behave as they do in groups; their vehicle is candor. Exhorted to "get in touch with their feelings" and to live in the "here-and-now," they sprawl on the floor . . . As they grow tired they rest their heads on rolled-up sweaters or corners of cot mattresses or each other's laps.[15]

An encounter group may meet for a few hours or a few days. Once increased interpersonal awareness is achieved, it is anticipated that attitudes and behaviors will change. For these changes to occur a three-phase process generally takes place: *unfreezing, change,* and *refreezing.*[16]

Unfreezing occurs in encounter groups through a deliberate process of nontraditional interaction. Our attitudes and behavior patterns have been developed through years of social experiences. Such patterns, following years of experimentation and refinement, have now become nearly automatic. The interpersonal style we develop through trial and error generally have considerable utility in our everyday interactions. Deep down, however, we may recognize a need for improvement, but we are reluctant to make an effort to seek im-

A SOCIALIZATION GROUP: A GROUP HOUSE FOR RUNAWAYS

New Horizons, located in an older home in a large midwestern city, is a private, temporary shelter where youths on the run can stay for two weeks. The facility is licensed to house up to eight youths; however, state law requires that parents be contacted and parental permission received before New Horizons can provide shelter overnight. Services include temporary shelter, individual and family counseling, and a twenty-four hour hotline for youths in crisis. Since the average stay at New Horizons is nine days, the population is continually changing. During their stay, youths (and often their parents), receive intensive counseling, which focuses on reducing conflicts between the youths and their parents, and on helping them make future living plans. The two-week limit conveys the importance to residents and their families of resolving the conflicts that keep them apart.

Every evening at seven, a group meeting allows residents to express their satisfactions and dissatisfactions with the facilities and program at New Horizons. All the residents and the two or three staff members on duty are expected to attend. The meetings are convened and led by the staff, most of whom are social workers. Sometimes, the group becomes primarily a "gripe" session, but the staff makes conscientious efforts to improve or change situations involving legitimate gripes. For example, a youth may indicate that the past few days have been "boring," and staff and residents then jointly plan activities for the next few days.

Interaction problems that arise between residents and between staff and residents are also handled during a group session. A resident may be preventing others from sleeping; some residents may refuse to share in domestic tasks; there may be squabbles about which TV program to watch; some residents may be overly aggressive. Since most of the youths face a variety of crises associated with being on the run, many are anxious and under stress. In such an emotional climate, interaction problems are certain to arise. Staff members are sometimes intensely questioned about their actions, decisions, and policies. For example, one of the policies at New Horizons is that each resident must agree not to use alcohol or narcotic drugs while at the shelter. The penalty is expulsion. Occasionally, a few youths use some drugs, are caught, and expelled. Removing a youth from this facility has an immense impact on the other residents and at the following meetings staff members are expected to clarify and explain such decisions.

The staff also presents material on topics requested by residents during meetings. Subjects often covered include sex; drugs; homosexuality; physical and sexual abuse (a fair number of residents are abused by family members); avoiding rape; handling anger, depression, and other unwanted emotions; legal rights of youths on the run; being more assertive; explaining running away to relatives and friends; and human services available to youths in the community. During such presentations, considerable discussion with residents is encouraged and generally occurs.

The final objective of the group is to convey information about planned daily activities and changes in the overall program at New Horizons.

provement, partly because our present style is functional and partly because we are afraid to reveal things about ourselves.

Steward L. Tubbs and John W. Baird describe the unfreezing process in sensitivity groups:

> Unfreezing occurs when our expectations are violated. We become less sure of ourselves when traditional ways of doing things are not followed. In the encounter group, the leader usually does not act like a leader. He or she frequently starts with a brief statement encouraging the group members to participate, to be open and honest, and to expect things to be different. Group members may begin by taking off their shoes, sitting in a circle on the floor, and holding hands with their eyes closed. The leader then encourages them to feel intensely the sensations they are experiencing, the size and texture of the hands they are holding, and so forth.
>
> Other structured exercises or experiences may be planned to help the group focus on the "here-and-now" experience. Pairs may go for "trust walks" in which each person alternately is led around with eyes closed. Sitting face to face and conducting a hand dialogue, or a silent facial mirroring often helps to break the initial barriers to change. Other techniques may involve the "pass around" in which a person in the center of a tight circle relaxes and is physically passed around the circle. Those who have trouble feeling a part of the group are encouraged to break into or out of the circle of people whose hands are tightly held. With these experiences, most participants begin to feel more open to conversation about what they have experienced. This sharing of experiences or self-disclosure about the here and now provides more data for the group to discuss.[17]

The second phase of the process involves making changes in attitudes and behavior, which are usually facilitated by spontaneous feedback as to how a person "comes across" to others. In everyday interaction spontaneous feedback seldom occurs, so ineffective interaction patterns are repeated. In sensitivity groups feedback is strongly encouraged, as the following interaction illustrates:

Carl: All right (*in a sharp tone*), let's get this trust walk over with and stop dillydallying around. I'll lead the first person around—who wants to be blindfolded first?

Judy: I feel uncomfortable about your statement. I feel you are saying this group is a waste of your time. Also, this appears to be your third attempt this evening to "boss" us around.

Jim: I also feel like you are trying to tell us peons what to do. Even the tone of your voice is autocratic and suggests some disgust with this group.

Carl: I'm sorry. I didn't mean it to sound like that. I wonder if I do that outside the group too.

Such feedback provides us with new insights on how we affect others. Once a member's problem interactions are identified, he or she is encouraged to try out new response patterns in the relative safety of the group.

The third and final phase involves "refreezing," a term that is not very descriptive since it implies rigidity within a new set of response patterns. On the contrary, by experimenting with new sets of behaviors, a group member becomes a growing, continually changing person who becomes increasingly effective in interacting with others. In terminating a sensitivity group, the leader may alert the participants to be "on guard" as old behavior patterns tend to creep back in.

Sensitivity groups usually generate an outpouring of emotions, as do therapeutic groups. Sensitivity groups provide an interesting contrast to therapy groups. In therapy groups, each member explores personal and emotional problems in depth, and then develops strategies to resolve them. Sensitivity groups generally do not directly attempt to identify and change specific emotional or personal problems such as drinking, feelings of depression, or sexual dysfunctions. The philosophy behind sensitivity groups is that by simply increasing personal and interpersonal awareness, people will be better able to avoid, cope with, and handle specific personal problems that arise.

Despite their popularity, sensitivity groups remain controversial. In some cases inadequately trained and incompetent individuals have become self-proclaimed leaders and have enticed people to join through sensational advertising. If handled poorly, the short duration of some groups may intensify personal problems; for example, a person's defense mechanisms may be stripped away without his developing adaptive coping patterns. Many authorities on sensitivity training disclaim the use of encounter groups as a form of psychotherapy and discourage those with serious personal problems from joining such a group. Carl Rogers, in reviewing his own extensive experience as leader/participant, echoes these concerns:

> Frequently the behavior changes that occur, if any, are not lasting. In addition, the individual may become deeply involved in revealing himself and then be left with problems which are not worked through. Less common, but still noteworthy, there are also very occasional accounts of an individual having a psychotic episode during or immediately following an intensive group experience. We must keep in mind that not all people are suited for groups.[18]

In some cases the popularity of sensitivity groups has led some individuals to enter harmful groups with incompetent leaders where normal ethical standards have been abused. Shostrom has identified some means by which those interested in encounter groups can prevent exploitation: (*a*) Never participate in a group of fewer than a half-dozen members. The necessary and valuable candor generated by an effective group cannot be dissipated, shared, or examined by too small a group, and scapegoating or purely vicious ganging up can develop. (*b*) Never join an encounter group on impulse—as a fling, binge, or surrender to the unplanned. (*c*) Never stay with a group that has a behavioral ax to grind. (*d*) Never participate in a group that lacks formal connection with a professional on whom you can check.[19]

After reviewing the research on the outcome of sensitivity groups, Lieberman, Yalom, and Miles provide an appropriate perspective for those interested in the intensive group experience:

> Encounter groups present a clear and evident danger if they are used for radical surgery to produce a new man [person]. The danger is even greater when the leader and the participants share this misconception. If we no longer expect groups to produce magical, lasting change and if we stop seeing them as panaceas, we can regard them as useful, socially sanctioned opportunities for human beings to explore and to express themselves. Then we can begin to work on ways to improve them so that they may make a meaningful contribution toward solving human problems.[20]

INITIAL DEVELOPMENT OF GROUPS

The process of establishing and conducting groups varies significantly, depending on the type of group and the specific purposes to be achieved. However, for a group to reach its

14

CONTRASTING GOALS OF THERAPY VS. SENSITIVITY GROUPS

THERAPY GROUPS

Step 1: Examine problem(s) in depth.

Step 2: Develop and select, from various resolution approaches, a strategy to resolve the problem.

SENSITIVITY GROUPS

Step 1: Help each person become more aware of herself and how she affects others in interpersonal interactions.

Step 2: Help a person develop more effective interaction patterns.

---

maximum potential, there are still some unifying or common elements to be addressed prior to establishing the group. These factors are described within this section and include determining a group's objectives, size, open-ended or closed-ended status, and duration. In addition, since specific pitfalls or dilemmas characterize certain types of groups, plans must be made to prevent or handle problems should they arise.

Determining Objectives

Careful consideration must be given to the reasons a group is being formed, or its objectives, in order to select effective members. For example, problem-solving groups often require the expertise of professionals in other disciplines—professionals whose skills and knowledge directly contribute to the accomplishment of group goals; some of these professionals may have backgrounds, training, and perceptions that differ from those of the social worker. While this approach produces a group with a wealth of expertise, it creates additional demands on the leader and other difficulties. When the members have diverse backgrounds and interests, these difficulties include problems encountered in setting goals, prioritizing goals, and determining tasks to be performed. Educational groups, on the other hand, are usually composed of members who share a common interest in a particular area, such as child-rearing skills. Individuals with similar needs join an educational group primarily to gain rather than dispense information. This tends to make leadership easier. Because potential members of therapeutic groups (unlike those of problem-solving or educational groups) often have diverse problems, and may in addition have interactional difficulties, a much more thorough screening of members is required. Therefore, it is essential that the objectives or purposes of each group be established at the beginning since these can have a significant impact on the process of membership selection and other aspects of functioning.

Size

The size of a group affects members' satisfactions, interactions, and the amount of output per member. Although smaller groups are generally rated more favorably, larger groups are often more successful in resolving complex problems.[21] While members in larger groups experience more stress and greater communication difficulties, they usually bring a greater number of problem-solving skills and resources to the group as a whole. Since each person has fewer opportunities to interact in a large group, some members feel inhibited and reluctant to talk. As the size of the group increases, discussion generally hinges on the input of the most frequent contributor, who assumes a dominant role. As a result, the gap in participation widens between the most frequent contributor and the other members of the group.

In his research on group size, Slater found that groups of five persons were considered most satisfactory by members themselves and

> most effective in dealing with an intellectual task involving the collection and exchange of information about a situation; the coordination, analysis, and evaluation of this information; and a group decision regarding the appropriate administrative action to be taken.[22]

In a group of five members, a number of different relationships can be formed with a moderate level of intimacy. Several individuals can also act as "buffers" who deal with strained situations or power plays. If a vote is needed to resolve a dispute, obviously a two-two split can be avoided. In groups smaller than five, Slater observed, the members were inhibited from expressing their ideas through fear of alienating one another and thereby destroying the group. In groups of more than five, members also felt inhibited and participated less often.

Groups with an even number of members tend to have higher rates of disagreement and antagonism than those with an odd number, apparently because of the possible division of the group into two subdivisions of equal size.[23] For each task to be accomplished, there is probably an optimal group size. The more complex the task, the larger the optimal size, so that the knowledge, abilities, and skills of many members are available to accomplish the task. A group should be large enough to allow members to speak freely without being inhibited and small enough to permit a moderate level of intimacy and involvement.

Open-Ended vs. Closed-Ended Groups

Whether the group will be open-ended, with new members added as old members leave, or whether the membership will remain constant until termination (closed-ended) should be determined at the outset. *Open-ended groups* provide a measure of synergism through the addition of new members. As new individuals join, they provide a different viewpoint, even though they usually are gradually socialized into group norms and practices by the older members. The impact of such changes is not all beneficial, however. The constant change in membership may inhibit openness and detract from the sense of trust needed before certain subjects are broached. In addition, open groups are likely to "have members at different levels of commitment to the process and members [who are not] at the same stages of development."[24]

A *closed-ended group* can often function more effectively because it has a relatively constant population and often operates within a specified time frame.[25] Although the premature loss of members can seriously damage such a group's effectiveness, a leader must deal with member termination in both open and closed groups and plan for this eventuality.

Duration

The duration of a group has two related components: the number of sessions and the length of each session. Many groups meet for one to two hours once or twice a week for a specified number of weeks. Meeting for one to two hours tends to optimize productive activity and behavior. Meeting lengths shorter than one hour usually do not allow sufficient time to thoroughly discuss the issues that are raised. In meetings that last longer than three hours, members tend to become drowsy, frustrated, and unable to concentrate. Although a meeting length of one to two hours appears to be a guideline for optimal functioning in many groups, at times pressing issues may necessitate a longer meeting to process and conclude group business. Obviously, if a crisis occurs five minutes before the end of the meeting, the group leader should not conclude the session. By the same token, some discussions can become so intense that they could last indefinitely and accomplish little. A pragmatic approach to terminating each meeting or series of meetings within a set time frame will enhance the group's respect for the leader and foster the group's development.

Setting meetings in which there are three or four (or more) days between meetings usually allows the members some time to work on tasks that are designed to accomplish their personal goals and the goals of the group. For example, in educational groups, members can study and complete homework assignments between meetings. In therapy groups, members can carry out homework assignments designed to reduce or resolve personal problems.

THE STAGES OF A GROUP

The steps involved in planning and implementing educational, therapeutic, and socialization groups are similar to the procedures followed by social workers who deal with individual clients:

Groups	**Individuals**
intake	intake
selection of members	assessment and planning
assessment and planning	intervention
group development and intervention	evaluation and termination
evaluation and termination	

Inexperienced group leaders usually expect a smooth transition from one stage to another and are disappointed if this does not occur. Therefore, many new practitioners tend to force the group out of one stage into another instead of allowing the natural growth process to evolve. Experience will demonstrate the futility of these efforts as, barring unforeseen circumstances, each group will move at its own pace and eventually arrive at the same destination. Groups that skip stages or whose development is otherwise thwarted will often return to a previous stage to complete unfinished business. While groups do sometimes become mired in one stage, these occurrences are less common than generally thought. The procedures for establishing socialization, educational, and therapeutic groups are briefly summarized in the following material and expanded upon throughout the text.

Intake

During intake, the presenting concerns and needs of prospective members are identified. Judgments that some or all of these persons could benefit from a group approach are made. An agreement is often formulated between the members of the group and the group leader about tentative group goals (see chapter 4). This stage may also be referred to as the contract stage, as the leader and the members make a commitment to pursue the situation to the next step.

Selection of Members

Individuals most likely to benefit from a group should be selected as members. Selecting a group requires attention to both descriptive and behavioral factors.[26] A decision needs to be made whether to seek homogeneity or diversity in these factors. There are few guidelines as to when diversity and when homogeneity of these factors will be most effective and efficient. Age, sex, and level of education are *descriptive factors* that may create homogeneity or foster diversity within the group. In groups of children and adolescents, the age span among members must be kept relatively small because levels of maturity and interests can vary greatly. Similarly, same-sex groupings may facilitate achieving group goals for pre-adolescents, but for middle-adolescent groups there may be specific advantages to having representation from both sexes.

The *behavioral attributes* expected of a group member will also have a major effect on the attainment of group objectives. For example, placing several hyperactive or aggressive youngsters in a group may be a prelude to failure. Members may be selected for their value as models for appropriate behavior or because they possess other personal characteristics expected to enhance the group. As a general rule the best judgment regarding a member's potential contribution to the group is obtained by looking at past behavioral attributes.[27]

Assessment and Planning

A more in-depth assessment and statement of goals and plans for action occur during this phase. In reality this step is completed only when the group ends, because the dynamic nature of most groups requires an ongoing adjustment of goals and intervention plans. Goals should be time-limited with a reasonable chance for attainment, and the leader should ensure that all goals are clearly stated to aid in later evaluations. Clarification of goals also eliminates hidden agendas.

Group Development and Intervention

Numerous models of group development have evolved. Three of these models are described in the section entitled "Models of Group Development Over Time."

Evaluation and Termination

To think of evaluation as a specific point in the life of a group is perhaps not realistic since evaluation must be an ongoing process. The decision to terminate a group may be based on the accomplishment of group or individual goals, the expiration of a predetermined period of time, the failure of the group to achieve desired ends, the leader of the group relocating, or a shortage of funds to keep the group going.

When a group is open-ended, the process of termination may be extended since members may be entering and leaving at different points. In other cases, closure occurs only in relation to specific tasks, since the group is intended to be an ongoing entity. Examples include a committee established to oversee the operation of a special program, a work group charged with developing and carrying out in-service training in an agency, or a board of directors of a community action program.

The termination of a group often produces the same reactions that characterize the termination of other significant relationships, including the feeling of being rejected. The group leader must be aware of these potential feelings and help group members terminate with a minimum of difficulty. Additional material on how to terminate a group is presented in chapter 32.

MODELS OF GROUP DEVELOPMENT OVER TIME

Groups change over time. Numerous models of frameworks have been developed to describe the changes that occur in groups over time. This text will describe the models of group development known as (1) the Garland, Jones, and Kolodny Model, (2) the Tuckman Model, and (3) the Bales Model.

Garland, Jones, and Kolodny Model

Garland, Jones, and Kolodny developed a model that identifies five stages of development in social work groups.[28] By describing and understanding the various kinds of developmental problems in groups, leaders can more effectively anticipate and respond to the reactions of group members. The conceptualization of Garland et al. appears particularly applicable to socialization, therapeutic, and encounter groups; to a lesser extent, the model is applicable to self-help, task, problem-solving and decision-making, educational, and recreation/skill groups.

Emotional closeness among members is the central focus of the model and is reflected in *struggles* that occur at five levels of group growth: preaffiliation, power and control, intimacy, differentiation, and separation.

Pre-Affiliation

In the first stage, *pre-affiliation*, members are ambivalent about joining the group, and interaction is guarded. Members test out, often through approach and avoidance behavior, whether they really want to belong. Because new situations are often frightening, members attempt to protect themselves from being hurt or taken advantage of, maintaining a certain amount of distance and attempting to get what they can from the group without taking many risks. Even though individuals are aware that group involvement will make demands that may be frustrating or even painful, they are attracted because of rewards and satisfying experiences in other groups. These former positive ramifications are transferred to the "new" group. During this first stage, the leader tries to make the group appear as attractive as possible "by allowing and supporting distance, gently inviting trust, facilitating exploration of the physical and psychological milieu, and by providing activities if necessary and initiating group structure."[29] This stage ends gradually as members begin to feel safe and comfortable within the group, and view its rewards as worth a tentative emotional commitment.

Power and Control

In the second stage, *power and control*, the character of the group begins to emerge. Patterns of communication, alliances, and subgroups begin to develop. Individuals assume certain roles and responsibilities, establish norms and methods for handling group tasks, and begin to ask questions. Although these processes are necessary to conduct meetings, they also lead to a power struggle in which each member attempts to gain greater control over the gratifications and rewards to be received from the group. A major source of gratification for any group is the leader, who influences the direction of the group and gives or withholds emotional and material rewards. At this point members realize that the group is becoming important to them. This second stage is transitional, with certain basic issues requiring resolution: Does the group or the leader have primary control? What are the limits of the power of the group and of the leader, and to what extent will the leader use his power?

This uncertainty results in anxiety and considerable testing by group members to gauge limits and establish norms for the power and authority of both the group and the leader. Rebellion is not uncommon, and the dropout rate in groups is often highest at this stage. During this struggle the leader should: (1) help the members understand the nature of the power struggle, (2) give emotional support to help members weather the discomfort of uncertainty, and (3) help to establish norms to resolve the uncertainty. Group members must trust the leader to maintain a safe balance of shared power and control.

When that trust is achieved, group members make a major commitment to become involved.

Intimacy

In the third stage, *intimacy*, the likes and dislikes of intimate relationships are expressed. The group becomes more like a family, with sibling rivalry exhibited and with the leader sometimes being referred to as a parent. Feelings are more openly expressed and discussed, and the group is viewed as a place where growth and change take place. Individuals feel free to examine and make efforts to change personal attitudes, concerns, and problems, and there is a feeling of "oneness" or cohesiveness. Members struggle to explore and make changes in their personal lives, and to examine "what this group is all about."

Differentiation

During the fourth stage, *differentiation*, members are freer to experiment with new and alternative behavior patterns because they recognize individual rights and needs, and they communicate more effectively. Leadership is more evenly shared, roles are more functional, and the organization itself is more efficient. Power problems are now minimal, and decisions are made and carried out on a less emotional and more objective basis. James Garland and Louise Frey note:

> This kind of individualized therapeutic cohesion has been achieved because the group experience has all along valued and nurtured individual integrity. . . .
> The worker assists in this stage by helping the group to run itself and by encouraging it to act as a unit with other groups or in the wider community. During this time the [social] worker exploits opportunities for evaluation by the group of its activities, feelings and behavior.[30]

The differentiation stage is analogous to a healthy functioning family in which the children have reached adulthood and are now becoming successful in pursuing their own lives. Relationships are more between equals, and members are mutually supportive and able to relate to each other in more rational and objective ways.

Separation

The final stage is *separation*. Group purposes have been achieved and members have learned new behavioral patterns to enable them to move on to other social experiences. Termination is not always easily accomplished, as members may be reluctant to move on and may display regressive behavior to prolong the existence of the group. Members may express anger or may psychologically deny that termination is approaching. Garland and Frey suggest the leader's (or social worker's) role:

> To facilitate separation the [social] worker must be willing to let go. Concentration upon group and individual mobility, evaluation of the experience, help with the expression of the ambivalence about termination and recognition of the progress which has been made are his major tasks. Acceptance of termination is facilitated by active guidance of members as individuals to other ongoing sources of support and assistance.[31]

21

Tuckman Model

Tuckman reviewed over fifty studies, primarily of limited-duration therapy and sensitivity groups, and concluded that these groups go through the following five predictable developmental stages: forming, storming, norming, performing, and adjourning.[32] Each of these stages will be briefly described.

Forming

In this stage members become oriented toward each other, work on being accepted, and learn more about the group. This stage is marked by a period of uncertainty in which members try to determine their places in the group and learn the group's rules and procedures.

Storming

In this stage conflicts begin to arise as members resist the influence of the group and rebel against accomplishing their tasks. Members confront their various differences, and the management of conflict often becomes the focus of attention.

Norming

In this stage the group establishes cohesiveness and commitment. In the process, the members discover new ways to work together. Norms are also set for appropriate behavior.

Performing

In this stage the group works as a unit to achieve group goals. Members develop proficiency in achieving goals and become more flexible in their patterns of working together.

Adjourning

In this stage the group disbands. The feelings that members experience are similar to those in the "Separation Stage" of the Garland, Jones, and Kolodny Model described on page 21.

Bales Model

The stages described in the Garland, Jones, and Kolodny Model and in the Tuckman Model are sequential-stage models, since both specify sequential stages of group development. In contrast, Robert F. Bales developed a recurring-phase model.[33] Bales asserted that groups continue to seek an equilibrium between task-oriented work and emotional expressions, in order to build better relationships among group members. (Task roles and social/emotional roles performed by members of a group are specified at some length in chapter 2.) Bales asserts that groups tend to oscillate between these two concerns. Sometimes a group focuses on identifying and performing the tasks that will lead to achievement of its goals. At other times, the group focuses on building the morale and improving the social/emotional atmosphere of the group.

The sequential-stage perspective and the recurring phase perspective are not necessarily contradictory. Both are useful for understanding group development. The sequential-stage perspective assumes that groups move through various stages while dealing with a series of basic themes that surface when they are relevant to the group's work. The recurring-phase perspective assumes that the issues underlying these basic themes are never completely resolved and tend to recur later.

GROUP COHESION

Group cohesion is the sum of all the variables influencing members to stay in a group. It occurs when the positive attractions of a group outweigh negative implications a member might encounter. The word *cohesion* is derived from Latin and can be translated literally as the "act of sticking together." A group's level of cohesion is constantly changing as events alter each member's feelings and attitudes about the group.

The extent of a member's attraction to and involvement in a group can be measured by his or her perceptions of the payoffs and costs. They are infinite because they vary from individual to individual, but the following lists offer a brief indication of possibilities:

Payoffs	Costs
companionship	being with people one dislikes
attaining personal goals	expending time and effort
prestige	criticism
enjoyment	distasteful tasks
emotional support	boring meetings

The higher the level of attraction (payoffs), the greater the attractive qualities of cohesion. Therefore, group leaders should constantly try to increase attractive qualities of a group.

An individual's willingness to risk and to become involved in a group depends to a large extent on the degree to which his needs for belonging are met. Often, members join groups to help meet the need to belong. Membership in a group or a person's willingness to share him- or herself often hinges on the degree of acceptance experienced in the group. The climate in a group is a crucial factor in determining the actual sense of belonging that members achieve. Clearly, the need for belonging can be a powerful factor in joining and remaining a member of groups.

Obviously, group members are most attracted to group meetings when friendly, pleasant interactions take place. Besides feeling relaxed, members are more apt to share their ideas and relate to others within the group. Initially, ice-breaker exercises can help members become more comfortable, and goals can be set that incorporate the personal goals of members (see chapter 4). The more members feel involved in making decisions, the more they will feel that their views are respected.

Highly cohesive groups have low rates of absenteeism and low turnover in membership. In addition, members are generally motivated to complete assigned tasks, and they are apt to conform to group norms. They are more willing to listen, accept suggestions, and defend the group against external criticism. Because a group provides a source of security, it often rewards members by becoming a support system that reduces anxiety, heightens self-esteem, adds meaning to living, and often helps members resolve personal problems. Therefore, membership in a cohesive group enhances a member's psychological health by transmitting feelings of being valued, accepted, and liked.

Members should be rewarded for jobs well done rather than coerced or manipulated, and a cooperative atmosphere, not a competitive one, should be created. Again, pleasing interactions, rather than a constant war of words or negative banter, increase a group's cohesion. If a difficult situation arises, a problem-solving approach should be used. A win-lose approach usually decreases cohesion (see chapter 9).

Trust among group members is another necessary condition for effective communication, cooperation, and cohesion. When distrust exists, individuals will not disclose sensitive personal information or commit their resources to accomplishing group goals. Even though some groups have "built-in" prestige, being a member of certain groups can potentially damage a member's reputation (for example, being a member of a board of directors of a nursing home beset by a well-publicized scandal involving extensive patient abuse).

A group's cohesion will generally decrease when there is a long-term disagreement on how to define or resolve a major problem. Unreasonable or excessive demands on members, such as forcing a shy person to give a speech, will also sharply reduce the group's attractiveness. Dominating members and those who engage in repulsive behavior are certainly not large drawing cards. Scapegoats, who are blamed for difficult situations, may react aggressively or drop out. Finally, cohesion can be decreased if outside activities of the members are curtailed because of the group. For example, a student group that meets two or three nights a week may interfere with study time, exercising, and socializing.

MEMBERSHIP AND REFERENCE GROUPS

A *membership group* is a group to which a person belongs. In a sense membership in a group is clearly defined: A person either belongs to a group or does not belong. However, some people are marginal members of a group. For example, everyone enrolled at a college campus is a member of the student body, but some students are only marginal members because they are not involved in any campus activities. Carol works nearly full time in the evening, does not live on campus, but does attend classes. She identifies primarily with the people she works with, and other students influence her very little. Carol, then, has limited psychological membership in the student body and only minor identification with the campus. Full psychological membership in a group occurs only when a person is positively attracted to the group and accepted as a member. The more fully a person is a member of a group, the greater will be that person's commitment to accomplishing group goals.

Individuals who aspire to membership in a group will act as the members act. Students who want to be admitted to a fraternity or sorority, for example, will act like members to increase their chances of being admitted. Aspiring members are psychologically identifying with the group, even though they are not members.

Voluntary membership is freely chosen while *involuntary membership* is required. Social workers often work with involuntary groups in prison settings, mental hospitals, residential treatment facilities, and schools, where members are often uninterested, hostile, or disruptive.

Practically all of us are members of a variety of groups. Jim, for example, is a family member, a Roman Catholic, a PTA member, plays forward on a basketball team, is a member of the National Association of Social Workers, and serves on the local board of Planned Parenthood. Occasionally there are conflicts, because the groups may schedule meetings at the same time and have different norms and values. Planned Parenthood's views on birth control and abortion, for example, differ from those espoused by the Catholic church. To resolve this dilemma, Jim can compartmentalize his values by accepting Planned Parenthood's views on abortion and birth control and most of the Catholic doctrine except the church's views on abortion and birth control. The resolution of conflicts resulting from multiple membership is often attained through much anxiety and great personal cost.

Reference groups are groups whose influence we accept and identify with. In the example given earlier, Carol is a member of a student body and of a work group. Since she primarily identifies with her work group, it serves as a reference group for her, but the student body does not. Reference groups have two distinct functions: (1) normative, in that members seek to conform to their positions and standards for behavior; and (2) decision-making, since members use group standards, or norms, as the basis for making and evaluating decisions.

Some members of a group are referents who influence and are influenced by other members. In a large group, only a small subgroup of members are referents. These referents "make sense" to other members (who identify with them) as they are viewed as experts or authorities, or have most of the power. Occasionally, people select a reference group in terms of an issue. For example, Jim uses Planned Parenthood as a reference group to express his feelings on birth control and abortion, while he uses the Catholic church as a reference group for his views on suicide, euthanasia, life after death, and morality.

BREAKING THE ICE

In most newly formed groups, the leader has the initial responsibility of seeking to create an atmosphere in which members feel comfortable. Members of a new group are apt to have a number of concerns: "Will I be respected and accepted?" "Will this group be worth my time and effort?" "Will I feel embarrassed or inferior?" "Will I be able to form new friendships?" "Are the other members the kind of people I will like?" "What will my roles and responsibilities be—and will I like them?" "Will I have a leadership role?" "Will others expect more of me than I am capable of giving?" "Will my personal goals or expectations be realized?" "If I find I do not like or enjoy this group, is there a nice way to get out?"

To help members become comfortable, the leader might use an ice-breaker exercise. (Several such exercises are described at the end of this chapter.) Such exercises are designed to help members become acquainted with one another, introduce themselves, reduce anxieties, and facilitate communication. Each group has a unique personality. In most social work groups, the leader attempts to create an atmosphere in which the members trust one another and want to share their thoughts and ideas. Ice-breakers are an important step in establishing such an atmosphere.

As a student, you have probably observed that each class has a unique personality. Norms are established in their first few sessions, for example, as to whether students will share and discuss their opinions and beliefs. If a norm of "silence" is established, the instructor generally ends up doing practically all the talking. Such a class becomes a "chore" for the instructor and also for the students. Many of the ingredients that go into determining whether a class will establish a norm of "talking" or of "silence" are unknown. Certainly, a norm of talking is facilitated by ice-breakers.

Ice-breaking exercises can also accomplish specific objectives, such as obtaining information on the members' expectations for the group. One such ice-breaker is described at the end of this chapter. Before we consider ice-breaker exercises, the pitfalls, ethics, and guidelines on conducting classroom exercises will be summarized.

EXPERIENTIAL LEARNING

It is important that social work students receive experiential training in classes to prepare them for the realities of social work practice. Social workers encounter many sensitive situations in the course of their work: divorce, suicide, child abuse and neglect, incest, and death. In a classroom a qualified instructor observes the level of psychological stress in participants, provides feedback on how to better handle sensitive situations, and intervenes if necessary. After students graduate and are working with clients, such guidance is seldom available. Therefore, it is vital that they develop their skills through practical classroom applications before they venture into real group counseling situations.

Classroom exercises offer a variety of payoffs. They can illustrate key theoretical concepts, clarify values, or help students develop skills such as assessment and intervention. They are generally fun and often teach students more effectively than other mechanisms. Exercises also help students get acquainted, build group cohesion, and increase group morale.

Pitfalls to Avoid in Conducting Class Exercises

1. Class exercises are not designed to solve emotional problems. Certainly the leader should not seek to meet his or her emotional needs through such exercises.
2. Class exercises should not be used simply to fill class time. They should have legitimate teaching objectives and value.
3. An exercise should not be used if there is insufficient time to discuss or process the activity.
4. Exercises should not replace other forms of instruction, such as lectures.
5. Although some students enroll in social work and psychology courses to solve their own personal problems, experiential exercises should *not* encourage students to disclose material they will later regret having divulged. If extremely personal information is revealed, the class atmosphere must be supportive. Subsequent discussion should be more generalized and objective.

Ethics and Guidelines for Conducting Exercises

1. The leader has the tasks of explaining the objectives, describing the steps, beginning the exercise, keeping the members on task and on time, modeling appropriate values and skills, leading the members in discussing and evaluating the exercise after it is conducted, and being alert to the emotional reactions of the members to the exercise.

2. Generally, the more enthusiasm the instructor displays for class exercises, the more enthusiasm the students will display.
3. Students learn in different ways. Some will be more responsive and learn more from exercises than others.
4. The learning needs of the students should determine the kinds of exercises used. Leaders may want to modify the exercises in this text to meet special learning needs. In designing or modifying an exercise, leaders should consider the following questions: Is this the best exercise to accomplish the learning objectives? Can the exercise be modified to meet the characteristics of the group? How can processing of the exercise be best accomplished? Is there sufficient class time to conduct the exercise? Is the group too large or too small for the exercise? Are the required materials available? What problems may arise? Is there sufficient time to process problems?
5. To allot enough time, the leaders should estimate how much time each step in the exercise will take.
6. When an exercise is introduced, group members should be informed of the objectives, given an overview of what will occur, and encouraged to ask questions. Members have a right to expect clear information before beginning the exercise. To build trust, the leader should not give false information or incorrect answers to questions. If an accurate answer will reveal information the exercise is designed to convey, the leader may say, "It is best to delay answering this question as the exercise is designed to reveal the answer."
7. The instructor should always be present when an exercise is being conducted.
8. The leader should have specific educational objectives for each exercise and be able to articulate these objectives. Students have the right to know what the objectives are. (If stating the objectives at the beginning will "give away" a point hidden in the exercise, the objectives should be carefully explained at the end.)
9. The leader should carefully plan each exercise and be qualified to conduct it. The exercises in this text are explained in considerable detail. The leader should prepare for each exercise by reading and visualizing the steps, and by thinking about how this specific class might respond.
10. A few exercises may arouse strong emotions because they may touch an area with which a student is struggling. The instructor should thus observe students closely, be prepared to talk privately with such students after class, and be aware of appropriate counseling resources for students whose psychological stress is severe.
11. The instructor should seek to establish a supportive, caring, and respectful atmosphere among the students.
12. The class should understand the importance of keeping sensitive personal information confidential.
13. Once the objectives and format of an exercise are explained, student participation should be voluntary. Students who do not wish to participate should be excused with the understanding that every student is expected to participate in most of the exercises.
14. No exercise should be so secretive or sensitive that other faculty could not be invited to observe.
15. It is generally better to use one or two exercises to demonstrate a point than to use several.
16. If a number of exercises are conducted during a term, the instructor should seek to have each student take an active role in at least some of them. Special efforts should be made to involve those students who are quiet and nonassertive.

17. The instructor should critique student skills or behavior in a positive way. The student should not be made to feel inferior, incompetent, or inadequate. When a shortcoming is pointed out, the student should also be praised for what she or he did well. The feedback should focus on behavior rather than on the person, on observations rather than on judgments. A problem-solving approach in which shortcomings are identified and alternatives for improvement provided works well. The feedback should focus on sharing ideas and information rather than on giving advice. The instructor should never embarrass a student in front of classmates, and sensitive subjects should be covered in a private meeting with that student.

18. The instructor should provide encouragement by being positive and by praising, at one time or another, each student for such actions as making positive contributions, putting forth effort, displaying progress, showing unique skills, or being perceptive and respectful of others.

19. After completion, each exercise should be discussed and evaluated in an open, relaxed atmosphere. Students must feel free to raise questions, express thoughts and concerns, and discuss the merits and shortcomings of the exercise. Such an evaluation brings about closure, which is important, and helps the leader improve the exercise for future use.

20. Even the most carefully designed exercises sometimes fail. An important instruction may have been left out. The students may be distracted by other concerns and fail to give the exercise their undivided attention. The exercise may be poorly designed. When an exercise flops, it is generally best to acknowledge that things did not go as planned. Attempting to cover up an obvious flop will only cause students to question the honesty and effectiveness of the leader. Humor can "take the edge off," and the leader may be able to achieve the learning objectives by using another closely related exercise. At times, an exercise may be a complete loss. How the instructor reacts will be a factor in determining the student's confidence in the instructor. In addition, an appropriate reaction will help students learn how to respond to failures in groups they lead. Since humans are fallible by nature, some exercises will not achieve the desired objectives, and instructors should learn from such mistakes.

GROUP EXERCISES

Goal: The following exercises are designed to help break the ice in new groups and are just a sample of the many ice-breaker experiences available. The group leader should select exercises appropriate to specific groups and should modify them as needed.

Exercise A: Getting Acquainted

The leader asks the members to sit in a circle and explains that the goal is to get acquainted. The group is asked to make a list of what they would like to know about each other, such as name, year in school, major, and reason for taking course. An interesting item the leader may decide to add is "most embarrassing moment." The list should be written on a blackboard or flip chart. One by one the members, including the leader, respond to the listed items. The leader should then ask if there is additional information the members want to know about him or her, including training and professional experience, and should answer all questions except those considered too personal.

Exercise B: Introducing a Partner

The same format is followed as in exercise A. The only variant is that after the items are listed, the members pair off and gather the information from their partners. If there is an uneven number of members, form a subgroup of three. Allow five minutes for information gathering. Partners then introduce each other to the group.

Exercise C: Personal Expectations for the Group

The leader asks the members to introduce themselves. Possible items that might be covered are:

Name
Year in school
Major
Paid experience in social work
Volunteer experience in social work
Most embarrassing experience (for humor)
Reason for taking course
Personal expectations for the class or group

This ice-breaker is useful as a first step in seeking to identify the personal goals of members. The leader's goals and objectives for the group should then be given. A discussion may well ensue, and it should focus on setting group goals. The leader should be flexible, seeking to set goals that meet legitimate expectations of the members. If one or more expectations are beyond the objectives of the group, the leader should tactfully indicate this and explain why.

Exercise D: Searching for Descriptors

The leader passes out a list of descriptors designed for a specific group. (A descriptor is a word or phrase that identifies an item.) Some possibilities are listed below. Each group member then finds three others who say "yes" to specific descriptors. (The number "three" may be increased or decreased.) Each member should then give a completed list to the leader. The exercise may be ended by asking the members what items of interest they learned about others.

Sample descriptors

Likes professional football
Is a Leo
Plays golf
Likes classical music
Has had a paid or volunteer
  job in social work
Is dating somewhat steadily
  or is married
Has received a speeding ticket

Owns a car
Has water-skied
Has traveled in Mexico
Has meditated
Likes to jog
Enjoys riding horses
Has flown airplanes
Attends church regularly

CHAPTER TWO

SOCIAL GROUP WORK AND SOCIAL WORK PRACTICE*

Goals: This chapter presents a conceptualization of social work practice. We will see that social work with groups is an integral component of social work practice. The chapter also summarizes the Curriculum Policy Statements of the Council on Social Work Education for baccalaureate degree programs and master's degree programs in social work.

31

What do social workers do? How is social work different from psychology, psychiatry, guidance and counseling, and other helping professions? What is the relationship between social work and social welfare? What knowledge, skills, and values do social workers need to be effective? This chapter will seek to address these questions. There have been a number of other efforts to address these same issues.[1] This chapter is largely an effort to integrate these prior conceptualizations. The purpose of this chapter is to describe social work as a profession and thereby assist social workers and other interested persons in understanding and articulating what social work is and what is unique about the social work profession.

DEFINITION OF SOCIAL WORK

Social work has been defined by the National Association of Social Workers (NASW) as follows:

> Social work is the professional activity of helping individuals, groups, or communities to enhance or restore their capacity for social functioning and to create societal conditions favorable to their goals.
>
> Social work practice consists of the professional application of social work values, principles, and techniques to one or more of the following ends: helping people obtain tangible services; providing counseling and psychotherapy for individuals, families, and groups; helping communities or groups provide or improve social and health services and participating in relevant legislative processes.
>
> The practice of social work requires knowledge of human development and behavior; of social, economic, and cultural institutions; and of the interaction of all these factors.[2]

The term *social worker* is generally applied to graduates (either with bachelor's or master's degrees) of educational programs in social work who are employed in the field of social welfare. A social worker is a *change agent*, a helper who is specifically employed for the purpose of creating planned change.[3] As a change agent a social worker is expected to be skilled at working with individuals, groups, families, and organizations, and in bringing about community changes.

RELATIONSHIP BETWEEN SOCIAL WORK AND SOCIAL WELFARE

The goal of social welfare is to fulfill the social, financial, health, and recreational requirements of all individuals in a society. Social welfare seeks to enhance the social functioning of all age groups, both rich and poor. When other institutions in our society (such

---

*The material in this chapter is adapted from *The Practice of Social Work*, by Charles Zastrow. Copyright © 1994, 1992, 1989, 1985, 1981 Brooks/Cole Publishing Company, a division of International Thomson Publishing Inc., Pacific Grove, CA 93950. By permission of the publisher.

as the market economy and the family) fail at times to meet the basic needs of individuals or groups of people, then social services are needed and demanded.

Barker defines social welfare as:

> A nation's system of programs, benefits, and services that help people meet those social, economic, educational, and health needs that are fundamental to the maintenance of society.[4]

Examples of social welfare programs and services are foster care, adoption, day care, Head Start, probation and parole, public assistance programs (such as Aid to Families with Dependent Children), public health nursing, sex therapy, suicide counseling, recreational services (Boy Scouts and YWCA programs), services to minority groups and veterans, school social services, medical and legal services to the poor, family planning services, Meals on Wheels, nursing home services, shelters for battered spouses, services to persons with acquired immune deficiency syndrome (AIDS), protective services for victims of child abuse and neglect, assertiveness training, encounter groups and sensitivity training, public housing projects, family counseling, Alcoholics Anonymous, runaway services, services to people with developmental disabilities, and sheltered workshops.

Almost all social workers are employed in the field of social welfare. There are, however, many other professional and occupational groups working in the field of social welfare, as illustrated in figure 2.1.

WHAT IS THE PROFESSION OF SOCIAL WORK?

The National Association of Social Workers defines the social work profession as follows:

> The social work profession exists to provide humane and effective social services to individuals, families, groups, communities, and society so that social functioning may be enhanced and the quality of life improved. . . .
>
> The profession of social work by both traditional and practical definition, is the profession that provides the formal knowledge base, theoretical concepts, specific functional skills, and essential social values which are used to implement society's mandate to provide safe, effective, and constructive social services.[a]

Social work is thus distinct from other professions (such as psychology and psychiatry) as it is the profession that has the responsibility and mandate to provide social services.

A social worker needs training and expertise in a wide range of areas to be able to effectively handle problems faced by individuals, groups, families, organizations, and the larger community. While most professions are increasingly becoming more specialized (for example, most medical doctors now specialize in one or two areas), social work continues to emphasize a generic (broad-based) approach. The practice of social work is analogous to the old general practice of medicine. A general practitioner in medicine (or family practice) has training to handle a wide range of common medical problems faced by peo-

---

a. Published 1982, National Association of Social Workers, Inc. Reprinted with permission, from *Standards for the Classification of Social Work Practice,* Policy Statement 4, p. 5. Copyright National Association of Social Workers, Inc.

Figure 2.1: Examples of Professional Groups Within the Field of Social Welfare

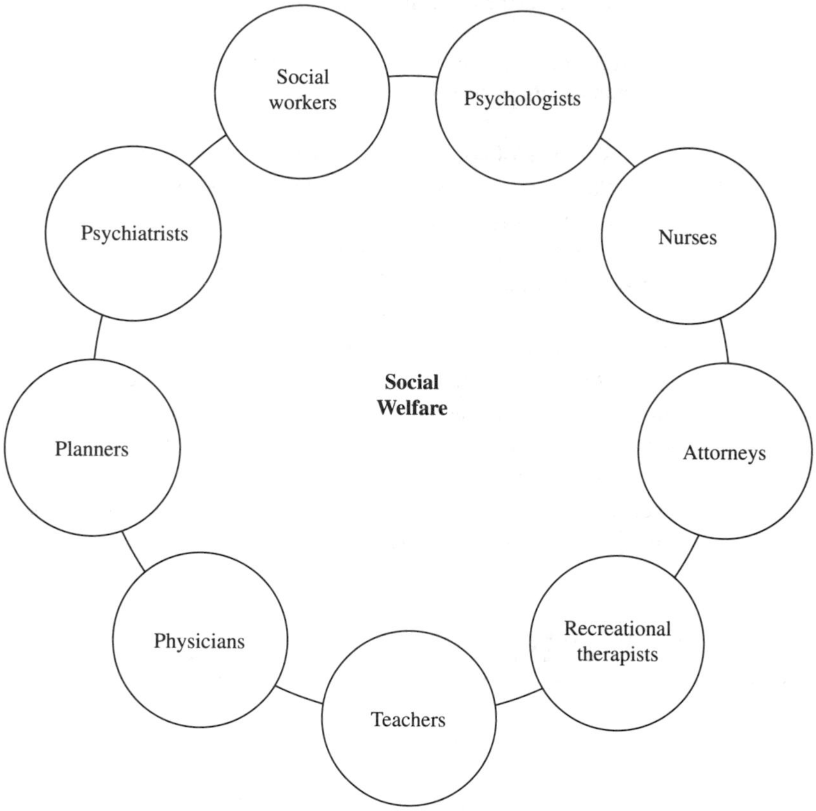

Professional people staffing social welfare services include attorneys providing legal services to the poor; urban planners in social planning agencies; physicians in public health agencies; teachers in residential treatment facilities for the emotionally disturbed; psychologists, nurses, and recreational therapists in mental hospitals; and psychiatrists in mental health clinics.

ple, while a social worker has training to handle a wide range of common social and personal problems faced by people.

GENERALIST SOCIAL WORK PRACTICE

There used to be an erroneous belief that a social worker was either a caseworker, a group worker, or a community organizer. Practicing social workers know that such a belief is faulty because every social worker is involved as a change agent in working with individuals, groups, families, organizations, and the larger community. The amount of time spent at each level varies from worker to worker, but every worker will, at times, be assigned and expected to work at these three levels and therefore needs training in all of them.

The Council on Social Work Education (the national accrediting entity for baccalaureate and master's programs in social work) requires all bachelor's level and master's level programs to train their students in generalist social work practice. (MSW programs, in addition, usually require their students to select and study in an area of specialization. MSW programs generally offer several specializations, such as family therapy, administration, corrections, and clinical social work.)

A generalist social worker is trained to use the problem-solving process to assess and intervene with the problems confronting individuals, families, groups, organizations, and communities. Anderson has identified three characteristics of a generalist social worker: (a) The generalist is often the first professional to see clients as they enter the social welfare system; (b) the worker must therefore be competent to assess clients' needs and to identify their stress points and problems; and (c) the worker must draw on a variety of skills and methods in serving clients.[5]

D. Brieland, L. B. Costin, and C. R. Atherton define and describe generalist practice as follows:

> The generalist social worker, the equivalent of the general practitioner in medicine, is characterized by a wide repertoire of skills to deal with basic conditions, backed up by specialists to whom referrals are made. This role is a fitting one for the entry-level social worker.
>
> The generalist model involves identifying and analyzing the interventive behaviors appropriate to social work. The worker must perform a wide range of tasks related to the provision and management of direct service, the development of social policy, and the facilitation of social change. The generalist should be well grounded in systems theory that emphasizes interaction and independence. The major system that will be used is the local network of services. . . .
>
> The public welfare worker in a small county may be a classic example of the generalist. He or she knows the resources of the county, is acquainted with the key people, and may have considerable influence to accomplish service goals, including obtaining jobs, different housing, or emergency food and clothing. The activities of the urban generalist are more complex, and more effort must be expended to use the array of resources.[6]

G. Hull (1990) defines generalist practice as follows:

> The basic principle of generalist practice is that baccalaureate social workers are able to utilize the problem solving process to intervene with various size systems including individuals, families, groups, organizations, and communities. The generalist operates within a systems and person-in-the-environment framework (sometimes referred to as an ecological model). The generalist expects that many problems will require intervention with more than one system (e.g., individual work with a delinquent adolescent plus work with the family or school) and that single explanations of problem situations are frequently unhelpful. The generalist may play several roles simultaneously or sequentially depending upon the needs of the client, (e.g.: facilitator, advocate, educator, broker, enabler, case manager, and/or mediator). They may serve as leaders/facilitators of task groups, socialization groups, information groups, and self-help groups. They are capable of conducting needs assessments and evaluating their own practice and the programs with which they are associated. They make referrals when client problems so dictate and know when to utilize supervision from more experienced staff. Generalists operate within the ethical guidelines prescribed by the NASW Code of Ethics and must be able to work with clients, coworkers, and colleagues from different ethnic, cultural, and professional orien-

tations. The knowledge and skills of the generalist are transferable from one setting to another and from one problem to another.[7]

The crux of generalist practice involves a view of the situation in terms of the person-in-environment conceptualization (described in an upcoming section in this chapter) and the capacity and willingness to intervene at several different levels, if necessary, while assuming any number of roles. The case example in the "Generalist Practice" box illustrates the approach of responding at several different levels in a variety of roles.

This text should facilitate readers' learning a generalist practice approach in social work by describing a variety of assessment and intervention strategies. Through learning these strategies, readers can then select those approaches that hold the most promise in facilitating positive changes in clients (who may be individuals, groups, families, organizations, or communities).

THE CHANGE PROCESS

A social worker uses a *change process* in working with clients. (Clients include individuals, groups, families, organizations, and communities.) The Council on Social Work Education, in its Curriculum Policy Statements, identifies the following eight skills needed for social work practice:

1. Defining issues
2. Collecting and assessing data
3. Planning and contracting
4. Identifying alternative interventions
5. Selecting and implementing appropriate courses of action
6. Using appropriate research to monitor and evaluate outcomes
7. Applying appropriate research-based knowledge and technological advances
8. Termination [8]

These eight skills, interestingly, provide an excellent framework for conceptualizing the phases of the change process in social work.

Phase 1: Defining Issues

Defining issues is the first step in the change process, and it often becomes complex. Let's examine the case example in the box entitled Generalist Practice Involves Options Planning. The example involves four teenagers who were expelled from high school for drinking beer at school during school hours. The school social worker, Jack Dawson, identifies a variety of issues (questions/concerns/problems), including the following: Do the youths have a drinking problem? Were the youths, disenchanted with the school system, displaying their discontent by breaking school rules? What short-term and long-term adverse effects may the expulsions have on the youths? Will the expulsions have an adverse labeling effect by marking these youths as "trouble makers," and thereby leading

CASE EXAMPLE: GENERALIST PRACTICE INVOLVES OPTIONS PLANNING

Jack Dawson is a social worker at a high school in a midwestern state. Four teenagers are expelled (consistent with school board policy) for being caught drinking alcoholic beverages at the school during school hours. Mr. Dawson assesses the situation and identifies the following potential courses of action. He can serve as an advocate for the youths by urging the school board and the administration to reinstate the youths. Mr. Dawson is aware that the expulsions are upsetting not only to the youths and their parents but also to the police department and the business community (because expelled youths tend to spend the day on the streets of the city). He can seek to involve the four teenagers in one-to-one counseling about their expulsion and their drinking patterns. He can involve these youths (along with others having drinking problems) in group counseling at the school. He can function as a broker to have the youths receive individual or group counseling from a counseling center outside the school

system. He can ascertain the willingness of the parents of these teenagers to become involved in family therapy and serve as a broker to link the interested families with a counseling center that offers family therapy. He can raise the issue (to parents, to the business community, to the police department, to the school administration, and to the school board) of whether expulsion from school for drinking alcoholic beverages is a desirable policy. (Perhaps a better school system policy, in cases like this, is to place the youths on "in school suspension," requiring them to stay in a study room for a few days.) Expulsion is a drastic measure that may adversely affect the future of these youths. Dawson can serve as an organizer and a catalyst to encourage interested parents and school staff to use the incident as a rationale for incorporating educational material on alcohol and other drugs into the curriculum. (The selected courses of action will depend on a variety of factors, including a cost-benefit analysis of each course.)

them into further delinquent behavior? How will the parents of these youths react to the drinking and to the expulsions? What effects will the expulsions have on other students at the school? (A possible positive effect: The expulsions may be a deterrent to other students who consider violating school rules. A possible negative consequence: The expulsions may encourage other students to violate school rules in order to be expelled and relieved of the obligation to attend school.) Will the expulsions create problems for merchants in the community if the expelled youths spend their days on the street? Is the school policy of expelling youths for drinking on school grounds constructive or destructive? Does the school system have a responsibility to add a drug-education component to the curriculum? Do certain aspects of the school system encourage youths to rebel? If so, should these aspects be changed?

The first step a social worker must take in a problematic situation is to identify the various issues raised by the situation. These issues will serve as a guide during the next phase (data collection and assessment).

During this initial phase (and during subsequent phases), it is essential that the worker seek to establish and continue a working relationship with the clients. A working relationship is facilitated when the worker reflects empathy, warmth, and sincerity.

Phase 2: Collecting and Assessing Data

This phase focuses on an in-depth collection and analysis of data to provide the social worker with answers to the issues raised in phase 1. On some of the issues, useful information can be obtained directly from the clients (including the youths in this example). For example, the question of whether the youths have a drinking problem can perhaps be answered by meeting individually with each of them, forming a trusting relationship, and then inquiring how often the youth drinks, how much the youth consumes when drinking, and what problems the youth has encountered while drinking. For other issues raised in phase 1, useful information must be collected from other sources. For example, the issue of short- and long-term adverse effects of the expulsion on the youths can perhaps be answered by researching the literature on this topic.

Assessment is the process of analyzing the data to make sense of it. Phase 2 also involves an assessment of the match, or fit, between the client's needs and the agency's eligibility requirements and resources. The service may be terminated for a lack of fit. The client may be referred elsewhere for service, perhaps because of the presumed superiority of some other agency's resources. Or, the fit may be deemed appropriate, and the social worker and the client then move on to the next phase.

Phase 3: Planning and Contracting

Planning includes formulating initial objectives (goals) and making decisions as to which objectives to pursue. An objective might be to seek to explore with the youths whether they have a drinking problem. Another objective might be to have the youths reinstated in school. Another might be to change the penalty for on-campus drinking from expulsion to in-school suspension. Or to add educational material about alcohol and other drug abuse to the curriculum. Often a strategy, such as cost-benefit analysis (comparing resources used to potential benefits), is used to decide which objective(s) to pursue. Rarely, in real-life situations, can social workers pursue *all* worthy objectives.

Contracting includes making arrangements with the client(s), or with organizations providing funding for the client(s), as to what services (with specified objectives) will be provided and at what cost (with specified financial arrangements).

Phase 4: Identifying Alternative Interventions

In phase 3, Jack Dawson, social worker at the high school from which four youths were expelled, selects as one of his objectives introducing the preventive approach. He will seek to add to the curriculum educational material about alcohol and other drugs. Numerous questions related to this objective now arise for Mr. Dawson. What specific material should be covered in a drug-education program? Which drugs should be included? (Mr. Dawson knows that describing certain drugs, such as LSD, may cause some parents to ask whether educational material about seldom-used drugs might encourage some youths to experiment.) *Where* should the drug-education component be added to the curriculum—in large assemblies with all students required to attend? In health classes? In social science classes? Will the school administration, teachers, school board, students, and parents affirm adding this component to the curriculum? What strategy will be most effective in gaining the support of these various groups?

As a first step in this phase, Mr. Dawson meets with his immediate supervisor, Dr. Maria Garcia, Director of Pupil Services at the high school, to discuss these issues and to generate a list of alternative strategies. Three strategies are discussed:

1. An anonymous survey could be conducted in the high school to discover the extent of alcohol and other drug use and abuse among students. Such survey results could document the need for drug education.
2. A committee of professional staff in the Pupil Services Department could develop a drug-education program.
3. The Pupil Services Department could ask the school administration and the school board to appoint a committee representing the school board, the school administration, the teachers, the students, the parents, and the Pupil Services Department. This committee would explore the need for and feasibility of a drug-education program.

Phase 5: Selecting and Implementing Appropriate Courses of Action

Mr. Dawson and Dr. Garcia decide that the best way to obtain broad support for the drug-education program is to pursue the third option listed in phase 4, above. Dr. Garcia meets with the high school principal, who—after some contemplation—agrees to explore the need for such a program. The principal, Mary Powell, requests the school board to support the formation of a committee. The school board agrees. A committee is eventually formed, and it begins holding meetings. Mr. Dawson is appointed by Dr. Garcia to be the Pupil Services' representative to this committee.

Phase 6: Using Appropriate Research to Monitor and Evaluate Outcomes

One of the first questions raised by some committee members during initial deliberations is, "If a drug-education program is developed, what specific drugs should it include?" Some committee members, as expected, are concerned that providing information about drugs not currently in use among young people in the community may encourage the use of such drugs. As a result, the Pupil Services Department is asked to conduct a student survey to identify the mind-altering drugs currently in use, and to discover the extent of such use.

A second (related) issue arising in the committee is the broader question of whether a drug-education program has preventive value, or whether such a program might promote illegal drug use. To obtain information on this issue, the Pupil Services staff research literature on the preventive value of drug-education programs across the nation. They also study the literature to find out what drug-education program formats are most effective.

After fourteen months of planning and deliberation, the committee presents to the school board its proposal for drug education. The program is designed as part of the health curriculum in the district's middle schools and high schools. One component of the proposal requires the Pupil Services Department to conduct an annual survey of a random sample of students to assess the extent of drug use/abuse and to elicit students' thoughts about the merits and shortcomings of the drug-education program. Such a survey offers a way to monitor and evaluate the program's outcomes.

Phase 7: Applying Appropriate Research-Based Knowledge and Technological Advances

The drug-education program added to the health curriculum contains the latest research-based knowledge about drugs commonly used by young people in the community. The information about these drugs includes the following: mind-altering effects, characteristics of physical and psychological dependency, and withdrawal and long-term health effects. The curriculum also contains research-based information on the most effective treatment approaches, methods of coping in a family with a drug-abusing member, ways to confront a friend or relative who is abusing, the dangers of driving under the influence of drugs, associations between drug use and sexually transmitted diseases (including AIDS), suggestions for people concerned about their own drug use, and practical ways to say "no" to drugs.

Helpful technological advances applied to this program include: computer databases that contain effective drug-education programs in other school systems, computer software for processing the surveys of student drug use and attitudes in the district, and current films and videotapes that offer age-appropriate drug-education material.

Phase 8: Termination

The committee that developed the drug-education program has its final meeting after the school board approves the proposal. At this point members may experience mixed emotions—delight that their task is successfully completed along with some regret that this group, now an important and meaningful part of their lives, has completed its task and will disband.

If a close working relationship has formed among committee members, termination is often a painful process. As issues were addressed, some dependency may have developed, and as a result members may experience a sense of loss when termination occurs.

A final evaluation is usually a part of terminating. It is extremely significant because it provides information about whether, for this situation, the committee's services have been beneficial.

A VARIETY OF ROLES

In working with individuals, groups, families, organizations, and communities, a social worker is expected to be knowledgeable and skillful in filling a variety of roles. The particular role selected should (ideally) be determined by what will be most effective, given the circumstances. The following material identifies some, but certainly not all, of the roles assumed by social workers.

Enabler

In this role a worker *helps* individuals or groups to articulate their needs, to clarify and identify their problems, to explore resolution strategies, to select and apply a strategy, and to develop their capacities to deal with problems more effectively. This role model is perhaps the most frequently used approach in counseling individuals, groups, and families. The model is also used in community practice—primarily when the objective is to help people organize to help themselves.

It should be noted that this definition of the term "enabler" is very different from the definition of "enabler" used in reference to chemical dependency. There the term refers to a family member or friend who facilitates the substance abuser in persisting in the use and abuse of drugs.

Broker

A broker links individuals and groups who need help (and do not know where to find it) with community services. For example, a wife who is physically abused by her husband might be referred to a shelter for battered women. Nowadays even moderate-sized communities have two or three hundred social service agencies/organizations providing community services. Even human services professionals are often only partially aware of the total service network in their community.

Advocate

The role of advocate has been borrowed from the law profession. It is an active, directive role in which the social worker represents a client or a citizens' group. When a client or a citizens' group is in need of help and existing institutions are uninterested (or openly negative and hostile), the advocate's role may be appropriate. The advocate provides leadership in collecting information, arguing the validity of the client's need and request, and challenging the institution's decision not to provide services. The purpose is not to ridicule or censure a particular institution but to modify or change one or more of its service policies. In this role the advocate is a partisan who is exclusively serving the interests of a client or of a citizens' group.

Empowerer

A key goal of social work practice is empowerment, the process of helping individuals, families, groups, organizations, and communities increase their personal, interpersonal, socioeconomic, and political strength and influence. Social workers who engage in empowerment-focused practice seek to develop the capacity of clients to understand their environment, make choices, take responsibility for those choices, and influence their life situations through organization and advocacy. Empowerment-focused social workers also seek a more equitable distribution of resources and power among different groups in society. This focus on equity and social justice has been a hallmark of the social work profession, as practiced by Jane Addams and other early settlement workers.

Activist

An activist seeks basic institutional change; often the objective involves a shift in power and resources to a disadvantaged group. An activist is concerned about social injustice, inequity, and deprivation. Tactics involve conflict, confrontation, and negotiation. Social action is concerned with changing the social environment in order to better meet the recognized needs of individuals. The methods used are assertive and action-oriented (for example, organizing welfare recipients to work toward improvements in services and increases in money payments). Activities of social action include fact-finding, analysis of community needs, research, dissemination and interpretation of information, organizing activities with people, and other efforts to mobilize public understanding and support on behalf of some existing or proposed social program. Social action activity can be geared toward a problem that is local, statewide, or national in scope.

Mediator

The mediator role involves intervention in disputes between parties to help them find compromises, reconcile differences, or reach mutually satisfactory agreements. Social workers have used their value orientations and unique skills in many forms of mediation (for example, divorcing spouses, neighbors in conflict, landlords and tenants, labor and management, and contenders for child custody). A mediator remains neutral, not siding with either party in the dispute. Mediators make sure they understand the positions of both parties. They may help to clarify positions, identify miscommunication about differences, and help both parties present their cases clearly.

Negotiator

A negotiator brings together people in conflict and seeks to bargain and compromise to find mutually acceptable agreements. Somewhat like mediation, negotiation involves finding a middle ground that all sides can live with. However, unlike a mediator (who maintains a neutral position) a negotiator is usually allied with one side or the other.

Educator

The educator gives information to clients and teaches them adaptive skills. To be an effective educator, the worker must first be knowledgeable. Additionally, the worker must be a good communicator so that information is conveyed clearly and is readily understood by the receiver. Examples include teaching parenting skills to young parents, instructing teenagers in job-hunting strategies, and teaching anger-control techniques to individuals with aggressive tendencies.

Initiator

An initiator calls attention to a problem or to a potential problem. It is important to recognize that sometimes a potential problem requires attention. For example, if a proposal is made to renovate a low-income neighborhood by building middle-income housing units, the initiator will be concerned that low-income residents could become homeless if the proposal is approved (because these current residents may not be able to afford middle-income units). Usually the initiator role must have some follow-up with other kinds of work. Calling attention to a problem does not usually resolve it entirely. For example, how can the low-income neighborhood be improved without displacing its residents?

Coordinator

Coordination involves bringing components together in an organized manner. For example, a multi-problem family may need help from several agencies to meet its complicated financial, emotional, legal, health, social, educational, recreational, and interactional needs. Frequently someone at an agency must assume the role of case manager to coordinate services from different agencies and avoid both duplication of services and conflict among the services.

Researcher

At times every worker is a researcher. Research in social work practice includes: reading literature on topics of interest, evaluating the outcomes of one's practice, assessing the merits and shortcomings of programs, and studying community needs.

Group Facilitator

A group facilitator serves as a leader for a group experience. This may be a therapy group, an educational group, a self-help group, a sensitivity group, a family therapy group, or a group with some other focus.

Public Speaker

Social workers occasionally talk to a variety of groups (e.g., high school classes; public service organizations such as Kiwanis; police officers, staff at other agencies) to inform them of available services, or to argue the need for new services. In recent years a variety of new services have been identified (for example, runaway centers, services for battered spouses, rape crisis centers, services for persons with AIDS, and group homes for youth). Social workers with public speaking skills are not only better able to interpret services to groups of potential clients, but probably also earn a few thousand dollars more each year.

A SYSTEMS PERSPECTIVE

Social workers are trained to take a systems perspective on their work with individuals, groups, families, organizations, and communities. A systems perspective emphasizes looking beyond the presenting problems of clients in order to assess the complexities and interrelationships of their problems. A systems perspective is based on systems theory. Key concepts of general systems theory are *wholeness, relationship*, and *homeostasis*.

The concept of *wholeness* means that the objects or elements within a system produce an entity greater than the additive sums of the separate parts. Systems theory is antireductionistic, asserting that no system can be adequately understood or totally explained once it has been broken down into its component parts. (For example, the central nervous system is able to carry out thought processes that would not be revealed if only the parts were observed.)

The concept of *relationship* asserts that the pattern and structure of the elements in a system are as important as the elements themselves. For example, Masters and Johnson have found that sexual dysfunctions primarily occur due to the nature of the relationship between husband and wife, rather than to the psychological makeup of the partners in a marriage system.[9]

Systems theory opposes simple cause-and-effect explanations. For example, whether a child will be abused in a family is determined by a variety of variables and the patterns of these variables: such as parents' capacity to control their anger, relationships between child and parents, relationships between parents, degree of psychological stress, characteristics of child, and opportunities for socially acceptable ways for parents to ventilate anger.

The concept of *homeostasis* suggests that living systems seek a balance to maintain and preserve the system. Jackson, for example, has noted that families tend to establish a behavioral balance or stability and to resist any change from that predetermined level of stability.[10] Emergence of the state of imbalance (generated either within or outside the marriage) ultimately acts to restore the homeostatic balance of the family. If one child in a family is abused, that abuse often serves a function as indicated by the fact that if that child is removed, a second child is often abused. Or, if one family member improves through seeking counseling, that improvement will generally upset the balance within the family; and other family members will have to make changes (such changes may be adaptive or maladaptive) to adjust to the new behavior of the improved family member.

Ecological theory is a subcategory of systems theory. Ecological theory has become prominent in social work practice, as discussed in the next section.

MEDICAL MODEL VS. ECOLOGICAL MODEL OF HUMAN BEHAVIOR

From the 1920s to the 1960s most social workers used a medical model approach to assessing and changing human behavior. This approach was initiated primarily by Sigmund Freud. It views clients as *patients*. The task of the provider of services is first to diagnose the causes of a patient's problems and then to provide treatment. The patient's problems are viewed as being inside the patient.

Medical Model

In regard to emotional and behavioral problems of people, the medical model conceptualizes such problems as *mental illnesses*. People with emotional or behavioral problems are then given medical labels, such as schizophrenia, paranoia, psychosis, and insanity. Adherents of the medical approach believe the disturbed person's mind is affected by some generally unknown internal condition. That unknown internal condition is thought to result from a variety of possible causative factors: genetic endowment, metabolic disorders, infectious diseases, internal conflicts, unconscious uses of defense mechanisms, and traumatic early experiences that cause emotional fixations and prevent future psychological growth.

The medical model has a lengthy classification of mental disorders that are defined by the American Psychiatric Association. The major categories of mental disorders are listed in table 2.1.

The medical model approach arose in reaction to the historical notion that the emotionally disturbed were possessed by demons, were mad, and were to be blamed for their disturbances. These people were "treated" by being beaten, locked up, or killed. The medical model led to viewing the disturbed as in need of help, stimulated research into the nature of emotional problems, and promoted the development of therapeutic approaches.

Table 2.1:

Major Mental Disorders According to the American Psychiatric Association

Disorders Usually First Diagnosed in Infancy, Childhood, or Adolescence
These include, but are not limited to, mental retardation, learning disorders, communication disorders (such as stuttering), autism, attention-deficit/hyperactivity disorder, and separation anxiety disorder.

Delirium, Dementia, and Amnestic and Other Cognitive Disorders
These include delirium due to alcohol and other drug intoxication, dementia due to Alzheimer's disease or Parkinson's disease, dementia due to head trauma, and amnestic disorder.

Substance-Related Disorders
This category includes mental disorders related to abuse of alcohol, caffeine, amphetamines, cocaine, hallucinogens, nicotine, and other mind-altering substances.

Schizophrenia and Other Psychotic Disorders
This category includes delusional disorders and all forms of schizophrenia (such as paranoid, disorganized, and catatonic).

Mood Disorders
This category includes emotional disorders such as depression and bipolar disorders.

Anxiety Disorders
This category includes phobias, post traumatic stress disorder, and other anxiety disorders.

Somatoform Disorders
This category includes psychological problems that manifest themselves as symptoms of physical disease (for example, hypochondria).

Dissociative Disorders
This category includes problems in which part of the personality is dissociated from the rest (for example, dissociative identity disorder—formerly called multiple personality disorder).

Sexual and Gender Identity Disorders
This category includes sexual dysfunctions (such as hypoactive sexual desire, premature ejaculation, male erectile disorder, male and female orgasmic disorders, and vaginismus), exhibitionism, fetishism, pedophilia (child molestation), sexual masochism, sexual sadism, voyeurism, and gender identity disorders (such as cross-gender indentification).

Eating Disorders
This category includes anorexia nervosa and bulimia nervosa.

Sleep Disorders
This category includes insomnia and other problems with sleep (such as nightmares and sleepwalking).

Impulse-Control Disorders
This category includes the inability to control certain undesirable impulses (for example, kleptomania, pyromania, and pathological gambling).

Adjustment Disorders
This category includes difficulties in adjusting to the stress created by such common events as unemployment or divorce.

Personality Disorders
A personality disorder is an enduring pattern of inner experience and behavior that deviates markedly from the expectations of the individual's culture, is pervasive and inflexible, has an onset in adolescence or early adulthood, is stable over time, and leads to distress or impairment. Examples include paranoid personality disorder, antisocial personality disorder, and obsessive-compulsive personality disorder.

Other Conditions
This category includes a variety of "other" disorders that may be the focus of clinical attention—parent-child relational problems; partner relational problems; sibling relational problems; child victims of physical abuse, sexual abuse, and neglect; adult victims of physical abuse and sexual abuse; malingering; bereavement; academic problems; occupational problems; identity problems; and religious or spiritual problems.

Source: *DSM–IV (The Diagnostic and Statistical Manual of Mental Disorders)*, 4th ed. (Washington, D.C.: American Psychiatric Association, 1994).

The major evidence for the validity of the medical model approach comes from studies suggesting that some mental disorders, such as schizophrenia, may be influenced by genetics (heredity). The bulk of the evidence for the importance of heredity comes from studies of twins. For instance, in a sample of over fifteen thousand twins, Hofer and Polin found a concordance rate (if one has it, both have it) for schizophrenia of 15.5 percent for identical twins and 4.4 percent for fraternal twins. Critics of such studies argue that the findings may be flawed, claiming that the physical similarity of identical twins leads their family and friends to treat them alike. However, there is some research suggesting a higher concordance rate for schizophrenia among identical twins even when they have been raised apart.[12]

Ecological Model

In the 1960s social work began questioning the usefulness of the medical model. Environmental factors were shown to be at least as important in causing a client's problems as internal factors. Research also was demonstrating that psychoanalysis was probably ineffective in treating clients' problems.[13]

In the 1960s social work shifted at least some of its emphasis to a *reform approach*. A reform approach seeks to change systems to benefit clients. The enactment of the anti-poverty programs (such as Head Start) in the 1960s is an example of an effort to change systems to benefit clients.

In the past several years social work has increasingly focused on using an *ecological approach*. This approach integrates both treatment and reform by conceptualizing and emphasizing the dysfunctional transactions between people and their physical and social environments. Human beings are viewed as developing and adapting through transactions with all elements of their environments. An ecological model gives attention to both internal and external factors. It does not view people as passive reactors to their environments, but rather as actively involved in dynamic and reciprocal interactions with them.

It tries to improve the coping patterns of people in their environments so that a better match can be attained between an individual's needs and the characteristics of his or her environment. One of the emphases of an ecological model is on the person-in-environment. The person-in-environment conceptualization is depicted in figure 2.2.

Figure 2.2 suggests that people interact with many systems. With this conceptualization, social work can focus on three separate areas. First, it can focus on the person and seek to develop his problem-solving, coping, and developmental capacities. Second, it can focus on the relationship between a person and the systems he or she interacts with and link the person with needed resources, services, and opportunities. Third, it can focus on the systems and seek to reform them to meet the needs of the individual more effectively.

The ecological model views individuals, families, and small groups as having transitional problems and needs as they move from one life stage to another. Individuals face many transitional changes as they grow older. Examples of some of the transitions are learning to walk, entering first grade, adjusting to puberty, graduating from school, finding a job, getting married, having children, having children leave home, and retiring.

Families also have a life cycle. The following are only a few of the events that require adjustment: engagement, marriage, birth of children, parenting, children going to school, children leaving home, and loss of a parent (perhaps through death or divorce).

Figure 2.2: Person-in-Environment Conceptualization

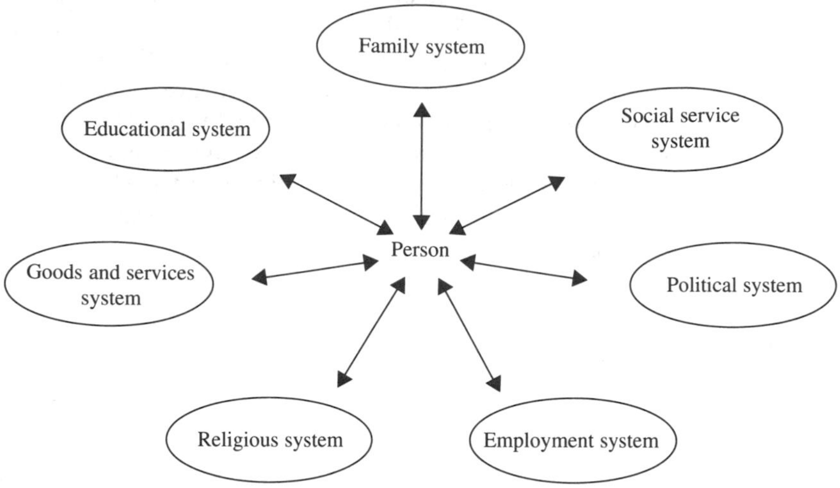

People in our society continually interact with many systems, some of which are listed in this figure.

Small groups also have transitional phases of development. Members of small groups spend time getting acquainted, gradually learn to trust each other, begin to self-disclose more, learn to work together on tasks, develop approaches to handle interpersonal conflict, and face adjustments to the group's eventual termination or to the departure of some members.

A central concern of an ecological model is to articulate the transitional problems and needs of individuals, families, and small groups. Once these problems and needs are identified, intervention approaches are then selected and applied to help individuals, families, and small groups resolve the transitional problems and meet their needs.

An ecological model can also focus on the maladaptive interpersonal problems and needs in families and groups. It can seek to articulate the maladaptive communication processes and dysfunctional relationship patterns of families and small groups. These difficulties cover an array of areas, including interpersonal conflicts, power struggles, double binds, distortions in communicating, scapegoating, and discrimination. The consequences of such difficulties are usually maladaptive for some members. An ecological model seeks to identify such interpersonal obstacles and then apply appropriate intervention strategies. For example, parents may set the price for honesty too high for their children. In such families children gradually learn to hide certain behaviors and thoughts, and even learn to lie. If the parents discover such dishonesty, an uproar usually occurs. An appropriate intervention in such a family is to open up communication patterns and help the parents to understand that if they really want honesty from their children, they need to learn to be more accepting of their children's thoughts and actions.

Two centuries ago people interacted primarily within the family system. Families were nearly self-sufficient. In those days, the *person-in-family* was a way of conceptualizing the main system which individuals interacted with. Our society has become much more complex. Today, a person's life and quality of life are interwoven and interdependent upon many systems, as shown in figure 2.2.

GOALS OF SOCIAL WORK PRACTICE

The National Association of Social Workers has conceptualized social work practice as having four major goals:[14]

Goal 1: Enhance the Clients' Problem-Solving, Coping, and Developmental Capacities

Using the person-in-environment concept, the focus of social work practice at this level is on the "person." With this focus a social worker serves primarily as an *enabler*. In the role of an enabler, the worker may take on activities of a counselor, teacher, care giver (i.e., providing supportive services to those who cannot fully solve their problems and meet their own needs), and behavior changer (i.e., changing specific parts of a client's behavior).

Goal 2: Link Clients with Systems That Provide Resources, Services, and Opportunities

Using the person-in-environment concept, the focus of social work practice at this level is on the relationships between persons and the systems they interact with. With this focus a social worker serves primarily as a *broker*.

Goal 3: Promote the Effective and Humane Operation of Systems That Provide Resources and Services

Using the person-in-environment concept, the focus of social work practice at this level is on the systems people interact with. One role a worker may fill at this level is that of an advocate. Additional roles at this level are:

Program developer: The worker in this role seeks to promote or design programs or technologies to meet social needs.
Supervisor: The worker in this role seeks to increase the effectiveness and efficiency of the delivery of services through supervising other staff.
Coordinator: The worker in this role seeks to improve a delivery system through increasing communications and coordination among human service resources.
Consultant: The worker in this role seeks to provide guidance to agencies and organi-

zations through suggesting ways to increase the effectiveness and efficiency of services.

Goal 4: Develop and Improve Social Policy

Similar to goal three, the focus of social work practice at this level is on the systems people interact with. The distinction between goal three and goal four is that the focus of goal three is on the resources available for serving people, while the focus of goal four is on the statutes and broader social policies that underlie such resources. Major roles of social workers at this level are *planner* and *policy developer*. In these roles, workers develop and seek adoption of new statutes or policies and propose elimination of ineffective or inappropriate statutes and policies. In these planning and policy development processes, social workers may take on an advocate role and, in some instances, an activist role.

A closely related, but somewhat different, conceptualization of the purpose (that incorporates the goals) of social work practice has recently been formulated by the Council on Social Work Education.[15] The Council on Social Work Education (CSWE) is the national accreditating body for social work education in the United States. CSWE defines the purpose of social work as follows:

> The profession of social work is committed to the enhancement of human well-being and to the alleviation of poverty and oppression. The social work profession receives its sanction from public and private auspices and is the primary profession in the provision of social services. Within its general scope of concern, professional social work is practiced in a wide variety of settings and has four related purposes:
>
> 1. The promotion, restoration, maintenance, and enhancement of the functioning of individuals, families, groups, organizations, and communities by helping them to accomplish tasks, prevent and alleviate distress, and use resources.
> 2. The planning, formulation, and implementation of social policies, services, resources, and programs needed to meet basic human needs and support the development of human capacities.
> 3. The pursuit of policies, services, resources, and programs through organizational or administrative advocacy and social or political action, so as to empower groups at risk and promote social and economic justice.
> 4. The development and testing of professional knowledge and skills related to these purposes.[b]

This definition of the purpose of social work differs from NASW's definition of the goals of social work practice in the following important ways. This definition emphasizes that social work has a commitment to "the enhancement of human well-being and to the alleviation of poverty and oppression." The definition identifies the client systems of social work practice as "individuals, families, groups, organizations, and communities." The

---

b. This material was first published by the Council on Social Work Education in the Curriculum Policy Statements for Baccalaureate Degree and Master's Degree Programs (1992). It is reprinted here with the permission of the Council on Social Work Education.

definition, in effect, adds two goals to NASW's listing of goals of social work practice: (1) "to empower groups at risk and promote social and economic justice," and (2) the "development and testing of professional knowledge and skills."

Readers of these two definitions of the goals (purposes) of social work should not view these definitions as inconsistent. Rather, each identifies important goals/purposes to which all social workers must attend.

A PROBLEM-SOLVING APPROACH

In working with individuals, families, groups, organizations, and communities, social workers use a problem-solving approach. Steps in the problem-solving process can be stated in a variety of ways. Below is a simple statement of this process:

1. Identify as precisely as possible the problem or problems.
2. Generate possible alternative solutions.
3. Evaluate the alternative solutions.
4. Select a solution or solutions to be used, and set goals.
5. Implement the solution(s).
6. Follow up to evaluate how the solution(s) worked.

(Note that another conceptualization of the problem-solving approach is the change-process view of social work practice, which was described earlier in this chapter.)

MICRO, MEZZO, AND MACRO PRACTICE

Social workers practice at three levels: (*a*) micro—working on a one-to-one basis with an individual, (*b*) mezzo—working with families and other small groups, and (*c*) macro—working with organizations and communities, or seeking changes in statutes and social policies.

The specific activities performed by workers include, but are not limited to, the following:

Social Casework

Aimed at helping individuals on a one-to-one basis to meet personal and social problems, casework may be geared to helping the client adjust to his/her environment, or to changing certain social and economic pressures that are adversely affecting an individual. Social casework services are provided by nearly every social welfare agency that provides direct services to people. Social casework encompasses a wide variety of activities, such as counseling runaway youths; helping unemployed people secure training or employment; counseling someone who is suicidal; placing a homeless child in an adoptive or foster home; providing protective services to abused children and their families; finding nursing homes for stroke victims who no longer need to be confined to a hospital; counseling individuals with sexual dysfunctions; helping alcoholics to acknowledge they have a drinking problem; counseling those with a terminal illness; being a probation and parole officer; providing services to single parents; and working in medical and mental hospitals as a member of a rehabilitation team.

Case Management

Recently a number of social service agencies have labeled their social workers *case managers*. The tasks performed by case managers are similar to those of caseworkers. The job descriptions of case managers vary from service area to service area. For example, case managers in a juvenile probation setting are highly involved in supervising clients, providing some counseling, monitoring clients to make certain they are following the rules of probation, linking clients and their families with needed services, preparing court reports, and testifying in court. On the other hand, case managers at a sheltered workshop are apt to be involved in providing job training to clients, counseling clients, arranging transportation, disciplining clients for unacceptable behavior, acting as an advocate for clients, and acting as liaison with the people who supervise clients during their nonwork hours (at a group home, foster home, residential treatment facility, or their parent's home). Hepworth and Larsen describe the role of a case manager as follows:

> Case managers link clients to needed resources that exist in complex service delivery networks and orchestrate the delivery of services in a timely fashion. Case managers function as brokers, facilitators, linkers, mediators, and advocates. A case manager must have extensive knowledge of community resources, rights of clients, and policies and procedures of various agencies, and must be skillful in mediation and advocacy.[16]

Barker defines case management as follows:

> A procedure to plan, seek, and monitor services for a variety of agencies and staff on behalf of a client. Usually one agency takes primary responsibility for the client and assigns a case manager, who coordinates services, advocates for the client, and sometimes controls resources and purchases services for the client. The procedure makes it possible for many social workers in an agency, or in different agencies, to coordinate their efforts to serve a given client through professional teamwork, thus expanding the range of needed services offered. Case management may involve monitoring the progress of a client whose needs require the services of many different professionals, agencies, health care facilities, and human service programs.[17]

Group Work

The intellectual, emotional, and social development of individuals may be furthered through group activities. In contrast to casework or group therapy, it is not primarily therapeutic, except in a broad sense. Different groups have different objectives, such as socialization, information exchange, curbing delinquency, recreation, changing socially unacceptable values, and helping to achieve better relations between cultural and racial groups. For example, a group worker at a neighborhood center may through group activities seek to curb delinquency patterns and change socially unacceptable values; or a worker at an adoption agency may meet with a group of applicants to explain adoption procedures and to help applicants prepare for becoming adoptive parents. Activities and focuses of groups vary: arts and crafts; dancing; games; dramatics; music; photography; sports, nature study; woodwork; first aid; home management; information exchange; and discussion of such topics as politics, sex, marriage, religion, and career selection.

Group Therapy

Group therapy is aimed at facilitating the social, behavioral, and emotional adjustment of individuals through the group process. Participants in group therapy usually have emotional, interactional, or behavioral difficulties. Group therapy has several advantages over one-to-one counseling, such as the operation of the *helper therapy* principle, which maintains it is therapeutic for the helper (who can be any member of a group) to feel he or she has been helpful to others.[18] In contrast to one-to-one counseling, group pressure is often more effective in changing maladaptive behavior of individuals, and group therapy is a time saver as it enables the therapist to treat several people at the same time. A few examples in which group therapy might be used are for individuals who are severely depressed, have drinking problems, are victims of a rape, are psychologically addicted to drugs, have a relative who is terminally ill, are single and pregnant, are recently divorced, or have an eating disorder.

Family Therapy

A type of group therapy aimed at helping families with interactional, behavioral, and emotional problems, family therapy can be used with parent-child interaction problems, marital conflicts, and conflicts with grandparents. A wide variety of problems are dealt with in family therapy or family counseling, such as disagreements between parents and youths on choice of friends, drinking and other drug use, domestic tasks, curfew hours, communication problems, sexual values and behavior, study habits and grades received, and choice of dates.

Community Organization

The aim of community organization is to stimulate and assist the local community to evaluate, plan, and coordinate efforts to provide for the community's health, welfare, and recreation needs. It perhaps is not possible to define precisely the activities of a community organizer, but such activities are apt to include encouraging and fostering citizen participation, coordinating efforts between agencies or between groups, public relations and public education, research, planning, and resource management. A community organizer acts as a catalyst in stimulating and encouraging community action. Agency settings where such specialists are apt to be employed include community welfare councils, social planning agencies, health planning councils, and community action agencies. The term *community organization* is now being replaced in some settings by such labels as *planning, social planning, program development, policy development*, and *macro practice*.

Barker defines community organization as:

> An intervention process used by social workers and other professionals to help individuals, groups, and collectives of people with common interests or from the same geographic areas to deal with social problems and to enhance social well-being through planned collective action. Methods include identifying problem areas, analyzing causes, formulating plans, developing strategies, mobilizing necessary resources, identifying and recruiting community leaders, and encouraging interrelationships between them to facilitate their efforts.[19]

Policy Analysis

Policy analysis involves the systematic evaluation of a policy and the process by which it was formulated. Those who conduct such an analysis consider whether the process and the result were clear, equitable, legal, rational, compatible with social values, superior to the alternatives, cost-effective, and explicit. Frequently such an analysis identifies certain shortcomings in the policy, and those conducting the policy analysis then usually recommend modifications designed to alleviate these shortcomings.

Administration

Administration is the activity that involves directing the overall program of a social service agency. Administrative functions include setting agency and program objectives, analyzing social conditions in the community, making decisions relating to what services will be provided, employing and supervising staff members, setting up an organizational structure, administering financial affairs, and securing funds for the agency's operations. Administration also involves setting organizational goals, coordinating activities toward the achievement of selected goals, and making and monitoring necessary changes in processes and structure to improve effectiveness and efficiency. In social work, the term administration is often used synonomously with management. In a small agency, administrative functions may be carried out by one person, while in a larger agency several people may be involved in administrative affairs.

Other areas of professional activity in social work include research, consulting, supervision, planning, program development, and teaching (primarily at the college level). The ability to study and evaluate one's own practice and to evaluate programs is an important skill for a social worker. Skills essential for social work practice are described further in the next section: Generalist social workers are expected to have an extensive knowledge base, to possess numerous skills, and to adhere to a well-defined set of professional social work values.

KNOWLEDGE, SKILLS, AND VALUES NEEDED FOR SOCIAL WORK PRACTICE

Knowledge

The knowledge needed for effective social work practice has been identified by NASW as follows:

- Knowledge of casework and group work theory and techniques
- Knowledge of community resources and services
- Knowledge of basic federal and state social service programs and their purposes
- Knowledge of community organization theory and the development of health and welfare services
- Knowledge of basic socioeconomic and political theory
- Knowledge of racial, ethnic, and other cultural groups in society—their values and lifestyles and the resultant issues in contemporary life
- Knowledge of sources of professional and scientific research appropriate to practice
- Knowledge of the concepts and techniques of social planning
- Knowledge of the theories and concepts of supervision and the professional supervision of social worker practice
- Knowledge of theories and concepts of personnel management
- Knowledge of common social and psychological statistical and other research methods and techniques
- Knowledge of the theories and concepts of social welfare administration
- Knowledge of social and environmental factors affecting clients to be served
- Knowledge of the theories and methods of psychosocial assessment and intervention and of differential diagnosis
- Knowledge of the theory and behavior of organizational and social systems and of methods for encouraging change
- Knowledge of community organization theory and techniques
- Knowledge of the theories of human growth and development and of family and social interaction
- Knowledge of small-group theory and behavioral dynamics
- Knowledge of the theories of group interaction and therapeutic intervention
- Knowledge of crisis intervention theories and techniques
- Knowledge of advocacy theory and techniques
- Knowledge of the ethical standards and practices of professional social work
- Knowledge of teaching and instructional theories and techniques
- Knowledge of social welfare trends and policies
- Knowledge of local, state, and federal laws and regulations affecting social and health services[c]

---

c. Published in 1982, National Association of Social Workers, Inc. Reprinted with permission, from *Standards for the Classification of Social Work Practice,* Policy Statement 4, p. 17. Copyright National Association of Social Workers, Inc.

The Council on Social Work Education has categorized the knowledge needed by social workers in ten broad content areas. Every accredited social work educational program is expected to provide the following content, which is excerpted from the 1992 curriculum policy statement.[20]

Liberal Arts Perspective

A liberal arts perspective enriches understanding of the person-environment context of professional social work practice and is integrally related to the mastery of social work content. The baccalaureate professional program in social work is built upon a liberal arts perspective.

A liberal arts perspective provides an understanding of one's cultural heritage in the context of other cultures; the methods and limitations of various systems of inquiry; and the knowledge, attitudes, ways of thinking, and means of communication that are characteristic of a broadly educated person. Students must be capable of thinking critically about society, about people and their problems, and about such expressions of culture as art, literature, science, history, and philosophy. Students must have direct knowledge about social, psychological, and biological determinants of human behavior and of diverse cultures, social conditions, and social problems.

Social Work Values and Ethics

Programs of social work education must provide specific knowledge about social work values and their ethical implications and must provide opportunities for students to demonstrate their application in professional practice. Students must be assisted to develop an awareness of their personal values and to clarify conflicting values and ethical dilemmas.

Diversity

Professional social work education is committed to preparing students to understand and appreciate human diversity. Programs must provide curriculum content about differences and similarities in the experiences, needs, and beliefs of people. The curriculum must include content about differential assessment and intervention skills that will enable practitioners to serve diverse populations.

Each program is required to include content about population groups that are particularly relevant to the program's mission. These include, but are not limited to, groups distinguished by race, ethnicity, culture, class, gender, sexual orientation, religion, physical or mental disability, age, and national origin.

Promotion of Social and Economic Justice

Programs of social work education must provide an understanding of the dynamics and consequences of social and economic injustice, including all forms of human oppression and discrimination. They must provide students with the skills to promote social change and to implement a wide range of interventions that further the achievement of individual and collective social and economic justice. Theoretical and practice content must be provided about strategies of intervention for achieving social and economic justice and for combatting the causes and effects of institutionalized forms of oppression.

Populations-at-Risk

Programs of social work education must present theoretical and practice content about patterns, dynamics, and consequences of discrimination, economic deprivation, and oppression. The curriculum must provide content about people of color, women, and gay and lesbian persons. Such content must emphasize the impact of discrimination, economic deprivation, and oppression upon these groups.

Each program must include content about populations-at-risk that are particularly relevant to its mission. In addition to those mandated above, such groups include, but are not limited to, those distinguished by age, ethnicity, culture, class, religion, and physical or mental ability.

Human Behavior and the Social Environment

Programs of social work education must provide content about theories and knowledge of human bio-psycho-social development, including theories and knowledge about the range of social systems in which individuals live (families, groups, organizations, institutions, and communities). The human behavior and the social environment curriculum must provide an understanding of the interactions between and among human biological, social, psychological, and cultural systems as they affect and are affected by human behavior. The impact of social and economic forces on individuals and social systems must be presented. Content must be provided about the ways in which systems promote or deter people in the maintenance or attainment of optimal health and well-being. Content about values and ethical issues related to bio-psycho-social theories must be included. Students must be taught to evaluate theory and apply theory to client situations.

Social Welfare Policy and Services

Social welfare policy and services content must include the history, mission, and philosophy of the social work profession. Content must be presented about the history and current patterns of provision of social welfare services, the role of social policy in helping or deterring people in the maintenance or attainment of optimal health and well-being, and the effect of policy on social work practice. Students must be taught to analyze current social policy within the context of historical and contemporary factors that shape policy. Content must be presented about the political and organizational processes used to influence policy, the process of policy formulation, and the frameworks for analyzing social policies in light of the principles of social and economic justice.

Social Work Practice

At the baccalaureate level, professional social work education prepares students for generalist practice with systems of all sizes. Practice content emphasizes professional relationships that are characterized by mutuality, collaboration, and respect for the client system. Content on practice assessment focuses on the examination of client strengths and problems in the interactions among individuals and between people and their environments.

Social work practice content must include knowledge, values, and skills to enhance the well-being of people and to help ameliorate the environmental conditions that affect people adversely. Practice content must include the following skills: defining issues; collecting and assessing data; planning and contracting; identifying alternative interventions; selecting and implementing appropriate courses of action; using appropriate research to monitor and evaluate outcomes; applying appropriate research-based knowledge and technological advances; and termination. Practice content also includes approaches and skills for practice with clients from differing social, cultural, racial, religious, spiritual, and class backgrounds and with systems of all sizes.

Research

The research curriculum must provide an understanding and appreciation of a scientific, analytic approach to building knowledge for practice and for evaluating service delivery in all areas of practice. Ethical standards of scientific inquiry must be included in the research content.

The research content must include quantitative and qualitative research methodologies; analysis of data, including statistical procedures; systematic evaluation of practice; analysis and evaluation of theoretical bases, research questions, methodologies, statistical procedures, and conclusions of research reports; and relevant technological advances.

Each program must identify how the research curriculum contributes to the student's use of scientific knowledge for practice.

Field Practicum

The field practicum is an integral component of the curriculum in social work education. It engages the student in supervised social work practice and provides opportunities to apply classroom learning in the field setting.

The baccalaureate practicum must provide the student with opportunities for:

a. The development of an awareness of self in the process of intervention.
b. Supervised practice experience in the application of knowledge, values and ethics, and practice skills to enhance the well-being of people and to work toward the amelioration of environmental conditions that affect people adversely.
c. Use of oral and written professional communications that are consistent with the language of the practicum setting and of the profession.
d. Use of professional supervision to enhance learning.
e. Critical assessment, implementation, and evaluation of agency policy within ethical guidelines.[d]

The curriculum at the master's level in social work must also be based on a liberal arts perspective. The statement of this perspective is very similar to the statement given above for the liberal arts perspective at the baccalaureate level. The curriculum at the master's level is mandated by the Curriculum Policy Statement of the Council on Social Work Education to be composed of: a) professional foundation content, and b) concentration content in an area. Each of these two components will be briefly described.

The professional foundation includes content on social work values and ethics, diversity, promotion of social and economic justice, populations-at-risk, human behavior and the social environment, social welfare policy and services, social work practice, research, and field practicum. The description of these areas in the Master's Level Curriculum Policy Statement is nearly identical to the description of these areas in the Baccalaureate Level Curriculum Policy Statement, and therefore will not be repeated.

Concentration content includes knowledge, values, and skills for advanced practice in an identifiable area. Identifiable areas frequently offered by master's programs include fields of practice, problem areas, populations-at-risk, and intervention methods or roles.

(This text provides material primarily in the "social work practice" content area. The text also includes material on social work values and ethics, diversity, promotion of social and economic justice, and populations-at-risk.)

---

d. This material was first published by the Council on Social Work Education and is reprinted here with the permission of the Council.

Core Practice Skills

There have been a number of efforts to articulate the essential skills for entry-level social work practice positions. A few of these conceptualizations will be presented to indicate contemporary thinking about core practice skills. It should be noted that there are a number of similarities between these conceptualizations, but there is *not* yet full agreement on these core skills.

Federico has indirectly described social work skills by outlining roles and activities:

1. *Outreach worker*—reaches out into the community to identify needs and follow up referrals to service contexts.
2. *Broker*—knows services available and makes sure those in need reach the appropriate services.
3. *Advocate*—helps specific clients obtain services when they might otherwise be rejected, and helps to expand services to cover more needy persons.
4. *Evaluation*—evaluates needs and resources, generates alternatives for meeting needs, and makes decisions between alternatives.
5. *Teacher*—teaches facts and skills.
6. *Mobilizer*—helps to develop new services.
7. *Behavior changer*—changes specific parts of a client's behavior.
8. *Consultant*—works with other professionals to help them be more effective in providing services.
9. *Community planner*—helps community groups plan effectively for the community's social welfare needs.
10. *Care giver*—provides supportive services to those who cannot fully solve their problems and meet their own needs.
11. *Data manager*—collects and analyzes data for decision-making purposes.
12. *Administrator*—performs the activities necessary to plan and implement a program of services.[21]

Baer has identified the following ten competencies as being essential for successfully performing the responsibilities of entry-level positions:

1. Identify and assess situations in which the relationship between people and social institutions needs to be initiated, enhanced, restored, protected, or terminated.
2. Develop and implement a plan for improving the well-being of people, based on problem assessment and the exploration of obtainable goals and available options.
3. Enhance the problem-solving, coping, and developmental capacities of people.
4. Link people with systems that provide them with resources, services, and opportunities.
5. Intervene effectively on behalf of populations most vulnerable and discriminated against.
6. Promote the effective and humane operation of the systems that provide people with services, resources, and opportunities.
7. Actively participate with others in creating new, modified, or improved service, resource, or opportunity systems that are more equitable, just, and responsive to consumers of services; work with others to eliminate unjust systems.

8. Evaluate the extent to which the objectives of the intervention plan were achieved.
9. Continually evaluate one's professional growth and development through assessment of practice behaviors and skills.
10. Contribute to the improvement of service delivery by adding to the knowledge base of the profession as appropriate and supporting and upholding the standards and ethics of the profession.[22]

These ten competencies were originally developed by Baer and Federico.[23]

NASW has identified the following skills as essential for social work practice:

Skill in listening to others with understanding and purpose.
Skill in eliciting information and in assembling relevant facts to prepare a social history, assessment, and report.
Skill in creating and maintaining professional helping relationships and in using oneself in relationships.
Skill in observing and interpreting verbal and nonverbal behavior and in using a knowledge of personality theory and diagnostic methods.
Skill in engaging clients in efforts to resolve their own problems and in gaining trust.
Skill in discussing sensitive emotional subjects in a nonthreatening supportive manner.
Skill in creating innovative solutions to clients' needs.
Skill in determining the need to end therapeutic relationships and how to do so.
Skill in interpreting the findings of research studies and professional literature.
Skill in mediating and negotiating between conflicting parties.
Skill in providing interorganizational liaison services.
Skill in interpreting or communicating social needs to funding sources, the public, or legislators.[e]

Closely related to conceptualizing essential skills, NASW has identified the following abilities as being needed for social work practice:

Ability to speak and write clearly.
Ability to teach others.
Ability to respond supportively in emotion-laden or crisis situations.
Ability to serve as a role model in a professional relationship.
Ability to interpret complex psychosocial phenomena.
Ability to organize a workload to meet designated responsibilities.
Ability to identify and obtain resources needed to assist others.
Ability to assess one's performance and feelings, and to use help or consultation.
Ability to participate in and lead group activities.
Ability to function under stress.
Ability to deal with conflict situations or contentious personalities.
Ability to relate social and psychological theory to practice situations.

---

e. Published 1982, National Association of Social Workers, Inc. Reprinted with permission, from *Standards for the Classification of Social Work Practice,* Policy Statement 4, p. 17–18. Copyright National Association of Social Workers, Inc.

Ability to identify the information necessary to solve a problem.
Ability to conduct research studies of agency services or one's practice.[f]

In its Curriculum Policy Statements for both the baccalaureate and master's degree programs, the Council on Social Work Education mandates social work programs that provide content on the following skills:

- Defining issues
- Collecting and assessing data
- Planning and contracting
- Identifying alternative interventions
- Selecting and implementing appropriate courses of action
- Using appropriate research to monitor and evaluate outcomes
- Applying appropriate research-based knowledge and technological advances
- Terminating[24]

These skills were discussed earlier in this chapter.

Values

Should the primary objective of imprisonment be rehabilitation or punishment? Should a father committing incest be prosecuted if publicity in the community is likely to lead to family breakup, or should an effort be made through counseling to stop the incest and keep the family intact? Should a wife who is occasionally abused by her husband be encouraged to remain with him? Should an abortion be suggested as one alternative for resolving the problems of someone who is single and pregnant? Should youths who are considered uncontrollable by their parents be placed in correctional schools? If a client of a social worker threatens serious harm to some third person, what should the worker do? If a client indicates he is HIV-positive and continues to persist in behavior that places his partner in danger of contracting the disease, but refuses to warn the partner of the peril, what should the social worker do? All of these questions involve making decisions that are largely based on values. Much of social work practice is dependent upon making such decisions.

NASW has identified the following broad-based values as necessary in social work practice:

Commitment to the primary importance of the individual in society.
Respect for the confidentiality of relationships with clients.
Commitment to social change to meet socially recognized needs.
Willingness to keep personal feelings and needs separate from professional relationships.
Willingness to transmit knowledge and skills to others.
Respect and appreciation for individual and group differences.

f. Published 1982, National Association of Social Workers, Inc. Reprinted with permission, from *Standards for the Classification of Social Work Practice,* Policy Statement 4, p. 18. Copyright National Association of Social Workers, Inc.

Commitment to developing clients' ability to help themselves.

Willingness to persist in efforts on behalf of clients despite frustration.

Commitment to social justice and the economic, physical, and mental well-being of all in society.

Commitment to a high standard of personal and professional conduct.[g]

The curriculum policy statements for both the baccalaureate and master's degree program in social work education further assert that:

Among the values and principles that must be infused throughout every social work curriculum are the following:

1. Social workers' professional relationships are built on regard for individual worth and dignity and are furthered by mutual participation, acceptance, confidentiality, honesty, and responsible handling of conflict.
2. Social workers respect people's right to make independent decisions and to participate actively in the helping process.
3. Social workers are committed to assisting client systems to obtain needed resources.
4. Social workers strive to make social institutions more humane and responsive to human needs.
5. Social workers demonstrate respect for and acceptance of the unique characteristics of diverse populations.
6. Social workers are responsible for their own ethical conduct, the quality of their practice, and seeking continuous growth in the knowledge and skills of their profession.[h]

Because values play a key role in social work practice, it is essential that social work educational programs (a) help students clarify their values, and (b) foster the development of values in students that are consistent with professional social work practice.

OBJECTIVES OF SOCIAL WORK EDUCATION

The Council on Social Work Education has specified objectives for baccalaureate and master's degree programs in social work education. These specified objectives highlight much of the knowledge, values, and skills needed in social work practice. Baccalaureate graduates from social work programs are expected to be prepared for beginning level social work practice, while master's graduates from social work programs are expected to be prepared for advanced level social work practice.

In addition, the Curriculum Policy Statement specifies that graduates of a baccalaureate social work program be able to:

---

g. Published in 1982, National Association of Social Workers, Inc. Reprinted with permission, from *Standards for the Classification of Social Work Practice,* Policy Statement 4, p. 18. Copyright National Association of Social Workers, Inc.

h. This material was first published by the Council on Social Work Education and is reprinted here with the permission of the Council on Social Work Education.

1. Apply critical thinking skills within the context of professional social work practice.
2. Practice within the values and ethics of the social work profession and with an understanding of and respect for the positive value of diversity.
3. Demonstrate the professional use of self.
4. Understand the forms and mechanisms of oppression and discrimination and the strategies of change that advance social and economic justice.
5. Understand the history of the social work profession and its current structures and issues.
6. Apply the knowledge and skills of generalist social work to practice with systems of all sizes.
7. Apply knowledge of bio-psycho-social variables that affect individual development and behavior, and use theoretical frameworks to understand the interactions among individuals and between individuals and social systems (i.e., families, groups, organizations, and communities).
8. Analyze the impact of social policies on client systems, workers, and agencies.
9. Evaluate research studies and apply findings to practice, and, under supervision, evaluate their own practice interventions and those of other relevant systems.
10. Use communication skills differentially with a variety of client populations, colleagues, and members of the community.
11. Use supervision appropriate to generalist practice.
12. Function within the structure of organizations and service delivery systems, and under supervision, seek necessary organizational change.[i]

The curriculum policy statement specifies the following objectives for graduates of a master's level program:

> Graduates of a master's social work program are advanced practitioners who can analyze, intervene, and evaluate in ways that are highly differentiated, discriminating, and self-critical. They must synthesize and apply a broad range of knowledge as well as practice with a high degree of autonomy and skill. They must be able to refine and advance the quality of their practice as well as that of the larger social work profession. These advanced competencies must be appropriately integrated and reflected in all aspects of their social work practice, including their ability to:
>
>   1. Apply critical thinking skills within professional contexts, including synthesizing and applying appropriate theories and knowledge to practice interventions.
>   2. Practice within the values and ethics of the social work profession and with an understanding of and respect for the positive value of diversity.
>   3. Demonstrate the professional use of self.
>   4. Understand the forms and mechanisms of oppression and discrimination and the strategies and skills of change that advance social and economic justice.
>   5. Understand the history of the social work profession and its current structures and issues.
>   6. Apply the knowledge and skills of a generalist social work perspective to practice with client systems of all sizes.
>   7. Apply the knowledge and skills of advanced social work practice in an area of concentration.

---

i. This material was first published by the Council on Social Work Education and is reprinted here with the permission of the Council.

8. Critically analyze and apply knowledge of bio-psycho-social variables that affect individual development and behavior, and use theoretical frameworks to understand the interactions among and between individuals and social systems (i.e., families, groups, organizations, and communities).
9. Analyze the impact of social policies on client systems, workers, and agencies and demonstrate skills for influencing policy formulation and change.
10. Evaluate relevant research studies and apply findings to practice, and demonstrate skills in quantitative and qualitative research design, data analysis, and knowledge dissemination.
11. Conduct empirical evaluations of their own practice interventions and those of other relevant systems.
12. Use complex communication skills differentially with a variety of client populations, colleagues, and members of the community.
13. Use supervision and consultation appropriate to advanced practice in an area of concentration.
14. Function within the structure of organizations and service delivery systems and seek necessary organizational change.[j]

These objectives (or competencies) can be viewed as yet another way of presenting the knowledge, values, and skills needed for beginning level and advanced level social work practice.

SOCIAL GROUP WORK AS A COMPONENT OF SOCIAL WORK PRACTICE

Social work practice involves providing humane and effective social services to individuals, families, groups, organizations, and communities. Social work with groups has considerable overlap in providing social services to individuals, families, organizations, and communities. The skills, knowledge, and values needed for effective social work practice with groups are very similar to the skills, knowledge, and values needed for effective social work practice with individuals, families, organizations, and communities.

The material in this text on verbal communication, nonverbal communication, problem solving, stress management, time management, interviewing, counseling, contracting, grief management, identity formation, de-sensitization to sexual issues, and improving interpersonal relationships is applicable to social work practice with both individuals and groups. A family, as described in chapter 24, is a subtype of a group. The close relationships between a group and an organization are described in chapter 12. Finally, the close relationships between a group and a community are described in chapter 13. Acquiring the skills, values, and knowledge needed for effective practice with groups will simultaneously increase a social worker's ability to work effectively with individuals, families, organizations, and communities.

---

j. This material was first published by the Council on Social Work Education and is reprinted here with the permission of the Council.

GROUP EXERCISES

Exercise A: Options Planning

Goals: This exercise is designed to help students gain an awareness of how generalist social workers generate options for combatting social problems.

Step 1. The leader briefly describes generalist social work practice and indicates that options planning is one important aspect. The leader should state the purpose of this exercise, ask students to form subgroups of about five students, then read the first vignette to the subgroup. Give them about ten minutes to arrive at their options. Then ask the subgroups to share their options with the class. Seek to stimulate class discussion of various options. Proceed with the remaining vignettes in the same manner.

VIGNETTE #1
Blackhawk High School has recently had significant increases in the number of female students who have become pregnant. Many of these students become single mothers. They face a number of obstacles in providing quality child care while trying to continue their education. The community is becoming increasingly concerned about the rising pregnancy rate and the difficulties these young mothers are encountering. The principal of the school requests that the school social worker, Ms. Gomez, do something to "fix" these problems. What are realistic options that she might initiate and pursue?

VIGNETTE #2
Milton College wants to better educate its students, faculty, and other staff about HIV and AIDS. Education is currently recognized as the best way to curb the spread of HIV and AIDS and combat HIV and AIDS discrimination. The president of the college requests that the social work department take the lead in developing educational approaches for use on campus. What realistic educational formats (such as peer education, workshops, and in-service training seminars) can be introduced to educate students, faculty, and other staff in these areas?

VIGNETTE #3
Mr. Komarek is a social worker for a public welfare department in a small rural community that has no shelter for homeless individuals or families. Community leaders have asked the county public welfare department to do something about the increasing number of homeless in the community. The director of the agency, responding to community pressure, assigns Mr. Komarek to head up a task force (i.e., a committee) to combat the homeless problem. What realistic options could be pursued by Mr. Komarek and this task force?

VIGNETTE #4
The mayor of a large city has appointed a task force to develop recommendations for improving living conditions in the inner city. The inner city has high rates of unemployment, crime, drug and alcohol abuse, births outside of marriage, substandard housing, high school dropouts, homeless individuals and families, gang activity, and homicides. A great

many people are receiving public assistance. Ms. Taylor, a social worker and social planner employed by United Way, is appointed to this task force. What realistic recommendations for improving living conditions should be advanced by this task force?

Exercise B: Social Work with Groups and Generalist Practice

Goal: This exercise is designed to help students acquire a working knowledge of key terms used in social work.

Step 1: The leader states the purpose of this exercise. Indicate that social workers must be able to describe to others what the profession of social work is and how it is distinct from other professions. Students form subgroups of about five students each. The leader asks each subgroup to discuss answers to the first of the following four questions. Give the subgroups about ten minutes to arrive at an answer. Then ask them to share their answers with the class. After this process is completed, the leader may summarize the answer to this question given in the text, and may compare it with the answers arrived at by the subgroups. The class's answers may be better than the text's.

Step 2: Proceed with the remaining three questions in a similar manner.

QUESTIONS
1. Define social work and social welfare, and describe the relationship between the two.
2. Define the profession of social work and describe how it is distinct from such other helping professions as psychology and psychiatry.
3. Define the terms "social worker" and "generalist social worker."
4. Describe how social work practice with groups is distinct from, but similar to, social work practice with other client systems—i.e., individuals, families, organizations, and communities.

PART TWO

LEADING GROUPS

CHAPTER THREE

LEADERSHIP ROLES, FUNCTIONS, AND GUIDELINES

Goal: Is the statement "He's a born leader" valid, or is leadership a learned characteristic rather than an inherited trait? This chapter describes four major approaches to leadership, including the trait approach, and defines effective group leadership functions, roles, and techniques. This chapter asserts that the use of power is a necessary component of group functioning. Five bases of power are described, and the different consequences of using these bases and the effects of unequal power in groups are also discussed. Material is presented here on how to start and lead a group.

Leadership occurs whenever one person in a group influences other members to help the group reach its goals. Because all group members influence each other at various times, each individual exerts leadership. However, a difference exists between being a designated leader—a president or chairperson—and engaging in leadership behavior. A *designated leader* has certain responsibilities, such as calling meetings and leading discussions, while *leadership* refers to influential behavior in general.

APPROACHES TO LEADERSHIP

Four major approaches to leadership theory—trait, position, leadership style, distributed functions—are summarized in the following sections.

The Trait Approach

Aristotle observed: "From the hour of their birth some are marked for subjugation, and others for command." This trait approach to leadership, which has existed for centuries, assumes that leaders have inherent personal characteristics, or traits, that distinguish them from followers. This approach asserts that leaders are born, not made, and emerge naturally instead of being trained. It has also been called the "great man" or "great woman" theory of leadership. According to Krech et al., who reviewed research studies on leadership traits, a leader needs to be perceived as: (1) a member of the group he is attempting to lead, (2) embodying to a special degree the norms and values central to the group, (3) the most qualified group member to accomplish the task at hand, and (4) fitting members' expectations about how he or she should behave and what functions he or she should serve.[1]

Some research on personality traits indicates that leaders tend to be better adjusted and more dominant, extroverted, "masculine," and interpersonally sensitive than their followers. Other traits, such as intelligence, enthusiasm, dominance, self-confidence, and egalitarianism, have also been found to characterize leaders.[2] Although potential leaders tend to have more positive attributes than other group members, they cannot be so successful that members perceive them as "different." For example, Davis and Hare found that "B" students were the campus leaders, while the more intelligent "A" students were considered "grinds" who occasionally were treated as outcasts for being "curve wreckers."[3] Also, the member who talks most has been found to win most decisions and so becomes the leader, unless he talks too much and antagonizes other group members.[4]

Two postulated leadership traits that have received considerable attention are: charisma and Machiavellianism. We will take a brief look at each of these traits.

Charisma

Charisma has been defined as "an extraordinary power, as of working miracles."[5] Johnson and Johnson give the following definition of a charismatic leader:

The charismatic leader must have a sense of mission, a belief in the social-change movement he or she leads, and confidence in oneself as the chosen instrument to lead the movement to its destination. The leader must appear extremely self-confident in order to inspire others with the faith that the movement he or she leads will, without fail, prevail and ultimately reduce their distress.[6]

Some charismatic leaders appear to inspire their followers to love and be fully committed to them. Other charismatic leaders offer their followers the hope and promise of deliverance from distress.

Charisma has not been precisely defined, and its components have not been fully identified. The qualities and characteristics that each charismatic leader has will differ somewhat from those of other charismatic leaders. The following leaders all have been referred to as charismatic, yet they differed substantially in personality characteristics: John F. Kennedy, Martin Luther King, Jr., Julius Caesar, General George Patton, Confucius, Gandhi, and Winston Churchill.

One difficulty with the charisma approach to leadership is that people who are viewed as having charisma tend to express this quality in a variety of ways. A second difficulty is that many persons do well as leaders without being viewed as having charisma. For example, many group therapists are effective in leading groups even though they are not viewed as charismatic.

Machiavellianism

Niccolò Machiavelli (1469–1527) was an Italian statesman who advocated the use of cunning, deceit, and duplicity as political methods rulers should use for increasing their power and control. Machiavelli was not the originator of such an approach; earlier theorists conceptualized leadership in terms of manipulation for self-enhancement. However, the term "Machiavellianism" has become associated with the notion that politics is amoral and that any means should be used to achieve political power. Machiavellian leadership is based on the concepts that people (1) are basically fallible, gullible, untrustworthy, and weak, (2) are impersonal objects, and (3) should be manipulated so that the leader may achieve his goals.

Christie and Geis conclude that Machiavellian leaders have four characteristics:

1. They have little emotional involvement in interpersonal relationships—it is easier to manipulate others if they are viewed as impersonal objects.
2. They are not concerned about conventional morality; they take a utilitarian view (what they can get out of it) rather than a moral view, of their interactions with others.
3. They have a fairly accurate perception of the needs of their followers, which facilitates their capacity to manipulate them.
4. They have a low degree of ideological commitment; they focus on manipulating others for personal benefit, rather than on achieving long-term ideological goals.[7]

While a few leaders may have Machiavellian characteristics, most do not. Very few groups would function effectively or efficiently with Machiavellian leaders.

In recent years the trait theory of leadership has declined in popularity, partly because research results have raised questions about its validity. For example, different leadership positions often require different leadership traits. The characteristics of a good leader in the military differ markedly from those of a good group therapy leader. Moreover, traits found in leaders have also been found in followers. Though qualities such as high intelligence and a well-adjusted personality may have some correlation with leadership, many highly intelligent people never get top leadership positions and some highly intelligent leaders (Adolf Hitler, for example) have been emotionally unstable. The best rule for leader selection involves choosing individuals with the necessary skills, qualities, and motivation to help a group accomplish its goals.

The Position Approach

In most large organizations, there are several levels of leadership, such as president, vice-president, manager, supervisor, and foreman. The position approach defines leadership in terms of the authority of a particular position and has focused on studying the behavior of people in high-level positions. At times, training and personal background of leaders have also been examined.

Studies using the position approach, however, have revealed little consistency in how people assume leadership positions. Obviously, individuals may become leaders with little related training (in family businesses, for example), while others spend years developing their skills. Also, individuals in different leadership positions have been found to display a variety of appropriate behaviors. For example, a drill sergeant in basic military training is not expected to be empathetic, but a sensitivity group leader is. It is difficult to compile a list of leadership traits by using this approach. Not surprisingly, the position approach has shown that what constitutes leadership behavior depends upon the particular requirements of the position.

Another problem with the position approach is that it is difficult to define which behavior of a designated leader is leadership behavior and which is not. Certainly not all of the behavior of a designated authority figure is leadership behavior. For instance, an inexperienced individual in a position of authority can mask incompetence with an authoritarian attitude. Also, the leadership behavior among group members who are not designated leaders is difficult for the position approach to explain, because this approach focuses its attention on designated leaders.

The Leadership-Style Approach

Because researchers on the trait and the position approaches were turning out contradictory results, Lewin, Lippitt, and White focused on examining leadership styles. Their research uncovered three: authoritarian, democratic, and laissez-faire.[8]

Authoritarian Leaders

These types of leaders, who have more absolute power than democratic leaders, set goals and policies, dictate the activities of the members, and develop major plans. The leader alone is the purveyor of rewards and punishments and knows the succession of future steps in the group's activities. Authoritarian leadership is generally efficient and decisive. One of the hazards, however, is that group members may respond out of necessity and not because of commitment to group goals. The authoritarian leader who anticipates approval from subordinates may be surprised to find that backbiting and bickering are common in the group. Unsuccessful authoritarian leadership is apt to generate factionalism, behind-the-scenes jockeying for position among members, and a decline in morale.

Democratic Leaders

In contrast, democratic leaders seek the maximum involvement and participation of every member in all decisions affecting the group and attempt to spread responsibility rather than concentrate it. Democratic leadership can lead to slow decision making and confusion, but it is frequently more effective because of the strong cooperation that emerges from group participation. Interpersonal hostilities between members, dissatisfactions with the leader, and concern for personal advancement all become issues that are discussed and acted upon. With democratic leadership, the private complaining that is kept behind the scenes in the authoritarian approach usually becomes public. When this occurs, such conflicts can be more openly and readily confronted and dealt with. Once this public conflict has been resolved in a democratic group, however, a strong personal commitment usually develops, which motivates members to implement group decisions rather than to subvert them. The potential for sabotage in an authoritarian group is high and therein lies the major advantage of the democratic style. The democratic leader knows that mistakes are inevitable and the group will suffer from them, but he or she must learn to stand back and allow the democratic process to continue without interference.

Depending on the situation, authoritarian or democratic leadership may be more effective, assuming members' expectations about appropriate behavior for each situation are met.[9] When group members anticipate a democratic style, as they do in educational settings or discussion groups, the democratic style is utilized well. When members anticipate forceful leadership from their superiors, as in industry or the military, individuals accept a more authoritarian form of leadership.

Laissez-Faire Leaders

These leaders participate very little, and group members are generally left to function (or flounder) with little input. Group members seldom function well under a laissez-faire style, which may be effective *only* when the members are committed to a course of action, have the resources to implement it, and need minimal leadership to reach their goals. For example, laissez-faire leadership may work well in a college department in which the faculty members are competent, conscientious, and responsible, and have the resources to meet their objectives.

The Distributed-Functions Approach

Because different leadership styles are required in different situations (even within the same group), research in recent years has focused more on how leadership functions are distributed. The distributed-functions approach disagrees with the "great man," or trait, theory of leadership and asserts that every member of a group will be a leader at times by taking actions that serve group functions. Leadership is defined as the performance of acts that help the group maintain itself and reach its goals. Leadership functions include setting goals, selecting and implementing tasks, and providing resources to accomplish group goals while maintaining the group's cohesion and satisfying the needs of individual members. The functional approach involves determining what tasks, or functions, are essential to achieve group goals and how different group members should participate.

With this approach, the demands of leadership are viewed as being specific to a particular group in a particular situation. For example, cracking a joke may be a useful leadership tactic in certain situations if it relieves tension. But when other members are revealing intense personal information in therapy, humor may be counterproductive and therefore inappropriate leadership behavior.

Many individuals who fear taking a leadership role are uncertain about leadership functions and feel they lack the proper qualities of a leader. Amazingly, even the most fearful and anxious students have already taken on many leadership roles and nearly everyone has assumed leadership responsibilities by adolescence. Functional leadership involves a learned set of skills that anyone with certain minimal capabilities can acquire. Responsible membership is the same thing as responsible leadership because both maintain the group's cohesion and accomplish its goals. Since people can be taught leadership skills and behaviors, the implication of this theory is that nearly everyone can be taught to be an effective leader.

LEADERSHIP ROLES

Task and Maintenance Roles

Through considerable research on problem-solving groups, Bales has identified two specific leadership functions: that of the task specialist and that of the social/emotional, or group maintenance, specialist.[10] All groups, whether organized for therapeutic reasons, problem solving, or other purposes, rely on members performing task roles and group maintenance roles satisfactorily. *Task roles* are those needed to accomplish specific goals set by the group. They have been summarized by David and Frank Johnson as follows:

> *Information and Opinion Giver:* Offers facts, opinions, ideas, suggestions, and relevant information to help group discussion.
> *Information and Opinion Seeker:* Asks for facts, information, opinions, ideas, and feelings from other members to help group discussion.
> *Starter:* Proposes goals and tasks to initiate action within the group.
> *Direction Giver:* Develops plans on how to proceed and focuses attention on the task to be done.
> *Summarizer:* Pulls together related ideas or suggestions and restates and summarizes major points discussed.
> *Coordinator:* Shows relationships among various ideas by pulling them together and harmonizes activities of various subgroups and members.
> *Diagnoser:* Figures out sources of difficulties the group has in working effectively and the blocks to progress in accomplishing the group's goals.
> *Energizer:* Stimulates a higher quality of work from the group.
> *Reality Tester:* Examines the practicality and workability of ideas, evaluates alternative solutions, and applies them to real situations to see how they will work.
> *Evaluator:* Compares group decisions and accomplishments with group standards and goals.

Group maintenance roles, which strengthen social/emotional bonds within the group, have also been identified by the Johnsons:

> *Encourager of Participation:* Warmly encourages everyone to participate, giving recognition for contributions, demonstrating acceptance and openness to ideas of others; is friendly and responsive to group members.
>
> *Harmonizer and Compromiser:* Persuades members to analyze constructively their differences in opinions, searches for common elements in conflicts, and tries to reconcile disagreements.
>
> *Tension Reliever:* Eases tensions and increases the enjoyment of group members by joking, suggesting breaks, and proposing fun approaches to group work.
>
> *Communication Helper:* Shows good communication skills and makes sure that each group member understands what other members are saying.
>
> *Evaluator of Emotional Climate:* Asks members how they feel about the way in which the group is working and about each other, and shares own feelings about both.
>
> *Process Observer:* Watches the process by which the group is working and uses the observations to help examine group effectiveness.
>
> *Standard Setter:* Expresses group standards and goals to make members aware of the direction of the work and the progress being made toward the goal, and to get open acceptance of group norms and procedures.
>
> *Active Listener:* Listens and serves as an interested audience for other members, is receptive to others' ideas, goes along with the group when not in disagreement.
>
> *Trust Builder:* Accepts and supports openness of other group members, reinforcing risk taking and encouraging individuality.
>
> *Interpersonal Problem Solver:* Promotes open discussion of conflicts between group members in order to resolve conflicts and increase group togetherness.[a]

Each of the foregoing task and maintenance functions may be required periodically within a group, and effective group members (and leaders) are sensitive to these needs.

A task leader emerges in many groups because he or she has the best ideas and does the most to guide discussions. Since this person concentrates on a task, and generally plays an aggressive role in moving the group toward the goal, hostility is apt to arise and the task leader may be disliked. Concurrently, a second leader may emerge: a social/emotional specialist who concentrates on group harmony and resolves tensions and conflicts within the group. In groups with an official leader, the leader is expected to be both the task specialist and the social/emotional specialist. In groups without an official leader, these two functions are generally assumed by two different emergent leaders. When social/emotional group maintenance needs are met, a group will continually improve its task effectiveness. However, when maintenance needs are ignored, a group's task effectiveness deteriorates.

Hersey and Blanchard have developed a situational theory of leadership that points out when leaders should focus on task behaviors, on maintenance behaviors, or on both.[11] In essence, the theory asserts that when members have low maturity in terms of accomplishing a specific task, the leader should engage in high-task behaviors and low-maintenance behaviors. Hersey and Blanchard refer to this situation as *telling*: the leader's behavior is most effective when the leader defines the roles of members and *tells* them how, when, and where to do needed tasks. The task maturity of members increases as their

---

a. David Johnson and Frank P. Johnson, Joining Together: Group Theory and Group Skills, pp. 26, 27. © 1975. Reprinted by permission of Prentice-Hall, Inc., Englewood Cliffs, N.J.

experience and understanding of the task increases. For moderately mature members, the leader should engage in high-task behaviors and high-maintenance behaviors. This combination of behaviors is referred to as *selling*: the leader should not only provide clear directions about role and task responsibilities, but also use maintenance behaviors to get the members to "buy into" the decisions that have to be made.

Hersey and Blanchard also assert that when the group members' commitment to the task increases, so does their maturity. When members are committed to accomplishing the task and have the ability and knowledge to complete the task, the leader should engage in low-task behaviors and high-maintenance behaviors. This is referred to as *participating*. Finally, for groups in which members are both willing and able to take responsibility for directing their own task behavior, the leader should engage in low-task and low-maintenance behaviors; this is referred to as *delegating*. Delegating allows members considerable autonomy in completing the task.

Other Roles

The designated group leader had a special obligation to assume, or to assist others in assuming, timely and appropriate task and maintenance roles. Each leader is also responsible for a variety of functions, which range from setting initial policies to planning for termination. To meet the needs and particular developmental stage of a group, a leader may be required to assume any of the previously described roles as well as:

Executive: coordinates the activities of a group.
Policy Maker: establishes group goals and policies.
Planner: decides the means by which the group shall achieve its goals.
Expert: offers ready source of information and skills.
External Group Representative: serves as official spokesperson.
Controller of Internal Relations: controls the group structure and in-group relations.
Purveyor of Rewards and Punishments: promotes, demotes, and assigns pleasant or unpleasant tasks.
Arbitrator and Mediator: acts as both judge and conciliator, and has the power to reduce or increase factionalism within the group.
Exemplar: serves as a model of behavior for other members.
Ideologist: serves as the source of group beliefs and values.
Scapegoat: serves as the target for members' frustrations and disappointments.

POWER AND INFLUENCE IN GROUPS

Although the use of power in human interactions is often viewed negatively, it is, in fact, a normal part of relationships because people are frequently influencing and being influenced by one another. The terms *power* and *influence* will be used interchangeably in this chapter. Both terms refer to the capacity of an individual to motivate others to carry out certain actions or to behave in a particular way. Earlier in this chapter, leadership was defined as one member of a group influencing other members to achieve group goals and promote group maintenance. In an effective group, each member at times takes a leadership role by performing task and maintenance functions. Task functions move the group forward; maintenance functions improve the social/emotional atmosphere of the group.

In making decisions, group members present their views and opinions in an effort to influence group members. For example, some members attempt to incorporate their personal goals into the group's goals or to promote the strategies for action they want implemented. Members influence each other to commit their time and resources to the group. Controversies are usually settled through mutual influence, as members seek acceptable compromises or solutions. The use of power is indeed a necessary component of effective group functioning, and it is natural and generally desirable for every member to influence other members in the pursuit of both personal and group goals.

Every group member has a need to control what happens in a group because people join groups to attain personal goals they cannot achieve individually. If members do not exert power, their chances of achieving their personal goals are minute, and they are apt to become apathetic and disengage themselves from the group.

When group members are cooperating, power is asserted in the same direction, and members encourage each other to put forth greater effort, as they would on a sports team. However, when members are competitive or have incompatible goals, their assertions of power conflict. Republican and Democratic congressional representatives, for example, are constantly competing with each other, and their efforts to influence frequently clash.

Group members in conflict sometimes resort to manipulation; that is, they influence others for their own purpose or profit. Often, this manipulation is dishonest or unfair, for it involves the use of power for one's own benefit at the expense of other members. When people say they do not want to have power over others, they usually mean they do not want to manipulate others. If group members feel coerced by threats or discover they are manipulated in other ways, they usually react with anger, distrust, resentment, and retaliation. Manipulation, then, is a destructive kind of power because it decreases cooperation and can cause serious maintenance problems. "Influencing with integrity" is in contrast to manipulation. In a group influencing with integrity involves seeking to influence the group in a direction that is in the group's best interests.

An effective group member is skillful in influencing others in a positive way. The amount of power a member has depends on how valuable his or her resources are. If a member has vital resources that are also available to others, that member will have less power. Interestingly, it is *not* a person's *actual* resources that determine power; instead, it is the *perception* of the other group members as to the value of a member's resources. It is possible to have vital resources but little power if these resources are ignored or unknown. It is also possible to have great power but few vital resources if members exaggerate the importance of such resources.

POWER BASES IN GROUPS

French and Raven have developed a framework for understanding the extent to which one group member influences another by identifying five bases of power: reward, coercive, legitimate, referent, and expert.[12] This framework allows group members to analyze the source of their power and offers suggestions on when, and when not, to use their power to influence others.

Reward Power

Rewards include such things as promotions, pay increases, days off, and praise. Reward power is based on B's (one member's) perception that A (another member or the entire group) has the capacity to dispense rewards or remove negative consequences in response to B's behavior. This power will be greater if the group members value the reward and believe they cannot get it from anyone else. Group members will usually work hard for someone who has high reward power and communicate effectively with him. Reward power can backfire, however, if group members feel they are being conned or bribed. If reward power is used by A in a conflict situation with B, B is apt to feel he is being bribed and controlled, and may eventually refuse to cooperate.

Coercive Power

The ability to fire a worker who falls below a given level of production is a common example of coercive power, which is based on B's perceptions that A can dispense punishments or remove positive consequences. Coercive power stems from the expectation on the part of B that he will be punished by A if he fails to conform to the required standards set by A. The distinction between reward and coercive power is important. French and Raven note that reward power will tend to increase the attraction of B toward A, while coercive power will decrease this attraction. If coercive power is used by A to attempt to settle a conflict, it often increases B's hostility, resentment, and anger. Threats often lead to aggression and counterthreats; for example, military threats often increase conflict between rival countries. Coercive power may exacerbate conflict by leading both A and B to distrust each other and to retaliate against each other. Therefore, whenever possible coercive power should not be used to settle conflicts.

Legitimate Power

Legitimate power is directly related to an internalized value or norm and is probably the most complex of the five power bases. Legitimate power is based on the perception by B that A has a legitimate right to prescribe what constitutes proper behavior for him and that B has an obligation to accept this influence. Cultural values constitute one common basis for legitimate power and include intelligence, age, caste, and physical characteristics as factors determining power. For example, in some cultures the aged are highly respected and are granted the right to prescribe behavior for others. The legitimate power inherent in a formal organization is generally determined by a relationship between positions rather than between persons. A supervisor in a factory, for instance, has the inherent right to assign work. A third basis for legitimate power is a legitimizing agent; for example, an election. The election process legitimizes a person's right to a position that already had a legitimate range of power associated with it.

The limits of legitimate power are generally specified at the time that power is assigned (e.g., in a job description). The attempted use of power outside of this range will decrease the legitimate power of the authority figure and decrease his attractiveness and influence.

Referent Power

Referent power occurs when one individual, A, influences another, B, as a result of identification. Identification in this context means either a feeling of oneness with A or a desire for an identity such as A's. The stronger the identification of B with A, the greater the attraction to A and the greater the referent power of A. A verbalization of referent power is "I am like A, and therefore I will believe or behave as A does," or "I want to be like A, and I will be more like A if I believe or behave as A does." In ambiguous situations (that is, situations where there are no objective right or wrong beliefs or opinions), B will seek to evaluate his thoughts, beliefs, and values in terms of what A thinks, believes, and values. In ambiguous situations B is apt to adopt the thoughts, beliefs, and values of the individual or group with which B identifies. French and Raven note that B is often not consciously aware of the referent power that A exerts.

Expert Power

Accepting a physician's advice in medical matters is a common example of expert influence, which is based on the perception that a person has knowledge or expertise that is the source of power. Another example would be accepting a counselor's suggestions. Experts can influence B (the responder) only if B thinks that A (the expert) has the right answer and B trusts A. The range of expert power is more limited than that of referent power because the expert is seen as having superior knowledge or ability only in specific areas. French and Raven note that the attempted exertion of expert power outside the perceived range will reduce that power because confidence in the expert seems to be undermined.

French and Raven theorize that for all five types, the stronger the basis of power, the greater the power. Referent power is thought to have the broadest range. Any attempt to use power outside the prescribed range is hypothesized to reduce the power.

EFFECTS OF UNEQUAL POWER

The effectiveness of a group is improved when: (a) power is based upon expertise and competence and (b) power is relatively equal among members. Members are more committed to implementing decisions when they feel they have had a fair say in making a decision. If a group is dominated by a few powerful members, the low-power members are likely to feel less committed to carrying out the decisions they perceive as being made by the powerful members. When power is relatively balanced, however, the members are generally more cooperative with each other.

Unequal power often leads to distrust between the high- and low-power members.

The low-power members fear they will be manipulated and are reluctant to share their thoughts completely with the high-power members, because they believe that if they express views in opposition to the views of the high-power members, they are apt to receive fewer rewards and may be coerced. High-power members avoid revealing weaknesses because they fear the low-power members may come to think they are undeserving of their power and seek to grasp it. The problem-solving capacity of groups is generally increased when members have fairly equal power or when the group has flexible and gradually changing power patterns that tend to equalize influence among group members.

Power based on authority or popularity can dramatically reduce the problem-solving capacities of groups when the tasks require expertise and competence. High-power people generally believe that low-power people really do like them because they see themselves as benevolent. They generally believe that low-power people communicate honestly with them and do not hide valuable information from them. When low-power members express dissatisfaction, however, high-power people frequently are not benevolent. Instead, they perceive that the low-power people are "making waves" and "not appreciating what is being done for them." In such situations high-power people may withhold rewards and use threats and coercion. These reactions usually intensify the conflict and polarize the two sides.

When threatened, high-power people may maintain power by instituting rules or norms that legitimize their power and make it illegal to change the status quo.[13] After the South lost the Civil War, for example, the white power structure in the South sought to maintain its power by keeping schools, restaurants, and public restrooms segregated. Processes were established that prevented many black people from voting, and few black persons were hired for high-status positions. Numerous state and local laws were enacted to legitimize this segregation.

High-power people may also maintain their position by creating severe penalties for attempting to change the status quo. Blacks in the South were lynched for such offenses as seeking to be served in white restaurants. In addition, high-power members may seek to deter low-power members from rebelling by dispensing a variety of rewards to those low-power members who support the status quo.

Halle has observed that the greater a person's power becomes, the less sufficient it seems because the requests and claims upon it increase faster than the capacity to fulfill them.[14] For example, although the United States has become very powerful in the past fifty years, requests for domestic and military help from other countries have increased more rapidly than the country's ability to fulfill them. The power of the United States thus seems insufficient.

How do low-power people relate to high-power people? There are a variety of strategies. One is to emphasize and exaggerate the degree to which high-power people like them, overestimating their goodwill.[15] Low-power people using this strategy direct much of their attention and communication to high-power people, seeking to remain on good terms with them.

A second strategy for low-power people is to become apathetic and submissive. Authoritarian leadership often breeds this reaction. A third strategy is to become angry and rebel; rebellion sometimes leads to destructive violence.

Low-power people can use a variety of strategies to change the distribution of power.[16] One is to endear themselves by frequently complimenting high-power people and agreeing with them. The hope is that high-power people will come to depend on them and reward them with more power. A second strategy is to develop personal resources and organizations so that they are less vulnerable to exploitation and less dependent upon high-power people. This strategy builds a separate power structure. A third strategy is to build coalitions with other parties. Right-to-life groups, for example, have formed a coalition with leaders in the Roman Catholic church in an attempt to make abortions illegal. A fourth strategy is to use existing legal procedures to bring pressures for change. The Civil Rights movement has used the court system extensively to force the power structure to make changes. A fifth strategy involves low-power members organizing and using confrontation techniques to force the power structure to change.

Perhaps the best known authority on using power confrontation techniques was Saul Alinsky.[17] Alinsky and his associates organized many citizens' groups to confront established power structures. For example, in the 1960s Alinsky was working with a citizens' group in the inner city of Chicago known as the Woodlawn Organization. City authorities had made commitments to this organization to improve several conditions in the neighborhood. When it became clear the commitments would not be honored, however, the Woodlawn Organization sought ways to pressure the city into meeting its commitments. The proposed solution was to embarrass city officials by tying up all the lavatories at O'Hare, one of the world's busiest airports. Alinsky describes this effort as follows:

> An intelligence study was launched to learn how many sit-down toilets for both men and women, as well as stand-up urinals, there were in the entire O'Hare airport complex and how many men and women would be necessary for the nation's first "shit-in."
>
> The consequences of this kind of action would be catastrophic in many ways. People would be desperate for a place to relieve themselves. One can see children yelling at their parents, "Mommy, I've got to go," and desperate mothers surrendering, "All right—well, do it. Do it right here." O'Hare would soon become a shambles. The whole scene would become unbelievable and the laughter and ridicule would be nationwide. It would probably get a front page story in the London *Times*. It would be a source of great mortification and embarrassment to the city administration. It might even create the kind of emergency in which planes would have to be held up while passengers got back aboard to use the plane's toilet facilities.
>
> The threat of this tactic was leaked (. . . there may be a Freudian slip here . . . so what?) back to the administration, and within 48 hours the Woodlawn Organization found itself in conference with the authorities who said they were certainly going to live up to their commitments and they could never understand where anyone got the idea that a promise made by Chicago's City Hall would not be observed.[18]

Community change efforts through group projects are often enjoyable!

GUIDELINES FOR FORMING AND LEADING A GROUP

The theory of leadership emphasized in this chapter is the distributed-functions approach, which asserts that every group member takes on leadership responsibilities at various times and that every effective action by a member is simultaneously an effective leadership action. Being a designated leader is not that different from taking on leadership roles. This section will summarize a number of suggestions for how to effectively form and lead a group.

Homework

The key to successful group leadership is extensive preparation. Even experienced leaders carefully prepare for each group and for each group session.

In planning for a new group, the following questions must be answered: What is the purpose or general goals of the group? How can these goals be achieved? What are the characteristics of the members? Do some members have unique individual goals or needs? What resources are needed to accomplish group goals? What is the agenda for the first meeting? What is the best way for members to suggest and decide on the specific goals of the group? Should an ice-breaker exercise be used? Which one? Should refreshments be provided? How should the chairs be arranged? What type of group atmosphere will best help the group accomplish its tasks? What is the best available meeting place? Why has the leader been selected? What do the members expect from the leader?

To plan the first meeting, a leader should view the group as a new member would. Here are a few questions a new member might have: What will be the goals of this group? Why am I joining? Will my personal goals be met? Will I feel comfortable? Will I be accepted? Will the other members be radically different in terms of backgrounds and interests? If I do not like this group, can I leave gracefully? Will other members respect what I have to say, or will they laugh and make fun of me? By considering such concerns, the leader can plan the first meeting to help other members feel comfortable and to clarify the goals and activities of the group.

Before the first meeting, it is *absolutely essential* that a leader identify the group's needs and expectations as precisely as possible. A group whose leader and members disagree on goals cannot succeed.

There are a variety of ways to identify what the members want. The leader might ask them before the first meeting. If that isn't possible, the leader might at least talk to the organizer of the meeting about the group's expectations. And, of course, the first meeting is a good time to clarify the group's goals. The leader also needs the answers to the following questions:

1. How many members are expected?
2. What are their characteristics: age, socioeconomic status, racial and ethnic background, gender, educational/professional background?
3. How knowledgeable are the members about the topics the group will be dealing with?
4. What are the likely personal goals of the various members?
5. How motivated are the members to accomplish the purposes for which the group is being formed? Voluntary membership usually indicates greater motivation. Individuals who have been ordered by a court to participate in an alcohol rehabilitation program, for example, have little motivation and may even be hostile.
6. What values are the members likely to have? While being careful to avoid stereotyping, a leader must understand, for example, that teenagers on juvenile probation will differ significantly from retired priests.

In planning a meeting, it is helpful for a leader to visualize how the meeting will go. For example, a leader may want to visualize the following first meeting:

The members will arrive at various times. I will be there early to greet them, introduce myself, assist them in feeling comfortable, and engage in small talk. Possible subjects of small talk that are apt to be of interest to these new members are _____, _____, and _____.

I will begin the meeting by introducing myself and the overall purpose of the group. I will use the following ice-breaker exercises for members to introduce themselves and get acquainted. I will ask the group to give me a list of four or five items they would like to know about the other members. Then the members will introduce themselves and respond to the items. I will also respond to the items and encourage the members to ask questions about me and the group.

After the ice-breaker exercise I will briefly state the overall purpose of the group and ask for questions. Possible questions are _____. My answers will be _____.

We will proceed to the agenda, which has been mailed to the members. During the discussion of each agenda point, the following questions may arise: _____. My answers are _____.

The kind of group atmosphere I will seek to create is democratic and egalitarian. Such an atmosphere is best suited for encouraging members to become committed to the group goals and to contribute their time and resources. I will create this atmosphere by arranging the chairs in a circle, by drawing out through questions those who are silent, by using humor, and by making sure I do not dominate the conversation.

I will end the meeting by summarizing what has been covered and the decisions that have been made. We will set a time for the next meeting. I will finally ask if anyone has any additional comments or questions. Throughout the meeting I will seek to establish a positive atmosphere, partly by complimenting the members on the contributions they make.

If a group has met more than once, the leader needs to review the following kinds of questions. Have the overall goals been decided upon and clarified? If not, what needs to be done in this clarification process? Is the group making adequate progress in accomplishing its goals? If not, what are the obstacles that must be overcome? Is the group taking the most effective course of action to reach its goals? What is the agenda for the next meeting? What activities should be planned? Will successful completion of these activities move the group toward accomplishing its overall goals? If not, which other activities will? Is each member, sufficiently motivated to help the group accomplish its goals? If not, why? What might be done to stimulate their interest?

Planning a Session

In planning a session, the leader must keep the group's overall goals—as well as those for that session—in mind. (For material on how to set group goals, see chapter 4.) To be effective, the leader must know exactly what should be accomplished in each session and make sure that all the items on the agenda contribute to the goals. Here is a checklist that may help leaders plan successful group sessions. An effective leader will:

1. Select relevant content. The material should not only be relevant to the specific goals for the session but also to the backgrounds and interests of the participants. Time-management advice for college students, for example, probably will be different from that for business executives. Time-saving tips for students will likely focus on improving study habits; business executives will be more interested in how to manage

time in an office setting. An excellent way to evaluate possible material is to define precisely how it will be valuable to members of the group. The leader should ask: "If a group member wants to know why he or she should know this, can I give a valid reason?" If that question cannot be answered precisely, the material should be discarded and replaced with more relevant material.

2. Use examples. Examples help to illustrate key concepts and stimulate the participants. People tend to remember examples more readily than statistics or concepts. Vivid case histories that illustrate the drastic effects of spouse abuse, for instance, will be remembered much longer than statistics on the extent of spouse abuse.

3. Present materials in a logical order. It is generally desirable to begin by summarizing the agenda items for the session. Ideally, one topic should blend into the next. Group exercises should be used in conjunction with related theoretical material.

4. Plan the time. Once the content of a session is selected and organized, the time each segment requires should be estimated. Accurate estimates will help determine whether planned material and activities are appropriate for the allotted time. A good leader also knows what material can be deleted if time is running short and what can be added if the session progresses more rapidly than planned. Substitute activities must also be available to replace speakers who fail to appear or films that fail to arrive.

5. Be flexible. A variety of unexpected events may make it desirable to change the agenda during a session. Interpersonal conflict between members may take considerable time, or it may become clear that subjects related to the group's overall purpose are more valuable for the group to focus on than the prepared agenda.

6. Change the pace. People pay attention longer if there is an occasional change of pace. Long lectures or discussions can become boring. Group exercises, films, guest speakers, breaks, debates, and other activities will help vary the tempo of a meeting or session. In group therapy, one way to change the pace is to move from one member's problems to those of another. Lectures can be more stimulating if the instructor:

- speaks extemporaneously instead of reading material
- walks around the room occasionally, rather than standing or sitting in one place
- draws out participants by asking questions

(An excellent way to learn how to give more stimulating presentations is to observe the nonverbal and verbal communication patterns of dynamic speakers.) It is critical to use appropriate transitions so that the topics blend into one another smoothly.

Relaxing Before You Start a Meeting

Before beginning a meeting, the leader is likely to be nervous about how the session may go. Some anxiety, in fact, is helpful because it increases alertness, and that will make the leader more attentive, producing a better meeting. Too much anxiety, however, reduces effectiveness. Relaxation techniques that can alleviate excessive anxiety are described in chapter 15. They are highly recommended and include walking, jogging, listening to music, meditating, and being alone to clear the mind. Effective group leaders generally learn they can reduce their level of anxiety through using one or more relaxation techniques. Practice in leading groups also builds confidence and reduces anxiety.

Cues upon Entering the Meeting Room

It is important that a leader be on time. Arriving early is even better because it allows the leader to see that materials, seating arrangements, refreshments, and any other needs are in place as planned. Being early also gives the leader an opportunity to observe the members. He or she can gain information about the interests of the participants from their age, sex, clothes and personal appearance, conversation, and interaction with one another. An effective leader observes such cues and uses them to create an initial bond with the participants. For example, this author was asked to give a workshop on suicide prevention to a high school class. Upon arriving, I was informed by the teacher that one of the students in the class had recently committed suicide. Instead of beginning with my planned presentation, I asked each student to write down, anonymously, one or two concerns or questions that they had about suicide. We then had a lively discussion based on their questions and concerns. Such a discussion was probably more valuable than the formal presentation (which I never gave) because it focused on their specific questions and concerns.

Seating Arrangements

Seating is important for several reasons. It can affect who talks to whom, influence leadership roles, and, as a result, affect group cohesion and morale. In most groups members should have eye contact with one another. The group leader must be able to make eye contact with everyone to obtain nonverbal feedback on what the members are thinking and feeling.

A circle is ideal for generating discussion, encouraging a sense of equal status for each member, and promoting group openness and cohesion. The traditional classroom arrangement, on the other hand, has the effect of placing the leader in a position of authority. It also tends to inhibit communication because members can easily make eye contact only with those closest to them.

Tables have advantages and disadvantages. They provide a place to write and to put work materials, and some members feel more comfortable at a table because they can lean on it. But tables restrict movement and may serve as barriers between people.

The leader should thus carefully consider the use of tables. In business meetings or other "working" sessions, for example, tables are probably necessary. In therapy groups, however, tables are seldom used. In some settings the tables themselves can be arranged to best meet the goals of the meeting. When work surfaces and serious communication are both required, small tables in a circle can be an effective arrangement.

The shape of the tables can influence the way group members interact with each other. If the table is rectangular, the leader traditionally sits at one end, which then becomes the "head" of the table. The head of the table is usually an "authority," tends to do more talking, and has a greater influence on the discussion than other group members. A round or square table, however, establishes a more egalitarian atmosphere. The "head of the table" effect can also be reduced by placing two rectangular tables together to make a square.

Where people sit at tables also affects interaction. People are most apt to talk to others sitting at right angles to them, then to those next to them, and finally to those sitting directly across from them. Group members seated elsewhere receive even less attention.

In new groups, or even established ones, members are likely to sit next to friends. If it is important for everyone in the group to interact, the leader may want to ask people to sit next to individuals they do not know.

Introductions

The leader's credentials should be summarized to give the group a sense of confidence that the leader can fulfill the expectations of the members. If the leader is being introduced, a concise summary of the leader's credentials *for the expected role* is desirable. If the leader is introducing himself, the important credentials should be summarized in an informative but modest way. The summary should be made in a way that helps create the desired atmosphere—whether it be formal or informal, fun or serious, or whatever. An excellent way to handle the introductions in many groups is to use an "ice-breaker" exercise as described in chapter 1.

It is highly desirable for the leader to learn the names of all group members as quickly as possible. This requires extra attention, and name tags can help everyone be more comfortable sooner. Members appreciate being called by name because it affirms their importance.

If the group is small, the members can introduce themselves individually, perhaps using an ice-breaker. In addition to the usual personal information, it is helpful for members to state their expectations for the group as they introduce themselves. This helps uncover hidden agenda that are incompatible with the goals of the group. If a stated expectation is beyond the scope of the group, the leader should tactfully discuss it to avoid later frustration or dissatisfaction.

Clarifying Roles

The leader of a group should be clear as to his or her roles and responsibilities. If they are unclear, the leader may want to discuss them with the group. One way of doing this is for the group to select goals and then make decisions about the tasks and responsibilities that *each* member will have in working toward the goals of the group. In most situations it is clearly a mistake for the leader to do the bulk of the work. Generally, the group will be most productive if all members make substantial contributions. The more members contribute to a group, the more likely they are to feel a part of the group. Such positive feelings will benefit everyone.

Even if the leader is certain of the appropriate roles, others may be confused or may have different expectations. If there is any doubt, the leader should explain the roles clearly. If group members indicate different expectations, the group should then make decisions about who will do what.

In explaining his or her role the leader should be modest about personal skills and resources, attempting to come across as a knowledgeable person rather than an authority figure who has all the answers. The leader must also be prepared to explain the reasoning behind exercises and other actions or activities. The leader's role will vary from group to group and from situation to situation.

Agenda

Most meetings are more effective if the leader provides an agenda several days beforehand. Ideally, all members of the group should have an opportunity to suggest items for the agenda. The agenda should be briefly reviewed at the start of the meeting to give each member a chance to suggest additions, deletions, or other changes. In some meetings it may be appropriate for the group to discuss, and perhaps vote on, the suggested changes in the agenda.

Additional Guidelines for Leading a Group

This section briefly summarizes additional suggestions for effectively leading a group. Future chapters will expand on these guidelines. Effective leaders:

1. Understand that leadership is a shared responsibility. Every member will take on leadership roles at times. Designated leaders should not seek to dominate a group or believe they are responsible for directing the group in all of its task and maintenance functions. In fact, productivity and group cohesion are substantially increased when everyone contributes.
2. Use decision-making procedures best suited for the issues facing a particular group. (See chapter 10 for a discussion of a variety of decision-making procedures and their consequences.)
3. Use a problem-solving approach to handle the issues and problems facing the group. (See chapter 9 for a summary of how to use the problem-solving approach.)
4. Create a cooperative atmosphere rather than a competitive one. (See chapter 4.)
5. View controversy and conflict as being natural and desirable for resolving issues and arriving at good decisions. In resolving conflicts, seek to use a no-lose, problem-solving approach rather than a win-lose approach. (See chapter 9.)
6. Generally, seek to confront members who are hostile or disruptive (chapter 5.)
7. Use appropriate self-disclosure (chapter 7.)
8. Seek to create an atmosphere of open and honest communication. (See chapter 7 for how to improve verbal communication and be an active listener, and chapter 8 for how to improve nonverbal communication.)
9. Provide stimulating, relevant content and exercises that illustrate the concepts and help members try out suggested new behaviors. In an assertiveness group, for example, theoretical material on how to be more assertive should be followed by practice in being more assertive. (The chapters in this text use this format.)
10. Give attention to how to end a session. A few minutes before the session is scheduled to conclude, or when the group has exhausted the subject, a brief summary emphasizing the major points to be remembered leaves the group with a sense of achievement and signals the end of the session. Additional ways to end a session are described in chapter 17.

Leaders are not born. They are made—through training, practice, and experience. By learning how to lead groups effectively individuals become more aware of themselves, grow as people, become more self-confident, feel good about themselves, develop highly marketable skills, learn to improve interpersonal relationships, and help themselves and others accomplish important tasks. Everyone reading this text has the potential to become an effective group leader. This chapter has sought to demystify leadership by describing what an effective leader does and is. It is now up to you to further develop your capacities in being a leader. You can do it!

GROUP EXERCISES

Exercise A: Desensitizing Fears of Leading a Group

Goals: To identify the specific fears about being a designated leader for a group and to provide information to reduce those fears.

Step 1. The group leader should state the purpose of this exercise. Each student should then be handed a sheet of paper and instructed to complete, anonymously, the sentence "My specific fears about being a designated leader of a group are . . ." The leader should emphasize that the completed statements are collected and discussed.

Step 2. The responses should be collected in a way that ensures anonymity and then read aloud. After a concern is read, the students should suggest ways of reducing the concern. If a concern involves handling hostile members, for example, the class, with help from the instructor, may suggest strategies for coping with them. If a member fears that he or she does not have the traits needed to lead a group, it may be pointed out that research has found that no specific traits distinguish leaders from followers and that the distributed-functions theory of leadership asserts that practically anyone can be trained to be a leader.

Step 3. After step 2 is completed, the group leader or the instructor may want to summarize key points on how to lead a group and explain that future sessions will explore these points in greater depth.

Exercise B: Task Functions and Group Maintenance Functions

Goal: To show that at times nearly everyone takes a leadership role in groups that involves performing task and group maintenance functions.

Step 1. The group leader should indicate that this exercise will elicit the class's thoughts on what criteria should be used for admitting students into the social work program at this campus. The leader should then explain that the Council on Social Work Education (the national organization that accredits social work programs) requires every program to have criteria for admitting students. There is considerable variation in criteria among the programs in this country. Common criteria include a minimum grade-point average and a vaguely defined "aptitude for social work."

Step 2. The class then forms subgroups of five or six students and each selects an observer. The observers then form a group in another room or hallway. The subgroups should not begin discussing their primary task until the observers return.

Step 3. The observers are told that their task is to record *significant* task and group maintenance functions performed by each member of their subgroup. The leader may need to explain that task functions are statements designed to help the subgroup accomplish its task and that group maintenance functions are statements made to strengthen the social/emotional aspects of group life. Observers should be given a handout that summarizes the task roles and group maintenance roles developed by David and Frank Johnson, which appear in this chapter. The observers will be asked after the exercise is over to summarize to their subgroup how each member contributed through certain task and group maintenance functions.

Step 4. The leader and observers return to the subgroups. The subgroups are informed that their task is to develop criteria for admitting students to the social work program at this campus. The subgroup is free to suggest various criteria but should probably begin by discussing: (1) whether a grade-point average should be used for admission and what it should be, and (2) how "aptitude for social work" should be defined and measured.

Step 5. The subgroups should work for twenty to thirty minutes, and each should then state and explain its proposed criteria. Time should then be called and each subgroup should be asked to indicate to the class what it arrived at.

Step 6. The group leader should indicate that one of the purposes of this exercise is to demonstrate that most members in a group assume leadership roles by carrying out task and group maintenance functions. The leader should then explain what task and group maintenance functions are.

Step 7. Each observer summarizes to his or her subgroup, but *not* to the whole class, the significant task and group maintenance functions performed by each member.

Step 8. End the exercise by asking members if they have any thoughts or comments.

Exercise C: Power Bases

Goal: To practice analyzing influence attempts in terms of power bases.

Step 1. The group leader explains the purpose of the exercise, describes the five bases of power developed by French and Raven, and briefly discusses the effects of using each base.

Step 2. The class divides into subgroups of three members each and answers the following questions:

1. What bases of power does the instructor of this course have?
2. What bases of power does a student in this class have?
3. What is the primary power base the instructor has?
4. What is the primary power base a student has?

Step 3. The subgroups share their answers to these questions by having one member from each subgroup write the answers on the blackboard. The class then discusses the reasons for the similarities and differences between the answers arrived at by the subgroups.

Step 4. In all likelihood the instructor will be seen as having much more power than students. The group leader should summarize the effects of unequal power on communication and on relationships within a group (as described in this chapter). Students then discuss how they feel when an instructor attempts to present himself on a level equal or superior to students. Further, what are the positive and negative aspects of each relationship?

Exercise D: Types of Influence

Goal: To increase awareness of feelings toward the following three types of influence: personal challenge, coercive power, and manipulation.

Step 1. The instructor explains the purpose of the exercise and asks students to visualize each of the following situations. The instructor should pause after each situation and allow students time to write their responses.

Narrative 1. Visualize an academic situation in which you worked hard on something because it presented a personal challenge and because you expected to grow as a person through meeting this challenge. Briefly, describe this situation on a sheet of paper and summarize your feelings about the challenge motivating you to work hard.

Narrative 2. Visualize a work situation in which someone sought to use coercive power to make you do something. Briefly, describe this situation on a sheet of paper and summarize your feelings about someone using coercive power to make you do something.

Narrative 3. Visualize a situation in which someone sought to manipulate or con you into doing something. Briefly, describe this situation on a sheet of paper and summarize your feelings when you discovered someone was attempting to manipulate or con you into doing something.

Step 2. The students then form subgroups of three members each to share what they wrote with each other and discuss how they felt about each situation. If any student does not wish to share these personal thoughts, that is acceptable.

Step 3. The students think of situations in which it would be desirable to use coercive power and manipulation, and then discuss them.

CHAPTER FOUR

PERSONAL GOALS, GROUP GOALS, AND THE NOMINAL GROUP

Goal: Just as a baseball team has a short-term goal of winning a game and a long-term goal of clinching a pennant, individuals and groups must identify short-term and long-term goals to function effectively. This chapter provides guidelines on setting goals, defines hidden agendas, describes the differences between competitive and cooperative groups, and presents an overview of the nominal group approach.

A goal is an end toward which an individual or group of people is working. It is an ideal or a desired achievement that people value. A personal goal is a goal held by a member of a group. A group goal is a goal held by enough members of a group that the group can be said to be working toward its achievement.

All groups have goals, and every individual who joins a group has personal goals. Groups generally have both short-range and long-range goals. The short-range goals should be stepping-stones to the long-range goals. Group goals are important for several reasons. The effectiveness and efficiency of the group and its procedures can be measured by the extent to which goals are achieved. Goals guide groups and their members by giving the group's programs and efforts direction. Conflicts between group members are often resolved according to which position is most helpful in achieving group goals. Group goals are also a strong motivating force that stimulates members to work together. Once members make a commitment to achieve a certain goal, they will feel an obligation to put forth their abilities, efforts, and resources to achieve it.

A member's commitment to a group goal will depend on: (1) how attracted this member is to the group, (2) how attractive the goal appears, (3) how likely it appears the group can accomplish the goal, (4) the ability to measure progress toward achieving the goal and the ability to measure when the goal is attained, (5) the rewards the group and the member will receive when the goal is attained, (6) the challenge presented by the goal is (a moderate risk of failure is usually more challenging than a high or low risk of failure,[1] and (7) the types of interactions the member will have with other group members in working toward the goal (some ways of interacting are more enjoyable and rewarding than others).

Setting group goals is the first step in measuring the effectiveness of a group. Once goals are set, the tasks necessary to accomplish the goals must be determined. Next, responsibilities for carrying out the tasks must be agreed upon or assigned, and deadlines for completing those tasks set. As the process proceeds, the extent to which deadlines have been met and tasks achieved must be evaluated. The final measurement is whether the group has achieved its goals. An effective group is one that has considerable success in achieving its goals. (The processes of setting group goals, determining the tasks for accomplishing the goals, assigning tasks to each member, and setting deadlines for accomplishing the tasks are, in reality, also the components of forming contracts with group members about expectations. Contracts and group goals should be reviewed periodically as the group progresses and revised if necessary.)

Group members will be more motivated to achieve group goals if they are involved in setting those goals. Through involvement, members will be (1) more likely to have their personal goals become a component of the group goals, (2) more aware of the importance of choosing these goals, and (3) more committed to providing their resources to achieve the goals.

PERSONAL GOALS

The personal goals of members may be *very* diverse. In a stress management group, for example, some members may join because they want to learn how to relax, others because they are lonely and want companionship, and still others because their spouses urge them to. Some may join because they have heard good things about the group leader and want to "check it out." A few may join because they do not believe stress is destructive and want to convince others of this belief.

While some members are acutely aware of their personal goals, others may not be. For example, freshman social work majors sometimes attend a meeting of the Student Social Work Club at the urging of a faculty member without having given much thought to their personal goals and objectives.

The more similarity there is between the personal goals of members and the goals of the group, the more attracted to the group the members are likely to be, and the more willing to provide their resources and energies to the group. If the personal goals of the group are homogeneous (alike), members are more apt to agree on group goals, to work together toward achieving those goals, and to be happier with the group. Heterogeneous personal goals do not necessarily spell failure for a group, but they do require special attention.

Hidden Agendas

When members have heterogeneous personal goals, hidden agendas are more likely to develop. (If members have homogeneous personal goals, these goals are apt to become group goals, and hidden agendas are less likely to arise.) A *hidden agenda* is a personal goal held by a member, but unknown to other group members, which interferes with the group's efforts. At times, hidden agendas can be very destructive. For example, I have participated in groups where an individual observed the comments and actions of others to obtain evidence to bring legal harassment charges. Usually, however, hidden agendas are less destructive than this and may consist of little more than a lonely person's wish to monopolize the group's "air time" with insignificant small talk. Because this type of behavior can slow progress severely, group goals should incorporate, to some extent, the personal goals of its members. Leaders can also minimize the effects of hidden agendas by making the group's goals clear at the outset.

Certain signals suggest hidden agendas. A member may fail to contribute or may say and do things that impede group activities. When hidden agendas appear to exist, the consequences of confronting a member about disruptive behavior must be evaluated. If the consequences appear beneficial, then the member should be confronted, either openly or privately. Whatever method of confrontation appears to be most beneficial should be used. Sometimes, however, hidden agendas are best left undisturbed. For example, a group member who has recently experienced the death of a spouse may use a nontherapy group to ventilate pain. In this situation, it may or may not be constructive to confront the person.

When confronting a member about a hidden agenda, avoid blaming or criticizing. The confrontation should lead to a trusting, open discussion of the issue. If the hidden agenda is rational and legitimate, extensive efforts should be made to help the member. Alternatives for resolving the concern could be explored and one or more implemented to resolve the problem. (See chapter 5 for further suggestions on confrontation.) Perhaps the goals of the group can even be revised to incorporate the more personal issue or perhaps the member can be helped to achieve the personal goal outside the group. A group member grieving over the death of a spouse, for example, may be referred to a counselor or to a survivors' group where the grief can be expressed and worked out more effectively.

93

ESTABLISHING GROUP GOALS

Although group goals can be developed in a variety of ways, the following procedures are recommended because they involve group members in the decision-making process. After the leader shares his or her views on the goals of the group, members are asked to explain their own reasons for joining—that is, their personal goals. Working together, the leader and group members discuss the merits of the goals presented and discuss additional goals, refining and rewording them until a final list is developed. Decision-making procedures as outlined in chapter 10 may be used to resolve conflicts and attain agreement. The final list should be typed and distributed to each member for reference.

Alternatively, the group leader may interview each member before the first meeting about personal and group goals, and then develop a composite list to present at the first meeting of the group. This list is then discussed and amended until a majority of members are satisfied. A less effective way to determine group goals is for the leader to attempt to "sell" the group a set of goals he believes is preferable. If group goals are prescribed in this manner or by the constitution of the group, they should still be fully discussed by members, who may refine and reword them.

Effective groups usually follow a variation of the following format. Long-range goals are set first, and efforts are made to state these goals in operational and measurable terms. Short-range goals are then established and prioritized as to their importance in achieving the long-range goals. Tasks are also identified to achieve short-range goals and then ranked according to their importance For high-priority tasks, specific responsibilities are assigned to group members, and deadlines are set for completion. Future evaluations then identify the progress being made in achieving the tasks and goals.

Operational and Measurable Goals

An *operational goal* is one that can be directly translated into courses of action to achieve the goal. A goal such as, "Each member of this class will be able to describe the difference between personal and group goals" is operational. Students could put this goal into action by studying the first part of this chapter and then taking a test that asks them to define both terms. The test scores measure whether the class reached the goal.

A *nonoperational goal* is one that cannot be achieved through specific actions. "Everyone in this class will learn how to cure all emotional and behavioral problems," for example, is nonoperational because treatment approaches have not been developed to treat successfully all people who have emotional and behavioral problems. A goal that is nonoperational is *much* harder to achieve. For instance, it may be centuries before we know whether it is possible to treat all emotional and behavioral problems successfully.

In practice, groups should strive to develop operational goals so that a course of action can be developed and the goal more readily achieved. "Helping students to better manage stress in their lives through instructing them in meditation," for example, is much more operational than "Seeking ways to help students better manage stress."

Group goals should also be measurable. For example, the goal "Having everyone in this class become a great group leader" is very difficult to measure *without* criteria to use in judging what constitutes a great leader. In contrast, the following goal is more measurable: "By the end of this semester, every student in this class will have demonstrated that she or he can lead a group at a level that the instructor deems *satisfactory*." One way to make this goal operational is by having the students take turns being a group leader. For each session, the instructor then rates the student who leads the group as doing a "satisfactory" or "less than satisfactory" job. Students who receive a "less than satisfactory" rating can be given additional opportunities to lead the class and have their performance rated again. Progress toward this goal is simply measured by counting the number of students who receive an overall "satisfactory" rating.

Operational, measurable goals are valuable for a variety of reasons. They help guide the members and the group in planning and working on tasks. A group that is unclear as to what its goals are will be even more confused as to what specific tasks are needed to reach those goals. Operational and measurable goals also measure the effectiveness of the leader because the leader's action can be judged in terms of movement toward group goals. Clear goals, in fact, often make leadership easier because the group knows what it is trying to achieve and is less likely to question a leader's actions that move the group toward its goals.

In addition, operational and measurable goals make it easier to communicate to other groups and to nonmembers what the group is about. Such goals also help evaluate progress. Each course of action can be assessed to determine its payoffs in attaining goals. The group can easily determine whether a course of action should be continued or abandoned. Clear goals and documented progress toward those goals are especially valuable when accountability is required by funding sources or others. A final advantage is that conflicts among members can often be resolved by determining which position appears to best help the group reach its goals. When conflicts arise in groups that do not have measurable and operational goals, there is no logical way to determine whose view has higher payoffs. As a result, the conflict is not apt to be resolved and may force the group to spend more time maintaining harmony than completing its work.

Forming clear goals that are operational and measurable is a lengthy, time-consuming process. The goal-setting stage is often when a group flounders the most. It occurs early in the life of a group, when members are also testing their interest and commitment and when interpersonal relationships are being formed. Arriving at goals the members can support often takes much longer than anticipated. The value of setting clear goals, however, far outweighs the time and effort saved by accepting goals that are vague and that may later be seriously challenged. David Johnson and Frank Johnson note, "The more time a group spends establishing agreement on clear goals, the less time it needs in achieving them—and the more likely it will be that the members will work effectively for the common outcome."[2]

Research has found groups have a better chance to be effective when:

1. The goals are clear, operationally defined, and measurable.
2. The members see the goals as being relevant, attainable, meaningful, and acceptable.
3. Both personal and group goals can be attained by the same activities and tasks.
4. The goals are viewed as challenging and have a moderate risk of failure.
5. The resources needed to accomplish the tasks are available.
6. There is high coordination among group members.
7. The group members maintain a cooperative rather than a competitive atmosphere.[3]

Competition vs. Cooperation

Groups tend to have either a cooperative or a competitive atmosphere. A cooperative group is marked by open and honest communication, trust, pooling of resources, and cohesion. Research into problem-solving groups has found a number of positive consequences of a cooperative group atmosphere. Cooperation among members increases creativity, coordination of effort, division of labor, emotional involvement in group accomplishment, helping and sharing, interpersonal skills, cooperative attitudes and values, positive self-attitudes, congeniality among group members, positive attitudes toward the group and tasks, divergent thinking, acceptance of individual and cultural differences, and problem-solving skills.[4]

A cooperative group atmosphere results when the personal goals of group members are perceived to be compatible, identical, or complementary. An example of a highly cooperative group is a football team where the main goal of each member is to win, and the main goal of the team is to win. In a cooperative group each member seeks to coordinate his or her efforts with those of other group members to achieve the goals of the group. In establishing a cooperative atmosphere, rewards to members must be based on the quantity and quality of group performance, rather than on individual performance.

In contrast, a competitive atmosphere is usually destructive. Competition exists when the members perceive their personal goals to be incompatible, different, conflicting, or mutually exclusive. In a highly competitive group, a member can achieve a goal only if the other group members fail to obtain their goals.[5] A group interview of several applicants for a job vacancy such as an audition for a play, for example, is intentionally competitive. Each member seeks to accomplish personal goals while seeking to block other group members from accomplishing theirs. The negative consequences of competition in problem-solving groups are numerous. Competition decreases creativity, coordination of effort, division of labor, helping and sharing, and cohesion. Competition promotes ineffective communication, suspicion and mistrust, high anxiety about goal accomplishment, competitive values and attitudes, negative self-attitudes, animosity among group members, and negative attitudes toward the group and its tasks. Competition also encourages the rejection of: differences of opinion, divergent thinking, and cultural and individual differences. A competitive atmosphere leads to low effectiveness in solving complex problems.[6]

Are there any situations in which competition is beneficial? There are a few. For example, in team sports coaches have discovered it is beneficial to have highly talented athletes compete for starting positions. Such competition generally encourages athletes to work harder. But even in team sports, successful coaches know that a key to winning is instilling a sense of team effort (that is, cooperative atmosphere), so that each player focuses not on individual recognition, but on helping the team win by playing the role he or she has been assigned.

Kelly and Stahelski examined the question of what happens when a competitive person joins a group that has a cooperative atmosphere.[7] Since cooperative groups are much more effective in solving problems than competitive groups, the question is significant. Three consequences were found to occur. The competitive behavior of the new member leads the other members to behave competitively. The competitive person views the former cooperative members as having always been competitive. The former cooperative members are generally aware that their competitive behavior is largely a consequence of the new member's competitiveness. Thus, it appears that one competitive person can change a cooperative group into a competitive group.

The positive characteristics of a cooperative group are readily destroyed by a competitive person. All of the following decrease when a competitive person joins a formerly cooperative group: trust, congeniality among members, openness of communication, and problem-solving orientation.[8] Why does a competitive person have such a strong, destructive effect? Apparently, the cooperative members realize the competitive person will, if given a chance, take advantage of their cooperativeness and use it to his or her personal advantage. In many situations their only recourse to prevent exploitation is to become competitive. Thus, even though cooperation is by far the most effective atmosphere in problem-solving groups, it takes only one competitive person to change the atmosphere to a destructive, competitive one. If a cooperative group is to survive, it must avoid introducing any competitive element.

THE NOMINAL GROUP APPROACH

The nominal group approach, developed by Andre Delbecq and Andrew Van de Ven, can be used as an aid in formulating group goals.[9] This approach is a problem-identification technique for designing or modifying programs and involves meeting with potential users to assess their needs. A nominal group is "a group in which individuals work in the presence of others but do not verbally interact."[10] By simply allowing group members to list their needs on paper *without group discussion*, each member's personal views can be ascertained. Too often in the past, new programs have been developed by "experts" who lacked a clear picture of the needs of their consumers, or by the most vocal members of a group; the result has been programs that do not effectively serve anyone. So, the prime objective of the nominal group approach is to identify the needs of the consumer group (that is, the potential users of a new service) in order to develop a program that serves them.[11]

A nominal group meeting can be conducted within a half-hour or an hour; it has often been used by university faculty to identify topics students wish to have covered in classes. For example, the nominal group approach was used by the social work department at the author's university in connection with an elective workshop in grief management.[12] Enrollment was limited to thirty students. At the first class meeting, the students were asked, using a nominal group approach, "What specific topics do you want covered in this course?" The specific steps in conducting a nominal group are described in exercise C at the end of this chapter. (The responses given in the grief management class appear in table 4.1.)

When a nominal group is used with a subgroup of a consumer group, care should be taken to obtain a representative cross section of the consumer group. Before using the nominal group approach, the subgroup should be informed of the purpose of the study. However, the researchers should generally *not* provide any information on what they think should be the results of using the nominal group approach so as not to bias the participants.

Research on the merits of the nominal group approach suggests that it is superior to brainstorming and to other types of group interaction for generating information relevant to a problem situation. It elicits more suggestions and covers more areas of interest.[13] (Brainstorming has the advantage that the items first suggested tend to set the direction for future items that are generated.) The nominal group is designed to receive input from all group members rather than just the more vocal or aggressive ones, as often happens in conventional group discussions. Evaluation of items is avoided, which substantially reduces the pressure against expressing minority opinions or unconventional ideas. Conflicting, in-

Table 4.1

Highest Ranking Topics for Grief Management Course

Topics	Number of Votes
1. Suicide	13
2. Getting over the loss and loneliness that result from the death of someone else	9
3. The terminally ill, and how to relate to them	9
4. Funeral director—guest speaker	9
5. AIDS	8
6. Getting over the loss of a close relationship	8
7. Coping skills for myself and others	8
8. Hospice movement—guest speaker	8
9. How to come to terms with your own death	7
10. Should one be permitted to take one's own life?	7
11. How to change fears and negative attitudes about death	6
12. Communication with survivors (that is, people who have had someone close to them die)	6
13. Sudden Infant Death Syndrome	6
14. Life after death	5
15. How to help others (parents) deal with the death of someone close (children)	4

compatible ideas are tolerated. Furthermore, the approach appears to save time, as it can be conducted faster than interacting group processes.[14] The nominal group approach has a gamelike quality, as the group generates creative tension, which appears to stimulate individuals to do their best in suggesting items.

GROUP EXERCISES

Exercise A: Setting Personal and Group Goals

Goal: To identify personal goals for this class and to set group goals.

Step 1. The group leader begins by explaining the purpose of the exercise. Then, the group leader should explain what operational and measurable goals are and summarize their importance.

Step 2. Each member makes a list of personal and group goals for the class on a sheet of paper. The instructor should also prepare a list of group goals for the class.

Step 3. A listing should be made on the blackboard of the personal and group goals suggested by each student (inform students that they have a right to privacy and do not need to identify their personal goals). The instructor's list of group goals should also be put on the blackboard.

Step 4. The class should then discuss the personal and group goals listed on the blackboard and decide what the goals for the class will be. (The group leader should have previously read chapter 10 on procedures for decision making.) In arriving at class goals, it should be made clear that since the instructor is responsible for the course, he or she may exclude or add any group goal.

Step 5. After group goals are established, the following questions should be discussed with the group:

1. Are all of these goals operational and measurable? If not, how can they be improved?
2. What difficulties were encountered in setting group goals?
3. Did it take longer than expected?
4. Did anyone become frustrated at some point? Why?
5. How satisfied is the group with the goals that were set?
6. How does the group feel about the instructor having a greater say as to what the group's goals should be?
7. Are these goals realistically attainable?
8. Are these group goals compatible with personal goals?
9. Are individuals committed to work toward attaining these group goals?

Exercise B: A Sphinx Foundation Grant

Goal: To observe what happens when some members are cooperative while others are competitive.

Step 1. The group leader explains that the exercise involves setting goals. Students are to assume that the Sphinx Foundation has awarded $100,000 to the students and faculty in this social work program to improve the program and/or social services in the community surrounding the campus. The task of the class is to arrive at recommendations as to how these funds should be used. The class is divided into three equal subgroups.

Step 2. Each subgroup meets for fifteen minutes to develop proposals. A representative then presents the proposals to representatives of the other two subgroups.

Step 3. The three representatives meet in the center of the room for fifteen minutes to present the proposals to each other and work toward a decision for the class. The three subgroups observe the negotiations. A subgroup cannot meet with the other subgroups, but members in a subgroup may talk among themselves. The subgroups may not talk with their representatives, but they may send written messages.

Step 4. The representatives should next confer with their subgroups for five minutes.

Step 5. The representatives then meet in the center of the room for five minutes to attempt to reach an agreement. Next, they meet with their subgroups for five minutes. And, finally, they meet again in the center of the room to seek to reach a final agreement.

Step 6. Discuss the following questions:

1. Was an agreement reached? Why or why not?
2. Did the representatives and the subgroups attempt to be cooperative or competitive? Why? What were the results of being primarily either cooperative or competitive?
3. Were the proposals primarily designed to benefit students, the department, or social services in the community? Why was this particular focus the major emphasis?
4. What are the representatives' feelings about this exercise? Did the representatives feel pressure from their subgroup? If so, what type of pressure?
5. How were decisions made within each subgroup, and how did the representatives make decisions?

99

Exercise C: The Nominal Group Approach

Goal: To show how to conduct a nominal group.

Step 1. The leader begins by describing what a nominal group is and how it can be used. The leader then explains that the goal of the exercise is to identify shortcomings in the university's social work program by obtaining the views of the participants as to their wants and needs. In a classroom setting it is not necessary to obtain a representative cross section of the group because the students compose the total population of potential users.

Step 2. The participants are randomly divided into small groups of five to eight students. Each group should be seated around a separate table. (When tables are not available, classroom desks can be arranged in groups of five to eight with only limited inconvenience.)

Step 3. The leader distributes a sheet of paper containing a question participants must answer in writing. (An alternative to distributing a sheet of paper is to write the question on the blackboard.) One question that might be used is the following:

> Without mentioning names, what do you see as the shortcomings of our social work program?
>
> Please—No talking

Step 4. For fifteen to twenty minutes, the participants privately list their responses to the question. No talking is permitted during this time.

Step 5. One member of each group is designated as recorder. The recorder asks each group member to state a shortcoming and lists each response on flip-chart sheets with a magic marker in full view of other members. This process continues until each member has given all of his or her responses. Listing is done separately for each group. Each response is recorded exactly as each member states it, and there is no discussion.

Step 6. The flip-chart sheets are then posted on the wall with masking tape near the group involved. A brief, informal discussion follows and focuses on clarifying what the ideas mean. There are two different approaches to reviewing the items: (1) all items are made known to the whole class, or (2) each group briefly reviews only the items recorded for its group. Both approaches appear to work. For smaller groups, the first is usually used. When the total number of listed items becomes very large, the second approach is generally more effective.

Step 7. Once the participants are familiar with the items on the flip-chart sheets, each is asked to list on index cards the five items he or she feels are most important.

Step 8. These items are handed in anonymously and then tabulated on the flip-chart sheets, or each student can simply check his or her five items on the flip-chart sheets with a magic marker. These results are then briefly discussed with the students. (The instructor may well find it desirable to share the results with the other faculty in the department, and a faculty meeting may be arranged to discuss and take action on the highly rated items.)

CHAPTER FIVE

GROUP NORMS AND PROBLEMS OF CONFORMITY

Goal: A nun chewing bubble gum in front of a class, or an administrator shouting at a group of employees, are both examples of individuals displaying behaviors that violate social norms. All groups have norms, and this chapter describes their importance, examines how they are formed, and discusses group pressures to conform. Various types of hostile or disruptive group members are identified, and methods are suggested for handling their uncooperative behavior.

Group norms are rules that specify proper group behavior. To be a norm, a rule must be accepted by a majority of the group. If a person recognizes a norm and believes the benefits of conforming outweigh the consequences of deviating, the norm can influence that person's behavior. At first members may conform because of pressures from the group. As time passes, though, members generally internalize norms and conform automatically. Norms provide one of the most important mechanisms of social control over members of groups and over society as a whole.

Every group has norms. If you frequently socialize with a certain group of students, for example, your group will gradually set norms as to what is acceptable and unacceptable behavior at gatherings. Your classes will have certain norms as well, covering smoking, chewing bubble gum, arriving late, absences, meeting deadlines, raising a hand before speaking, and cheating on exams.

Some norms are set formally—bylaws and constitutions of organizations, for instance, specify responsibilities for the officers. Other norms are set informally. During a department meeting the department chair may frown at a faculty member who is reading his mail. If that faculty member responds to the nonverbal communication and puts aside his mail, other faculty members may observe the nonverbal interaction and decide never to read their mail during meetings. Through this process a norm against reading mail has informally been established.

Norms have an "ought to" or "must" quality, and they vary in importance. There are strong pressures to obey and, in some cases, severe penalties for violating *important* norms—confidentiality in therapy groups, for example. If a member violates confidentiality by revealing personal information about another member to others outside the group, he may be penalized by expulsion from the group. Failure to obey less important norms, such as not belching at meetings, generates only mild disapproval and little or no penalty.

Members are often only subconsciously aware of many of the norms that are guiding their behavior. If one were to ask a group member to define his group's norms, he would probably be able to list only a few because many norms are taken for granted. Norms relating to dress, promptness, or foul language are often given little thought by group members.

When a person enters a new group, he generally feels strange and uncomfortable because he is unaware of the norms. So he searches for clues to norms, asking himself such questions as: What is appropriate to disclose, and what is not? Who is in the "in" group, and who is left out? Is smoking permissible? Can I tell a joke? Do members raise their hands before speaking? What role does each member play? Is the group competitive or cooperative? Are there hidden agendas? Are there coalitions? Which members are more powerful?

HOW NORMS ARE LEARNED AND DEVELOPED

Some group norms are fairly universal, so new members who have worked in groups before will be aware of many norms that are likely to be operating. For example, an individual who joins a therapy group can expect other members to be honest, open, and self-disclosing. Many groups have the following norms: reciprocity (if someone does something positive for you, you should do something positive in return); fair play (don't lie or cheat to get what you want); social responsibility (you should help those who need it); and shared air time (everyone should have a chance to talk and no one should monopolize the conversation).

New members learn norms by talking privately with a group member they trust. They may ask questions such as: Who has the power? Is it acceptable to say or do such and such? Are there coalitions in the group? Do some members have hidden agendas? Are there personal matters that some members are sensitive about? Someone who is overweight, for example, may express discomfort with comments on dieting, and other members may individually decide not to mention dieting when the overweight person is present.

Although norms are learned in a variety of ways, the most common way is through positive and negative reinforcement. Through a process of trial and error, members identify which of their behaviors are accepted and rewarded by the group and which are judged inappropriate or destructive. Another way members identify norms is through "modeling," which involves learning through observing another member's behavior.

Some norms are in the bylaws, constitution, minutes, and/or other documents of a group or organization. For example, there may be guidelines for placing an item on the agenda, the duties and responsibilities of the officers, and the decision-making procedures for resolving crucial issues. Furthermore, norms can take the form of role expectations that can be official or unofficial. Officially, the chair of a group is expected to call and run meetings; the secretary keeps minutes. Unofficially, a wealthy member is expected to make donations when the group needs funds. Likewise, a member who is skilled at reducing tension is expected to ease the tension level when it gets too high.

Some norms develop less formally through nonverbal communications. For example, the leader of a therapy group may shake his head in disapproval of one member mimicking another. The other members note the gesture and then individually (without discussion) decide not to mimic anyone in the group in the future.

Some norms become known only after they are violated. Rodney Napier and Matti Gershenfeld give an example.

> A minister may preach about justice and racial equality and may urge his congregation to live according to these principles, all of which they accept from him. However, when he marches in a picket line, the congregation may rebuke him for transcending his position. He may be sanctioned with a statement to the effect that ministers may preach about justice and equality, but action on social issues is for others. In this situation, neither the minister nor the congregation knew the norm existed until an action took place that was contrary to the norm; the congregation then made known the violation by the threat of sanctions.[1]

New norms may develop from suggestions on group policy or procedures made by group members. For example, a member may suggest, "In order for an item to be placed on the agenda, the members must be informed of it at least forty-eight hours prior to the meeting to give them an opportunity to think about it." If the group approves of the suggestion, it becomes a policy and a norm.

CONFORMITY

Conformity means yielding to group pressure. To conform, a group member must experience conflict between the influences exerted by the group (group norms) and his or her personal values. A member experiencing this type of conflict has two options: announce an independent position or conform by agreeing with the group's position in either an expedient or a true manner. The *expedient conformer* can outwardly agree but inwardly disagree, while a *true conformer* agrees both outwardly and inwardly.

There have been a number of classic studies of conforming behavior. Muzafer Sherif examined what has been called the "autokinetic effect" of conformity.[2] In his experiment subjects in a darkened room were asked to judge how far a dot of light moved. Although the light *appeared* to move, it actually did not (the autokinetic effect). Each subject saw the dot of light and made a series of individual judgments as to how far it moved. The subjects were then brought together in groups of three to judge how far the light moved. Their judgments tended to converge into a group standard. Later, when they again viewed the light by themselves, they tended to retain the group standard as their answer. The essential finding was that when a situation is ambiguous and there is no objective way of determining the "right" answer, members rely on the group to help define reality. In real life this finding means that membership in a group determines much of what individuals will see, learn, think about, and do.

S. E. Asch also examined conforming behavior and investigated what happens when an individual's judgment conflicts with that of other group members.[3] The experiments involved two sets of cards, as shown in figure 5.1.

Subjects from psychology classes who volunteered for the experiment were arranged in groups of seven to nine. They were seated at a table and asked to state in turn which line was closest in size to the standard. In the control groups, practically all subjects chose line 2. The responses in the experimental groups, however, were of greater interest. In the experimental groups all of the group members except for *one subject* were accomplices of the experimenter. The *subject* was always seated so that he would give his opinion last. All of the accomplices chose the same wrong line. When it came to the subject's turn, he was faced with relying on his own judgment or conforming to the group's judgment, even though he probably perceived it as wrong. In a variety of similar studies, Asch found that more than one-third of the subjects conformed to the group judgment. Such a high level of conformity is amazing considering there was no overt group pressure to conform, the situation was not ambiguous, and the subjects did not know each other.

According to Stanley Schachter, everyone has a need to evaluate the "rightness" of feelings, opinions, values, and attitudes as well as the extent of abilities. He conducted studies to demonstrate that in the absence of objective, nonsocial means of evaluation, a

Figure 5.1: Cards in Asch Conformity Studies

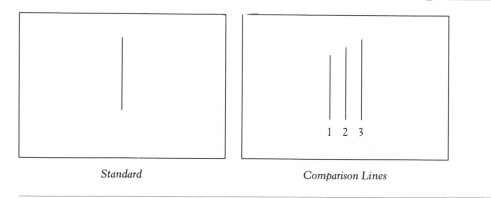

Standard   Comparison Lines

person will rely on other people as comparative points of reference. He called this the theory of social comparison. A study by Schachter and Singer provides support for the theory.[4] Subjects were aroused by an injection of adrenaline and then exposed to the actions of a peer. In some cases, the peer (actually the experimenter's confederate) behaved in a highly euphoric manner, while for other subjects he acted as if he were angry. The experimenters predicted that those subjects who did not have an appropriate explanation for the physiological sensations aroused by the drug (because they had been uninformed or misinformed about the drug and its effects) would imitate the inappropriate behavior of the confederate and interpret their feelings in a manner consistent with the confederate's behavior. The predictions were confirmed, Furthermore, the control subjects, who were either informed of the effects of adrenaline or did not receive the injection, displayed few imitative responses of the confederate. To a large extent, then, the peer defined social reality for the experimental subjects, that is, those subjects injected with adrenaline who did not receive an explanation of the physiological sensations aroused by the drug.

A number of conclusions have been drawn from conformity research and are summarized as follows.[5]

1. Group pressure influences behavior, even when the bogus group consensus is obviously wrong. In one study, for example, fifty military officers were asked to indicate which of two figures shown side by side, a star and a circle, was larger in area. The circle was clearly about one-third larger but under group pressure 46 percent of the officers agreed with the bogus group consensus that the star was larger.

2. Many people can be pressured into yielding on attitudes and opinions even on personally significant matters. For example, the same fifty military officers were asked, first privately and then later under group consensus conditions, to consider the statement: "I doubt whether I would make a good leader." In private none of the officers expressed agreement, but under unanimous group pressure, 37 percent expressed agreement.

3. Although yielding occurs more often on difficult, subjective items than on easy, objective ones, there are extremely large individual differences. A few people yield on almost all items, a few on none. Most yield on some and not on others.

4. When people are retested privately on the same items some time later, a major part of the yielding effect disappears because the person tends to rely on personal judgment. Yet, a small part of the yielding effect remains, indicating group pressure can change attitudes.

5. As a group increases in size, the pressure to yield increases, and more yielding occurs. When a person is opposed by only one other person, there is very little yielding. Yielding is markedly reduced when a person has the *support* of one other person (a partner) in the group.

Apparently a dissident opinion has a tremendous effect in strengthening the independence of like-minded people.

In a dramatic study involving conformity Milgram demonstrated that subjects in an experimental situation would administer electric shocks of dangerous strength to another person when instructed to do so by the experimenter.[6] (The other person, unknown to the subject, did not actually receive the electrical shocks.) Even when they were instructed to give increasingly strong shocks and the victim protested in anguish, most subjects followed the experimenter's orders. This series of studies on obedience demonstrated that people will yield to "authoritative" commands even when the behavior is incompatible with their own normal moral standards of conduct. Milgram suggested that his studies help us understand why the German people complied with the unethical commands of Hitler. Group pressures, especially when viewed as authoritative, have a tremendous effect on a person's actions, attitudes, and beliefs.

Idiosyncrasy Credits

Every member of a group gains credits (and increased status) by exhibiting competence and conforming to the expectations applicable at a given time. Eventually, these credits allow a person to break the norms and rules of the group without being chastised. To some extent, after credits have been accumulated, nonconformity to general procedures or expectations serves as a confirming feature of one's status and further enhances one's position. Yet there is a limit to the number of idiosyncrasy credits awarded. Nonconformity beyond this limit will result in a dramatic decrease in status and perhaps even in rejection by the other group members.[7]

DOS AND DON'TS OF NORMS

Norms should be established that will improve the capacity of the group to function effectively, such as starting meetings on time or cooperating rather than competing. Because norms exist only to allow the group to function effectively, nonfunctional norms should be identified and then either discarded or replaced with more appropriate standards. In some settings, it is desirable to write down crucial norms. In group homes, for example, all the rules about smoking, drinking, curfew hours, attending school, and domestic duties should be posted so that the residents are fully aware of them. The consequences of violating these norms should also be clearly written out.

Important norms should be enforced immediately after a violation and as consistently as possible. If norms are not enforced, they will lose their power, and a new norm (that it's OK to break such a rule) may begin to emerge. In most social service settings, social workers *must* follow through on consequences when clients violate important norms. Social workers lose their credibility with clients when consequences do not follow violations. Most centers serving runaways, for example, clearly spell out that residents cannot use alcohol or drugs while at the center. Residents who do are asked to leave. In one center, workers failed to expel a resident caught using alcohol, and the next day most of the residents were drinking beer.

Group leaders should personally attempt to model the norms they believe are important. At a group home, for example, residents will not keep their rooms clean if the group leader's office is a mess.

PROBLEMS OF CONFORMITY

Hostile or disruptive members who fail to conform to group norms may be present in any group, even in those where membership is voluntary. However, they are more likely to be found in involuntary groups. Involuntary members often (at least at initial group meetings) wish they were a thousand other places than at the meeting. They may be angry and believe the time spent in the group will be a complete waste.

An involuntary client is one who is compelled to be a recipient of a social worker's

THE CONFORMITY POWER OF GROUPS

The power of groups over individuals is great, as shown by the following examples.

On February 4, 1974, Patty Hearst, a college student and daughter of a wealthy publishing magnate, was kidnapped by the Symbionese Liberation Army, an ultraradical group. She was forcibly dragged from her home in Berkeley, California, taken to a house by her abductors, and placed in a closet. For several days, she remained in this closet with no lights. She was blindfolded, her hands were bound, and she was given food but was unable to dispose of her body wastes. Besides making constant threats against her life, her captors told her that her family had abandoned her by not complying with the kidnap demands. She was informed that her parents said it was all right with them if she was put to death. At times, Patty was also sexually assaulted by her captors. After a number of weeks passed, she was released from the closet. A few days later she was taken to a bank where (according to Ms. Hearst) her captors forced her to participate in a bank robbery. She was given a gun to use during the robbery, and one of her captors (armed with a gun) kept an eye on her. After this robbery, she was taken back to her place of captivity and informed that she was now guilty of bank robbery and murder, and that the FBI would shoot her on sight. For the next several months, Ms. Hearst conformed because of this pressure and joined her captors in committing additional crimes and in trying to avoid apprehension by the police. After her apprehension nineteen months later, she claimed that she had committed bank robbery and other crimes because she was brainwashed by her captors. She was given a light prison sentence for her role in the robberies.

In the 1960s Jim Jones, a minister, started a religious commune called the People's Temple Movement in San Francisco, California. Gradually, the members were asked to give all their personal property to the People's Temple. In return, the Temple provided food, shelter, social services, and social and spiritual programs. Jones had considerable charisma and was successful in seducing the members to center their whole lives around the Temple and its activities. To further gain control over his followers, Jim Jones took them to an isolated area in the jungles of Guyana, South America. Rumors that the members were being sexually and physically abused and were being treated as slaves filtered back to California. In response to these complaints, a congressman with a small staff went to Guyana to investigate the People's Temple Movement. Jim Jones ordered the congressman killed so that he could not report on the abuses he saw. The congressman was shot to death. Jim Jones then concluded that the United States would take strong retaliatory action and urged his followers to take their own lives en masse so they could be reunited in paradise. More than nine hundred men, women, and children committed mass suicide by drinking a fruit punch containing cyanide.

The power of conformity is also exhibited in religious cults such as Hari Krishna, the Moonies, and Scientology, whose members are able to convince typical white, middle-class college youths to join and forgo their education, career goals, families, and material possessions.

Source: Adapted from "Patty's Own Story," *Wisconsin State Journal*, Sept. 24, 1975, pp. 1-2.

(or another professional person's) services. For example, an individual may be required to be a recipient by a court order, by the fact of incarceration, or by family or employer pressure.

There are a variety of settings in which social workers encounter involuntary clients: at correctional institutions, protective services, mental-health facilities, certain public schools, group homes, residential treatment facilities, nursing homes, and hospitals. In each of these settings, social workers may be expected to lead groups of unwilling clients.

Types of Disruptive Behavior

Unwilling group members can display counterproductive behavior. To more vividly describe some of these disruptive behaviors, we will look at the behaviors as if they were characters or personalities.

The Bear

This person openly expresses anger, rage, frustration, resentment, and hostility. The bear may be unhappy as a member of the group or with what is happening in the group. Discontent can be expressed in a variety of ways: verbally, by attacking other members of the group; nonverbally, by facial expressions; or physically, by aggressively pushing and shoving another member.

The bear who directly expresses unhappiness in an active fashion can also express unhappiness in passive-aggressive ways through indirect aggression. George Bach and Peter Wyden have called indirect aggression "crazy-making."[8] Indirect aggressors maintain a front of kindness but find subtle, indirect ways of expressing their anger, rage, or frustrations. Bach and Wyden label direct aggression "clean fighting" because feelings are expressed openly and can be identified and resolved. "Dirty fighters" use indirect tricks and never clearly express their feelings, which often causes a great deal of pain and can destroy effective communication in a group. Most disruptive behaviors involve an element of indirect aggression.

If you have a relationship with a "dirty fighter," he or she will identify what will "press your buttons" (that is, "get your goat"). When the "dirty fighter" is angry or frustrated with you, he or she will casually and subtly "press these buttons" to get you going.

The Eager Beaver

This person volunteers to do crucial tasks but has little intention of completing them, simply seducing other members into believing he or she is a willing contributor. The eager beaver may partially perform some of the tasks to show good faith but then employ a variety of excuses to explain why the tasks cannot be completed on time.

The Clown

This disrupter is rarely serious. He or she is always joking and clowning around, even when the other members want to be serious. A clown inhibits other members from expressing their thoughts and feelings because they fear they may be ridiculed.

The Psychoanalyzer

Continual analysis of what other members are doing and saying is the psychoanalyzer's forte. He or she often uses psychological terms and delights in analyzing what others really mean and what's wrong with them. The psychoanalyzer often slows down a group by getting members to engage in mind-reading rather than task completion. Other members are inhibited from expressing their thoughts and feelings; they fear they may be analyzed as having psychological problems

The Withholder

A withholder has important information or resources that would help the group accomplish its task but intentionally withholds assistance. He or she is more interested in watching the group struggle and spin its wheels.

The Beltliner

Everyone has a psychological "beltline" under which are subjects that he or she is extremely sensitive about. Beltline items may include physical characteristics, intelligence, past behavior, past unhappy events, or personality characteristics. An overweight person, for example, may be highly sensitive about comments related to obesity. Members who make subtle negative comments about the sensitive areas of other members threaten group cohesion and morale. A beltliner is a dirty fighter.

The Guiltmaker

A group member may attempt to control others by making them feel guilty. The guiltmaker traps the group into helping him or her with personal needs and goals, rather than working toward group goals. The guiltmaker uses such common expressions as, "You never do anything for me" and "All I've done for you and this is the thanks I get," to trigger the guilt response.

The Catastrophe Crier

By exaggerating the seriousness of a problem, a catastrophier would have group members believe that consequences will be not minor but disastrous. Since the catastrophier focuses only on examining the severity of the problem and not on developing and implementing problem-solving approaches, he or she intensifies a problem rather than solving it.

The Subject Changer

This person does not want a group to deal with crucial issues or with controversy and conflict. When difficult situations arise, he or she tries to change the subject. If successful, a subject-changer prevents the group from dealing with crucial topics. There are a variety of reasons for seeking to change a subject; for example, the changer may detest heated debates or may fear the debate will reveal something he or she wishes to keep hidden.

The Whiner

A whiner continually complains about one thing or another without taking action to resolve the problem. Because the whiner seeks attention and sympathy from other members, he or she slows down a group in accomplishing its tasks.

The Benedict Arnold

If a group is competing with another group, a betrayer, or Benedict Arnold, supplies confidential information to the other group. This person may encourage people outside the group to ridicule or disregard it or slyly have the group's funding cut back. Inside the group this member may attempt to prevent the group from accomplishing its goals. People appointed to head departments at state and federal levels, for example, are expected by the public to be voices for the growth and progress of that department. But some appointees have betrayed this trust by a hidden agreement with the appointers to be a "hatchet man" and cut the services and funding requests of their departments.

The Trivial Tyrannizer

Instead of honestly sharing concerns, frustrations, and discontent, this member annoys a group with constant interruptions and digressions. He or she may arrive late for meetings and leave early, fail to show up for crucial meetings requiring everyone's attendance, or bring up concerns that the group has already acted on. Besides raising trivial questions about the wording of the minutes, for instance, this person may yawn or read something when other members are speaking.

The Shirker

A group member may be disruptive simply by failing to do anything for the group. When assigned certain tasks, the shirker will evade these responsibilities by using a variety of excuses.

The Power Grabber

A power grabber may attempt to become the group leader or the power source behind the group leader by convincing other members that he or she has more expertise than any one else in the group or by buying the support of others with money, favors, or promises. A power grabber may create conflicts that make the leader look bad, and sabotage the efforts of the leader, even though he or she may not assume leadership power.

The Paranoiac

Because he or she is excessively or irrationally suspicious and distrustful of others in the group, the paranoiac always feels picked on. Much of this person's time is spent defending him- or herself and finding fault with other group members. Paranoiac individuals often feel that other members must be discredited before they can amass enough evidence to discredit the paranoiacs.

It should be noted that some disrupters are intentionally aware of the effects of their behavior. Most of the above examples are of this type. On the other hand, some disrupters are acting out of unconscious personal needs and therefore may not be aware their behavior is having a disruptive effect. The following suggestions on handling disruptive behavior apply whether the disrupter is aware or unaware of the effects of his or her behavior.

Handling Disruptive Behavior

Hostile and disruptive behavior can be handled in three basic ways: (1) members can be allowed to continue to be disruptive and the effects can be ignored or minimized; (2) the leader can confront members about their disruptive behavior; and (3) other group members can confront the disruptive behavior. The approach chosen should be based on what method will be most helpful to the group.

Minimizing Disruptiveness

If a disruptive group member is allowed to express discontent to the group, he or she may become less disruptive as time goes on through a ventilating process. When a member is disruptive, it is often helpful for the leader to ask the person tactfully to express his or her concerns. The group may then decide to deal with the concerns, especially those that are legitimate. With some concerns resolved, the disruptive group member may become more satisfied with the group and begin to feel the group has something to offer.

Let us assume, for example, that a man is angry and embarrassed about being sent to "Group Dynamics," a group consisting of people found guilty of driving while intoxicated. This man may be angry that he got a ticket while others who drink and drive have not been caught and "sentenced" to the group by a judge. At the initial meetings, he may aggressively ask a litany of questions: "What is the purpose of the group?" "What evidence is there that the group will do any good?" "What does one have to do in the group to pass?" "What qualifications does the group leader have for leading this group?" "Has the group leader ever been intoxicated while driving?" "If not, how can the leader understand what the members are thinking and feeling?" "If so, how can the leader be hypocritical by attempting to 'play therapist' when he or she has similar problems?" "Will members be forced to reveal personal things?" "What is the purpose of each of the group exercises?" "Does the leader believe the people in this group are drunks?"

The leader can handle these concerns by allowing this man to air his views and by providing honest answers. Furthermore, the group leader may acknowledge that he would also be angry if placed in that member's position. This approach seeks to allow members to ventilate their concerns, to answer their questions, and to convey understanding of their unhappiness. The goal is to create an atmosphere in which the group will be receptive to the content and exercises that will make the group effective.

Leader Confrontation

The group leader can confront the member about his disruptive behavior with other group members present or at a private meeting. The choice of private or group confrontation should be based on which will be most beneficial. If other members are present, they may be able to elaborate on the ways in which the member's behavior is disrupting the group and emphasize the seriousness of the problem. A disadvantage of group confrontation is that a hostile member may feel he or she is being "ganged-up on."

During a confrontation, the group leader should seek to fully and assertively express concerns in a nonblaming way by using "I"-messages (see chapter 7 for "I"-messages and chapter 22 for assertiveness).[9] Some confronters make the mistake of primarily using the two types of "you"-messages: solution and put-down messages. Solution messages order, direct, command, warn, threaten, preach, moralize, or advise. Put-down messages blame, judge, criticize, ridicule, or name-call.

"I"-messages consist of a nonblaming description of the effects of the disruptive member's behavior on the group or on the leader. The group leader simply tells the member which behavior is disruptive and then leaves it up to that member to take responsibility for changing it. "I"-messages generally lead to honesty and openness in a relationship, while "you"-messages usually reduce communication and polarize relationships.

Sometimes, simply confronting a member with his disruptive behavior will lead to a change because he may not be aware of the behavior's negative effects. Once informed, he may alter the behavior or reveal reasons for being disruptive. For example, the disruptive member may be resentful because he has not been assigned more responsibilities in the group. Assigning that person more tasks may lead not only to a cessation of the disruptive behavior, but also to his becoming a contented, productive member. When concerns underlying the disruptive behavior are resolved, it often ceases. In such a confrontation, the leader must tactfully ask questions to identify the reasons for the disruptive behavior.

However, confrontation may not always stop the behavior, for the disrupter may either continue along the same line or switch to another method of disruption. A "clown," for example, may become a "subject changer" or a "betrayer." If the disruptive behavior continues after a confrontation, the group leader can ignore the disruptive behavior as much as possible and minimize its effects, or confront the member again. In choosing the second alternative, the group leader must clearly inform the member that adverse consequences will result, explain those consequences, and follow through on implementing them if disruptive behavior continues.

For example, a group leader may inform a disruptive member in a court-imposed Group Dynamics class that he has four choices: (1) to participate in meetings and get as much out of them as possible; (2) not to participate but to attend in order to meet the court's requirement; (3) to attend and continue disrupting the class, with the court then being informed of his disruptive behavior; or (4) not to come to class, in which case the lack of attendance will be documented, the court notified, and that person's driver's license possibly suspended.

Another example can be drawn from my observations of students. Some tend to monopolize a class by rambling on about topics only remotely connected to what is being discussed. Usually, simply informing them privately about the rambling and the need to share "air time" solves the problem. However, a few students continue rambling even after the first confrontation. They are then informed privately that they must raise their hands before talking and will be called on only once or twice each session, depending on the class. Furthermore, I indicate that if they try to talk before raising their hands, I will ask the class members if they believe some people are using up too much class time. If the answer is "yes," the class will then be asked to set rules for sharing class time. The second confrontation has always resulted in less rambling.

Group Confrontation

The third approach is to have another group member, rather than the leader, confront the disruptive member; the same guidelines apply here that were described earlier for such a confrontation. There are certain situations in which the confrontation is best handled by someone other than the leader. For example, several years ago the social work department at a large eastern university recruited someone from another university to chair the department. A faculty member in that department had wanted the position and felt cheated. When the new chair came, this faculty member refused to do any departmental tasks and was at times verbally disruptive during faculty meetings. Two other faculty members in this department met with the disgruntled party to explain the reasons he was not selected, to allow him to express his resentment, and to politely request that he seek to be more cooperative because it was in everyone's best interests. This confrontation was quite successful and changed the disgruntled faculty member's attitude.

If confrontation is necessary, a decision has to be made by the group leader and by other concerned members about who should do it. Generally, the decision should be based on who appears to have the best chances of influencing the disruptive member.

Reducing the Likelihood of Disruptive Behavior

Group members are less apt to be disruptive when their personal goals are identified and incorporated into the group goals. By involving all group members in setting goals and making decisions, the group's communication, cohesion, and problem-solving effectiveness are likely to increase. An autocratic leadership style discourages commitment while a democratic style promotes it. Moreover, autocratic leadership is less satisfying to members and may lead to disruptive behavior. Group goals that are clear, operational, and measurable also tend to increase members' satisfaction with and commitment to the group, and to reduce frustrations (see chapter 4).

A cooperative atmosphere leads to higher morale, open and honest communication, more effective problem solving, and increased group cohesion and satisfaction. A competitive atmosphere is more apt to lead to disruptive behavior (see chapter 4).

If some members are disruptive in similar ways, the group can discuss the effects of the disruptions in a nonblaming way and set "house rules" for handling disconcerting behavior. For example, three or four people who are smoking may be irritating the nonsmokers. House rules may be established as to when and where smoking may take place. Or some members may be habitually late. This problem can be discussed, and the group can agree on some rules regarding meeting times and tardiness.

Disruptive behavior usually decreases if the group leader is well organized, covers relevant and interesting material, and effectively helps the members reach decisions and accomplish goals. A group leader should also pay attention to meeting the social/emotional needs of members and actively strive to have all members participate in making decisions. He or she cannot play favorites and must follow through on what is initiated. If the group leader has serious problems in one or more of these areas, discontent and disruptive behavior will probably increase.

The more assertively and competently the leader presents him- or herself, the more trust and confidence the group members will display. If the leader is aggressive, the members will usually feel angry or intimidated and respond either aggressively or passive-aggressively. If the leader is nonassertive, the members will tend to have a low level of confidence in the leader and may begin asking whether a new leader should be selected.

If a group is not functioning well, the leader should confront the group with his or her concerns and ask the group to help identify the reasons so that changes can be made. Depending on the circumstances, these can be identified at a group meeting or through written reports that ensure anonymity. Using this confrontational approach, the leader commits him- or herself to working with the group to make changes. For example, I taught a practice course in which hardly anyone was asking questions or making comments. During the fifth week of the class, I confronted the class in the following manner: "I think we've got a problem. This is the fifth week of this practice class, and no one is saying anything. To make this class go, we need to start talking. One of the first skills that social workers need is the ability to talk. I'm not convinced that people in this class can talk. So far, it's been mainly me that's been talking. Now, I'm going to shut up and let you talk. I want you to tell me why you're not talking. I'm a big boy. I can take whatever you have to say." After a few minutes of silence, some students began talking, and we ended up having a lively discussion. Basically, the students said I was primarily lecturing, which led them to be passive, and they requested exercises to try out the theories and principles I was presenting. In future classes, I adjusted my teaching approach to include exercises. After this confrontation, the students became more verbal in future sessions (though still not as verbal as I desired).

When members are forced to attend a group they do not want to attend, as in the case of involuntary clients, the group leader may begin by saying something like, "I know most of you really don't want to be here, and I wouldn't either if I were forced to come. I wonder if we might begin by talking about your anger and unhappiness about being here?" Then the group leader should attempt to convey the purposes of the group, what is going to happen, and how the members can satisfy the minimal requirements for "passing." The group leader can mention that members can: (1) choose to actively participate and get as much out of the group as possible, (2) remain silent and listen to what others have to say, (3) vent their anger and unhappiness in disruptive ways (which will probably anger and alienate others in the group) or, (4) refuse to come, which will have certain consequences. The group leader can then indicate that he or she cannot control their behavior, so the choice among these alternatives is up to each member. Such an approach almost always leads the involuntary clients to choose either the first or second alternative, perhaps because such an approach leads these clients to conclude that the leader is understanding of their anger—and they then focus on making the best choices in this predicament.

Sometime during the life of the group, one or more members may struggle with the leader for control. There are a variety of ways to handle a power struggle. (1) The person (or persons) may be given limited leadership responsibilities. This "second-in-command" approach may satisfy the member, who may become very helpful. He or she may accomplish important group tasks or, in therapy groups, prove to be a useful "co-counselor." (2) The group leader and the member desiring to be the leader can meet privately and work out a shared leadership arrangement to present to the group, or identify the changes that the member would like to see made. (3) The leader may display in a tactful manner (through words and actions) that he is the person best qualified to lead the group. (Following this strategy a political campaign-like atmosphere sometimes occurs, with the leader and the aspiring leader acting as competing candidates, each seeking to impress other group members with superior qualifications.) (4) The group leader can resign, ask the members whom they wish to have as their leader, and indicate that he or she would again take the position if the group so desired. (5) Another strategy is to ask for a vote of confidence. If a majority vote of support is not received, the group leader promises to step down. By rallying his resources and supporters in a display of strength, a group leader can usually show the aspiring leader that a take-over attempt is futile. (6) Finally, the group leader can threaten the aspiring leader with certain adverse consequences. Sometimes, these threats boomerang and motivate the aspiring leader to work harder, or are used to convince other group members that the present group leader lacks moral integrity.

GROUP EXERCISES

Exercise A: The Autokinetic Effect

Goal: To show that in ambiguous situations individuals will rely on the group to help define reality.

Note: This exercise is a variation of the study on the autokinetic effect discussed earlier in the chapter.

Step 1: For this exercise the group will need a room that can be completely darkened. The group leader explains that this study will determine each student's capacity to judge how far a dot of light moves in a darkened room. The class sits at the back of the room with pencils and paper ready to record their answers. With all lights off, the leader places a small flashlight at the front of the room and secures it so it will *not* move. The flashlight is then turned on for thirty seconds, then off, and students are asked to record how far they think the light moved. (The room remains dark.) The process is conducted two more times. During this part of the exercise, the students are asked not to talk with each other and to save their answers for later discussion. The lights are then turned on.

Step 2: The students form subgroups of three members toward the back of the room, and the room goes dark. The light is turned on three separate times for approximately thirty seconds. However, after each time the light is turned off, the students discuss and arrive at a group consensus as to how far the light moved. Each student records his group's consensus.

Step 3: With the lights back on, the students are informed that they will again be tested individually and that they are not to talk with anyone during this part of the exercise. The process is repeated as above. Each time the flashlight is turned off, the students are to record (in the dark) how far the light moved.

Step 4: Nine or ten volunteers write their answers to the nine trials on the blackboard: the first three done individually, the second three through group consensus, and the final three again individually.

Step 5: The class discusses whether these results are consistent with previous studies on the autokinetic effect, where the final three judgments tend to converge to a group standard. (In making this comparison, note whether the final three judgments are closer to the middle three group judgments than were the first three judgments.)

Step 6: The leader may, or may not, summarize at this point the results of the Asch studies and other studies done on conformity.

Exercise B: Identifying and Changing Group Norms

Goals: To give practice in identifying norms that exist in a group and to assess whether some of these norms should be changed.

Step 1. The group leader explains what group norms are and states the purpose of this exercise. The class then forms subgroups of three or four students. Each subgroup makes a list of norms that exist in the class.

Step 2. From this list, the subgroups identify a few of the norms that they would like to see altered and propose changes.

Step 3. A representative from each subgroup writes its list of norms on the blackboard, circling the norms the subgroup wants changed.

Step 4. A class discussion follows. Are the subgroups generally in agreement or disagreement as to the norms that exist in the class? For the norms that are circled, a representative from each subgroup should state why the subgroup would like to see these norms changed and present the subgroup's suggestions for replacing these norms. The class should then discuss whether the changes are desirable. (Since the instructor has primary responsibility for how the class is conducted, the instructor has the right to veto any suggested change.)

Exercise C: An Ornery Instructor

Goals: To help develop an awareness of norms that exist in the group and to look at what happens in a group when the leader acts under a new set of norms.

Step 1. This exercise is perhaps best done by the instructor. The instructor begins the class in a fashion very different from what he or she generally does. For example, the instructor may dress much more or much less formally. If chairs are generally in a circle, they should be put in rows. If the instructor generally engages in small talk before starting the class, this should be avoided. If the instructor comes across as a warm person, he or she should attempt to come across as a cold person. The instructor may take roll call, for instance, and announce that from this point forward a student's grade will be dropped one full grade for each missed class period. The instructor may openly criticize students who arrive late or who otherwise disrupt the class in minor ways. The instructor may indicate he or she is unhappy with the way the class is going, and therefore new rules will be implemented: roll call will be taken each day; there will be a quiz every week; each student's attitude and participation in the class will now count 30 percent of the final grade; any student who fails to take an exam at the scheduled time or who does not get a paper in on time will receive no higher than a D in the course; and the students will be graded down severely if they do not participate in class.

Step 2. After ten or fifteen minutes of this uncharacteristic behavior, the instructor should explain the real purpose of the exercise, which involved the intentional violation of existing norms. The instructor then asks what the class was thinking and feeling when he or she applied a new set of norms in the class. The instructor may conclude by stating that norms are very important in guiding the direction of a group and that significant changes in norms often lead to confusion and resistance.

Exercise D: How Group Decisions Affect Values

Goals: To show how group decisions affect individual values.

Step 1. The group leader explains that the purpose of this exercise is to help students assess their values. He then distributes the following questionnaire, explains that the results will be anonymous, and instructs students *not* to talk while filling it out. The class then forms subgroups of five or six members. The questions are as follows:

1. Do you believe homosexual teachers should be allowed to teach young children?
   a. Definitely
   b. Probably
   c. Undecided
   d. Probably not
   e. Definitely not
2. Do you believe severely and profoundly retarded people who will never function beyond a six-month age level should be kept alive at taxpayers' expense?
   a. Definitely
   b. Probably
   c. Undecided
   d. Probably not
   e. Definitely not
3. Do you believe people have a right to take their own lives?
   a. Definitely
   b. Probably
   c. Undecided
   d. Probably not
   e. Definitely not
4. Should teenage females be allowed to have an abortion on demand without the consent of a parent?
   a. Definitely
   b. Probably
   c. Undecided
   d. Probably not
   e. Definitely not

5. Would you want your child to attend classes in a school that a child who has AIDS is attending?
   a. Definitely
   b. Probably
   c. Undecided
   d. Probably not
   e. Definitely not

Step 2. The questionnaires are collected and kept separate for each subgroup. The subgroups are then asked to discuss each topic and arrive at a single answer for each question. Each subgroup should be given an additional questionnaire on which to record its answers.

Step 3. After the subgroups have completed Step 2, each member should again fill out the questionnaire anonymously. Again, the questionnaires for each subgroup should be kept separate.

Step 4. Prior to conducting this exercise, the group leader should arrange to have the instructor tabulate the results. The results should be recorded according to the following format:

Subgroup A

Number of students selecting this alternative

		Prediscussion Replies	*Group Decision Replies*	*Postdiscussion Replies*
Question 1	a.			
	b.			
	c.			
	d.			
	e.			
Question 2	a.			
	b.			
	c.			
	d.			
	e.			
Question 3	a.			
	b.			
	c.			
	d.			
	e.			
Question 4	a.			
	b.			
	c.			
	d.			
	e.			
Question 5	a.			
	b.			
	c.			
	d.			
	e.			

Step 5. During a break, the responses for all the subgroups are put on the blackboard or entered on a transparency according to the format listed in Step 4. The following questions should then be discussed: Do the prediscussion replies differ from the postdiscussion replies? If "yes," what are the reasons some members changed their views? Do group discussions and group decisions appear to influence value judgments by students? When students answered the individual questionnaire after the group decision did they feel a conflict between the group view and their personal values? If "yes," how did they feel about this conflict, and how did they attempt to resolve it?

Exercise E: Confrontation and I-Messages

Goals: To practice confrontation and using I-messages.

Step 1. The group leader begins by explaining the goals of the exercise. Then, I-messages should be described. I-messages are a nonblaming description of the effects of another's behavior on you. In using I-messages, the sender does not necessarily have to use the term "I"; the key is to describe the effects of another's behavior on you in a *nonblaming way,* without being critical or suggesting solutions. (See chapter 7 for a more detailed description of I-messages.)

Step 2. The following situations involving confrontation use role playing, and the "confronter" is urged to use I-messages. Two different students should be asked to volunteer for each role play and are given the following instructions.

> *Role play 1.* You're a group leader, and a member of your group has been ten to fifteen minutes late for every meeting. His habitual tardiness has been disruptive, and you fear that other members may follow this person's example and also arrive late. Your task is to confront this member about being late.
>
> *Role play 2.* You're a group leader, and there has been interpersonal conflict in the group that is not being dealt with because each time efforts are made to deal with the conflict, Jim (or Jill) either makes a joke of it or changes the subject. Your task is to confront Jim (or Jill) about this.
>
> *Role play 3.* You're a nonsmoker, along with most other group members. Jean (or John) usually sits next to you and frequently smokes a cigarette, which you find increasingly irritating. Your task is to confront Jean (or John) about this.
>
> *Role play 4.* You're a group member, and the group has been going nowhere because goals have not been established. The leader appears confused and uncertain about group procedures. The group is composed of students who are supposed to advise the social work faculty on curriculum and departmental policies. You are aware that this is the first group the leader has led. Your task is to confront the leader and explain that you and other members feel confused and frustrated because it appears that the group has been floundering.

Step 3. After each role play, discuss how well each confronter: (1) assertively expressed his or her concerns, and (2) used I-messages to express the concerns.

Exercise F: Confronting and Being Confronted by Others

Goals: To practice tactfully confronting a partner about his or her group performance and to receive feedback on group performance.

Note: The instructor should lead this exercise, because it may generate strong emotions in the participants.

Step 1. The group leader explains the purposes of the exercise. Before beginning, the group leader indicates that some members need to work on controlling their disruptive behavior. The group leader should also explain that other issues may be brought up in the confrontation. The group leader briefly summarizes the following ways in which members are disruptive, to suggest areas that the confronting student may want to mention tactfully to his or her partner.

The Bear	The Eager Beaver
The Psychoanalyzer	The Beltliner
The Guiltmaker	The Withholder
The Clown	The Catastrophe Crier
The Subject Changer	The Whiner
The Benedict Arnold	The Trivial Tyrannizer
The Shirker	The Power Grabber
The Paranoiac	

Step 2. Next, each member pairs up with another. The instructor explains that the task of each student is to confront his or her partner tactfully about behavior related to group performance that he or she might work on. First, one student is the confronter and the other the listener; then roles are reversed. The group leader should emphasize the importance of: (1) first complimenting the partner on demonstrated strengths to balance out the negative feelings that may result from the confrontation, (2) using I-messages, and (3) being tactful and making the confrontation as positive as possible.

Step 3. After the confrontations, the instructor asks the students how they felt about the experience and encourages discussion of the positive and negative aspects of the exercise.

CHAPTER SIX

WORKING WITH MINORITY GROUPS

Goal: Social work practice, whether it includes working with individuals or groups, must take into account the enormous diversity of clients and consumers of social services. The goal of this chapter will be to present some ideas and information regarding various minority groups, which will be useful for group workers and should enhance their ability to work with people whose backgrounds and experiences are substantially different from their own.

The profession of social work has had a long tradition of seeking to protect the rights of minority groups and advocating equal opportunities for their members. For example, the Code of Ethics of the National Association of Social Workers states:

> The social worker should act to prevent and eliminate discrimination against any person or group on the basis of race, color, sex, sexual orientation, age, religion, national origin, marital status, political belief, mental or physical handicap, or any other preference or personal characteristic, condition, or status.[1]

The code also states that a social worker should not practice, facilitate, condone, or collaborate with any form of discrimination against any member of a minority group.

Unfortunately, there has been a long history of prejudice, discrimination, and oppression against minority groups in our culture. Some definitions may be useful.

Prejudice means prejudging, making a judgment in advance of due examination. Prejudice is a combination of stereotyped beliefs and negative attitudes, so that prejudiced individuals think about members of a minority group in a predetermined, usually negative, categorical way.

Discrimination involves taking action against people because they belong to a category. Discriminatory behavior often derives from prejudiced attitudes.

Robert Merton, however, notes that prejudice and discrimination can occur independently of each other. Merton describes four different "types" of people:

1. The *unprejudiced nondiscriminator*, in both belief and practice, upholds American ideals of freedom and equality. This person is not prejudiced against other groups and, on principle, will not discriminate against them.
2. The *unprejudiced discriminator* is not personally prejudiced but may sometimes, reluctantly, discriminate against other groups because it seems socially or financially convenient to do so.
3. The *prejudiced nondiscriminator* feels hostile to other groups but recognizes that law and social pressures are opposed to overt discrimination. This person does not translate prejudice into action.
4. The *prejudiced discriminator* does not believe in the values of freedom and equality and consistently discriminates against other groups in both word and deed.[2]

An example of an unprejudiced discriminator is the owner of a condominium complex in an all-white, middle-class suburb who refuses to sell a condominium to a minority family because he fears that doing so will reduce the value of the remaining units. An example of a prejudiced nondiscriminator is a personnel director of a fire department who believes Hispanics are unreliable and poor fire fighters, yet complies with affirmative action efforts to hire and train Hispanic fire fighters.

It should be noted that it is difficult to keep personal prejudices from eventually leading to some form of discrimination. Strong laws and firm informal social norms are necessary to break the causal relationship between prejudice and discrimination.

Discrimination is of two types: *de jure* and *de facto*. De jure discrimination is legal discrimination. The so-called Jim Crow laws in the South in the last century gave force of law to many discriminatory practices against blacks, including denial of the right to trial, prohibition against voting, and prohibition against interracial marriage. Today, in the United States, there is practically no de jure discrimination, as such laws have been declared unconstitutional and have been removed.

De facto discrimination refers to discrimination that actually exists, whether legal or not. Housing patterns in many cities are an example of de facto discrimination. Wealthy whites tend to live in affluent suburbs, non-whites in inner-city ghettos. The effects of such segregation tend to carry over to other areas: for example, sharp discrepancies in the quality of educational systems between affluent suburbs and inner city areas.

Oppression is the unjust or cruel exercise of authority or power. Members of minority groups in our society are frequently victimized by oppression from segments of the white power structure. Oppression and discrimination are closely related, as all acts of oppression are also acts of discrimination.

A *minority group* is a group that has a subordinate status and is subjected to discrimination. It is not size that is critical in defining a group as a minority, but rather lack of power. Women, even though in the majority in our society, are a minority according to this definition.

Chapter 2 indicated that "Professional social work education is committed to understand and appreciate human diversity."[3] The population groups that compose human diversity "... include, but are not limited to, groups distinguished by race, ethnicity, culture, class, gender, sexual orientation, religion, physical or mental ability, age, and national origin."[4]

Populations-at-risk are diverse populations that are currently being victimized (or are in danger of being victimized in the future) by discrimination, economic deprivation, or oppression. Chapter 2 also indicated that social workers have an obligation to advance social and economic conditions for populations-at-risk.

Social justice is an ideal condition in which all members of a society have the same basic rights, protection, opportunities, obligations, and social benefits.[5] Economic justice is also an ideal condition in which all members of a society have the same opportunities for attaining material goods, income, and wealth.[6]

Stereotypes are fixed mental images of a group that are applied to all its members. Stereotyping is the attribution of a fixed and usually inaccurate and unfavorable conception to a category of people.

In working with diverse groups, a social worker needs: (1) to be aware of personal stereotypes and preconceptions about minority groups, (2) to have a knowledge about the minority groups that he or she is working with and the special needs of those groups, and (3) to be aware of which intervention techniques are apt to be effective with those groups and which will not. These areas will briefly be described.

YOUR STEREOTYPES AND PRECONCEPTIONS

Our society has had a long history of discriminating against minority groups. The extent of the discrimination has changed with time for some minority groups. Italian Americans and Chinese Americans, for example, were victimized by discrimination to a greater extent last century than they are currently.

All of us have some prejudices against minority groups because we were socialized in a society where prejudices abound. Abraham Lincoln is recognized as the person who was most responsible in our society for ending slavery. But Lincoln had prejudices against African Americans, as illustrated in the following statement:

> I will say, then, that I am not, nor ever have been in favor of bringing about in any way the social and political equality of the white and black races; that I am not, nor ever have been, in

favor of making voters or jurors of Negroes, nor of qualifying them to hold office, nor to inter-marry with White people . . . and in as much as they cannot so live, while they do remain together there must be the position of superior and inferior, and I as much as any other man am in favor of having the superior position assigned to the White race.[7]

As social workers it is critically important for each of us to recognize our personal prejudices and stereotypes against some minority groups. It is important for three reasons. First, social workers have taken a professional value position to combat discrimination as stated in the NASW Code of Ethics. Second, in working with minority groups it is important for us to be aware of our stereotypes and prejudices so that we do not subtly discriminate against minority groups. Third, by being aware of our prejudices and stereotypes, we can work on reducing and eliminating them.

Currently there are a number of commonly accepted myths and stereotypes about homosexuals, both male and female. Some of these myths will be summarized and then followed with factual information. As you read these myths, examine whether you believe any of them.

Myth 1—Appearance and Mannerisms. All male homosexuals are effeminate; they have a "swishy" walk, talk with a lisp, and are limp wristed. Correspondingly, all lesbians are masculine; they have short hair, dress mainly in men's clothes, and appear manly.

Fact. Because of these stereotypes, many people erroneously believe it is easy to identify gays and lesbians. The fact is that most homosexuals dress, look, and behave just like everyone else. Except for a small percentage of individuals, it is impossible to recognize a homosexual simply by his or her appearance or mannerisms.[8]

Myth 2—Gender Identity. Male homosexuals desire to be women, and female homosexuals desire to be men.

Fact. This myth confuses *gender identity* (masculine or feminine) with *choice of sexual partner* (homosexual or heterosexual). The fact is that while homosexuals generally choose a sexual partner of the same gender, their gender identity is identical to that of heterosexuals. A male homosexual views himself as male and does not desire to be a female. A female homosexual views herself as female and does not desire to be a male.[9]

Myth 3—Sexual Roles. In a homosexual couple one partner will assume the dominant (sometimes called masculine) role and the other will play the submissive (sometimes called feminine) role.

Fact. Such role playing occurs infrequently since most homosexuals engage in many forms of behavior and do not restrict themselves to one or another role. Homosexual partners often switch roles during the sexual act or engage in mutual oral-genital stimulation. In regard to role playing outside the sexual act itself, the vast majority of male homosexuals do not attempt to play the female role, and the vast majority of female homosexuals reject the entire practice of male-female role playing.[10]

Myth 4—Child Molesters. Male homosexuals are child molesters.

Fact. The vast majority of child molesting is done by heterosexual men to young girls.[11] Parents should be more fearful that heterosexual male teachers will try to seduce their young girls than that the homosexual male teachers will molest their young boys. There is no reason to assume that a homosexual is more apt to be a child molester than is a heterosexual.

Myth 5—Homosexual or Heterosexual. People are either homosexual or heterosexual.

Fact. Kinsey and his colleagues demonstrated that it is a mistake to conceptualize homosexuality and heterosexuality as comprising two separate categories. Instead, these researchers found that many people have had some heterosexual and some homosexual experiences, to varying degrees.[12] Their seven-point continuum is shown in figure 6.1 Probably a majority of adults have either had a homosexual experience or at least fantasized about having one.

Myth 6—Mental Illness. Homosexuals are mentally ill.

Fact. Research has found no evidence that homosexuals are less well-adjusted than heterosexuals. Personality tests reveal no differences (except for sexual preferences) between homosexuals and heterosexuals.[13] In 1973, the American Psychiatric Association voted to remove homosexuality from its list of mental disorders, and thus homosexuality is no longer officially classified as a psychiatric disorder.

Myth 7—AIDS. Homosexuals are to blame for the AIDS epidemic.

Fact. Although men who are gay are a high-risk group for the AIDS virus in our society, practically no cases have been reported among lesbians. (Gay men are at high risk for acquiring AIDS due to the transfer of bodily fluids that occurs during anal intercourse.) AIDS is not a life-threatening disease only for gay men; the incidence of the disease is increasing rapidly among heterosexuals. In many African countries the majority of people afflicted with AIDS are heterosexuals.

Homosexuals are not the cause of AIDS. Blaming a deadly disease on the group who, in the United States, has suffered and died disproportionately from AIDS, is a classic case of blaming the victim. While it is true that the largest single "risk group" of persons with AIDS is gay men, it is ludicrous to conclude that this group caused this health crisis. AIDS is caused by a virus. It is also ludicrous to assert that gay men want to deliver the disease to the world after first delivering it to themselves. Quite to the contrary, the gay male community in the United States has been in the forefront of educating people about behavior that minimizes the transmission of the disease. Gay men have radically altered their sexual behavior patterns, as evidenced by a substantial drop in the rate of transmission of the disease among this group in the past few years.

Figure 6.1: Sexual Orientation

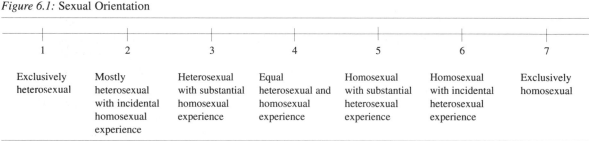

1	2	3	4	5	6	7
Exclusively heterosexual	Mostly heterosexual with incidental homosexual experience	Heterosexual with substantial homosexual experience	Equal heterosexual and homosexual experience	Homosexual with substantial heterosexual experience	Homosexual with incidental heterosexual experience	Exclusively homosexual

Myth 8—Sexual Preference. People choose to be homosexual.

Fact. Recent research shows that sexual orientation is established early in life, perhaps long before adolescence.[14] While every person has the potential to behave sexually in the manner he or she may choose, one's true sexual orientation may be set before birth or at a very early age, and then no longer influenced by the environment. Many homosexually oriented persons behave as if they are heterosexual in this society because there are so many sanctions against homosexuality. However, their true sexual orientation and preferred sexual partner, in the absence of these negative sanctions, would be someone of the same gender. Human beings certainly have the ability to respond sexually to persons who are not their preferred sexual partners, but to do so requires going against the current of their innermost inclinations. The question of what causes a person's sexual orientation to be set (either as homosexual or heterosexual) has not as yet been answered. It appears that some people are naturally heterosexual in orientation and others are naturally homosexual, just as some people are naturally left-handed and others are naturally right-handed.

KNOWLEDGE ABOUT MINORITY GROUPS

Social workers sometimes make the mistake of using their own social, cultural, or economic values as the norm. The following is an example of this mistake by an adult services worker for a public welfare department. (Names and other identifying information have been changed.)

Bill Ridder received an anonymous call that a seventy-nine-year-old male, Vern Broadcort, was living in abysmal conditions. Ridder made a home visit. Vern Broadcort lived alone in a rural area in northern Minnesota. The house was a mess. There was nearly an inch of dirt and newspapers on the floor. The house had no running water or toilet facilities, and Broadcort's clothes were filthy. He had not taken a bath for over a year. The house was heated, even in winter, by a small wood stove in the kitchen. The refrigerator had a rancid odor because some of the food had spoiled. There were no clean dishes; a green mold was growing on some that had been used but not washed. Broadcort mentioned he occasionally washed his dishes in rainwater. The dishwater that was in a large bowl had a muddy, dark brown color to it.

Ridder also visited some of Broadcort's neighbors, who expected the house to catch fire one of these days. They said Broadcort frequently drank himself into a stupor and then would smoke cigarettes. When he coughed, which he often did (according to the neighbors), hot ashes from the cigarette would be blown several feet away. Broadcort did appear mentally alert, however, and he stated his doctor felt he was in fair health. He did suffer from emphysema, arthritis, and an occasional occurrence of gout.

Ridder decided that the best place for Broadcort to live was in a nursing home and found one with an available bed. He then asked Broadcort if he would be interested in moving there. The reply from Broadcort shocked Ridder. "No way am I moving to a nursing home," he said. "This is my home. I was born and raised here, and I intend to die here. If you should get a court order to send me to a nursing home, I'll give up the will to live and soon die there. I personally don't believe you can get a court order to make me move out of here. I own this place, and I'm mentally alert and not hurting anyone. Who do you think you are that you can come in here and tell me where to live!"

Ridder went back to his supervisor to discuss the case. The supervisor informed Ridder that Broadcort, if mentally competent, had the right to live where he chose, as long as he was not hurting anyone else in the process. The supervisor then tactfully asked Ridder to think about whether he was seeking to force his values onto Broadcort, who obviously was content with his living environment. Ridder thought a while and agreed that he probably was.

If a social worker has experienced the prejudices that a client is exposed to and was raised in an environment similar to a client's, that worker may be more perceptive about and empathetic to that client. An African-American social worker, for example, may better understand what African-American clients are saying and experiencing than a white social worker would. Similarly, a worker with a disability may be more perceptive to what a client with a disability is thinking and feeling. Conversely, clients who are members of a minority group may initially feel they are being better understood when the worker is a member of the same minority group.

On the other hand, a social worker does not need to be a member of the client's minority group in order to work effectively with that client. The problematic nature of cross-cultural social work does not preclude its effectiveness. Mizio has noted, for example, that effective white workers can establish viable working relationships with nonwhite clients and that some nonwhite workers are less effective with others of the same race or culture than white workers.[15] The following example illustrates this point:

> In answering the question of whether a white middle-class psychiatrist can treat a black family, I cannot help but think back over my own experiences. When I first came to New York and decided to go into psychotherapy I had two main thoughts: (1) that my problems were culturally determined, and (2) that they were related to my Catholic upbringing. I had grown up in an environment in which the Catholic Church had tremendous influence. With these factors in mind, I began to think in terms of the kind of therapist I could best relate to. In addition to being warm and sensitive, he had to be black and Catholic. Needless to say, that was like looking for a needle in a haystack. But after inquiring around, I was finally referred to a black Catholic psychiatrist.
>
> Without going into too much detail, let me say that he turned out to be not so sensitive and not so warm. I terminated my treatment with him and began to see another therapist who was warm, friendly, sensitive, understanding and very much involved with me. Interestingly enough, he was neither black nor Catholic. As a result of that personal experience, I have come to believe that it is not so much a question of whether the therapist is black or white but whether he is competent, warm and understanding. Feelings, after all, are neither black nor white.[16]

Perhaps it is helpful to state the obvious. We are all human, and we all have some uniquenesses and differences. But being human, we also have a lot in common. As with any client, the social worker who is working with a minority client needs the skills that will lead to positive changes. Such skills include listening, relationship building, competence, empathy, and problem solving. A worker's effectiveness is also increased substantially by knowledge of a client's minority group and its unique characteristics.

There are an *immense* number of different minority groups in our society: several racial groups, numerous ethnic groups, women, gays and lesbians, many religious groups, people with mental or physical disabilities, the elderly, and others. It is beyond the scope of this chapter to describe the unique characteristics of these diverse groups. Instead, a few characteristics of some minority groups will be summarized to illustrate the importance of learning about the minority group of a client.

When working with Native Americans (American Indians) it is considered rude—an attempt to intimidate, in fact—to maintain direct eye contact.[17] Social workers and other professionals need to respect this cultural pattern by seeking to substantially reduce direct eye contact with Native Americans.

If a male client begins talking about his partner, it is a mistake to assume the partner is a woman and refer to the person as "she" or "her."[18] The client may be gay. Such an erroneous assumption could lead the client to terminate the interview and further contact. Obviously, this caution applies to women clients as well. Most helping professionals have also come to realize that attempts to change a client's sexual orientation are usually unsuccessful. In the past, some heterosexual therapists attempted to change homosexual orientation, with poor results. As explained previously, sexual orientation appears to be established early in life.

Chicano men, in contrast to Anglo men, have been described as exhibiting greater pride in their maleness.[19] Machismo—a male's sense of personal virility—is highly valued among Chicano men and is displayed by males to portray dominance and superiority. Machismo is demonstrated differently by different people. Some may seek to be irresistible to women and to have a number of sexual partners. Some resort to weapons or fighting. Others boast of their achievements, even those that never occurred. Recent writers have noted that the feminist movement, urbanization, upward mobility, and acculturation are contributing to the decline of machismo.[20] Chicanos also tend to be more familistic than Anglos. Familism is the belief that the family takes precedence over the individual. Schaefer notes:

> Familism is generally regarded as good because an extended family provides emotional strength at times of family crisis. . . . The many significant aspects of familism include: (1) importance of the *compadrazo* (godparent–godchild relationship); (2) benefits of financial dependency of kin; (3) availability of relatives as a source of advice; and (4) active involvement of the elderly within the family.[21]

On the negative side, familism may discourage youth from pursuing opportunities that will take them away from the family. It should be noted that the differences between Chicanos and Anglos with regard to machismo and familism are ones of degree, not of kind. Later in this chapter we will examine how the concept of familism can be utilized in providing services to Chicanos.

Some subcultures of African Americans have communication styles and vocabularies that differ from those of the dominant white culture. Children raised in these subcultures often have difficulty in understanding the English language spoken in school. Black American dialects appear to be the result of a creolized form of English that was at one time spoken on Southern plantations by black slaves.[22] (*Creolization* is the development of a language based on two or more languages. This new language then serves as the native language of its speaker.) Most African Americans in the United States speak a "radically nonstandard" English.[23] Present-day black English is a combination of the linguistic remnants of its Southern plantation past and a reflection of the current African-American sociocultural situation. As such, it is a dialect in its own right and not simply a distortion of standard English. Most adult African Americans are thus bilingual, being fluent in a black American dialect and in standard English.

Our culture places a high value on physical beauty. Americans spend large proportions of their budgets on clothes, cosmetics, exercise programs, and special diets to look more attractive. Beauty is identified with goodness and ugliness with evil. Movies, television, and books portray heroes and heroines as physically attractive and villains as ugly. Snow White, for example, was beautiful, while the evil witch was ugly. Unfortunately, this emphasis on the body beautiful has caused those with a disability to be the object of cruel jokes and has occasionally resulted in persons with a disability being shunned or being treated as inferior. Wright has noted that the emphasis on the body beautiful has also led society to believe that those with a disability "ought" to feel inferior.[24] Wright has coined the term *the requirement of mourning* for this expectation of society. An able-bodied person who spends a great deal of time, money, and effort to be physically attractive psychologically wants a person with a disability to mourn the absence of physical perfection. The able-bodied person needs feedback that it is worthwhile and important to strive to have an attractive physique.

Another consequence of the body-beautiful cult is that persons with a disability are sometimes pitied. Most resent such pity and the accompanying condescension. They want to be treated as equals. Our society also tends to equate a specific disability with general incompetence. Weinberg has noted that people talk louder in the presence of someone who is blind, assuming that people who cannot see cannot hear either.[25] Persons with a physical disability at times are assumed to be mentally and socially retarded.[26]

In seeking to participate fully in our society, persons with a disability must face not only the obstacles created by their disabilities, but also the additional obstacles created by society's reaction to disability. When working with persons with a disability, helping professionals need to provide assistance in both areas. Social workers also need to advocate for eradicating prejudices and discrimination against persons with a disability to ensure equal rights and opportunities for them.

WHICH INTERVENTION TECHNIQUES WORK?

Imagine you and a friend are traveling in Russia. In a medium-size city in central Russia your knapsacks are stolen, and they contain your passports, other forms of identification, travelers checks, and money. Won't you be terrified? Won't you worry that without identification and money you might be thrown into jail or victimized in some other way? If you decide to go to a social service agency for help, won't you be wary of how you will be treated? Won't you be worried that the staff will not believe your story, and will refuse help or even turn you over to the police? Because you do not speak Russian, won't you also be worried about how you will communicate your predicament?

Such feelings are similar to those of many members of racial and ethnic groups when they seek help from a social service agency in this country. They probably have been victimized by Anglo prejudice and discrimination in the past. Perhaps they have even been victimized by entire systems—education, law enforcement, and health care, for example. When they seek help they may display their fears and concerns through anxiety, fear, and visible stress. Some may appear depressed, nonassertive, and passive because they feel overwhelmed and seek to be compliant. Others may be extremely sensitive to the slightest evidence of unjust treatment and may respond aggressively to such normal procedures as waiting or filling out forms.

White workers with nonwhite clients need to be aware that the emotional reactions displayed by clients will probably be a combination of their reactions to their problems and to their distrust of agencies they view as part of the white power structure. If clients are highly anxious and fearful, workers need initially to focus on putting them at ease by conveying warmth, competence, calmness, and interest. They need to listen carefully to clients, convey understanding, and identify specific fears so those fears can be alleviated.

If clients appear depressed, a worker needs to be warm and empathetic. The worker should also seek out the reason behind the depression and then help the client combat it (see chapter 21). It may be useful to help passive clients be more assertive in obtaining what they need and want, and in gaining greater control over their lives (see chapter 22).

Social workers should not personalize the outbursts of angry or hostile clients. Clients may display anger for a variety of reasons over which the individual worker has little or no control. Ventilation can sometimes reduce anger, and the worker can be available for that process. Often it is helpful for the worker to identify the source of the anger and attempt the deal with that. Sometimes anger can be dissipated simply by conveying warmth and understanding, and helping the client solve a problem. If a worker believes the client may become violent, he or she should invite one or more co-workers to participate in sessions. If a worker is making a home visit and senses danger, it may be advisable to say something such as, "I think we need some time to cool off in order to take a more objective look at this. I'll be back tomorrow at this same time." If the visit involves investigation of child abuse or some other potentially volatile situation, a police officer might be asked along for the return visit.

There is a limit to the verbal abuse that a worker should take from a client. To maintain credibility the worker must have the respect of the client and that means limiting verbal abuse. A variety of statements can be used. For example: "I realize you are angry. But I've reached the limit of listening to your verbal abuse. Either we are going to discuss this calmly, or I'm going to have to ask you to leave. Which do you prefer?"

In working with adult clients who are not fluent in English, it is better to avoid using the client's bilingual children as interpreters.[27] Using the children as interpreters embarrasses parents, because it makes them partially dependent on their children and suggests they are ignorant of essential communication skills. In addition, children probably will not communicate well because of their limited vocabulary and experience. When an interpreter is used, another important guideline is that the worker should talk to the client, not to the interpreter. Talking to the translator places the client in the position of bystander rather than central figure in the relationship.

Workers should use their own patterns of communication and avoid the temptation to adopt the client's accent, vocabulary, or speech.[28] Mistakes in pronunciation or usage may be offensive or make the worker appear insincere.

Space limitations do not permit a complete listing of which intervention techniques work with specific minority groups. The following examples, however, demonstrate the need for a worker to learn the techniques appropriate to a particular client or group.

As mentioned earlier, Chicanos tend to have a strong sense of familism. Delgado and Humm-Delgado suggest that natural support systems are a useful resource in providing assistance to Chicanos.[29] These support systems include: extended family, folk healers, religious institutions, and merchant and social clubs. The extended family includes the family of origin, nuclear family members, other relatives, godparents, and those considered to be like family. Folk healers are prominent in Chicano communities. Some use treatments that blend natural healing methods with religious or spiritual beliefs. Religious institutions (especially the Roman Catholic church) provide such services as pastoral counseling, emergency money, job-locating, housing assistance, and some specialized programs, such as drug-abuse treatment and prevention. Merchant and social clubs can provide such items as native foods, herbs, referral to other resources, credit and information, prayer books, recreation, and the services of healers. The reluctance of Chicano clients to seek help from a social welfare agency can be reduced by greater use of these natural support systems. Outreach can be done through churches and community groups. If a social welfare agency gains a reputation for utilizing such natural support systems in the intervention process, Chicanos will have greater trust in the agency and be much more apt to seek help. Utilizing such natural support systems also increases the effectiveness of the intervention process.

Religious organizations that are predominantly African American usually have a social and spiritual mission. They are apt to be highly active in efforts to combat racial discrimination. Many prominent African-American leaders, such as the late Martin Luther King, Jr., and Jesse Jackson, have been members of the clergy. African-American churches have served to develop leadership skills. They have also served as social welfare organizations to meet such basic needs as food, clothing, and shelter. African-American churches are natural support systems that workers need to utilize to serve troubled African-American individuals and families.

A worker with an urban background employed in a small rural community needs to live his or her life consistent with community values and standards. A violator of community norms will not be effective in a small community because he or she will not have the necessary credibility. A worker in a small community needs to identify community values regarding: religious beliefs and patterns of expression, dating and marriage patterns, values related to domestic and wild animals (for example, opposing deer hunting in rural communities may run counter to strong local values), drug usage, political beliefs and values, and sexual mores. Once such values are identified, the worker should attempt to achieve a balance between the kind of lifestyle he or she wants and the kind of lifestyle the community expects.

Kadushin recommends that workers in initial meetings with adult clients of diverse racial and ethnic groups should observe all formalities.[30] Such usage would include a formal title (Mr., Miss, Mrs., Ms.), the client's proper full name, greeting with a handshake, and other common courtesies. In initial contacts workers should also show their agency identification and state the reasons for the meeting.

In addition, agencies and workers should establish working hours that coincide with the needs of the groups being served. Doing so might mean evening and weekend hours to accommodate working clients.

In the area of group services to racially diverse clients, Davis recommends that membership be selected in such a manner that no one race vastly outnumbers the others.[31] Sometimes it is necessary to educate clients about the processes of individual or group counseling. Using words common to general conversation is much better than using sophisticated technical jargon that clients are not likely to comprehend.

Native Americans place a high value on the principle of self-determination.[32] This sometimes presents a perplexing dilemma for a worker who wonders "How can I help if I can't intervene?" Native Americans will request intervention infrequently, and the worker needs to have the patience to wait for the request. How long this will take varies. During the waiting period the non-Native American worker should be available and may offer assistance as long as there is no hint of coercion. Once help is accepted, the worker will be tested. If the client believes the worker has been helpful, the word will spread and the worker is likely to have more requests for help. If the worker is not helpful, this assessment will also spread, and the worker will face increased difficulties.

To establish rapport with African Americans, Hispanics, Native Americans, or clients of other groups who have suffered from racial oppression, a peer relationship should be sought in which there is mutual respect and mutual sharing of information. An attitude of superiority is offensive and should be avoided.

When working with gay people, it is not uncommon for workers to experience homophobia—the irrational fear of homosexuality—because homosexuality has traditionally been viewed negatively as an illness, an emotional disturbance, a deviance, a criminal act, a sin. Personal homophobia must be confronted and resolved, however. One way is to apply social work values to gay clients. It is a serious mistake for a worker to convey a negative evaluation of a client's being gay because it contradicts the basic social work value of the client's right to self-determination. Another suggestion is for a worker to become familiar with the gay lifestyle and gay community. Such knowledge is essential in helping gay clients to identify and evaluate the various alternatives available to them.[33] Knowing resource people within the gay community will also enable a worker to be more aware of available services, activities, and events. Many services that focus on specific aspects of gay life are needed by gay people. These include support groups for gay men who are in the process of recognizing their homosexuality, legal advice for gay parents seeking child custody, counseling for gay couples, information on safer sex practices to avoid acquiring AIDS, and lesbian support groups.

Social workers have an obligation to help protect the civil rights of people who are gay through education and advocacy. Sexual orientation should be respected instead of criticized. Political candidates who are advocates of gay rights should be supported. Agencies that discriminate against gay people need to be confronted and educated to provide their services in a fair and just manner. Social workers should encourage the development of local support groups for gays, if such groups have not as yet been developed in the community. Gramick has suggested that social workers need to refuse to accept homophobic behavior from colleagues and states that such actions should be pointed out as a violation of the NASW Code of Ethics.[34] As stated earlier, social workers have an obligation to advance social and economic justice for all populations-at-risk.

THE RAP FRAMEWORK FOR LEADING MULTIRACIAL GROUPS

Whenever people of different races interact in a group, the leader should assume that race is an issue, but not necessarily a problem. Race is an issue in a multiracial group because it is a very apparent difference among participants and one that is laden with considerable social meaning. The leader of a multiracial group should not attempt to be colorblind because being colorblind leads to ignoring important dynamics related to race.

In leading a multiracial group, Davis, Galinsy, and Schopler urge that the leader use the RAP framework.[35] RAP stands for: *recognize, anticipate*, and *problem solve*. Each of these elements will be briefly described.

Recognize

Recognizing crucial ethnic, cultural, and racial differences in any group requires the leader to be both self-aware and aware of the racial dynamics of the group. A leader of a multiracial group needs to:

- Be aware of his or her own values and stereotypes
- Recognize racial, ethnic, and cultural differences among the members
- Respect the norms, customs, and cultures of the populations represented in the group
- Become familiar with resources (community leaders, professionals, agencies) in the

community that are responsive to the needs of the racial components of the group. These resources can be used as consultants by the leader when racial issues arise and may also be used as referral resources for special needs of particular members.

- Be aware of various forms of institutional discrimination in the community and of their impact on various population groups
- Be aware of racial tensions in the community that may concern members of the group. Such tensions may directly impact interactions among members of different races in the group.

Anticipate

Anticipating how individual members will be affected by racial issues prepares the leader to respond preventively and interventively when racial issues arise. The leader should anticipate potential sources of racial tension in the group when the members formulate their group goals, and when the leader structures the group's work. Because relationships among members and race-laden outside issues (i.e., outside of the group) change over time, anticipating racial tensions is an ongoing leadership responsibility. To anticipate tensions and help members deal effectively with them, the leader should:

- Seek to include more than one member of any given race. If the group has a solo member, the leader should acknowledge the difficulty of this situation for that member and should make it clear that that member is not expected to serve as the representative of his or her race.
- Develop a leadership style that is culturally appropriate to the group's specific racial configuration. This requires that the leader become knowledgeable about the beliefs, values, and cultures of the various racial components of the group.
- Treat all members with respect and equality in both verbal and nonverbal communications
- Help the group formulate goals responsive to the concerns and needs expressed by all the members
- Seek to empower members to obtain their rights, particularly if they are being victimized by institutional discrimination or by other forms of racism in the community
- Acknowledge in initial contacts with members and in initial sessions that racial and ethnic differences do exist in the group and that any issues that arise in the group regarding race must be openly discussed—even if discussing such issues and differences is uncomfortable
- Encourage the development of norms of mutual respect and appreciation of diversity
- Announce in initial sessions that at times people do and say things that are racially inappropriate. When this occurs, these comments and actions will be thoroughly discussed in order to resolve the issues and to work toward appreciation of differences.

Problem Solve

When incidents related to racial issues do arise, the leader must intervene to resolve the issues. The leader should:

- Use a problem-solving approach (described in chapter 9). Briefly, this approach involves identifying the issues and needs of each party, generating alternatives to meet those needs, evaluating the merits of each of these alternatives, and selecting and implementing the most promising alternative.
- Use conflict-resolution approaches (described in chapter 9). These approaches include role reversal, empathy, inquiry, I-messages, disarming, stroking, and mediation.
- Use interventions and goals that are culturally acceptable and appropriate for all members of the group
- Provide some rules when involving members in problem solving and conflict resolution (for example, no name calling).
- Assist members in being assertive in confronting and dealing with problems related to race
- Be prepared to advocate outside the group on a member's behalf when that member is being victimized by discrimination and oppression in the community

GROUP EXERCISES

Exercise A: Whom Wouldn't You Marry?

Goal: To identify personal stereotypes and prejudices.

Step 1: The following questionnaire is distributed to the students.

MARRIAGE QUESTIONNAIRE
Assume that you are single. Place an X at the description of anyone you would be hesitant to marry. To maintain anonymity, do not write your name on this sheet.

____ Person who is bisexual	____ a Native American
____ Person who is blind	____ a Puerto Rican
____ Person who is deaf	____ an Italian
____ Person who has cerebral palsy	____ a German
____ Person who is elderly	____ a Yugoslav
____ Person who has genital herpes	____ a Norwegian
____ Person who is mildly retarded	____ a Samoan
____ Person who has been hospitalized for an emotional problem	____ an Arab
	____ an Israeli
	____ a Chinese
____ a Russian	____ a Japanese
____ an American	____ a Filipino
____ a Cuban	____ an Eskimo
____ a French person	____ a Brazilian
____ a Mexican	____ a Hungarian
____ a White Protestant	____ a Vietnamese
____ a Roman Catholic	____ a Pakistani
____ a Jew	____ a Korean
____ a Muslim	____ a White American
____ an African American	

Step 2. After completing the first step, the students write the reasons they would be hesitant to marry the indicated people. The instructor explains that this part of the exercise is very important because it helps students clarify their values. The explanations should be complete and specific. Statements such as "It wouldn't work out," for example, or "My parents would object" are not acceptable without elaboration.

Step 3. The students hand in their responses anonymously, and the instructor reads many of them. (If a member of a group represented on the list is present, the instructor must use discretion in deciding which responses are read aloud.) A discussion of how to maintain objectivity in the face of personal prejudice should then be initiated. The instructor may conclude the exercise with the following question: "If you checked one or more of these groups, does it suggest that you hold negative stereotypes and prejudices toward these groups?"

Exercise B: Coming Out of the Closet

Goal: To identify stereotypes and myths that you may hold about gays and lesbians.

Step 1: The students assume they have a homosexual orientation, which they have been hiding. Each student then writes a letter to his or her parents revealing this sexual orientation and asking for acceptance and support.

Step 2: As the students are writing their letters the leader observes their verbal and nonverbal communication and makes notes on apparent stereotypes. (Students are apt to express stereotypes in conversations with students seated next to them.) A few volunteers are asked to read their letters to the class.

Step 3: After a few letters are read, the leader summarizes apparent stereotypes he observed.

Step 4: As an optional step, the myths and facts about homosexuality may be summarized. A summary of this material is in the chapter.

Step 5: If negative stereotypes are expressed, the leader should seek to initiate a discussion of how a heterosexual worker who has negative stereotypes about homosexuality can seek to be objective in working with clients who are homosexual.

Exercise C: Spaceship to Futura

Goal: To clarify your feelings about groups that have been discriminated against.

Step 1: The group leader indicates that one of the purposes of this exercise is to help students clarify their values related to the continuation of the human race after a nuclear war. The class forms subgroups of five or six, and the following vignette is read to the students:

The United States has discovered in another galaxy a planet, Futura, whose environment is very similar to the earth's. There is every indication that the planet will be able to support human life, although no human life has been detected on Futura. The United States has just completed a spaceship that will be able to travel to Futura. The spaceship is being built on a remote island in the Pacific Ocean and will hold only a total of seven people. Your subgroup has been appointed by the government to select the first seven people to go to Futura. Your subgroup is in frequent contact with the chief scientist for this project. The spaceship is remarkable in that it has a new computer system that has already been programmed to automatically guide the spaceship to Futura without requiring a pilot.

Suddenly, a nuclear war breaks out among the world powers. It is New Year's Eve. Russia, China, the United States, and Israel are already launching their nuclear warheads. It looks like the nuclear destruction may eliminate human civilization on this planet. The chief scientist frantically calls. The spaceship must take off in fifteen minutes to Futura, or it will be destroyed. She and your subgroup believe that the seven people who go may be the only people left to start the human race again.

There are thirteen people at the spaceship. Your subgroup must decide who will be selected. (If the thirteen people themselves decide, they are likely to become irrational and begin fighting.) Your subgroup has only fifteen minutes to make a decision. If a decision is not made in fifteen minutes, a nuclear warhead is apt to hit the island and destroy the spaceship. All you know about the thirteen people is the following:

1. The chief scientist, female, forty-seven years old
2. A Hispanic peasant, female, four months pregnant
3. An African-American male, third-year medical student
4. A white female, prostitute, twenty-seven years old, a Communist
5. A white male, homosexual, Olympic athlete, twenty-four years old
6. A white biology professor, sixty-seven years old
7. A rabbi, twenty-seven years old
8. A white female, on general relief, twenty-eight years old, has been arrested for several felonies, has never been employed
9. A female home economist, twenty-four years old, white, has cerebral palsy
10. A Korean child, male, eight years old
11. A white male, moderately retarded due to a lack of oxygen at birth, thirty-three years old
12. A white female elementary schoolteacher, twenty-seven years old, has genital herpes
13. A twenty-eight-year-old white farmer, has had a vasectomy

Step 2. The group leader distributes copies of this list to the students and the subgroups begin their discussions. The group leader informs the subgroups when ten, five, three, and one minutes remain. At the end of fifteen minutes, the discussions end.

Step 3. Each subgroup shares its selections and reasoning. The leader then conducts a discussion that explores what values underlie the selections, why certain individuals were rejected, how a social worker can be objective when faced with personal prejudice or stereotypes, and what students think they have learned.

PART THREE

COMMUNICATION IN GROUPS

CHAPTER SEVEN

CHAPTER SEVEN

VERBAL COMMUNICATION

Goals: In order to be effective, group members and social workers must be able to communicate their thoughts and feelings accurately. This chapter presents a model of communication, describes factors that interfere with the communication process, and offers guidelines on how to communicate more effectively.

All cooperative group interaction, whether verbal or nonverbal, depends upon effective communication. Through communication members argue, trade insults, debate issues, arrive at group goals, assume tasks and responsibilities, laugh, and work out differences. Effective communication occurs between two or more people when the receiver interprets the sender's message in the way the sender intended. The meaning of a communication is the response it elicits in the receiver, regardless of the intent of the sender.

A MODEL OF COMMUNICATION

Although most people think they understand what communication is all about, they are not fully aware of the process that goes on whenever people share ideas. This section will briefly summarize the process. We'll begin by assuming that you, a sender, want to express a thought or a feeling.

The first thing you do is translate your thoughts and feelings into symbols (usually spoken words, but also nonverbal signals) that others can understand. This process is called *encoding*. Finding the precise symbols to express what you think or feel can be difficult. The next step is to *send the message*. There are a number of ways of sending a message: by letter, telephone, note, spoken word, touch, posture, gestures, and facial expressions. When your message reaches a receiver, the receiver *decodes* the message by interpreting it in terms of thoughts or feelings that mean something to the receiver. The completed process is shown in figure 7.1

This process is one-way communication, in which a sender directs a message to a receiver. Most communication is a two-way process, however, as the initial sender directs a

Figure 7.1: A Model of Communication

Figure 7.2: A Model of Two-Way Communication

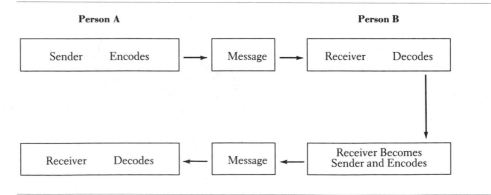

message to a receiver and the receiver responds. Two-way communication is diagrammed in figure 7.2.

With effective communication, what the receiver decodes is what the sender sends. However, frequently something goes wrong. A friendly joke is taken as an insult. A subtle request is missed. A constructive suggestion is taken as a put-down.

Our model identifies the areas in which misinterpretations may occur. First, the sender may have difficulty putting into symbolic form the thoughts and feelings he or she wishes to express. Second, the message may not be sent effectively. There may be too much noise for the sender to be fully heard, or the sender may not speak loudly enough. Although non-verbal cues tend to be ambiguous, words also have a variety of meanings and may connote something different from what the sender intends. Third, during the decoding process the receiver may misunderstand the sender's message as a result of several factors, including: physiological factors; individual attitudes, values, beliefs, defense mechanisms, and stereotypes; and perceptual factors, such as not listening. Later in this chapter we will take a closer look at how each of these factors influences communication.

One-Way Communication

Some groups and many corporations use one-way communication. The boss or group leader gives instructions and orders, or makes announcements to the other group members, who are not allowed to respond with their thoughts, feelings, and ideas. In one-way communication, the listener's role is only to receive the sender's messages and to carry out instructions and orders. The advantages of one-way communication are that messages and instructions are given quickly, and the boss does not have to deal with the questions and concerns of the listeners. In authority hierarchies, messages are often passed down through several levels.

Some studies have examined what happens when information is passed through several people using one-way communication.[1] As the message is passed along, it tends to become more simplified and distorted because of the three psychological processes of leveling, sharpening, and assimilation. First, receivers reduce or *level* the amount of information because they recall less information than they receive. In successive messages, fewer details are mentioned and fewer words are used. Second, a few high points become dominant and readily remembered or *sharpened*, while much of the remainder is forgotten. Third, the receivers interpret or *assimilate* much of the message in terms of their own unique personalities and reference frames. This process involves changing the unfamiliar to some known context, leaving out material that seems irrelevant, and substituting material that gives meaning in terms of the receiver's frame of reference.

Directive or Coercive Communication

A variation of one-way communication involves feedback, which McGregor has labeled *directive* or *coercive* communication.[2] With this approach, a chairperson delivers a message, and group members have an opportunity to seek clarification. The feedback is limited to determining how well the members understand the message. When the chair determines that the members understand the message, communication ceases. This type of communication is based on the premise that the chair's view on an issue is in the best in-

ERRONEOUS INTERPRETATIONS OF WORDS

Language is symbolic, and meanings often rest more in people than in words themselves. Moreover, each word in any language can be interpreted in a variety of ways, which often leads to misunderstandings. A tragic example concerns Japan during the summer of 1945. In late July, Japanese governmental leaders knew they had been beaten and wanted to end the war. When the Potsdam Declaration issued by the Allied Forces called upon Japan to surrender, Premier Suzuki informed the Japanese press on July 28 that his response was "mokusatsu." He apparently intended this word to mean "to withhold comment," which was supposed to be a signal to the Allied Forces that Japan was preparing to surrender. Unfortunately, the word "mokusatsu" can also be translated into "to ignore." The Japanese press hastily translated Premier Suzuki's statement into English and chose the wrong meaning, and Radio Tokyo broadcast to the world that the Suzuki cabinet had decided to ignore the Potsdam ultimatum. Suzuki's cabinet was furious about his choice of words and the message that was broadcast. The United States government responded on August 6 by dropping an atomic bomb on Hiroshima, and a few days later on Nagasaki. Hundreds of thousands of people were needlessly killed.

Source: William J. Coughlin, "The Great Mokusatsu Mistake," in *Looking Out/Looking In*, by Ronald B. Adler and Neil Towne, 3rd ed. (New York: Holt, Rinehart, and Winston, 1981), pp. 303–305.

terest of the group or organization. Directive or coercive communication has an advantage over simple one-way communication in that there is a process in place to determine whether members understand the message.

Problems with One-Way Communication

Some serious drawbacks exist to one-way and directive communication. The members may have valuable information that could improve the group's productivity, but because it is not communicated to the chair, it is never considered. In addition, details of the original message are lost, and the original message is distorted as it is passed from one level to another. These distortions will reduce the coordination between hierarchy levels and sometimes result in ineffective implementation of the chair's directives. In addition, the morale of the group and the commitment of members to carry out the directives are substantially reduced when the members have no input into the decision-making process. A major defect of American corporations has been that communication is usually a one-way process. Japanese corporations produce higher quality products at lower cost, partially as a result of the positive two-way communication between workers and management. In Japanese companies, workers identify their concerns and offer suggestions for improving productivity in periodic meetings with management. (Many American corporations are now moving toward implementing two-way communication between workers and management.)

Two-Way Communication

Some groups use two-way communication, which allows all members to participate fully. There are numerous benefits to be gained through this type of interaction. Since minority opinions are encouraged and often expressed, two-way communication improves cohesion, group morale, trust, and openness. Conflicts and controversies are resolved through higher quality solutions as the resources and ideas of all the members are pooled. Although two-way communication is almost always more productive and effective than one-way communication, it is much more time-consuming.

Problems with Two-Way Communication

The authority hierarchy also affects two-way communication because high-status people tend to talk more, and most of the messages are directed to these high-status members. Often members with little power take few risks and avoid frank remarks because they fear the consequences. High-authority members are often reluctant to reveal their limitations and vulnerabilities for fear of appearing weak and undeserving of their status. This tendency of high-authority members also reduces honest and open communication.

When there are sharp differences in status and authority among members, a cooperative atmosphere should be established to encourage the full participation of all members. Also, if the group is to be effective, group norms must indicate that the ideas and opinions of all group members are valuable and essential.

PERCEPTION

Let's go back to the model of communication presented at the beginning of the chapter. Among the areas in which communication can go awry is the receiver's perception of the sender's message. The message perceived by the receiver depends not only on the encoding processes of the sender, but also on the receiver's decoding, or interpretation. For example, the receiver may *add* to the sender's message. If a student of the opposite sex tells you, "You really look nice today," you may perceive that the sender is really saying, "I'd like to be romantically involved with you." A receiver also may *not fully comprehend* everything the sender is saying, just as an undergraduate may not fully grasp all the details of a sophisticated, abstract lecture given by a senior faculty member. Finally, a receiver may *distort* portions of the message because, for example, it cannot be heard clearly.

What a receiver perceives, then, *becomes the message.* This message may be fully accurate, partially accurate, or completely inaccurate. An ink blot test demonstrates that there are huge variations in what individuals perceive in an ill-defined or nebulous communication. The perception of any sender's message is based on the receiver's experiences, the receiver's needs, and the sender's actual message. Because a receiver's response is always a combination of what is seen, heard, *and* happening within the receiver at that moment, it is unlikely that two people will ever perceive the same thing in exactly the same way.[3] This response process can be easily demonstrated by counting the number of triangles in figure 7.3.

The number of triangles that you count will depend on the number of ways you look at

Figure 7.3: How Many Triangles Can You Count in this Diagram?

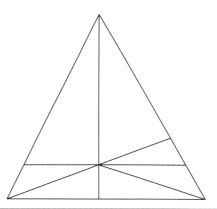

the diagram and define a triangle. People count as few as one triangle and as many as twenty. Obviously, then, more complex messages are even more difficult to interpret accurately.

The Perceptual Process

Since receivers are exposed to much more input than they can possibly handle, perceptions are organized to attach meaning to individual experiences. The first step of this process is to *select* data considered important enough to interpret.

Several factors cause receivers to select certain messages and ignore others. For example, stimuli that are *intense* (loud, large, or bright) stand out; someone who laughs loudly at a party will attract more attention than people who are quiet. *Repetitious* stimuli also attract attention and are widely used by advertisers. For example, Smokey the Bear—who reminds people to be careful to avoid starting forest fires—has become a symbol through repetitive advertising. Since a *change in stimuli* attracts attention, the constant noise level of cars going by will be tuned out, but any unusual sound will get our attention. *Motives* often determine the information selected from an environment. If an individual is hungry while traveling, he is much more apt to notice billboards advertising food and restaurants. If a person has a hobby or becomes an expert in some area, relevant information is also more likely to be observed. A group member sensitive about a certain subject is much more likely to pay attention to a comment even remotely related to his sensitive area.

The second step of the perceptual process is to *organize* data in some meaningful way. To make sense of human behavior, for example, people will interpret a specific behavior in terms of their favorite theories. If we believe in psychoanalytic theory, we will attempt to understand or interpret behavior according to a psychoanalytic model. If we believe in the principles of cognitive behavior theory, our interpretation of the same behavior will be very different. A psychoanalyst would say that a single woman who becomes pregnant has an unconscious desire (such as wanting to hurt her father or mother) that leads her to become pregnant. In contrast, a cognitive behavioral specialist would say that she decided to have intercourse because she believed that the anticipated rewards outweighed the potential consequences.

Group members constantly select what is important to remember and respond to, and organize messages in order to interpret and react to them. In the organizational process, past experiences, knowledge of human behavior, beliefs, values, attitudes, stereotypes, and defense mechanisms lead individuals to hear and see what they want. Information that supports a person's views is remembered, while information that forces individuals to question their firm beliefs and attitudes is often ignored or forgotten.

Physiological Influences

Each individual perceives the world in a unique way because of a number of physiological factors. Although only one world exists "out there," each person perceives a somewhat different world because of his or her own perceptual hardware.

Taste

There are fairly wide variations in the ways people experience taste. Although there are four basic types of taste—sweet, sour, salty, and bitter—individual taste buds permit considerable variation. Experiments have shown that litmus paper treated with PTC phenyl-thio-carbamide) will taste salty, bitter, sweet or sour, or have no taste at all, depending on who tastes it.[4] Arguments and discussions concerning the palatability of food often center on which food tastes better, but the simple fact is that the same food tastes different to different people.

Smell

There are also wide variations in the sense of smell. Odors pleasing to one person are repulsive to others. Such variations in perception thus affect communication.

Temperature

Sensitivity to temperature also varies greatly. Some people may be perspiring at 70°F, while others may be shivering. When a person has a fever, his or her perception of the "ideal" temperature changes, for example, and disagreements over appropriate temperatures in offices and houses are frequent.

Hearing

Noisy environments (factories, rock clubs, airports) have contributed to hearing loss, and people with significant uncorrected hearing losses are apt to miss parts of communications in a group. Often, they are forced to "fill in" by guessing the sounds they can't hear, reading lips, and observing nonverbal communication.

Vision

People who are color blind, far-sighted, near-sighted, or otherwise visually impaired perceive objects differently from people who have good vision. Sherri Adler briefly describes how her poor vision affected communication with her husband, Ron:

Since I've known Ron we've had some experiences that have caused communication problems because of our differences in vision: He has perfect eyesight, and even when I'm wearing contacts he can see better than I can.

A few summers ago we drove to Colorado. I would get angry (and frightened) when he continuously passed cars on narrow two-lane roads, and he would get mad at me for following slow-moving cars for thirty minutes without passing. When I explained that I just couldn't see as far up the road as he could, we realized that we didn't see things the same way and that our safety would be threatened if I was to drive the way he wanted me to.[5]

Other Physiological Factors

Other physiological factors also influence our perception. If we are relaxed and well rested, we are apt to perceive a joke played on us by a friend as being humorous, and we are likely to laugh heartily. However, if we are in ill health, under high stress, fatigued, tired, hungry, thirsty, or nearly asleep that same joke may not seem funny. All of these physiological factors have a substantial effect on our perceptions and the way we relate to people. For some women, the menstrual cycle plays a role in shaping moods and perceptions, and thus it may affect communication. There is some evidence that men may also have a four- to six-week physiological cycle of high periods and low periods.[6] Both males and females have a daily cycle in which a number of changes occur in sexual drive, body temperature, alertness, tolerance to stress, and mood, largely due to hormonal cycles.[7] Because of these daily changes, prime time for productive work varies with individuals.

Sociopsychological Influences

Sociopsychological factors, including defense mechanisms, beliefs, attitudes, values, and stereotypes, influence what we perceive.

Defense Mechanisms

A defense mechanism is a psychological attempt to avoid or escape from painful conditions such as anxiety, frustration, hurt, and guilt. An individual's defense mechanisms are usually activated when he or she faces information that conflicts with his or her self-image. Defense mechanisms preserve self-concept and self-esteem, and soften the blows of failure, deprivation, or guilt. Common defense mechanisms will be briefly summarized in the following sections.

Rationalization. One of the most common defense mechanisms is rationalization, the development of a logical but false explanation that protects a person's self-concept. Group members who use this mechanism actually believe the excuses they have dreamed up. For example, a student who fails an exam may blame it on poor teaching or having to work outside of classes rather than acknowledging the real reasons, such as not studying.

Projection. By using this defense mechanism, group members can unconsciously attribute their unacceptable ideas and impulses to others. An example would be a person who wanted to make himself look good by making others look bad. Psychologically, this person does not want to admit to himself that he has such self-

146

ish motives. So, he projects the selfishness onto others by believing they are trying to make him look bad, which then justifies his own negative behavior.

Denial. An individual can escape psychic pain by rejecting or denying reality. When people are confronted with a serious loss, they are likely to deny it. For example, a person can deny that a loved one has died. Many alcoholics deny they have a drinking problem.

Reaction Formation. Group members can avoid facing an unpleasant truth by acting opposite to the way they feel. Individuals who are angry and cannot admit it to others or themselves often act as if there is nothing wrong. By using the reaction-formation defense mechanism, sad and lonely individuals can act as if they are the life of the party, laughing and telling jokes. Also, people at funerals who are grieving deeply may behave as if everything is fine. The defense mechanism of denial is generally involved in reaction formation, as the individual seeks to deny painful facts, events, or feelings.

Compensation. This mechanism involves offsetting a real or fancied defect or inferiority by creating a real or fancied achievement or superiority. A divorced father may attempt to soften his children's pain by buying them expensive toys. Also, just as unhappily married college students can avoid dealing with their marriage by putting all their energies into their studies, persons who have "failed" in their careers and personal life can compensate for their failure by getting "high" on alcohol and drugs.

Identification. When you were seven or eight you had heroes or heroines that you idealized and imitated. Some adults hide their real feelings in certain situations and instead of being themselves imitate someone they admire. The problem with this mechanism is that people "hooked" on identification cannot respond to a situation genuinely. They deny their real feelings and instead act as their hero would.

Fantasy. The pain of reality can be reduced by fantasizing, and it is not uncommon, for example, for an unhappy adopted child to fantasize that his natural parents are exalted, loving people who will one day rescue him. Everyone daydreams, but most people soon return to reality. Some fantasies, however, endure and have destructive effects. For example, a former client of mine thought he could bring his deceased mother back to life by bringing female corpses to his home. After digging up several graves, he was arrested.

Regression. Some adults regress to an infantile or childlike state when ill or in trouble, with the subconscious goal of receiving more care and attention. When certain group members are confronted about their failings, they shed tears in an attempt to be excused for not fulfilling crucial commitments.

Apathy and Emotional Insulation. Individuals can protect their self-esteem by not getting involved in certain situations or pretending they don't care. A soured romantic relationship sometimes causes a person to withdraw into a shell of non-involvement. Faculty members turned down for promotion sometimes become apathetic and avoid productive work for fear of "failing" again. Unfortunately, emotional insulation prevents individuals from being involved in rewarding relationships, and apathy prevents them from achieving what they really desire.

Displacement. This mechanism occurs when hostile or aggressive feelings are vented against safer objects or people rather than against those who caused the feelings. A husband who has had a frustrating day at work, for example, may verbally or physically abuse his wife, children, or family pets.

Undoing. When a person feels guilty about some act or wish, he can undo his guilt by acting in a manner that reflects the reverse of this act or wish. The classic example is an unfaithful spouse who lavishes attention on his or her mate.

Although everyone uses defense mechanisms to cope with unpleasant situations, defense mechanisms can become destructive when perception of reality becomes seriously distorted. The following example illustrates how defense mechanisms can severely distort a message. (Names have been changed in this example.)

Dr. Nystrom was recruited from a different university to chair the social work department at a medium-sized midwestern university. Three weeks after the start of the first semester, four students came to Dr. Nystrom's office to complain about the teaching of Dr. Weller, a new faculty member. Dr. Nystrom asked the students to present their concerns to Dr. Weller, but the students wanted to remain anonymous. Dr. Nystrom then asked the students to specify their concerns. Next, he informed Dr. Weller of the concerns. Weller appeared stunned and said little.

The next day Dr. Weller barged into Dr. Nystrom's office. "I know my teaching is good," she declared. "I spent most of last night trying to figure out what's happening. It is clear to me there is nothing wrong with my teaching. I've concluded that you are turning students against me." (This is rationalization and projection.) Dr. Nystrom was unable to convince Dr. Weller that he was not turning students against her, and their relationship deteriorated. Ever since then, Dr. Weller has been convinced that Dr. Nystrom is seeking to have her contract terminated. Dr. Weller has continued to receive low student evaluations but has rationalized them with excuses, such as ill-health and claiming that faculty in the department are turning students against her. This paranoia has had a destructive effect on departmental morale.

Communication that Fosters Defensiveness

Jack Gibb has found that we are more likely to respond defensively to certain types of communication and that defensiveness is *reciprocal*.[8] If a sender begins to respond defensively, the receiver will react by putting up defenses, which will then increase the sender's defensiveness. Gibb has identified six types of messages that increase a receiver's defensiveness: evaluative, controlling, manipulative, indifference, superiority, and certainty.

Any message perceived as *evaluative* or *judgmental* increases the receiver's defensiveness. When an individual is being evaluated or rated, he or she is more on guard. In contrast, nonblaming communication reduces defensiveness.

Communication meant to *control* behavior or thoughts also increases defensiveness. For example, when a salesperson aggressively attempts to sell a product, many customers react defensively. Gibb indicates that defensiveness is decreased when the sender projects a willingness to share in the solution of a problem, for example, "Let's find a solution that works for both of us."

Defensiveness also increases when people discover that someone is trying to *manipulate* them. Since people would rather be asked to do something directly than be tricked into doing it, manipulative communication leads to distrust and defensiveness. An honest request may not always produce an immediate positive response, but it will lead to more open and honest communication and support in crucial situations.

Indifference to another person's feelings and thoughts increases defensiveness by conveying a lack of concern and implying that the person involved isn't important. Defense mechanisms then allow the receiver to maintain a sense of value to offset the indifference. Gibb has found that empathy reduces defensiveness and is much more beneficial to relationships than indifference is.

When someone relates to us in a *superior* way, we often become angry, tune that person out, or use defense mechanisms to maintain our self-respect. Some individuals go to great lengths to cut the superior person "down to size." Relating on an *equal basis* is much more conducive to openness, sharing, and reducing defensiveness. Instructors who relate to students as equals, for example, are using better educational and communication methods than instructors who attempt to impress students with their superior position and knowledge.

The final type of communication that, as Gibb notes, increases defensiveness is *certainty*. This type involves messages from people who steadfastly assert that their way of doing things is the *only* way, or who act as if they have all the answers. Gibb notes that people who work hard at demonstrating certainty usually feel insecure and inferior; their certainty is a reaction formation. In this case, defensiveness can be reduced when openness to new information and ideas is communicated.

Defensiveness is probably the greatest barrier to effective communication and should be avoided. Messages should be sent in ways that do not make either senders or receivers defensive.

Beliefs, Values, and Attitudes

Individuals use their beliefs, values, and attitudes to select, interpret, and organize information. If a member in a group is liked, his comments receive more attention and support. Dislike sparks disagreement or strenuous opposition. Sometimes a group member will dislike another so intensely that he automatically votes against every motion that person makes, even those to his direct benefit.

The importance of beliefs and values in communication can be illustrated with just a few examples. If parents are conservative and strongly opposed to interracial marriages, they will probably be opposed to interracial dating. A Roman Catholic who strongly opposes abortions will feel close to a speaker who supports that belief and be repelled by someone who favors choice. Deeply religious individuals often become threatened when someone professes that some other religion than theirs is the one, true religion. Finally, people with different sexual values will usually avoid discussing sexuality with each other.

Beliefs have a major impact on perception and sometimes lead to inaccurate interpretations of a message. For example, some people incorrectly believe that others are generally attempting to control them or put them down. Under this system of belief, they are apt to misinterpret general statements, jump to conclusions, and become defensive. Open and honest communication is unlikely to occur. This type of misinterpretation of messages has also been called the tendency to *personalize* messages.

Stereotypes

Stereotypes are fixed mental images of a group that are applied to all its members. Stereotypes may be partially accurate or completely erroneous. You can discover the stereotypes you hold by considering the mental images you get in response to the following phrases: "a macho male," "a Republican," "a welfare mother," "a policeman," "a homosexual," "a handicapped person," "an ex-con." For most of these phrases, you probably were able to get a mental picture of what such people look like, and you probably have beliefs about their lifestyles, values, interests, and attitudes. During your first interaction with someone who fits into one of these categories, you are apt to respond in terms of your preconceived expectations. For example, if you distrust and fear police officers, you would probably be guarded in what you said and did if you met an officer, and you would be apt to end the interaction as rapidly as possible.

SELF-DISCLOSURE

One of the main reasons we are not fully understood when we communicate is that we do not fully express what we are thinking and feeling. We often ponder how much we should share about our thoughts and feelings. What are the costs and benefits of self-disclosure?

Self-disclosure has been defined as "the process of deliberately revealing information about ourselves that is significant and that would not normally be known by others."[9] Some people are *over*disclosers in that they either talk too much about themselves or they talk revealingly about themselves at inappropriate times. If a student social work club is discussing a proposal for a new course on aging, for example, it would be inappropriate for a student to indicate that he has periodically thought about suicide. *Under*disclosers don't want others to know them intimately and speak very little about themselves even when the situation calls for it. An underdiscloser may encourage friends to share their personal concerns but then refuse to talk personally about herself. Appropriate self-disclosure can be defined as the right amount of self-revelation at the right time.

The risks of self-disclosure have been described by Sidney M. Jourard: "When you permit yourself to be known, you expose yourself not only to a lover's balm, but also to a hater's bombs. When he knows you, he knows just where to plant them for maximum effect."[10] The risks of self-disclosure include subsequent criticism, laughter, disapproval, or rejection, as well as a danger that the information may be used against the individual involved. If a student discloses to a class that he has a drinking problem or homosexual thoughts, there is always the danger that someone in the class may inform a potential employer.

People fail to disclose appropriately for many reasons. Some may fear closeness, rejection, and criticism, or they may be ashamed of their thoughts, feelings, or past actions. In certain instances, disclosure will put pressure on a group member to change; for example, a person may be reluctant to acknowledge that he has a drinking problem because he knows that if he acknowledges the problem there will be pressure put on him to give up drinking (which he doesn't want to do). Jourard asserts that self-disclosure is necessary for psychological health and growth because people can't be themselves unless they know themselves.[11] Through self-disclosure a person can know him- or herself better; nonetheless, many cannot or will not face troubled parts of themselves and so resist self-disclosure.

If thoughts and feelings are not shared, an individual is not accurately communicating what he is really thinking and feeling and will not be fully understood. Honest and open relationships that are meaningful are based on self-disclosure with people accepting individuals as they are. A close, meaningful relationship is probably not possible without mutual self-disclosure.

The question of whether to disclose can be answered by following a simple guideline. Individuals should self-disclose when the potential benefits outweigh the potential risks; making realistic judgments about the potential benefits and risks is the hard part. A leader of a therapy group usually should self-disclose if the information will be therapeutic for group members. For example, if members have drinking problems, a leader who shares her personal experiences with drinking could provide useful information and make group members feel less guilty. On the other hand, a leader who is still emotionally involved with a problem usually *should not* self-disclose, or group members may view her as a client rather than a therapist. If a leader of a group of battered women tearfully relates a sexual assault, members may feel that she cannot be objective in dealing with their situations.

It is also important to remember that there are degrees of self-disclosure; you don't have to tell everything. It is possible to share some opinions, feelings, thoughts, or experiences while reserving riskier information. By observing the reactions of the receivers, a sender can better determine whether it is in his or her best interests to reveal more.

What is disclosed should be relevant to the present relationship with the receivers. For example, a romantic relationship could disintegrate if past sexual relationships were disclosed. Most people know their partners have had previous sexual experiences, but few want to hear the intimate details.

The Johari Window

Joe Luft and Harry Ingram developed a graphic model of self-disclosure in groups known as the *Johari* (taken from the authors' first names) *Window*.[12] The diagram in figure 7.4A represents everything there is to know about you: your needs, dislikes, past experiences, goals, desires, secrets, beliefs, values, and attitudes. However, you do not know everything about yourself. You are aware of some things and unaware of other things, as diagrammed in figure 7.4B. In addition, the frame can be divided to show what others know about you and what others do not know about you. This is shown in figure 7.4C.

By combining parts *b* and *c* of figure 7.4, we get a Johari Window, as illustrated in figure 7.4D. A Johari Window divides everything about you into four parts. Quadrant 1 is the *open* area of yourself, the part of which both you and others are aware. This area has been referred to as the "public self," as it represents how one knowingly presents himself. Quadrant 2 is your *blind* area, which represents the part of yourself that others are aware of but that you aren't. It has been called the "bad breath" area because while others may know you have bad breath, you don't. Quadrant 3 is the *hidden* area, the part you are aware of but others aren't. This part has been called the "secret" area, as you know all kinds of things about yourself that you are not telling to the group. Quadrant 4 is your *unknown* area, which represents that part of you of which neither you nor others are aware. A Johari Window can be individualized by moving the boundaries into the position that best describes a single personality. For example, the Johari Window in figure 7.5 describes a man who is very aware of himself but who tends to hide much of himself from others.

Communication in a group generally follows certain principles. Initially, group members tend to be guarded and seldom self-disclose; quadrant 1 of their Johari Window will be small. Members test the rules for behavior by barely speaking, giving short answers, and being careful about what they reveal. But as the group continues, group members usually begin revealing more about themselves. One of the common characteristics of groups is that an environment is generally created in which members feel safe and protected. After a feeling of trust develops, members begin to disclose more personal aspects of their lives. As secret, private information is made public, quadrant 1 is enlarged and quadrant 3 becomes smaller.

A key characteristic of the Johari Window is that a change in any one quadrant will affect all other quadrants. For example, the more personal information is shared, the larger quadrant 1 becomes. Quadrant 2 immediately becomes smaller as others know more about an individual from his self-disclosure. Quadrant 3 may become smaller because others offer feedback, which reduces the size of the blind area as the individual gets to know more about himself. Through this self-disclosure and feedback process, parts of an individual that are unknown may be discovered, which will alter the size of quadrant 4.

The implications of the Johari Window are that the more information is shared, the more others know and the greater the feedback. This feedback often leads to greater self-awareness, more sharing about ourselves, and more sharing on the part of others.

It should be cautioned, however, that self-disclosure is usually best done gradually. If the first bits of self-disclosure are well received and accepted, the individuals can feel that it is safe to reveal more. It is generally a mistake to try to build a relationship by immedi-

Figure 7.4: A Johari Window

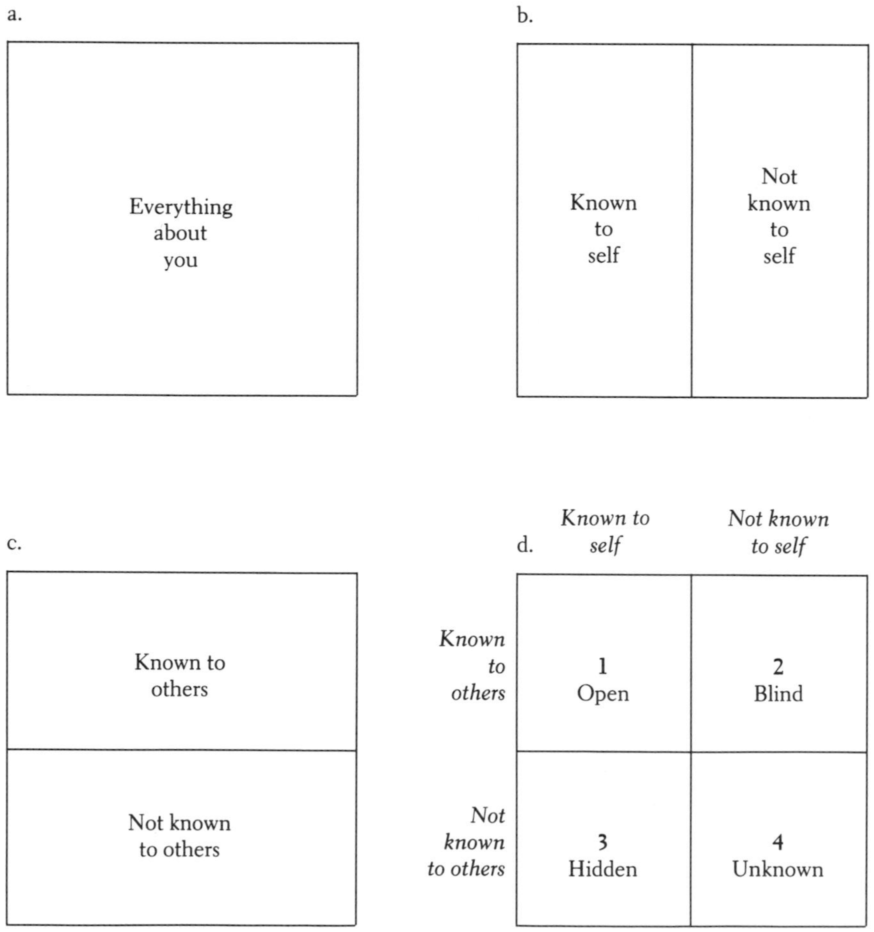

Figure 7.5: Johari Window Showing Hidden Personality Type

	Known to self	Not known to self
Known to others	1 Open	2 Blind
Not known to others	3 Hidden	4 Unknown

ately divulging all the secrets and private details about oneself. Besides the risk of hurt, hasty "undressing" of ourselves is apt to scare others away.

HOW TO COMMUNICATE EFFECTIVELY

Given all the factors that can lead to garbled messages, it is important that everyone attempt to send messages effectively. A number of suggestions will be given for improving communication for both a sender and a receiver.

Sender

If nonverbal and verbal messages match, a receiver can better interpret the information. Double and often contradictory messages are sent when nonverbal and verbal messages don't agree. Messages should be complete and specific. If you have to request a special favor of someone, it is usually desirable to explain why. Also, it is important to specify what you are requesting. Vague or incomplete messages are often misinterpreted.

"Own" your messages by using personal pronouns such as "I" to show that you are clearly taking responsibility for your thoughts and feelings. When group members "dis-own" messages by saying "someone said" or "most people would feel," it is difficult to determine whether *they* think and feel this way, or whether they are simply repeating the thoughts and feelings of others.

Each message should be phrased in a way that is appropriate to the receiver's frame of reference. The words you use in explaining the Johari Window to a child should be quite different from those you use with classmates. Also, supporting verbal messages with handouts, pictures, and written messages will help the receiver understand them. Always ask for feedback when you're unsure whether the receiver has accurately perceived the message.

Express your concerns to others in nonblaming rather than judgmental or evaluative terms. Judgmental or evaluative words make others defensive. Note the immense difference between "I feel put down by what you just said" and "I'm really getting tired of your running me into the ground—watch it." The first is apt to foster communication, the second, defensiveness.

Physical factors that interfere with effective communication and should be reduced include: chairs in a row rather than in a circle, poor acoustics, loud outside noises, an unacceptable room temperature, ineffective lighting, uncomfortable chairs, and too little time allotted to discuss issues.

Receiver

Communication is often halted when the receiver takes a message personally. Instead of jumping to the wrong conclusions, a receiver should ask questions that will clarify the sender's intentions and reasoning. Clarification can be ascertained by paraphrasing the sender's message in a question: "Are you saying . . . ?" or "Are you feeling . . . ?" If the receiver immediately disagrees, then the sender may become cautious and defensive, which will interfere with open and honest communication. It is important to remember that communication is fostered if you speak up for yourself *only after* you are accurately aware of the sender's message. In resolving an argument, a group leader can use the principle of *role reversal*. The receiver restates the ideas and feelings of the sender accurately and to the sender's satisfaction before proceeding to present his own views. The receiver should express the sender's feelings and ideas in his own words rather than parroting or mimicking the words of the sender. Before indicating approval or disapproval, a receiver should place him- or herself in the sender's shoes in order to understand what the sender is thinking and feeling.

Social workers should be aware that a sender may not have communicated his or her feelings or meaning accurately or fully. The sender may have chosen the wrong words or used words that were ambiguous. For example, the phrase "I care about you" has meanings ranging from "I care about you as much as I care about any human being" to "I'm in love with you." In such situations it is extremely important to seek clarification by asking questions in a nonblaming, nonevaluative fashion.

Listening Skills

To communicate effectively it is essential to develop good listening skills. Unfortunately, many people are caught up in their own interests and concerns, and they are distracted by those thoughts when someone is speaking to them. Kadushin explains why it is difficult for an interviewer to develop good listening skills:

> The nature of spoken communication presents a special hazard, seducing the interviewer into an easy nonlistening. The hazard lies in the great discrepancy between the number of words that are

normally spoken in one minute and the number of words that can be absorbed in that time. Thought is much more rapid than speech. The average rate of spoken speech is about 125 words per minute. There is, then, a considerable amount of dead time in spoken communication, during which the listener's mind can easily become distracted. The listener starts talking to herself to take up the slack in time. Listening to the internal monologue may go on side by side with listening to the external dialogue. More often, however, it goes on at the expense of listening to the external dialogue. The interviewer becomes lost in some private reverie—planning, musing, dreaming.[13]

Kadushin gives the following suggestions on how to listen effectively:

> Rather than becoming preoccupied as a consequence of the availability of the spare time between the slow spoken words, the good interviewer exploits this time in the service of more effective listening. The listener keeps focused on the interviewee but uses the time made available to the mind by slowness of speech to move rapidly back and forth along the path of the interview, testing, connecting, questioning: How does what I am hearing now relate to what I heard before? How does it modify what I heard before? How does it conflict with it, support it, make it more understandable? What can I anticipate hearing next? What do I miss hearing that needs asking about? What is he trying to tell me? What other meanings can the message have? What are his motives in telling me this?[14]

ACTIVE LISTENING EXAMPLE IN A GROUP SESSION AT A RUNAWAY CENTER

Sixteen-year-old youth: I hate school. I'm no longer going to go.

Counselor: You're so unhappy with what's happening at school that you're thinking about dropping out.

Youth: Yes, my home life is a shambles, and school isn't going well either.

Counselor: It's real depressing to have both your home life and school not going well.

Youth: Sometimes, like now, I feel like giving up. I've tried pretty hard to make things better at home and at school.

Counselor: You're feeling bad because the things you've done haven't worked out the way you'd like.

Youth: Yes, I got an F on the English paper I got back yesterday.

Counselor: You're feeling especially bad because of the grade you got on your English paper.

Youth: Since the commotion at home, my grades have started to fall.

Counselor: You're thinking that your problems at home may be affecting your schoolwork.

Youth: I don't really want to admit it to myself, but I guess it's true. For the past several weeks it's been harder for me to concentrate on school.

Counselor: You feel your grades are slipping because you haven't been able to concentrate because of what is happening at home.

Youth: I guess when I'm at school I have to focus more on my schoolwork. Maybe if I talked to some of my teachers and let them know what I'm going through, they might be more understanding. I guess I really don't want to drop out of school.

Active Listening

Thomas Gordon has developed four techniques that are designed to improve communication: active listening, I-messages, collisions of values, and no-lose problem solving.[15] No-lose problem solving is described in chapter 9.

Active listening is recommended when listening to a problem. A member in a therapy group says, "I'm fat and ugly—all my friends have boyfriends and not me." For such situations Gordon recommends that the group leader (or another member) use active listening. The steps involved in active listening are (a) the receiver of a message tries to understand what the sender's message means or what the sender is feeling, and then (b) the receiver puts this understanding into his own words and restates it for the sender's verification. An active listening response to the above might be, "You want very much to have a boyfriend and think the reason you don't is related to your physical appearance." An active listening response involves either *reflecting feelings* or *restating content.*

Gordon lists a number of advantages of active listening. It facilitates problem solving by the person with the problem, which fosters the development of responsibility. By talking a problem through instead of only thinking about it, a person is more apt to identify the root and arrive at a solution. When a person feels that others are listening, he or she will be more likely to listen to them in the future. In addition, the relationships between group members will probably improve, because when individuals feel they are heard and understood, positive emotions toward others increase. Finally, active listening helps a person with a problem to explore, recognize, and express feelings.

When first using the technique, receivers may make some mistakes. One is to use the technique to guide the person with the problem to a solution preferred by the receiver. The sender will usually then feel manipulated, and the approach may be counterproductive. A second mistake is to parrot back the words rather than paraphrase the intended meanings or feelings. For instance, if a member shouts at a group leader, "You stupid jerk," an appropriate response would be "You're angry with me," not "You think I'm a jerk."

I-Messages

Active listening is used when someone else has a problem. Many occasions arise when another group member causes a problem for you. For example, another group member may irritate or criticize you. You may remain silent and irritated or send a "you-message." There are two types of you-messages: a *solution* message and a *put-down* message. A solution message orders, directs, commands, warns, threatens, preaches, moralizes, or advises. A put-down message blames, judges, criticizes, ridicules, or name-calls. Examples of you-messages include, "You stop that," "Don't do that," "Why don't you be good," "I hate you," and "You should know better."

Gordon advocates that I-messages are better. For example, if a member is loudly tapping a pencil on a table, an I-message might be, "The tapping of the pencil is irritating to me."

I-messages, in essence, are nonblaming messages that simply communicate how the sender of the message believes the receiver is affecting the sender. I-messages do not provide a solution, and they do not criticize. It is possible to send an I-message without using the word I. The essence of I-messages involves sending a nonblaming message of how the

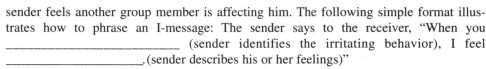
sender feels another group member is affecting him. The following simple format illustrates how to phrase an I-message: The sender says to the receiver, "When you _____ (sender identifies the irritating behavior), I feel _____.(sender describes his or her feelings)"

You-messages are generally counterproductive because people do not like to be ordered or criticized. You-messages frequently result in an ongoing struggle between the two people involved.

In contrast, I-messages communicate much more honestly the effect of behavior. I-messages tend to be more effective because they help the other group member to assume responsibility for his or her behavior. An I-message says that you trust the group member to respect your needs and to handle the situation constructively. I-messages are much less likely to produce an argument. They tend to facilitate honesty, openness, and more cordial relationships within the group.

Collisions of Values

Collisions of values between group members are common. Likely areas of conflict include values about abortion, sexual behavior, clothing, religion, use of drugs, hairstyles, and conscientiousness in carrying out assigned group tasks.

Gordon asserts that there are three constructive ways to resolve value conflicts. The first is to model the values you hold as important. If you value honesty, be honest. If you value openness, be open. If you are not living according to the values you profess, then you need to change either your values or your behavior. Congruence between behavior and values is important if you want to be an effective model.

The second way is to attempt to be a consultant to the members with whom you are in conflict. There are some dos and don'ts for a good consultant. First of all, a good consultant inquires whether the other person would like to hear his or her views. If the answer is no, then do not proceed to consult because the other group member will react negatively. If the answer is yes, be sure you have all the pertinent facts. Then share these facts once so the other person understands them. Let the other group member have the responsibility of deciding whether to follow the suggestions. To continue consulting, a person must be neither uninformed nor a nag.

The third way to reduce tensions over a values issue is to modify your values. By examining the values held by the other group member, you may realize they have merit, and you may move toward those values or increase your understanding of why the person holds his or her values.

GROUP EXERCISES

Exercise A: The Johari Window

Goal: To introduce the Johari Window and demonstrate how it can be used to further self-awareness.

Note: The instructor should lead this exercise, and students should be told **not to disclose personal information.**

Step 1: The group leader describes what the Johari Window is and how increased self-disclosure generally leads to greater self-awareness and more meaningful relationships. The group leader may also describe why group members are initially reluctant to self-disclose but gradually begin to do so. With appropriate self-disclosure in groups, cohesion and group morale generally increase. The group leader should note that personal information should *not be* disclosed during this exercise.

Step 2. The members pair up into subgroups. Each member draws a Johari Window representing him- or herself and then his or her partner. These drawings should be made privately.

Step 3. The partners share their drawings with each other. Each describes the reasons for drawing the window in the form that is displayed. The two partners discuss the similarities and differences in their drawings; for example, why did A draw him- or herself as not being very open while B drew A as being a very open person?

Step 4. The class discusses thoughts about the merits and shortcomings of the Johari Window and what they learned from the exercise.

Exercise B: Defense Mechanisms

Goal: To become more aware of the use of defense mechanisms.

Step 1. The group leader begins by stating the purpose of the exercise and giving brief descriptions of common defense mechanisms (see "Defense Mechanisms," p. 146).

Step 2. Each member lists on a sheet of paper the three defense mechanisms a *friend* uses most often and then describes one or two examples of each. The leader explains that students will be asked to share what they write with two other students.

Step 3. After Step 2 is completed, the class forms subgroups of three students, and each member is asked to share what he or she wrote. The two listeners should provide feedback on whether the defense mechanisms have desirable or undesirable consequences. For the undesirable, the members discuss more effective approaches.

Step 4. The class discusses what they learned from the exercise and how they feel about it.

Exercise C: Distortions in Transmitting Information

Goal: To demonstrate the effects of transmitting information through a series of one-way and two-way communications among group members.

Step 1. The leader explains the purpose of the exercise, asks ten students to step outside, and informs them that their task will be to repeat to someone else what they hear. The remaining students are observers. The first five students will use one-way communication, and the second five will use two-way communication. A copy of the following story is distributed to the observers, who are asked to record: (a) what each participant adds to the communication and (b) what each participant leaves out of the communication.

Step 2. The first participant returns, and the leader slowly reads the following story to him.

> A farmer in western Kansas put a tin roof on his barn. Then a small tornado blew the roof off, and when the farmer found it two counties away, it was twisted and mangled beyond repair.
>
> A friend and lawyer advised him that the Ford Motor Company would pay him a good price for the scrap tin, and the farmer decided he would ship the roof up to the company to see how much he could get for it. He crated it up in a very big wooden box and sent it off to Dearborn, Michigan, marking it plainly with his return address so that the Ford Company would know where to send the check.
>
> Twelve weeks passed, and the farmer didn't hear from the Ford Company. Finally, he was just on the verge of writing them to find out what was the matter, when he received an envelope from them. It said, "We don't know what hit your car, mister, but we'll have it fixed for you by the fifteenth of next month."[16]

The story is read once and no questions are allowed. The second participant enters, the first repeats the story to the second, and so on. The fifth participant should repeat the story to the observers, *and this fifth repetition should be tape-recorded to play back later.*

Step 3. The sixth participant enters and is told that he may ask questions about the story he is about to hear. The story is read and questions answered. The process is repeated until the tenth participant repeats the story to the observers. The tenth repetition should be tape-recorded to play back later.

Step 4. The group leader explains the effects of leveling, sharpening, and assimilation on the transmission of information. Some observers summarize verbally what each participant added to and left out of the story.

Step 5. The group leader describes why two-way communication is generally superior to one-way communication. The group leader should then play back the fifth and tenth participants' descriptions of the story. A discussion should then follow as to which version was closer to the original story.

Exercise D: The Intruder

Goals: To present a model for communication and to demonstrate that there are fairly wide variations in what students perceive.

Step 1. Prior to the meeting the group leader arranges for a friend or acquaintance to barge into the class and create a scene. This accomplice should not be known to anyone in class.

Step 2. The group is informed that the purpose of this exercise is to become aware of factors that reduce or prevent effective communication. The group leader describes the communication model presented at the beginning of this chapter. When the group leader is nearly finished, the leader should *unobtrusively* signal the accomplice to enter. The accomplice should barge in, create a ruckus, say some disparaging things about the group leader, threaten the group leader, and then leave angrily.

Step 3. The leader explains that the purpose of this exercise is to see how closely the students' perceptions match. Ask each student to write down on a sheet of paper the following information:

a. The intruder's height and weight
b. What the intruder was wearing
c. What the intruder looked like
d. What the intruder said and did

Step 4. Several descriptions are read aloud and differences discussed. If there are sharp differences, why did they occur? The leader explains that perceptual differences among people are a major barrier to effective communication.

Exercise E: Active Listening

Goal: To develop active-listening skills.

Step 1. The leader explains the purpose of the exercise and describes what active listening is and what it is designed to accomplish. The leader indicates that active listening involves using two types of statements—reflecting feelings and restating content.

Step 2. Students pair off. (If there is someone without a partner, the leader should participate.) One member of each pair selects a topic to discuss for about ten minutes. The topic may involve: (a) a philosophical or moral issue such as abortion, (b) a problem with a friend or a relative, or (c) a problem at school.

Step 3. The member who selects a topic discusses the issue for about ten minutes. The listener should try to respond solely with active-listening statements.

Step 4. After the discussion, the presenter should discuss with the listener the quality of the active-listening statements. Did the listener make the mistake of making suggestions, asking questions, or beginning to talk about personal experiences? Did active listening motivate the presenter to continue talking? Did the presenter perceive the active-listening statements to be primarily "natural" or "artificial"?

The listener should then discuss with the presenter his or her thoughts and feelings about using active-listening statements. Did the listener want to make other types of statements? If so, what?

Step 5. The roles should then be reversed and the process repeated.

Step 6. Students form a circle and discuss the merits and shortcomings of active listening. Did any unique or unusual events occur?

CHAPTER EIGHT

NONVERBAL COMMUNICATION

Goals: Sigmund Freud noted, "He that has eyes to see and ears to hear may convince himself that no mortal can keep a secret. If his lips are silent, he chatters with his finger tips; betrayal oozes out of him at every pore."[1] This chapter summarizes material on nonverbal communication and demonstrates how nonverbal communication can be used to better understand others.

It is impossible not to communicate. No matter what we do, we transmit information about ourselves. Even an expressionless face at a funeral communicates something. As you are reading this, stop for a minute and analyze what nonverbal messages you would be sending if someone were observing you? Are your eyes wide open or are they half closed? Is your posture relaxed or tense? What are your facial expressions communicating? Are you occasionally gesturing? What would an observer deduce you are feeling from these nonverbal cues?

Nonverbal cues often reveal feelings a person is intentionally trying to hide. Bodily reactions such as sweating, stammering, blushing, and frowning often reveal the presence of emotions—fear, embarrassment, or discomfort—that people would rather hide from others. By developing skills in reading nonverbal cues, group leaders can become more aware of what others are feeling and how to interact with them more effectively. Since feelings stem from thoughts, nonverbal cues that reveal what people are feeling also transmit information about what people are thinking.

In literature, perhaps the greatest reader of nonverbal cues was Sherlock Holmes. In this exchange Holmes deduces the following about his friend Watson:

> "How do I know that you have been getting yourself very wet lately, and that you have a most clumsy and careless servant girl?" . . .
>
> "It is simplicity itself," said he; "my eyes tell me that on the inside of your left shoe, just where the firelight strikes it, the leather is scored by six almost parallel cuts. Obviously they have been caused by someone who has very carelessly scraped round the edges of the sole in order to remove crusted mud from it. Hence, you see, my double deduction that you had been out in vile weather, and that you had a particularly malignant boot-slitting specimen of the London slavey."[2]

FUNCTIONS OF NONVERBAL COMMUNICATION

Nonverbal communication interacts with verbal communication and can repeat, substitute for, accent, regulate, or contradict what is spoken.

Repetition

Nonverbal messages may *repeat* verbal ones. A husband may say he is really looking forward to becoming a father and repeat this happy anticipation with glowing facial expressions.

Substitution

Nonverbal messages may *substitute* for verbal ones. If you know a close friend has just failed an important exam, even though he may not talk about it, you can get a fairly good idea what he is thinking and feeling by watching him.

Accentuation

Nonverbal messages may *accent* verbal messages. If someone you are dating says she is angry and upset with something you did, she may emphasize the depth of these feelings by pounding a fist and pointing an accusing finger. (Accentuation and repetition are closely related, although accentuation usually involves greater emphasis.)

Regulation

Nonverbal messages may serve to *regulate* verbal behavior. Looking away from someone who is talking to you indicates that you are not interested in talking.

Contradiction

Nonverbal messages may *contradict* verbal messages. An example is someone with a red face, bulging veins, and a frown yelling, "Angry! Hell no, what makes you think I'm angry?" When nonverbal messages contradict verbal messages, the nonverbal messages are often more accurate. When receivers perceive a contradiction between nonverbal and verbal messages, they usually believe the nonverbal.[3]

The Risk of Misinterpretation

While nonverbal messages can be revealing, they can also be unintentionally misleading. Think of the times when people have misinterpreted your nonverbal messages. Perhaps you tend to say little when you first wake up, and others have interpreted this as meaning that you are angry or troubled. Perhaps you have been quiet on a date because you were tired or because you were thinking about something that happened recently—has your date at times misinterpreted your behavior to mean you are bored or unhappy with the relationship? While deep in thought, have you had an expression on your face that others have interpreted as a frown? Nonverbal behavior is often ambiguous. A frown, for example, may represent a variety of emotions: anger, rejection, confusion, unhappiness, fatigue, or boredom. *Nonverbal messages should be interpreted not as facts but as clues to be checked out verbally to determine what the sender is thinking and feeling.*

FORMS OF NONVERBAL COMMUNICATION

Nonverbal communication may take many forms. We communicate by the way we move, the expressions we make, the clothes we wear, even by the way we arrange our homes and offices. The following discussion examines the different avenues of nonverbal expression, including posture and body orientation, gesture, touch, choice of clothing, control of personal space and setting of boundaries, facial expression, voice tone and level, personal appearance, and design of personal environments.

Posture

An indication of how much posture can communicate is the large number of phrases that have posture as a metaphor:

"He is able to stand on his own two feet."
"I've got a heavy burden to carry."
"She's got a lot of backbone."
"Stand tall."

In picking up nonverbal cues from posture, it is important to note both the overall posture of a person and changes in posture. People tend to be relaxed in nonthreatening situations and to tighten up when under stress. Some people never relax, and their rigid posture shows it.

The degree of physical tenseness can reveal status differences. In interactions between a higher- and a lower-status person, the higher-status person is usually more relaxed, the lower-status person more rigid and tense.[4] For example, note the positions that are usually assumed when a faculty member and a student are conversing in the faculty member's office.

Teachers and public speakers often watch the posture of students or people in the audience to gauge how a presentation is being received. If people in the audience are leaning forward in their chairs, it is a sign the presentation is going well. If the audience members are slumping in their chairs, the presentation is probably beginning to bomb.

Body Orientation

Body orientation is the extent to which we face toward or away from someone with our head, body, and feet. Facing someone signals an interest in starting or continuing a conversation, while facing away signals a desire to end or avoid conversation. The phrase "turning your back" concisely summarizes the message that is sent when you turn away from someone. Can you remember the last time someone signaled a wish to end a conversation with you by turning away?

Facial Expressions

The face and eyes are generally selected as the primary source of nonverbal communication because facial expressions often are mirrors that reflect thoughts and feelings. Ekman and Friesen have identified six basic emotions that facial expressions reflect—fear, surprise, anger, happiness, disgust, and sadness.[5] These expressions appear to be recognizable in all cultures; people seeing photos of such expressions are quite accurate in identifying the emotions behind them.

Yet, facial expressions are a complex source of information. They can change rapidly; slow-motion films have found that a fleeting expression can come and go in a fifth of a second. In addition, there are at least eight distinguishable positions of the eyes and lids, at least eight positions for the eyebrows and forehead, and at least ten for the lower face.[6] Multiplying these different combinations leads to several hundred possible combinations. Therefore, it is almost impossible to compile a directory of facial expressions and their corresponding emotions.

Because people are generally aware that their facial expressions reflect what they are feeling and thinking, they may mask them. For example, a person who is angry and doesn't want others to see the anger may hide this feeling by smiling. In using facial expressions to interpret feelings, social workers must be aware that the sender may be concealing his or her real thoughts and feelings.

Eye Contact

When you want to end a conversation, or avoid a conversation, you look away from the other person's eyes. If you want to start a conversation, you often seek out the receiver's eyes. You may wait until the receiver looks at you: when he does, it is a signal that he is ready to begin talking.

NONVERBAL BEHAVIOR AMONG POKER PLAYERS

Oswald Jacoby has noted that poker players use nonverbal messages extensively and has divided poker players into three classes: naive players, tricky players, and unreadable players.

Naive players are usually beginning players who possess few skills. When they look worried, they probably are. When they have a mediocre hand, they take a long time to bet. They bet quickly on a good hand, but frown and scowl and look like bad luck has bitten them if they are dealt poor cards. A bluff is accompanied by a guilty look; when they raise a bet, everyone else folds. Naive players reveal their hands by body language that is seldom apparent in veteran poker buffs. Players of this type usually quit poker at an early stage because of their "bad luck."

Most poker players are "tricky" players and act exactly the opposite of the way they really feel. When they have a poor hand, they exude confidence, and when they have a good hand they tremble a little and look nervous as they bet. Sometimes, they do a triple cross, by acting the way they really feel.

Unreadable players show no consistency in their behavior. They will randomly exude confidence or look nervous, and these nonverbal messages will give no clue as to the nature of their hand. Unreadable players are the most successful.

Source: Adapted from Oswald Jacoby, *Oswald Jacoby on Poker* (New York: Doubleday, 1974).

The eyes can also communicate dominance or submission. When a high-status person and a low-status person are looking at each other, the low-status person tends to look away first. Downcast eyes often signal submission or giving in. Of course, downcast eyes may also signal sadness, boredom, fatigue, remorse, or disgust.

Good salespeople are aware that eye contact is a sign of involvement and often manage to catch our eyes. Then they begin their pitch and maintain "courteous" eye contact. They know social norms require a receiver to hear what a person has to say once the person is allowed to begin speaking. These social norms trap us into listening to the sales pitch once eye contact has been made. Salespeople in stores utilize eye contact in another way. They determine which items a customer is looking at most and then emphasize these items in their sales pitch.

The importance of eyes in communication is reflected in these common phrases:

"He could look right through you."
"She has an icy stare."
"He's got shifty eyes."
"Did you see the gleam in her eye?"

Eye expressions suggest a wide range of human feelings. Wide-open eyes imply wonder, terror, frankness, or naiveté. Lowered eyelids may mean displeasure. A constant stare connotes coldness; eyes rolled upward suggest the person believes another's behavior is strange or unusual.

When we become emotionally aroused or interested in something, the pupils of our eyes dilate. Some counselors are sufficiently skilled in reading pupil dilation to tell when they touch a sensitive area by watching a client's eyes. E. H. Hess and J. M. Polt measured the amount of pupil dilation while showing men and women various kinds of pictures.[7] The greater the subject's interest in the pictures, the more the eyes dilated. Women's eyes dilated an average of 20 percent when looking at pictures of nude men. Men's eyes dilated an average of 18 percent when looking at pictures of nude women. Surprisingly, the greatest increase in pupil size occurred when women looked at a picture of an infant and mother.

Gestures

Most of us are aware that our facial expressions convey our feelings. When we want to hide our true feelings, we concentrate on controlling our facial expressions. We are less aware that our gestures also reveal our feelings, however, and as a result, gestures are sometimes better indicators of feelings.

People who are nervous tend to fidget. They may bite their fingernails, tap their fingers, rub their eyes or other parts of their body, bend paper clips, or tap a pencil. They may cross and uncross their legs, rhythmically swing a crossed leg back and forth, or rhythmically move a foot up and down.

There are many other gestures that provide clues to a person's thoughts and feelings. Clenched fists, whitened knuckles, and pointing fingers signal anger. When people want to express friendship or attraction, they tend to move closer to each other. Hugs can represent a variety of feelings: physical attraction, "good to see you," "best wishes in the future," and friendship. Shaking hands is a signal of friendship, and a way of saying "Hello" or "Goodbye."

Albert Scheflen notes that a person's sexual feelings can be signaled through gestures. He describes "preening behavior," which sends a message that the sender is attracted to the receiver. Preening includes rearranging one's clothing, combing or stroking one's hair, and glancing in a mirror. Scheflen cites a number of invitational preening gestures that are specific to women: Exposing a thigh, protruding a breast, placing a hand on a hip, exhibiting a wrist or palm, or stroking a thigh.[8] Naturally these gestures do not always suggest sexual interest. (It is interesting that comparable research has not been conducted on males. Conducting this research only on women may indicate a sexist bias.)

Gestures are used in relation to verbal messages to repeat, substitute, accent, contradict, and regulate. Some people literally speak with their hands, arms, and head movements. Their gestures may be so automatic that they are surprised when they see themselves on videotape and observe the number of gestures they use.

Touching

Rene Spitz has demonstrated that young children need direct physical contact, such as being cuddled, held, and soothed. Without direct physical contact, the emotional, social, intellectual, and physical development of children will be severely stunted.[9] Spitz observed that in the nineteenth century high proportions of children died in orphanages and other child-care institutions. The deaths were not found to be caused by poor nutrition or inadequate medical care but by lack of physical contact with parents or nurses. From this research came the practice of "nurturing" children in institutions—picking babies up, holding them close, playing with them, and carrying them around several times a day. With this practice, the infant mortality rate in institutions dropped sharply. Ashley Montagu describes research findings that suggest that eczema, allergies, and certain other medical problems are in part caused by a person's lack of physical contact with a parent during infancy.[10]

Adults also need physical contact. People need to know that they are loved, recognized, and appreciated. Touching (through holding hands, hugging, pats on the back) are ways of communicating warmth and caring. Unfortunately, most American men and some American women have been socialized to refrain from touching, except in sexual contexts. Sidney Simon has noted:

> In our now more than slightly cockeyed world, there seems to be little provision for someone to get touched without having to go to bed with whoever does the touching. And that's something to think about. We have mixed up simple, healing, warm touching with sexual advances. So much so, that it often seems as if there is no middle way between "Don't you dare touch me!" and "Okay, you touched me, so now we should make love!"[11]

Our language is a mirror of our culture. Common phrases suggest that more importance is placed on the senses of sight and hearing than on touch:

"Seeing is believing."
"It's good to see you again."
"It's really good to hear from you."
"I've got my eye on you."

We have coined few phrases that include words for touch. For example, when leaving someone we say, "See you again soon," rather than "Touch you again soon." If we should say the latter, it would be apt to be interpreted as having sexual connotations.

Touching someone is in fact an excellent way of conveying a variety of messages, depending on the context. A hug at a funeral will connote sympathy, while a hug when meeting someone says, "It's good to see you." A hug between parent and child means, "I love you," while a hug on a date may have sexual meanings. A number of therapists have noted that *communication and human relationships would be vastly improved if people reached out and touched others more—with hugs, squeezes of the hand, kisses, and pats on the back.* Touch is crucial for the survival and development of children, and touch is just as crucial for adults to assure them that they are worthwhile and loved.

There is a danger that a hug by someone who wants to send a message of nonsexual love and support may be misinterpreted by the receiver as being an incident of sexual harassment. One way of avoiding this predicament is for the person who wants to give a hug to ask the receiver: "Would you like a hug?"

Clothing

Clothes keep us warm, protect us from illness, and cover certain areas of our body so we are not arrested for indecency. But clothes have many other functions. Uniforms such as those worn by police officers or fire fighters tell us what a person does and what services he or she can render. People intentionally and unintentionally send messages about themselves by what they wear. Clothes give messages about occupations, personalities, interests, group norms, social philosophies, religious beliefs, status, values, mood, age, nationality, and personal attitudes. There are numerous "wardrobe engineers" (tailors, manufacturers, sellers of clothes) who assert that a person can obtain what he wants by improving his wardrobe, and there is some truth to the phrase "clothes make the person."

The importance of clothes in determining judgments that people make about strangers was demonstrated in a study by Hoult. Hoult began by having 254 female students rate the photos of male models on qualities such as "best-looking," "most likely to succeed," "most intelligent," "most likely to date or double date with," and "best personality." For these photos, Hoult obtained independent ratings of clothes and models' heads. Hoult then placed higher-ranked outfits on models with lower-ranked heads. Lower-ranked clothing was placed on models with higher-ranked heads. He found that, regardless of how the model's head was ranked, higher-ranked clothing was associated with an increase in rank while lower-ranked clothing was associated with loss of rank.[12]

Ronald Adler and Neil Towne have described an experiment in which a student spent a week hitchhiking back and forth from Los Angeles to Santa Barbara, a distance of one hundred miles. On Tuesday, Thursday, and Saturday, the student wore stay-pressed slacks, well-shined leather shoes, and an ironed shirt; on Monday, Wednesday, and Friday, he wore old blue jeans, sandals, and a tie-dyed sweatshirt. Other than the clothes, the student kept other factors constant, such as where he stood and at what time of day. The student described the results:

> It was incredible! On my three grubby days I got rides from people who looked just like I did. Two of them drove old VW buses, and the third had a '55 Ford pickup truck. They all wore Levis, boots, et cetera, and all had pretty much the same life style. On the days when I dressed

up, I got rides in shiny new Oldsmobiles and Cadillacs from people who were completely opposite from the ones I'd driven with the day before.[13]

Any given item of clothing can convey several different meanings. For example, the tie a person selects to wear may reflect "sophistication" or "nonconformity." In addition, the way the tie is worn (loosened, tightly knotted, thrown over one's shoulder, soiled and wrinkled) may provide additional information.

Clothes also affect our self-image. If a person feels appropriately dressed, he is usually more self-confident, assertive, and outgoing. If not, he becomes more reserved, less confident, and less assertive.

With clothes (as with other forms of nonverbal communication), there is a real danger of misreading nonverbal messages. We often judge others based on the basis of skimpy information, and frequently these interpretations are in error. Sometimes we get "burned" by our misinterpretations. Several years ago I had a client who for the previous ten years had lived elegantly, traveling all over Europe and North America, staying in the finest hotels. He financed his lifestyle by writing bad checks. When he needed money he would dress in an expensive suit because, he explained, people took his check much more readily when he was well dressed.

Personal Boundaries

Each of us wears a kind of invisible "bubble" of personal space wherever we go. The area inside this bubble is strictly private; only people who are emotionally close to us are allowed inside. You can sometimes tell how people are feeling toward each other by noting the physical distance between them. In fact, Edward Hall has identified four distinct distances, or zones, in people's daily interactions that guide their relations with others. These zones are intimate, personal, social, and public.[14] The particular zone chosen depends upon the context of the interaction, feelings toward the person, and interpersonal goals. Boundary behavior, like other nonverbal signals, provides group leaders with important information. For example, the distance maintained by group members should indicate to the group leader the members' personal preferences in individual interactions. These preferences, which may change considerably as the group progresses toward its goals, should be respected; otherwise, leaders are likely to encounter problems, such as resistance or distrust.

Intimate Zone

This zone begins with skin contact and extends out about eighteen inches. Only people who are very close emotionally enter this zone, primarily in private situations—comforting, conveying caring, making love, and showing love and affection. When a person voluntarily allows someone to enter this distance, it is a sign of trust because defenses are lowered. On the other hand, if a person maintains a "safe" distance of two or more feet, it probably means that the person is still sorting out the relationship.

When an uninvited intruder moves into this intimate zone, a person usually feels invaded and threatened. His posture becomes more upright, his muscles tense, and he may move back and avoid eye contact as a way of signaling he wants a less intimate relationship. When people are forced to stand close to strangers on crowded buses and elevators, they generally avoid eye contact and try not to rub against others, probably to say "I'm sorry I'm forced to invade your territory—I'll try not to bother you."

Personal Zone

This zone, which ranges from approximately eighteen inches to four feet, is the distance at which a couple stands apart from each other in public. Interestingly, if someone of the opposite sex stands close to someone we are dating or married to, we tend to wonder whether this person is trying to "move in" on us. If we see our spouse or date move close to someone of the opposite sex, we may become suspicious and jealous.

The far range of the personal zone (from about two and a half to four feet) is a distance at "arm's length," just beyond the other person's reach. Interactions occurring at this distance may still be reasonably close, but they are much less personal than those at the near range of the personal zone. Sometimes, communication at "arm's length" represents a test by people to determine whether they want the relationship to become emotionally closer.

Social Zone

This zone, which ranges from about four feet to twelve feet, usually encompasses business communications. The nearer part of this zone (from about four to seven feet) is the distance at which co-workers usually converse and at which salespeople and customers usually interact. Hall indicates that the seven- to twelve-foot range is used for more impersonal and formal situations. For example, this is the distance at which your boss talks to you when seated behind a desk. If you were to pull your chair around to the side of the boss's desk, a different kind of relationship would be signaled. The way furniture is arranged and the plants and wall hangings that people have in an office also convey signals about their values and interests and the type of relationship they want to establish. If the desk is placed between the office-owner and the customer, client, or student, the desk acts as a barrier and suggests that the office-owner wants formal and impersonal interaction. An office in which a desk is not used as a barrier and one that has plants suggests the office-owner wants warmer, less formal interactions.

Public Zone

This zone extends outward from twelve feet. Teachers and public speakers generally use the nearer range of public distance. In the farther range (beyond twenty-five feet), two-way communication is very difficult. Any speaker who voluntarily places considerable distance between himself and the audience is not interested in having a dialogue.

Territoriality

Territoriality is behavior characterized by identification with an area in a way that indicates ownership and a willingness to defend it against those who may invade it.[15] Many birds and small animals (including dogs, geese, snakes, and skunks) will strike out at much larger animals if they feel their territory is being invaded.

Territoriality also exists in human interactions. Traditionally, Dad and Mom have their

170

chairs, and each child has his or her own bedroom. The feeling of territorial ownership is sometimes extended to objects that are not really owned. Students in a class tend to select a certain seat to sit in. If someone else should happen to sit in that seat, the first student may feel that ownership rights are being violated, even though clearly the school campus owns the chairs.

Acquired properties—cars, homes, leisure-time equipment, plants, and clothes—are strong indicators of interests and values and often become topics of conversation. Material objects also communicate status messages, since wealthy people own more property than the poor. Generally, more personal space and greater privacy is granted to people of higher status. Before entering your boss's office, for example, you knock and then wait for an invitation. With people of an equal or lower status, you frequently walk right in.

Voice

Depending on emphasis, a word or phrase may carry many meanings. For example, look at how the meanings of the following sentences are changed by changing the word that is emphasized:

He's giving this money to Herbie.
(HE is the one giving the money; no one else.)

He's *giving* this money to Herbie.
(He is GIVING, not lending, the money.)

He's giving *this* money to Herbie.
(The money being exchanged is not from any other source; it is THIS money.)

He's giving this *money* to Herbie.
(MONEY is the unit of exchange, not a check or wampum.)

He's giving this money to *Herbie.*
(The recipient is HERBIE, not Eric or Bill or Rod.)[16]

Usually a person raises his voice at the end of a question and lowers it at the end of a declarative statement. Sometimes, an individual intentionally manipulates his voice to contradict the verbal message.

In addition to emphasizing particular words, our voices communicate in other ways. These include length of pauses, tone, pitch, speed, volume, and disfluencies (such as stammering or saying "uh," "um," and "er"). Taken together, these factors have been called paralanguage, which deals with *how* something is said and not with what is said.[17]

By using paralanguage, group members can contradict their verbal messages. For example, by simply changing the tone or inflection in his or her voice, a person can convey the following messages literally or sarcastically:

"I really like you."
"I'm having a perfectly wonderful time."
"You're really terrific."
"There's nothing that I like better than liver sausage."

171

Albert Mehrabian has found that when the paralanguage and the verbal message are contradictory, the paralanguage carries more meaning.[18] When there is a contradiction between words and the way something is said, receivers usually interpret the message by the way it was said.

An excellent way to learn more about how a group uses paralanguage is to videotape a meeting and then watch the replay. This process also provides valuable feedback about group members' use of other forms of nonverbal communication.

Physical Appearance

While it is common to hear people say that it is only inner beauty that really counts, research shows that outer beauty (physical attractiveness) influences responses for a broad range of interpersonal interactions. Singer found that college professors tended to give higher grades to females who were physically attractive than to those who were less attractive.[19] According to Mills and Aronson, attractive females could modify attitudes of male students more than less attractive females could.[20] Widgery and Webster have determined that attractive persons, regardless of sex, will be rated high on credibility, which greatly increases their ultimate persuasiveness in a variety of areas—sales, public speaking, changing attitudes, being recognized as a credible counselor, and so on.[21] An attractive applicant for a position is much more apt to receive an employment offer than an unattractive applicant.

Unattractive defendants are more likely to be judged guilty in courtrooms and to receive longer sentences.[22] The evidence is clear that *initially* we respond much more favorably to physically attractive people. Attractiveness serves to open doors and create greater opportunities.

Physically attractive people outstrip less attractive people on a wide range of socially desirable evaluations, including personality, popularity, success, sociability, persuasiveness, sexuality, and often happiness.[23] Attractive women, for example, are more apt to be helped and less likely to be the objects of aggressive acts.[24] Less attractive people are at a disadvantage from early childhood. Teachers, for example, interact less (and less positively) with unattractive children.[25] Physical attractiveness is also a crucial factor in determining the number of personal interactions. Practically everyone prefers the most attractive date regardless of his or her own attractiveness and regardless of rejection by the most attractive date.[26]

Interestingly, unattractive men seen with attractive women are judged higher in a number of areas than attractive men seen with attractive women.[27] They are judged as making more money, being more successful, and having more intelligence. Apparently, the evaluators reasoned that unattractive males must compensate for their appearance in other areas to obtain dates with attractive women.

Our weight suggests certain stereotypes, which may or may not be accurate. People who are overweight are judged to be older, more old-fashioned, less strong physically, more talkative, less good-looking, more agreeable and good-natured, more sympathetic, more trusting, more dependent, and more warmhearted. Muscular individuals are rated as being stronger, better-looking, younger, more adventurous, more self-reliant, more mature in behavior, and more masculine. A person with a thin physique is rated as younger, more suspicious of others, more tense and nervous, less masculine, more pessimistic, quieter, more stubborn, and more inclined to be difficult.[28] Overweight and very thin people have been discriminated against when attempting to obtain jobs, purchase life insurance, adopt children, or enter college.[29] There are stereotypes (which may be erroneous) that people

172

who are severely overweight have a low self-image. The important point here is that even our body weight communicates messages.

Being physically attractive does not mean that a person will be more intelligent, more successful, better adjusted, and happier than less attractive people. Attractiveness initially opens more doors to success, but after a door is opened, it's performance that determines outcome. It should also be noted that everyone has the ability to improve his physical appearance. Dieting, exercising, managing stress, learning to be assertive, adequate sleep, and good grooming habits will substantially improve a person's physical appearance.

Environment

Perhaps all of us have been in immaculate homes that have "unliving rooms" with furniture coverings, plastic lamp coverings, and spotless ashtrays that send nonverbal messages of "Do not get me dirty," "Do not touch," "Do not put your feet up," and "Stay alert to avoid a mistake." Owners of these homes wonder why guests cannot relax and have a good time. They are unaware that the environment is communicating messages that lead guests to feel uncomfortable.

A study by Maslow and Mintz found the attractiveness of a room shapes the kind of communication that takes place and influences the happiness and energy of people working in it.[30] The researchers used an "ugly" room, which looked like a janitor's closet, and a "beautiful" room, which was furnished with drapes, carpeting, and comfortable furniture. To gauge the subjects' energy levels and feelings of well-being, researchers asked them to rate a series of pictures of models' faces. When subjects were in the ugly room, they became tired and bored sooner, taking longer to complete their task. They described the room as producing fatigue, headaches, monotony, and irritability. When the subjects moved to the beautiful room, they displayed a greater desire to work. They also rated the faces they were judging higher and communicated many more feelings of comfort, importance, and enjoyment. This experiment provides evidence supporting the commonsense notion that workers do a better job and generally feel better when they are in an attractive environment.

Wall decorations, types of furniture, and placement of furniture in a meeting area convey messages as to whether the group leader wants informal, relaxed communications, or formal, to-the-point communications. A round table, for example, suggest egalitarian communication, while a rectangular table suggests status and power differences. At a rectangular table, high-status people generally sit at one end of the table, while low-status individuals sit at the other. If sides of equal strength hold a meeting around a rectangular table, each side sits at opposite ends, rather than intermingling. A classroom in which the chairs are in a circle suggests the instructor wants to create an informal atmosphere. A classroom with the chairs in rows suggests the instructor wants to create a formal atmosphere.

When clients come into the offices of helping professionals, the offices communicate messages. A clean, neat waiting room with comfortable chairs, plants, and soft background music communicates warmth, caring, and a professional approach. Negative messages are sent by an unclean room, hard chairs, few wall decorations, and loose paint on walls. A messy office may suggest to a client that the worker is overwhelmed, perhaps burning out, and therefore is unlikely to be of much help. A worker can *tell* his clients he wants them to feel comfortable by providing comfortable padded chairs instead of hard wooden ones, by providing tissues and ash trays, by having plants and wall decorations that suggest the worker really likes his job, and by arranging the furniture to facilitate communication.

Other Nonverbal Cues

Social workers need to be aware of other nonverbal cues: skin color, breathing patterns, muscle tension, and hand temperature.

When people become anxious, angry, embarrassed, or otherwise emotionally excited, the color of the skin reddens. This color change is particularly evident in the face, neck, and chest. Some people, when emotionally excited, have a pronounced facial blush or extensive reddening of the chest and neck. Such reddening is a cue to a worker that a group member or client is emotionally excited. In therapy, such a cue may signal that the client is focusing on emotionally charged material, which often needs to be explored.

The breathing pattern of a group member is another cue. When a member is anxious or emotionally excited, breathing rate increases, which can be observed by watching the person's chest.

Another cue commonly observed by psychotherapists, educators, and others is a change in muscle tension. When you become acquainted with someone, a common cue that you often use (and frequently are not aware of) to tell whether that person is relaxed or tense (or emotionally excited) is the degree of tenseness of muscles in that person's face, neck, and arms.

When a person is relaxed, the temperature on the surface of his or her hands is normally ten to fifteen degrees warmer than when the person is tense. As part of the reaction to stress, blood flows inward. When a person is relaxed, blood flows outward, and warms the hands and skin. When you shake hands with someone, you are able to tell whether that person is relaxed or under stress. (It should be noted that other variables will cause a person's hand to feel colder. The person may have been outside in cold weather or recently held a cold drink.)

GROUP EXERCISES

Exercise A: Chairs, Stickpins, and Coat Hangers

Goals: To identify and observe nonverbal messages that people respond to and to give feedback on the ways in which nonverbal messages are used constructively.

Step 1. The leader describes the purpose of the exercise. She asks the class to identify various types of nonverbal behaviors on the blackboard. A partial list would include:

Muscle tension	Breathing patterns
Eye contact	Clothes
Smiles	Distance between people
Eyebrow movements	communicating
Gestures	Touch
Voice tone	Silence and pauses
Facial color	Facial expressions

Step 2. The class forms groups of three students each. Each subgroup member picks out of a hat or box an unimportant topic to talk about. Possible topics include a chair, a stickpin, a coat hanger, or a bar of soap. Insignificant topics are suggested so that the focus will be on nonverbal communication.

Step 3. Each group member talks a minute and a half to his or her small group on the selected topic. The two who are observing in each group should note the speaker's nonverbal signals. The leader should inform the subgroups when it is time for each member to start and to stop talking.

Step 4. After all three group members have spoken, group members share what they liked about the way each communicated nonverbally.

Step 5. Group members are then asked to think about their nonverbal communication *privately* and about what they could change to communicate more effectively nonverbally.

Exercise B: Nonverbal Cues

Goals: To learn the kinds of nonverbal cues that (a) should be used to obtain social work employment and (b) establish a relaxed nonthreatening atmosphere for clients.

Step 1. The group leader states the goals of the exercise. The first task for each member of the class is to assume that he or she is a director of a social service agency interviewing applicants for a social work position. As director, which nonverbal cues might enter into the decision as to which applicant to hire? (Responses should be listed on the blackboard.)

Step 2. The second task for each student is to assume the role of a client who is emotionally upset and has painful decisions to make, such as whether to get a divorce. As a client, which nonverbal cues by a counselor would establish a relaxed, nonthreatening atmosphere that would increase the chances of the client fully sharing concerns? As responses are given, they are also listed on the blackboard.

Step 3. The similarities and differences between the two lists are discussed. For the differences, the possible reasons for these discrepancies are also discussed.

Exercise C: A Popular Faculty Member

Goal: To become more aware of using nonverbal communication in assessing human behavior.

Step 1. The group leader selects a popular faculty member whom the students are familiar with. The class indicates the specific nonverbal cues used by this instructor to increase his or her effectiveness. The following clues should be considered: clothing, eyes, facial expressions, posture, physical appearance, gestures and other body movements, and paralanguage.

Step 2. With this same instructor in mind, the class focuses on the appearance of this faculty member's office and imagines that this is the only information they have about the instructor. The class then discusses the nonverbal messages sent by the types of objects, arrangement of objects, and general conditions of the office. Next, the class discusses which of these nonverbal messages give an impression different from what the instructor is like. Which are consistent? Finally, the class discusses the types of interaction the office atmosphere suggests should take place—for example, whether the communication is expected to be formal and businesslike, or relaxed and informal.

Exercise D: Double Messages

Goal: To understand how verbal messages can contradict nonverbal messages.

Step 1. The class divides into two groups of equal size and is informed that this is an exercise in keeping conversations going. One group leaves for a separate room or the hallway.

Step 2. The remaining, or first, group is told that this is really an exercise in learning more about how people react when someone seems to be saying one thing verbally and another nonverbally. Each member's task is to pick a topic to discuss with another person in the other group for ten minutes. The topic may be anything, such as politics, movies, sports, whatever. While discussing the topic, each person should periodically *nonverbally* contradict his or her verbal message by using facial expressions, gestures, laughter, and voice fluctuations. Furthermore, each person should note and observe the partner's nonverbal reactions to these double messages.

Step 3. The second group is told that each person will be paired with someone in the first group. The partner in the first group will start a conversation on a topic. The task of each person in this second group is to keep the discussion going and to inject controversial topics into the conversation.

Step 4. The room should be large enough to allow individuals to spread out and carry on conversations. Perhaps two rooms can be used. Individuals from both groups pair off, and discuss the topic for approximately ten minutes.

Step 5. The real purpose of the exercise is now explained to the second group. The first group discusses the following questions with the second group listening. What nonverbal cues did they use to contradict their verbal messages? Was sending a double message hard to do? What were the reactions to these double messages?

Then, the second group discusses the following: How did they feel about their partners during this exercise? Did they believe what their partners were saying verbally? How did they cope with the double messages they were receiving? When nonverbal messages conflicted with verbal messages, which were they more likely to believe?

Exercise E: The Flat Tire

Goal: To become more aware of individual differences and skills in using nonverbal cues to relay messages.

Step 1. The leader explains that the exercise involves students relaying messages nonverbally. Four students volunteer to leave the room. Then, the following is read to a fifth volunteer who must try to remember and communicate it nonverbally to the first student who returns. That student will then nonverbally communicate it to the second student, and so on.

> You are driving a car and your right front tire goes flat. You get out and kick the tire. You go to the trunk, open it, and there's no spare. You angrily slam the trunk shut. You then attempt to hitchhike to a gas station you recently passed. A motorcyclist stops to give you a ride to the gas station.

The volunteers receiving the message may ask questions, but the senders must communicate their answers nonverbally.

While these five volunteers are acting out this exercise, the remainder of the class responds to the following questions on paper each time the message is relayed: What did the relayer add to or delete from the message? If there was a communication breakdown as a result of a weakness in a nonverbal cue, how could this have been avoided by using a better one?

Step 2. The person who receives the final message states it verbally. This message is compared to the original and the whole class discusses the two questions in Step 1.

Exercise F: Communicating While Blindfolded

Goal: To better understand how communication is affected when the sense of sight is not used.

Step 1. The leader explains that nonverbal communication is heavily dependent on the sense of sight. We watch other people's facial expressions, eyes, posture, hand gestures, and body movements. The leader describes the goal of the exercise and asks for five or six volunteers. These volunteers sit in a circle in the middle of the class. The volunteers are given a controversial topic to discuss (for example, whether the elderly who have a terminal illness and are in severe pain have a right to take their own lives). All volunteers are either blindfolded or asked to keep their eyes tightly shut while discussing the topic. The topic is discussed for ten to fifteen minutes.

Step 2. At the end of ten or fifteen minutes, the discussion ends. The volunteers remove their blindfolds or open their eyes, and discuss the following questions;

1. How did it feel to be blindfolded?
2. How did not being able to see affect the communications?
3. Did having a blindfold on interfere with being able to concentrate on what was said?
4. Was it difficult to hear?
5. Do they think they gestured more or less than they usually do?
6. During this exercise, did they become aware of anything they had not noticed before?
7. Does not being able to see the people you are talking to substantially hamper communication? If yes, in what ways?

Step 3. As an additional optional step, this exercise may be repeated with a new group of volunteers.

Exercise G: Giving and Receiving Feedback about Nonverbal Communication

Goals: To observe nonverbal communication in others and receive feedback about nonverbal communication.

177

Step 1. The group leader states the purpose of the exercise and divides the class into two groups of equal size. If there is an uneven number, the group leader can participate. Each member in one group should pair up with someone in the other group.

Step 2. One group sits in an inner circle, and the other group members sit in an outer circle to observe the nonverbal communication of their partners. The inner circle discusses a controversial topic that will arouse strong emotions. The topic could be abortion or whether a male and female who are both severely retarded should legally be permitted to marry and to have children. The discussion should continue for ten to twenty minutes. People in the outer circle observe the nonverbal communication of their partners—gestures, body movements, eye behavior, paralanguage, facial expressions, and so on.

Step 3. After the discussion, the observing partner informs his or her partner as to what nonverbal cues were used and what messages communicated. After the observing partner is finished, the partner who was observed should have an opportunity to discuss his or her degree of agreement with the observer's interpretations.

Step 4. The roles of the partners are reversed and steps 2 and 3 repeated.

Step 5. The class discusses what they learned from this exercise.

Exercise H: Zones of Personal Space

Goal: To observe how the distance between communicators affects what people are thinking and feeling.

Step 1. The leader explains the purpose of the exercise. Two people volunteer for an exercise to illustrate these effects.

Step 2. The volunteers stand at the farthest corners of the room, away from each other. Their task is to slowly, very slowly, move toward each other. As they are slowly moving toward each other, they engage in small talk about topics of their choosing. They should continue slowly walking and conversing until they touch. When they touch they should slowly start moving away from each other but continue to converse. At the point when they are most comfortable in conversing, they should stop.

Step 3. Other volunteers may be selected to repeat the exercise until interest wanes.

Step 4. The volunteers involved in this exercise should then determine the distances between partners that were most comfortable and least comfortable for conversing. The leader of the exercise should note the points at which the various pairs were most comfortable in conversing, and then make some statements about the extent of the congruence between these "most comfortable points" and the theoretical material in the chapter as to the "most comfortable point" for conversing in this type of situation.

PART FOUR

PROBLEM-SOLVING AND DECISION-MAKING GROUPS

CHAPTER NINE

PROBLEM SOLVING, CONTROVERSY, AND CONFLICT RESOLUTION

Goals: Perhaps the most important activity performed by social workers is problem solving, a process that involves several stages. This chapter describes that process and instructs students in using brainstorming to help define problems and generate solutions. This chapter also describes both the merits and pitfalls of controversy and conflict, illustrating that controversy often fosters creativity, and details the following approaches for resolving conflicts: no-lose problem solving, role reversal, mediation, empathy, I-messages, disarming, stroking, and inquiry.

PROBLEM-SOLVING APPROACH

In a nutshell, practically all of the work done by social work practitioners involves problem solving. Social workers use a problem-solving approach extensively to help individuals, families, small groups, organizations, and community groups. Problem solving has been defined by David Johnson and Frank Johnson:

> *Problem solving* is the process of resolving the unsettled matters, of finding an answer to a difficulty; it is a process that results in a solution to a problem, and it involves changing the actual state of affairs until it is identical with the desired state of affairs.[1]

Problem solving can be broken down into six steps: (1) identifying and defining the problem; (2) assessing the size and causes of the problem; (3) developing alternative strategies or plans for solving it; (4) assessing the merits and shortcomings of these alternative strategies; (5) selecting and implementing the most desirable strategy or strategies; and (6) evaluating the success of the strategies used.

Identification and Definition

The more precisely and accurately a problem is defined, the easier it is to solve. Contrast the following two statements describing problems: "Fifty-seven young children in a six-block-square area of this city are in need of care during the daytime because their parents are working." Here the terms of the problem are defined concretely. Because the problem group, its locale, and a time period are specified, the problem can be easily addressed. Now consider another example: "Some children in some school systems in this city seem to be becoming more apathetic about the way their lives are going, and something should be done about it." Since no particular group and no clear symptoms have been identified, there is no way to determine a solution.

When using the problem-solving approach, a group should initially (1) determine the actual or current state of affairs and (2) specify the desired state of affairs. The differences between the actual and desired state of affairs should be thoroughly discussed and agreed upon. If the group concludes that there are serious negative consequences associated with the actual state of affairs, then members' commitment to reach the desired state of affairs is apt to be high.

Arriving at a group definition of a workable problem can be difficult. Brainstorming, which is described in this chapter, can help to develop descriptions of the problem. These descriptions are then rephrased until an agreed-upon definition is reached. It should include a precise statement of both the actual and the desired state of affairs.

Assessment of Size and Causes

Once a definition of the problem is arrived at, the group next gathers information to help it assess the magnitude and causes of the problem. In assessing the magnitude, the following questions arise: Who is affected? How many people are affected? How seriously? Where are they located?

Often, identifying the causes of a problem will suggest strategies for resolving it. If high unemployment is a problem in a state and most of the unemployed are untrained for available jobs, for example, this information suggests that programs to train the unemployed for available jobs will alleviate unemployment. Only rarely is it possible to resolve a problem without knowing its causes. For example, some urban renewal projects have rebuilt blighted areas without knowing all the causes that led to the deterioration of housing and living conditions.

Development of Alternative Strategies

The third problem-solving step is to formulate alternative ways to solve the problem. Brainstorming is a useful technique for generating a wide range of strategies. Sometimes, the wildest ideas suggested may stimulate other members to come up with one or more pragmatic alternatives. If group members cannot produce workable strategies, outside experts may be consulted.

Assessment of Strategies

Next, the merits and shortcomings of each strategy must be assessed, and often a cost-benefit analysis of each strategy is done. Costs include money, time, material resources, and professional fees. Although the actual costs and benefits of each strategy are often difficult to assess objectively, reasoned judgments must be made as to what resources will be needed and what the outcomes of applying these resources will be. For example, if racial segregation is a problem in a large city, judgments must be made as to whether the costs of school busing to achieve school integration (such as transportation costs and movement away from the benefits of the neighborhood school concept) justify this type of busing.

Selection and Implementation

The fifth step involves two separate processes. The first is *decision making*, in which the group selects one of the proposed alternatives. (Decision making in a group can be done in a variety of ways. Many of these approaches are described in chapter 10.) After a strategy is selected, the group must *implement* the strategy. Generally, the more solid the group support for the selected strategy, the greater the chances for its successful implementation. Required tasks must be identified, jobs assigned, and deadlines set for starting and completing each task.

Evaluation

In evaluating the strategy's success two areas need to be examined: Was the strategy fully implemented, and what were its effects? The main criterion is the extent to which the strategy has narrowed the discrepancy between the actual and desired state of affairs. This is why precise descriptions of each are necessary in the problem definition.

If the strategy was not fully implemented, then additional efforts may be required. If the strategy has been fully implemented without achieving the desired state of affairs, however, perhaps new strategies are in order. In addition, implementation of a strategy may expose other problems. For example, the 1960s civil rights movement focused on reducing racial discrimination. But it also generated awareness that many other groups are discriminated against: women, homosexuals, and persons with a disability.

The evaluation phase should demonstrate the extent to which the problem has been resolved, what yet remains to be resolved, and what new problems have been identified. Not surprisingly, the evaluation phase often leads to another problem-solving effort. The old problem is redefined or another problem is identified. The steps of the problem-solving approach are then repeated.

BARRIERS TO EFFECTIVE PROBLEM SOLVING

There are several barriers to effective problem solving: inadequate definitions; invalid hypotheses; poor communication; and lack of trust, skills, resources, and motivation within the group.

Inadequate Definitions

If a problem is stated imprecisely, individual group members are apt to vary in their interpretations of the problem. For example, take the following problem statement: "Children are under too much pressure in our school systems." Possible interpretations of "too much pressure" include "academic pressure," "pressure to use alcohol and drugs," "religious pressure," "pressure from teachers and parents," "pressure resulting from racial tensions," "pressure to have sexual experiences," and "pressure to break the law." Unless the problem is defined more precisely, group members will probably disagree on how to solve it.

Invalid Hypotheses

Closely related to inadequate definitions, invalid hypotheses and theories about the causes of a problem also erect a formidable barrier. Emotionally disturbed people were once thought to be possessed by demons, for example, and in the early 1900s, criminals were considered to be mentally retarded.[2] Two hundred years ago physicians thought that bloodletting (through using leeches) would help heal people who were physically ill. If a group has faulty theories about the causes of a problem, the members may develop ineffective strategies to solve it. For example, we know today that seeking to drive demons out of someone who has emotional problems will not alleviate his or her emotional trauma.

184

Inadequate Communication

Poor communication in the group may exist for a variety of reasons. Group members may not possess well-developed communication skills, or some may withhold information to attempt to manipulate others in the group. Interpersonal conflict between group members may inhibit them from participating effectively. With poor communication, a group will generate fewer alternative strategies and inadequately assess their potential consequences. In addition, enthusiasm and commitment to implement the proposed group strategy will be diminished.

Lack of Skills

A group may lack the skills to define and solve a problem. A group may not have the expertise to design and conduct a necessary research study, for instance, or the skills to write a grant proposal to obtain needed resources. When the group lacks an essential skill, the group must acquire the skill by recruiting appropriate new members or retaining an outside consultant.

Lack of Resources

There never seem to be sufficient financial resources to accomplish everything that is desired. A planning group to combat the homeless problem, for example, may be partially stifled by lack of funds to build a sufficient number of low-cost housing units for the homeless.

Lack of Motivation

Some groups fail to solve problems because their members are not motivated to do so. By creating a supportive, trusting, cooperative atmosphere, a leader can encourage unmotivated members to participate. Unmotivated members could be asked to share their reasons for not participating, and perhaps changes could be made to encourage their input. The motivated members could also carry the group to some initial successes in the hope that the unmotivated members would be inspired to participate more. Relatively easy tasks could be delegated to these individuals, who should be complimented for their efforts.

BRAINSTORMING

Brainstorming is a procedure designed to generate ideas in quantity through the full participation of all group members. The procedure helps individuals share their ideas without the interruption of discussion or evaluation. By allowing members to present any idea that comes to mind, more and often better ideas are generated than if the same persons had worked independently. Brainstorming was developed by Alex Osborn, who outlined the following ground rules nearly half a century ago.[3] Brainstorming can last anywhere from about one minute to half an hour. The session continues as long as ideas are being generated. Each session is to be freewheeling and open. The wilder and more absurd the ideas the better, as these ideas may lead to a breakthrough or a new course of action. Criticism or evaluation of any idea is not allowed. The ideas are simply listed for the group as rapidly as possible without any comment, discussion, or clarification.

The quantity of ideas counts, not quality. A greater number of ideas will increase the likelihood of usable ideas. Members are encouraged to build on the ideas of other group members whenever possible, so that thoughts are expanded and new combinations of ideas are formulated. The focus is always on a single issue or problem. Members should not skip from problem to problem, or try to brainstorm a multiproblem situation.

A relaxed, congenial, cooperative atmosphere should be promoted, and all members, no matter how shy and reluctant to participate, should be encouraged to contribute. It is often advisable to limit members to one idea at a time so that less vocal individuals will feel encouraged to express their ideas. For new members unfamiliar with brainstorming, the rationale and rules for brainstorming should be explained. If groups are being formed specifically for brainstorming, members should have some diversity of opinion and background. After the brainstorming session is over, the group selects the best ideas (or a synthesis of these ideas) related to the issue or problem.

Brainstorming has a number of advantages because it increases involvement of all members, reduces a group's dependency upon a single authority figure, and provides a procedure for obtaining a large number of ideas in a relatively short period of time.

The pressure to say the "right things" to impress others in the group is reduced, and the process is interesting, fun, and stimulating. An open sharing of ideas within a nonevaluative climate allows each group member to build upon the ideas of others to create unique combinations.

Many people find brainstorming a strange experience, however, and it may lead initially to a sense of discomfort.[4] In a restricted, self-conscious group, brainstorming may actually hinder participation, because it forces members into patterns of behavior that are felt to be "uncomfortable."[5]

In some situations, brainstorming may be used as an "ice-breaker" to open up a stuffy and inhibited group.[6] What effect brainstorming will have on the group depends partially on the group leader's skills and timing in using the approach.

CONFLICT

Conflict, which is an antagonistic state of action involving divergent ideas or interests, is inevitable in groups. David Johnson and Frank Johnson summarize the potential merits and dangers of a conflict in a group:

> A conflict among group members is a moment of truth in group effectiveness, a test of the group's health, a crisis that can weaken or strengthen the group, a critical event that may bring creative insight and closer relationships among members—or lasting resentment, smoldering hostility, and psychological scars. Conflicts can push members away from one another or pull them into closer and more cooperative relationships. Conflicts may contain the seeds of group destruction or the seeds of a more unified and cooperative unit. . . . They have the potential for producing both highly constructive and highly destructive consequences for group functioning.[7]

Our society maintains an erroneous belief that conflicts produce negative results and should be avoided. Conflict is seen as a cause of divorces, low work morale, deterioration of friendships, psychological trauma, violence, and social disorder. In reality, the cause of these destructive events is the ineffective and harmful management of conflicts. Since people have divergent interests, beliefs, values, and goals, it is inevitable that conflicts will occur in interpersonal relationships.

Conflicts are not only a natural part of any relationship within a group, they are also desirable because, when handled effectively, they have a number of payoffs. Without conflict, members would become bored because disagreements often spark the interest and curiosity of group members and produce lively discussions. Conflicts motivate members to define issues more sharply, search harder for resolution strategies, and work harder in implementing solutions. Conflict can also lead to greater commitment, cohesion, communication, and cooperation and can revitalize stagnant groups. By expressing and working out their dissatisfactions, group members can assess their beliefs, values, and opinions. Therefore, verbal conflicts can also lead to personal growth and encourage innovation and creativity.

CONTROVERSY

Controversy is a debate, dispute, or discussion involving differences in beliefs, information, opinions, ideas, or assumptions among group members. Emotional reactions to controversy may be positive (curiosity, liking for other members, excitement, exhilaration, stimulation, involvement, commitment) or negative (frustration, disgust, anger, fear, resentment, rejection, apathy, paranoia), depending on how the group handles the controversy. People react differently to controversy. Some shy away from it. Others take a difference of opinion personally and are hurt or angered. Others find controversies to be stimulating and fun, and hope to find a few each day. Still others view controversy in groups as a constructive way for members of each side to express themselves, ventilate concerns, and work out differences.

When handled effectively, controversy can be healthy and invigorating. However, some ineffective groups do not manage controversy well and tend to suppress and withdraw from it. These groups have norms that urge members to suppress conflicts and to express group consensus outwardly, even when some members have serious misgivings about group decisions. When controversy does arise in ineffective groups, members may view the opposing positions in terms of "right vs. wrong" or "we vs. they."

Win-Lose Approach

In ineffective groups, resolutions of controversy between opposing positions become "win-lose" situations. In many competitive fields, such as sports, business, and politics, individuals or teams are pitted against each other. In groups, controversies are often cast in the same competitive mold. Because each side denies the legitimacy of the other's interests and concerns, members attempt to sell their position without really listening to the other side. Power blocks are formed to support one position against another. The original goals and objectives of the group may fade into the background as a "win" on issues becomes the objective of the warring sides.

In win-lose situations, the group as a whole loses because it fails to achieve its long-range goals and objectives. The losing side is not motivated to carry out the winning decision. The losers resent the winners and may attempt to reverse their decision or impede its implementation. In such an atmosphere, distrust increases between opposing sides, communication becomes more limited and inaccurate, and group cohesion decreases. Members' unresolved feelings often result in biased judgments and actions; members will frequently refuse to vote for a good idea simply because they dislike the person who suggested it.

Obviously, communication is severely hampered in groups that handle controversy in a win-lose fashion. Conflict in win-lose situations leads to the denial or distortion of unpleasant facts and information, as each side is apt to deny, hide, or distort information inconsistent with its position in an effort to win.[8] Members misinterpret the ideas and actions of those perceived as being opponents, causing "blind spots" in communication. A win-lose approach leads to deceitful expression of ideas and feelings at times because winning sometimes receives higher priority than honesty. Disagreement tends to be interpreted as personal rejection on the part of opposing group members, and the group's future decisions are generally poor.

Problem-Solving Approach

A more effective approach to use in resolving conflicts is the problem-solving approach described earlier in this chapter. Through the use of this approach, members tend to listen to one another, recognize the legitimacy of another's interests, and influence one another with rational arguments. Instead of a competitive environment, problem solving encourages an atmosphere of cooperation.

The differences between a win-lose strategy and a problem-solving strategy can be summarized as follows:

Win-Lose Strategy	Problem-Solving Strategy
The conflict is defined as a win-lose situation.	The conflict is viewed as a mutual problem.
Each side seeks solutions to meet only its needs.	Each person seeks to find solutions to meet the needs of all members.
Each side attempts to force the other side into submission.	Each person cooperates with others to find mutually acceptable compromises.
Each side increases its power by emphasizing its independence from the other, and the other's dependence upon itself.	Each person equalizes his power by emphasizing interdependence.
Each side inaccurately, deceitfully, and misleadingly communicates its goals, needs, and ideas; information inconsistent or harmful to one's position is not shared.	Each person honestly and openly communicates his goals, needs, and ideas.

No expression of empathy or understanding is made of the views, values, and opinions of the other side.

Threats are used to attempt to force the other side into submission.

Rigid adherence to one's position is expressed.

Changes in position are made very slowly, in an effort to force concessions from the other side.

No suggestions are sought from third parties as the focus is on forcing the other side to give in.

Efforts are made to convey empathy and understanding of the views, values, and opinions of others.

Threats are avoided to reduce the defensiveness of others.

A willingness to be flexible is expressed.

Positions are changed readily to help in problem solving.

Third parties are sought to help in problem solving.

CREATIVITY

A cooperative, problem-solving approach in a group also promotes creativity. Creativity is a process of bringing something new into existence; it results from productive controversy. Because a problem is viewed from new perspectives, new alternatives can be suggested and formulated for resolving the problem.

Deutsch has identified three means of fostering creativity in a group.[9] First, an appropriate level of motivation for finding a viable solution must be aroused. Second, there must be a cooperative, problem-solving atmosphere in the group that allows members to reformulate the problem once an impasse has been reached. Third, diverse ideas must be suggested or available that can be flexibly put together into new and varied solutions.

Groups are most creative when the motivational level is high enough for members to maintain problem-solving efforts despite frustrations and dead ends. However, this level should not be so high that it overwhelms the group by causing members to become too tense to concentrate. Excessive tension leads to defensiveness and reduces receptiveness to innovative approaches. Too much anxiety inhibits members from fully expressing their views, interferes with their listening to the views of others, and often leads to closed-mindedness.

Creative group members seek out different ways of looking at the problem and innovative ways of resolving it in a way that is open minded. That is, a member assesses relevant information based on its *own* merits, not on how it resembles or differs from his own ideas, opinions, and assumptions. When conflict occurs between two members, each can listen to the other's criticisms, judge their validity fairly, and suggest new strategies that take into account both members' concerns. This leads to a creative solution to the problem.

In contrast, a closed-minded person views relevant information from his own assumptions, beliefs, and frame of reference.[10] Closed-minded members emphasize the differences between what they believe and do not believe, ignoring or denying information contrary to their value system. They tend to have contradictory beliefs that they fail to question, and in their efforts to defend these beliefs, they stifle creativity.

NO-LOSE PROBLEM SOLVING

The no-lose problem-solving approach asserts that it is almost always possible for both sides to have their needs met in a conflict situation. This approach, which is a variation of the problem-solving approach described earlier in this chapter, was developed by Thomas Gordon and is based on two basic premises: (1) all persons have the right to have their needs met, and (2) what is in conflict between the two sides is almost never their *needs* but their *solutions* to those needs.[11]

The distinction between "needs" and "solutions" is all-important. For example, assume that a student social work club is arguing over whether to fund a graduation party for seniors or a campus day-care center in danger of being closed. An analysis of "needs" and "solutions" in this discussion would reveal that the club is arguing over solutions rather than needs. There is a need to honor the graduating seniors and a need for the day-care center to receive operating funds. However, there are a variety of ways of meeting both needs. The club may spend its funds on a graduation party and hold a fund raiser for the day-care center, or fund the center and hold a graduation party by having members donate food, refreshments, and a few dollars at the party. Half of the club's funds could go to the center, and the remainder to a reduced-cost graduation party. In addition, many other solutions could be generated to meet these needs.

The six steps to the *no-lose problem-solving approach* are:

1. Identify and define the needs of each opposing side.
2. Generate possible alternative solutions.
3. Evaluate the alternative solutions.
4. Decide on the best acceptable solution.
5. Work out ways of implementing the solution.
6. Evaluate how it worked.[12]

The first step is by far the most difficult because group members often view conflicts in terms of win-lose and attempt to identify and meet primarily their own needs. When each side's needs in a conflict are identified, however, what usually is in conflict are not the *needs* of each side, but their *solutions*. No-lose problem solving will generally lead to creative solutions, after *all six steps* are followed.

The advantages of this approach are that both sides fulfill their needs, and group harmony and cohesion are increased. The resentment, hostility, and subversive actions of a win-lose situation are also eliminated. Actually, it is in each group member's best interest to resolve conflicts in a way that will help all members achieve their short-term goals and needs and increase the long-term effectiveness of the group, so that the long-term goals and needs of *all* members have a better chance of being achieved. Frequently, with groups that function in terms of win-lose, the winning side may win some battles, but the effectiveness of the group may diminish. All members may thus fail to accomplish their long-term goals and satisfy their needs.

INTERGROUP CONFLICT

Just as there is a conflict within groups, conflicts often arise *between* groups. Within a single organization, various groups are often forced to vie for funding, human resources, and power. For example, in a university, members of different department faculties (e.g., sociology, psychology, social work) may conflict over: which department will receive authorization to add a new course (such as human sexuality); which department will be given a new faculty position; what will be the budget allocation for each department; and which department will use which human service agencies for field placements for students.

As with intragroup conflict, the sides involved in intergroup (or between-group) conflict can use either a win-lose approach or a no-lose problem-solving approach to attempt to resolve the conflict. The same advantages and disadvantages described for intragroup conflicts hold true for those conflicts occurring between competing groups.

When the conflicts are formulated in terms of win-lose situations, the results are both predictable and destructive.[13] Each group becomes much more cohesive as members join together to defend their group against attack; members will close ranks and frequently put aside intragroup conflicts. Group members become more willing to accept autocratic leadership since rapid, consistent decisions must be made and "a solid front" presented. The groups in conflict tend to become more polarized as each perceives its position as "right" and "moral," while the opposing groups are belittled and devalued. Members' satisfaction with the group increases because they feel an increased sense of identity with their group and an increased sense of belonging.

Hostility increases between the two groups. Distortions in perceptions increase, since each group highlights the best parts of itself and the worst parts of the other group. Communication and interaction between the groups decrease, as each group assigns inaccurate and uncomplimentary stereotypes to the opposing group and views it as distinctly inferior.

Because group members often misinterpret the other side's position, distrust is heightened, and negotiators are often selected from each group to work out differences. These negotiators tend to be among the most militant leaders of each group and tend to assert their group's position rather than work toward a creative agreement that will meet the needs of all sides. They want at any cost to avoid giving in so that they are not branded as "losers" or "traitors." If a third party is brought in to decide the dispute, the winning side will view the third party as fair and objective, while the losing side will view the third party as being biased, thoughtless, and irrational.

There are two usual outcomes when intergroup conflict is cast in a win-lose mold. One outcome is a stalemate, in which the opposing groups continue doing battle and remain deadlocked, perhaps for years. In the other outcome, one side wins and the other side loses.

The side that loses initially loses cohesiveness and may even disband. Members analyze the reasons for losing, often place blame, and then quarrel among themselves. Previous unresolved conflicts surface and tension increases. The group often finds a scapegoat, such as the leader, the third-party negotiator, or the least conforming members of the group. If an "ineffective" leader is blamed for the defeat, he may be replaced. Through a reassessment of the loss, the group reshapes some of its goals and reexamines its positive stereotypes of itself and its negative stereotypes of the opposing groups. This, in effect, may lead to a more realistic assessment of itself and of the opposing groups. Once a loss has been accepted, a losing group that sees hope of victories in the future may reorganize and again become effective. If future victories appear impossible, members may become so demoralized, depressed, and apathetic that they drift away from the group, or become uninvolved and nonproductive.

The group that wins generally celebrates and feels a strong sense of cohesion. It becomes self-satisfied, loses its fighting spirit, and members tend to become casual, even playful, while putting forth little effort for group work. Because they have won, they feel little need to evaluate the positive stereotypes of their group or the negative stereotypes of the losing group. Therefore, the winning group makes few changes—it is content.

In contrast to the win-lose approach, a problem-solving strategy can be used to resolve intergroup conflict through a variety of structural arrangements. One arrangement is for the leaders or representatives of each group to meet, or, if the groups are small enough, a meeting of *all* the members involved can be scheduled. If necessary, a mediator can be chosen to call a meeting of representatives from the groups, or an ongoing committee of representatives from each group can be selected to work on present conflicts and new issues.

Calling a meeting is the easy part; the hard part is to convince each side that it is in the best interest of everyone to use a problem-solving approach. The benefits of using a problem-solving approach for intergroup conflict are the same as those described for intragroup conflict in this chapter. One way of pointing the conflicting groups in this direction is to: (1) briefly summarize the disadvantages and likely future problems in using a win-lose approach, (2) indicate the potential benefits to all sides in using a problem-solving approach, and (3) ask the groups in conflict to try the problem-solving approach.

The most important point about intergroup conflict is that it is much better if each side uses a cooperative, problem-solving approach rather than a win-lose approach. Group leaders must be aware that it is very difficult to undo the negative feelings and resentments that result from a competitive, win-lose situation. If need be, third-party mediators or arbitrators should be brought in early in a win-lose conflict to turn the situation around.

The win-lose strategy and the no-lose problem-solving strategy are frequently mutually exclusive. If two groups are in conflict, negotiators for each side cannot be both honest and deceitful at the same time. They cannot simultaneously convey and withhold empathy and understanding or use threats to win and avoid threats in order to reduce defensiveness. Moreover, these negotiators cannot simultaneously be flexible and rigid.

Although the problem-solving approach is by far the most desirable, a win-lose approach may be necessary when an opposing side refuses to use a problem-solving strategy. Being open, flexible, and willing to make concessions to a group using a win-lose strategy may increase the chances of being exploited and of losing.

TECHNIQUES FOR RESOLVING CONFLICTS

The no-lose problem-solving approach has already been described. Additional techniques that have value in resolving conflicts are: role reversal, empathy, inquiry, I-messages, disarming, stroking, and mediation.

Role Reversal

A useful strategy in resolving both intragroup and intergroup conflict is role reversal. The basic rule for role reversal is: *Each person expresses his or her opinions or views only after restating the ideas and feelings of the opposing person.* These ideas and feelings should be restated in one's own words rather than parroted or mimicked in the exact words of the other person. It is advisable to begin the restatement with words such as "Your position is . . . ," "You seem to be saying . . . ," or "You apparently feel. . . ." Approval or disapproval, blaming, giving advice, interpreting, or persuading should be avoided.

In addition, nonverbal messages should be consistent with the verbal paraphrasing and convey interest, openness, and attentiveness to the opposition's ideas and feelings. Above all, role reversal should be the expression of a sincere interest in understanding the other person's feelings, ideas, and position.

Role reversal can result in a re-evaluation and a change of attitude concerning the issue by both parties, for the group members involved are apt to be perceived as people who are understanding, willing to compromise, cooperative, and trustworthy.[14] The approach has also been found to increase cooperative behavior between role reversers, to clarify misunderstandings, to change win-lose situations into problem-solving situations, and most important, to allow the issue to be perceived from the opponent's frame of reference.

Empathy

A technique closely related to role reversal is the expression of empathy. Empathy involves putting yourself in the shoes of the person you are in conflict with and expressing your understanding of what she is thinking and saying. Some examples of phrases that are useful in helping you express empathy are:

"What you seem to be saying is. . . ."
"I take it that you think. . . ."
"I sense that you feel _____ ____ about this issue."

When expressing empathy it is essential to mirror what was said in a non-judgmental way that will help you grasp the essence of what the other person is thinking or feeling.

Similar to role reversal, empathy is used to facilitate open communication, assist in clarifying misunderstandings, increase cooperative behavior, and facilitate the process of no-lose problem solving.

Inquiry

If you are in conflict with someone and you are confused regarding his thoughts and feelings, the inquiry technique may be useful. This technique involves using gentle, probing questions to learn more about what the other person is thinking and feeling. Tone of voice is very crucial in inquiry because asking a question sarcastically or defensively is apt to draw defensive responses from the person you are in conflict with.

I-Messages

As described in chapter 7, the technique of using I-messages also facilitates more open and honest communication between parties in conflict. In contrast, you-messages tend to increase defensiveness between parties in conflict.

Disarming

When you are in conflict with someone, the disarming technique is frequently an effective strategy in resolving the conflict. The disarming technique involves finding some truth in what the other person (or side) is saying and then expressing your "agreement"—even if you feel that the other person is largely wrong, unreasonable, irrational, or unfair. There is always a grain of truth in what the other person says, even if it sounds obnoxious and insulting. When you disarm the other person with this technique, she will recognize that you respect her. Once disarmed, the other person won't feel so dogmatic and will be less likely to insist that she is entirely right and you are entirely wrong. As a result, she is apt to be more willing to examine the merits of your point of view. If you want respect, *give* respect first. If you want to be listened to, disarming helps you listen to the other person first and facilitates open (rather than defensive) communication. Friendly responses facilitate open communication, while hostile responses usually produce defensive communication.

In using the disarming technique, it is important to be genuine in what you say and to express your agreement sincerely.

Stroking

Closely related to disarming, stroking is saying something genuinely positive to the person (or side) you are in conflict with, even in the heat of battle. Stroking tells the other person that you respect him, even though both of you may be angry. During an argument or conflict, you are apt to feel the need to reject the other person before you get rejected (to "save face"). Often, people overreact and differences of opinion are blown out of proportion. To prevent this rejection, simply let the other person know that, although you are at odds, you still think highly of him. This makes it easier for him to open up and to listen, because he will feel less threatened.

Mediation

In the past two decades, mediation has increasingly been used to resolve conflicts between disputing groups. The federal government as far back as 1913 established federal mediators to help resolve issues between employers and employees.[15] It was expected that mediated settlements would prevent costly strikes or lockouts for workers and employers alike, and that the welfare and safety of Americans would be protected. Federal use of mediation in labor disputes set a precedent for many states to pass laws and train a cadre of mediators to handle intrastate labor conflicts.

Mediation is currently being used in a variety of ways. The Civil Rights Act of 1964 created the Community Relations Service of the U.S. Department of Justice to use mediation to resolve disputes relating to discriminatory practices based on race, color or national origin.[16] Diverse private agencies, civil rights commissions, and state agencies now use mediation to handle charges of sex, race, and ethnic discrimination. The federal government funds Neighborhood Justice Centers that provide free or low-cost mediation services to the public to resolve disputes, informally, inexpensively, and efficiently.[17] Disputes settled through mediation are resolved much more efficiently and creatively than those resolved in court. Mediation is also used in schools and colleges to settle disputes: between students, between students and faculty, between faculty members, and between faculty and administration. The criminal justice system uses mediation to resolve disputes in correctional facilities; for example, for prison riots, hostage negotiations, and institutionalized grievance procedures.

Mediation is also used extensively in family disputes involving child custody and divorce proceedings, disputes between parents and children, conflicts involving adoption and the termination of parental rights, and domestic violence situations. Moore states "In family disputes, mediated and consensual settlements are often more appropriate and satisfying than litigated or imposed court outcomes."[18]

Mediation is used to settle disputes between business partners, private individuals, governmental agencies and individuals, landlords and tenants, businesses and customers, and in personal injury cases.

Many professionals now occasionally act as mediators to help people or groups in conflict to resolve their concerns. Such professionals include attorneys, social workers, psychologists, and guidance counselors. A few social workers, attorneys, and other professionals are working full time as mediators—often in public or private mediation agencies.

Moore defines mediation as follows:

> Mediation involves the intervention of an acceptable, impartial, and neutral third party who has no authoritative decision-making power to assist contending parties in voluntarily reaching their own mutually acceptable settlement of issues in dispute. . . . Mediation leaves the decision-making power in the hands of the people in conflict. Mediation is a voluntary process in that the participants must be willing to accept the assistance of the intervenor if the dispute is to be resolved. Mediation is usually initiated when the partners no longer believe that they can handle the conflict on their own and when the only means of resolution appears to involve impartial third-party assistance.[19]

There are various models of the mediation process.[20] As an illustration, the one developed by Joan Blades will be summarized.[21] Blades views the mediation process as involving five stages:

1. *Introduction/Commitment.* This first stage usually is accomplished in a one- to two-hour session. The mediator sets ground rules, describes mediation, answers questions, discusses fees, and seeks to gain a commitment to the process from the two parties. The mediator also seeks to develop an understanding of the more pressing issues, gains a sense of the personal dynamics of the two parties, and tries to ascertain whether they are ready and willing to mediate. If one or both of the parties are not willing to mediate, then the mediation probably should not proceed. If one or both of the parties are hesitant to proceed, the mediator usually describes the alternatives to mediation—such as a lengthy and expensive court battle.
2. *Definition.* The two parties, with the mediator's assistance, define the areas in which they already agree and disagree. Certain disputes, such as division of property issues in divorce mediation, are apt at this stage to require a considerable amount of information.
3. *Negotiation.* Once the two parties agree on the issues in conflict and relevant factual information on these issues is obtained, the two parties are ready to begin negotiating. At this stage the mediator seeks to have the parties focus on one issue at a time. A

problem-solving approach is used in which the needs of each party are first identified and alternatives are generated. The mediator recedes into the background when discussions are proceeding well and steps in when emotions intensify or when the two parties are overlooking creative solutions that will meet their needs.

4. *Agreement.* Once alternatives are generated and related facts are evaluated, the two parties are ready to begin making agreements on the issues. The role of the mediator is to maintain a cooperative atmosphere and to keep the two parties focused on a manageable number of issues. The mediator summarizes areas of agreement and provides legal or other information necessary to a discussion. The mediator helps the two parties examine the merits and shortcomings of the options. During this stage the mediator praises the parties for the progress they are making and gets them to praise themselves for progress made. A mediator seeks to create a positive atmosphere.

5. *Contracting.* In this final stage of mediation the two parties review the agreements and clarify any ambiguities. The agreements are almost always written in the form of a contract, which is available for future reference. Either party, the mediator, or everyone together may do the actual writing of the contract. The contract expresses what each party agrees to do and may set deadlines for the diverse tasks to be completed. It also specifies consequences if either party fails to meet the terms of the contract. Mediators seek to have specific agreements stated in concrete form to prevent future controversies. The ultimate goal of mediation is a contract in which no one is a loser and which both parties willingly abide by.

One of the major techniques a mediator uses is a caucus.[22] At times a mediator or either party may stop the mediation and request a caucus. In a caucus the two parties are physically separated from each other, and there is no direct communication between them. In a caucus the mediator meets with one of the parties or with both parties individually. There are a wide variety of reasons for calling a caucus. A caucus may be used to vent intense emotions privately, to clarify misperceptions, to reduce unproductive or repetitive negative behavior, to seek clarification of a party's interests, to provide a pause for each party to consider an alternative, to convince an uncompromising party that the mediation process is better than going to court, to uncover confidential information, to educate an inexperienced disputant about the processes of mediation, or to design alternatives that will later be brought to a joint session.

Some parties are willing, in a caucus, to privately express possible concessions. Usually such concessions are conditional upon the other party making certain concessions. By the use of caucuses, a mediator can go back and forth relaying information from one party to the other and seek to develop a consensus.

GROUP EXERCISES

Exercise A: Suspended from High School

Goal: To learn how to use the problem-solving approach in a group.

Step 1. The group leader describes the stages of the problem-solving approach:

1. Identifying and defining the problem
2. Assessing the size and causes of the problem
3. Developing alternative strategies or plans for solving it
4. Assessing the merits and shortcomings of these alternative strategies
5. Selecting and implementing the most desirable strategy or strategies
6. Evaluating the success of the strategies used

Step 2. The class divides into subgroups of four or five students each. Each subgroup is to apply the problem-solving approach to the following situation.

> Five students have been suspended for a four-day period for drinking alcoholic beverages at their high school, which is located in a small city of 5,400. It has been the policy of the school board to suspend any student caught drinking at school. In the past five months a total of sixteen students have been suspended. The police department is unhappy with the suspensions because when the students are suspended they usually loiter on the city streets during school hours. The school social worker contacted the parents of the five suspended students, and only one couple indicated an interest in receiving counseling for their daughter. The other parents stated they weren't sufficiently concerned to talk further about the suspensions.

The task of each subgroup is to arrive at answers (and reasons for their answers) to each of the following five questions:

1. What do you see as being the most serious problem to deal with?
2. What do you believe are the causes of this problem?
3. What possible strategies could combat this problem?
4. What do you see as the merits and shortcomings of each of these strategies?
5. Which of these strategies would you select to combat the problem you have identified?

Step 3. Each subgroup shares its answers and reasoning with the class. After all of the subgroups have presented their answers, the class discusses why different problems and strategies were defined and selected by the subgroups.

Exercise B: Brainstorming

Goal: To show how to use brainstorming.

Step 1. The leader describes the purpose of brainstorming and its ground rules, as explained in this chapter.

Step 2. The leader gives the class an issue or problem to brainstorm. If the class is very large, subgroups of ten to fifteen students may be formed. The issue or problem should be one that the class has some awareness of and background on. One possible topic: "What do you see as the major problem (without naming any person) in our social work program?"

Step 3. The most important problem should be singled out after the brainstorming is completed. For example, each class member could list his or her choices for the five most serious problems on a notecard. A tally could then be made, and the problem receiving the most votes would then be declared the most serious problem.

Step 4. After the most serious problem is determined, a second brainstorming exercise is conducted to generate a list of strategies to resolve it. Following this brainstorming, the most viable strategies should be identified.

Step 5. A discussion elicits the view of the class as to the strengths and shortcomings of brainstorming.

Exercise C: Busing to Achieve Racial Integration

Goal: To observe and negotiate intergroup conflict.

Step 1. The group leader provides the following background information.

All of you live in a middle-class suburb of Middletown, which has had no racial problems. Your suburb is located next to the big city of Skyscraper. A recent study by the federal government has found that four public schools in the inner city of Skyscraper are racially segregated, as 98 percent of the students are African-American. This inner-city school district is spending only half as much money per child on education as is your suburb of Middletown. The dropout rate in these inner-city schools is 55 percent compared to 10 percent in Middletown. Only 15 percent of the graduates from the inner-city schools in Skyscraper go on to college, while 65 percent of the graduates from Middletown go on to college. The federal government has ruled that the school districts in Middletown and Skyscraper must become racially integrated through busing between the systems. Three groups—concerned parents, civil rights activists, and school staff—have been asked by the Middletown school board to arrive at some recommendations to present to the school board on how to integrate the school districts. The school board of Middletown will act on these recommendations and then propose them to the Skyscraper School Board as a way of implementing the federal government's declaration that the school districts in the two communities must become racially integrated.

Step 2. The class is randomly divided into the three groups. Each group receives a handout that describes the group's views and tasks. (No group should be informed of the views of the other two.) The views and tasks are further described in the following material.

Concerned parents. You want what is best for your child. You do not want your child to associate with children from inner-city areas. You are vehemently opposed to a busing system that would send your children to an inner-city school. You are less opposed to students being bused from Skyscraper to Middletown, but you want to keep the number of children who are bused to Middletown as small as possible. You are also concerned that your taxes will increase because of busing. Your group has two tasks:

198

(1) to develop two to four proposals for possible presentation to the Middletown School Board that will get the federal government off your back while minimizing any possible changes in your child's education, and (2) to select a negotiator who will represent your group in negotiations with the other two groups in arriving at a set of proposals to present to the school board.

School staff. Your group is composed of teachers, school administrators, and school social workers. Value-wise you are in favor of racial integration. You are also in favor of the neighborhood school concept in which the school is a center that serves students and parents in the neighborhood. Therefore, you are unsure whether to support school busing. Some of your staff members fear that juvenile crime, vandalism, and racial clashes will increase if busing occurs. Your tasks are: (1) to develop two to four proposals for possible presentation to the Middletown School Board that will creatively further racial integration while interfering very little with the neighborhood-school concept in Middletown, and (2) to select a negotiator who will represent your group in negotiations with the other two groups in arriving at a set of proposals to present to the school board.

Civil rights activists. Your group is delighted that the federal government has declared that the school districts in Skyscraper and Middletown must become racially integrated. You believe such integration will be highly valuable in reducing racial prejudice and racial discrimination in the future. You are ambivalent about using school busing, but you are unaware of other strategies to integrate schools. Your group is composed of a number of community leaders, generally with a liberal orientation. Members of your group include clergy, social workers, directors of social service agencies, and concerned business leaders. You fear that members of the other two groups may seek to minimize efforts to integrate the school systems. Your tasks are: (1) to develop two to four proposals that will fully integrate the school systems, and (2) to select a negotiator who will represent your group in negotiations with the other two groups in arriving at a set of proposals to present to the school board.

Step 3. After each group has prepared a set of proposals, the negotiators for the three groups meet to arrive at a consistent set of proposals to present to the Middletown School Board. The other class members observe the negotiations.

Step 4. The group leader defines the win-lose and problem-solving strategies and describes the following techniques that are useful in resolving conflicts: role reversal, stroking, disarming, empathy, I-messages, and inquiry. The class then discusses the following five questions:

1. Did the negotiators arrive at a consistent set of proposals? Why or why not?
2. Did the negotiators use primarily a win-lose or a problem-solving strategy?
3. Did any of the negotiators use the techniques of role reversal, stroking, empathy, I-messages, disarming, or inquiry?
4. How creative were the proposals arrived at by the three groups and the three negotiators?
5. What did the students learn from this exercise?

199

Exercise D: Creative Thinking

Goal: To gain experience in coming up with answers that require creative thinking.

Note: In doing these exercises on creativity, the group leader is encouraged to add or substitute exercises of his or her own.

Step 1. The group leader explains that questions will be asked that require innovative thinking. The leader may want to create competition and a gamelike atmosphere by dividing the class into two or more subgroups and recording a tally mark on the blackboard when a subgroup shouts out the correct response. (The correct answers are given in appendix A.)

1. In counting from zero to one hundred, how many nines do you come across?
2. Two women are playing checkers. They play five games, and each woman wins the same number of games. How come?
3. You're told to take five pills, one every half hour. How many hours will they last?
4. A yacht in the harbor has a ten-foot ladder hanging over the side. If the tide rises two feet an hour, how many hours will it take for the water to reach the top of the ladder?
5. Do they have a Fourth of July in England?
6. Why can't someone living in Washington, D.C., be buried west of the Mississippi River?
7. How many outs are there in a baseball inning?
8. A man builds a rectangular house with all four exposures facing south. Then he goes outside and kills a bear. What color is the bear? Where is the house located? (Award a correct response for each answer.)
9. If it takes three minutes to boil an egg, how long will it take to boil seven eggs?
10. Assume two cars start to travel toward each other from a distance of 2,000 miles. If car A travels at a rate of 150 mph and car B at 100 mph, how far will each car be from its origin when they meet?
11. A farmer had three two-thirds size haystacks in one field and six three-fifths size haystacks in another field. He put them all together. How many did he have then?
12. "Jill is my niece," said Paul to his sister Karen. "She is not my niece," said Karen. Explain this.
13. If you had twelve dollars and spent all but four dollars, how much would you have left?

Exercise E: The Manhattan Glass

Goal: To interact in small groups to resolve problems that require creativity.

Step 1. The class divides into subgroups of three students each and receives the necessary material (such as matches and handouts) for resolving the problems. After one subgroup completes the problem, it is declared a winner and all subgroups receive another problem. A tally of which subgroup arrives at the correct answer first for each problem is kept on the blackboard.

Task 1: These twelve matches are positioned to form one large square and four small squares. By changing the position of exactly three matches, reduce the number of squares to three small squares.

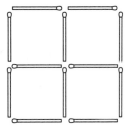

Task 2: These four full-sized matches form a Manhattan glass. The half-match is a cherry. By moving just two matches, make another Manhattan glass of the same shape and size with the cherry on the outside. Do not move the cherry.

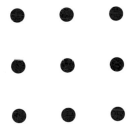

Task 3: connect all nine dots with only four straight lines without lifting your pencil from the paper.

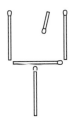

Task 4: By drawing only two straight lines, divide this shape into four equal parts with two dots in each part.

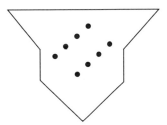

Task 5: Place the numbers one through eleven in the eleven circles shown so that every three numbers in a straight line add up to eighteen.

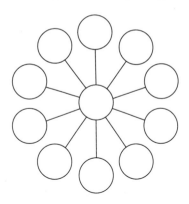

Exercise F: Brainteasers

Goal: To creatively arrive at answers to twenty-five "brainteasers."

Step 1. The group leader gives the following twenty-five brainteasers (page 203) to each student. The class divides into subgroups of about five persons. The groups have twenty minutes to arrive at answers. The leader starts by indicating that the first answer is "sand-box" and instructs each subgroup to write its answers on a sheet of paper.

Step 2. The subgroups exchange papers for grading. The leader reads the right answers and then asks each subgroup how many correct answers it produced.

1	2	3	4	5
SAND	MAN / BOARD	STAND / I	R/E/A/D/I/N/G	WEAR / LONG

6	7	8	9	10
R ROADS A D S	T O W N	CYCLE CYCLE CYCLE	LE VEL	O / M.D. Ph.D. B.S.

11	12	13	14	15
KNEE / LIGHTS	II IIII / OO	CHAIR	DICE DICE	T O U C H

16	17	18	19	20
GROUND / feet feet feet feet feet feet	MIND / MATTER	He's/Himself	ECNALG	DEATH/LIFE

21	22	23	24	25
G.I. / CCC CC	_____ Program	B L O U S E (C)	J YouUMe S T	mt

Exercise G: Resolving Conflicts

Goal: To practice using techniques to resolve conflicts in real-life situations.

Step 1. The leader describes each of the following techniques that are useful in resolving conflicts: role reversal, stroking, no-lose problem solving, disarming, empathy, I-messages, and inquiry. The students are then instructed to try to use one or more of these techniques to resolve interpersonal conflicts that arise in their daily lives during the next seven days. (To facilitate their remembering details of their efforts to use these techniques in conflict situations, students are instructed to record the details of the incidents in a journal (for example, a notebook).

Step 2. After a week or so, the leader asks in class for volunteers to: (a) describe which techniques they used, (b) briefly summarize the details of the conflict they encountered, and (c) reveal the extent to which the techniques were useful in resolving the conflict. (If no one volunteers, the leader should cite one or two examples of how she used these techniques to resolve interpersonal conflicts in the recent past. Such sharing by the leader may lead others to share their experiences.)

CHAPTER TEN

DECISION MAKING

Goals: Almost every day, we react to some sort of decision made by several individuals working together in a structured setting. Congressional subcommittees, managerial boards, and community groups debate the merits of new approaches and strategies. This chapter presents the bases for making decisions, the different procedures groups can use, and the likely consequences of using these procedures.

The effectiveness of a group is largely dependent upon its ability to make good, sound decisions: when to meet, how meetings will be conducted, why the group is meeting, and what it will do. Decisions almost always involve choosing among several different options and reaching a consensus. Members of some groups are only vaguely aware of how decisions are made, while others spend hours debating how decisions will be made. Seldom is the same procedure used for arriving at all decisions in a group, since different circumstances warrant varied decision-making processes. In our society, important decisions are usually made by groups rather than individuals. If a problem or issue is complex, a group usually makes a better decision than an individual.[1]

THE BASES OF DECISIONS

Most people tend to believe that decisions are made primarily on the basis of objective facts and figures. In fact, values and assumptions form the bases of most decisions, and facts and figures are used only in relation to these subjective, learned experiences. Consider the following list of questions. What do they indicate about how we make our most important decisions?

1. Should abortions be permitted or prohibited during the first weeks following conception?
2. Should homosexuality be viewed as a natural expression of sexuality?
3. When does harsh disciplining of a child become child abuse?
4. When should confidentiality be violated?
5. Should the primary objective of imprisonment be rehabilitation or retribution?

Answers to these questions are not usually based on data uncovered after careful research; they are based on individual beliefs about the value of life, personal freedom, and protective social standards. Even everyday decisions are based largely on *values*.

Practically every decision is also based on certain *assumptions*. Without assumptions, nothing can be proven. Assumptions are made in every research study to test any hypothesis. In a market survey, for example, analysts assume that the instruments they use (such as a questionnaire) will be valid and reliable. It cannot even be proven the sun will rise in the east tomorrow without assuming that its history provides that proof. The same holds true for groups involved in decision making. For example, if a local group decides that busing should be used to facilitate racial integration, it is probably assuming busing will have certain benefits. On the other hand, if a group decides not to use school busing, it is probably assuming the probable costs will outweigh the predicted benefits. In either case, the assumption cannot be proven beforehand. Proof comes only when the decision is implemented and its effects are evaluated.

The purpose of statistical information and research studies is to test assumptions, hypotheses, and beliefs. All of the following are beliefs held by many Americans:

- The death penalty has a deterrent effect on persons who are considering committing serious crimes such as homicide.
- Most welfare recipients are able to work but would rather live it up on welfare.
- Mental patients are more likely to commit a crime than other people.

- Male homosexuals are apt to display "feminine" mannerisms.
- Crimes committed by the lower class are the most costly in our society.

That each of these beliefs has been invalidated by research shows the importance of scientifically testing beliefs. Research demonstrates that a country's adoption of a death penalty generally does not result in a decrease in homicide rates or in rates of other serious crimes.[2] Only a small fraction of welfare recipients are able to work—the vast majority cannot work because they are children, are elderly, have a disability, or are homebound mothers with young children.[3] People labeled as mentally ill are no more likely to commit crimes than people considered sane.[4] Male homosexuals are no more apt to be effeminate than male heterosexuals,[5] and white-collar crime appears to be the most costly in our society.[6]

APPROACHES TO DECISION MAKING

Before discussing an issue leading to a decision, a group must know what decision-making approach it will use, because different approaches lead to diverse consequences for the future operation of the group. An effective group is aware of these consequences and must choose the best approach considering the amount of time available, the nature of the decision to be made, and the kind of atmosphere the group wants to create. The nature of the task, the history of the group, and the kind of setting in which the group is working must also be considered. Six decision-making approaches will be discussed:

1. Consensus of the group
2. Simple majority vote
3. Two-thirds or three-fourths majority vote
4. Delegated decisions
5. Multiple voting
6. Averaging individual opinions

Consensus

This approach is the most effective one for motivating all of the members to support and work for the decision, because everyone comes to agree with the final decision. This approach is also the most time consuming, since the concerns of each member have to be recognized. David Johnson and Frank Johnson describe consensus as follows:

> Consensus is more commonly defined as a collective opinion arrived at by a group of people working together under conditions that permit communications to be sufficiently open—and the group climate to be sufficiently supportive—so that everyone in the group feels he has had his fair chance to influence the decision. When a decision is made by consensus, all members understand the decision and are prepared to support it. Operationally, consensus means that all members can rephrase the decision to show that they understand it, that all members have had a chance to tell how they feel about the decision, and that those members who continue to disagree or have doubts will, nevertheless, say publicly that they are willing to give the decision an experimental try for a period of time.[7]

To use consensus effectively, the group must have a trusting, cooperative atmosphere. Members must feel free to present their views but must do so as clearly and logically as possible. They must refrain from blindly arguing their own individual views and listen to and respect the views of other members. Members should also *avoid* going along with the group if they believe the majority opinion is a mistake. It is dangerous to yield to the majority if the only reason is to avoid conflict and to appear united. This type of conforming can lead to dangerous groupthink, as described later in this chapter. Members, however, should yield to the majority opinion if that position appears to have merit and has a fair chance of having positive outcomes.

Differences of opinion should be sought and dealt with respectfully. Divergent views are advantageous because they increase the chances of reviewing all crucial aspects of an issue, building upon the views of others, and making viable decisions.

The participation of all members is encouraged, with emphasis placed on finding the best solution that everyone can agree on and support. If a group becomes stalemated over two alternatives, a third alternative is often sought to incorporate the major desires of both subgroups. In this way, the group avoids the kind of divisiveness that can occur with other types of decision making, such as voting.

Consensus is difficult to achieve because it requires that members be flexible. They must also understand that the thorough discussion of divergent points of view should lead to a synthesis of ideas, resulting in an innovative, creative, and high-quality decision. Active participation, equally distributed power, and a substantial amount of time are necessary to analyze divergent views and cooperatively synthesize ideas that will be agreeable to everyone.

Because consensus resolves controversies and conflicts, it increases the group's ability to make high-quality decisions in the future. Other forms of decision making do not resolve conflicts and controversies. When group members feel they have participated in the decision and support it, they may contribute more of their resources to implement the decision. Consensus is useful in making important, serious, and complex decisions in which the success of the decision depends upon all members being committed to it.

Simple Majority Vote

Most groups use a simple majority-vote approach. Issues are discussed until they are clarified and it appears a simple majority of the members has arrived at an alternative. A vote is then taken.

There are several advantages to this type of decision making. Decisions are arrived at much faster. Most decisions do not warrant the full support of all members. Even groups without trust, open communication, and willingness on the part of members to give up favorite positions can become operational by using this approach.

However, shortcomings of the simple majority approach are numerous. Minority opinions are not always safeguarded. Racial groups, women, certain ethnic groups, homosexuals, and persons with a disability have received the brunt of many adverse decisions made by simple majority voting. Majority voting frequently splits a group into "winners" and "losers," and sometimes, the number of losers is nearly as great as the number of winners, representing as much as 49 percent of the vote. These losers may feel their concerns are not receiving attention, refuse to support group efforts, and work to subvert or overturn the decision. Obviously, if voting alienates a minority, the future effectiveness of the group is diminished. There is a danger that a majority rule may be interpreted by a minority as being an unfair means of control and manipulation. Therefore, to maintain its effectiveness, groups that use majority voting should create a climate in which members feel they have had their day in court and feel an obligation to support the final group decision.

Two-Thirds or Three-Fourths Majority Vote

A high-percentage majority vote, such as two-thirds or three-fourths, is used primarily for decisions of substantial consequence, such as enacting amendments to the U.S. Constitution or changing the bylaws and constitution of an organization. A high-percentage majority vote is also often used by governmental decision-making units to pass emergency requests for special funds.

This type of vote is a compromise between the consensus and simple majority approaches. A high-percentage majority vote takes more time than a simple majority because more votes are needed, but less time than consensus because not everyone must agree. A strong minority can block a decision, so a small majority cannot force its views on them. However, a small minority may still feel controlled and manipulated by a majority rule. A high-percentage majority vote will generally draw stronger support from group members than a simple majority, but it will not generate as much support as consensus. Psychologically, the losing side on a 76 to 24 percent vote under a three-fourths majority system is more apt to go along with the winning side than if the winning side won by 51 percent under a simple majority system.

For crucial decisions that require the support of practically all members, it is advisable to reach as strong a majority agreement as possible. A decision not to grant a faculty member tenure, for example, is less likely to be appealed and to win an appeal if the vote in a department is twenty to one rather than eleven to ten.

Delegated Decisions

Because large groups cannot carefully debate and make all daily decisions, many groups delegate less important decisions to an expert, the group leader, or a subgroup. Subgroups include executive, temporary, or standing committees. However, the types of decisions to be delegated must be well defined to avoid potential conflicts and to limit the authority of those group members who have been selected to make less important decisions. In many groups, conflicts and disagreements arise when these limits are not clarified. It is common for group members and leaders to differ on which decisions should be made by the leader and which should be made by the group as a whole. When a leader's decision-making authority is in doubt, the group as a whole should deal with the question. Otherwise, the leader may be criticized for overextending his authority.

Expert

Authority can be delegated to the person in the group with the most expertise in a particular area. The expert can review the issues and inform the group of the decision. A major problem is that it is often difficult to determine which member has the most expertise. Personal popularity and power often interfere with the accurate selection of the most expert member. Since the group is leaving the decision to a single member, there is often little or no discussion of options. This may limit the number of viable options that the expert considers. Finally, a decision made by one person may not receive the support of other members to implement it.

Group Leader

A group may allow the leader to make certain decisions. Before making some of these decisions, however, the leader may call a meeting of the group, describe the issues, and use the discussion to arrive at a decision. A chancellor or president of a university often uses this approach by seeking the advice and suggestions of various subgroups. Actually, the most time-efficient method is when the leader makes a decision without any group discussion. This procedure works best for uncomplicated, less important issues. Although efficient, it may not be effective. Since the group may not understand the issues, members may disagree with the decision and withhold resources to implement it. If members feel that the leader is overstepping his authority, they may retaliate by limiting his authority or by replacing him. In addition, without input from the group, a leader is less likely to be fully aware of all the viable courses of action. By involving the group, the leader will hear a variety of options and give group members an opportunity to express their views. Still, if the leader's decision is unpopular, support for implementation will be limited.

Subgroup

Another approach to delegating decisions is to allow a subgroup, such as an executive committee or a temporary committee, to make certain decisions. When a subgroup makes a decision, it should consider the views of the larger group because unpopular decisions are generally not supported. If the subgroup continually makes unpopular decisions, the larger group can retaliate by reviewing the decisions, changing the membership of the subgroup, reducing its decision-making powers, or disbanding it. Subgroups are especially effective when a group has a large number of minor decisions to make and limited time.

Multiple Voting

If an organization has a number of alternatives before it, a series of ballots may be taken until one alternative receives the required number of winning votes. Multiple voting may be done in a variety of ways. In selecting a presidential candidate, both the Republican and Democratic conventions ballot until one candidate receives a majority. Another approach is to keep narrowing the number of choices. For example, if there are fifty options, each member may first vote for five options. The ten options receiving the most votes are considered in the second round, with members voting for three options. In the third round the top four options are considered with members voting for two options each. In the fourth and final round, the top two options are considered, and members vote for one option. With this type of multiple voting, it is essential that the members agree on the voting rules prior to voting. Otherwise, those who want a choice that is not selected may charge, *after* reviewing the results of the voting, that the group leader is arbitrarily and capriciously excluding their favorite choices.

Averaging Individual Opinions

In an emergency, it may not be possible to get the members together for a meeting. In this situation the group leader may contact each individual member to obtain his vote. The alternative chosen is the one receiving the most votes. Fewer than 50 percent of the votes could pass the motion, since the other votes may be spread over a variety of options. This approach may also be used for making decisions the leader does not believe are important enough for a group meeting.

However, there are a number of disadvantages to this approach. Without group discussion, many of the members may not be fully aware of all the issues, alternatives, or consequences of the proposal. A poor decision may result because the votes of the least informed members may cancel out the votes of the most knowledgeable. With little involvement, members are unlikely to have much commitment toward implementing the decision. There is also a danger that a subgroup opposed to the decision may feel it has been left out and may work hard to overturn the decision or impede its implementation. Another danger is that the person conducting the vote may influence the members to vote for his position.

GROUP VS. INDIVIDUAL DECISION MAKING

In theory, the task of making a decision within a group should follow a rational problem-solving process: identify the problem, generate proposed solutions, weigh the merits and shortcomings of proposed solutions, and select the alternative with the fewest risks and the greatest chance of success. In practice, however, subjective influences can impede this process.

We have all heard our share of amusing, yet halfway serious anecdotes about "runaround meetings," "inconclusive conclusions," and "slower-than-snails committees." While group-made decisions have the advantage of being based on a wider variety of information and a greater variety of expertise, they are also susceptible to subjective influences in the group. Without awareness of these subjective obstacles, groups will not necessarily make better decisions than individuals.

Each group member brings not only his objective knowledge and expertise to the decision-making process, but also his subjective experience: his unique attitudes, feelings, biases, and vested interests. These will probably not be expressed at the start of a meeting but will be triggered in the course of the ensuing discussion. As the decision-making process continues, there is an increasing tendency for individuals to allow their reactions to one another to interfere with objective thought.

Is group decision making inferior or superior to individual decision making? Individual decision making occurs when decisions are made without group interaction. A leader, an expert, or a poll of individuals make a decision that must be implemented by the group. There is overwhelming evidence that group decision making is usually superior.[8] This conclusion applies even when the individual decision is made by an expert.

There appear to be several reasons why group decision making is usually superior.[9] Through group interaction, the knowledge, abilities, and resources of each member are pooled. An individual acting alone often lacks information, skills, or resources needed to arrive at the best decision. Also, working in the presence of others motivates a person to put forth more effort, be more careful, and increase the quality of his or her work. Having more people working on a problem increases the probability that someone in the group will suggest a viable solution. Through group interaction, the members can build on each other's ideas, develop a decision based on this building-block approach, and identify the positive and negative consequences of each alternative. Since it is always easier to identify other people's mistakes than our own, the problem areas in the favorite alternatives of others can be identified and analyzed. In addition, different ways of looking at problems and tasks are more likely to result when different individuals are contributing. Also, when group members have participated in making a decision, they will be more likely to accept and support it.

It should be noted, however, that subjective influences can substantially reduce the quality of group decision making. Some group members may alter their actual opinions or hold back relevant information because they do not want to displease others in the group. One or several members may begin to contribute so much to the discussion, or state their opinions so forcefully, that others begin to resign themselves to being inactive. Arguments that are not pertinent to the issue at hand may take on major significance. For some group members, winning such arguments becomes more important than reaching a decision. Interpersonal attractions and repulsions among group members also influence decision making; some members are inclined to support alternatives of lower quality that are advocated by members they are attracted to, and they are also inclined to reject higher quality alternatives advocated by group members that they dislike. Sometimes a combination of subjective influences results in the development of *groupthink*.

Groupthink

Irving Janis first identified "Groupthink" as a result of a study done on groups of U.S. presidential advisors.[10] During this study, he found that powerful social pressures were often exerted when a dissident began to voice objections to what otherwise appeared to be a group consensus. Groupthink is a problem-solving process in which proposals are accepted without a critical, careful review of the pros and cons of the alternatives, and in which considerable social pressure is brought to bear against those expressing opposing points of view. Groupthink occurs partially because the norms of the group hold that it is more important to bolster group morale than to evaluate all alternatives critically. Another group norm that increases groupthink is that members should remain loyal by sticking with the policies to which the group is already committed, even when those policies are not working.

Janis has listed a number of factors that promote groupthink:

1. Members have an illusion of being invulnerable, which leads them to become overly optimistic about their selected courses of action, leads them to take extraordinary risks, and causes them to fail to respond to clear warnings of danger.
2. Members have an unquestioning belief in the moral rightness of their group, which leads them to ignore the ethical consequences of their decisions.

212

3. The group applies social pressures to display disapproval toward any member who momentarily questions the basic policies of the group or who raises questions about a policy alternative favored by the majority.
4. The group constructs rationalizations to discount warnings and other forms of negative feedback that would, if taken seriously, lead the members to rethink basic assumptions about policies that are not working.
5. Group members hold stereotyped views of the leaders of opposing groups. These leaders are viewed either as being so evil that it would be a mistake to genuinely try to negotiate differences or as so stupid or so weak that they will not be able to prevent the group from attaining its objectives.
6. Members sometimes assume "mind guard" roles in which they attempt to protect their leader and the group from negative information that might lead them to question the morality and effectiveness of past decisions.
7. Members keep quiet about their misgivings and even minimize to themselves the importance of these misgivings. Through self-censorship members avoid deviating from what appears to be group consensus.
8. The members believe practically everyone in the group fully agrees on the policies and programs of the group.

Groupthink spawns a number of poor decision-making practices. The group limits its discussion to those courses of action consistent with past decisions and policies; as a result, more divergent strategies (some of which are viable) are not considered. The group fails to reexamine a selected course of action, even when risks, drawbacks, and unintended consequences become clear. The group makes little effort to get cost-benefit information on possible strategies from appropriate experts. Members seek primarily to obtain facts and listen to opinions that support their preferred policy and tend to ignore facts and opinions that do not. The group fails to work out contingency plans to cope with foreseeable setbacks, and it spends little time considering how the chosen strategy might be sabotaged by political opponents or hampered by bureaucratic red tape.

In order to prevent the development of groupthink, a group has to be "on guard" about its dangers. Members must realize their selected courses of action may fail. Members must be aware of the ethical consequences of their decisions. The group should welcome the questioning of basic policies by members. The group should realistically assess the merits and shortcomings of the views being expressed by opposing groups. Members should feel free to express their misgivings about basic policies and strategies of their group. The group should welcome the advancement of new and novel strategies for resolving the problems that it is combatting. Finally, the group needs to consistently apply the problem-solving approach in assessing problems, in generating alternatives, in evaluating these alternatives, and in selecting and implementing strategies.

GROUP EXERCISES

Exercise A: Hard Choices—Funding Social Programs

Goals: To analyze how decisions are made, to understand that most decisions are based on values and assumptions, and to realize that setting budgets for social programs involves hard choices because of scarce resources.

Step 1. The group leader states that funding sources (such as the federal, state, and local governments, and United Way) have to make difficult choices about how much money to allocate to diverse social programs. Financial resources to fund all social programs are simply unavailable, and some people suffer greatly because they do not receive the needed services and funds.

Step 2. The group divides into subgroups of five or six students. A person from each subgroup volunteers to be an observer for that group. The observer's role is to record information during the exercise related to the following four questions.

1. Which decision-making procedures were used by the group? Possible procedures include consensus, simple majority voting, two-thirds or three-fourths majority voting, and multiple voting. (These procedures should be briefly defined for the observers; the definitions may be given on a handout.)
2. What values and assumptions were expressed as reasons for the decision the subgroup made?
3. Which members appeared to have the most influence in arriving at a decision?
4. What did the influential members say or do to influence the subgroup?

After the exercise is over, the observers will be asked to share this information with the class. The observers should not vote or participate in the discussion of the subgroup.

Step 3. Each subgroup is informed that it is the funding source for a local community and that it has $10 million to allocate for the following social programs, which need a total of $15 million. Each subgroup has the task of deciding how much money to allocate to each agency. No subgroup can go over the $10-million limit. (The group leader should distribute the following information on a handout.)

The Center for Developmental Disabilities needs $1.5 million to care for severely and profoundly retarded adults. All of these adults are so retarded that they are unable to walk. It costs $70,000 a year to care for each adult. If the center does not receive its requested funds, there is a danger that some of these clients may not receive the necessary medical care and may die.

The Anti-Poverty Agency needs $3.5 million to maintain families at an income level of only 80 percent of that defined as the poverty line. It costs $12,000 per year to maintain a family of three (generally a single parent with two children). If the agency does not receive its requested funds, there is a danger that many of these families will go hungry, have inadequate shelter, and lack essential clothing for winter.

Protective Services needs $1 million to combat abuse, neglect, and incest. If the agency does not receive all of its needed funds, there is the danger that a number of children will continue to be exposed to abuse, neglect, or incest, which could severely affect them for the rest of their lives.

The Mental Health Center needs $2.5 million to help clients with severe emotional problems, some of whom are so depressed they are suicidal. If the center does not receive all of its needed funds, inadequate services will be provided to clients, and there is a danger that the problems of many clients will intensify. A few may even take their own lives.

The Alcohol and Drug Abuse Treatment Center needs $2 million to help chemically dependent clients and their families. If the center does not receive all of its needed funds, inadequate services will mean the problems experienced by the clients and their families are apt to intensify. Since alcohol and drug abuse are contributing factors to many other problems (such as poverty, mental illness, and family violence), there is a danger these problems will also intensify.

The Shelter for Battered Women, which is located in a house in a residential area, is requesting $500,000. If funds are cut back, the shelter staff assert they will have to turn away some of the battered women and their children who need shelter and other services.

Group Homes for Youths runs four group homes—two for young women and two for young men. It needs $500,000. If needed funds are cut back, this agency will have to reduce the number of youths it is serving. Some will be transferred to more expensive residential treatment programs, some returned to an unhealthy home environment, and some will simply run away.

The Red Cross needs $1 million for its blood bank and for disaster relief. If funds are cut back, there is a danger there will be an insufficient supply of blood available for transfusions, and many of the families who are hit by disasters (such as tornadoes and floods) will not be served.

The Sheltered Workshop provides work training and sheltered work to clients with a variety of physical or mental disabilities. It needs $2 million, or it will be forced to turn away clients. If clients are turned away, they will lose hope of becoming productive and perhaps self-supporting, and will also end up requesting assistance from the Mental Health Center and from the Anti-Poverty Agency.

Equal Rights is an agency providing a wide range of services to racial minorities in the area: work training, job placement, and housing location. It also investigates and takes legal action against employees and landlords charged with racial discrimination. The agency needs $500,000. If funds are cut back, there is a danger that discrimination against racial minorities will increase.

Step 4. Each subgroup shares with the class its decisions for allocating funds and the reasons behind them. (The cuts that are made can be summarized on the blackboard by having the leader list the names of the agencies, and then having a representative from each subgroup list the amount of money that was cut—totaling $5 million—from the requested allocations.) Ask the subgroup members to share their feelings about the exercise. After each subgroup finishes, the observer for that subgroup should inform the class of the answers to the four questions listed in Step 2. The leader should ask if anyone noted that the Shelter for Battered Women, which has one house, was requesting the same amount of money as Group Homes for Adolescent Youth, which runs four group homes.

Exercise B: Consensus

Goal: To learn about the complexities of arriving at a consensus on an issue when people hold strongly divergent views.

Step 1. The group leader explains what a consensus is and describes the group atmosphere necessary to a consensus.

Step 2. The class is given a controversial issue to discuss and bring to a consensus. For example, the class may be asked whether it supports legalized abortions during the first several weeks following conception.

Step 3. After the exercise is over, the students discuss their feelings about the pressure to arrive at a consensus in the face of strongly divergent views and why the class was, or was not, able to arrive at a consensus.

Exercise C: Subjective Influences on Merit Raises

Goal: To demonstrate that group decisions are often substantially affected by subjective influences.

Step 1. Six students volunteer to play the roles of social work faculty members on a merit committee at a university. The department has eighteen faculty members, and six of these members have applied for "superior" merit increases. The committee has a total of $12 thousand, all of which must be distributed to these six applicants. The three areas of recognizing merit increases are: teaching excellence, research and publishing, and services to the campus and to the community.

The decision on how much money to distribute to each applicant rests entirely with this committee. The committee may recommend that all, or nearly all, of the $12 thousand be distributed to one or two applicants, with the others receiving little or none, or the committee may distribute the money fairly evenly among the applicants. The committee is provided with the information in table 10.1 about the meritorious activities of the applicants. (This information may be displayed on the chalkboard or on individual sheets distributed to the class.)

Step 2. The leader hands out an individual "additional information card" to each role player. Each card has a one sentence description of one of the applicants. The other role players are not allowed to see the information on the card. (These cards should be prepared in advance.) Each card provides information likely to foster a strong personal reaction toward the respective faculty member. The role players are told they are free to bring up the information on their cards during the role playing or to disregard the information. The leader is free to be creative in writing the additional information on the cards. The following are some appropriate examples:

"Garcia is planning to retire next year, so a significant merit increase would not only recognize his years of public service to the community, but would also substantially

Table 10.1

Faculty Member	Summary of Meritorious Activities	Teacher Rating*
Juan Garcia	Served on university budget committee. Is president of the Board of Directors of the United Way in the community.	4.1
Karen Pagel	Attended two professional conferences. Is the faculty advisor to the Student Social Work Club.	4.2
Dale Riesen	Published a social work textbook and two articles in professional journals.	3.5
Jean Duvey	Is chair of the department and did the bulk of the work needed to achieve reaccreditation of the social work program by the Council on Social Work Education.	4.0
Kevin Aaron	Wrote and received a grant on "Long Distance Social Work Education" that brought $150 thousand to the program for using communication technology to provide social work education classes to other communities in the state.	3.9
Joyce Jackson	Presented three papers on child abuse intervention at national conferences.	4.3

*Based on student course evaluations (5 = highest, 1 = lowest)

increase the pension he will receive after retirement since monthly payments from the pension plan are based on a teacher's last three earning years."

"Pagel, single mother with three young children, is working on her doctorate and is by far the lowest paid member of the department; in fact, she's barely able to financially provide for her family."

"Riesen is married, but is also secretly dating one of the female students in the social work program; he refuses to advise students or to serve on departmental committees."

"Duvey works many more hours for the department than any other faculty member, but much of the work that she does (paperwork and advising of prospective students) goes unnoticed by the other faculty members."

"Aaron is addicted to alcohol (he was recently involved in a drunk driving accident and left the scene of the accident in which someone was injured); he refuses to acknowledge his alcohol abuse, and has hidden the drunk driving incident from the other social work faculty members and the university administration."

"Jackson has been extremely helpful to you and the other young instructors in the department, but her mentoring of young faculty members has not been recognized financially by the campus."

Step 3. The role players discuss the applicants for merit awards. The role players are given an opportunity to share their additional information about one faculty member. Also, if they desire, they can fabricate and share additional information (which may be positive or negative in nature) about the faculty member listed on their card. The role players then end up making decisions about how much money to assign to each of the six applicants.

Step 4. The role players and the class then process the decisions that were arrived at by discussing the following kinds of questions:

1. Did the additional information—and/or any other subjective information that was fabricated—play an important role in determining the amount of the merit raises assigned to the six applicants?
2. Did the role players reveal the additional information on their cards in the group discussions? Why, or why not?
3. What were the key values (such as quality teaching or family values) that contributed to the decisions that were made?
4. In making group decisions, such as this one, which tends to have greater weight—objective information or subjective information?

CHAPTER ELEVEN

PARLIAMENTARY PROCEDURE*

Goals: A basic familiarity with parliamentary procedure is essential to conduct the business of most groups and organizations, whether the group be a neighborhood body, tenants' union, or a chapter of the National Association of Social Workers. This chapter briefly describes the rules and procedures that apply to various groups, identifies the functions of various officers, and defines key terms.

Parliamentary procedure is a term used to describe the process by which many groups transact business. Large groups such as state and national legislatures and delegate assemblies, and smaller groups such as Boards of Directors and many task groups need a set of rules and procedures to handle their work. Perhaps the most well known and frequently used guidelines are called *Robert's Rules of Order*. While the title *Robert's Rules of Order* is familiar to most social workers, not everyone knows what it is.[1] Over one hundred years ago, General Henry M. Robert published his first guide to parliamentary law. The book became so popular that to this day it is used as the final authority on the fair and orderly operation of meetings. Although revised substantially since 1876, it remains the bible for those charged with chairing or presiding over meetings. The material contained in this chapter draws heavily from the work of Robert and other parliamentarians as well as from the author's own experiences.

BASIC RULES

The process of considering, discussing, and acting on ideas, proposals, and plans is usually facilitated when a group adopts a set of procedures that are effective and efficient. Regardless of the type of group with which one is dealing, a firm knowledge of parliamentary procedure is essential. Think of the confusion, for example, if there were no agreement on how many votes would be needed to pass a motion or how many people were needed before a group could act formally. To minimize disagreements and further the purposes of the group, most organizations choose a relatively standard method of accomplishing their goals. Called parliamentary procedure, this method addresses significant issues such as what constitutes a quorum, in what order items should appear on the agenda, and how elections should be held. Without agreement on these and other basic points, few organizations would ever accomplish their goals, and group members would become bogged down and frustrated because they lack a means of facilitating their work.

Most small groups choose to utilize less formal procedures to conduct their business than do larger organizations and bodies. Thus, while much of what is covered in the succeeding pages is applicable regardless of group size, it should be realized that the needs of the individual group will determine *if or how strictly rules are followed*. The sole purpose of parliamentary procedure is to facilitate the business of the group, and the procedures should not become barriers to action by the body. A number of parliamentary terms are listed and defined in appendix B of this text.

MOTIONS

In general, the business of a group is brought before it in the form of motions. Motions are basically proposals for action suggested by members of the group. An example of a motion would be: "I move we donate the proceeds of our fund-raiser to the Bolton Refuge

---

*This chapter was written by Grafton H. Hull, Jr., professor and director, School of Social Work, Southwest Missouri State University.

House." To ensure that frivolous motions are not used to impede a group, most motions require a second. Seconds are simply verbal indications that an idea or proposal has the support of another individual. The seconder simply says, "I second the motion." After a member has stated a motion and it has been seconded by another, the chairperson repeats the motion for the benefit of all members of the body.

If no one seconds a motion, it is appropriate for the chair to inquire, "Is there a second?" If there is no second, the motion is dead. If the motion does receive a second, discussion or debate of the proposed motion normally follows. The person who made the motion is usually given the first opportunity to speak in favor of the motion, and all who wish to speak on either side of the issue are allowed to do so. In order to speak for or against a motion, the speaker must ask for the floor. This is done simply by raising one's hand or asking to speak. The debate, however, must be related to the motion on the floor.

If desired, members may propose to amend or change the motion on the floor or to take other action such as sending the proposal to a committee. These secondary motions also help the group accomplish its tasks. Normally, when all who wish have had a chance to speak, a vote is taken on the motion. The method of taking the vote may vary from group to group, but voice voting or voting by a show of hands are common. Once the vote is taken, the chairperson or president announces the outcome and the body moves on to other business.

Primary and Secondary Motions

There are two major classes of motions: *primary motions*, which bring business to the floor, and *secondary motions*, which are often used to take action on the primary motion. Technically speaking, no item of business requiring a decision may be acted upon until it has first been stated in the form of a motion and opened to discussion. Using the correct motion to accomplish the body's goal thus becomes very important.

Types of Motion	**Purpose**
Primary:	
Main Motion	To bring a proposal before the group for action.
Incidental Motions (main)	To adjourn, amend the bylaws or constitution, repeal an action already taken.
Secondary:	
Amend or Refer	To modify or change a main motion or refer it to a committee.
Postpone or Table	To defer action on a motion. Postponements are usually to a certain time.
Call or Move the Question	To end debate on a motion and go ahead with a vote.
Reconsider	To consider a motion a second time.
Point of Order (or Information)	To raise a question about procedure or seek information.
Take from the Table	To bring a previously tabled item up for discussion.

Additional motions are used from time to time but do not occur often enough to justify their inclusion here. (See *Robert's Rules of Order* for an extended list of motions and their purposes.)

Debating and Voting on Motions

The most important principle to follow in debating a motion is that all who wish to be heard must be given the opportunity. As mentioned earlier, the maker of the motion is usually given the first opportunity to speak on the proposal, as well as the right of speaking last before a vote is taken. A person who has spoken once on a topic and wishes to speak again must wait until others have their first chance to be heard. The debate must be germane to the motion or else the presiding officer may rule the speaker out of order. After all who wish to speak have been heard, the chairperson often asks, "Is there any further debate?" If there is none, the vote may commence. In certain instances, a group may wish to limit debate on a topic. "Calling the question" on the motion is a secondary motion whose purpose is to cease debate. Stopping debate requires agreement by two-thirds of those present; a simple majority (51 percent) is not sufficient. The right of bodies to deliberate is so important that only substantial agreement from the body can limit the right. It should be noted that some motions do not allow debate. Among these are motions to adjourn, to take a recess, to appeal a decision by the chair, to table a motion under consideration, or to refer a matter to committee. In addition, some motions require no second. They include point of order or information, and withdrawal of a motion by its maker.

When debate has ended, as indicated either by no further comments or by calling the question, the motion must be voted on. Most motions must receive a simple majority of votes to pass. Amendments to bylaws or a constitution are common exceptions. Usually a voice vote will be adequate, although a show of hands is also quite frequently used. Paper ballots are seldom used, except for elections, although they can be requested by consensus or majority vote. Votes that result in a tie automatically fail and the chairperson may vote to break a tie in most groups. The choice to vote or not to vote is up to the chair. After the vote has been taken and tabulated, it is the responsibility of the presiding officer to announce the results.

For new chairpersons there are five rules or steps to remember when taking the vote:

1. State the motion upon which the group will be voting.
2. State how the group may vote (i.e., show of hands, voice vote, etc.) and what the vote will mean.
3. Call for the vote.
4. Announce the results of the vote.
5. State what action will, or will not, be taken as a result of the vote.

For voice votes, a simple statement will suffice: "All those in favor say aye." "All those opposed say no." The result may be announced by stating, "The ayes have it" or, "The motion is carried."

If there is any doubt in the chairperson's mind as to whether one side or the other carried the question, it is appropriate to say, "The chair is in doubt. Will those in favor of the motion please raise their hands?" This will usually settle the matter. Occasionally, a group will allow voting by mail or by the use of proxies, whereby someone who is not present allows another who is, to vote on his or her behalf. If proxies are to be used, this must be agreed to before the vote is taken.

OTHER RULES AND PROCEDURES

Quorum

A quorum is the minimum number of members who must be present before a group can take any official action. Frequently, this figure is established in the body's bylaws or constitution. If it is not included or otherwise provided for, the usual rule of thumb is to require a simple majority of the membership. If no quorum is present, the only official action a body can take is to set the time to meet again, adjourn, or recess.

Agenda

The "order of business," or agenda, is another important concept. It is customary to follow the order of business noted below when setting the agenda:

1. Reading of minutes of the previous meeting and approving them
2. Reports of standing committees
3. Reports of special committees (if any)
4. Unfinished business from previous sessions
5. New business
6. Establishing time for next meeting
7. Announcements
8. Adjournment

While this order is not set in concrete, most groups do follow it, since it provides a logical progression from past to present to future.

Elections

Often a group establishes a special nominations committee to prepare a slate of candidates for various organizational offices (such as president, vice-president, secretary, and treasurer). In addition, most groups provide for a process whereby nominations may be received from the floor. When one member states, "I nominate Jim for secretary," no second is required. Some groups prepare a double slate with two or more candidates for each position while others provide only a single candidate. Regardless of which system is used, voting for nominees is usually done by secret ballot. This lessens any embarrassment to the losing candidate and helps maintain the decorum of the group.

Constitution and Bylaws

A constitution and bylaws are helpful mechanisms for guiding a group over time. Unfortunately, many smaller groups do not have these documents and must develop their own procedures and processes. If a group does have a constitution and bylaws, it is necessary for the members and leaders to become familiar with their contents. Changes in the constitution or bylaws must be approved by two-thirds of the membership, which is an exception to the usual 51 percent rule.

THE ROLES OF OFFICERS

Most organizations assign specific duties and responsibilities to designated individuals. These duties include presiding over meetings, maintaining a record of actions taken by a body, ensuring that decisions that have been made are carried out, and managing the organization's funds. In addition, usually one or more persons are assigned the task of carrying out routine responsibilities between meetings of the body. These tasks and many others are usually left to the officers or elected representatives of the body.

Chairperson

The responsibility for ensuring that the organization operates smoothly and in accordance with the interests of the membership falls on the shoulders of the chairperson or president. Among the tasks normally assigned to this person are the following:

1. Opening the session
2. Announcing the business to be transacted
3. Recognizing and calling upon members who want to speak
4. Stating motions for the benefits of the group
5. Putting all questions to a vote
6. Assisting in accomplishing the business of the group
7. Maintaining the decorum and proper procedure of the group
8. Keeping the group informed of issues relevant to the body's deliberations
9. Authenticating actions taken by the group (signing letters, checks, or other documents pursuant to actions of the body)
10. Voting only to create or break a tie
11. Remaining impartial whenever possible

If this list seems impressive, it represents only a portion of the tasks expected of the chairperson. Each person who assumes this role should be reasonably conversant with parliamentary procedure and be able to assist the membership by suggesting appropriate motions and procedures and providing information about past actions by the group that have a bearing on matters under consideration. Fortunately, the chairperson has the assistance of other officers who can help in this effort.

Secretary

The secretary is charged with responsibility for maintaining minutes of the group, keeping a list of members and committees, and, in larger groups, determining the agenda. As recording officer, the secretary should prepare a file of correspondence and establish a record of any actions taken by the group. Since the minutes of a group's meeting constitute its permanent record, they assume great importance. Among the items to be included in the minutes are:

1. The name of the group
2. When the group met
3. Where the group met
4. The kind of meeting (special or regular)
5. Who chaired the meeting
6. Which members were in attendance
7. Whether previous minutes were approved
8. All main motions that were presented and the results of those motions
9. When the body adjourned

Some minutes also indicate whether those who were absent were excused or not. Still other minutes may include *only* motions approved by the body and/or major points in the debate on a topic. Each organization will eventually develop its own style or method of recording this information. Whatever information is included, the minutes remain an indispensable record of what a group did or did not do. They should be accurate and submitted for approval by the body at a subsequent meeting to ensure that the group accepts the minutes as its official record.

Treasurer

The office of treasurer may or may not exist depending upon the needs of the individual group. For groups that handle money, such as professional organizations, fund-raising committees, and the like, the treasurer is an important position. In some organizations the position is combined with that of the secretary. It is up to the particular group to decide which approach best meets its own needs.

THE OPERATION OF COMMITTEES

Most organizations rely on committees to produce the preliminary work of the assembly. This practice has evolved in part because of the difficulty of working in large groups and arriving at a product that can be debated and then modified, adopted, or defeated. The use of committees varies among organizations. Some groups establish a series of standing committees that have the responsibility for handling all matters arising in a specific area. Examples include nominations committees, in-service training committees, and personnel committees, to name a few. Most groups also establish, as needed, special or ad hoc committees to deal with a specific task for which no other committee has been appointed. Examples might be a committee to plan the retirement party for a co-worker, or one to put together a resource manual for the agency. On rare occasions, a large group will function as a Committee of the Whole. (As a Committee of the Whole, the entire body acts as one large committee to discuss and act on a subject not yet in sufficient form to be voted upon by the original body. Often, time limits are established for operating as a Committee of the Whole.)

When a committee is established, it is customary for the presiding officer to appoint a chairperson for the committee. In addition, it is usually good practice to give the committee sufficient instructions to allow it to accomplish its purpose as carefully and expeditiously as possible.

Most committees operate less formally than the bodies that established them. Thus, there will be less reliance on parliamentary procedure and more decision by consensus in many groups. Some committees will establish subcommittees to handle certain topics and prepare the preliminary work for the committee's consideration. When a committee has completed its deliberations or has a report for the larger body, it should notify the organization chair so that the committee's report may be placed on the agenda. The chair of a committee should be prepared to provide a report to the larger group and answer questions regarding the report. If the committee's report calls for specific action, a motion to accomplish this action should be made after the report has been given and any questions answered.

GROUP EXERCISES

Exercise A: Running a Meeting Using Parliamentary Rules

Goal: To increase understanding of parliamentary rules and procedures through practice.

Step 1. The class can be operated as a Committee of the Whole with either the instructor or a student assuming the role of chairperson. The group might be asked to discuss a topic such as the college's general education requirements, recommendations for improving the social work program, changes in the legal drinking age, designing a better social service agency, or admission requirements for social work programs. Whatever topic is selected, the group can be broken into subcommittees to develop proposals for consideration by the entire group. After reconvening, the entire group can operate by parliamentary procedure, making and amending motions, limiting debate, tabling where appropriate, and voting on various proposals.

A useful format to follow after the discussion is for the instructor to be the acting chairperson to receive nominations from the students for the office of chairperson. After nominations are received, the nominees are given an opportunity to summarize their experience with parliamentary procedure. A ballot vote is then taken and the results announced. After the vote, the elected chairperson leads the group in using parliamentary procedure to receive and consider the motions that the subgroups have prepared. During this process, the instructor should act as an advisor to the group on appropriate parliamentary procedure. This exercise gives students an opportunity to learn by doing and will facilitate the process of understanding parliamentary rules and procedures.

Exercise B: Parliamentary Bingo

Goal: To increase understanding of parliamentary terms and concepts.

Step 1. Each class member is given, *at least one period in advance*, a list of parliamentary terms and their definitions. (Appendix B contains an extended list.) Upon arriving in class, each student is given a bingo sheet with the names of various terms or concepts entered into each square. The group leader or instructor then draws randomly from an envelope the definitions of these terms and reads them aloud. When a student recognizes the definition as corresponding to a term on her or his sheet, the student then places an X through that square. The rest of the game continues as in bingo until one player has a complete row of Xs. The exercise may be done for extra credit points with the first five to ten players who get bingo winning the points. Other variations are possible.

The following are four sample bingo cards. Additional cards can be prepared simply by using parliamentary terms taken from appendix B, "Definitions of Parliamentary Terms."

Sample Parliamentary Bingo Card A

Repeal	Point of Order	Withdraw	Floor	Take from the Table
Adjourned Meeting	Committee	Aye	Minutes	Agenda
Annul	Second	Expunge	Convene	Adjourn
Nomination	Quorum	Roll Call	Main Motion	Limit Debate
Recommit	Filibuster	Recess	Debate	Appeal

Sample Parliamentary Bingo Card B

Ad Hoc Committee	Committee	Point of Order	Incidental Motion	Proxy
Aye	Reconsider	Recess	Lay on the Table	Call the Question
Nomination	Amend	Main Motion	Take from the Table	Limit Debate
Debate	Appeal	Rescind	Expunge	Adjourned Meeting
Filibuster	Convene	Minutes	Bylaws	Precedence

Sample Parliamentary Bingo Card C

Main Motion	Lay on the Table	Expunge	Appeal	Log Rolling
Debate	Amend	Minutes	Point of Order	Adopt
Reconsider	Privileged Motions	Recess	Limit Debate	Credentials
Refer to Committee	Roll Call	Withdraw	Annul	Adjourn
Aye	Suspend	Main Motion	Take from the Table	Proxy

Sample Parliamentary Bingo Card D

Expunge	Withdraw	Amend	Take from the Table	Floor
Repeal	Chair	Agenda	Rescind	Recess
Table	Reconsider	Minutes	Adjourn	Committee
Second	Limit Debate	Quorum	Main Motion	Nomination
Recommit	Precedence	Appeal	Privileged Motion	Point of Order

PART FIVE

ORGANIZATIONS AND COMMUNITIES

CHAPTER TWELVE

ORGANIZATIONS AND GROUPS

Goals: This chapter provides an introduction to social work practice with organizations. The close relationship between the terms "group" and "organization" are examined. Several models of organizations are presented. The chapter ends with a presentation of guidelines for helping professionals to survive and thrive in a bureaucracy.

An organization is defined here as a collectivity of individuals gathered together to serve a particular purpose. The types of purposes (or goals) that people organize to achieve are infinite in number, ranging from obtaining basic necessities to eliminating the threat of worldwide terrorism or attaining world peace. In each case an organization exists because people working together can better accomplish tasks and achieve goals than one individual can.

Etzioni described the importance of organizations in our lives:

We are born in organizations, educated by organizations, and most of us spend much of our lives working for organizations. We spend much of our leisure time paying, playing, and praying in organizations. Most of us will die in an organization, and when the time comes for burial, the largest organization of all—the state—must grant official permission.[1]

The importance of organizations for social work practice has been summarized by Netting, Kettner, and McMurtry:

As social workers, our roles within, interactions with, and attempts to manipulate organizations define much of what we do. Clients often come to us seeking help because they are not able to obtain help from organizations that are critical to their survival or quality of life. In turn, the resources we attempt to gain for these clients usually come from still other organizations. . . . Social workers with little or no idea of how organizations operate, how they interact, or how they can be influenced and changed from both outside and inside are likely to be severely limited in their effectiveness.[2]

Many disciplines (including business, psychology, political science, and sociology) have produced a prodigious amount of theory and research on organizations. However, in spite of the importance of organizations to social work practice, the amount of social work literature devoted to organizations is limited. One significant reference in this area is *Social Work Macro Practice*.[3]

THE RELATIONSHIP BETWEEN A GROUP AND AN ORGANIZATION

In chapter 1 a group was defined as:

Two or more individuals in face-to-face interaction, each aware of his or her membership in the group, each aware of the others who belong to the group, and each aware of their positive interdependence as they strive to achieve mutual goals.[4]

An organization, as previously stated, is a collectivity of individuals gathered together to serve a purpose. How do these two terms relate?

There is considerable overlap between these two terms. Some organizations can also be considered "groups" and vice versa. For example, a social work student club can be considered to be both an organization and a group. Another example of both a group and an organization is a parent-teacher association at an elementary school.

However, a large organization is generally not considered a group. For example, the General Motors Corporation is considered an organization, but not a group. One of the reasons it is not referred to as a group is that its employees and owners (including stockholders) are so large in number that no one has personal contact with all the other members of the organization. In similar manner, most other large organizations (such as the National Rifle Association and the American Medical Association) are not considered "groups." Such associations are "gathered together" for a specific purpose. However, the term "gathered together" does not mean that everyone has personal contact with everyone else as do the members of a group.

Most small, informal groups with no specific purpose are not considered organizations. For example, a group of neighborhood children who occasionally meet to play with one another is not considered an organization.

MODELS OF ORGANIZATIONS*

The Autocratic Model

The autocratic model has been in existence for thousands of years. During the Industrial Revolution, this model was the prominent model of how an organization should function. The model depends on *power*. Those who are in power act autocratically. The message to employees is "You do this—or else," meaning that an employee who does not follow orders is penalized, often severely.

An autocratic model uses one-way communication—from the top to the workers. Management believes that it knows what is best. The employee's obligation is to follow orders. Employees have to be persuaded, directed, and pushed into performance, and this is management's task. Management does the thinking, and the workers obey the directives. Under autocratic conditions, the workers' role is *obedience* to management.

The autocratic model does work in some settings. Most military organizations throughout the world are formulated on this model. The model was also used successfully during the Industrial Revolution; for example, in building great railroad systems and in operating giant steel mills.

The autocratic model has a number of disadvantages. Workers are often in the best position to identify shortcomings in the structure and technology of the organizational system, but one-way communication prevents feedback to management. The model also fails to generate much of a commitment among the workers to accomplish organizational goals. Finally, the model fails to motivate workers to put forth effort to further develop their skills (skills that often would be highly beneficial to the employer).

The Custodial Model

Many decades ago when the autocratic model was the predominant model of organizational behavior, some progressive managers began to study their employees and soon

---

*Material in this section is adapted from *The Practice of Social Work*, by Charles Zastrow. Copyright © 1994, 1992, 1989, 1985, 1981, Brooks/Cole Publishing Company, a division of International Thomson Publishing Inc., Pacific Grove, CA 93950. By permission of the publisher.

found that the autocratic model often caused the employees to be filled with insecurity, frustration, and feelings of aggression toward management. Since the employees could not directly express their discontent, it was expressed indirectly. Some employees vented their anger on their families and neighbors, and the entire community suffered. Others sabotaged production. Davis and Newstrom described sabotage in a wood-processing plant.

> Managers treated workers crudely, sometimes even to the point of physical abuse. Since employees could not strike back directly for fear of losing their jobs, they found another way to do it. They *symbolically* fed their supervisor to a log-shredding machine! They did this by purposely destroying good sheets of veneer, which made the supervisor look bad when monthly efficiency reports were prepared.[5]

In the 1890s and 1900s some progressive employers thought that if these feelings could be alleviated, employees might feel more like working, which would increase productivity. To satisfy the employees' security needs, a number of companies began to provide welfare programs. Examples include pension programs, child-care centers at the workplace, health insurance, and life insurance.

The custodial approach leads to employee dependence on the organization. According to Davis and Newstrom, "If employees have ten years of seniority under the union contract and a good pension program, they cannot afford to quit even if the grass looks greener somewhere else!"[6]

Employees working under a custodial model tend to focus on their economic rewards and benefits. They are happier and more content than under the autocratic model, but they do not have a high commitment to helping the organization accomplish its goals. They tend to give *passive cooperation* to their employer. The model's most evident flaw is that most employees are producing substantially below their capacities. They are not motivated to advance to higher capacities. Most such employees do not feel fulfilled or motivated at their place of work. In summary, contented employees (which the custodial model is designed to generate) are not necessarily the most productive employees.

The Scientific Management Model

One of the earliest and most important schools of thought on the management of functions and tasks in the workplace was based on the work of Frederick Taylor.[7] Taylor was a mechanical engineer, an American industrialist, and an educator. He focused primarily on management techniques that would lead to increased productivity. He asserted that many organizational problems in the workplace involved misunderstandings between managers and workers. Managers erroneously thought that workers were lazy and unemotional, and they mistakenly believed they understood workers' jobs. Workers mistakenly thought that managers cared most about exploiting them.

To solve these problems, Taylor developed the *scientific management model*, which focused on the need for managers to conduct scientific analyses of the workplace. One of the first steps was to conduct a careful study of how each job could best be accomplished. An excellent way to do this, according to Taylor, was to identify the best worker for each job and then carefully study how he or she effectively and efficiently did the work. The goal of this analysis was to discover the optimal way of doing the job—in Taylor's words, the "one best way." Once this best way was identified, tools could be modified to better complete the work, workers' abilities and interests could be fitted to particular job assignments, and the level of production that the average worker could sustain could be gauged.

Once the level of production for the average worker was determined, Taylor indicated the next step was to provide incentives to increase productivity. His favorite strategy for doing this was the piece-rate wage, in which workers were paid for each unit they produced. The goals were to produce more units, reduce unit cost, increase organizational productivity and profitability, and provide incentives for workers to produce more.

Taylor's work has been criticized as having a technicist bias, since it tends to treat workers as little more than cogs in a wheel. No two workers are exactly alike, so the "one best way" of doing a job is often unique to the person doing it. In fact, forcing the same work approach on different workers may actually decrease both productivity and worker satisfaction. In addition, Taylor's approach has limited application to human services. Since each client is unique—with unique needs, unique environmental impact factors, and unique strengths and capacities—each human services case has to be individualized, and therefore it is difficult (if not impossible) to specify the "one best way" to proceed.

The Human Relations Model

In 1927 the Hawthorne Works of the Western Electric Company in Chicago began a series of experiments designed to discover ways to increase worker satisfaction and worker productivity.[8]

Hawthorne Works manufactured telephones on an assembly-line basis. Workers needed no special skills and performed simple, repetitive tasks. The workers were not unionized, and management sought to find ways to increase productivity. If job satisfaction could be increased, employees would work more efficiently and productivity would increase.

The company tested the effects on productivity of a number of factors: rest breaks, better lighting, changes in the number of work hours, changes in the wages paid, improved food facilities, and so on. The results were surprising. Productivity increased, as expected, with improved working conditions; but it also increased when working conditions worsened. This latter finding was unexpected and led to additional study.

The investigators discovered that participation in the experiments was extremely attractive to the workers. They felt they had been selected by the management for their individual abilities, and so they worked harder, even when working conditions became less favorable. In addition, the workers' morale and general attitude toward work improved, since they felt they were receiving special attention. By participating in this study, the workers were able to work in smaller groups and became involved in making decisions. Working in smaller groups allowed them to develop a stronger sense of solidarity with their fellow workers. Being involved in decision making decreased their feelings of meaninglessness and powerlessness about their work.

In sociological and psychological research, the results of this study have become known as the "Hawthorne effect." In essence, when subjects know they are participants in a study, this awareness may lead them to behave differently and substantially influence the results.

The results of this study, and of other similar studies, led some researchers to conclude that the key variables impacting productivity are social factors. Etzioni summarized some of the basic tenets of the human relations approach:

- The level of production is set by social norms, not by physiological capacities.
- Noneconomic rewards and sanctions significantly affect the behavior of the workers and largely limit the effect of economic incentive plans.
- Workers do not act or react as individuals but as members of groups.
- The role of leadership is important in understanding social factors in organizations and this leadership may be either formal or informal.[9]

Numerous studies have provided evidence to support these tenets.[10] Workers who are capable of greater productivity often will not excel because they are unwilling to exceed the "average" level set by the norms of the group, even if this means earning less. These studies have also found that attempts by management to influence workers' behavior are often more successful if targeted at the group as a whole, rather than at individuals. Finally, the studies have documented the importance of informal leadership in influencing workers' behavior in ways that can either amplify or negate formal leadership directives. This model asserts that managers who succeed in increasing productivity are most likely responsive to the workers' social needs.

One criticism of the human relations model is (surprisingly) that it tends to manipulate, dehumanize, oppress, and exploit workers. The model leads to the conclusion that management can increase productivity by helping workers become content, rather than by increasing economic rewards for higher productivity. The human relations model allows for concentrated power and decision making at the top. It is not intended to empower employees in the decision-making process or to assist them in acquiring genuine participation in the running of the organization. The practice of dealing with people on the basis of their perceived social relationships within the workplace may also be a factor in perpetuating the "good old boys" network; this network has disadvantaged women and people of color over the years. Another criticism of the human relations approach is that a happy work force is not necessarily a productive work force, because the norms for worker production may be set well below the workers' levels of capability.

Theory X and Theory Y

Douglas McGregor developed two theories of management.[11] He theorized that management thinking and behavior are based on two different sets of assumptions, which he labeled Theory X and Theory Y.

Theory X managers view employees as being incapable of much growth. Employees are perceived as having an inherent dislike for work and attempting to evade work whenever possible. Therefore, X-type managers believe they must control, direct, force, or threaten employees to make them work. Employees are also viewed as having relatively little ambition, wishing to avoid responsibilities, and preferring to be directed. Theory X managers therefore spell out job responsibilities carefully, set work goals without employee input, use external rewards (such as money) to force employees to work, and punish those who deviate from established rules. Because Theory X managers reduce responsibilities to a level at which few mistakes can be made, work usually becomes so structured that it is monotonous and distasteful. These assumptions, of course, are inconsistent with what behavioral scientists assert are effective principles for directing, influencing, and motivating people. (Theory X managers are, in essence, adhering to an autocratic model of organizational behavior.)

In contrast, *Theory Y managers* view employees as wanting to grow and develop by exerting physical and mental effort to accomplish work objectives to which they are committed. These managers believe that the promise of internal rewards, such as self-respect and personal improvement, are stronger motivators than external rewards (money) and punishment. They also believe that under proper conditions, employees will not only accept responsibility but seek it. Most employees are assumed to have considerable ingenuity, creativity, and imagination for problem solving. Therefore, they are given considerable responsibility to test the limits of their capabilities. Mistakes and errors are viewed as necessary phases of the learning process, and work is structured so employees have a sense of accomplishment and growth.

Employees who work for Y-type managers are generally more creative and productive, experience greater work satisfaction, and are more highly motivated than employees who work for X-type managers. Under both management styles, expectations often become self-fulfilling prophecies.

The Collegial Model

A useful extension of Theory Y is the collegial model, which emphasizes the team concept. It involves employees working closely together and feeling a commitment to achieve a common purpose. Some organizations—such as university departments, research laboratories, and most human services organizations—have a goal of creating a collegial atmosphere to facilitate achieving their purposes. (Sadly, many such organizations are unsuccessful in creating such an atmosphere.)

Creating a collegial atmosphere is highly dependent on management building a feeling of partnership with employees. When such a partnership develops, employees feel needed and useful. Managers are then viewed as joint contributors rather than as bosses. Management is the *coach* who builds a better team. Davis and Newstrom described some of the approaches to developing a team concept:

> The feeling of partnerships can be built in many ways. Some organizations have abolished the use of reserved parking spaces for executives, so every employee has an equal chance of finding one close to the workplace. Some firms have tried to eliminate the use of terms like "bosses" and "subordinates," feeling that those terms simply create perceptions of psychological distance between managers and nonmanagers. Other employers have removed time clocks, set up "fun committees," sponsored company canoe trips, or required managers to spend a week or two annually working in field or factory locations. All of these approaches are designed to build a spirit of mutuality, in which every person makes contributions and appreciates those of others.[12]

If the sense of partnership is developed, employees produce quality work and seek to cooperate with co-workers, not because management directs them to do so, but because they feel an internal obligation to produce high-quality work. The collegial approach thus leads to a sense of *self-discipline*. In this environment, employees are more apt to have a sense of fulfillment, to feel self-actualized, and to produce higher-quality work.

Theory Z

William Ouchi described the Japanese style of management in his 1981 best-seller *Theory Z*.[13] In the late 1970s and early 1980s, attention in the U.S. business world became focused on the Japanese approach to management, as markets long dominated by American firms (such as the automobile industry) were taken over by Japanese industries. Japanese industrial organizations had rapidly overcome their earlier reputation for poor quality work and were setting worldwide standards for quality and durability.

Theory Z asserted that the theoretical principles underlying Japanese management went beyond Theory Y. According to Theory Z, a business organization in Japan is more than the profitability oriented entity that it is in the United States. It is a way of life. It provides lifetime employment. It is enmeshed with the nation's political, social, and economic network. Furthermore, its influence spills over into many other organizations, such as nursery schools, elementary and secondary schools, and universities.

The basic philosophy of Theory Z is that involved and committed workers are the key to increased productivity. Ideas and suggestions about how to improve the organization are routinely solicited and implemented, where feasible. One strategy for accomplishing this is the *quality circle*, where employees and management routinely meet to brainstorm about ways to improve productivity and quality.

In contrast to American organizations, Japanese organizations tend not to have written objectives or organizational charts. Most work is done in teams and decisions are made by consensus. The teams tend to function without a designated leader. Cooperation within units and between units is emphasized. Loyalty to the organization is also emphasized, as is organizational loyalty to the employee.

Experiments designed to transplant Japanese-style management to the United States have resulted in mixed success. In most cases American organizations have concluded that Theory Z probably works quite well in a homogeneous culture that has Japan's societal values, but some components do not fit well with the more heterogeneous and individualistic character of the United States. In addition, some firms in volatile industries (such as electronics) have difficulty balancing their desire to provide lifetime employment with the need to adjust their work forces to meet rapidly changing market demands.

Management by Objectives

Fundamental to the core of an organization is its purpose; that is, the commonly shared understanding of the reason for its existence.

Management theorist Peter Drucker proposed a strategy for making organizational goals and objectives the central construct around which organizational life is designed to function.[14] In other words, instead of focusing on employee needs and wants, or on organizational structure, as the ways to increase efficiency and productivity, Drucker proposed beginning with the desired outcome and working backward. The strategy is first to identify the organizational objectives or goals and then to adapt the organizational tasks, resources, and structure to meet those objectives. This management by objectives (MBO) approach is designed to focus the organization's efforts on meeting these objectives. Success is determined, then, by the degree to which stated objectives are reached.

This approach can be applied to the organization as a whole, as well as to internal divisions or departments. When the MBO approach is applied to internal divisions, the objectives set for each division should be consistent and supportive of the overall organizational objectives.

In many areas, including human services, the MBO approach can also be applied to the cases being serviced by each employee. Goals are set with each client, tasks to meet these goals are then determined, and deadlines are set for the completion of these tasks. The degree of success of each case is then determined at later date (often when a case is closed) by the extent to which stated goals were achieved.

An adaptation of the MBO approach, called strategic planning and budgeting (SPB), has become popular in the 1990s. The process involves first specifying the overall vision or mission of an organization, then identifying a variety of more specific objectives or plans for achieving that vision, and finally adapting the resources to meet the specific high-priority objectives or plans. Organizations in the 1990s often hire outside consultants to assist in conducting the SPB process.

One major advantage of the MBO approach for an organization (or its divisions) is that it produces clear statements (made available to all employees) about the objectives and the tasks that are expected to be accomplished in specified time periods. This type of activity tends to improve cooperation and collaboration. The MBO approach is also useful because it provides a guide for allocating resources and a focus for monitoring and evaluating organizational efforts.

An additional benefit of the MBO approach is in the area of diversity in the workplace. Prior to this approach, those responsible for hiring failed to employ women and people of color in significant numbers. As affirmative action programs were developed within organizations, the MBO approach was widely used to set specific hiring goals and objectives. The result has been significant changes in recruitment approaches that have enabled a number of women and other minorities to secure employment.

Total Quality Management

Total quality management (TQM) has been defined as:

> . . . the integration of all functions and processes within an organization in order to achieve continuous improvement of the quality of goods and services. The goal is customer satisfaction.[15]

TQM is based on a number of ideas. It means thinking about quality in terms of all functions of the enterprise and is a start-to-finish process that integrates interrelated functions at all levels. It is a systems approach that considers every interaction among the various elements of the organization. TQM asserts that management, in many businesses and organizations, makes the mistake of blaming what goes wrong in an organization as the fault of individual people, not of the system. TQM, instead, believes in the *85/15 Rule*, which asserts that 85 percent of the problems can be corrected only by changing systems (structures, rules, practices, expectations, and traditions that are largely determined by management) and fewer than 15 percent of the problems can be solved by individual workers. When problems arise, TQM asserts that management should look for causes in the system and work to remove them before casting blame on workers.

TQM asserts that quality includes continuously improving all the organization's processes that lead to customer satisfaction. Customer satisfaction is the main purpose of the organization. The customer is not the "point of sale." The customer is part of the design and production process, as the customer's needs must continually be monitored.

In recent years numerous organizations have adopted a TQM approach to seeking to improve their goods and services. One of the reasons that quality is being emphasized more is that consumers are increasingly shunning mass-produced, poorly made, disposable products. Companies are realizing that in order to remain competitive in global markets, high quality is essential in their products and services. Ford's motto of "Quality Is Job One" symbolizes this emphasis on quality.

There are a variety of approaches to TQM, because numerous theoreticians have advanced their own diverse approaches. A summary of these approaches is contained in *Principles of Total Quality*.[16] A description of all these approaches is beyond the scope of this text, but one approach to TQM has been summarized by David Hower, as containing the following twelve principles:

- employees asking their external and internal customers what they need, and providing more of it
- instilling pride into every employee
- concentrating on information and data (a common language) to solve problems, instead of concentrating on opinions and egos
- developing leaders, not managers, and knowing the difference
- improving every process (everyone is in a process), checking this improvement at predetermined times, then improving it again if necessary
- helping every employee enjoy his or her work while the organization continues to become more productive
- providing a forum or open atmosphere so that employees at all levels feel free to voice their opinions when they think they have good ideas
- receiving a continuous increase in those suggestions, and accepting and implementing the best ones
- utilizing the teamwork concept, since teams often make better decisions than individuals
- empowering these teams to implement their recommended solutions and learn from their failures
- reducing the number of layers of authority to enhance this empowerment
- recognizing complaints as opportunities for improvement[17]

This approach gives the reader a "flavor" of TQM.

SURVIVING IN A BUREAUCRACY*

A bureaucracy is a subcategory (or type) of organization. A bureaucracy can be defined as a form of social organization whose distinctive characteristics include a vertical hierarchy

---

*Material in this section is adapted from *The Practice of Social Work*, by Charles Zastrow. Copyright © 1994, 1992, 1989, 1985, 1981, Brooks/Cole Publishing Company, a division of International Thomson Publishing Inc., Pacific Grove, CA 93950. By permission of the publisher.

with power centered at the top; a task specific division of labor; clearly defined rules; formalized channels of communication; and selection, compensation, promotion, and retention based on technical competence.

There are basic structural conflicts between helping professionals and the bureaucratic systems in which they work. Helping professionals place a high value on creativeness and changing the system to serve clients. Bureaucracies resist change and are most efficient when no one is "rocking the boat." Helping professionals seek to personalize services by conveying to each client that "you count as a person." Bureaucracies are highly depersonalized, emotionally detached systems that view every employee and every client as a tiny component of a large system. In a large bureaucracy employees *don't* count as "persons," but only as functional parts of a system. Additional conflicting value orientations between a helping professional and bureaucratic systems are listed in Exhibit 1.

Any of these differences in value orientations can become an arena of conflict between helping professionals and the bureaucracies in which they work. Knopf summarized the potential areas of conflict between bureaucracies and helping professionals:

> The trademarks of a BS (bureaucratic system) are power, hierarchy, and specialization; that is, rules and roles. In essence, the result is depersonalization. The system itself is neither "good" nor "bad"; it is a system. I believe it to be amoral. It is efficient and effective, but in order to be so it must be impersonal in all of its functionings. This then is the location of the stress. The hallmark of the helping professional is a highly individualized, democratic, humanized, relationship-oriented service aimed at self-motivation. The hallmark of a bureaucratic system is a highly impersonalized, valueless (amoral), emotionally detached, hierarchical structure of organization. The dilemma of the HP (helping person) is how to give a personalized service to a client through a delivery system that is not set up in any way to do that.[18]

Numerous helping professionals respond to these orientation conflicts by erroneously projecting a "personality" onto the bureaucracy. The bureaucracy is viewed as being "red tape," "officialism," "uncaring," "cruel," "the enemy." A negative personality is sometimes also projected onto the officials, who may be viewed as being "paper shufflers," "rigid," "deadwood," "inefficient," and "unproductive." Knopf states:

> The HP (helping person) . . . may deal with the impersonal nature of the system by projecting values onto it and thereby give the BS (bureaucratic system) a "personality." In this way, we fool ourselves into thinking that we can deal with it in a personal way. Unfortunately, projection is almost always negative and reflects the dark or negative aspects of ourselves. The BS then becomes a screen onto which we vent our anger, sadness, or fright, and while a lot of energy is generated, very little is accomplished. Since the BS is amoral, it is unproductive to place a personality on it.[19]

A bureaucratic system is neither good nor bad. It has neither a personality nor a value system of its own. It is simply a structure developed to carry out various tasks.

A helping person may have various emotional reactions to these conflicts in orientation with bureaucratic systems.* Common reactions are anger at the system, self-blame

---

*This description highlights a number of negatives about bureaucratic systems, particularly their impersonalization. In fairness, an advantage of being part of a large bureaucracy is that the potential is there for changing a powerful system to the clients' advantage. In tiny or nonbureaucratic systems, the social worker may have lots of freedom but little opportunity or power to influence large systems or mobilize extensive resources on behalf of clients.

EXHIBIT 1: VALUE CONFLICTS BETWEEN A HELPING PROFESSIONAL AND BUREAUCRACIES

Orientations of a Helping Professional

Desires democratic system for decision making.

Desires that power be distributed equally among employees (horizontal structure).

Desires that clients have considerable power in the system.

Desires a flexible, changing system.

Desires that creativity and growth be emphasized.

Desires that focus be client-oriented.

Desires that communication be on a personalized level from person to person.

Desires shared decision making and shared responsibility structure.

Desires that decisions be made by those having the most knowledge.

Desires shared leadership.

Believes feelings of clients and employees should be highly valued by the system.

Orientations of Bureaucratic Systems

Most decisions are made autocratically.

Power is distributed vertically.

Power is held primarily by top executives.

System is rigid and stable.

Emphasis is on structure and the status quo.

System is organization-centered.

Communication is from level to level.

A hierarchical decision-making structure and a hierarchical responsibility structure are characteristic.

Decisions are made in terms of the decision-making authority assigned to each position in the hierarchy.

System uses autocratic leadership.

Procedures and processes are highly valued.

("It's all my fault"), sadness and depression ("Poor me," "Nobody appreciates all I've done"), and fright and paranoia ("They're out to get me," "If I mess up I'm gone").

Knopf identified several types of behavior patterns that helping professionals choose in dealing with bureaucracies.[20] The *warrior* leads open campaigns to destroy and malign the system. A warrior discounts the value of the system and often enters into a win-lose conflict. The warrior generally loses and is dismissed.

The *gossip* is a covert warrior who complains to others (including clients, politicians, and the news media) how terrible the system is. A gossip frequently singles out a few officials for criticism. Bureaucratic systems often make life very difficult for the gossip by assigning distasteful tasks, refusing to promote, giving very low salary increases, and perhaps even dismissing.

The *complainer* resembles a gossip, but confines complaints to other helping persons, to in-house staff, and to family members. A complainer wants people to agree in order to find comfort in shared misery. Complainers desire to stay with the system, and generally do.

The *dancer* is skillful at ignoring rules and procedures. Dancers are frequently lonely, often reprimanded for incorrectly filling out forms, and have low investment in the system or in helping clients.

The *defender* is scared, dislikes conflict, and therefore defends the rules, the system,

244

and bureaucratic officials. Defenders are often supervisors and are viewed by others as "bureaucrats."

The *machine* is a "bureaucrat" who takes on the orientation of the bureaucracy. Often a machine has not been involved in providing direct services for years. Machines are frequently named to head study committees and policy groups and to chair boards.

The *executioner* attacks persons within an organization with enthusiasm and vigor. An executioner usually has a high energy level and is impulsive. An executioner abuses power by indiscriminately attacking and dismissing not only employees but also services and programs. Executioners have power and are angry (although the anger is disguised, denied). They are not committed to either the value orientation of helping professionals or to the bureaucracy.

Knopf listed 66 tips on how to survive in a bureaucracy.[21] A number of the most useful suggestions are summarized here:

1. Whenever your needs, or the needs of your clients, are not met by the bureaucracy, use the following problem-solving approach: (a) Precisely identify your needs (or the needs of clients) that are in conflict with the bureaucracy; this step is defining the problem. (b) Generate a list of possible solutions. Be creative in generating a wide range of solutions. (c) Evaluate the merits and shortcomings of the possible solutions. (d) Select a solution. (e) Implement the solution. (f) Evaluate the solution.

2. Obtain a knowledge of how your bureaucracy is structured and how it functions. This knowledge will reduce fear of the unknown, make the system more predictable, and help in identifying rational ways to best meet your needs and those of your clients.

3. Remember that bureaucrats are people who have feelings. Communication gaps are often most effectively reduced if you treat them with as much respect and interest as you treat clients.

4. If you are at war with the bureaucracy, declare a truce. The system will find a way to dismiss you if you remain at war. With a truce, you can identify and use the strengths of the bureaucracy as an ally, rather than having the strengths be used against you as an enemy.

5. Know your work contract and job expectations. If the expectations are unclear, seek clarity.

6. Continue to develop your knowledge and awareness of specific helping skills. Take advantage of continuing education opportunities (for example, workshops, conferences, courses). Among other advantages, your continued professional development will assist you in being able to contract from a position of competency and skill.

7. Seek to identify your professional strengths and limitations. Knowing your limitations will increase your ability to avoid undertaking responsibilities that are beyond your competencies.

8. Be aware that you can't change everything, so stop trying. In a bureaucracy, focus your change efforts on those aspects that most need change and that you have a fair chance of changing. Stop thinking and complaining about those aspects you cannot change. It is irrational to complain about things that you cannot change or to complain about those things that you do not intend to make an effort to change.

9. Learn how to control your emotions in your interactions with the bureaucracy. Emotions that are counterproductive (such as most angry outbursts) particularly need to be controlled. Doing a rational self-analysis of unwanted emotions (see chapter 21) is one way of gaining control of your unwanted emotions. Learning how to respond to stress in your personal life will also prepare you to handle stress at work better.

10. Develop and use a sense of humor. Humor takes the edge off adverse conditions and reduces negative feelings.

11. Learn to accept your mistakes and perhaps even to laugh at some of them. No one is perfect.

12. Take time to enjoy and develop a support system with your co-workers.

13. Acknowledge your mistakes and give in sometimes on minor matters. You may not be right, and giving in sometimes allows other people to do the same.

14. Keep yourself physically fit and mentally alert. Learn to use approaches that will reduce stress and prevent burnout (see chapter 15).

15. Leave your work at the office. If you have urgent unfinished bureaucratic business, do it before leaving work or don't leave.

16. Occasionally take your supervisor and other administrators to lunch. Socializing prevents isolation and facilitates your involvement with and understanding of the system.

17. Do not seek self-actualization or ego-satisfaction from the bureaucracy. A depersonalized system is incapable of providing this. Only you can satisfy your ego and become self-actualized.

18. Make speeches to community groups that accentuate the positives about your agency. Do not hesitate to ask after speeches that a thank-you letter be sent to your supervisor or agency director.

19. If you have a problem involving the bureaucracy, discuss it with other employees; focus on problem solving rather than on complaining. Groups are much more powerful and productive than an individual working alone to make changes in a system.

20. No matter how high you rise in a hierarchy, maintain direct service contact. Direct contact keeps you abreast of changing client needs, prevents you from getting stale, and keeps you attuned to the concerns of employees in lower levels of the hierarchy.

21. Do not try to change everything in the system at once. Attacking too much will overextend you and lead to burnout. Start small and be selective and specific. Double-check your facts to make certain they accurately prove your position before confronting bureaucratic officials.

22. Identify your career goals and determine whether they can be met in this system. If the answer is no, then (a) change your goals, (b) change the bureaucracy, or (c) seek a position elsewhere in which your goals can be met.

GROUP EXERCISES

Exercise A: Analyzing a Human Services Organization

Goals: This exercise is designed to give students a framework for analyzing organizations.

Step 1. The leader divides the class into subgroups of five or six students. Each subgroup has to select a human services agency to analyze. (Each subgroup should select a different agency.) Each subgroup will gather information through interviews at its agency and then give a report at a future class session covering the following questions:

a. What is the agency's mission statement?

b. What are its clients' major problems?

c. What services does the agency provide?

d. How are client needs determined?

e. What percentage of clients are people of color, women, gays or lesbians, elderly, or members of other at-risk populations?

f. What was the total cost of services for the past year?

g. How much money is spent on each program?

h. What are the agency's funding sources?

i. How much and what percentage of funds are received from each source?

j. What types of clients does the agency refuse?

k. What other agencies provide the same services in the community?

l. What is the organizational structure of the agency? For example, is there a formal chain of command?

m. Is there an informal organization (that is, people who exert a greater amount of influence on decision making than would be expected for their formal position in the bureaucracy)?

n. How much decision-making input do the direct service providers have on major policy decisions?

o. Does the agency have a board that oversees its operations? If yes, what are the backgrounds of the board members?

p. Do employees at every level feel valued?

q. What is the morale among employees?

r. What are the major unmet needs of the agency?

s. Does the agency have a handbook of personnel policies and procedures?

t. What is the public image of the agency in the community?

u. In recent years what has been the rate of turnover among staff at the agency? What were the major reasons for leaving?

v. Does the agency have a process for evaluating the outcomes of its services? If yes, what is the process, and what are the outcome results?

w. What is the subgroup's overall impression of the agency? For example, if members of the subgroup needed services that this agency provides, would they want to apply at this agency? Why, or why not?

Exercise B: Understanding and Applying Models of Organization

Goal: This exercise is designed to increase students' knowledge of organizational models and to teach them how to apply the models.

Step 1. The leader should summarize the models of organizations described in this chapter: the autocratic model, the custodial model, the scientific management model, the human relations model, Theory X, Theory Y, the collegial model, Theory Z, management by objectives, and total quality management. (As an alternative, assign the students to read this material in the text.)

Step 2. Ask the students to form subgroups of about five members. Ask each subgroup to decide which models are currently most applicable to describing organizational behavior within the organization of social work faculty in the program. (If the number of social work faculty members is very small, the class may instead be asked to decide which models are currently most applicable to describing the organizational behavior of the departmental faculty of which the social work program is a component).

Step 3. Have the members of each subgroup state their views on which models are most applicable and the reasons for their decisions. Seek to have a class discussion among the subgroups, because there are apt to be differences of opinion.

Exercise C: Theory X and Theory Y

Goal: To become more aware of Theory X and Theory Y styles of management.

Step 1. The leader explains the purpose of this exercise and describes both theories of management, providing personal examples of employment under a manager who used one or the other style.

Step 2. Class members describe examples of their own employment held under these styles of management and then discuss their feelings about working under each system.

Step 3. Since Theory Y is apparently superior to Theory X in motivating employees to be creative and productive, students should discuss why Theory X is used by so many managers.

CHAPTER THIRTEEN

COMMUNITIES AND GROUPS

Goals: This chapter provides an introduction to social work practice with communities. The close relationship between the terms "group" and "community" is examined. Organizations such as Habitat for Humanity exemplify the concepts of both a group and a community. A framework for analyzing a community is presented, along with three models a social worker can use in seeking constructive community changes.

Acommunity has been defined as, "a group of individuals or families that share certain values, services, institutions, interests or geographic proximity."[1] The term "institution" in this definition is sometimes rather difficult to comprehend. Barker has defined institution as "an organization established for some public purpose and the physical facility in which its work occurs, such as a prison."[2]

The reader will note that the terms *organization* and *community* are closely related. An organization was defined in chapter 12 as a collectivity of individuals gathered together to serve a particular purpose. Some communities are also organizations. A nursing home can be considered both an organization (the residents and staff form a collectivity of individuals having a specific purpose) and a community (the residents and staff share certain values, services, physical facilities, interests, and geographic proximity).

But not all communities are institutions, and vice versa. The residents of a large city form a community, as they share certain services and institutions, and have geographic proximity; but a large city is not an organization, as its residents are not gathered together to serve a particular purpose.

The owners and employees of a large multinational corporation (such as Philip Morris Corporation which has offices in many countries and sells a variety of products including tobacco and groceries) form an organization. However, the Philip Morris Corporation is not considered a community, because the corporation is so large that its vast number of owners and employees do not engage sufficiently in "sharing" with one another to be considered a community.

THE RELATIONSHIP BETWEEN A GROUP AND A COMMUNITY

The terms "community" and "group" are closely related. As noted in chapter 1, a group is:

> . . . two or more individuals in face-to-face interaction, each aware of his or her membership in the group, each aware of the others who belong to the group, and each aware of their positive interdependence as they strive to achieve mutual goals.[3]

A distinguishing characteristic of a group is that its members have personal contact with one another. A community, as stated earlier in this chapter, is "a group of individuals or families that share certain values, services, institutions, interests, or geographic proximity."[4]

In many cases a group and a community overlap and the group can also be considered a community. The congregation of St. Peter's Catholic Church in Madison, Wisconsin, is both a group and a community. The members have personal contact with one another (characteristic of a group) and share the religious values of the Catholic Church (characteristic of a community).

There are a number of other examples in which a group is also a community. The small unincorporated village of Little Chicago, Wisconsin, is composed of one bank, three stores, one tavern, a restaurant, and five residential homes. The village is a community (its residents share geographic proximity, services, values, and interests) and have personal contact with one another (a key characteristic of a group). Some of the interests and values that are shared are hard work, helping neighbors out in times of trouble, a belief in Christianity, and the cherishing of country living in rural America.

Many communities are so large that their members do not have personal contact with one another, and therefore are not a group. For example, Roman Catholics throughout the world have a common set of values, and therefore can be considered to be a community. However, no one has personal contact with everyone else, so they are not considered a group. The residents of New York City form a community, as they share geographic proximity (in fact, distinct geographic boundaries). But this community is not a group since no resident has personal contact with everyone else.

FRAMEWORK FOR ANALYZING A COMMUNITY

A variety of frameworks have been developed for analyzing a community. The following framework presents an elementary approach:

1. *Community Members.* Who are the members of this community? How many members are there? What unique or distinct characteristics do these members have? What is their ethnic or racial composition? What is the age composition? Do the members have pride in their community? If "yes," what aspects do the residents have pride in?
2. *Economic Characteristics.* What are the principal economic characteristics of the community? What are the principal types of employment? What are the major industries? Have there been recent changes in the economic base? What is the unemployment rate?
3. *Community Values.* Does the community have a distinct set of values? If "yes," what are these values? Who set these values and why were they selected, or how did they develop? Have there been changes in these values over time? If "yes," what changes have occurred and for what reasons?
4. *Needs and Social Problems.* What do the members perceive as their most critical needs? Why are these needs perceived as critical? How effectively do the members perceive that their community is responding to their needs? Closely related to the above questions are the following: What major social problems affect the members? Are subgroups of the population experiencing social problems of critical proportions? What data is available on these identified social problems, and what are the sources of this data?
5. *Oppression and Discrimination.* Are some subgroups of the population being victimized by oppression and discrimination? (Oppression can be defined as the unjust or cruel use of authority or power.) If "yes," the following questions are important: Why are oppression and discrimination occurring? How is the power structure in the community responding to the oppression and discrimination? What efforts are being made to combat this oppression and discrimination? Who are the leaders in these efforts?
6. *Power Structure.* Who holds the power in the community? What is the nature of the power—such as financial, military or police strength, election processes? How does the power structure maintain its power? Is the power fairly evenly distributed among the members, or is the power in the hands of a small segment of the members? What are the attitudes of the power structure toward those in the community with little or no power?
7. *Human Services.* What existing human service agencies and organizations are seen as the major service providers in the community? What primary human services are provided? Who are the major beneficiaries of these services? Are subgroups with critical needs being ignored? If "yes," why are their needs being ignored? What is the image of the social work profession in the community?

8. *Educational Services.* What are the major educational resources in the community? What educational services are being provided? Who are the major beneficiaries of these services? Are there subgroups whose educational needs are being ignored? If "yes," why are these needs being ignored?

MODELS OF COMMUNITY PRACTICE*

A variety of approaches have been developed for community practitioners to bring about community change. In reviewing these approaches, Jack Rothman and John Tropman have categorized them into three models: locality development, social planning, and social action. It should be noted that these models are "ideal types." Actual approaches to community change have tendencies or emphases that categorize them in one of the above models; yet most approaches also have components characteristic of one or both of the other models. Advocates of the social planning model, for example, may at times use community change techniques (such as wide discussion and participation by a variety of groups) that are characteristic of the other two models. At this point we will not attempt to deal with the mixed forms, but for analytical purposes will instead view the three models as "pure" forms.

Locality Development Model

The first model, locality development (also called community development), asserts that community change can best be brought about through broad participation of a wide spectrum of people at the local community level. The model seeks to involve a broad cross section of people (including the disadvantaged and the power structure) in identifying and solving their problems. Some themes emphasized in this model are democratic procedures, a consensus approach, voluntary cooperation, development of indigenous leadership, and self-help.

The roles of the community practitioner in this approach include enabler, catalyst, coordinator, and teacher of problem-solving skills and ethical values. The approach assumes that conflicts that arise between various interest groups can be creatively and constructively handled. It encourages people to express their differences freely but assumes people will put aside their self-interests in order to further the interests of their community. The approach assumes people will put aside their self-interests through appeals to altruism. The basic theme of this approach is "Together we can figure out what to do and do it." The approach seeks to use discussion and communication between different factions to reach consensus about the problems to focus on and the strategies or actions to resolve these problems. A few examples of locality development efforts include neighborhood work programs conducted by community-based agencies; Volunteers in Service to America; village-level work in some overseas community development programs, including the Peace

*This section is adapted from *Introduction to Social Work and Social Welfare*, by Charles Zastrow. Copyright © 1992, 1988, 1982, 1978, Brooks/Cole Publishing Company, a division of International Thomson Publishing Inc., Pacific Grove, CA 93950. By permission of the publisher.

CASE EXAMPLE OF THE LOCALITY DEVELOPMENT MODEL

Robert McKearn, a social worker for a juvenile probation department, noticed in 1985 that an increasing number of school-age children were being referred to his office by the police department, school system, and parents from a small city of 11,000 people in the county served by his agency. The charges included status offenses (such as truancy from school) and delinquent offenses (such as shoplifting and burglary). Mr. McKearn noted that most of these children were from single-parent families.

Mr. McKearn contacted the community mental health center, the self-help organization Parents Without Partners, the pupil services department of the public school system, the county social services department, some members of the clergy, and the community mental health center in the area. Nearly everyone he contacted saw an emerging need to better serve children in single-parent families. The pupil services department mentioned that such children were performing less well academically in school and tended to display more serious disciplinary problems.

Mr. McKearn arranged a meeting of representatives from the groups and organizations that were contacted.

At the initial meeting a number of concerns were expressed about the problematic behaviors being displayed by children who had single parents. The school system considered these children to be "at risk" for higher rates of truancy, dropping out of school, delinquent activities, suicide, emotional problems, and unwanted pregnancies. Although a number of problems were identified, no one at this initial meeting was able to suggest a viable strategy to better serve single parents and their children. The community was undergoing an economic recession; therefore, funds were unavailable for an expensive new program.

Three more meetings were held. At the first two a number of suggestions for providing services were discussed, but all were viewed as either too expensive or impractical. At the fourth meeting of the group, a single parent representing Parents Without Partners mentioned that she was aware that Big Brothers and Big Sisters programs in some communities were of substantial benefit to children who were raised in single-parent families. This idea seemed to energize the group. Suggestions began to "piggy back." The group, however, determined that funds were unavailable to hire staff to run a Big Brothers and Big Sisters program. However, Rhona Quinn, a social worker in the pupil services department, noted that she was willing to identify at-risk younger children in single-parent families and that she would be willing to supervise qualified volunteers in a "Big Buddy" program.

Mr. McKearn mentioned that he was currently supervising a student in an undergraduate field placement for an accredited social work program from a college in a nearby community. He noted that perhaps arrangements could be made for undergraduate social work students to be "Big Buddies" for their required volunteer experience. Rhona Quinn said she would approve of the suggestion if she could have the freedom to screen interested applicants for being "Big Buddies." Arrangements were made over the next two months for social work students to be "Big Buddies" for at-risk younger children from single-parent families. After a two-year experimental period, the school system found the program sufficiently successful that it assigned Ms. Quinn half-time to supervise the program, which included selecting at-risk children, screening volunteer applicants, matching children with Big Buddies, monitoring the progress of each matched pair, and conducting follow-up to ascertain the outcome of each pairing.

CASE EXAMPLE OF THE SOCIAL PLANNING MODEL

In the mid-1960s the U.S. Department of Health, Education and Welfare mandated (for several years) that every community in the nation had to provide information and referral (I&R) services about social services. If the I&R services met federal guidelines, the federal government would reimburse local communities for 75 percent of the cost. In Wisconsin, the State Department of Human Services met with local planning agencies and encouraged them to develop I&R services in their local communities. The state agreed to reimburse local communities for an additional 12.5 percent of the cost. This reimbursement schedule meant local communities could provide I&R services for only 12.5 percent of the total cost.

The board of directors of Lincoln County Social Planning Agency authorized its staff to do a feasibility study on establishing a centralized information and referral center. Donald Levi (social planner on the staff) was assigned to direct the study. Mr. Levi collected the following data:

> There were over 350 community service agencies and organizations in this largely metropolitan county. Not only clients but also service providers were confused about what services were available from this array of agencies.
>
> There was a confusing array of specialized information and referral services being developed. (Specialized information and referral services provided I&R services in only one or two areas.) There were specialized information and referral services developing in suicide prevention, mental health, mental retardation, day care, adoption services, and alcohol and drug treatment.

Mr. Levi then designed a program model for providing a centralized information and referral service. The model involved a service that would provide I&R services on *all* human and community services in the county. For example, I&R would provide information not only on available day-care services but also on where to find public tennis courts and whom to call to remove a stray cat killed in front of your house. The centralized information and referral service number would be widely publicized on television, radio, and billboards, in newspapers and telephone directories, and so on. A budget was developed by Mr. Levi for the program costs.

The board of directors of the Lincoln County Social Planning Agency concluded that such a centralized information and referral service would be more efficient and economical than the confusing array of specialized information and referral services that had been developing. The board therefore authorized Mr. Levi to pursue the development of a centralized I&R service.

Mr. Levi conducted a questionnaire survey of all the human service agencies in the county and of all the clergy in the county. The results showed that both groups strongly supported the development of a centralized I&R service. In addition, the Easter Seal Society felt so strongly that such a service was needed that they contacted Mr. Levi to indicate that the organization was willing to donate funds for the new program. Mr. Levi was delighted, and an arrangement was worked out for the Easter Seal Society to fund the program for a three-year demonstration period.

The only remaining barrier was that federal and state guidelines required that the program be approved by the county welfare board before reimbursement would be made. Mr. Levi and two members of the board of the Lincoln County Social Planning Agency presented the new program proposal to the county's welfare board. The presentation included graphs showing the savings of a centralized I&R service over specialized I&R services and contained written statements of support from a variety of sources, including city council members, the United Way, human service agencies, and members of the clergy. It was also indicated there would be no cost to the county for a three-year demonstration period. At the end of the demonstration project there would be an evaluative study of the merits and shortcomings of the program. Mr. Levi fully ex-

CASE EXAMPLE OF THE
SOCIAL PLANNING MODEL *(con't.)*

pected approval. He was speechless when the county welfare board said no. They indicated that they turned the proposal down because they felt a centralized I&R would mean that more people would be referred to county social service agencies, which would raise costs to the county, and because they thought there would be

pressure on the county to fund the program after the three-year demonstration project ended.

The county continued to be served by less efficient and less effective specialized I&R services. This case example realistically illustrates that some planning efforts are unsuccessful.

Corps; and a variety of activities performed by self-help groups. A case example of the locality development model is presented in the first box ("Locality Development Model").

Social Planning Model

The second model, the social planning approach, emphasizes a technical process of problem solving. The approach assumes that community change in a complex industrial environment requires highly trained and skilled planners who can guide complex change processes. The role of the expert is stressed in this approach to identifying and resolving social problems. The expert or planner is generally employed by a segment of the power structure, such as area planning agency, city or county planning department, mental health center, United Way board, Community Welfare Council, and so on. Because the social planner is employed by a segment of the power structure, there is a tendency for the planner to serve the interests of the power structure. Building community capacity or facilitating radical social change is generally not an emphasis in this approach.

The planner's roles in this approach include gathering facts, analyzing data, and serving as program designer, implementer, and facilitator. Community participation may vary from little to substantial with this approach, depending on the community's attitudes toward the problems being addressed. For example, an effort to design and obtain funding for a community center for the elderly may or may not result in substantial involvement by interested community groups, depending on the politics surrounding such a center. Much of the focus of the social planning approach is on identifying needs and on arranging and delivering goods and services to people who need them. The change focus of this approach is "Let's get the facts and take the next rational steps." A case example of this approach is presented in the second box ("Social Planning Model").

Social Action Model

The third model, the social action approach, assumes there is a disadvantaged (often oppressed) segment of the population that needs to be organized, perhaps in alliance with others, in order to pressure the power structure for increased resources or for treatment more in accordance with democracy or social justice. Social action approaches at times seek basic changes in major institutions or seek changes in basic policies of formal organizations. Such approaches often seek redistribution of power and resources. Unlike in the vision of a unified community held by locality developers, the power structure or opposition is the target of action. Perhaps the best-known social activist was Saul Alinsky, who advised, "Pick the target, freeze it, personalize it, and polarize it."[5]

The roles of the community practitioner in this approach include advocate, agitator, activist, partisan, broker, and negotiator. Tactics used in social action projects include protests, boycotts, confrontation, and negotiation. The change strategy is one of "Let's organize to overpower our oppressor."[6] The client population is viewed as being a "victim" of the oppressive power structure. Examples of the social action approach include boycotts during the civil rights movement during the 1960s, strikes by unions, protests by anti-abortion groups, and protests by African-American and Native American groups.

The social action model is not widely used by social workers at present. Many workers find that being involved in social action activities may lead their employing agencies

CASE EXAMPLE OF THE SOCIAL ACTION MODEL

Saul Alinsky, a nationally noted social action strategist, provides an example of a creative social action effort. The example also shows that social action efforts are often enjoyable.

I was lecturing at a college run by a very conservative, almost fundamentalist Protestant denomination. Afterward some of the students came to my motel to talk to me. Their problem was that they couldn't have any fun on campus. They weren't permitted to dance or smoke or have a can of beer. I had been talking about the strategy of effecting change in a society and they wanted to know what tactics they could use to change their situation. I reminded them that a tactic is doing what you can with what you've got. "Now, what have you got?"

I asked. "What do they permit you to do?" "Practically nothing," they said, "except—you know—we can chew gum." I said, "Fine. Gum becomes the weapon. You get 200 or 300 students to get two packs of gum each, which is quite a wad. Then you have them drop it on the campus walks. This will cause absolute chaos. Why, with 500 wads of gum I could paralyze Chicago, stop all the traffic in the Loop." They looked at me as though I was some kind of nut. But about two weeks later I got an ecstatic letter saying, "It worked! It worked! Now we can do just about anything so long as we don't chew gum."

Source: Saul Alinsky, *Rules for Radicals* (New York: Random House, 1972), pp. 145-146.

to penalize them with unpleasant work assignments, low merit increases, and denial of promotions. Many agencies will accept minor and moderate changes in their service delivery systems but are threatened by the prospect of radical changes that are often advocated by the social action approach.

An example of the social action approach is presented in the third box ("Social Action Model"). Table 13.1 presents a summary of the three models that have been discussed: locality development, social planning, and social action.

Table 13.1

Characteristics of Three Models of Community Planning

Characteristic	Locality Development	Social Planning	Social Action
1. Goals	Self-help; improve community living; emphasis on process goals	Use problem-solving approach to resolve community problems; emphasis on task goals	Shifts power relationships and resources to an oppressed group; create basic institutional change; emphasize task and process goals
2. Assumptions concerning community	Everyone wants community living to improve and is willing to contribute to that improvement.	Social problems in the community can be resolved through the efforts of planning experts.	The community has a power structure and one or more oppressed groups, so social injustice is a major problem.
3. Basic change strategy	Broad cross section of people involved in identifying and solving problems	Experts using fact-gathering and problem-solving approach.	Members of oppressed groups organizing to take action against the power structure—i.e., the enemy
4. Characteristic change tactics and techniques	Consensus: communication among community groups and interests; group discussion	Consensus or conflict	Conflict or contest: confrontation, direct action, negotiation
5. Practitioner roles	Catalyst; facilitator; coordinator; teacher of problem-solving skills	Expert planner; fact gatherer; analyst; program developer; and implementor	Activist; advocate agitator; broker; negotiator; partisan
6. Views of power structure	Members of power structure are collaborators in a common venture.	Power structure is employers and sponsors.	Power structure is external target of action, oppressors to be coerced or overturned.
7. Views of client population	Citizens	Consumers	Victims
8. Views of client role	Participant in a problem-solving process	Consumer or recipient	Employer or constituent

GROUP EXERCISES

Exercise A: Analyzing a Community

Goal: This exercise is designed to instruct students in understanding and analyzing communities.

Step 1. The leader begins by defining the term "community." Subgroups of three or four students are then formed. Each subgroup selects a different community to analyze.

Step 2. Using the framework presented in this chapter (or some other framework chosen by the subgroup) each subgroup gathers information on the community it selected. At future class sessions, each subgroup makes a presentation to the class on its selected community.

Exercise B: Analyzing Community Change

Goal: This exercise is designed to have students learn how to analyze community change efforts.

Step 1. The leader should describe the three models of community change developed by Rothman and Tropman. These models are: locality development, social planning, and social action. In addition to describing these approaches, the leader should instruct the students to read the related material in this chapter.

Step 2. Have the class form subgroups of about three students each. Each subgroup should select a different community change or community planning effort to report on to the class. An example of a planning effort is a project by the social work student organization to plan an educational conference or workshop on a topic such as AIDS. Another example is the efforts of a community group to establish a homeless shelter.

Step 3. Each subgroup should gather information to answer the following questions about its selected community change effort. One way to gather the information is for the subgroup to interview the planners. In future class sessions each subgroup should give a presentation to the class on its selected planning effort.

QUESTIONS
 a. What are the goals of the planning effort? How many planners are involved? Who are the planners, and what are their planning credentials? Why is this planning effort being undertaken?
 b. Which of the three community change models is this planning group primarily using? What characteristics of this model (see table 13.1) are being displayed by the planners? Does this planning effort have any characteristics of these other two models? If "yes," what characteristics of the other two models are being displayed?
 c. What are the results of this planning effort—that is, to what extent are the goals being accomplished? What are the strengths and shortcomings of this planning effort?

PART SIX

SELF-HELP AND EDUCATIONAL GROUPS

CHAPTER FOURTEEN

SELF-HELP GROUPS

TO ALL THE SIGNS THAT MAKE
DRIVING A LITTLE SAFER,
WE'D LIKE TO ADD ONE MORE.

Even though your ability to drive a car is seriously impaired at a
blood alcohol level of .08, most states only prosecute at .10 or higher.
We'd like every state to make .08 the blood alcohol limit.
If you want to help, please call or write your state legislators.
Together we can make this a sign of life.

MADD
Mothers Against Drunk Driving

Goal: Self-help groups constitute one alternative to coping alone by assisting members to meet their specific needs through the understanding and help of others who have had similar experiences. This chapter describes the objectives of self-help groups, outlines some of the therapeutic principles they use, and discusses the reasons self-help groups are effective.

MENDED HEARTS: AN EXAMPLE

Founded by four patients recovering from heart surgery in a Boston hospital, Mended Hearts is now a national organization for heart surgery patients and their families.[1] The four patients shared their concerns about their uncertain future, and the pain and changes in life style they faced. They also focused on the positives—new feelings of well-being, their plans and hopes for the future, and the happiness they experienced from having "mended hearts." From these experiences, they concluded such conversations would be immensely helpful to others facing heart surgery. With the assistance of a heart surgeon, Dr. Dwight Harken, they formed the first Mended Hearts group in 1951. They adopted the slogan, "It's great to be alive and to help others." Mended Hearts was formally incorporated in 1955, and a constitution and bylaws were adopted. As hospitals began performing heart surgeries in other regions in the country in the 1960s, chapters of Mended Hearts were formed in these regions. With the number of heart surgeries sharply increasing since the 1960s, the number of chapters and members has grown dramatically.

Meetings are typically held in the hospitals where heart surgeries are performed. At a typical meeting, a physician or medical expert will speak on an aspect of heart disease, surgery, and the recovery process. Other meetings will feature other topics and speakers on exercise, social security, nutrition, insurance, employment, or related topics. A question-and-answer period usually follows. Light refreshments are then generally served. The meetings are open to heart patients, their spouses, and professionals.

Local chapters generally have a monthly newsletter with a variety of information: advances in heart surgery, inspirational material, anniversaries of members' heart surgeries, and announcements of the activities of the local and national organizations.

An important service provided by Mended Hearts is accredited visitors who visit heart patients before and after surgery to offer support, information, and encouragement. To become accredited, visitors, who have all had heart surgery, attend a series of seminars (involving eight to ten hours of training) that consist of lectures, role plays, and discussions of visitor guidelines. They are then tested on their knowledge of functions of the heart, various heart problems, and the corresponding treatment approaches. Before visiting by themselves, prospective visitors accompany accredited visitors on their hospital rounds. This process screens potential visitors to ensure an effective, high-quality program.

In a study of the impact of Mended Hearts, Borman and Lieberman conclude:

> Our findings with Mended Hearts . . . indicate that those patients who are forced into early retirement seem to benefit the most from their service responsibilities as Mended Heart visitors. At the same time, from the perspective of those about to undergo heart surgery, such visits from those who have had the experience seem to be most welcome.[2]

DEFINITION AND CHARACTERISTICS

Self-help groups are diverse. Some are small, grassroots affiliations unrelated to external structures. Others are part of large, well-organized, national organizations. The diversity of self-help groups has been summarized by Lieberman and Borman:

Self-help groups have been seen as support systems; as social movements; as spiritual movements and secular religions; as systems of consumer participation; as alternative care-giving systems adjunct to professional helping systems; as intentional communities; as subcultural entities that represent a way of life; as supplementary communities; as expressive-social influence groups; and as organizations of the deviant and stigmatized.[3]

Hepworth and Larsen define self-help groups this way:

Self-help groups consist of people who share common conditions, experiences, or problematic situations (e.g., obesity, alcoholism, child abuse, minority status, history of mental disorders, parents of developmentally disabled children, or single parents) and mutually seek to assist each other to enhance their coping capacities related to their common factors. The help these groups provide is available without charge and is based on the experiences of members rather than professional expertise. Largely self-governing and self-regulating, self-help groups generally have effective communication networks among members that, in addition to regular group meetings, provide opportunities for both telephone and face-to-face contacts.[4]

Self-help groups emphasize peer solidarity rather than hierarchical governance. They tend to disregard in their organizational structure the usual institutional distinctions between board of directors, professionals, and consumers, as members (at various times) give and receive help and share responsibility for performing leadership tasks and for accomplishing the goals of the group. Self-help groups tend to be self-supporting and thrive largely on donations from friends and relatives rather than on government funds, foundation grants, or fees from the public.

Riessman summarizes the distinctive characteristics of self-help groups as follows:

- a noncompetitive, cooperative orientation;
- an anti-elite, antibureaucratic focus;
- an emphasis on the indigenous—people who have the problem and know a lot about it from the inside, from experiencing it;
- an attitude of do what you can, one day at a time. You can't solve everything at once.
- a shared, often revolving leadership;
- an attitude of being helped through helping (the helper-therapy principle) . . .;
- an understanding that helping is not a commodity to be bought and sold;
- a strong optimism regarding the ability to change;
- an understanding that although small may not necessarily be beautiful, it is the place to begin and the unit to build on;
- a critical stance toward professionalism, which is often seen as pretentious, purist, distant, and mystifying. Self-helpers like simplicity and informality.
- an emphasis on the consumer, or, in Alvin Toffler's term, the "prosumer." The consumer is a producer of help and services;
- an understanding that helping is at the center—knowing how to receive help, give help, and help yourself. . . .
- an emphasis on empowerment.[5]

When people help each other in self-help groups, they tend to feel empowered, as they are able to control important aspects of their lives. When help is given from the outside (from an expert or a professional), there is a danger that dependency may develop, which is the opposite effect of empowerment. Empowerment increases motivation, energy, personal growth, and an ability to help that goes beyond helping oneself or receiving help.

TYPES OF SELF-HELP GROUPS

Two different classifications of self-help groups will be summarized in order to convey the varieties and focuses of self-help groups that now exist. The first classification is by Katz and Bender, and the second, by Powell.

Katz and Bender Classification

Katz and Bender have formulated the following classification of self-help groups:[6]

1. Groups that focus on self-fulfillment or personal growth. Examples are Alcoholics Anonymous; Recovery, Inc. (for former mental patients); Gamblers Anonymous; and Weight Watchers.
2. Groups that focus on social advocacy. Examples are Welfare Rights Organizations, MADD (Mothers Against Drunk Drivers), and The Committee for the Rights of the Disabled. Katz and Bender note that the advocacy "can be both on behalf of broad issues, such as legislation, the creation of new services, change in the policies of existing institutions and so on; or it can be on behalf of individuals, families, or other small groups."[7]
3. Groups whose focus is to create alternative patterns for living. Examples are Gay Liberation and certain religious cults such as the Moonies.
4. "Outcast haven" or "rock-bottom" groups. Katz and Bender define this type as follows:

   These groups provide a refuge for the desperate, who are attempting to secure personal protection from the pressures of life and society, or to save themselves from mental or physical decline. This type of group usually involves a total commitment, a living-in arrangement or sheltered environment, with close supervision by peers or persons who have successfully grappled with similar problems of their own.[8]

   Examples include Synanon, at least in its early years, and many other ex-drug addict organizations.
5. Groups of mixed types that have characteristics of two or more categories. An example is Parents Without Partners, which focuses on personal growth, advocacy, and providing social events.

Powell Classification

Powell classifies self-help groups into the following five categories:[9]

1. *Habit disturbance organizations.* These organizations focus on a problem that is specific and concrete. Examples of this category include Alcoholics Anonymous, Smoke-

stoppers, Overeaters Anonymous, Gamblers Anonymous, Take Off Pounds Sensibly (TOPS), Women for Sobriety, Narcotics Anonymous, and Weight Watchers.

2. *General purpose organizations.* These organizations address a wide range of problems and predicaments. Examples of this category are Parents Anonymous (for parents of abused children), Emotions Anonymous (for persons with emotional problems), the Compassionate Friends (for persons who have experienced a loss through death), and GROW, an organization that works to prevent the hospitalization of mental patients through a comprehensive program of mutual aid. In contrast to habit disturbance organizations, general purpose organizations address a wider range of problems and predicaments.

3. *Lifestyle organizations.* These organizations seek to provide support for, and advocate for, the lifestyles of people whose members are viewed by society as being different (the dominant groups in society are generally indifferent or hostile to that difference). Examples of this category include Widow-to-Widow Programs, Parents Without Partners, ALMA (Adoptees' Liberty Movement Association), Parents/FLAG (Parents and Friends of Lesbians and Gays), National Gay and Lesbian Task Force, and the Gray Panthers, an intergenerational group that advocates for the elderly.

4. *Physical handicap organizations.* These organizations focus on major chronic diseases and conditions. Some are for people with conditions that are relatively stable, some for conditions that are likely to get worse, and some for terminal illnesses. Examples of this category include Make Today Count (for the terminally ill and their families), Emphysema Anonymous, Lost Chord clubs (for those who have had laryngectomies), stroke clubs, Mended Hearts, the Spina Bifida Association, and Self-Help for Hard of Hearing People.

5. *Significant other organizations.* The members of these organizations are parents, spouses, and close relatives of troubled and troubling persons. Very often, members of significant other groups are last-resort care-givers. Significant others contend with dysfunctional behavior. Through sharing their feelings, they obtain a measure of relief. In the course of sharing, they may also learn about new resources or new approaches. Examples of such organizations include Al-Anon, Gam-Anon, Toughlove, and the National Alliance for the Mentally Ill.

WHY SELF-HELP GROUPS ARE BENEFICIAL

Many direct service self-help groups stress: (1) a confession to the group that they have a problem; (2) a testimony to the group recounting their past experiences with the problem and their plans for handling the problem in the future; (3) the requirement that when a member feels an intense urge of a recurrence (such as to drink or to abuse a child), she calls another member of the group who comes over to stay with the person until the urge subsides.

There appear to be several other reasons such self-help groups are successful. The members have an internal understanding of the problem, which helps them to help others. Having experienced the misery and consequences of the problem, they are highly motivated and dedicated to finding ways to help themselves and their fellow sufferers. The participants also benefit from the "helper therapy principle"; that is, the helper gains psychological rewards by helping others.[10] Helping others makes a person feel "good" and worthwhile, and enables the helper to put his own problems into perspective. Others have problems that may be as serious or more serious than his.

Some self-help groups (such as parents of the mentally retarded) raise funds and operate community programs. Many people with a personal problem use self-help groups in the same way that others use social agencies. An additional advantage of self-help groups is that they generally operate with a minimal budget. As discussed earlier, self-help groups often empower their members. Hundreds of self-help groups are now in existence.

Many people who have problematic behaviors (such as abusing their children) have few friends and relatives they can turn to for help and are thus socially isolated. Those who join a self-help group soon become aware that associating with caring others who have experienced similar problems is a source of immense support. Hepworth and Larsen summarize some of the benefits of a self-help group for members:

1. Having a reference group wherein one shares common problems or concerns with others and is accepted by them.
2. Gaining hope based on the knowledge that other members have experienced similar difficulties and are coping (or have coped) successfully with them.
3. Confronting problems head-on and accepting responsibility for them as a result of confrontations by other members.
4. Putting their problems in perspective and applying knowledge and skill derived from the experiences shared by others.[11]

Borman found five therapeutic factors of direct service self-help groups:

1. *Cognitive restructuring.* Members develop a new perspective on themselves and their problems.
2. *Hope.* Members develop hope that their life will get better as they see the lives of others with similar problems have improved.
3. *Altruism.* Members feel good about themselves for helping others.
4. *Acceptance.* Members feel they will not be rejected or blamed for their problems.
5. *Universality.* Members become aware that they are not alone in having the problems they face.[12]

LINKAGE WITH SOCIAL WORKERS

Because self-help groups are often more effective than one-to-one counseling or group therapy in treating problematic behaviors, it is vitally important that social workers relate to them constructively. Social workers need to be aware of the self-help groups available in the community in which they work so they can function as brokers or case managers in making appropriate referrals for clients. Social workers also need to be knowledgeable about how self-help groups function so that they work in synergy, rather than in competition, with such programs.

Another major function that social workers can perform with self-help groups is to be consultants. There is a myth that self-help groups are antiprofessional. In reality, many were started with the help of one or more professionals, and most continue to receive professional consultation. Professionals can provide support and consultation on organiza-

EXAMPLES OF SELF-HELP GROUPS

ORGANIZATION	SERVICE FOCUS
Abused Women's Aid in Crisis	For battered wives and other abused women
Adoptee's Liberty Movement Association	For adoptees searching for their natural parents
Alcoholics Anonymous	For adult alcoholics
American Diabetes Association	Clubs for diabetics, their families, and friends
Brain Tumor Support Group	For persons with brain tumors or their loved ones
Burns Recovered	For burn victims
Caesarian Birth Association	For those expecting a cesarean birth
Candlelighters	For parents of young children with cancer
Checks Anonymous	For persons in debt
Concerned United Birthparents	For parents who have surrendered children for adoption
Depressives Anonymous	For depressed persons
Divorce Anonymous	For divorced persons
Emotions Anonymous	For persons with emotional problems
Emphysema Anonymous	For those with emphysema
Fly Without Fear	For people who are afraid of flying
Fortune Society	For ex-offenders and their families
Gam-Anon	For families of gamblers
Gray Panthers	An intergenerational group
Make Today Count	For persons with cancer and their families
Naim Conference	For widowed persons
The National Conference of Stutterers	For adult stutterers
National Organization for Women	For women's rights
Overeaters Anonymous	For overweight persons
Parents Anonymous	For parents of abused children
Phobia Self-Help Groups	For persons with phobias
Prison Families Anonymous	For family members of prisoners
Resolve	A support group for infertile people
Stroke Clubs	For those who have had strokes and their families
Survivors of Suicide Victims	For the relatives and friends of suicide victims
We Care	Support group for divorced and separated persons

Note: Alan Gartner and Frank Riessman in *Help: A Working Guide to Self-Help Groups* (New York: Franklin-Watts, 1980) describe more than two hundred self-help groups. Thomas J. Powell in *Self-Help and Professional Practice* (Silver Spring, MD: National Association of Social Workers, 1987) also describes a number of self-help groups.

tional issues, resources for members in unique circumstances, fund-raising activities, efforts to enact or change legislation, and social advocacy efforts to change the service policies of one or more agencies. Maguire has provided a partial list of the ways in which a professional can assist a self-help group:

1. Help arrange a meeting place.
2. Help locate funds.
3. Refer members to the group.
4. Arrange or provide training of members and of leaders.
5. Accept referrals from the group.
6. Help provide credibility of the group within the professional community and within the community.[13]

Another important function that social workers can serve is to help form needed self-help groups in a community. Hepworth and Larsen note:

Practitioners can also serve as organizers where resources are sparse and appropriate self-help groups do not exist. By working with clients who demonstrate leadership potential, a practitioner may stimulate them, assisting them as needed, to contact a national or regional self-help organization for the purpose of establishing a local chapter. If a national organization does not exist, the practitioner may serve as a catalyst and consultant in organizing a local group, which necessitates working with selected lay leaders in recruiting members, developing objectives and bylaws (if needed), arranging facilities, planning refreshments, and developing an organizational meeting.[14]

STARTING A SELF-HELP GROUP

Starting a self-help group is similar to starting any group. If there is a national organization, it is essential to contact this organization to get its material on guidelines for establishing a local chapter. If a national organization does not exist, then it may be necessary to start from "scratch." The following kinds of questions need to be answered:

1. What are the goals of the group?
2. What kinds of services should be provided to meet the goals?
3. What are the criteria for membership?
4. What are the costs; for example, will dues be charged?
5. Where will the group meet?
6. How will potential members be contacted?
7. What are the procedures for joining and leaving the group?
8. What kind of organizational structure should the group have?

Answers to these questions should not be arrived at by the professional alone. Self-help groups tend to work best when concerned and motivated individuals who are facing a problem meet and arrive at answers to these questions. Most self-help groups have evolved as circumstances warrant rather than being carefully planned from the start.

A few comments will be made about some of these questions. Usually the nature of the problem will determine how to contact potential members. For example, if former

ALCOHOLICS ANONYMOUS: A SELF-HELP GROUP

In 1929, Bill Wilson was a stock analyst. When the stock market crashed, he lost most of his money and took to the bottle. A few years later his doctor warned him that his continual drinking was jeopardizing his health and his life. Bill W. underwent what he perceived was a spiritual experience, and he made a commitment to stop drinking. He had discovered that discussing his drinking problem with other alcoholics helped him to remain sober. One of the people he discussed his problem with was Robert Smith, an Ohio doctor and an alcoholic. Together they formed Alcoholics Anonymous, a self-help group composed of recovering alcoholics.

AA stresses: (a) an admission to the group that the member has a drinking problem; (b) a testimony to the group recounting past experiences with the drinking problem and plans for handling the problem in the future; and (c) support from another member of the group, who will even stay with a person who feels an intense urge to drink until the urge subsides. Today, AA has chapters in over one hundred countries.

The term "recovering" is used because AA believes there is no such thing as a permanently recovered alcoholic. The local chapters (usually from ten to thirty persons per chapter) meet once or twice a week for discussion sessions. These groups resemble traditional group therapy meetings without the presence of a trained professional leader.

Bill W. and Dr. Bob, as they are known within AA, remained anonymous until their deaths. Local chapters still follow the treatment procedures they initiated—the sharing of similar experiences in order to abstain from the first drink that is too many and the thousand drinks that are not enough.

AA is still widely regarded as the treatment approach that has the best chance of helping an alcoholic. In testimony to its value are hundreds of other self-help groups with treatment programs based on the AA model—Weight Watchers, Prison Families Anonymous, Parents Without Partners, Debtors Anonymous, Gamblers Anonymous, Emotions Anonymous, Emphysema Anonymous, and many more.

1. Alan Gartner and Frank Riessman, *Help: A Working Guide to Self-Help Groups* (New York: Franklin-Watts, 1980), p. 8.

---

heart surgery patients want to start a Mended Hearts chapter, they should first contact heart surgeons to explain the group and to determine if the surgeons would like a local chapter of Mended Hearts at the hospital. The surgeons can be a valuable resource by providing access to new patients facing heart surgery. For other groups, prospective members may be contacted in a variety of ways: radio and television announcements, notices in church buildings and social service agencies, flyers to service providers, door-to-door solicitation, flyers mailed to target groups, and notices in local newspapers.

Generally, it is best to hold meetings at a public agency, business, church, or private agency. If meetings are held in the home of a member, that member may eventually decide that regular meetings are too much of an inconvenience. Rotating meetings in the homes of individual members is generally not a good idea either because members may find it frustrating to continually locate new places. New members may get so discouraged with changes in the meeting place that they drop out.

In the process of starting a self-help group Lieberman and Borman note:

There is an early zig-zag process of groping, trying out various approaches, dropping some, and developing new ones. Changes occur on a number of fronts . . .: (1) organizational size; (2) organizational structure; (3) program focus; (4) nature of membership; (5) nature of leadership; (6) articulation with professionals and agencies; and (7) sources of financial support.[15]

GROUP EXERCISES

Exercise A: Alcoholics Anonymous

Goal: To increase awareness of how a self-help group functions.

Step 1. Local chapters of Alcoholics Anonymous usually hold some open meetings that anyone may attend. The leader contacts a local chapter, inquires whether the class may attend, and makes the necessary arrangements—including time, date, and place. If these arrangements cannot be made with AA, the leader contacts other self-help groups in the community.

Step 2. At the class period following the meeting of the self-help group, the leader leads a discussion of the students' thoughts about the meeting they attended. The class also discusses the merits and shortcomings of this self-help group.

Exercise B: Combatting AIDS

Goal: To increase awareness of how a social action self-help group functions.

Step 1. The leader explains the purpose of the exercise and indicates AIDS may be the most serious disease ever faced by the human race. The students are told that their function is to serve as a social action self-help group. The class forms subgroups of five or six persons. Each subgroup has the task of developing recommendations that this self-help group will then pursue to protect humans from the spread of AIDS. (If the leader thinks it advisable, some other topic may be chosen.)

Step 2. Each subgroup selects its top three recommendations for combatting AIDS.

Step 3. The class reassembles. Each subgroup presents its three recommendations, and they are listed on the blackboard. The students then select the top five recommendations their self-help group ought to pursue. A discussion should then follow on how this self-help group can realistically seek to implement these recommendations.

CHAPTER FIFTEEN

STRESS MANAGEMENT

Goals: Stress is considered to be a contributing factor or cause of most physical illnesses and many emotional and behavioral problems. This chapter presents material on the nature, causes, and effects of stress and describes burn-out as one of the reactions to stress. A variety of ways to manage stress and prevent burn-out are included. (In regard to the types of groups described in chapter 1, a stress management group is an educational group.)

It is essential that students, social workers, and other helping professionals learn how to manage stress in themselves and how to help their clients manage stress. Stress is a contributing factor in a wide variety of *emotional and behavioral problems,* including anxiety, child abuse, spouse abuse, temper tantrums, feelings of inadequacy, physical assaults, explosive expressions of anger, feelings of hostility, impatience, stuttering, suicide attempts, and depression.[1]

Stress is also a contributing factor in most physical illnesses. These illnesses include hypertension, heart attacks, migraine and tension headaches, colitis, ulcers, diarrhea, constipation, arrhythmia, angina, diabetes, hay fever, backaches, arthritis, cancer, colds, flu, insomnia, hyperthyroidism, dermatitis, emphysema, Raynaud's disease, alcoholism, bronchitis, infections, allergies, and enuresis. Stress-related disorders have now been recognized as our number-one health problem.[2]

Becoming skillful at relaxation is important in treating and facilitating recovery from both emotional and physical disorders. The therapeutic value of learning how to manage stress has been dramatically demonstrated by Simonton and Simonton, who have reported success in treating terminal cancer patients by instructing them on stress management.[3] People who have AIDS tend to live longer if they utilize stress management techniques.[4]

In fact, the increased recognition of the importance of stress management in treating physical and emotional disorders is gradually altering the traditional physician-patient relationship. Instead of being passive participants in treatment, patients are increasingly being taught (by social workers and other health professionals) how to prevent illness and how to speed up recovery by learning stress management strategies.

People who are successful in managing stress have a life expectancy several years longer than those who are continually at high stress levels.[5] Moreover, effective stress management is a major factor that enables people to live fulfilling, healthy, satisfying, and productive lives.[6]

CONCEPTUALIZING STRESS

Stress can be defined as the physiological and emotional reactions to stressors. A *stressor* is a demand, situation, or circumstance that disrupts a person's equilibrium (internal balance) and initiates the stress response. Every second people are alive their bodies are responding to stressors that call for adaptation or adjustment. Their bodily reactions are continually striving for *homeostasis,* or balance. There are an infinite variety of possible stressors: loss of a job, loud noise, toxic substances, value conflicts, arguments, death of a friend, getting engaged, getting married, heat, cold, pollutants, serious illness, moving away from home, lack of purpose in life.

Reactions to Stress

Hans Selye, one of the foremost authorities on stress, found that a person's body reacts to stressors in the same way regardless of the source of stress.[7] This means an individual's body reacts to positive stressors (e.g., a romantic kiss) in the same way it reacts to negative stressors (e.g., an electric shock).

Selye found a three-stage physical reaction to stress: an alarm phase, a resistance phase, and an exhaustion phase.[8] Selye called this three-phase response the General Adaptation Syndrome.

In the *alarm phase* the body recognizes the stressor and responds by preparing for fight or flight. The body's reactions are numerous and complex, and will be only briefly summarized here.[9] The hypothalamus (located in the brain) sends a message to the pituitary gland to release its hormones. These hormones trigger the adrenal glands to release adrenaline. The release of adrenaline and other hormones results in the following:

1. Increased breathing and heartbeat rates
2. A rise in blood pressure
3. Increased coagulation of blood, which minimizes potential loss of blood in case of physical injury
4. Diversion of blood from the skin to the brain, the heart, and contracting muscles
5. A rise in serum cholesterol and blood fat
6. Decreased mobility of the gastrointestinal tract
7. Dilated pupils

These changes result in a huge burst of energy, improved vision and hearing, and increased muscular strength—all changes that increase a person's capacity to fight or to flee. A major problem of the fight-or-flight reaction is that a threat cannot always be dealt with by fighting or fleeing. In our complex civilized society, fighting or fleeing generally runs counter to sophisticated codes of acceptable behavior. The fight-or-flight response was once appropriate and functional for humans, but now it seldom is.

In the *resistance phase*, bodily processes attempt to return to homeostasis, and the body tries to repair any damage caused by the stressors. In handling most stressors, the body generally goes through only the two phases of alarm and repair. During a lifetime these two phases are repeated thousands of times.

The third phase of *exhaustion* occurs only when the body remains in a state of high stress for an extended period of time and is unable to repair damage. If exhaustion continues, a stress-related illness, such as high blood pressure, ulcers, or migraine headaches, may develop.

Stressors

A stressor has two components: (1) the experience or event encountered, and (2) our self-talk about the event.[10] Figure 15.1 presents a model of a stress response indicating both a sequence of events and reactions as they occur.

The following example shows how a person's thinking can turn a potentially positive event into a source of negative stress.

Stressor $\Bigg\{$ **Event:**

Self-talk:

Sharon Kempers is asked out for a date by someone she has wanted to date for a long time.

I'm really worried he won't like me. I'm not a good conversationalist, and he will now notice all the other faults I have. I really don't know what I should wear. He wants me to meet some of his friends, and I'm afraid they won't like me. I'm afraid I'm going to really blow this.

Stress {	**Emotions:** ↓	Anxiety, worry, alarm, tension
	Physiological Reactions:	The alarm stage of the General Adaptation Syndrome is occurring. If sustained and intensive, conditions exist for a stress-related illness to develop.

The model in figure 15.1 suggests two broad approaches for reducing stress: (1) either change the distressing event, or (2) change the self-talk about the event. (These two approaches will be discussed at greater length in a later section.)

It should certainly be noted that not all stress is bad. Life without it would be boring. Hans Selye indicates that stress is often "the spice of life" and that it is impossible it live without experiencing stress.[11] Even dreaming produces stress. At times stress is beneficial, because it stimulates and prepares individuals to perform tasks.

Optimal Levels of Stress

Virtually every task or activity requires some response from the alarm stage of the General Adaptation Syndrome, and for each task there is an optimal level of response. Students, for example, sometimes find that they need to be under moderate stress to study effectively for an exam. At too low a level of alarm stage response, they may have trouble concentrating and may even fall asleep. At too high a level of alarm stage response, they

Figure 15.1: A Model of Stress Response

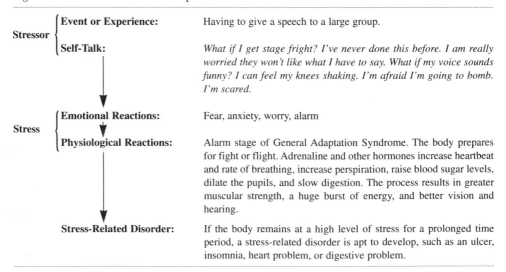

Stressor {	**Event or Experience:**	Having to give a speech to a large group.
	Self-Talk:	*What if I get stage fright? I've never done this before. I am really worried they won't like what I have to say. What if my voice sounds funny? I can feel my knees shaking. I'm afraid I'm going to bomb. I'm scared.*
Stress {	**Emotional Reactions:** ↓	Fear, anxiety, worry, alarm
	Physiological Reactions:	Alarm stage of General Adaptation Syndrome. The body prepares for fight or flight. Adrenaline and other hormones increase heartbeat and rate of breathing, increase perspiration, raise blood sugar levels, dilate the pupils, and slow digestion. The process results in greater muscular strength, a huge burst of energy, and better vision and hearing.
	Stress-Related Disorder:	If the body remains at a high level of stress for a prolonged time period, a stress-related disorder is apt to develop, such as an ulcer, insomnia, heart problem, or digestive problem.

Figure 15.2: Levels of Alarm Stage Response and Efficiency in Performing Tasks

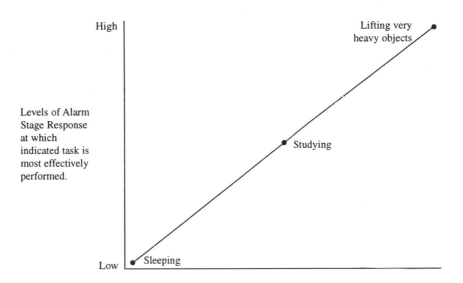

become anxious—which also interferes with concentration. Maximum levels of alarm stage response are needed only during emergencies when great physical strength is required—e.g., when a heavy object has fallen on someone. At the opposite extreme, falling asleep requires relaxation—that is, an almost-zero level of alarm stage response. People who suffer from insomnia are not relaxed. They are still thinking about things which generate a moderate level of alarm stage response and keep them from dozing off. For a graphic illustration of this concept, see figure 15.2

Grasping this concept is important, because self-talk can be altered to increase or decrease levels of alarm stage response and bring it to an optimal level.

LONG-TERM DISTRESS

Dr. Selye calls harmful stress "distress."[12] Long-term distress generally results in a stress-related physical illness. Distress occurs when the stressors are prolonged so that a person enters the exhaustion phase of the General Adaptation Syndrome. There are a number of signals, presented in figure 15.3, that we can use to measure our level of stress. Most of us use the signals identified in figure 15.3 to judge whether our friends are under too much stress. But most of us fail to use these same signals to determine when our own stress level is too high. For our emotional and physical health, we need to give more attention to monitoring these signals in ourselves.

Long-term distress occurs when we think negatively about events that have happened to us. When unpleasant events occur, we always have a choice to react negatively or positively. If we continue to think negatively about the situation, our thinking keeps our body under a high level of stress—which can then lead to a stress-related illness. On the other hand, if we think positively about the situation, our thinking enables the body to relax and repair any damage that was done. In addition, when we are relaxed, our natural immune system is much more effective in combating potential illnesses. There is substantial evidence that our self-talk (that is, our thinking processes) has immense interaction with the functioning of our immune system. Our self-talk can function as both a slayer and a healer. If we *awfulize* (that is, think negative thoughts), we set off the alarm stage of the General Adaptation Syndrome. When we are in the alarm stage, our immune systems are depressed and do not function well. As a result, we are more susceptible to infections and diseases. On the other hand, when we think positive and relaxing thoughts, our bodies are in the re-

Figure 15.3: Indicators of Stress Level

Note: You have to use your own judgment based on these signals to determine whether a stress level is too high.

Positive Level	*Level Too High*
1. Behaviors	
Creative, making good decisions	High-pitched nervous laughter
Friendly	Not creative
Generally successful	Poor work quality
Able to listen to others	Overdrink or overeat
Productive, getting a lot done	Smoke to excess
Appreciate others, sensitive to others, and	Stutter
recognize contributions of others	Unable to concentrate
Smile, laugh, joke	Easily startled by small noises
	Impatient
	Let little things bother you
	Unpleasant to be around
	Put others down, irritable
	Engage in wasteful activity
2. Feelings	
Confident	Resentful, bitter, dissatisfied, angry
Calm, relaxed	Timid, tense, anxious, fearful
Pleasure and enjoyment	Paranoid
Excitement and exhilaration	Weary, depressed, fed up
	Feeling inadequate
	Confused, swamped, overwhelmed
	Feeling powerless or helpless
3. Body Signals	
Able to sleep well	Loss of appetite, diarrhea, or vomiting
Absence of aches and pains	Accident proneness
Coordinated body reactions	Sweating, frequent need to urinate
Unselfconsciousness about body functioning	Trembling, nervous tics
In good health, stress-related illnesses absent	Feeling dizzy or weak
	Frequent colds and flu
	High blood pressure
	Tight or tense muscles
	Asthma or breathing irregularities
	Skin irritations, itches, and rashes
	Problems sleeping
	Upset stomach or ulcers
	Various aches and pains—muscle aches,
	backaches, neck aches, and headaches

sistance stage of the General Adaptation Syndrome, as a result, our immune syst functioning at their optimal level and can fight off diseases and infections and assis pairing any damage caused when our bodies were in the alarm stage.

Earlier it was indicated that our bodies react to positive stressors the same wa react to negative stressors. The reason negative stressors are much more likely to res stress-related disorders is that we tend to stop thinking intensely about positive stres (such as a romantic kiss) within a few hours after they occur, while we tend to inten and dwell on negative stressors for several hours (or even days) after they occur. By thi ing intensely about negative stressors, we keep our bodies under a moderate or high lev of stress.

BURN-OUT

Burn-out is increasingly recognized as a serious problem affecting many people, particularly professionals employed in human services, and several books have been published on this subject.[13] Maslach and Pines have conducted extensive studies of burn-out among social workers, psychiatrists, psychologists, prison personnel, psychiatric nurses, legal-aid attorneys, physicians, child-care workers, teachers, ministers, and counselors, and have summarized a number of symptoms:

> Burn-out involves the loss of concern for the people with whom one is working. In addition to physical exhaustion (and sometimes even illness), burn-out is characterized by an emotional exhaustion in which the professional no longer has any positive feelings, sympathy, or respect for clients or patients. A very cynical and dehumanizing perception of these people often develops, in which they are labeled in derogatory ways and treated accordingly. As a result of this dehumanizing process, these people are viewed as somehow deserving of their problems and are blamed for their own victimization and thus there is a deterioration in the quality of care or service that they receive. The professional who burns out is unable to deal successfully with the overwhelming emotional stresses of the job, and this failure to cope can be manifested in a number of ways, ranging from impaired performance and absenteeism to various types of personal problems (such as alcohol and drug abuse, marital conflict, and mental illness). People who burn out often quit their jobs or even change professions, while some seek psychiatric treatment for what they believe to be their personal failings.[14]

Freudenberger describes the symptoms of burn-out as follows:

> Briefly described, burn-out includes such symptoms as cynicism and negativism and a tendency to be inflexible and almost rigid in thinking, which often leads to a closed mind about change or innovation. The worker may begin to discuss the client in intellectual and jargon terms and thereby distance himself from any emotional involvement. Along with this, a form of paranoia may set in whereby the worker feels that his peers and administration are out to make life more difficult.
>
> Another sign is that the worker takes on a superior "know-it-all" attitude that borders on the condescending. He hardly communicates with others and tends to become a loner or withdrawn. On the other hand, he may go to the other extreme and hardly do any work because he is socializing most of the time. Other workers experiencing burn-out may begin to limit their contact with their clients. They begin to speak of being bored with the work. . . . All is becoming too routine. They may also begin to verbalize a sense of helplessness as well as hopelessness about the clients and begin to speak of them in derogatory or flip terms.[15]

Personal Difficulties

Another important factor contributing to high stress and burn-out at work is personal difficulties at home. Home responsibilities (for example, caring for a terminally ill parent, having a child who is getting into trouble with the police, or dealing with an unhappy marriage) are stressful and may lead to burn-out.

Other Causes

Additional causes include poor time management, inability to work effectively with other people, lack of purpose or undefined goals in life, and inability to handle emergencies effectively.[20]

APPROACHES TO MANAGING STRESS AND PREVENTING BURN-OUT

The following approaches have been useful for helping group members reduce stress and prevent burn-out. It is up to each individual to select the ones he believes will be most helpful. Managing stress is similar to dieting: it will work for those who put forth the effort. (For further reading on these approaches, see the notes for this chapter.)

Goal Setting and Time Management

Stress and burn-out can come from the feeling of "too much to do and too little time in which to do it." Often, this feeling is due to not having clear short-term and lifetime goals and not knowing how to manage time effectively to achieve them. Realistic goals and a plan for achieving them lead to increased self-confidence, improved decision making, a greater sense of purpose, and an improved sense of security.

One technique for stress management is to help group members define short-term and lifetime goals and to teach them how to prioritize the tasks necessary to achieve them.[21] High-priority tasks should be accomplished first, and low-priority (low-payoff) tasks should generally be ignored because they can interfere with the accomplishment of high-priority tasks. (For a fuller discussion of time management, see chapter 16.)

Relaxation

Deep breathing relaxation, imagery relaxation, progressive muscle relaxation, meditation, and biofeedback are effective techniques for reducing stress and inducing the "relaxation response" (becoming relaxed).[22] Each of these techniques is facilitated by sitting in a comfortable position in a quiet place and closing one's eyes.

Deep breathing relaxation involves stopping thoughts about day-to-day concerns and concentrating on breathing processes. For five to ten minutes, a group member may slowly and gradually inhale deeply and exhale, while telling himself something like "I am relaxing, breathing smoother. This is soothing, and I'm feeling calmer, renewed, and refreshed." *Continued practice* of this technique will enable a person to become more relaxed when confronting a tense situation.

By using *imagery relaxation,* a group member can switch his thinking from daily concerns to focusing on an ideal relaxation place for ten to fifteen minutes. This ideal setting might include lying on a beach by a scenic lake in the warm sun or relaxing in warm water in a bathtub while reading a magazine. The group member should savor all the pleasantness, the peacefulness, focusing on everything that he finds calming, soothing, and relaxing. He will sense his whole body becoming refreshed, revived, and rejuvenated.

Progressive muscle relaxation is based on the principle that a person whose muscles are relaxed cannot be anxious.[23] The group leader instructs members to tighten and then relax a set of muscles. As they relax their muscles, they are asked to concentrate on the relaxed feeling while noting that the muscles are becoming less tense. The following is an excerpt of the first part of rather lengthy instructions to a group for progressive muscle relaxation:

> Make a fist with your dominant hand (usually right). Make a fist and tense the muscles of your (right) hand and forearm; tense it until it trembles. Feel the muscles pull across your fingers and the lower part of your forearm. . . . Hold this position for five to seven seconds, then . . . relax. . . . Just let your hand go. Pay attention to the muscles of your (right) hand and forearm as they relax. Note how these muscles feel as relaxation flows through (twenty to thirty seconds).[24]

The procedure of tensing and then relaxing the hand and forearm is repeated three or four times until they are relaxed. Next, other muscle groups are tensed and relaxed in the same manner, one group at a time. In succession, the muscle groups might include left hand and forearm, right biceps, left biceps, forehead muscles, upper lip and cheek muscles, jaw muscles, chin and throat muscles, chest muscles, abdominal muscles, back muscles between shoulder blades, right and left upper leg muscles, right and left calf muscles, and toes and arches of the feet. With practice, a group member can gradually develop the capacity to relax whenever anxious simply by visualizing the muscles relaxing.

There are a variety of *meditative approaches:* imagery relaxation and deep breathing relaxation are two examples. Herbert Benson has identified four basic components in meditative approaches that induce the relaxation response.[25] These components are: (1) being in a quiet environment free from external distractions, (2) being in a comfortable position, and (3) having an object to dwell on, such as a word, sound, chant, phrase, or imagery of a painting,* and (4) assuming a passive attitude and not thinking about day-to-day concerns. This last component Benson asserts is the key element in inducing the relaxation response.

Biofeedback equipment provides mechanical feedback to a person about his or her level of stress. This equipment can inform people about levels of stress they are usually unaware of—until a markedly higher level is reached. For example, a person's hand temperature may vary ten to twelve degrees in an hour's time, with an increase in temperature indicating increasing calm and relaxation. With biofeedback equipment, numerous physi-

---

*Since any neutral word or phrase will work, Herbert Benson, in *The Relaxation Response* (New York: Avon, 1975), suggests repeating the word *one* silently to oneself.

cal conditions can be measured and fed back, such as blood pressure, hand temperature, muscle tension, heartbeat rate, and brain waves. With biofeedback training, a client is first instructed in using the equipment to recognize high levels of anxiety or tenseness. Then, he or she is instructed on how to reduce such high levels either by closing the eyes and adopting a passive, "letting go" attitude or by thinking about something pleasant and calming. Often relaxation approaches are combined with biofeedback to elicit the relaxation response.

Exercise

Stress prepares our body to move or become involved in large-muscle activity (including fight or flight). Large-muscle activity refers to the kinds of exercise involving many muscle groups at the same time, such as jumping rope. Through exercise, a group member can use up fuel in the blood, reduce his or her blood pressure and heart rate, and reverse the other physiological changes set off during the alarm stage of the General Adaptation Syndrome. Exercising helps a person keep physically fit and have more physical strength to handle crises. It also reduces stress, and relieves tension. For these reasons group members should be encouraged to have a daily exercise program. A key to adhering to a daily exercise schedule is to select an enjoyable program. Many activities are available: walking, stretching, jogging, isometric exercises, jumping rope, swimming, playing tennis, dancing, housework, sex, gardening, golf.

Taking Care of Your Physical Self

In addition to exercising, it is important to have a nourishing diet, to take appropriate care of oneself, and to get enough sleep. Not only does a nourishing diet help keep people fit to resist stress, but research shows there are direct links between what individuals eat and how they feel emotionally. Some foods (such as coffee) produce tension, while overeating causes individuals to feel drowsy and even ill. Staying slim and trim helps a person feel good about him- or herself. Appropriate medical care also is a way to strengthen weak physical links that are vulnerable to stress-related illnesses.

Social Support Groups

Everyone needs to feel close to others. Support groups allow people to share their lives, have fun with others, and let their hair down. These groups are also a resource for help when emergencies and crises arise. There are a variety of possible support groups that center on: co-workers, a hobby or sports, a service (such as Rotary), a family, an extended family, a church, a community organization, a social club (such as Parents Without Partners), and so on. Essential characteristics of support groups are: (1) the group meets regularly, (2) the same people attend, (3) there is an opportunity for spontaneity and informality, and (4) a feeling of closeness develops among members.[26]

Talking to Others

Every human needs someone with whom to share good times as well as personal difficulties. Sharing concerns with someone helps to vent emotions, and talking a concern through often generates constructive strategies for resolving it. A good listener is someone who conveys caring and understanding, keeps the information confidential, is empathic, helps explore the difficulty in depth, helps arrive at alternatives for resolving the difficulty, and encourages the person to select and try out a resolution strategy.

Positive Thinking

When anticipated and unanticipated events occur, people can choose to take either a positive or negative view of the situation. If they take a negative view, they are apt to experience more stress and alienate friends and acquaintances. If they take a positive view, they are likely to maintain their equilibrium, stay relaxed, and cope with the situation quickly and easily, minimizing negative consequences. (This approach is described in the box "Positive Thinking.")

POSITIVE THINKING

Give a smile to everyone you meet (smile with your eyes)—and you'll smile and receive smiles. . . .

Give a kind word (with a kindly thought behind the word)—you will be kind and receive kind words. . . .

Give appreciation (warmth from the heart)—you will appreciate and be appreciated. . . .

Give honor, credit, and applause (the victor's wreath)—you will be honorable and receive credit and applause. . . .

Give time for a worthy cause (with eagerness)—you will be worthy and richly rewarded. . . .

Give hope (the magic ingredient for success)—you will have hope and be made hopeful. . . .

Give happiness (a most treasured state of mind)—you will be happy and be made happy. . . .

Give cheer (the verbal sunshine)—you'll be cheerful and cheered. . . .

Give encouragement (the incentive to action)—you'll be cheerful and cheered. . . .

Give a pleasant response (the neutralizer of irritants)—you will be pleasant and receive pleasant responses. . . .

Give good thoughts (nature's character builder)—you will be good and the world will have good thoughts for you. . . .

Source: W. Clement Stone, "Be Generous," in *A Treasury of Success Unlimited,* edited by Og Mandino (New York: Hawthorne Books, 1966), pp. 9–10.

Akin to positive thinking is having a philosophy of life that allows you to take crises in stride and to maintain a relaxed pace. When work is approached in a relaxed fashion, greater creativity is generated and stress is reduced. Leisure time should be enjoyed and used to develop oneself more fully as a person and to find enjoyment in each day.

When distressing events happen to you, it is psychologically therapeutic to view the event with the perspective of "Good luck? Bad luck? Who knows?" This perspective is indicated by the following story related by Anthony de Mello, S. J.:

> There is a Chinese story of an old farmer who had an old horse for tilling his fields. One day the horse escaped into the hills and when all the farmer's neighbors sympathized with the old man over his bad luck, the farmer replied. "Bad luck? Good luck? Who knows?" A week later the horse returned with a herd of wild horses from the hills and this time the neighbors congratulated the farmer on his good luck. His reply was, "Good luck? Bad luck? Who knows?" Then, when the farmer's son was attempting to tame one of the wild horses, he fell off its back and broke his leg. Everyone thought this very bad luck. Not the farmer, whose only reaction was, "Bad luck? Good luck? Who knows?" Some weeks later the army marched into the village and conscripted every able-bodied youth they found there. When they saw the farmer's son with his broken leg they let him off. Now was that good luck? Bad luck? Who knows?[27]

Changing Stress-Producing Thoughts

It is often erroneously believed that emotions, including feelings of tenseness and anxiety, are primarily determined by experiences—that is, by events that occur. However, cognitive therapies have shown the primary source of a person's emotions to be what he tells himself about his experiences.[28] An example will help clarify this important concept:

Event: Vicki Vogel is promoted to unit supervisor at a large insurance company.

Ms. Vogel's Thinking: *This promotion will make others jealous and lead to conflict with the people with whom I work. I don't believe I'm prepared to handle these new responsibilities. If I fail, I'll be demoted and will be a failure. My career will end.*

Emotion: Worry, alarm, tension, anxiety.

On the other hand, if Ms. Vogel tells herself something else, her emotions will be quite different.

Event: Vicki Vogel is promoted to unit supervisor at a large insurance company.

Ms. Vogel's Thinking: *This is really great that the company is recognizing the skills I have. I've been working here for six-and-a-half years and thoroughly know how to do the work in this unit. Supervising peo-*

ple will be a challenge, but I've supervised people before in some of the church's projects I've headed up. This kind of challenge will help me grow in my career and as a person. I have a number of ideas I want to try here to improve what we do.

Emotion: Excitement, a feeling of self-worth, mild anxiety accompanied by self-confidence.

This example illustrates two important concepts. First, a person's thoughts primarily determine his or her emotions. Second, by challenging and changing negative and irrational thinking, individuals can eliminate an unwanted emotion. Frequently, events cannot be changed, but individuals have the power to view such events rationally and positively, and to control, to a large degree, what their emotions are.[29] (See chapter 21 for a fuller discussion.)

Changing or Adapting to Distressing Events

There are an infinite number of distressing events: the death of someone close, the breakup of a romantic relationship, being fired, having an unfulfilling job, failing some courses, getting into an argument, having unresolved religious questions. When distressing events occur, group members should be encouraged to confront them directly to try to improve the situation. If a person is grieving because of the death of someone else, he or she might find it helpful to talk about it within the group or seek professional private counseling. Terminated or fired employees should find out the reasons they were dismissed so they can deal constructively with them and begin to seek another job. If a person has unresolved religious questions, group discussion followed by talking to a member of the clergy or taking a course on the philosophy of religion may help.

Most distressing events can be improved by confronting them head on and taking constructive action to change them. However, a number of events cannot be changed. Group members may not be able to change the irritating habits of others. If a situation cannot be changed, the only constructive alternative is to accept it. It is counterproductive to nag, complain, and become upset. Acceptance of things that cannot be changed will leave an individual more relaxed and calm.

Personal Pleasures

Personal pleasures relieve stress, provide a change of pace, are enjoyable, make us feel good, and are (in reality) personal "therapies." What is pleasurable to one person may not be to another. Common pleasures are being hugged, listening to music, going shopping, taking a hot bath, going to a movie, having a glass of wine, family and religious get-togethers, taking a vacation, singing, and so on. Such "treats" remind individuals that they have worth; they also add spice to life.

Enjoyable activities beyond work and family responsibilities are also pleasures that relieve stress. Research has found that "stress reduces stress"; that is, an appropriate level of stressful activities in one area helps reduce excessive stress in others.[30] Getting involved in enjoyable outside activities switches a person's negative thinking about his daily concerns to positive thoughts about the enjoyable activities. Therefore, it is stress reducing to become involved in enjoyable activities such as golf, tennis, swimming, scuba diving, taking flying lessons, traveling, and so on.

Personal pleasures can also be used as "payoffs" to ourselves for jobs well done. Most of us would not shortchange others for doing well; we ought not to shortchange ourselves. Such rewards make us feel good and motivate us to move on to new challenges.

"Mental-health time" is an indulgence that should be used when one is under extended stress. When a stress level has been too high for too long, relaxation is crucial to one's physical and emotional health. One should take a day off and do only what one wants to do. (A number of agencies now allow employees a certain number of paid mental-health days.)

GROUP EXERCISES

Exercise A: Resolving Current Stressors

Goal: To identify and work on resolving current stressors.

Step 1. The leader describes what stressors are and indicates the goal of this exercise. The leader then instructs students to write their answers to the following questions. (These questions may be written on the blackboard.) The leader should inform students to feel free to write responses they want to keep private, as they will not be required to reveal anything they do not want to share.

    a. What are the three most serious, unresolved stressors that you are currently facing?
    b. What attempts have you made to resolve each of these stressors?
    c. Why have you not as yet been able to resolve each of these stressors?
    d. Are you currently awfulizing about these stressors?
    e. What constructive actions do you think you should now take to resolve each of these stressors?

Step 2. After the students write their answers to these questions, they form subgroups of three persons. In the subgroups each member shares those responses that they are comfortable in sharing. While a member is sharing his or her responses, the other two members focus on suggesting alternatives to resolving the stressors being discussed.

Step 3. After the subgroups finish their discussions, the leader asks if anyone (or any subgroup) has a complicated situation that he or she would like to share with the class. Such situations are discussed, with efforts being made to suggest alternatives to resolve the stressors. (If a distressing event cannot be changed, it is usually possible for the person involved to change his or her cognitions about the distressing event.) The exercise ends when no one has additional complicated situations to share.

Exercise B: Relaxation Through Meditation

Goal: To relax through meditating, thereby reducing stress and preventing burn-out.

Step 1. The leader briefly describes what stress is and its causes and effects. He then explains that burn-out is one of the reactions to high levels of stress and summarizes approaches for reducing stress and preventing burnout. (Preparing a handout that summarizes these approaches would be helpful.) The leader notes that it is important for each person to learn some ways to reduce stress.

Step 2. The leader explains that meditating is one way to reduce stress and states the following:

I will now lead you in a meditation exercise. The purpose is to show you that through meditating you can reduce stress and anxiety. You can do this exercise by yourself whenever you are anxious or want to relax. You can do it, for example, before giving a speech in class, taking a crucial exam, or going to bed at night.

Herbert Benson, who wrote the book, *The Relaxation Response,* has identified four key elements common to meditative approaches that help people to relax. These four elements are: (1) being in a quiet place; (2) getting in a comfortable position; (3) having an object to dwell on, such as your breathing or a phrase that you continually repeat silently to yourself; and (4) having a passive attitude in which you let go of your day-to-day concerns by no longer thinking about them. Having a passive attitude is the key element in helping you to relax.

Now, I want you to form a circle. (Wait until a circle is formed.) I will lead you in three types of meditation. First, we will do a deep breathing exercise. Then, we will move into repeating the word "relax" silently to ourselves. Third, I'll have you focus on visualizing your most relaxing place. We will move directly from the first to the second, and then from the second to the third without stopping. When we do this exercise, don't worry about anything unusual happening. There will be no tricks. Concentrate on what I'm telling you to focus on, while taking a passive attitude where you let go of your everyday thoughts and concerns. Everyday thoughts and concerns may occasionally enter your mind, but seek to let go of them when they do.

Before we start, I want each of you to identify one of your most relaxing scenes. It may be lying in the sun on the beach or by a lake. It may be sitting in warm water in a bathtub reading a book. It may be sitting by a warm fireplace. Is there anyone who hasn't identified a relaxing scene? (Wait until everyone has identified one.)

OK, we're ready to start. (If possible, dim the lights, or turn out some of them.) First, I want you to close your eyes and keep them closed for the entire exercise. Next, get in a comfortable position. If you want, you can sit or lie on the floor. (Take five or six minutes for each of the three meditative exercises. Speak softly and slowly. Pause frequently, sometimes for twenty seconds or more without saying anything. Feel free to add material to the following instructions.)

First, I want you to focus on your breathing. Breathe in and out slowly and deeply. . . . Breathe in and out slowly . . . as you breathe out feel how relaxing it feels. . . . While exhaling, imagine your concerns are leaving you . . . as you're breathing in and out, feel how you're becoming more calm, more relaxed, more refreshed. . . . Just keep focusing on breathing slowly in and out. . . . Don't try to be in sync when I'm talking about breathing in and out. . . . Find a breathing rhythm that's comfortable for you. . . . Breathe in slowly and deeply, and then slowly breathe out. . . . You've got the power within you to get more and more relaxed. . . . All you have to do is focus on your breathing. . . . Breathe in slowly and deeply, and then slowly breathe out. . . . If other thoughts happen to enter your mind, just let them drift away as effortlessly as possible. . . . The key to becoming more relaxed is to let go of your day-to-day concerns. . . . To do this, all you need to do is simply focus on your breathing. . . . Breathe in slowly and deeply, and then breathe out.

Now, we will switch to repeating silently to yourself the word "relax." Keep your eyes closed . . . just keep repeating to yourself the word "relax." . . . Keep repeating "relax" to yourself silently and slowly. . . . If day-to-day thoughts enter your mind, let them. . . . Keep repeating "relax" to yourself. . . . All of us encounter daily stressors. . . . It is impossible to avoid daily stressors. . . . The important thing to remember about stress management is not to seek to avoid daily stressors but to find ways to relax when we are under high levels of stress. . . . An excellent and very simple way to learn to relax is to sit in a quiet place, in a comfortable position, and silently repeat to yourself the word "relax" . . . "relax" . . . "relax." . . . By simply repeating the word "relax" to yourself, you have the power within you to become more and more relaxed. . . . Find a nice comfortable pace for repeating the word "relax" to yourself. . . . The pace should be slow enough so that you can relax. . . . But not be so slow that thoughts about your day-to-day concerns enter your mind. . . . Remember, the key to relaxing is letting go of your day-to-day concerns. . . . If such concerns begin to enter your mind, focus more of your attention on repeating "relax" silently and slowly to yourself. . . . By repeating "relax" to yourself, you will find it will appear to have magical powers for you, as you will find yourself becoming more and more relaxed and refreshed. . . . [Have the members repeat "relax" for five or six minutes.]

Now, we will switch to focusing on your most relaxing scene. Don't open your eyes. . . . Focus on being in your most relaxing place. . . . Feel how good and relaxing it feels. . . . Just dwell on how relaxing it feels. . . . Enjoy everything about how calm and relaxing this place is. . . . Feel yourself becoming calmer, more relaxed. . . . Enjoy the peacefulness of this place. . . . Feel yourself becoming more relaxed, more renewed and refreshed. . . . Enjoy all the sights and sounds of this special place for you. . . . Notice and cherish the pleasant smells and aromas. . . . Feel the warmth, peacefulness, and serenity of this very special place for you. . . . Whenever you want to become more relaxed, all you have to do is close your eyes, sit quietly, and visualize yourself being in this very relaxing place. . . . The more you practice visualizing being in your relaxing place, the quicker you will find yourself become relaxed. . . . It will appear to you that your relaxing place has magical, relaxing powers for you, but in reality you are simply relaxing yourself by letting go of your day-to-day concerns and instead focusing on enjoying the peacefulness of your most relaxing place. . . . If you have to give a speech, or are facing some other stressful situation, you can learn to reduce your level of anxiety by simply closing your eyes for a short period of time and focusing your thoughts on being in your most relaxing place. . . . You always have the power within you to reduce your level of anxiety. . . . All you have to do is close your eyes and visualize being in your very special relaxing place. . . . Continue to visualize, now, being in this very relaxing place. . . . Feel yourself becoming more relaxed, refreshed, and calm. . . . If you're feeling drowsy, that's fine. . . . Feeling drowsy is an indication that you're becoming more and more relaxed. . . . You're doing fine. . . . Just keep on visualizing being in your very relaxing place. . . . You will become more and more relaxed by simply letting go of your day-to-day concerns and by enjoying this very special relaxing place. . . . (Pause, then continue this exercise for five or six minutes.)

Unfortunately, in a minute or so it will be time to return to this class. But there is no hurry. I will slowly count backwards from five to one, and then ask you to open your eyes shortly after we reach one. . . . (5) Enjoy how relaxed you feel. You may now feel warmer, drowsy, and so relaxed that you feel you don't even want to move a muscle. . . . Enjoy this very special feeling. . . . It is healthy to become this relaxed as your immune system functions best when you are relaxed. . . . (4) Slowly begin to return to this class. . . . There is no rush. . . . There is no hurry. . . . Take your time to become more alert. Anytime you want to relax, all you need to do is use one of these three meditative approaches. With practice you will gradually get better at relaxing by using these approaches. . . . (3) You should now focus on returning in a short time to this class. . . . Take your time . . . we still have a half-minute or so. . . . Examine whether you want to make a commitment to use relaxation exercises to reduce the daily stress you encounter. . . . (2) We are nearly at the time to return to this class. . . . You should now work towards becoming more and more alert. . . . (1) Slowly open your eyes. . . . There is no hurry. . . . Take your time to get oriented. A word of caution: if you have to drive some place soon, please walk around for several minutes before trying to drive a car, as you may be so relaxed now that you may not be alert enough to drive safely.

Step 3. The leader then asks question such as: What do you think of these three approaches? How relaxed did you get? Did any of you have trouble getting relaxed? If yes, why? Which of the three approaches did you like better and why? (If the members are very relaxed and drowsy, they may feel they do not have the energy to respond to these questions. The leader should respect such a "mood," and not pressure members to respond.) Note: As an additional relaxation technique, the leader might play a muscle relaxation tape so that the class can experience this type of relaxation technique as well.

WHAT MAKES A GROUP?

What is a group?

"A plurality of individuals who are in contact with one another, who take one another into account, and who are aware of some significant commonality—an essential feature of a group is that its members have something in common and that they believe that what they have in common makes a difference."

Michael S. Olmstead, *The Small Group* (New York: Random House, 1959, pp. 21–22).

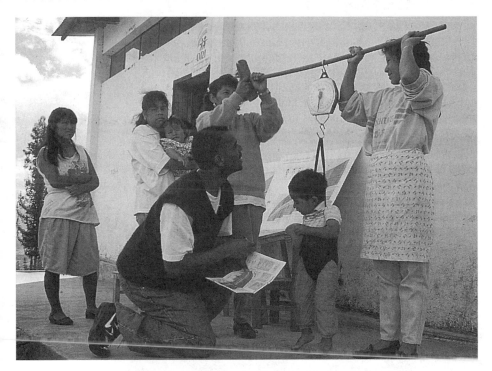

What is a group's purpose?

This Peace Corps worker helps an Ecuadorian family. How does the worker know what the family needs? Are this family's needs the same as that of other families with which the worker interacts? How does the worker know the group dynamics in a foreign country?

What are a group's goals?

Who sets them? In successful groups, the goals tend to be set by all members, thus ensuring that the group's goals account for each member's personal goals. These Habitat for Humanity volunteers have formed a self-help group so that they can focus their individual concerns into a collective program for a better quality of life for future home owners.

What factors contribute to a group's cohesion?

In an encounter group, the level of cohesion among members is high as a result of the strong bonds that are forged by the participants as they learn to communicate with openness.

Who should belong to a group?

Who joins a group or is chosen for it depends on the group's purpose. These young people volunteered to attend a safe sex lecture given by a social worker who, coincidentally, is pregnant. A group's composition, once it is settled, raises many issues concerning the social worker's approach to the group. This sex education lecture targeted underprivileged urban neighborhoods. How might these teenagers' particular social, cultural, or ethnic circumstances determine the kinds of issues that were discussed?

What can each member contribute to a group's success?

Like players on a winning sports team, each member of a successful group takes a position that contributes in some way to achieving the group's goals. Whether the goal is immediate—winning more points—or long term—learning to live with a disability—each member can help by performing a group-oriented function.

What does group leadership involve?

Leadership means that one member influences other members in order to help the group achieve its goals. To influence others, each member needs to be aware of what kind of power he or she possesses and of how that power may be used in the service of the group. How can the social worker see to it that each member realizes and uses his or her special power? How might that task determine the social worker's own style of leadership?

CHAPTER SIXTEEN

TIME MANAGEMENT

Goal: Time is the most valuable commodity we have. It cannot be renewed, recycled, or otherwise recovered. This chapter describes the principles of time management, presents time-saver tips, and summarizes suggestions for overcoming procrastination. (In regard to the types of groups described in chapter 1, a time management group is an educational group.)

To waste our time is to waste our life. Time is life. When our time is gone, we are gone. Time management focuses on helping people become more effective. It emphasizes the importance of selecting the best task to do and then doing it in the most productive way. Unfortunately, time is a non-renewable resource that, as Harold Taylor adds,

> is measured in past accomplishments. Those who look back and see few goals accomplished, few achievements, few times when they felt proud of what they have done—those people feel that life has sped by too quickly. They feel cheated.
>
> But those who look back and are flooded with memory after memory of satisfying activities, achievements, relationships, feel they have lived a long and fruitful life.[1]

When people fail to accomplish important tasks in their lives, it is often because they are not well-organized. As we will see, time management can help group members set goals in their lives and organize their time and resources to reach these goals. However, too much organization is as ineffective as too little. Overly organized people are too busy making "to do" lists, updating, losing, and redoing them.

Time management begins with setting goals. What do you really want from life? Answer that question to find your lifetime goals. People who do not set lifetime goals are apt to be bored, unhappy, depressed, confused, and unfulfilled. They haven't figured out what they want out of life, so they really do not know what will be fulfilling and satisfying to them. They "muddle through." Generally, they are followers who let others make decisions and then are frustrated and angry when a decision doesn't work out for them. Such muddlers frequently become complainers and have difficulty making major decisions. When asked to marry, they delay. When a new job presents itself, they vacillate. When an opportunity arises for moving to another geographic area, they hesitate. And when a "big" decision is made, they second-guess themselves—all because they have no meaningful goals to guide them.

A TIME-MANAGEMENT APPROACH

Setting life goals is not an easy task. It requires considerable contemplation, reflection, and sifting through numerous options. But, people who set life goals are generally more comfortable, happy, contented, and fulfilled. They know what brings them enjoyment and fulfillment, and, therefore, can work toward accomplishing those goals. They tend to make decisions for themselves, rather than having decisions made for them. When confronted with making major decisions (such as marriage, having children, or a new job opportunity), they compare alternatives in terms of their life goals and arrive at a decision that will likely be in their long-term best interests.

Set Goals

The first step in a time-management process is for individual group members to set personal goals. They should answer two questions:

1. What are my long-term goals?
2. What are my goals for the next six months?

Answers to each of these questions should be listed on separate sheets of paper. In identifying these goals, group members should recognize that their short-range and long-range goals will change over time. That is to be expected. Trapping themselves into working toward goals they no longer want is a mistake. As time passes, certain goals will be dropped or altered, and others will be replaced.

In specifying short-range and long-range goals, group members should consider a variety of areas, including career, financial position, marital status, family goals, community involvement, religious goals, education, exercise, stress-reduction, self-improvement, relationships, vacations, retirement, hobbies, and recreation and leisure.

Prioritize Goals

The next step is to prioritize these goals. Alan Lakein recommends using three categories: assigning the letter "A" to high-value goals, "B" to medium-value goals, and "C" to those with low values.[2] Prioritizing should be done separately for both the short-range and the long-range goals. The A, or high-value goals, should be further prioritized by ranking them in order: A-1, A-2, A-3, A-4, and so on. With this process, group members will have identified just what it is they want to do with their lives at this time.

Long-term goals tend to change for a variety of reasons. A person could accomplish a number of them, such as graduating from college, getting married, or finding a career position. Some of the unattained goals may no longer be important or valuable. Therefore, it is advantageous to review and refine long-term goals periodically (perhaps annually). Since short-term goals are generally for six-month periods, they should be reviewed semi-annually.

List Tasks for A Goals

The most important goals are A goals, and these should receive the bulk of attention and time. Since a group member cannot *do* a goal, the next step in the planning process is to list specific tasks that will help him or her move toward each short-range and long-range A goal.

A junior majoring in social work, for example, might have chosen "obtaining a social work job after graduation" as one of his or her longer-range goals. Specific tasks for reaching this goal might be listed as follows:

1. Studying carefully for exams and writing quality papers to get good grades.
2. Doing volunteer work in social service agencies.
3. Writing a resumé.
4. Identifying areas in social work where vacancies are located and then taking elective courses related to these areas.
5. Actively participating in the social work organization at this campus.

6. Asking a social work faculty member that I trust to give me feedback on my strengths and deficiencies for obtaining social work employment and on what I need to work on to improve my chances of getting a job.

7. Selecting a field placement that will (a) best help me to develop my social work skills and knowledge, and (b) establish contacts with people who can help me get a job.

Prioritize Tasks

If group members were conscientious in listing possible tasks for each goal, they would have too many tasks and not enough time for all of them. Therefore they should prioritize each task into A, high-value tasks; B, medium-value tasks; and C, low-value tasks. A tasks for each A goal should then be further prioritized into A-1, A-2, A-3, A-4, and so on.

Schedule Tasks

If group members have faithfully followed the above process, they will have a clear vision of their important short-range and long-range goals, and of the specific tasks that will help them to achieve these goals. Daily work on each A task for each A goal is not possible, so group members need to select one or two (or a few more) daily tasks to focus on. If the A tasks a person selects seem too overwhelming (such as writing quality papers for each of his courses), they should be divided into smaller segments (such as doing library research for a policy paper).

In planning a schedule, time to achieve A tasks should be blocked out by designating specific hours or days for each task. Alan Lakein suggests setting aside a special A time each day and banishing all C tasks and interruptions during this time period.[3] A weekly reminder calendar can help to schedule meetings, exam dates, paper due dates, and other important tasks. By using a calendar, group members can block out times to do A tasks in a place free from interruptions and distractions.

Each person has an *internal prime time*, which is when that person is most effective and productive. Each group member should find his own internal prime time since it varies considerably among individuals. For some it is the morning; for others it is the afternoon or evening. Group members should schedule their A tasks during their internal prime time.

In scheduling daily time, members may be flexible to accommodate whatever emergencies may arise. Therefore, it is important to leave an hour or so each day uncommitted. Too rigid a schedule will lead to high stress. Built into each daily schedule should be time for exercising, relaxing, and rewards.

In scheduling time, it is crucial to list high-value tasks and to avoid listing low-value tasks. Lakein has adapted the 80/20 rule to time management:

> If all items were arranged in order of value, 80 percent of the value would come from 20 percent of the items, while the remaining 20 percent of the value would come from 80 percent of the items. . . . The 80/20 rule suggests that in a list of ten items, doing two of them will yield most (80 percent) of the value. Find these two, label them A, get them done. Leave most of the other eight undone.[4]

This rule is not carved in stone, Lakein explains, as some items have more or less value than the 80/20 rule suggests. He illustrates the rule with the following examples:

80 percent of sales from 20 percent of customers.
80 percent of production is in 20 percent of the product line.
80 percent of sick leave is taken by 20 percent of employees.
80 percent of file usage is in 20 percent of files.
80 percent of dinners repeat 20 percent of recipes.
80 percent of dirt is on 20 percent of floor areas that are highly used.
80 percent of dollars is spent on 20 percent of the expensive meat and grocery items.
80 percent of the washing is done on the 20 percent of the wardrobe that is well-used items.
80 percent of TV time is spent on 20 percent of programs most popular with the family.
80 percent of reading time is spent on 20 percent of the pages in the newspaper (front page, sports page, editorials, columnists, feature page).
80 percent of telephone calls come from 20 percent of all callers.
80 percent of eating out is done at 20 percent of favorite restaurants.[5]

TIME-SAVER TIPS

A number of time-saver ideas for college students are presented here. Select those of value to you.

Planning Tomorrow

At the end of each day, write down on a calendar the essential tasks you will do tomorrow. Planning in this way organizes tomorrow and enables you to relax today, your mind free from worries about tomorrow. This "to do" list could contain mostly A tasks, discussed earlier, but it can also include B and C tasks, such as "buy tickets for a ball game this weekend."

Concentrated Study

One or two hours of intensive, concentrated study time is more effective than four or five hours of slight concentration, daydreaming, and socializing. Using this approach of intense concentration in my senior year in college, I studied only one-third as much and received better grades. In lectures, I focused intensely on what the instructor was saying, studied intensely for only one or two hours at a time, and accomplished much more.

Best Use of Time

People who use time effectively monitor themselves throughout the day by asking: "What's the best use of my time right now?" Many of us squander our time by doing C tasks instead of A tasks. For example, if we have an important, distasteful exam to study for, we may waste our time cleaning our apartment or room and rationalize that that is important, too. Doing C tasks as a way of avoiding doing A tasks has been called "productive avoidance." Ask yourself, "Would anything terrible happen if I didn't do this task?" If the answer is "No," then don't do it.

Writing Papers and Reports

When writing a term paper or a report, complete it in as few planning, research, and writing sessions as possible. Do not switch back and forth from writing a little on the paper and then doing something else. Much time is wasted in getting reoriented when you return to working on a partially completed paper.

When writing letters or answering mail, handle each piece of paper only once. Substantial time is wasted (through getting reoriented) by returning to write partially completed letters.

Physical Environment

Close your door when you do not want to be disturbed. Place your lists of high value goals and tasks where you can see them, so they remind you what you should be working on. Be prepared to carry study material at all times. Then you can take advantage of unexpected delays during a commute, in a physician's office, or waiting for a friend.

Saying "No" Assertively

Learn to say "No" as a time saver when friends and relatives suggest an activity that will interfere with your plans to do an A task. Seek to end unproductive activities as quickly as possible.

Deadlines

Set deadlines and stick to them. Avoid typewritten messages when handwritten messages will suffice. Ideas for how to complete A tasks can be written down with a deadline attached to them, rather than trusting to memory. Meetings started and ended on schedule do not waste people's time.

Avoid "Shoulds"

Avoid running your life by "shoulds." Somehow we never do many of our shoulds, as they are often interpreted as distasteful. Reinterpret the "shoulds" to be items you either will do or won't do. The "won'ts" you no longer have to do, and the "wills" are psychologically much more desirable to do than "shoulds."

Be Optimistic

Be an optimist. Don't waste time regretting or worrying about events that have not turned out well. Give yourself time off and special rewards when you successfully accomplish major projects.

Amount of Sleep

Can you reduce the amount of time you sleep? For most people, sleep takes up the largest single block of time during a day, and many get more than they need. Try reducing your sleep time by half an hour to see if you are as effective as before. In addition, have a light lunch rather than a big meal at noon so you won't become drowsy in the afternoon.

Relaxation

Try not to think of work on weekends. Learn to "let go" of negative events that happened earlier in the day and relax each evening. It is important to "do nothing" now and then to refresh yourself. A person who manages time effectively does not work harder, just smarter. (Relaxation techniques are described in chapter 15.)

Other Study Hints

By taking a speed-reading course you will learn to read faster and probably increase your comprehension. Marking the important points in a book with a pen, pencil, or marker during the first or second reading will save you time later during a review for an exam.

OVERCOMING PROCRASTINATION

Procrastination is intentionally putting off doing something that should be done; it is the thief of time. Once we develop the procrastination habit, we find plenty of ways to support it. We know we should be doing a certain A task, but instead we delay getting at it. We often squander our time by doing lesser-value tasks. For example, we know a paper is due in two days, but instead of writing it, we go shopping, spend hours talking to friends, wash clothes, or watch television. Sound familiar?

Procrastination is a major barrier to achieving short-range and long-range goals. Most people procrastinate doing an A task because it seems overwhelming or unpleasant. Overwhelming tasks are viewed as too complex or too time-consuming. For example, you put off starting to write a twenty-page paper due in one week because it seems that little can be accomplished in the short study time available. Unpleasant tasks, of course, generate negative emotions that may be difficult to deal with. For example, you put off telling your parents that you're failing a course because you fear their reactions and because you dread how you will feel after you inform them.

Swiss Cheese Approach

The key to getting an overwhelming A task under control is to poke holes in it by breaking it down into smaller tasks—the Swiss cheese approach. Completion of the smaller tasks nibbles away at the larger task until it is finally eliminated altogether.

For example, you have a research proposal to write for a class, and you feel overwhelmed because you have never written a proposal before and because you have little idea what topic to write the proposal on. Divide the task into smaller tasks. Begin by making a list of three or four research topics you're interested in. The next step is to formulate a research hypothesis in each of the areas. The third step might be to meet with your instructor to get his or her thoughts about the hypotheses. The fourth step might be to go to the library to examine what research has been done related to your hypotheses and to review what kinds of research designs have been used. Once you have done this, you will be ready to select a topic. And, in reviewing the literature, you will in all probability have come across a design that you can adapt for writing your proposal. At this point, you may want to make a rough outline of your design that you can take to your instructor for feedback. After you make the changes suggested by your instructor, you are ready to sit down and write the research proposal.

Other Suggestions

Begin research. Unpleasant tasks can sometimes be made less unpleasant simply by learning more about them. Library research and interviews with experts or others knowledgeable in the field are good ways to begin.

Isolate parts of a task that can be done immediately. Completing several tasks early in the process provides initial success and motivation.

Set deadlines. Reasonable deadlines are a good way to avoid procrastination and build motivation.

Plan ahead. As parts of the project are completed, know the next step. This will keep the work moving forward.

Change of scene. If the work becomes boring or fatiguing, a change of pace or scene can often help. This approach simply means working for a while in the library, then in a dormitory room or even a student lounge. Such changes add variety and reduce boredom.

Attack fear. Fear of failure or of a specific task can be a deterrent to even beginning work on a project. That fear can be attacked through a rational self-analysis (see chapter 21). This process can effectively neutralize fears and enable the project to proceed.

> *Consider the consequences.* Delaying work can mean missed deadlines, hurried and thus inferior work, and poor grades. It can also mean missed opportunities. Contemplating the consequences of procrastination can be an effective motivator.
>
> *Consider the benefits.* A personal reward system for completing a task—or parts of a task—is a good way to begin moving forward on a project.
>
> *Cut off escape routes.* Common escapes from work include socializing, daydreaming, sleeping, and watching television programs. Escape routes can be blocked by removing the temptation or by working in a place or at a time when the temptations will not be available.

ADVANTAGES OF TIME MANAGEMENT

While most of the material in this chapter is directed toward college students, time management and time-saver principles are applicable to work situations throughout life.[6] Time management is a *way* of life. People who are effective time managers are easy to identify. They accomplish major projects with quality and within deadlines. They show little hesitation, indecision, or confusion. They are successful people who have confidence in themselves. They are smooth, calm, appear in control, and display little wasted motion. They have a calming effect on others. They know when and how to relax. They're the kind of people you like to do business with. They don't procrastinate.

Harold L. Taylor says:

> Time management is not a finite skill or a body of knowledge that can be studied for two days, two weeks or two years, learned, and then put into practice. Like time itself, it is never ending. It is a continuing process of managing yourself more and more effectively with respect to time.
>
> Search out ideas, new methods, new techniques, and adapt them to your use. Investigate timesaving products. Wage a campaign against bad habits which rob you of precious time. Form new habits. Keep your goals in mind—*and* on paper—and refer to them constantly. Review them. Revise them. Make sure everything you do relates to them.[7]

GROUP EXERCISES

Exercise A: Setting High-Value Goals and Tasks

Goal: To set short-range and long-range goals and to identify high-value tasks for accomplishing these goals.

Step 1. The leader begins by defining time management and describing the purpose of this exercise.

Step 2. Group members are asked to list their goals for the next six months on one sheet of paper and their long-range goals on another. A variety of areas should be considered, such as career, exercise and health, and education.

Step 3. After Step 2 is completed, group members prioritize their goals by assigning A to high-value goals, B to medium-value goals, and C to low-value goals, further ranking high-value goals in order: A-1, A-2, A-3, and so on.

Step 4. Group members then list the tasks needed to achieve the specific A goals.

Step 5. Group members then prioritize each task's value in achieving their A goals using the A, B, C approach. The leader explains that if this process is conscientiously followed, a person will have a clear vision of his or her important short-range and long-range goals, and of the specific tasks that will help to achieve these goals.

Step 6. The class discusses the merits and shortcomings of this process and what they learned from this process.

Exercise B: Time Diagram

Goal: To use a time diagram to determine how you are spending your time and whether this is the way you want to spend your time.

Step 1. The group leader explains that the way we spend our time can be viewed as a revolving stage with each setting being a section. These settings can be diagrammed according to the amount of time we invest in each. The following examples should be provided.

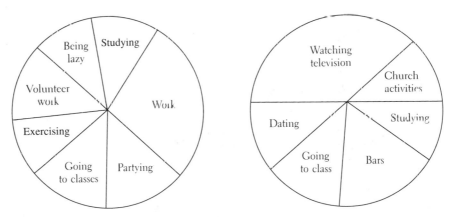

Note that the time spent sleeping is usually excluded from such diagrams, unless it is a specific time-management problem.

Step 2. Students prepare diagrams showing how they spent their time for the past month. Each diagram should include the settings in which time was spent and the amount of time spent.

Step 3. The class forms subgroups of three or four to share diagrams and comment on the following information:

1. Was this a typical month? If not, explain why.
2. Is this the way you *really want* to spend your time and energies?
3. Are you primarily directing your life, or is someone else? If someone else is primarily directing your life, who is this person, and what are your feelings about it?
4. If Exercise A has been done, the class discusses the extent to which the amount of time they are spending on high-value tasks is correlated to their use of time during the past month.

Exercise C: Putting an End to Procrastination

Goal: To develop strategies for doing the important tasks you are putting off.

Step 1: The group leader defines procrastination and explains that the main reasons people procrastinate are that tasks are viewed as overwhelming or unpleasant. The leader then summarizes a number of strategies for ending procrastination. The leader may want to distribute a handout listing these strategies.

Step 2. Each person writes down answers to the following three questions on a sheet of paper.

1. What important tasks are not getting done because you're procrastinating?
2. Why are you procrastinating?
3. What specific strategies do you intend to use to stop procrastinating and to start doing these tasks?

Step 3. The class forms subgroups of three or four to share their responses and to suggest additional strategies for overcoming procrastination.

Step 4. The class discusses what they learned from this exercise.

Exercise D: Internal Prime Time

Goal: To identify and more effectively utilize internal prime time.

Step 1. The leader explains the concept of internal prime time. The leader instructs each person to take a sheet of paper and draw the following outline for a graph. Members are then instructed to map their daily energy cycle on this graph. In this mapping process, members first place dots, representing their energy levels, at each two hour interval. (This mapping process should be done separately for weekdays and for weekends.) After dots are placed, lines are drawn to connect the points. A solid line is used to represent a weekday, and a dotted line is used to represent a weekend. The high point on each line is then marked with an X and the low point with an O.

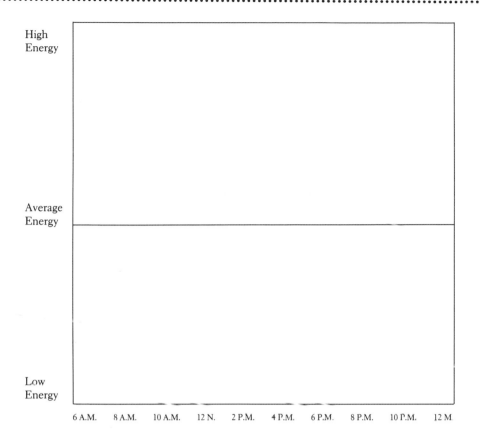

High
Energy

Average
Energy

Low
Energy

6 A.M.   8 A.M.   10 A.M.   12 N.   2 P.M.   4 P.M.   6 P.M.   8 P.M.   10 P.M.   12 M.

Step 2. Members form subgroups of three or four persons. Each member is asked to share his or her graph and respond to the following questions. (These questions may be written on the blackboard.)

1. How does my internal prime time relate to my daily work schedule? Am I doing my most creative and taxing work at my high energy points during the day?
2. How does my weekend cycle differ from my weekday cycle? If there is a difference, why does it exist?
3. What changes do I need to make in my work schedule to more effectively utilize my internal prime time?

Step 3. The exercise may be ended by having members reassemble in a large group and asking them what they learned from this exercise.

PART SEVEN

THERAPEUTIC GROUPS

CHAPTER SEVENTEEN

STARTING AND LEADING THERAPY GROUPS

Goal: This chapter summarizes a number of guidelines for starting, leading, and ending therapy groups. A number of aspects are covered, including: preparation and homework, relaxing before starting a session, cues upon entering the meeting room, seating arrangements, introductions, clarifying roles, building rapport, exploring problems in depth, exploring alternative solutions, ending a session, ending a group, co-facilitating a group, legal safeguards for group facilitators, and professional boundaries with clients.

Counseling people with personal problems is neither magical nor mystical. Although training and experience in counseling are beneficial, everyone has the potential to help another by listening and talking through difficulties. This is not to say that everyone will be successful at counseling. Helping professionals (such as social workers, psychiatrists, psychologists, and guidance counselors) have a higher probability of being successful. But competence and empathy rather than degree or certificates, are the keys to effective counseling.

This chapter seeks to present a number of suggestions for how to effectively start, lead and end therapy groups. Since experienced group therapists may find this material to be rather obvious, the primary intended readers are those therapists who are planning to lead their first groups and therapists who have already led some groups but are seeking additional suggestions for improving their group skills.

PREPARATION AND HOMEWORK

Extensive preparation is needed for leading therapeutic groups. The leader should have considerable training in: (1) assessing human behavior and human problems; (2) comprehensive therapeutic intervention approaches—such as reality therapy, behavior therapy, rational therapy, transactional analysis, feminist intervention, and client-centered therapy.[1]*; (3) specialized therapeutic intervention techniques, such as assertiveness training and relaxation techniques; (4) interviewing and counseling; and (5) principles of group dynamics, such as cohesion, task roles, social-emotional roles, and effects of authoritarian versus democratic styles of leadership. Baccalaureate and masters programs in social work generally provide considerable material in these areas.

For any therapy group, the leader also needs to study the literature on: the causes of problems that members are experiencing, the most effective intervention strategies for these programs, the prognosis for positive changes, and expectations as to the length of time the intervention strategies need to be applied to induce positive changes.

When leading a group, extensive preparation is key to a successful group experience for the members (including yourself). Even experienced leaders have to carefully prepare for each group and for each time the group meets.

In planning for a new group, answers to the following questions need to be formulated. What are the overall purpose and general goals of the group? What are the ways in which these general goals might be accomplished? What are the characteristics of the members? What are the unique and individual needs of each member? What resources do the members need to have in order to help them better handle their personal problems? What should be the format for the first meeting? What are the individual therapeutic goals for each member? When the group first meets, should an ice-breaker exercise be used? If so, what? Should refreshments be provided? How should the chairs be arranged? What type of group atmosphere will best help the members solve their personal problems? What is the best available meeting place? Why have you been selected to lead the group? What do the members expect you to do?

As you plan for the first meeting, it is very helpful to view the group as a new mem-

---

*These therapy approaches are summarized in chapters 18 through 23.

ber would view it. Questions and concerns that a new member may have are the following: Why am I joining? Will my personal goals be met in this group? Will I feel comfortable in this group? Will I be accepted by other members? Will the other members be radically different in terms of background and interests? If I do not like this group, can I get out of attending meetings? Will other members respect what I have to say, or will they laugh and make fun of me? What exactly will be discussed during these meetings? What will I be expected to say and do? Will pressures be put on me to make changes that I do not want to make? Through considering such concerns, the leader can plan the first meeting in a way that will assist the other members to feel comfortable and that will help clarify the members' questions as to the format and activities of the group.

When you are going to be a leader, it is *absolutely essential* that you do your homework prior to the first meeting to identify as precisely as possible what the members' needs and expectations are. The quickest way to fail as a leader is to allow a group to go in a different direction than the members desire.

There are a variety of ways to identify what the members want. It may be possible to discuss with each member, prior to the first meeting, what his or her expectations are and what each member can realistically expect to achieve in the group. If you are asked by someone else to lead the group, it is essential to ask that person what the expectations for the group are. The members should generally be asked at the first meeting to give their views as to what they desire to get out of the group. Another way to determine group members' expectations (which needs to be done for preparatory reasons anyway) is to "scout" the following about the group:

1. How many members are expected?
2. What are their characteristics (personal problems, ages, socioeconomic status, racial and ethnic backgrounds, gender mix, educational and professional backgrounds, and so on)? If you are involved in selecting who will be in the group, you will have to make some judgments regarding whom to include and whom to exclude. Two important criteria for including members in a therapy group are: (a) the potential benefit of the group experience for each member, and (b) the degree to which each member's presence is potentially beneficial to the other members in the group.
3. How knowledgeable and informed are the members about the issues the group will be dealing with?
4. What are apt to be the personal goals and agendas of the members?
5. How motivated are the members to accomplish the purposes for which the group is being formed? This can partly be determined by examining how voluntary the membership is. Involuntary members in a group (for example, members who have been court ordered to attend due to a conviction for driving while intoxicated) are apt initially to have little motivation to participate and perhaps may even be hostile that they are being forced to attend.
6. What are apt to be the underlying value systems of the members? A group of teenagers who have an eating disorder is apt to differ significantly from a group of adult parents who are grieving the death of a child. (However, it is important to remember to view the members in terms of being unique persons rather than in terms of stereotypes.)

In planning for the first (and additional) sessions, it is helpful to visualize (imagine) how you, as leader, want to the session to go. For example, at the first session, the following may be visualized:

The members will arrive at various times. I will be there early to greet them, to introduce myself, to assist them in feeling comfortable, and to engage in small talk. Possible subjects of small talk that are apt to be of interest to these new members are _____, _____, and _____.

I will begin the session by introducing myself and the overall purpose of the group. I will use the following ice-breaker exercise for members to introduce themselves and to get acquainted with each other. I will ask the group to give me a list of four or five items that they would like to know about the other members. Then members will introduce themselves and give answers to the four or five items. I will also answer these items and encourage the members to ask further questions that they have about me and the group.

After the ice-breaker exercise I will briefly state the overall purpose of the group and ask if the members have questions about this. Possible questions that may arise are _____. If such questions arise, my answer will be _____.

We will then proceed to an introductory exercise that is designed to encourage the members to begin sharing the personal problems they are experiencing. If this exercise fails to elicit much discussion after considerable probing on my part, I will present theoretical material on some of the psychological and societal dynamics of the personal problems they are experiencing.

The kind of group atmosphere I will seek to create is a democratic, egalitarian one. Such an atmosphere is best suited for encouraging members to share and problem solve the issues they are experiencing. I will seek to do this by arranging the chairs in a circle, by drawing out through questions those who are silent, by using humor, and by making sure that I do not dominate the conversation.

I will end the session by summarizing what has been covered and what is planned for future sessions. During this summary I will encourage members to give their suggestions for what should be dealt with in future sessions. We will set a time for the next session. Finally, I will ask if anyone has any additional comments or questions. Throughout the session I will seek to establish a positive atmosphere, partly by complimenting the members on the contributions they make.

If a group has met one or more times, the leader needs to review the following kinds of questions:

- Has the overall format for the group been sufficiently decided upon and clarified? If not, what needs to be done in this clarification process?
- Is each member making adequate progress in problem solving? If not, what obstacles are preventing these members (and perhaps the group) from sufficiently progressing? Do these obstacles need to be confronted?
- Are there more effective courses of action that might be considered that would benefit the group and certain members?
- What should be the format for the next session? What activities should be planned?
- Will successful completion of these activities move the group and the members toward accomplishing their overall goals? If not, perhaps other activities need to be selected.
- Does each member seem sufficiently interested and motivated to work on his or her problems, or are there some members that appear disinterested? If so, why do they appear disinterested, and what might be tried to stimulate their interests?

RELAXING BEFORE STARTING A SESSION

Prior to starting a session, you are apt to be nervous about how the session may go. Some anxiety is helpful in order to be mentally alert and to facilitate your attending to what is being communicated during the session. Some leaders, however, have too high a level of anxiety, which reduces their effectiveness. If your anxiety is too high, you can reduce it by engaging in activities that you find relaxing. Relaxation techniques are highly recommended (see chapter 15). Other suggestions include taking a walk, jogging, listening to music you find relaxing, and finding a place where you can be alone to clear your mind. Effective group leaders generally learn they can reduce their level of anxiety through using one or more of these techniques. Through practice in leading groups, you will gradually build up your confidence.

CUES UPON ENTERING THE MEETING ROOM

It is important for you as leader to be on time—perhaps even a little early. By being early, you can check to see that everything is as you planned. You'll be able to do what needs to be done—such as checking to see that refreshments are available (if refreshments are planned), erasing the blackboard, arranging the chairs in the way you desire, and so on.

By being early you will also have an opportunity to observe the moods of the members. If it is a group you have not previously met, being early gives you an opportunity to gain information about the interests of the participants from their: age, gender, clothes and personal appearance, small-talk, and the way they interact with one another. An effective leader observes such cues and generally finds a way to "join" such participants.

SEATING ARRANGEMENTS

The seating arrangement is important for several reasons. It can affect who talks to whom and have an influence on who will play leadership roles. As a result, it can have an effect on group cohesion and group morale.

It is important in most groups for the members to have eye contact with one another. It is even more important that the group leader be able to make eye contact with everyone, in order to obtain nonverbal feedback on what the members are thinking and feeling. A circle is ideal for generating discussion, for encouraging a sense of equal status for each member, and for promoting group openness and group cohesion.

When a group meets for the first time (and often later) members are apt to sit next to friends. If it is important that everyone in the group interact with one another, it may be desirable to ask people to sit next to people they do not know in order to counteract any cliquishness in the group and to encourage members to get to know each other.

INTRODUCTIONS

During the introduction, the leader's credentials should be summarized in such a way that members gain a sense of confidence that he or she can fulfill their expectations. If the leader is introduced by someone, a brief concise summary of the leader's credentials *for the expected role* is desirable. If the leader is introducing him- or herself, important credentials are summarized in a nonarrogant fashion. The summary is also delivered in a way that creates the desired atmosphere—informal or formal, fun or serious, and so on. An excellent way in many groups to handle the introductions is to use an "ice-breaker" exercise.

In meeting with a group, it is highly desirable to learn the members' names as quickly as possible. This requires extra attention on the leader's part. Name tags facilitate this process for everyone. Members appreciate being addressed by name—it helps convey to them that they have importance.

It is generally advantageous for each member to introduce him- or herself, perhaps through using an ice-breaker. It is often desirable during introductions that members state their expectations for the group. This helps uncover hidden agendas. If a stated expectation is beyond the scope of the group, the leader tactfully states and discusses it in order to prevent an unrealistic expectation becoming a source of frustration or dissatisfaction for that member.

In group therapy, as in individual therapy, there are two types of members; voluntary and involuntary. In voluntary groups, the therapist can take a more casual, less directive approach to begin with. In such groups the therapist may begin by involving members in small talk. This preliminary chit-chat may be about the weather, parking problems, baseball, something currently in the news, and so on. Casual conversation has the advantage of letting group members become acquainted with the therapist and the other group members.

In involuntary groups, the therapist may begin by introducing him- or herself and making a formal statement about the purpose of the group. Then members may be asked to introduce themselves. Generally, in involuntary groups, less is left up to the members themselves, since they have less motivation for being there and less commitment to the group.

With both voluntary and involuntary groups, it is sometimes helpful (after introductions) to begin a session with some factual information. This can be done in a brief presentation by the group leader or by showing a short film or videotape. For example, if the group members are involuntary clients who have been convicted of operating a motor vehicle while intoxicated, the leader may choose to show a film that vividly shows that as alcohol consumption increases, reaction times slow, and the chance of serious accidents occurring dramatically increases. Such factual information is designed not only to provide educational material, but also to serve as a "trigger" to start a discussion. After factual information is presented, it is sometimes useful to involve the group members in an exercise related to the factual material.

If the group has met previously, the leader may choose to begin by bringing up for discussion a topic that was not fully discussed at the last meeting. Or, if "homework" assignments were given to some members, the leader may begin by saying, "Jim, at the last meeting you indicated you were going to do (such and such). How did that work out?"

CLARIFYING ROLES

As leader of a group, you must understand clearly your roles and responsibilities. In most situations it is a mistake for the leader to do the majority of the work. The group generally is most productive if all members make substantial contributions. The more members contribute to a group, the more they are apt to psychologically feel a part of the group.

The helper therapy principle is generally operative in groups.[2] With this principle, members at times interchange roles and sometimes become the helper for someone else's problems. In the helper role, members receive psychological rewards for helping others. Groups also help members to put their problems into perspective as they realize others have problems as serious as their own.

Even if you are fairly clear about what you would like your role to be, the other group members may be confused about what your role is, or may have different expectations of you. If there is a chance that the other members are puzzled about your role, you should explain carefully what you perceive your role to be. If members indicate they have different expectations, time should be devoted to clarifying the roles and responsibilities of the designated leader and of the other group members.

In explaining what you perceive your role to be, it is generally desirable to be straightforward about your skills and resources. Generally speaking, you want to come across as a knowledgeable person rather than as an authority figure who has all the answers.

Be prepared to explain the reasoning behind the things you do. For example, if you are doing an exercise, inform the group about the goals or objectives of that exercise. (If questions arise about whether the goals for the exercise are consistent with the overall goals for the group, be prepared to provide an explanation.)

The role that the leader assumes in a group will vary somewhat from situation to situation. For example, there are apt to be substantial differences in the responsibilities of the leader in an eating disorders group for teenagers versus an assertiveness group in a shelter for battered women.

Remember that leadership is a shared responsibility. Every member at times will take on leadership roles. Designated leaders should not seek to dominate a group, nor should they believe they are responsible for directing the group in all of its task functions and group maintenance functions. In fact, productivity and group cohesion are substantially increased when everyone contributes.

BUILDING RAPPORT

The therapist tries to establish a nonthreatening group atmosphere, wherein the members feel accepted and safe enough to communicate their troubles fully. During the initial contacts, the therapist "sells" him- or herself (but not arrogantly) as a knowledgeable, understanding person who may be able to help and who wants to try. The tone of the therapist's voice conveys the message that he or she understands and cares about group members' feelings. The therapist is calm and never expresses shock or laughs when members begin to open up about problems. Emotional outbursts, even if subtle, lead group members to believe that the therapist is not going to understand or accept their difficulties, and they will usually stop discussing them.

A therapist views group members as equals. New therapists sometimes make the mistake of thinking that because someone is sharing intimate secrets with them, they (the therapists) must be very important, and end up assuming a superior position vis-à-vis their clients. If members feel that they are being treated as inferiors, they will be less motivated to reveal and discuss personal issues.

The therapist should use a "shared vocabulary" with the members. This does not mean that the therapist uses the same slang and the same accent as group members. If clients perceive the therapist is mimicking their speech patterns, they may feel seriously offended. In order to communicate effectively, the therapist uses words that members understand and do not find offensive.

The therapist (and other members) need to keep what members say confidential. Unfortunately, many people have nearly irresistible urges to share "juicy secrets" with someone else. If a group member discovers that confidentiality has been violated, that member's trust in the group will be quickly destroyed. It is essential that the therapist explain the importance of "what is said in the group, remains in the group."

EXPLORING PROBLEMS IN DEPTH

The therapist and group members examine such areas as the extent of the problem, how long the problem has existed, what the causes are, how the member feels about the problem, and what physical and mental capacities and strengths the member has to cope with the difficulty, prior to exploring alternative solutions. A problem area is often multidimensional; that is, there are usually a number of problems involved. Explore all of them. A good way to decide which problem to handle first is to ask the group member which problem he or she perceives as most pressing. If it is a problem that can be solved, start with exploring it in depth and together develop a solution. Success in solving one problem will increase each group member's confidence in the leader and thereby further improve rapport.

Therapists should convey *empathy,* not sympathy, and encourage group members to do so, too. Empathy is the capacity to understand and to share in another person's feelings. Sympathy also involves sharing feelings, but it results in offering pity. The difference is subtle. Empathy usually encourages problem-solving, while sympathy usually encourages group members to dwell on the problem without taking action to improve the situation. For example, if a leader offers sympathy to a depressed person, that person will keep telling his or her sad story over and over, each time having the emotional outpouring reinforced by the leader's sympathy, without taking any action to improve the situation. Telling the story over and over only reopens old wounds and prolongs the depression.

Therapists should "trust their guts." The most important resources that therapists have are their own feelings and perceptions. Therapists should continually strive to place themselves in members' shoes, understanding that members' values and pressures may be different from their own. It probably never happens that a group leader is 100 percent on target in an appraisal of a client's pressures, problems, and perspectives, but 70 to 80 percent is usually sufficient to allow the therapist to be helpful. Empathizing is very useful in helping the therapist to determine what additional areas may need to be explored, what should be said, and what possible solutions might be effected.

When a therapist believes that a client has touched upon an important area of concern, further communication can be encouraged in a number of ways. Showing interest nonverbally (by making and continuing eye contact, leaning forward, and raising eyebrows slightly) encourages further sharing. Allowing for pauses is important. New therapists usually become anxious when there is a pause and hasten to say something—anything—to keep the conversation going. This is usually a mistake, especially when it leads to a change in the topic. Although a pause often makes a group member anxious, it gives him or her time to think about what areas of concern are most important, and then usually motivates the member to continue the conversation in that area.

Neutral probes that do not control the direction of conversation but encourage further communication are helpful. For example, "Could you tell me more about it?," "Why do you feel that way?," and "I'm not sure I understand what you have in mind" all ask for further information, but just what kind is left up to the member. Reflecting feelings—for example, "You seem angry" or "You appear to be depressed about that"—works the same way. Summarizing what a group member is saying shows not only that you are listening but also that you have received the message the group member sent. An example is, "During this past hour, you made a number of critical comments about your spouse; it sounds like you're fairly unhappy about certain aspects of your marriage."

Approach socially unacceptable topics tactfully. Tact is an essential quality of a competent therapist. Try not to ask a question in such a way that the answer will put the respondent in an embarrassing position.

When pointing out a limitation that a group member has, also mention and compliment the member on any assets. When a limitation is mentioned, the person will feel that something is being laid bare or taken away. Therefore, compliment him or her in another area to give something back.

A competent therapist watches for nonverbal cues and uses them to identify a sensitive subject, as the client will generally display anxiety by a changing tone of voice, fidgeting, yawning, stiff posture, or a flushed face. Some therapists claim that they can tell when the pupils of his or her eyes dilate.

Therapists should be honest. An untruth may be discovered. If that happens, the group member's confidence in the therapist will be seriously damaged and the relationship seriously jeopardized. Being honest goes beyond not telling lies. For example, the therapist should point out shortcomings that are in the group member's best interest to correct. If a client is fired from jobs because of poor grooming habits, this should be brought to the person's attention.

EXPLORING ALTERNATIVE SOLUTIONS

After a problem is explored in depth, the next step is to consider alternative solutions. The therapist begins by asking something like, "Have you thought about ways to resolve this?" The merits, shortcomings, and consequences of the alternatives thought of by the member are then tactfully and thoroughly examined. Next, the therapist seeks to involve other group members by asking them if they are aware of alternatives that may work for this situation. Those members who do suggest alternatives temporarily assume a "helper" role. In such a role the "helper therapy" principle operates as the member receives psychological rewards from helping others. If the therapist has additional viable alternatives to suggest, they should then be mentioned. The merits, shortcomings, and consequences of the alternatives suggested by group members and by the therapist are then thoroughly explored.

Group members usually have the right to self-determination, that is, to choose one course of action from possible alternatives. The therapist's role is to help individuals clarify and understand the likely consequences of each available alternative, but usually not to give advice or choose the alternative for them. If a therapist were to select an alternative, there are two possible outcomes: (1) the alternative may prove to be undesirable for the group member, in which case he or she will probably blame the therapist for the advice and their future relationship will be seriously hampered; or (2) the alternative may prove to be desirable for the person involved. This immediate outcome is advantageous. But the danger is that the group member will become overly dependent on the therapist, seeking the therapist's advice for nearly every decision in the future and generally being reluctant to make decisions.

The guideline of not giving advice does *not* mean that the therapist should not suggest alternatives that a client has not considered. On the contrary, it is the therapist's responsibility to suggest and explore all viable alternatives with a client. A good rule to follow is that when a therapist believes a client should take a certain course of action, this should be phrased as a suggestion—"Have you thought about . . . ?"—rather than as advice, "I think you should . . ."

Group therapy is done *with* group members, not *to* or *for* them. Each member should have responsibility for doing many of the tasks necessary to improve a situation. A good rule to follow is that each member should take responsibility for those tasks that he or she has the capacity to carry out. Doing things *for* group members, similar to giving advice, brings with it the risk of creating a dependent relationship. Successful accomplishment of tasks by clients leads to personal growth and better prepares them for taking on future responsibilities.

A group member's right to self-determination should be taken away only if the selected course of action has a high probability of seriously hurting the client or others. For example, if it is highly probable that a parent will continue to abuse a child, the therapist should intervene and have the child removed from the home, even if this is done against the client's will. For most situations, however, the group member should have the right to select a course of action even when the therapist believes that another alternative is better. Frequently, a client is in a better position to know what is best, and if it turns out not to be the best, he or she will probably learn from the mistake.

When a group member selects an alternative, he or she should clearly understand what the goals are, what tasks need to be carried out, how to accomplish the tasks, and who will carry them out. Frequently, it is desirable to write a "contract" for future reference, with a time limit set for the accomplishment of each task.

If a group member fails to meet the terms of the "contract," the therapist should not criticize or accept excuses. Excuses let people off the hook; they provide temporary relief, but they eventually lead to more failure and to a failure identity. Simply ask, "Do you still wish to try to fulfill your commitment?" If the person answers affirmatively, another time deadline acceptable to the member is set.

Perhaps the biggest single factor in determining whether a group member's situation will improve is his or her motivation to carry out essential tasks. A therapist tries to motivate apathetic group members. One way to increase a members's motivation is to clarify what will be gained by meeting a goal. When individuals meet commitments, therapists should reward them, verbally or in other ways. Never criticize members for failing. Criticism usually increases hostility and rarely leads to positive, lasting change. Also, criticism serves only as a temporary means of obtaining different behavior; when a person believes that he or she is no longer under surveillance, that person will usually return to the destructive behavior.

If a group member lacks confidence or experience, it may be helpful to role play a task before the person actually attempts it. For example, if a pregnant single woman wants help in telling her partner about the pregnancy, role playing the situation within the group assists the woman in selecting words and developing a strategy for informing him. The therapist or another group member plays the woman's role and models an approach, letting the woman play the partner's role. Then, the roles are reversed so that the woman practices telling her partner.

ENDING A SESSION

Ending is not always easy. Ideally, the therapist and group members accept the fact that the session is ending, and subjects being discussed are not "left hanging." Abrupt endings are apt to be perceived by the group members as discourteous and rejecting.

There are some useful guidelines on how to terminate a therapy session. Initiate preparation for ending the session at the beginning of the session. Inform the members explicitly the time the session will end. Unless an unusual situation develops, the leader assertively seeks to terminate at the scheduled time. When the allotted time is nearly up, the therapist informs the group members by saying something like: "I see our time is just about up. Is there anything you'd like to add before we look at where we've come to, and where we now go from here?"

It is often helpful to summarize what was discussed during the session. If the session focused only on exploring problems that the members have, another session can be set up for fuller exploration and to begin looking at alternatives for resolving the problems.

It is helpful to give members "homework" assignments between sessions. A couple who are having trouble communicating with each other might be encouraged to set aside a certain amount of time each evening to discuss their thoughts with each other. At the next session this "homework" assignment may be reviewed.

Ideally, the group members are emotionally at ease when the session ends. Therefore, the therapist should not introduce emotionally charged content at the end of the session but should reduce the intensity of emotion. Just as it is sometimes advisable to begin a session with small talk, a short social conversation at the end may provide a transition out of the session. If a group member displays a reluctance to end a session, it is sometimes helpful to directly confront this by saying, "It appears to me that you wish we had more time." The reasons for the person's reluctance can then be discussed.

At times, a group session can be ended with a restatement of the way both the therapist and group have agreed to proceed. Or, a more explicit summation may be made by the group leader of what was discussed, what decisions were arrived at, what questions remain to be resolved, and what actions will be taken. A somewhat different approach is to ask each group member to state one item that was discussed or learned from the session and/or what he or she now plans to do.

Some therapy groups end by each member "leaving" a bad feeling and "taking home" a good one to be acted upon during the week. Sometimes concerns that were alluded to but not fully discussed might be mentioned in closing as topics that will be taken up at the next session. Some members reveal their most serious concerns for the first time at the end of a session, perhaps because they are ambivalent about whether they are ready to fully explore these concerns with the group. In these instances the therapist has to make a professional judgment about whether to extend the session beyond the allotted time or to set up an appointment to discuss these concerns privately or to wait until the next group session.

Sometimes it is helpful to end a group session with a relaxation exercise (described in chapter 15). A relaxation exercise helps members not only to relax, but also to reduce their level of stress so that they can more objectively view and work on resolving their problems after they leave.

Closing is especially important because what occurs during this last phase is likely to determine the members' impressions of the session as a whole. Leave enough time for closing so that the members do not feel rushed, as that might create the impression that they are being evicted.

ENDING A GROUP

The ending phase of a group frequently offers the greatest potential for powerful and important work. Group members may feel a sense of urgency as they realize there is little time left, and this can lead them to reveal their most sensitive and personal concerns. Because the work remaining to be done is usually clearly identified at this point, members can focus their efforts on completing it. However, the relationship dynamics are also heightened in this phase, as the members prepare to move away from each other, and the termination of the group may evoke powerful feelings in members.

If group members have grown emotionally close to each other, the ending of a group will be interpreted as a loss and produce a variety of emotions. Kübler-Ross stages of emotional reactions that people display when terminally ill resemble the reactions that people have to other important losses, including the ending of a successful and cohesive group.[3] Members may display denial through ignoring the imminent end of the group, anger and rage, or sadness and depression. They may attempt to bargain for an extension of the group in a variety of ways, such as urging that the group deal with additional problems. Ideally, members will ventilate and work through such feelings, and gradually come to accept the ending of the group. (Kübler-Ross stages are more fully described in chapter 25).

Other emotions may also be displayed. Some members may feel guilty because of adverse comments they made or because they believe they failed to take certain actions that would have benefited themselves or other members in the group. If a member left prematurely, some members may feel the group let him or her down. Members may want to share their feelings about the support system they will lose when the group ends. If certain members want the group to continue, they may interpret the ending of the group as a personal rejection. On the other hand, members who feel that the group was very successful may want to have a celebration to give recognition to the successes and to say goodbye.

In many ways the concluding sessions are the most difficult for the therapist and the group members. Strong emotions are often generated and should be ventilated and worked through. It is painful to terminate a group when members have formed relationships to share their most personal and important concerns and feelings. Our society has done little to train us to handle such separations; in fact, some segments in our society have a norm of being "strong" and not expressing feelings.

The therapist can help members accept the ending of a group in a number of ways. The process of terminating a group should begin during the early stages of the group. This guideline is particularly relevant for time-limited groups. The therapist should attempt to prevent the formation of dependency relationships between the members and the therapist. The goal is independence and better functioning, and this should be reiterated whenever appropriate during group sessions.

The therapist may summarize the emotional reactions that people have to group endings. An appropriate point for a discussion occurs when members display denial, anger, guilt, bargaining, or sadness. When discussing these feelings, the therapist shares his or her personal feelings and recollections, since the ending of the group has meaning for the therapist as well. The therapist can provide a model that may help members to express both their positive and negative concerns about the group ending. A problem-solving approach may be used to alleviate concerns; for example, if a group member is apprehensive about future problems, the therapist might provide the member with several other counseling resources.

The ending process should provide enough time for the therapist and the members to sort out their feelings and use the ending productively. A sudden ending cuts short necessary work and may not allow enough time for members to work through feelings and complete the remaining work. Sometimes, members indirectly express their anger by being late, appearing apathetic, being sarcastic, or battling over minor issues. In these situations the therapist should respond directly to the indirect cues by saying something like, "I wonder if your recent critical remarks are related to your anger that this group is ending? I know you have invested a lot in this group and may dislike that our meetings are coming to an end." By helping members to recognize and articulate their feelings, a therapist can help them express and work through those feelings. Once such feelings are dealt with, member will be more productive during the remaining time.

At or near the end of a group, members may test new skills and do things independently. They may report having tackled a tough problem or dealt with an issue by themselves. The therapist should acknowledge their independence and make positive remarks about the member's ability to "go it alone."

At times, the therapist may be the person leaving the group, perhaps to take a job elsewhere. In this situation, the therapist should create a smooth transition. If appropriate, involve the members in selecting the new leader. It may be helpful for the former leader and the new leader to be co-leaders for a brief period of time.

The ending of a group is a transition to something else. The important element during the ending phase of a group is to work with all members to help them develop a game plan so that the transition enables them to work toward new goals. The transition should not stifle members; rather, it should help them to progress. It may be valuable to note that life is full of transitions and passages; from early childhood to kindergarten; from kindergarten to elementary school; from childhood to puberty; from puberty to dating; from school to the work world; from being single to being married; from having responsibility only for oneself to becoming a parent; from working to retirement; and so on. In a transition phase we have the potential to make choices that will affect our future; the choices we make and the efforts we put forth determine whether the transition is constructive or destructive for us. Helping each member to make productive, realistic plans for the future is a goal of the ending phase of many groups.

During the process of terminating a group it is important that the therapist spend time obtaining feedback on how to improve future groups. Usually this is done by having members fill out a brief evaluation at the last (or next-to-last) session. This evaluation is done anonymously by the members. The following questions apply to a variety of therapeutic groups. For the first seven questions use the following scale: (1) Strongly disagree, (2) Disagree, (3) Neutral or uncertain, (4) Agree, (5) Strongly agree.

1. I am very satisfied with what this group accomplished.

   1   2   3   4   5

2. My personal goals in this group have been attained.

   1   2   3   4   5

3. I truly enjoyed being a member of this group.

   1   2   3   4   5

4. The therapist has done a superb job in leading the group.

   1   2   3   4   5

5. This has been one of the most rewarding groups I have participated in.

   1   2   3   4   5

6. I have grown extensively as a person through participating in this group.

   1   2   3   4   5

7. I have made substantial progress in resolving those personal problems which led me to join this group.

   1   2   3   4   5

The next three questions are open-ended:

8. The strengths of this group are:
9. The shortcomings of this group are:
10. My suggestions for changes in this group are:

At the final session it is also desirable for the members to discuss what they got out of the group, the merits of the group, and suggestions for improving it. Members should be given a chance to bring up unfinished business. In some cases an extra session may be held to complete unfinished business items.

One final important suggestion will be given. Occasionally, a therapist refers an individual to another group or therapist, or discusses a group member with another professional therapist. The reason may be: (a) the therapist feels that he or she is unable to empathize with that group member; (b) the therapist has extreme personal difficulty in accepting the fact that a member is choosing alternatives that the therapist finds disgusting (such as continuing to abuse a family member); (c) the member's problems are of such a nature that the therapist feels unable to provide the therapeutic help; and (d) a working relationship is not established with the member. A competent therapist knows that he or she can work with and help some people but not all. It may be in an individual's and a therapist's best interests to refer a group member to someone else who can help.

CO-FACILITATING GROUPS

Even though many settings do not have the resources to allow two leaders to facilitate a group, some programs can afford this type of group facilitation. Also, many students in internships are given opportunities to co-facilitate groups with either their field instructor or some other professional at their agency. The co-facilitator approach has many advantages, including the following:

- Each facilitator can grow from working with, observing, and learning from the other.
- Group members can benefit from the different life experiences, insights, and perspectives of the two facilitators.
- The two facilitators can complement each other, thereby benefiting the group.
- The two facilitators can provide valuable feedback to each other, including by discussing what happened in a session and how to approach a complex issue.
- The two facilitators can serve as models for the members with respect to how they relate and communicate to each other and to the group.
- If one of the leaders is female and the other is male, barriers that some members have involving gender can be more effectively confronted, explored, and resolved.
- While one facilitator is working with a particular member, the other facilitator can scan the group to get a sense of how the other members are reacting.
- Co-leading offers a certain safety, especially when practitioners are leading a group for the first time, since it is typical for beginning group facilitators to experience self-doubt and anxiety. Facing a group for the first time with a co-facilitator whom you respect and trust can turn what initially seems a frightening task into a delightful learning experience.

It should be noted that major disadvantages to co-facilitating a group occur when the facilitators fail to develop and maintain an effective working relationship. In order to develop such a working relationship, it is essential that the two facilitators respect each other. The two facilitators are likely to have some differences in leadership style and may not always agree or share the same perceptions and interpretations. However, when there is mutual respect, they will generally be able to communicate and discuss these differences, trust each other, and work cooperatively instead of competitively. If trust and respect between the facilitators are lacking, the members are bound to sense disharmony and the group is apt to be negatively affected. Power struggles between two incompatible co-facilitators may divide the group. Friction between the two facilitators can serve as a model for the other members to focus on negatives within the group and to subtly or overtly verbally hurt one another.

It is important for group facilitators to learn whom they can co-facilitate with and whom they cannot. Even secure, competent, and experienced facilitators who respect one another may not be able to work effectively together if their styles clash. For example, a facilitator who believes in leading by giving a great many suggestions aimed at providing quick answers for every problem expressed by group members is likely to clash with a facilitator who believes members best learn and grow by struggling and arriving at their own answers to their personal issues. If two facilitators discover that they cannot effectively work together, it does not necessarily mean that one is right and the other wrong, or that one or both are incompetent. It may simply mean that their styles clash and that each would be better off making arrangements to work with someone who has a similar style.

It is important for co-facilitators to get together regularly (ideally shortly after the end of each session) to discuss where the group has come and where the group needs to go. Additional areas to be discussed include: how the facilitators view the group and the individual members, how the facilitators feel about working with each other, and how to approach any complex issues that have arisen related to the group. The facilitators also need to make plans for the next session.

LEGAL SAFEGUARDS FOR GROUP FACILITATORS

Unfortunately, filing lawsuits has become a national pastime. In order to avoid a malpractice suit or to provide a defense if a lawsuit arises, a group facilitator should maintain reasonable, ordinary, and prudent (marked by wisdom or judiciousness) practices. Following are some guidelines for group leaders that are useful in translating the terms *reasonable, ordinary,* and *prudent* into concrete actions:

- Screen candidates for a group experience carefully. Many potential problems can be avoided by effective screening practices. The facilitator should select group members whose needs and goals are compatible with the goals of the group, who will not impede the group process, and whose well-being will not be jeopardized by the group experience.
- Adequately inform the members about the group process. Entrance procedures, time parameters of the group experience, expectations of group participation, goals of the group, intervention methods that will be used, rights of members, responsibilities of members and facilitator, methods of payment (where appropriate), and termination procedures should be explained at the outset of the group.
- Obtain written parental consent when working with minors.
- Obtain written informed-consent procedures at the outset of a group. Contracts signed by both the facilitator and the members are an example of such a procedure.
- Have a clear rationale for the techniques and exercises you employ in group sessions. Be prepared to concisely explain and defend the theoretical underpinnings of your techniques and exercises.
- Consult with your supervisor or an attorney on issues involving complex legal and ethical matters.
- Avoid becoming entangled in social relationships with group participants.
- Be aware of those situations in which you are legally required to break confidentiality.
- Carry malpractice insurance.
- Actively engage in keeping up with the theoretical and research developments that have a direct application to group therapy.
- Be knowledgeable about, and abide by, the codes of ethics for social workers. (In the United States, refer to the *NASW Code of Ethics* and in Canada refer to the *Canadian Association of Social Workers' Code of Ethics.*)
- Be aware of when it is appropriate to refer a group member for another form of treatment, and also be aware when group therapy might be inadvisable.
- Instruct members on how to evaluate their progress toward their individual goals. Also, routinely assess the general progress of the group.
- Write and maintain adequate records on the needs and goals of each member and the progress (or lack of it) made by each member in the group.
- Avoid promising members magical cures. Create reasonable expectations about what the group can and cannot achieve.
- Practice within the boundaries of your state and local laws.
- If you work for an agency, have a contract that specifies the agency's legal liability for your professional functioning.
- Abide by the policies of the agency that employs you. If you strongly disagree with agency policies and if they interfere with your ability to do your job, seek first to change these policies. If the policies cannot be changed, consider resigning.

• Define clearly to the members what confidentiality means and why it is important, and stress that what the members disclose should be kept confidential—even though the members should be aware that confidentiality cannot be guaranteed because some members may intentionally or unintentionally breach confidentiality.

SETTING PROFESSIONAL BOUNDARIES WITH CLIENTS

Is it appropriate for a social worker to have lunch or dinner with a client? Is it appropriate to attend a party (where alcoholic drinks are being served) where clients may be present? Is it appropriate to hug a client who is experiencing emotional distress? These are examples of boundary questions that arise in interactions with clients. Over the years I have seen a number of social workers and a number of social work interns subjected to severe disciplinary actions for failing to establish and maintain appropriate professional boundaries with clients. For example, a female intern was terminated at her field placement at a halfway house for chemically addicted correctional residents after she began dating one of the residents. A male social worker in a high school was dismissed for relating sexually explicit stories to the female clients he was working with.

Social workers have an obligation to establish appropriate boundaries in professional relationships with clients. *The NASW Code of Ethics* contains the following statements on boundary issues:

> The social worker should not condone or engage in any dual or multiple relationships with clients or former clients in which there is a risk of exploitation of or potential harm to the client. The social worker is responsible for setting clear, appropriate, and culturally sensitive boundaries.
>
> The social worker should under no circumstances engage in sexual activities with clients.[4]

Another section of the *NASW Code of Ethics* states:

> The social worker should not exploit relationships with clients for personal advantage.[5]

It is impossible to develop additional guidelines that will answer all the questions that may arise when social workers set boundaries with clients. The following guidelines may be useful in resolving some boundary dilemmas:

• In your professional *and* personal life, try to be a role model for the values and principles of the social work profession.
• In relationships with clients, try to gain their respect and to exemplify the values and principles of the social work profession, rather than establish a friend-to-friend relationship.
• Never try to meet your personal needs or wants in relationships with clients.
• Try to increase your awareness of your own needs, feelings, values, and limitations so you become increasingly aware of how such factors may impact client relationships.
• When questions arise about the appropriateness of certain interactions with a client (such as whether to go to lunch), try to arrive at an answer by gauging whether the interaction will have a constructive impact on the client and your relationship. If a

concrete beneficial impact cannot be objectively specified, do not engage in the interaction.

- Constructive professional relationships with clients require a certain amount of distance. If you have questions about whether contemplated social interactions will interfere with the boundaries of a professional relationship, consult your supervisor or a respected colleague.
- In your professional social work role with clients, be aware of any inappropriate behavior, verbal communications, and dress your part. For example, sharing details of your "wild" parties with teenage clients is probably unprofessional.

GROUP EXERCISES

Exercise A: Developing Counseling Skills with Role Playing

Goals: To develop counseling skills through role-playing counseling situations.

Step 1. The leader summarizes the following five phases of group counseling: (1) starting the meeting; (2) building a relationship; (3) exploring problems in depth; (4) exploring alternative solutions with clients and then trying one or more of the alternatives; and (5) ending the meeting. The purpose of the exercise is explained.

Step 2. Two students volunteer to be clients with personal problems. These two students may be allowed to come up with their own contrived problem or be given one. An infinite number of personal problems are possible, for example:

1. Two siblings are concerned about their dad living alone. Dad's wife recently died, and he has difficulty in getting around because of his arthritis. He tends to be gruff and not easy to live with.
2. A married couple has three children and is fairly content. The wife, however, wants to be a surrogate mother for a couple who wants a child. The husband does not want his wife to be a surrogate.
3. Two males or females have become sexually involved with each other. They do not know what the future will hold for their relationship and wonder whether they should inform their close friends and relatives.
4. A wife sometimes becomes so irritated at her two children that she physically abuses them. The husband wants the abuse to stop but does not know why the abuse is occurring or what he can do to prevent it.
5. One person who does not drink is concerned that his friend has a drinking problem. The second person denies a problem exists. Both are seeking counseling to resolve this conflict.
6. A sixteen-year-old female has informed her mother that sexual relations have been occurring frequently for the past three years with her stepfather. The mother is shocked;

the teenager is embarrassed and afraid. Both are seeking counseling on how they can emotionally cope and what they should do.

Step 3. The group leader may do the counseling or ask one or two students to role play the counselor. (If the group leader does the counseling, she or he should not be told what situation is being role played prior to the interview.) It is useful to have two counselors for the role play, so that one counselor isn't "stuck" not knowing what to say.

Step 4. Role play the interview.

Step 5. The class discusses the merits and shortcomings of the counseling. The counseling may be analyzed in terms of the guidelines presented in the chapter.

Step 6. Additional situations may be role played and then discussed.

Exercise B: Group Therapy in Action

Goal: To give an experiential awareness of being in a group therapy session.

Step 1. The leader announces that at the next class period a simulated group therapy session will be conducted, and states the goal of the exercise. Each student is given the "homework assignment" of identifying one or two personal problems that a friend or relative currently has. Students are told that they should not reveal the identity of the person having the problem and that the personal problem should be that of a friend or relative *and not of themselves*.

Step 2. At the next class period, the leader begins by stating ground rules:

> Today, we will have a simulated group therapy session in order to give you an experiential awareness of being in group therapy. Because this is a class, I strongly request that you do not reveal any personal information about any dilemmas or difficulties you are experiencing. Instead, describe one or two complicated personal dilemmas that a friend or relative is currently facing. For confidentiality reasons, please do not reveal the identity of the person whose problems you talk about. Remember, for reasons of confidentiality, what is said here stays here. Are there any questions about what we are going to do, or about the ground rules?

> If there are questions, try to answer them.

Step 3. Ask students to begin sharing concerns being faced by a friend or relative. If the class is reluctant to start, the leader initiates the process by specifically asking a normally vocal student to begin. When a student is sharing, the leader encourages the other students to probe with questions in order to further explore the problem, and then encourages them to suggest realistic and creative courses of action to resolve the problem. (In group therapy sessions, each member at times takes on the role of therapist.)

Step 4. After the dilemma revealed by one student is fully discussed and problem solved, other students share dilemmas that are currently being experienced by their friends and relatives. The exercise continues until the end of the class period, or until no one has anything further to share. At the end of the exercise, students are asked their thoughts about the benefits and shortcomings of the exercise, and their suggestions for changes in the format of the exercise when it is again used. During the exercise, one or more of the students may begin talking about a personal problem he or she is facing. The leader at this point has to make a judgment as to whether to let the student continue. The leader should not allow students to divulge personal information that they are apt to later regret sharing.

CHAPTER EIGHTEEN

CLIENT-CENTERED THERAPY IN GROUPS

Goal: Client-centered therapy has excellent suggestions for building rapport between the therapist and other group members. This therapy approach relies on clients to find solutions to their problems. This chapter summarizes client-centered therapy and describes how to use this approach in groups.

The founder of client-centered therapy* was Carl Rogers.[1] Client-centered therapy rests squarely on the assumption that everyone has a *self-actualization motive*. This motive is defined as the inherent tendency of each person (and organism) to develop his or her capacities in ways that serve to maintain or enhance the person.

Formulating theories of personality development and of psychopathology have not been a primary focus of client-centered theorists. Rogers was more interested in investigating the manner in which personality *changes* come about than in identifying the *causes* of present personality characteristics.

The driving force in personality development is theorized as the self-actualization motive, which seeks to optimally develop a person's capacities. Emotional and behavioral problems are thought to develop in childhood when the child *introjects* (takes on) those values of others which are inconsistent with his or her self-actualizing motive. Introjecting values inconsistent with one's self-actualizing motive causes "incongruences" between one's self-concept and the experiences that one has. For example, if a male child introjects the values that it is morally wrong to date or dance until age twenty, these introjected values will be part of his self-concept. As a teenager he may experience that peers relate to him in this area as being a prude with archaic values. When a person experiences incongruencies between his or her self-concept and experiences, that person will feel tension, anxiety, and internal confusion.

A person can respond to this "incongruence" in a variety of ways. One way is to use various defense mechanisms. A person may *deny* that experiences are in conflict with his or her self-concept. Or, the person may distort or rationalize the experiences so that they are then perceived as being consistent with his or her self-concept. If a person is unable to reduce the inconsistencies through such defense mechanisms, the person is forced to directly face the fact that incongruences exist between self and experiences which will lead the person to feel unwanted emotions (such as anxiety, tension, depression, guilt, or shame). If a person has a large or significant degree of incongruence between self and experiences which the defense mechanisms cannot cope with, "disorganization of self" generally occurs (for example, a "psychotic" breakdown).

THEORY OF THERAPY

The focus of client-centered therapy is to help clients become aware of incongruences between their self-concept and their experiences. Once this insight is achieved, the self-actualizing motive fosters a reorganization of the self-concept to be more congruent with experiences. Because of this self-actualizing motive, client-centered therapists are nondirective. They do not even suggest possible resolution approaches to clients.

Client-centered therapy asserts that the following three therapist attitudes are necessary and sufficient conditions to effect positive change in the client: empathy, positive regard, and genuineness or congruence. It is theorized that whenever a therapist displays these three attitudes toward a client, the actualizing potential of the client will begin to change and grow.

---

*Rogers and his colleagues now prefer the term *person-centered* therapy to client-centered, as they believe this name describes more adequately the human values their way of working incorporates.

Empathy is the capacity of the therapist to "put him- or herself in the shoes" of the client so that the therapist is able to understand what the client is thinking and feeling. Empathy also involves communicating this understanding to the client.

Unconditional positive regard means that the therapist fully accepts the client and conveys a genuine caring for the client. Positive regard requires a nonjudgmental attitude. Also, the therapist does not express approval or disapproval, does not make interpretations, and does not probe unnecessarily. The therapist conveys that he or she fully trusts the client's resources for increased self-understanding and positive change. With this attitude the client concludes: "Here is someone who repeatedly tells me in one way or another that she believes in my ability to find my way in the process of growth. Perhaps I can begin to believe in myself.[2]

Genuineness or *congruence* is the capacity of the therapist to trust his or her own gut reactions, and then convey those feelings or reactions that the therapist believes have relevance in the relationship. This willingness of the therapist, to express thoughts and feelings, provides the client with a reality base that the client can trust. It also takes away some of the risk of sharing hidden secrets with another.

For Rogers the *nature* of the relationship between client and therapist is seen as *the* key variable in producing positive changes. Rogers states:

> The more the therapist is perceived by the client as being genuine, as having an empathetic understanding, and an unconditional regard for him, the greater will be the degree of constructive personality change in the client.[3]

Rogers indicates two conditions are necessary before therapy can occur. First, the client needs to be uncomfortable or anxious because of incongruences between self and experiences. (Client-centered therapy will not work well with clients who deny a problem exists or who are unmotivated to change.) Second, a therapist must create a nonthreatening atmosphere where the client feels that he or she is fully accepted and understood and that the therapist genuinely cares about the client.

In such a relationship a client feels free (perhaps for the first time) to explore incongruences between self and experiences. (For example, a client begins to examine the inconsistency between believing that sex is sinful while enjoying the physical sensations of sex.) The client then comes face to face with the awareness that there is incongruence. The client begins to examine this incongruence and to think about what it would mean if other values were held (for example, having a value that responsible sexual experiences are desirable). During this process the client usually experiences feelings which have in the past been denied, repressed, or otherwise kept from consciousness. If and when this occurs, the concept of self becomes reorganized to include those experiences which in the past have been kept from consciousness. In addition, the client's concept of self becomes increasingly congruent with his or her experiences and also more consistent with the self-actualizing processes.

The role of the therapy is best characterized as being *nondirective*. The therapist's role is to create a permissive, nonthreatening psychological atmosphere where the client feels accepted by the therapist and feels free to explore his or her defenses and the incongruences between self and experiences. If growth of the individual is to occur, it is postulated that it is necessary for each person to assume responsibility for his or her actions, decisions, and behavior. Change that is significant and enduring, Rogers said, must be self-initiated. Therefore, complete responsibility for the direction of treatment sessions rests with the client. A client-centered therapist *does not* bring up subjects to discuss, give advice, make interpretations, or provide suggestions. Rogers believed that a person's self-actualization motive knows what courses of action the person should take, and therefore the focus of client-centered therapy is to help the client gain insight into values that are inconsistent with this motive, and then to allow the self-actualizing processes to make decisions and determine future directions.

During therapy, a client centered therapist seeks to help the client clarify personal thoughts and feelings. Three types of statements are primarily, and continually, used in the interview: clarification or reflection of feeling, restatement of content, and simple acceptance.

Clarification or Reflection of Feelings

If a client begins an interview by making critical statements about his or her boss, spouse, and the weather, the therapist might help the client better understand feelings by saying something like "You seem angry today" or "You're really upset about something today."

It should be noted that when client-centered therapists reflect feelings, they at times add to the reflection by expressing their own feelings at the moment, as indicated in the following excerpt:

Client: I think I'm beyond help.
Therapist: Huh? Feel as though you're beyond help. I know. You feel just completely hopeless about yourself. I can understand that. I don't feel hopeless, but I can realize that you do. Just feel as though nobody can help you and you're really beyond help.[4]

Restatement of Content

If a woman goes into a twenty-minute outburst about how her husband is not supporting the family, not being affectionate, and frequently coming home intoxicated, the therapist might say, "You're pretty unhappy with the way your husband is treating you and the children"—which is designed to help the wife take an overall look at her marriage.

Simple Acceptance

The therapist responds with "I see" or "Hmmm" to something the client has said. The therapist's words are said in a tone that conveys that the therapist understands and fully accepts what the client has said.

The use of these types of statements is illustrated in the following excerpt from a group therapy session with a client, a twenty-one-year-old male college student:

Client: I'm going to drop out of school. I'll never make it in college anyway, with the grades I'm getting.

Therapist: You're really down on college and thinking about dropping out because you believe you may not graduate due to your grades.

Client: I just received a D on my first exam in math, and I really studied for it.

Therapist: I see.

Client: It's a required course for my business major. I expected I'd do much better.

Therapist: You're feeling discouraged this evening because you anticipated you'd do much better.

Client: When I took the exam two days ago, I left thinking I was going to get at least a B on it. It didn't seem that hard.

Therapist: You were shocked when you received your exam back earlier today. You thought you had done much better.

Client: Yeah. I made some dumb mistakes in multiplying and dividing, which screwed up four of my answers.

Therapist: I see.

Client: If I don't pass this course, I'll never graduate. I've never received a D before in college.

Therapist: Your grades, overall, at this college have been fairly good. Certainly good enough to graduate. Tonight, however, you're kind of in a state of shock over the D you received earlier today.

Client: That's true. I guess I'm upset and making things worse than they are. It would be a mistake to toss away three years of college here.

Therapist: You're now concluding that getting one D does not mean you should drop out.

Client: I need to focus on what I can do to get a better grade on the next exam. Perhaps I can talk to the instructor to get her suggestions for studying for the next exam.

The theoretical objective of therapy is to enable the client to become fully functioning. A fully functioning person is a mature individual who has achieved complete congruence, hence, he or she is psychologically adjusted. This individual is not in a static state, but is a person in process—a person who is continually changing.[5]

Therapy frees clients of their faulty learning so that they can be what they are innately suited to be. This is not to say that therapy will produce an optimally adjusted person, but the therapeutic experience can help a person start the development of a new pattern of adjustment.

USING CLIENT-CENTERED THERAPY IN GROUPS

Rogers conceptualized the role of the therapist or facilitator in a group as having the same characteristics as the role of the therapist in one-to-one therapy. These characteristics are empathy, unconditional positive regard, and congruence. In addition, the group therapist should be nondirective, and use the following three types of statements: clarification or reflection of feelings; restatement of content; and simple acceptance. Rogers has further asserted that it is important for the facilitator to accept and to respect the group as a whole, as well as the individual members.[6]

The central hypothesis of group therapy using a client-centered approach is that group members have within themselves vast resources for self-understanding and for altering their behaviors, attitudes, and self-concepts. These resources become operative in a facilitative psychological climate. Such a climate is apt to be created by a group therapist who is empathetic, caring, and genuine.

Rogers can be praised for the outstanding contributions he made in articulating the components of a therapeutic relationship. Rogers emphasized the importance of the following concepts in building a helping relationship: *nonthreatening atmosphere, nonjudgmental attitude, empathy, genuineness,* and *client as problem solver.* Rogers also developed techniques involving therapist's responses that have facilitated the development of a constructive relationship: *clarification or reflection of feeling, restatement of content,* and *simple acceptance.* The relationship between the social worker and the client, partly due to Rogers' emphasis, has become recognized as the keystone of social work practice.[7]

Fischer reviewed a large number of studies conducted on the three attitudes hypothesized by Rogers as being necessary and sufficient conditions for producing positive changes in clients—the three attitudes of empathy, genuineness, and positive regard or warmth. Fischer concludes:

> The findings from these studies have been remarkably consistent. Taken together, this research strongly supports the view that the level of therapist or helper empathy, warmth, and genuineness and associated interpersonal skills is related to positive change in client personal and social functioning. Practitioners who are relatively high on these core conditions of interpersonal helping tend to be effective practitioners. These findings hold with a wide variety of types of practitioners regardless of training, background, or theoretical orientation.[8]

These findings dramatically suggest that regardless of the theoretical orientation of a counselor, a successful outcome of counseling is highly dependent on a counselor conveying empathy, warmth and genuineness!

In spite of these strengths, there are some limitations of client-centered therapy. Eysenck found that outcome studies on client-centered therapy generally *fail* to demonstrate that clients receiving the therapy improve at a higher rate than control groups with similar problems.[9] Why these rather discouraging results? It would seem that while developing a helping relationship and helping clients to gain insight into their problems are an essential part of counseling, these elements do not constitute the total counseling process. Clients not only need to gain an understanding of the nature and causes of their problems, they also need to be made aware that there are various courses of action that they can take to resolve the problems. Client-centered therapists do not inform clients of available resolution strategies, as they believe it is the responsibility of clients to figure this out for themselves. Many other theorists, such as Glaser, have pointed out the importance of having the counselor suggest various alternatives, and then having clients make commitments (contracts) to try one of these alternatives.[10]

Examples of the importance of exploring alternatives are easily listed. People who are depressed may understand why they are depressed (for example, a broken romance), but may not know how to resolve the depression. A person who knows he or she has a drinking problem, is addicted to narcotic drugs, or is a chain smoker may be unaware of the various programs and approaches to resolve these addictions. A mother who is aware she is an ineffective parent may be unaware of what she can do to be more effective. A person who knows he or she is shy or aggressive may be uninformed about specific assertive training techniques. A person who has a phobia (for example, high test anxiety) knows a problem exists, but is often unaware of how to resolve the fear and anxiety.

While empathy, warmth, and genuineness may well be an essential part of counseling,

Prochaska notes that Rogers "seems to have gone too far and concluded that what may be necessary conditions for therapy to proceed are also sufficient conditions for therapy to succeed."[11]

GROUP EXERCISE

Exercise A: Client-Centered Therapy in Action

Goal: To understand the merits and shortcomings of client-centered therapy.

Step 1. Prior to explaining client-centered therapy, ask for two volunteers to come up with a contrived problem that they jointly have (e.g., a "brother" and "sister" disagree on whether they should seek to place their mother in a nursing home—the mother is living alone and has recently been diagnosed as having Alzheimer's disease). Ask for two students to volunteer to be counselors. Instruct the "clients" to go out in the hallway to select and develop their contrived problem. While the "clients" are out in the hallway, inform the counselors they can use only statements that: (a) clarify or reflect feelings, (b) restate content, or (c) convey simple acceptance. Briefly give examples of these statements. Inform the "counselors" that they should not ask questions, make interpretations, or provide suggestions. Indicate that in theory, client-centered therapists use only the above three types of statements.

Step 2. Ask the "clients" to return, and have the counselors then counsel the "clients."

Step 3. After the counseling is completed, ask the counselors to discuss their feelings about being limited to these three types of statements. Ask the "clients" and the other students in class to discuss their thoughts about this type of counseling.

Step 4. Review the principles of client-centered therapy.

CHAPTER NINETEEN

TRANSACTIONAL ANALYSIS
IN GROUPS

Goal: Two key conceptualizations of Transactional Analysis that are particularly useful in group therapy and group work are game analysis and script analysis. Game analysis and script analysis are described in this chapter, and the applications of these conceptualizations to groups are summarized.

The founder of Transactional Analysis was Eric Berne.[1] A transaction is a unit of social intercourse. A transaction is composed of a transactional stimulus (verbal and nonverbal messages sent by one individual) and a transactional response (verbal and nonverbal messages by another individual, who is reacting to a transactional stimulus). The following is an example of a transaction:

Husband: What are we going to have for dinner tonight?
Wife: It's up to you. Whatever you'd like to make for us.

Transactional Analysis focuses much of its attention on analyzing the communications and interactions between clients and significant others in their lives.

Transactional Analysis has numerous conceptualizations. It is an elaborate approach to therapy. Fully describing this approach is beyond the scope of this chapter. The interested reader is referred to the references in the notes for this chapter.[2]

The two treatment conceptualization of Transactional Analysis that probably have the most useful applications to groups are game analysis and script analysis. Game and script analyses can be used by social workers in therapy groups to help members identify interpersonal and intrapersonal problems and then to develop more effective behavioral patterns. Because group members often exhibit or discuss the games they play, destructive games can be analyzed and new patterns of behavior can be tested with the supportive feedback of other group members.

GAMES

A game can be defined as a set of transactions with a gimmick (a hidden scheme for attaining an end).[3] In a game, participants are consciously or unconsciously striving to achieve an ulterior outcome by using a hidden scheme. For example, in the following exchange a salesman uses a gimmick to sell his product:

Salesman: This one is better, but you can't afford it.
Male customer: That's the one I'll take.

The salesman arouses the customer's pride by telling him that he is unable to afford the better but more expensive item. Psychologically, the customer says to himself, "I'll buy the expensive item just to show that arrogant fellow I'm as good as any of his customers."

People who are attempting to achieve a hidden outcome may or may not be aware of their intentions—or of the gimmick they are using. For instance, a husband who has a vague fear his wife may desert him may not be aware he is playing a game when he says to her, "Honey, why don't you quit work and stay home to take care of the house? I can earn enough to support both of us." Although some games may lead to substantial financial loss or mental anguish for some participants, not all games are necessarily undesirable. An individual with a strong need for social approval, for example, may perform many "altruistic" and "charitable" deeds.

A game may be repeated frequently. For some group members, playing a certain game may become so much a part of their personality that it can aptly be called their style of life. A male alcoholic who denies to himself and to others that he has a drinking problem is an example. The alcoholic's payoffs for denying his drinking problem are the rewards he receives from drinking—such as feeling high and temporarily escaping his problems.

The "alcoholic" game also illustrates another aspect of games: several people may be involved. In the alcoholic game described by Berne, there may be a nagging, masochistic wife who literally drives her husband to drink so that he will abuse her when inebriated.[4] This wife receives two payoffs. First, the abuse is a form of recognition or attention.* Second, on the day after a drunken episode, the wife has ammunition to belittle and berate her husband and to get him to do things to atone for his behavior. The alcoholic may also have companions who frequently invite him to "have a drink—a drink will be good for you." Their payoff is the fun they have partying. Then, there is the sympathetic listener, perhaps a bartender who listens in order to persuade the alcoholic to buy more drinks.

Social and Psychological Levels

There are often two levels of communication involved in games: social and psychological. The *social level* is the overt or manifest, and the *psychological level* is the covert or latent. Prochaska gives the following example of these two levels of communication in a game:

> For example, if a woman asks a man, "Why don't you come by my place to see my collection of sculpture?" and the man responds, "I'd love to. I'm really interested in art," they may be . . . communicating a message at a different level, such as . . . "Boy, I'd really like to get you alone in my apartment" and "I'd sure love to look at your curves."[5]

Payoffs

As a game progresses, one or more of the participants may switch behavior to receive a payoff. An example is provided by Prochaska:

> For the payoff to occur, one of the players has to pull a switch. In this case, after fixing drinks and sitting close on the couch examining a reproduction of Rodin's *The Kiss,* the woman still seems to be sending a seductive communication. The man's vanity convinces him to proceed, and he puts his hand on her leg, only to be rebuffed by a slap on the face and an irate "What kind of woman do you think I am?"[6]

As Prochaska describes, each player sets up a response that will satisfy his or her psychological needs:

---

*Transactional Analysis makes an important psychological point by asserting that in the absence of receiving positive "strokes"—forms of human recognition—a person will seek negative ones. In other words, this approach holds that even negative human attention may be desired over no attention at all. Positive strokes include greetings, smiles, approval, cheers, and applause. Negative strokes include cold looks, disapproval, criticism, and frowns.

Besides gaining mutual recognition, excitement, and some structured time together, there is also a strong emotional payoff for each. The woman is able to proudly affirm her position in life that she is OK, while feeling angry toward men for not being OK, just as her mother always said. The payoff for the man is to feel depressed and thereby reaffirm his conviction that he is not OK.[7]

Types of Games

Eric Berne lists a large number of psychological games in his book, *Games People Play*.[8] Although the number of different games that can be played is infinite, people tend to have a repertoire of favorites. In fact, many group members base their social relationships upon finding suitable partners to play the corresponding opposite roles. The following are common games that are often encountered in group therapy.

In the game "Why Don't You? Yes, But . . . ," a group member consistently asks for suggestions or advice, and then rejects it. The other participants in this game assume the principal player is attempting to solve a real problem, so they offer suggestions. The principal player in this game is able to get at least two payoffs—one is attention from other group members; the other is the feeling of superiority that comes from being able to put others down by implying, "That's really a dumb suggestion." The other participants may get a payoff through telling themselves, "I must be a warm, caring person as this person respects and trusts me enough to share this problem with me."

In the "One Up" game, one group member attempts to top whatever someone else says. If the conversation is about big fish, the One Upper always has a story about how he caught a record-breaker. If the topic is about poor grades, the One Upper explains how his are "the worst." If jokes are being told, the One Upper begins by saying, "I've got one that'll top that. Have you heard about . . ."

"Wooden Leg" is a game in which a group member attempts to manipulate others to expect less of him because of such "wooden legs" as having a physical disability, being raised in a poor home, having had a tragic romance, having emotional problems such as being depressed, and so on. Closely related, "If It Weren't For . . ." is a cop-out game in which players seek to rationalize not succeeding at a variety of tasks and goals to absolve themselves of personal responsibility.

A group member who plays "Poor Me" is seeking sympathy and may at times try to get others to do things for him. Closely related is someone who plays "Ain't It Awful" by often taking a negative view of events in order to receive attention and sympathy. In the game "There I Go Again," the player tries to excuse ineffective behavior without taking responsibility; the payoff is that others are less apt to pressure the player to be responsible.

Some group members enjoy playing "Confession," in which they reveal all their personal troubles in the hope of receiving recognition and help. Some unhappily married men enjoy discussing "Wives Are a Pain" as a way of ventilating their unhappiness. Some unhappily married wives enjoy discussing "Men Aren't Worth It" as a way of ventilating their frustrations. Parents claim "Look How Hard I've Tried" when a home situation is particularly unsettled and hostile as a way to relieve their frustrations that their family goals have not been achieved.

Some group members who have received few positive strokes end up seeking a lot of negative strokes, which to them is better than receiving no strokes. One game played to receive negative strokes is "Kick Me," in which the player seeks negative reactions from others. Group members who enjoy creating trouble for others are apt to play "Let's You and Him Fight"; the payoff is the pleasure they receive from watching others tangle.

People who receive psychological rewards for analyzing others and giving advice often play "Psychiatry." A group member who tries to see how many different sexual relationships he can have often plays "Love 'Em and Leave 'Em"; the payoff is a variety of sexual experiences and the hedonistic pleasure of sexual conquests. Many males in our society are socialized to play "Mr. Macho," and many females are socialized to play "Miss America." "Monday Morning Quarterbacks" attempt to make themselves feel important by telling others what they should have done differently *after* things have not turned out well.

GAME ANALYSIS

Game analysis is a treatment technique intended to help clients gain insight into their interactions through the use of game concepts. The kinds of games that are the main focus of such analysis are those that lead to undesirable outcomes for group members or others.

In group game analysis, the counselor or leader serves several functions. Initially, he or she introduces members to the concept of games and to the process of game analysis by taking members step-by-step through the analysis of a game. The counselor points out early on that games are commonly played by everyone and that not all games are bad; game analysis in the group tends to focus on those games that are destructive for individuals or impede group functioning. "Game playing" carries a negative connotation for many people, suggesting deception and exploitation. Therefore, members may resist examining their personal games out of distaste or guilt. By reassuring the group that games are common and often positive, the counselor will reduce members' resistance and encourage their participation in game analysis.

The group counselor also helps members identify their games by assigning names to them. The names (for example, "Poor Me") are frequently colloquial and describe the behavior itself, so that members find them understandable and meaningful.[9] By naming their behaviors, group members can more easily identify similar interactions when they occur in the future.

Changing destructive game behavior is ultimately what members are trying to achieve, and the group counselor works toward helping them to achieve this end. In helping members recognize how their roles in such games lead to negative consequences, the counselor also helps them to consider other games they could play that would have positive outcomes and satisfy their goals. Most people have positive goals; they simply haven't identified the best strategies for achieving them. Often these individuals can be instructed on what to do by using game concepts. For example, a person seeking a job may need to learn "How to Get an Interview" and "How to Sell Yourself in an Interview." Or a couple who are frequently feuding may need to learn "How to Fight Fairly" and "How to Give in a Relationship to Get What You Want."

Once group members recognize and understand a game that is causing them difficulty, they are in a better position to stop their destructive behavior and to explore alternative modes of behavior. Analyzing behavior in terms of games may be intriguing to clients, lead to greater personal involvement in therapy, and increase their motivation to resolve their difficulties. Also, game analysis provides group members with a method of analyzing certain problematic interactions. After learning how to analyze such interactions, they should be better able to analyze problematic games other than those specifically discussed at meetings.

LIFE SCRIPTS

Every person has life scripts (plans) formed during childhood and based upon early beliefs about themselves and others. These plans are developed from early interactions with parents and others and are largely determined by the pattern of human recognition, or "strokes" in Transactional Analysis terminology, that are received.

Many details of a life script are supplied by parental opinions, suggestions, and encouragements. Examples include, "She's such a cute girl, everyone loves her," "He's stupid and will never amount to much," "He'll be famous some day," "He's sure nutty," "All the girls want to date him." Fairy tales, myths, TV shows, early life experiences, and children's stories are also important sources of life scripts. While parental influences and fairy tales are important contributing factors, the life script is still the creation of the young child. One's life script may involve either winning or losing and be exciting or banal. Each script also includes specific roles, such as heroes and heroines, villains, persecutors, innocent bystanders, and victims.

Harris has identified four general life scripts that a person chooses that determine how the person views himself or herself in comparison to others.[10] These four positions are: (1) I'm OK—You're OK; (2) I'm OK—You're not OK; (3) I'm not OK—You're OK; and (4) I'm not OK—You're not OK.

Group members who decide "I'm OK—You're OK," tend to be productive, law-abiding, successful individuals who have positive, meaningful relationships with others.

Group members who decide "I'm OK—You're not OK," predispose themselves to exploit, cheat, rob, or succeed at the expense of others. This type of person may be a criminal, a ruthless business executive, or a destructive lover who "loves 'em and leaves 'em."

Individuals who decide, "I'm not OK—You're OK" feel inferior in the presence of those they judge as superior. This life script frequently leads to withdrawal from others as a way to avoid being reminded of not being OK. Withdrawal is not the only alternative. The person can write a counterscript based on lines borrowed from early authority figures: "I can be OK if . . ." The person is then driven to achieve the "if" contingencies. Examples of such contingencies include making huge sums of money, being submissive, being entertaining by making others laugh, and so on. This individual then strives to meet these contingencies in order to receive strokes and approval from others.

People who decide "I'm not OK—You're not OK" tend to be the most unhappy and disturbed. Prochaska states:

> The extreme withdrawal of schizophrenia or psychotic depression is their most common fate. They may regress to an infantile state in the primitive hope that they may once again receive the strokes of being held and fed. Without intervention from caring others, these individuals will live out a self-destructive life or institutionalization, irreversible alcoholism, senseless homicide, or suicide.[11]

James and Jongeward provide the following example of how a life script is played:

> . . . a woman, who had taken the position "Men are bums," marries a "sequence of bums." Part of her script is based on "Men are not OK." She fulfills her own prophecy by nagging, pushing, complaining, and generally making life miserable for her husband (who has his part to play). Eventually, she manipulates him into leaving. Then she can say, "See, I told you. Men are bums who leave you when the going gets rough."[12]

Most life scripts are learned at an early age. As children grow, they learn to play roles—villains, law enforcers, heroes, heroines, victims, rescuers—and find others to play complementary roles. Through playing roles, children integrate new themes and parts into their roles and gradually develop their life scripts. The particular scripts that are developed are substantially influenced by the reactions they receive from significant people in their lives. James and Jongeward provide an incident in the life of a client, now forty-three, that led her to conclude, "I'm not OK, and men are not OK either."

> My father was a brutal alcoholic. When he was drunk, he would hit me and scream at me. I would try to hide. One day when he came home, the door flew open and he was drunker than usual. He picked up a butcher knife and started running through the house. I hid in a coat closet. I was almost four years old. I was so scared in the closet. It was dark and spooky, and things kept hitting me in the face. That day I decided who men were—beasts, who would only try to hurt me. I was a large child and I remember thinking, "If I were smaller, he'd love me" or "If I were prettier, he'd love me." I always thought I wasn't worth anything.[13]

Playing out this script, she married an alcoholic at twenty-three and for the next twenty years lived her life feeling worthless and at the mercy of a "beast."

A life script and a theatrical script have many similarities. Each has a cast of characters, dialogue, themes and plots, acts and scenes, and generally both move toward a climax. Often, however, a person is unaware or only vaguely aware of the life scripts he is acting out. Public stages on which people act out their scripts include home, social gatherings, church, school, office, and factory.

Individuals follow scripts, and so do families and cultures. Cultural scripts are expected patterns of behavior within a society. In the U.S. culture, for example, only men are expected to fight in military conflict; in others, such as Israel, both sexes are expected to fight wars. In regard to cultural scripts, James and Jongeward note:

> Script themes differ from one culture to another. The script can contain themes of suffering, persecution, and hardship (historically, the Jews); it can contain themes of building empires and making conquests (as the Romans once did). Throughout history some nations have acted from a "top-dog" position of the conquerer; some from an "underdog" position of the conquered. In early America, where people came to escape oppression, to exploit the situation, and to explore the unknown, a basic theme was "struggling for survival." In many cases this struggle was acted out by pioneering and settling.[14]

Historically, women were socialized in our society to have different life scripts from men. American women traditionally were expected to be affectionate, passive, conforming, sensitive, intuitive, dependent, and "sugar and spice and everything nice." They were supposed to be primarily concerned with domestic life, to be nurturing, instinctively to love caring for babies and young children, to be deeply concerned about their personal appearance, and to be

THEMES FOR LIFE SCRIPTS

There are an infinite number of script themes. A few of the more common ones are:

I must be loved by everyone.
I've got to be perfect.
I've got to be the best at what I do.
My purpose in life is to save sinners.
When people tell me their problems, I have to rescue them.
I will take my life some day.
To be noticed I must play tricks on people.
People will love me only if I make them laugh.
I'll also be a victim.
I'm a martyr.
I can always get what I want by being pushy.

I'll eventually go crazy.
My life will always be one big party.
I'm cut out to be a leader.
I'm a failure and always will be.
I'll never get anywhere.
I've got to save for a rainy day.
If I acquire a lot of money, I'll be popular.
I'm always the life of a party.
I'm always miserable.
Life has always shortchanged me.
I should always be silent as it is wrong to rock the boat.
Men are animals.
I will never let anyone get the best of me.
I'm headed for fame and fortune.

self-sacrificing for their family. They were not to appear to be ambitious, aggressive, competitive, or more intelligent than men. They were expected to be ignorant and uninterested in sports, economics, or politics. In relationships with men, they were not to initiate forming a relationship and were expected to be tender, feminine, emotional, and appreciative.

There are also a number of traditional sex role expectations for males in our society. A male was expected to be tough, fearless, logical, self-reliant, independent, and aggressive. He was expected to have definite opinions on the major issues of the day and make authoritative decisions at work and at home. He was expected to be a strong individual who was never depressed, vulnerable, or anxious. He was never supposed to display "sissy" or feminine behavior, and he was expected not to cry or show emotion openly. A male was the provider, the breadwinner, the competent force in all situations, who was also physically strong, self-reliant, athletic, daring, aggressive, brave, and forceful. He was supposed to initiate relationships with women and dominate in relationships with them. As a result of the women's movement and a number of other factors, these sex role scripts are being changed.

In our society (as well as in other large and complex societies), there are a number of subcultures—street gangs, Chicanos, Texans, Presbyterians, Jews, professional baseball players, dentists, farmers, college students—and each subculture has its own scripts. Common scripts for college students, for example, include cramming at the last moment for exams, procrastination, partying, idealism, shortage of money, and expectation of success and happiness after graduation. Families also have scripts, which provide a set of directions for family members:

"We Winships have always been pillars of the community."
"We Schoemakers have always been gamblers."
"We Hepps have never had to ask for a handout from anyone."
"We Watsons have all gone to college."
"We Rices have always been Democrats."

If a family member does not live up to the script, he or she is often viewed as a "deviant" or a "black sheep."

The importance of scripts in determining human behavior is emphasized by Berne:

Nearly all human activity is programmed by an ongoing script dating from early childhood, so that the feeling of autonomy is nearly always an illusion—an illusion which is the greatest affliction of the human race because it makes awareness, honesty, creativity, and intimacy possible for only a few fortunate individuals. For the rest of humanity, other people are seen mainly as objects to be manipulated. They must be invited, persuaded, seduced, bribed or forced into playing the proper roles to reinforce the protagonist's position and fulfill his script.[15]

Often people play games as part of their life scripts. A group member who has a script of being a Casanova often plays the game "Love 'Em and Leave 'Em." A person whose script is "I won't let anyone get the best of me" may play "One Up." A person whose script involves being an advisor to others may play "Monday Morning Quarterback." A group member whose script is "I'll always find a way to seduce people into helping me" is apt to play "Poor Me."

SCRIPT ANALYSIS

Script analysis, like game analysis, is a treatment intended to help clients gain insight into the life roles they set for themselves through scripts. Here again, the counselor and clients focus on scripts that are negative and counterproductive for the client or others.

The counselor serves the same basic function in script analysis as in game analysis. Briefly, the counselor introduces members to the concept of life scripts and shows them how their scripts can be identified and analyzed, reassures them that not all scripts are bad, thereby reducing members' resistance to and encouraging their participation in script analysis; helps members assign names to their scripts and understand how these are counterproductive to achievement of goals; and helps members find new, more successful scripts for the future. Group members then have the opportunity to practice and test out their new scripts in group interactions.

GROUP EXERCISES

Exercise A: Game Analysis

Goal: To understand the concepts of game analysis and learn to identify and describe games that are played.

340

Step 1. The leader begins by summarizing how games are defined and by giving examples of a number of different games.

Step 2. Each person describes on a sheet of paper a destructive game that he or she has either played or observed others play.

Step 3. The class forms subgroups of three or four persons, so that the members can share the descriptions of the games they identified. (*Students should know that they may choose not to share the game they wrote down.*) After a member shares what he or she has written, the other members of the subgroup discuss with this person what might be done to stop the destructive game from being replayed.

Step 4. As a class, the students discuss the merits and shortcomings of analyzing destructive interactions in terms of game concepts.

Exercise B: Destructive Life Scripts

Goal: To identify destructive scripts that someone close to them (either a family member or a friend) is acting out.

Step 1. The leader explains what life scripts are and gives a number of examples of common life scripts (see "Life Scripts" in this chapter).

Step 2. Each person describes as fully as possible on a sheet of paper a destructive life script that a family member or a friend is acting out. *Important: The person should not be identified.* The following example is read to illustrate the kind of description desired.

> I know a person who was brought up to believe that a marriage vow should never be broken, no matter how difficult the situation may become. This woman has a number of scripts associated with this view. Some of these are that it is the wife's role to do the domestic tasks around the home, that she has the main responsibility for raising the children, that it is her duty to cover up for her husband's drinking, that God will reward her in the afterlife for her trials and tribulations in this present life, that it is her duty to work outside the home to meet financial needs, and that she should put up with the abuse that her husband dishes out. With these scripts this woman is now in her sixties and has been married for thirty-four years. She has raised three children and has worked as a nurse all the years of her marriage. Her husband is an alcoholic, was a construction worker, but has not worked for the past nineteen years because he has cirrhosis of the liver and has had one stroke. He continues to drink. For all the years of the marriage, he has been verbally and physically abusive to her. She recently retired. The three children moved away from home several years ago and now have families of their own. The husband comes home drunk three or four times a week, is now incontinent, and the wife is increasingly becoming frustrated and angry about having to be nursemaid to her husband who continues to berate her. The husband has been in a number of alcoholic treatment programs, including Alcoholics Anonymous, but none of these has curbed his drinking. His health problems are now such that he

needs extensive attention that is currently being provided by the wife. The wife does not want to place the husband in a nursing home as this would wipe out the money she has worked hard to save for retirement. She does not want to separate or get a divorce, while at the same time she is feeling at her wits' end about being nursemaid to an alcoholic who is abusive and incontinent. What should she do?

Step 3. The students form subgroups of three or four persons and share the life scripts that were written. The subgroups discuss what can be done to help people who are playing out these destructive life scripts.

Step 4. The class discusses the merits and shortcomings of analyzing destructive interactions in terms of life scripts.

Exercise C: Analyzing Your Own Life Scripts

Goal: To identify and reflect upon life scripts.

Step 1. As in Exercise B, the instructor reviews what life scripts are and gives examples.

Step 2. The instructor explains that life scripts are generally formed at a young age and asks the students to imagine what their childhood years were like. Each person writes down one or two sentences or phrases in regard to what their parents said about the following. (The instructor reads each of the following, giving students time to write down their responses.)

Your intelligence	*Your worth*	*Your abilities*
Your health	*Your morals*	*Your friends*
Your looks	*Your sexuality*	*Your future*

Step 3. Each person reflects upon whether their current assessments of themselves in these areas are consistent or inconsistent with what their parents told them.

Step 4. The class discusses the merits and shortcomings of this exercise.

CHAPTER TWENTY

REALITY THERAPY
IN GROUPS

Goal: Reality therapy is a commonsense approach that is widely used. It emphasizes establishing rapport with clients and then using a problem-solving approach. This chapter summarizes reality therapy and describes how to use reality therapy in groups.

The founder of reality therapy is William Glasser.[1] Reality therapy is based on the premise that there is a single basic psychological need faced by everyone: the need for an identity. Glasser and Zunin define the need for an identity as:

> the need to feel that each of us is somehow separate and distinct from every other living being on the face of the earth and that no other person thinks, looks, acts, and talks exactly as we do.[2]

Although identity can be viewed in several ways, Glasser believes that from a therapeutic vantage point it is most useful to conceptualize identity in terms of people who develop a *success identity* versus those who develop a *failure identity*.

People who develop a success identity do so through the pathways of *love* and *worth*. People who view themselves as successful must feel that at least one other person loves them, and that they also love at least one other person. They must also feel that at least one other person feels they are worthwhile, and they must feel they (themselves) are worthwhile.

In order to develop a success identity a person must experience both love and worth. Glasser and Zunin state:

> In reality therapy, we see *worth* and *love* as two very different elements, consider, for example, the extreme case of the "spoiled" child. One may fantasize that a child, if showered with "pure love," whose parents' "goal" was never to frustrate or stress or strain this child in any way, and when he was faced with a task or difficulty always had his parents to perform this task for him, this child always relieved of responsibility would develop into an individual who would feel loved but would not experience worth. Worth comes from accomplishing tasks and achieving success in the accomplishment of those tasks.[3]

A person can also feel worthwhile through accomplishing tasks (for example, a successful business person), but believe he is unloved because he cannot name someone whom "I love and who loves me." Experiencing only one of these elements (worth or love) without the other can lead to a failure identity.

A failure identity is likely to develop when a child has received inadequate love or been made to feel worthless. People with failure identities express their sense of failure by: (a) developing emotional or behavioral problems, (b) engaging rather extensively in delinquent or criminal activities, or (c) withdrawing. Reality therapy agrees with the commonsense notion that those with a positive self-concept are apt to be responsible and productive citizens, while those with a negative self-concept are apt to display their feelings of inferiority in one or more of the following ways: emotional problems, behavioral problems, criminal activities, suicide, or withdrawal.

A success identity or a failure identity is not measured by finances or labels, but rather in terms of how a person perceives him- or herself. It is possible for individuals to regard themselves as failures while others view them as being successful. Formation of a failure identity usually begins during the years when children first enroll in school. It is at about this age (five or six) that children develop the social and verbal skills and the thinking capacities to define themselves as being either successful or unsuccessful. Children, as they grow older, then tend to associate with others having a similar identity; those with failure identities associating with others having a failure identity, and success identities associating with other successful people. As the years pass, the two groups associate less and less with each other. Glasser and Zunin note:

For example, it is indeed rare for a person with a success identity to have, as a close and personal friend, someone who is a known criminal, felon, heroin addict, and so forth.[4]

People with success identities tend to compete constructively, meeting and seeking new challenge. Also, they tend to reinforce one another's successes. On the other hand, people with failure identities find facing the real world to be uncomfortable and anxiety producing, and therefore choose either to withdraw, to distort reality, or to ignore reality.

THEORY OF THERAPY

In counseling clients (both individually and in groups), reality therapy advances the following fourteen principles:

Responsible Behavior

The main goal of reality therapy is to help clients reject irresponsible behavior and to learn improved ways of functioning. A responsible person is defined as one who has the ability to fulfill personal needs and to do so in a way that does not deprive others of the ability to fulfill their needs. (Glasser indicates the above description of a responsible person is also an excellent guide to use in determining whether actions are moral or immoral.)

One of the therapist's tasks is to confront clients with their cop-outs. Reality therapists do not excuse clients' irresponsible behavior through theoretical interpretations that blame personal problems on the past actions of parents or on other excuses. Responsibility is emphasized because, in order for clients to feel worthwhile, they must feel they are maintaining a satisfactory standard of behavior.

Mental Illness Labels Are Destructive

Glasser agrees with Szasz that mental illness is a myth.[5] Glasser presents his view:

> In consonance with our emphasis on responsibility and irresponsibility, we who practice Reality therapy advocate dispensing with the common psychiatric labels, such as neurosis and psychosis, which tend to categorize and stereotype people. Limiting our descriptions to the behavior which the patient manifests, we would, for example, describe a man who believes that he is President Johnson as irresponsible, followed by a brief description of his unrealistic behavior and thinking. Calling him psychotic or schizophrenic immediately places him in a mental illness category which separates him from most of us, the label thereby serving to compound his problem. Through our description it can immediately be understood that he is unsuccessful in fulfilling his needs. He has given up trying to do so as John Jones and is now trying as President Johnson, a logical delusion for a man who feels isolated and inadequate. The description *irresponsible* is much more precise, indicating our job is to help him to become more responsible so that he will be able to satisfy his needs as himself."[6]

Glasser urges that the word *irresponsible* be used in place of medical model labels, such as "insane," "psychotic," and "schizophrenic."

Glasser raises the question: If we relate to people who have emotional problems as if they are insane and lock them up in a mental institution, how can we expect them to learn to be responsible and productive? Those who adjust to the routine in a mental hospital are in no way learning how to make it in the real world, as a mental institution is an artificial environment in which dysfunctional behavior is expected and excused. Glasser asserts that labeling people as "mentally ill" sidetracks them into dwelling on the erroneous notion that they have a "disease of the mind," which no one as yet knows how to treat. Instead, Glasser asserts it would be far better to relate to people with emotional and behavioral problems as people who have an excellent potential (as everyone does) to improve and resolve their personal problems. It is well known that the way people are treated is the way they come to perceive themselves. If people are treated as mentally ill, they are apt to perceive themselves as being mentally ill and to play that role (perhaps for the rest of their lives). On the other hand, if people with emotional problems are related to as being sane, with a high potential to solve their own problems, they are much more likely to become responsible and productive.

Involved Relationship

The identity we develop is largely dependent on our involvement with others. In therapy it is important for the therapist to help a client clarify and understand him- or herself, including beliefs, values, opinions, and self-concepts.

For a therapist to become involved is also important; as every person at all times must have at least one person who cares about him or her. Cool detachment and aloofness are not considered helpful. Reality therapists seek to become involved through conveying warmth, understanding, and concern.

Reality therapists are *personal* in therapy; that is, they seek to present themselves as real people. They do not project an image of omnipotence, but reveal themselves. When appropriate and constructive, reality therapists will personalize the counseling by self-disclosing their own experiences.

Focus on Present and Future

Reality therapists believe that what we want now and in the future, along with our motivation to achieve what we want, is more important (than our past experiences) in determining what our future will be. The past is fixed; it cannot be changed. All that can be changed is the present and the future. Past experiences brought us to the present, but in no way should be used as justification for irresponsible behavior now and in the future. Permitting a person to dwell on the past is a waste of time. If the past is discussed it is always related to current behavior. For example, if a person describes a broken romance that occurred several years ago, the therapist will ask how that event is related to the client's present behavior.

DOES MENTAL ILLNESS EXIST?

Thomas Szasz, in the 1960s, was one of the first authorities to assert that mental illness is a myth—that it does not exist.[1] Beginning with the assumption that the term *mental illness* implies a "disease in the mind," Szasz categorizes all of the so-called mental illnesses into three types of emotional disorders and discusses the inappropriateness of calling such human difficulties "mental illnesses":

1. *Personal disabilities,* such as excessive anxiety, depression, fears, and feelings of inadequacy. Szasz says such so-called mental illnesses may appropriately be considered "mental" (in the sense that thinking and feeling are considered "mental" activities), but he asserts they are not diseases.
2. *Antisocial acts,* such as bizarre homicides and other social deviations. Homosexuality used to be in this category but was removed from the American Psychiatric Association's list of mental illnesses in 1974. Szasz says such antisocial acts are only social deviations, and he asserts they are neither "mental" nor "diseases."
3. *Deterioration of the brain with associated personality changes.* This category includes the "mental illnesses" in which personality changes result following brain deterioration from such causes as arteriosclerosis, chronic alcoholism, Alzheimer's disease, general paresis, or serious brain damage due to an accident. Common symptoms are: loss of memory, listlessness, apathy, and deterioration of personal grooming habits. Szasz says these disorders can appropriately be considered "diseases," but are diseases of the *brain* (that is, brain deterioration specifies the nature of the problem) rather than being diseases of the *mind*.

Szasz, in "The Myth of Mental Illness," asserts that the notion that people with emotional problems are mentally ill is as absurd as the belief that the emotionally disturbed are possessed by demons:

The belief in mental illness as something other than man's trouble in getting along with his fellow man, is the proper heir to the belief in demonology and witchcraft. Mental illness exists or is real in exactly the same sense in which witches existed or were real. (P. 67)

The point that Szasz and many other writers are striving to make is that people do have emotional and behavioral problems, but they do not have a mystical mental illness. These writers believe that terms that describe unwanted emotions and dysfunctional behaviors are very useful: for example, *depression, anxiety, obsession, compulsion, excessive fear, hallucinations,* and *feelings of being a failure.* Such terms describe personal problems that people have. But mental illness terms, they assert (such as schizophrenia and psychosis), are not useful, because there is no distinguishing symptom that would indicate whether a person has, or does not have, the "illness."

1. Thomas Szasz, "The Myth of Mental Illness," in *Clinical Psychology in Transition,* ed. John R. Braun (Cleveland, OH: Howard Allen, 1961).

Focus on Behavior Rather Than on Feelings

Feelings and actions are considered to be interrelated and mutually reinforcing. Reality therapists assume that humans have only limited control over their feelings. Changing actions of clients is considered to be the most productive way to help clients feel better.

Reality therapists believe it is important for clients to become aware of what they are doing that is leading them into difficulty. If a client states, "I have really felt sad and miserable the last few weeks," a reality therapist will say, "What are you doing to make yourself depressed?" Or, if a client indicates at some length that he is unhappily married, the reality therapist will ask such questions as "What are you doing that contributes to the unhappiness?" and "What are you planning to do about your unhappiness?"

Value Judgments

Reality therapists believe people need to learn to evaluate their own behavior and assess what they are doing to contribute to their failures before they can be assisted. This therapy is persistent in guiding clients to explore their actions for signs of irresponsible behavior. Therapists repeatedly ask clients what their current behavior is accomplishing and whether it is meeting their needs. Reality therapists believe people do not change irresponsible behavior unless they first understand what they are doing.

A major task for reality therapists is to help clients face the morality of their behavior. Reality therapists seek to help clients judge whether their behavior is irresponsible. Clients are assisted in seeing that their behavior is irresponsible whenever they are hurting themselves or hurting others—and this judgment is to be made by clients. Therapists generally do not make value judgments for clients as this would relieve them of the responsibility for their behavior.

By questioning *what* the person is doing now and *what* he can do differently, the therapist conveys a belief in the person's ability to behave responsibly.

Planning

Reality therapists seek to explore problems in depth with clients and to then explore alternative solutions and their consequences. If a client cannot develop a personal plan for future action, the therapist will help develop one. Once the plan is worked out, a contract is drawn up and signed by the client and the therapist. The plan is usually a minimal, realistic plan for behaving differently in matters in which the client admits to acting irresponsibly. If the contract is broken, a new one is designed and agreed upon. Plans are also generally made for the contract to be reviewed periodically.

Commitment is a keystone in reality therapy. It is only from making and following through with plans that people gain a sense of self-worth and maturity.

Reject Excuses

Glasser is aware that not all plans and commitments made by clients will be achieved. But he does not encourage searching for reasons to justify irresponsible behavior: to do so would support a belief that clients have acceptable reasons for not doing what they have agreed was within their capabilities. Excuses let people off the hook; they provide temporary relief, but they eventually lead to more failure and to a failure identity.

When a client fails to meet a commitment, the therapist simply asks "Are you planning to meet your commitment?" If the answer is in the affirmative, the therapist asks "When?" Or, if the client says he no longer intends to meet the commitment, the therapist may suggest working together to develop a new contract.

In not accepting excuses, the therapist does not seek to deprecate or demean the client for failing, but seeks to convey that a reasonable plan for improvement is always possible.

Eliminate Punishment

Punishing persons when they fail to meet a commitment reinforces a failure identity. It also usually leads to more hostility without producing positive, lasting changes. It serves as only a temporary means of forcing different behavior. When the client no longer believes he is under surveillance, he will usually return to exhibiting irresponsible behavior.

Eliminating punishment is quite different, according to Glasser, from following through on the natural consequences of behavior involved in contractual planning.* For example, if a runaway youth contracts to receive shelter at a runaway center on the condition that he will remain drug-free, and then is caught smoking pot, the center must follow through on the consequences spelled out in the contract, which may include removal from the shelter. Not following through on such consequences would only reinforce the irresponsible behavior.

Do Not Offer Sympathy

Sympathy does little more than convey the therapist's lack of confidence in the client's ability to act more responsibly. Listening to long, sad stories about the client's past, or sympathizing with a person's misery will do nothing to improve that person's ability to lead a responsible life.

---

*Glasser has a minor conceptual problem in this area as learning theory defines following through on consequences as being a form of punishment.

CASE EXAMPLE: REALITY THERAPY

Several years ago when I [the author] was employed as a social worker at a maximum security hospital for the criminally insane, my supervisor asked me to develop and lead a therapy group. When I wondered aloud who should be in the group and what its objectives should be, my supervisor indicated those decisions would be mine. He added that no one else was doing group therapy at the hospital and that the hospital administration thought it would be desirable to develop such a program.

Being newly employed at the hospital and wary because I had never been a group leader before, I asked myself, "Who is in the greatest need of group therapy?" and "If the group members do not improve, or even deteriorate, how will I be able to explain this—that is, cover my tracks?" I concluded that I should select those identified as being most ill (those labeled as chronic schizophrenics). Because such patients are generally expected to show little improvement, I felt I would not be blamed if group members did not improve. However, if they did improve, I thought it would be viewed as a substantial accomplishment.

First I read the case records of all the residents (eleven) who were diagnosed as chronic schizophrenics. I then met individually with each of these residents to invite them to join the group. (To my surprise, each of the residents appeared to be very different from the impressions I received from reading the case records.) I explained the purpose of the group and the probable topics to be covered. Eight of the eleven who were contacted decided to join; some frankly stated they would join primarily because it would look good on their records and increase their chances for an early release.

In counseling these group members, the approach I used was based on reality therapy. I began the first group meeting by stating I knew what the "key" was to their being discharged from the hospital and asked if *they* knew what that might be. This statement got their attention. I indicated that the key was very simple— they had to learn to "act sane" so that the medical staff would think they had recovered. At the first meeting the

purpose and the focus of the group was presented and described. Our purpose was not to review the past, but to make life in the present more enjoyable and meaningful and to plan for the future. Various topics would be covered: how group members could convince the hospital staff they no longer needed hospitalization; how they could prepare for returning to their home community (for example, learning an employable skill while at the institution); and what to do when they felt depression or some other unwanted emotion or had an urge to do something that would get them into trouble again after their release. Occasionally films covering some of these topics would be shown and discussed. The group would meet for about one hour each week for twelve weeks.

This focus on improving the current circumstances of the group members stimulated their interest, but soon they found it uncomfortable and anxiety-producing to examine what the future might hold for them. They also became uncomfortable after being told they had considerable control over their future. They reacted to this discomfort by stating that they were "mentally ill" and therefore had some internal condition that was causing their strange behavior. Further, since no cure for their schizophrenia had yet been found, they believed they could do little to improve.

I told them that their excuses were "garbage" (stronger terms were used) and spent a few sessions convincing them that the term "chronic schizophrenic" was a meaningless label. I spent considerable time in explaining the myth of mental illness; that people do not have a "disease of the mind," though they may have emotional problems. I went on to explain that what had gotten them locked up was their deviant behavior. The only way for them to get out was to stop such behavior and convince the staff that they would not exhibit it if released.

The next excuse they tried was that the broken homes or ghetto schools or broken romances or other misfortune had "messed up" their lives for good, and they could do little about their situation. "Garbage," I

CASE EXAMPLE: REALITY THERAPY (con't.)

---

told them. True, their past experiences were important. But, I emphasized, what they *wanted* out of their future and the motivation they had to achieve their goals were more important in determining the future.

Finally, after working through a number of excuses we focused on how they could better handle specific problems: how to handle being depressed, how to stop exhibiting behavior considered "strange," how to present themselves as being "sane" in order to increase their chances of an early release, and how to adjust to returning to their home communities. Besides determining what kind of work or career they desired upon their release, they prepared themselves by learning a skill or trade while at the institution. By examining what they wanted out of the future, we could outline specific steps to help them achieve their goals. It was

also important to stress that they continue to take the psychoactive medication that had been prescribed.

The results of this approach were encouraging. Instead of idly spending much of the time brooding about their situation, group members became motivated to take action. At the end of the twelve weeks, the eight members spontaneously stated that the meetings were making a positive change in their lives and requested that another social worker from the hospital be assigned to continue the group after I left to return to school. This was arranged. Three years later on a return visit to the hospital, I was informed that five of the eight group members had been released to their home communities and two of the others had shown improvement. One group member's condition was described as "unchanged."

Rarely Ask Why

Asking a client the reasons for irresponsible actions implies that such explanations make a difference. The reality therapist believes that irresponsible behavior is just that, regardless of the reasons. Listening to explanations for irresponsible behavior is not only time-consuming, but may also be counterproductive as it may lead the client to conclude that the irresponsible behavior can continue by coming up with (often contrived) explanations. By giving little attention to such explanations, the reality therapist conveys that responsible behavior is expected.

Praise Responsible Behavior

People need recognition for their positive accomplishments and for their positive efforts in *trying* to accomplish something even though they may not succeed. Such responsible behavior is reinforced and praised by reality therapists.

Reality therapists also seek to convey that they believe people are capable of changing their irresponsible behavior. It is easier to do things well when others are encouraging and realistically optimistic.

351

Question Traditional Case Histories

Traditional case histories emphasize the failures, shortcomings, problems, and traumas which the client has to cope with. Such case histories are often tragic and notorious misrepresentations. They usually tell more about the theoretical orientation of the writer than about the client, as they try to reinterpret client's behaviors and feelings in terms of diagnostic labels and the writer's favorite theory of personality development. Rarely do case histories provide an assessment of the person's successes and personality strengths, which are at least as important in understanding a person as that person's shortcomings and failures.

Foster Success Experiences

In helping clients to develop plans to improve their circumstances, the reality therapist strives to help clients achieve *realistic* goals and helps them to understand and master the tasks (means) involved in accomplishing these goals. To counteract failure identities, clients need to begin to take risks and experience successes. Gradually such successes lead clients to perceive themselves more positively.

USING REALITY THERAPY IN GROUPS

Reality therapy is a commonsense approach to therapy. The approach has been found to be effective with clients in one-to-one situations and in groups. It emphasizes a problem-solving approach to therapy. In summary form, the basic format of reality therapy involves three phases for the therapist:

1. Developing a relationship with clients.
2. Exploring problems in depth.
3. Exploring alternatives for resolving these problems, with clients then selecting one or more alternatives to implement.

There is overlap between these phases.

Reality therapy emphasizes the concept that clients are personally responsible for their own behavior. It affirms a belief in the dignity of people and their ability to improve their situation. The goal of therapy is to help clients identify their irresponsible behavior and then learn to be more responsible. The concepts of reality therapy are relatively simple to learn and apply. The use of reality therapy is demonstrated in the box "Case Example: Reality Therapy."

GROUP EXERCISES

Exercise A: Counseling with Reality Therapy

Goal: To practice using the concepts of reality therapy in counseling situations.

Step 1. Describe the purpose of this exercise. Summarize the fourteen principles of reality therapy which are described in this chapter. Indicate that in summary form the basic emphasis of a reality therapist is on the following three phases:

1. Developing a relationship with clients.
2. Exploring problems in depth.
3. Exploring alternatives for resolving these problems.

(There is overlap among these three phases).

Step 2. Have two volunteers make up a contrived problem that they jointly have. (For example, a husband wants to have children and wants his wife to stay home to raise them, while the wife wants a career and does not want to have children.) Ask for two more volunteers to be "counselors" and to use the principles of reality therapy. Have the "counselors" counsel the "clients."

Step 3. Have the class discuss the merits of the counseling that was given and how well the "counselors" used the principles of reality therapy.

Exercise B: Mental Illness Debate

Goal: To identify the arguments as to whether or not mental illness exists.

Step 1. At a class session some students in the class form two panels—one that will argue that mental illness exists, and the other that will argue that mental illness is a myth. Panel members are given a few days to gather information and to prepare their arguments. Panel members may interview counselors and therapists in the community and also read reference materials.

Step 2. At the selected class date, a debate is held. At the end of the debate, the students uninvolved in the debate summarize the strong points made by the debaters.

CHAPTER TWENTY-ONE

RATIONAL THERAPY IN GROUPS

Goal: Rational therapy asserts that unwanted emotions and dysfunctional behaviors are primarily determined by our thought processes, rather than by external events. This chapter summarizes rational therapy and describes how to use rational therapy in groups.

354

The two main developers of rational therapy are Albert Ellis and Maxie Maultsby.[1] The approach has the potential to enable those who become skillful in rationally analyzing their self-talk to control or get rid of their undesirable emotions and dysfunctional behaviors.

THEORY OF THERAPY

It is erroneously believed by most people that our emotions and our actions are primarily determined by our experiences (that is, by events that happen to us). On the contrary, rational therapy has demonstrated that the primary cause of all our emotions and actions is what we tell ourselves about events that happen to us.

All feelings and actions occur according to the following format:

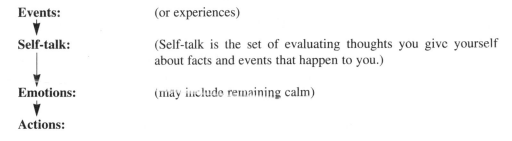

Events:	(or experiences)
Self-talk:	(Self-talk is the set of evaluating thoughts you give yourself about facts and events that happen to you.)
Emotions:	(may include remaining calm)
Actions:	

An example will illustrate the above process.

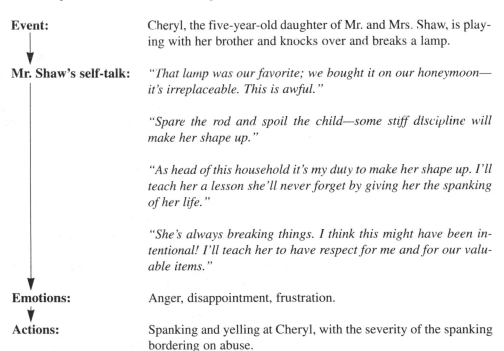

Event:	Cheryl, the five-year-old daughter of Mr. and Mrs. Shaw, is playing with her brother and knocks over and breaks a lamp.
Mr. Shaw's self-talk:	*"That lamp was our favorite; we bought it on our honeymoon—it's irreplaceable. This is awful."*
	"Spare the rod and spoil the child—some stiff discipline will make her shape up."
	"As head of this household it's my duty to make her shape up. I'll teach her a lesson she'll never forget by giving her the spanking of her life."
	"She's always breaking things. I think this might have been intentional! I'll teach her to have respect for me and for our valuable items."
Emotions:	Anger, disappointment, frustration.
Actions:	Spanking and yelling at Cheryl, with the severity of the spanking bordering on abuse.

If, on the other hand, Mr. Shaw gives himself a different set of self-talk, his emotions and actions will be quite different.

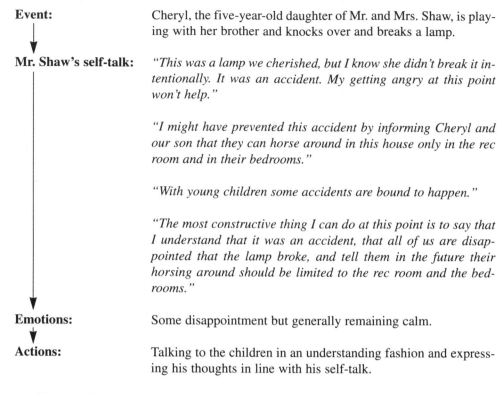

Event:	Cheryl, the five-year-old daughter of Mr. and Mrs. Shaw, is playing with her brother and knocks over and breaks a lamp.
Mr. Shaw's self-talk:	*"This was a lamp we cherished, but I know she didn't break it intentionally. It was an accident. My getting angry at this point won't help."*
	"I might have prevented this accident by informing Cheryl and our son that they can horse around in this house only in the rec room and in their bedrooms."
	"With young children some accidents are bound to happen."
	"The most constructive thing I can do at this point is to say that I understand that it was an accident, that all of us are disappointed that the lamp broke, and tell them in the future their horsing around should be limited to the rec room and the bedrooms."
Emotions:	Some disappointment but generally remaining calm.
Actions:	Talking to the children in an understanding fashion and expressing his thoughts in line with his self-talk.

The most important point about the above process is that our self-talk determines how we feel and act; by changing our self-talk, we can change how we feel and act. Generally, we cannot control events that happen to us, but we have the power to think rationally and thereby change *all* of our unwanted emotions and ineffective actions.

The rehabilitative aspect of this conceptualization of self-talk is that any unwanted emotion and any ineffective behavior can be changed by identifying and then changing the underlying self-talk.

The self-talk we give ourselves about specific events that happen to us is often based on a variety of factors, including our beliefs, attitudes, values, wants, motives, goals, and desires.[2] For example, the self-talk a married woman might give herself on being informed by her husband that he wants a divorce would be influenced by her desire (or lack of desire) to remain married, by her values and beliefs about being a divorcée, by her attitudes toward her husband, by how she believes getting a divorce would be consistent or inconsistent with her present goals, and by her beliefs about the reasons why her husband says he wants a divorce.

Another important thing about self-talk is that with repeated occurrences of an event, a person's emotional reaction becomes nearly automatic because the person rapidly gives himself or herself a large set of self-talk gradually acquired through past experiences. For example, a few years ago I counseled a woman who became intensely upset and depressed every time her husband came home intoxicated. In examining her emotional reactions it became clear that because of the repeated occurrences she would rapidly tell herself the following on seeing him inebriated:

"He's making a fool of himself and of me."

"He's foolishly spending money we desperately need."

"For the next few hours I'm going to have to put up with his drunken talk and behavior—this is awful."

"He loves drinking more than he loves me because he knows I do not want him to get drunk."

"Woe is me."

CHANGING UNWANTED EMOTIONS

Rational therapy is increasingly being used to change unwanted emotions. Because this is a primary focus of rational therapy, the methods used to change unwanted emotions will be specified in this section.

Rational therapy asserts that all emotions are primarily determined by self-talk, even the emotion of love. Individuals often believe that love is a feeling beyond their control. The language of love reinforces this erroneous belief: "I just *couldn't help it*, he swept me off my feet," "I *fell* in love," and "*It was* love at first sight." In reality, even the emotion of love is based primarily on self-talk. The following format illustrates this process.

Event: A woman's ideal date is a man who is tall and athletic, has dark hair, is a good conversationalist, and likes pop music. She meets a man in one of her classes who is six feet tall, a football player, has dark hair, is personable, and likes pop music.

Her Self-Talk: *I can hardly believe I've finally met someone I'm really attracted to. This person is really handsome, charming, the kind of person I'd really like to get to know better and to go out to dinner with.*

Her Emotion: Feelings of infatuation.

There are five ways to change an unwanted emotion. Three are constructive: getting involved in a meaningful activity; changing the negative and irrational thinking underlying the unwanted emotion; and changing the distressing event. Each can be learned and practiced within a group setting. Two are destructive: abuse of alcohol, drugs, and food; and suicide. We will discuss each of the five in turn.

Meaningful Activity

Practically everyone encounters day-to-day frustrations and irritations—having a class or two that isn't going too well, working at a job that's unpleasant, or coping with a dull social life. Dwelling on such irritations will spawn such unwanted emotions as depression, anger, frustration, despair, or feelings of failure. Which of these emotions a person has will directly depend upon the person's self-talk.

Meaningful, enjoyable activity, however, produces satisfaction and a healthful distraction from unwanted emotions. Group members can learn the value of meaningful activity by writing an "escape" list, a list of activities they find motivating, energizing, and enjoyable: taking a walk, playing golf or tennis, going to a movie, shopping, doing needlework, visiting friends, and so on. By having an "escape" list of things they enjoy doing, group members can nip unwanted emotions in the bud. By getting involved in things they enjoy, they can use enjoyable activities to take their minds off their day-to-day concerns and irritations. The positive emotions they experience will stem directly from the things they tell themselves about the enjoyable things they are doing.

In urging group members to compile and use an escape list, rational therapy is not suggesting that members avoid doing something about unpleasant events. If something can be done to change a distressing event, all constructive efforts should be tried. However, we often do not have control over unpleasant events and cannot change them. Although we cannot change unpleasant events, we always have the capacity to control and change what we tell ourselves about the unpleasant events. It is this latter focus that is often helpful in learning to change our unwanted emotions.

Changing Self-Talk

A second approach to changing unwanted emotions is to identify and then alter the negative and irrational thinking that leads to them. Maultsby has developed an approach entitled Rational Self-Analysis (RSA) that is useful for learning to challenge and change irrational thinking.[3] An RSA has six parts, as shown in figure 21.1.

The goal in doing an RSA is to change an unwanted emotion (anger, love, guilt, depression, hate) by recording the event and one's self-talk on paper. Under part A (facts and events), group members state the facts or events that occurred. Under part B (self-talk), they write all of their thoughts about the events in part A. Group members number each statement in order (1, 2, 3, 4, and so on), and write "good," "bad," or "neutral" after each self-talk statement to show themselves how they believe each part B statement reflects on themselves as individuals. Under part C (emotional consequences), they write simple statements describing their gut reactions/emotions stemming from the self-talk in part B.

Figure 21.1: Format for Rational Self-Analysis (RSA)

A Facts and events	**D(a)** Camera check of A
B Self-talk 1. _____ 2. _____ etc.	**D(b)** Rational debate of B 1. _____ 2. _____ etc.
C Emotional consequences of B	**E** Emotional goals and behavioral goals for similar future events

Part D(a) is to be written *only* after parts A, B, and C have been completed; part D(a) is a "camera check" of part A. Group members reread part A and ask themselves, "If I had taken a moving picture of what I wrote was happening, would the camera verify what I have written as fact?" A moving picture would probably have recorded the facts, but not personal beliefs or opinions. Personal beliefs or opinions belong in part B. A common example of a personal opinion mistaken as a fact is: "Karen made me look like a fool when she laughed at me while I was trying to make a serious point." Under D(a), camera check of A, group members correct any opinions by stating only the factual part: "I was attempting to make a serious point when Karen began laughing at what I was saying." Then, the personal opinion part of the statement should be added to B (that is, "Karen made me look like a fool").

Part D(b) determines whether the self-talk statements in B are rational. Each B statement should be taken separately. Group members read B–1 first and ask themselves if it is consistent with rational thinking. It is *irrational* if it does one or more of the following:

1. *Does not fit the facts.* For example, when a person *feels* unloved after a lover has ended their relationship, even though several close friends and relatives love that person.
2. *Endangers one's life.* For example, when someone takes drugs to escape from a problem.
3. *Keeps one from achieving short- and long-term goals.* For example, when a person wants to do well in college but decides to go out socializing instead of studying before exams.
4. *Causes significant trouble with other people.* For example, when a person challenges others to a fight when feeling insulted.
5. *Leads one to feel emotions that one does not want to feel.*

If the self-talk statement is rational, group members should merely write "that's rational." If, on the other hand, the self-talk statement is irrational, group members should then think of an alternative self-talk to that B statement. This new self-talk statement is of crucial importance in changing an undesirable emotion and needs to be: (1) rational, and (2) a self-talk statement a group member is willing to accept as a new opinion for himself. After jotting down this D(b)–1 self-talk in part D(b), group members consider B–2, B–3, and so on in the same way.

Under part E, the new emotions group members desire in similar, future A situations should be noted. In listing these new emotions, members should keep in mind that they will follow from their self-talk statements in part D(b). This part may also contain a description of specific actions they intend to take to help them achieve their emotional goals when they encounter future A events.

To make a rational self-analysis work, group members must challenge their negative and irrational thinking with rational debates. With effort, they can learn to change any unwanted emotion, and this capacity is one of the most important abilities a person can have. (Once members become adept in RSA, they will be able to do the process without having to write it out.)

Challenging negative and irrational thinking *will* change unwanted emotions if members put the needed effort into it. Just as dieting is guaranteed to result in a loss of weight, so this approach is guaranteed to change unwanted emotions. Both, however, require effort and a commitment to use the processes in order to make them work.

Changing the Distressing Event

A third way to change unwanted emotions is to change the distressing event. There are an infinite number of distressing events: losing a job, the breakup of a romantic relationship, receiving failing grades, being in an automobile accident, and so on. In some cases, constructive action can be taken to change the distressing event. For example, if a man is terminated from a job, he can seek another; when he finds one he will feel better. If a student is getting failing grades, a conference with the instructor may give the student some ideas about how to improve the grades. If the suggestions appear practical and have merit, the student will feel better.

Not all distressing events can be changed. For example, a woman may have a job that she needs and be forced to interact with other employees who display behaviors she dislikes. If that individual cannot change the behaviors of the others, the only other constructive option is to "bite the bullet" and adapt to the circumstances. However, when it is practical to change distressing events, they should be changed. When constructive changes in events are made, a person is then apt to feel better because he or she will then (in all likelihood) be having more positive self-talk related to the constructive changes that have been made.

Destructive Ways of Dealing with Unwanted Emotions

There are two destructive ways to deal with unwanted emotions which, unfortunately, some people use. I want to make it clear that I strongly discourage using either of the following two ways. I present them only in order to complete the list of ways to deal with unwanted emotions. One of these methods is to temporarily relieve intense unwanted emotions through the use of alcohol, other drugs, or food. Many people seek relief in the use of mind-altering drugs such as alcohol, cocaine, tranquilizers, and so on. When the effects of the drug wear off, the person's problems and unwanted emotions remain, and there is a danger that through repeated use the person will become dependent on the drug. Some people overeat for the same reasons—loneliness, insecurity, boredom, and frustration. The process of eating and the feeling of having a full stomach provide temporary relief from intense unwanted emotions. Such people are apt to become overweight or bulimic—or both.

The other destructive way to relieve unwanted emotions is suicide. This is the ultimate destructive approach to dealing with unwanted emotions. If you know of someone who is contemplating suicide, you have a legal right and an ethical obligation to seek to connect that person with professional help—even when the suicidal person requests that you do not inform anyone else of his or her intentions.

ASSESSING AND CHANGING DYSFUNCTIONAL BEHAVIOR

Our self-talk is the primary determinant not only of our emotions, but also of our actions, as illustrated in the following diagram:

EXAMPLE OF RATIONAL SELF-ANALYSIS

A.   **Facts and Events**

A.   I dated a guy steadily for two months that I really thought I liked. I knew something was not quite right with our relationship. I was unable to figure out what it was until he finally said that he had been dating another girl for two years and was still seeing her. However, he promised that they would break up soon and urged me to "hang on" for a little while. Three weeks passed, and then I saw them speaking to each other one night. When she left, I went over to talk to him and he seemed to be in a bad mood. I tried to get out of him what was the matter. Then, we began to talk about the other girl, and he said he could not break up with her for a while and we were not going to see each other at all for a while. Then, I started to yell at him for various things, and the crying began.

B.   **Self-Talk**

B-1.   I hate him! (bad)

B-2.   How could I be such a sucker for the last two months? (bad)

B-3.   All guys are jerks. (bad)

B-4.   I'll never date anyone else again. (bad)

B-5.   I'm glad I know now where I stand for sure. (good)

B-6.   What did I ever do to him to be treated like this? (bad)

D(a).   **Camera Check of A**

D(a).   All of this is factual.

D(b).   **My Rational Debates of B**

D(b)-1.   I don't really hate him. He was good to me and we did enjoy the times we had together.

D(b)-2.   I should not feel as if I was a sucker because I did not know about the other girl until he finally told me.

D(b)-3.   Guys are not all jerks. I have many male friends who are far from being jerks. In fact, I do not even know what a "jerk" is. I've never seen a jerk. Guys are humans, not jerks. It is irrational to label someone a "jerk" and then to relate to that person as if the label were real.

D(b)-4.   I know I will date again, since I always have after other breakups.

D(b)-5.   That's rational.

D(b)-6.   He told me I never did anything to have this happen. It was just a situation he got himself into and he now needs time to work things out.

(continued next page)

361

EXAMPLE OF RATIONAL SELF-ANALYSIS *(con't.)*

B-7. No one loves me. (bad)

D(b)-7. How can I say that! I have a lot of close friends and relatives, and I know several guys that think highly of me.

B-8. I'm a failure. (bad)

D(b)-8. I'm not a failure. I'm doing well in college and at my part-time job.

B-9. I'll never find anyone I loved as much as him to date. My life is ruined. (bad)

D(b)-9. My life is certainly not ruined. I'm accomplishing many of my goals in life. With two million eligible guys in the world there are certainly many other worthy guys to form a relationship with. I told myself the same erroneous things a few years ago when I broke up with someone else. I will eventually get involved in another relationship with someone else I love. I need to think positively and dwell on the positive things I've learned in this relationship.

B-10. This guy just used me and took what he could get. (bad)

D(b)-10. Neither of us "used" each other. I'm even uncertain what "used" means. We enjoyed being together and had a lot of good times. He told me he has a lot of positive feelings toward me. He was forced to make a choice between two people, both of whom he enjoyed being with.

B-11. My life is over. I'll never find happiness again. (bad)

D(b)-11. My life is certainly not over. I have many positive things happening to me right now, and there are many things I enjoy doing. I also have a number of close relatives and friends who'll be there when I need them.

B-12. This is awful! This is the worst thing that could happen to me. (bad)

D(b)-12. Life is full of ups and downs. It is a mistake to "awfulize" and to exaggerate how this breakup will affect my future. There are many other more dreadful things that could happen—such as a terminal illness.

C. **My Emotions**
Outward emotions were crying and yelling. Inner emotions of feeling angry, hurt, depressed, embarrassed, a failure, and unloved.

E. **My Emotional and Behavioral Goals**
To be able to change my unwanted emotions so that I no longer am angry, depressed, and hurt about this breakup. Also, I would like to talk to him in private and apologize for my behavior. After I become more comfortable with this breakup, I will gradually be interested in dating someone else in the future.

Events

↓

Self-talk

↓

Emotions

↓

Actions

In a nutshell, our actions are primarily determined by our self-talk (cognitions). Our thoughts determine our actions. To demonstrate this principle, reflect on the last time you did something bizarre or unusual. What self-talk statements were you giving yourself (that is, What were you thinking) prior to and during the time when you did what you did?

Rational therapy maintains that the reasons for any dysfunctional act (including crime) can be determined by examining what the offender was telling him- or herself prior to and during the time when the act was being committed. Two examples of cognitions that lead to dysfunctional behavior are the following:

Cognition: A sixteen-year-old sees an unlocked Firebird and thinks, "Hey, this is the ultimate car to drive. Let me cross the starting wires and take it for a ride."

Behavior: Car theft.

Cognition: A twenty-three-year-old male is on his third date with the same woman. He brings her to his apartment and thinks, "She is really sexy. Since I've wined and dined her three times, it's now time for her to show her appreciation. I'll bet she wants it as much as I do. I'll show her what a great lover I am. If she says, 'Don't,' I know she really means 'Don't stop.' I'll use a little force if I have to. When it's over, she'll really love me."

Behavior: Date rape.

It should be noted that the cognitions underlying each dysfunctional behavior may vary considerably among perpetrators. For example, possible cognitions for shoplifting a shirt might be the following. "This shirt would look really nice for the wedding I'm going to on Saturday. Since I'm buying a number of other items from this store, they still will make a profit from me even if I take this without paying for it." Another may be: "This will be a challenge to see if I can get away with taking this shirt. I'll put it on in the fitting room and put my own shirt and coat on over it, and no one will even see me walk out of the store with it. Since I've taken a number of things in the past, I'll act real casual as I walk out of the store." Or: "My son really needs a decent shirt. He doesn't have any nice ones to wear. I don't get enough money from AFDC to buy my children what they need. I know my son is embarrassed to wear the rags that he has. I'll just stick this shirt under my coat and walk out with it."

Assessing human behavior is largely a process of identifying the cognitions that underlie unwanted emotions or dysfunctional behavior. The stages of this process are as follows:

1. Identify as precisely as possible the unwanted emotions and/or dysfunctional behavior that a client has.

2. Identify the cognitions or thinking patterns that the client has during the time when the client is having unwanted emotions or is displaying dysfunctional behavior. There are two primary ways of identifying these cognitions. One way is to ask the client what he was thinking prior to and during the time when the client was having unwanted emotions or displaying dysfunctional behavior. If this approach does not work (perhaps because the client refuses to divulge what he was thinking), a second approach is to obtain information about the client's life circumstances at that time. Once these life circumstances are identified, the professional conducting the assessment needs to place herself mentally into the life circumstances of the perpetrator, and then reflect on the kinds of cognitions that would lead this client to have his specific unwanted emotions or dysfunctional behavior. For example, if the client is a sixteen-year-old female who has run away from home and is unemployed, it is fairly easy to identify (to some extent) the kinds of cognitions that would lead such a person to turn to prostitution.

A deduction of the principle that thinking processes determine dysfunctional behaviors and unwanted emotions is that *in order to change dysfunctional behaviors or unwanted emotions it is necessary for the affected person to change his thinking patterns.* These concepts are illustrated in the box on page 365.

WHAT REALLY CAUSES PSYCHOLOGICAL CHANGES VIA PSYCHOTHERAPY?

Client-centered therapy, psychoanalysis, rational therapy, feminist intervention, behavior therapy, transactional analysis, reality therapy, hypnosis, meditation, and crisis intervention have all been used to treat a wide range of emotional and behavioral problems. Practically all of these approaches have been used to treat people who are depressed, or lonely, or have marital or other interpersonal relationship problems, or who have disabling fears and phobias, or are overly aggressive, or have drinking problems, or who suffer from grief, shame, or guilt. Each of the above therapies differs substantially from every other in treatment techniques and in terms of explaining why therapeutic change occurs. Yet, each of these approaches is used by various practitioners who are able to provide case examples that each of these approaches leads to positive changes.

How can all these distinct and diverse psychotherapeutic approaches produce positive changes in clients? What is it that produces positive changes in therapy? Is there a single explanation that will describe psychotherapy changes that are produced by diverse therapies? (The explanation presented here is one that is advanced by rational therapists. This explanation has not as yet been universally accepted.)

Rational therapy asserts that unwanted emotions and dysfunctional actions arise primarily from our self-talk, generally self-talk that is negative or irrational. If this conceptualization is accurate, an important corollary is that *any therapy technique that is successful in changing emotions or actions is effective primarily because it changes a person's thinking from self-talk that is negative or irrational to self-talk that is more rational*

OUR THINKING DETERMINES OUR BEHAVIORS AND OUR EMOTIONS

A few years ago I was describing to a class the concept that our thinking primarily causes our emotions and our actions. A male student voluntarily self-disclosed the following:

What you're saying makes a lot of sense. It really applies to something that happened to me. I was living with a female student whom I really cared about. I thought, though, that she was going out on me. When I confronted her about it, she always said I was paranoid and denied it.

Then one night I walked into a bar in this town and I saw her in a corner in a "clutch" position with this guy. I told myself things like "She really is cheating on me. Both of them are play-

ing me for a fool." Such thinking led me to be angry.

I also told myself "I'm going to set this straight. I'm going to get even with them. I'll break the bottoms off these two empty beer bottles and then jab each of them with the jagged edges." I proceeded to knock off the bottoms on the bar, and then started walking toward them. I got to within eight feet of them and they were still arm in arm and didn't see me. I began, though, to change my thinking. I thought that if I jabbed them, the end result would be that I would get eight to ten years in prison, and I concluded she isn't worth that. Based on this thinking I decided to drop the beer bottles, walk out, and end my relationship with her—which is what I did.

and *positive*. In other words, self-talk appears to be the key therapeutic agent in all approaches that produce positive changes in our emotions and our behaviors.

USING RATIONAL THERAPY IN GROUPS

Rational therapy asserts that learning how to think rationally (and thereby countering unwanted emotions and dysfunctional behaviors) is an educational process. Clients can learn how to analyze and change irrational self-talk in a variety of ways: instructions by the therapist; viewing videotapes and films on rational therapy; reading books and pamphlets; and attending workshops or seminars on rational therapy.

In group therapy, the therapist first teaches clients the basic concepts of rational therapy. Group members are then assisted in: identifying their unwanted emotions and dysfunctional behaviors; identifying the irrational and negative self-talk that causes their unwanted emotions and dysfunctional behaviors; and developing more rational and positive thinking processes to counter their negative and irrational self-talk. Group members also are assisted in other ways to change their unwanted emotions and dysfunctional behaviors—for example, by getting involved in meaningful activities and by changing distressing events. One common strategy in rational therapy groups is to give each member the homework assignment of writing a Rational Self-Analysis (RSA) on an unwanted emotion or dysfunctional behavior that he or she wants to change. At future group sessions, these RSAs are shared and discussed.

365

GROUP EXERCISES

Exercise A: Changing Unwanted Emotions with Self-Talk

Goal: To learn that unwanted emotions stem primarily from negative and irrational self-talk and that they can be relieved by positive, rational self-talk.

Note: It is advised that the instructor be the designated leader for the exercises in this chapter, as the exercises may generate strong emotions in the participants. Students should not divulge sensitive personal information.

Step 1. Ask the students to think about the last time they were depressed or angry and then to relate what made them depressed or angry. List three or four responses on a blackboard under the two headings "Angry" and "Depressed." (I've run the exercise over fifty times, and people will always provide events or experiences that they believe cause their unwanted emotions.) After making the list, point out that events cannot generate an emotion; instead a person's thoughts about these events cause the unwanted emotions.

Elaborate on this by suggesting certain self-talk statements that may have led students to be angry or depressed. For example, if someone says "I became depressed because my boyfriend didn't send me flowers on Valentine's Day," you might say, "Was your self-talk something like, 'He really doesn't love me. He didn't even remember me on Valentine's Day. This is the pits. This is awful. I feel so hurt. I put so much time into this relationship and it appears he doesn't think very much of me'?" (As an alternative to guessing at self-talk, you can ask students to tell the class what their thoughts were about the events.) Diagram the self-talk process to the class, illustrating that unwanted emotions arise from our self-talk about events.

Step 2. Ask the students what their self-talk would be if the following event occurred: Someone they have been dating for three years says the relationship is over. This event is listed on the blackboard under the heading "A-Event." List each of the self-talk statements given by the students on the blackboard under a B section (B-1, B-2, etc.). For each self-talk statement, the students discuss what emotions would result. (For example, if a student says, "I'll never find anyone else," the resulting emotions might be depression and despair.) Write the emotions on the blackboard under a C section (C-1, C-2, etc.).

Step 3. Explain that all unwanted emotions can be changed by challenging each negative and irrational self-talk statement with a rational debate. Ask the students to give a rational debate for each of the negative and irrational self-talk statements listed in the B section.

Exercise B: Writing a Rational Self-Analysis

Goal: To demonstrate how to write a Rational Self-Analysis.

Step 1. Explain that all emotions arise primarily from self-talk and that unwanted emotions can be changed by identifying the negative and irrational self-talk and then challenging this self-talk with rational debates. Distribute a handout of a Rational Self-Analysis (the example in this chapter will work) to show how an RSA is done. Have each person in the class write an RSA on an unwanted emotion they have experienced in the recent past. Then, complete the exercise by having the students discuss the merits and shortcomings of doing a Rational Self-Analysis.

Exercise C: Positive Affirmations

Goal: To provide another way to change negative and irrational thinking.

Step 1. Indicate that some people find writing a Rational Self-Analysis to be too time-consuming and cumbersome. An alternative is to use a positive affirmation, a positive assertion that helps one achieve emotional and behavioral goals. The process of writing a positive affirmation also enables a person to identify negative and irrational thinking that the person may not be aware of.

Step 2. Each student selects a realistic emotional or behavioral goal that he or she wants to achieve. The following are examples:

"I believe I am a person of worth."
"I will no longer be depressed about _____ _____."
"I will no longer get angry and aggressive when _____ occurs."
"I will lose fifteen pounds in two months."
"I will stop smoking today."
"I will limit my drinking of alcohol to two drinks when I go out."
"I will no longer feel guilty about _____."
"I believe I am an attractive person."
"I will assertively express myself when _____ occurs."

Step 3. Have each student start writing (on a sheet of paper) one positive affirmation over and over. When negative thoughts enter their minds, have them record those thoughts, and then continue writing the positive affirmation according to the following format:

Positive Affirmation	Negative Thoughts
I will lose 15 pounds in two months.	
I will lose 15 pounds in two months.	
I will lose 15 pounds in two months.	I overeat when I'm bored, depressed, or lonely.
I will lose 15 pounds in two months.	
I will lose 15 pounds in two months.	I will need to develop an exercise program, which I hate to do.
I will lose 15 pounds in two months.	One reason I'm fat is because I snack between meals.
I will lose 15 pounds in two months.	I will have to limit the number of beers that I have, when I go out—beer is putting a lot of weight on me.
I will lose 15 pounds in two months.	I wonder if I really want to make all the changes that I will have to make to lose 15 pounds.

I will lose 15 pounds in two months.
I will lose 15 pounds in two months.
I will lose 15 pounds in two months.

Step 4. Allow the students to write for ten to fifteen minutes. Ask for volunteers to share what they wrote. Have the class discuss the merits and shortcomings of writing positive affirmations. One advantage of repeated writing of the affirmation, for example, is that it trains the mind to more readily accept the positive affirmation.

Exercise D: Assessing and Changing Dysfunctional Behavior

Goal: To facilitate students' learning how to assess and change dysfunctional behavior.

Step 1. The leader indicates that rational therapy asserts that thinking processes primarily determine behavior. This approach maintains that the reasons for unusual or dysfunctional behavior can always be identified by determining what the perpetrator was thinking prior to and during the time when the act was being committed. Divide the class into subgroups of about four persons. Hand each subgroup a card that identifies a perpetrator who has engaged in dysfunctional behavior. Each subgroup should have a different dysfunctional behavior to focus on. Examples of character types to distribute to students include:

1. Alcoholic
2. Spouse abuser
3. Child abuser
4. Bulimic
5. Anorexic

6. Date rapist
7. Compulsive gambler
8. Embezzler
9. Adulterer
10. Arsonist

Step 2. Each subgroup seeks to specify the cognitions that would lead its assigned perpetrator to engage in the indicated dysfunctional behavior. After the subgroups identify the cognitions through a discussion, each subgroup is instructed to specify the interventions that it believes would be most effective in changing the thinking patterns of its assigned perpetrator and curbing the dysfunctional behavior. (Examples of interventions include individual and group therapy, support groups, legal intervention, and family therapy.) The subgroup then selects a spokesperson to summarize the cognitions and list of interventions for the class.

Step 3. Each subgroup specifies to the whole class the type of perpetrator it was assigned to focus on, and the spokesperson then summarizes the cognitions and interventions listed. After each subgroup presents this information, the remainder of the class has an opportunity to suggest cognitions and interventions that the subgroup may have overlooked.

Step 4. The exercise is ended by the class discussing the merits and shortcomings of the assertion by rational therapy that cognitions determine behavior, and changing negative and irrational cognitions in a positive and rational direction is the key psychotherapeutic agent in changing dysfunctional behavior.

CHAPTER TWENTY-TWO

BEHAVIOR THERAPY
IN GROUPS

Goal: Behavior Therapy approaches are based on learning theories. This chapter begins by describing three learning processes and then summarizes the following behavior intervention techniques that are used by social workers in groups: assertiveness training, token economies, contingency contracting, and cognitive behavior techniques.

No one person is credited with the development of behavioral approaches to psychotherapy. Behavior therapists vary considerably in both theory and technique. The main assumption of this therapy system is that maladaptive behaviors are primarily acquired through learning and can be modified through additional learning.

Historically, learning theory has been the philosophical foundation for behavior therapy, even though there has never been agreement as to which learning theory is the core of behavior therapy. A number of authorities have advanced somewhat different theories of how people learn. Pavlov, a Russian who lived between 1849 and 1936, was one of the earliest. Other prominent learning theorists include Edward Thorndike, E. R. Guthrie, C. L. Hull, E. C. Tolman, and B. F. Skinner.[1]

A large number of behavior therapists have achieved international recognition for developing therapy approaches based on learning principles. Some of these therapists include R. E. Alberti and M. L. Emmons, A. Bandura. B. F. Skinner, J. B. Watson and R. Rayner, and J. Wolpe.[2]

In spite of the wide variation in behavioral therapy approaches and techniques, there are some common emphases. One is that the maladaptive behavior (such as bed-wetting) is the problem and needs to be changed. This approach is in sharp contrast to the psychoanalytic approach which views the problematic behavior as being a *symptom* of some underlying, subconscious causes. While psychoanalysts assert the underlying, subconscious causes must be treated to prevent the substitution of new symptoms or the return of old symptoms, behavior therapists assert that treating the problematic behavior will not result in symptom substitution.

Another common emphasis of behavior therapists is the assertion that therapy approaches must be tested and validated by rigorous experimental procedures. Such a focus requires that the goals of therapy be articulated in behavioral terms that can be measured. Baseline levels of problematic behaviors are established prior to therapy in order to measure whether the therapy approach is producing the desired change in the rate or intensity of responding.

TYPES OF LEARNING PROCESSES

The three major types of learning processes postulated by learning theory are operant conditioning, respondent conditioning, and modeling. These three learning processes will be briefly described.

Operant Conditioning

Much of human behavior, according to learning theory, is determined by positive and negative reinforcers. A *positive reinforcer* is any stimulus that, when applied following a behavior, increases or strengthens that behavior. Common examples of such stimuli are food, water, sex, attention, affection, and approval. The list of positive reinforcers is inexhaustible and highly individualized. Praise, for example, is a positive reinforcer when, and only when, it maintains or increases the behavior with which it is associated (for example, efforts to improve one's writing skills).

A synonym for negative reinforcer is aversive stimulus. A *negative reinforcer* (or aversive stimulus) is any stimulus which a person will terminate or avoid if given the opportunity. Common examples of negative reinforcers are frowns, electric shock, and criticism. (It should be noted that the same stimulus—for example, the smell of Limburger cheese—can be a positive reinforcer for one person, while it may be a negative reinforcer for another.)

There are four basic learning principles involving positive reinforcers and aversive stimuli:

1. If a positive reinforcer (for example, food) is presented to a person following a response, the result is positive reinforcement. With positive reinforcement the occurrence of a given behavior is strengthened or increased.
2. If a positive reinforcer is withdrawn following a person's response, the result is punishment.
3. If an aversive stimulus (for example, an electric shock) is presented to a person following a response, the result is punishment. (As can be seen, there are two types of punishment.)
4. If an aversive stimulus is withdrawn following a person's response, the result is negative reinforcement. In negative reinforcement, a response (behavior) is increased through removing an aversive stimulus (for example, fastening one's seat belt in a car to turn off the obnoxiously loud and annoying buzzer).

In sum, positive and negative reinforcement increase behavior, and punishment decreases behavior. Principles of operant conditioning are used in three behavioral techniques which are described in this chapter (assertiveness training, token economies, and contingency contracting). Operant conditioning principles are also used in aversive techniques (such as administering an electric shock when a client engages in maladaptive behavior). Aversive techniques will not be described in this chapter, as they are seldom, if ever, used by social workers. *Positive reinforcement (reward) approaches are generally more effective than those based on punishment. Punishment is often counterproductive as it can lead to the client becoming hostile about the treatment procedures.* Also, punishment may have only temporary effects. When the client realizes she is no longer under surveillance, she may return to exhibiting the maladaptive behavior.

Respondent Conditioning

Respondent learning has also been called classical or Pavlovian conditioning. A wide range of everyday behaviors are considered to be respondent behaviors—including many anxieties, fears, and phobias. A key concept in respondent learning is "pairing"; that is, behaviors are learned by being consistently and over time paired with other behaviors or events. In order to explain respondent conditioning, we will begin by defining the following key terms:

Neutral stimulus (NS): A stimulus that elicits little or no response.
Unconditioned stimulus (UCS): A stimulus that elicits an unlearned or innate response.

Unlearned or innate response (UR): A response that is innate; for example, the response of salivating to having food in the mouth.

Conditioned response (CR): A new response that has been learned.

Conditioned stimulus (CS): An originally neutral stimulus which through pairing with an unconditioned stimulus now begins to elicit a conditioned response.

Respondent learning asserts that when a neutral stimulus *(NS)* is paired with an unconditioned stimulus *(UCS)*, the neutral stimulus will also come to elicit a response similar to that being elicited by the UCS. That new response is called a *conditioned response (CR)* because it has been learned; the originally neutral stimulus, once it begins to elicit the response, becomes the conditioned stimulus *(CS)*. Thus, it is possible for an event that originally elicited no fear whatsoever (for example, being in the dark) to come to elicit fear when it is paired with a stimulus that does elicit fear (for example, horrifying stories about being in the dark). This learning process is indicated in the following paradigm:

a. *UCS* (horrifying stories about being in the dark)   elicits *UR* (fear)

b. *NS* (being in the dark)
   ↓
   (paired with)
   UCS → elicits → *CR* (fear)

c. *NS* becomes *CS* → elicits *CR* (fear)

The *CS* → *CR* bond can be broken by *respondent extinction* or by *counterconditioning*. Respondent extinction involves continuing presentation of the conditioned stimulus without any further pairing with the unconditioned stimulus. Respondent extinction gradually weakens, and eventually eliminates, the CS–CR bond.

Counterconditioning is based on the principle that the CS–CR bond can be broken by using new responses that are stronger than and incompatible with old responses that are elicited by the same stimulus. For example, it is possible to teach a person to relax (new response) instead of becoming anxious (old response) when confronted with a particular stimulus (for example, the prospect of flying in a small plane).

Modeling

Modeling refers to a change in behavior as a result of the observation of another's behavior; that is, learning by vicarious experience or imitation. Much of everyday learning is thought to take place through modeling—using both live models and symbolic models (such as films). Modeling has been used in behavior modification to develop new behaviors that are not in a person's repertoire; for example, showing a youngster how to swing a bat. Modeling has also been used to eliminate anxieties and fears; for example, through using a model in assertiveness training. Anxieties and fears are reduced or eliminated through modeling in assertiveness training by exposing fearful observers to modeled events in which the model performs feared activity without experiencing any adverse effects and even enjoys the process.

THEORY OF BEHAVIOR THERAPY

Behavior therapy is based on the assumption that all behavior occurs in response to stimulation, internal or external. The first task of the behavior therapist is to identify the probable stimulus-response (S–R) connections that are occurring for the client. This part of the therapy process is called the behavioral or functional analysis. The following is an illustration of an S–R connection: For a person who has a fear of heights the stimulus (S) of flying in a small plane would have the response (R) of intense anxiety and seeking to avoid the stimulus.

Prior to, and during the time when the therapists is doing the behavioral analysis, the therapist is also attempting to establish a working relationship. During the behavioral analysis, the therapist attempts to determine the stimuli that are associated with the maladaptive responses. Through this analysis both the client and the therapist arrive at an understanding of the problem and generally how it developed. This insight, although it does not treat the problem, is useful because it reduces some of the client's anxiety and the client no longer feels possessed or overwhelmed by unknown, mysterious forces. It should be noted that errors about hypothesized S–R connections at this diagnostic stage usually lead to ineffective treatment, as the treatment will then be focused on treating S–R connections that are *not* involved in perpetuating the maladaptive behavior.

The therapist begins a behavioral analysis by taking a detailed history of the presenting problem, its course, and particularly of its association with current experiences. In making such an analysis it is crucial to obtain specific, concrete details about the circumstances in which the presenting problem arises. If, for example, a client is shy in some situations, it is important to identify the specific interactions in which the client is shy. Furthermore, it is important to determine the reasons why the client is shy: Is it because the person does not know how to express him- or herself, or is it because the person has certain fears? The treatment chosen depends on such information.

If the clients do not know how to express themselves, a *modeling* approach through role-playing might be used. On the other hand, if clients have the response potential but are inhibited because they do not think they have the right to assertively express themselves, reframing (described later in this chapter) might be used to change their thinking processes so that they realize that everyone has the right to express thoughts and feelings.

The objective in doing a behavioral analysis is to identify the antecedent stimuli that are generating the maladaptive responses. Once these connections are identified, they are discussed with the client to help the client gain insight and to obtain the client's feedback on possible erroneous connections. The client and the therapist then agree upon the goals for the treatment. The process of how therapy will proceed (along with the techniques to be used) are described to the client. This provides the client with an idea of his or her role in treatment, and Orne and Wender have found that this knowledge fosters positive outcomes and reduces the dropout rate.[3]

Chambless and Goldstein describe the sources of information for making a behavioral analysis:

> The behavior therapist may base the functional analysis on interviews with the client and important people in the client's life or on information gained by having the client keep a journal. Questionnaire data are often useful. Interpersonal problems may be more clearly defined if the therapist and client role play interactions with which the client reports difficulty. When the therapist has a difficult time making the analysis, observing the client in the situation where the

problem occurs may lead to a wealth of information. Obviously, there are times when this would be impossible or in poor taste, but direct observation is used much less frequently than it should be.[4]

The remainder of this chapter is focused on presenting behavior therapy techniques that are commonly used by social workers. These techniques include: assertiveness training, token economies, contingency contracting, and cognitive behavior techniques.

ASSERTIVENESS TRAINING

Assertiveness training has become the most frequently used method in modifying unadaptive interpersonal behavior. It is particularly effective in changing both timid behavior and aggressive behavior. Wolpe originally developed this approach,[5] and it has been further developed by a variety of authors, including Alberti and Emmons, and Fensterheim and Baer.[6]

Assertiveness problems range from extreme shyness, introversion, and withdrawal to inappropriate rages that can alienate others. A nonassertive person is often acquiescent, fearful, and afraid of expressing his real feelings spontaneously. Frequently, resentment and anxiety build up, which may result in general discomfort, feelings of low self-esteem, tension headaches, fatigue, and perhaps a destructive explosion of anger and aggression. Some people are overly shy and timid in nearly all interactions; however, most encounter occasional problems in isolated areas where it would be to their benefit to be more assertive. For example, a young man might be quite effective and assertive in his job as a store manger but still be awkward and timid in a social situation.

Nonassertive, Aggressive, and Assertive Behaviors

There are three basic styles of interacting with others—nonassertive, aggressive, and assertive—and they have been summarized by Alberti and Emmons as follows:

> In the *nonassertive* style, you are likely to hesitate, speak softly, look away, avoid the issue, agree regardless of your own feelings, not express opinions, value yourself "below" others, and hurt yourself to avoid any chance of hurting others.
> In the *aggressive* style, you typically answer before the other person is through talking, speak loudly and abusively, glare at the other person, speak "past" the issue (accusing, blaming, demeaning), vehemently expound your feelings and opinions, value yourself "above" others, and hurt others to avoid hurting yourself.
> In the *assertive* style, you will answer spontaneously, speak with a conversational tone and volume, look at the other person, speak to the issue, openly express your personal feelings and opinions (anger, love, disagreement, sorrow), value yourself equal to others, and hurt neither yourself nor others.[7]

The following examples describe two typical situations in which an assertive response could be used effectively. In the first situation, the level of intimacy is low since the situation occurs with a business associate. However, in the second instance, the social situation involves a husband and wife and a much more intimate relationship. Group leaders should note that just as it is more difficult to say "no" to a friend than to a stranger who wants to borrow $50, it is more difficult to deal with assertive behavior on an intimate than on a superficial level.

1. You are driving with a business associate to a distant city for a conference. The associate lights up a pipe; you soon find the smoke irritating and the odor somewhat stifling. What are your choices?

   Nonassertive response: you attempt to carry on a cheery conversation for the three-hour trip without commenting about the smoke.
   Aggressive response: you become increasingly irritated until you explode, "Either you put out that pipe or I'll put it out for you—the odor is sickening."
   Assertive response: in a firm, conversational tone, you look directly at the associate and state, "The smoke from your pipe is irritating me. I'd appreciate it if you would put it away."

2. At a party with friends, your husband subtly puts you down by stating, "Wives always talk too much." What do you do?

   Nonassertive response: you don't say anything, but feel hurt and become quiet.
   Aggressive response: you glare at him and angrily ask, "John, why are you always criticizing me?"
   Assertive response: you carry on as usual, waiting until the drive home to calmly look at him and say, "When we were at the party tonight, you said that wives always talk too much. I felt you were putting me down when you said that. What did you mean by that comment?"

Assertiveness training is designed to lead one to realize, feel, and act on the assumption that one has the right to be oneself and express one's feelings freely. Assertive responses are generally not aggressive responses, and the distinction between these two types of interactions is important. If, for example, a woman has an overly critical mother-in-law, the woman may intentionally do things that will upset her (not visiting, serving food she dislikes, not cleaning the house), urging her husband to tell his mother to "shut up," and getting into loud arguments with her. On the other hand, an effective assertive response would be to counter criticism by saying: "Jane, your criticism deeply hurts me. I know you're trying to help when you give advice, but I feel that you're criticizing me. I know you don't want me to make mistakes: but to grow, I need to make my own errors and learn from them. If you want to help me the most, let me do it myself and be responsible for the consequences. The type of relationship I'd like to have with you is a close adult relationship and not a mother–child relationship."

Assertiveness Training in Groups

All of us are nonassertive in some situations where it would be to our benefit to be assertive. Many of us are aggressive in some situations in which it would be more constructive to be assertive. Assertiveness training groups are ideal settings to learn to be more assertive, for they allow members to test new assertive behaviors through interactions with others. Assertiveness training groups also allow members to learn new assertive strategies through observing effective assertive responses that are modeled by other group members. The following material summarizes a step-by-step approach for facilitating an assertiveness training program within a group setting.[8]

Examining Group Interactions

The first step to implementing assertiveness training in a group is for each member to examine his or her interactions. Aggressive, assertive, and nonassertive behavior are defined by the group leader, and examples are provided. Then, group members are asked by the leader to silently and privately arrive at answers to the following questions:

1. Are there situations that you would like to handle more assertively?
2. Are there situations in which you habitually withhold opinions and feelings that you want to express?
3. Are there situations in which you habitually become angry and lash out at others, only to regret your aggression later?

Selecting Areas for Improvement

Group members individually and privately select interactions (identified in the preceding step) in which it would be to their benefit to be more assertive. These may include situations in which they were overpolite, too apologetic, timid, or allowed others to take advantage of them while inwardly harboring feelings of resentment, anger, embarrassment, fear, or self-criticism for not having the courage to express themselves; and overly aggressive interactions in which they exploded in anger or walked over others. For *each* set of nonassertive or aggressive interactions, group members can become more assertive, as shown in the next steps. The group leader should add at this point that the members will not be required to reveal the situations in which they have habitually been nonassertive or aggressive.

Visualizing an Incident

Group members are instructed to concentrate on a specific incident involving their problematic interactions. They close their eyes for several minutes and vividly imagine the details, including specific conversations and feelings. As part of this visualization process, the leader indicates that non-verbal communication is as important as verbal communication. The leader then asks the members to silently arrive at answers to the following questions:

1. *Eye contact:* "Did you look directly at the other person in a relaxed, steady manner? Looking down or away suggests a lack of self-confidence. Glaring is an aggressive response."
2. *Gestures:* "Were your gestures appropriate, free-flowing, relaxed, and used to emphasize your message effectively? Awkward stiffness suggests nervousness; other gestures, such as an angry fist, signal an aggressive reaction."

3. *Body posture:* "Did you show the importance of your message by facing the other person, leaning forward, holding your head up, and sitting or standing appropriately close?"
4. *Facial expression:* "Did your facial expression show the firmness of purpose and self-confidence consistent with an assertive response?"
5. *Voice tone and volume:* "Was your response stated in a firm, conversational tone? Shouting may suggest anger. Speaking softly suggests shyness, a cracking voice nervousness."
6. *Speech fluency:* "Did your speech flow smoothly, clearly, and slowly? Rapid speech or hesitation in speaking suggests nervousness."
7. *Timing:* "Were your verbal reactions to a problem stated at the appropriate time? Generally, spontaneous expressions are the best, but certain situations should be handled at a later time—for example, challenging some of your boss's erroneous statements in private rather than in front of the group he is addressing."
8. *Message content:* "Which of your statements were aggressive, which assertive, and which nonassertive? Why do you believe you responded nonassertively or aggressively? Have you habitually responded nonassertively or aggressively in this situation?"

Visualizing an Assertive Model

The leader instructs the group members to continue to keep their eyes closed. The leader states: "We will now focus on coming up with some alternative approaches for being assertive that you can use in your problematic situation. One way to do this is to visualize how someone you view as being fairly assertive would handle this situation. What would this assertive model say? How would this person be assertive nonverbally in this situation?" (Pause)

Alternative Assertive Approaches

The leader continues the visualization exercise by asking group members to come up with several alternative approaches for being assertive in this situation. Members then are instructed to visualize using each of these approaches. For each approach, members should think through what the full set of interactions would be, along with the consequences. (The leader pauses frequently while group members are visualizing these alternatives.) The leader then instructs members to select an approach, or combination of approaches, that each believes will work best in his or her situation. Through imagery, members should continue practicing this approach until they feel comfortable with it.

If anyone has difficulty in thinking of a strategy to use, the leader indicates that it may be helpful after this visualization exercise ends to have someone else in the class role play an assertive approach for this situation. Group members continue, through imagery, to practice their chosen strategy until they feel ready to use it when their problematic situation occurs again. The leader informs the members that when a real-life situation occurs they should expect to be somewhat anxious as they first try to be assertive. Members are also informed that after trying out their assertive strategy in a real-life situation, they should reflect on its effectiveness by asking themselves the following questions:

1. Considering the nonverbal and verbal guidelines for being assertive, which component of your responses were assertive, which were aggressive, and which were nonassertive?

2. What were the consequences of your effort?
3. How do you feel after trying out this new set of interactions?

The leader explains that some success is to be expected, but not complete personal satisfaction with these initial efforts. Learning to be more assertive is a continuing process. Also, group members should be told: "Pat yourself on your back for the progress you made in being more assertive—you've earned it! Learning to be more assertive is an exhilarating experience. But you should also identify the areas where you need to improve and continue to use the process." Finally, members should be informed that the visualization exercise is drawing to a close and should now open their eyes.

Role Playing

The leader distributes note cards and asks members to write down anonymously one or two problematic situations they would like others in the class to role play. After the cards are handed in the leader selects an interesting situation and asks volunteers to role play it. Generally, there are two people in the situation, and one role involves using an assertive strategy. After the situation is role played, the class discusses what was done well and what else might have been done. Another role play situation is then selected, and the process continues.

The Assertiveness Model

After several situations are role played, the leader summarizes how one becomes more assertive:

1. Identify a problematic situation in which you are habitually nonassertive or aggressive.
2. Visualize a problematic incident and identify your nonverbal and verbal communication.
3. Develop alternative approaches for being assertive in this situation. A few approaches may be arrived at by visualizing how an assertive model would act.
4. Select an assertive strategy and continue to practice it through imagery.
5. Role play an assertive strategy to gain confidence or watch someone else role play the strategy. After watching someone else, role play the approach yourself.
6. Try out the assertive strategy in a real-life situation.
7. Analyze what you did well and what you still need to work on to become more assertive.

Comments

The leader may want to supplement the above material by showing one or more films or videotapes on assertiveness training. If a group member is still afraid of attempting assertive behavior, he or she should repeat the modeling, visualizing, and role-playing steps. For those few individuals who fail to develop the needed confidence to try out being assertive, seeking professional private counseling is advised, since being able to express oneself and have effective interactions with others is essential for personal happiness.

The leader should add it is a mistake to seek to be assertive in all situations. There are some situations in which it is best to be nonassertive. For example, if two large muscular people are physically fighting, it may be a mistake for a small-sized individual to assertively intervene. There are also some situations where it is best to be aggressive. For example, if you observe someone being sexually assaulted, it may be advantageous to intervene by aggressively seeking to stop the perpetrator.

The structure of the technique in assertiveness training is relatively simple to comprehend. Considerable skill (common sense and ingenuity), however, is needed to determine what will be an effective assertive strategy when a real-life situation arises. The joy and pride obtained from being able fully to express oneself assertively is nearly unequaled.

TOKEN ECONOMIES

Tokens are symbolic reinforcers, such as poker chips or points on a tally sheet, which can later be exchanged for items that constitute direct forms of reinforcement, such as candy or increased privileges (for example, an adolescent in a group home being allowed to go to movies). An economy involves an exchange system that specifies exactly what the tokens can be exchanged for, and how many tokens it takes to get particular items or privileges. The economy also specifies the target behaviors (such as going to school or making a bed) that can earn tokens, and the rate of responding that is required to earn a particular number of tokens. For example, attending school every day for two weeks earns ten tokens at an adolescent group home, and ten tokens can be exchanged for attending a sports event.

Token economies have been successfully used in a wide variety of institutional settings, including: mental hospitals, training schools for delinquents, classrooms for students with emotional problems, schools for persons with a cognitive disability, sheltered workshops for persons with a physical or cognitive disability, and group homes for adolescents. There is more evidence to support the effectiveness of token economies than for almost any other behavioral technique.[9] Token economies have been used to effect positive changes in a wide variety of behaviors, including: personal hygiene, social interactions, job attendance and performance, academic performance, domestic tasks such as cleaning, and personal appearance. At times, clients not only earn tokens for desired behaviors, but also lose tokens for undesired behaviors (for example, instigating a fight).

Effective token economies are much more difficult to establish than it appears at first glance. Prochaska summarizes some of the most important factors that need to be given attention in establishing a token economy:

> Some of the more important considerations include staff cooperation and coordination, since the staff must be more observant and more systematic in their responses to clients than in a non-contingent system. A variety of attempts at establishing token economies have failed because the staff did not cooperate adequately in monitoring the behavior of residents. Effective token economies must also have adequate control over reinforcements, since an economy becomes ineffective if residents have access to reinforcements by having money from home or being able to bum a cigarette from a less cooperative staff member. Problems must be clearly defined in terms of specific behaviors to be changed in order to avoid conflicts among staff or patients. Improving personal hygiene, for example, is too open to interpretation by individuals, and patients may insist that they are improving their hygiene even though staff members may disagree. There is much less room for misunderstandings if personal hygiene is defined as clean finger-

nails, no evidence of body odor, clean underwear, and other clear-cut rules. Specifying behaviors that are positive alternatives to problem behavior is very critical in teaching residents what positive actions they can take to help themselves, rather than relying on just a negative set of eliminating responses. Perhaps most important for more lasting effectiveness of token economies is that they be gradually fade out as problem behaviors are reduced and more adaptive responses become well established. Obviously the outside world does not run according to an institution's internal economy, and it is important that clients be prepared to make the transition to the larger society. Using an abundance of social reinforcers along with token reinforcers helps prepare clients for the fading out of tokens, so that positive behaviors can be maintained by praise or recognition rather than by tokens. Also encouraging patients to reinforce themselves, such as by learning to take pride in their appearance, is an important step in fading out tokens. Some institutions use transitional wards where clients go from token economies and learn to maintain adaptive behaviors through more naturalistic contingencies, such as praise from a fellow patient. In such transitional settings, backup reinforcers are available if needed, but they are used much more sparingly than in the token economies. Without the use of fading, token economies can become nothing more than hospital management procedures that make the care of patients more efficient without preparing patients to live effectively in the larger society.[10]

CONTINGENCY CONTRACTING

Closely related to token economies is contingency contracting. Contingency contracts provide the client with a set of rules that govern the change process. Contracts may be unilateral; that is, a client may make a contract with him- or herself. For example, a woman with a weight problem may limit herself to a certain calorie intake, with a system of rewards being established for staying within the calorie limit. Contracts may also be bilateral and specify the obligations and the mutual reinforcements for each of the parties.

Kanfer notes a good contingency contract should contain the following seven elements:

1. A clear and detailed description of the required instrumental behavior should be stated.
2. Some criterion should be set for the time or frequency limitations which constitute the goal of the contract.
3. The contract should specify the positive reinforcements, contingent upon fulfillment of the criterion.
4. Provisons should be made for some aversive consequence, contingent upon nonfulfillment of the contract within the specified time or with the specified frequency.
5. A bonus clause should indicate the additional positive reinforcements obtainable if the person exceeds the minimal demands of the contract.
6. The contact should specify the means by which the contracted response is observed, measured, recorded; and a procedure should be stated for informing the client of his achievements during the duration of the contract.
7. The timing for delivery of reinforcement contingencies should be arranged to follow the response as quickly as possible.[11]

Helping professionals are increasingly finding it very useful to develop contingency contracts (also called *behavioral change contracts*) with clients. Such contracts specify:

the desired goals, the tasks to be performed to meet these goals, the tasks that will be done by the client and those that will be carried out by the therapist, and the deadline for completing these tasks.

Kanfer indicates that using contingency contracts in marriage counseling is one area where contracts are increasingly being used.[12] In such a contract each spouse agrees to change behaviors that irritate the other, with a system of reinforcements and consequences being specified that will be applied according to the extent to which the contract provisons are met.

Formulating contracts with clients in both one-to-one settings and group settings has a number of advantages. The contracts serve as guides to clients as to the specific actions they need to take in order to improve their problematic situations. Contracts tend to have a motivational effect, because when people commit to the terms of a contract, they usually feel a moral obligation to follow through on the commitments they make. In addition, reviewing whether or not commitments made in contracts are being met provides therapists and clients with one method for measuring progress. If a client's commitments are usually fulfilled, positive changes are probably occurring. If commitments are generally unfulfilled, it suggests positive changes are not occurring.

COGNITIVE BEHAVIOR TECHNIQUES

A major trend in behavior therapy in the past two decades has been recognition of the role of cognition (thinking processes) in human behavior. Following the observations of cognitive therapists such as Albert Ellis and A. T. Beck, cognitive behavior therapists have accepted the notion that changing one's thoughts will often change one's feelings and behavior.[13]

The traditional paradigm of behavior therapy has been S (stimulus) → (response). Cognitive behavior therapists insert an additional step in this paradigm:

$$S \text{ (stimulus)} \to O \text{ (cognitions of organism)} \to R \text{ (response)}^*$$

This section summarizes the following techniques that have been developed to change cognitions: thought stopping and covert assertion, diversion techniques, and reframing.

Thought Stopping and Covert Assertion

Though stopping is used by clients whose major problems involve obsessive thinking and ruminations about events which are very unlikely to occur (such as worrying that a plane they will be taking in two weeks will crash, or worrying that they are becoming mentally ill).

In thought stopping, the client is first asked to concentrate on and express out loud ob-

---

*It is very interesting to note that the paradigm of cognitive behavior therapists [S (stimulus) → O (cognitions of organism) → R (response)] is very similar to the following paradigm of rational therapists [Events → Self-Talk → Emotions and Actions].

sessive, anxiety-inducing thoughts. As the client begins to express those thoughts, the therapist suddenly and emphatically shouts "Stop." This procedure is repeated several times until the client reports that the thoughts are being successfully interrupted. Then the responsibility for the intervention is shifted to the client, so that the client now says "Stop" out loud when he or she begins to think about the troubling thoughts. Once the overt shouting is effective in stopping the troubling thoughts, the client then begins to practice saying "Stop" silently whenever the troubling thoughts begin.

Rimm and Masters supplemented the thought-stopping technique with a *covert assertion* procedure.[14] In addition to interrupting obsessive thoughts by saying "Stop," the client is encouraged to produce a positive, assertive statement that is incompatible with the content of the obsession. For example, a client who worries about becoming mentally ill (when there is no basis for such thinking) may be encouraged to add the covert assertion "I'm perfectly normal" whenever he or she interrupts the obsessive thinking with "Stop."

Mahoney successfully used thought stopping and covert assertion as part of a comprehensive program for overweight clients.[15] Mahoney first instructed clients to become aware of such self-statements as, "I just don't have the will power" and "I sure can taste eating a strawberry sundae." The clients were then trained to use thought stopping and covert assertion to combat these thoughts.

Diversion Techniques

Diversion techniques are used with clients who have strong, unwanted emotions—such as loneliness, bitterness, depression, frustration, and anger. As indicated in chapter 21, unwanted emotions stem primarily from negative and irrational thinking. By becoming involved in physical activity, work, social interactions, or play, these clients will usually switch their negative cognitions to cognitions related to the diversion activities they are involved in. Once they focus their thinking on the diversion activities that they find meaningful and enjoyable, they will experience more pleasing emotions.

Diversion techniques are used in both rational therapy (see chapter 21) and cognitive behavior therapy. Rational therapy and cognitive behavior therapy are closely related. In fact, rational therapy is sometimes classified as a cognitive-behavioral approach.

Reframing

Reframing involves assisting a client to change those cognitions that are causing unwanted emotions or dysfunctional behaviors. As the following material describes, there are a variety of categories of cognitions that may be reframed.

One focus of reframing is on *positive thinking*. When unpleasant events occur (such as receiving a lower grade on an exam than anticipated), we can choose to think positively or to think negatively. If we take a positive view and focus on problem solving, we are apt to identify and initiate actions to improve the circumstances. On the other hand, if we think negatively, we develop unwanted emotions (such as depression and frustration) and fail to focus on problem solving. With negative thinking, we generally do not do anything constructive and may even engage in destructive behavior.

When a client is thinking negatively, a therapist can use reframing to assist the client in realizing that he or she is thinking negatively. At times it is helpful to say to the client that both negative and positive thinking often become self-fulfilling prophecies (see chapter 29). Then, through asking the client to name some positive aspects of the situation, the therapist seeks to assist the client in thinking more positively. (If the client is unable to identify any positives, the therapist may suggest some positive aspects). The client may be encouraged to tell him- or herself to "stop" whenever negative thinking occurs and instead to focus on self-talk about positive aspects of the situation.

Some people take a negative view of most events that happen to them; for such people, reframing through using positive cognitions is more difficult and time consuming. However, if they are successful in learning to think positively, they often make substantial gains.

A second closely related way in which reframing is used is "*deawfulizing.*" When distressing events occur, most of us tend to "awfulize"—we exaggerate the negatives. Think about how you reacted when someone with whom you were romantically involved broke up with you or when you received a parking or speeding citation. Did you awfulize the situation and as a result feel angry, hurt, or depressed? When we awfulize, we focus only on the negatives and do not identify constructive actions to improve the situation. When a client is awfulizing, a therapist can usually help the client identify such thought processes by simply inquiring, "I wonder if you're awfulizing?" The therapist can then assist the client, as described in the above material on reframing with positive thinking, to give cognitions that are more positive and oriented toward problem solving.

A third reframing focus involves *de-catastrophizing.*[16] De-catastrophizing is used when clients are worrying about anticipated feared events. De-catastrophizing involves continually asking clients "what if" an anticipated, undesired consequence occurs. For example, the following is a dialogue with a twenty-one-year-old college student who feared expressing his thoughts and feelings in class:

Therapist: What do you think will happen if you begin expressing your views in your classes?

Client: My voice may crack, and the others may laugh at me.

Therapist: It is unlikely that your voice will crack. But even if it does and the students happen to laugh a little, is that really worse than your anger and frustration over not sharing your thoughts?

Client: I don't know.

Therapist: Which is worse when you're asked a question in class: Shrugging your shoulders and appearing tongue-tied, or responding as best as you can even though your voice may crack?

Client: I hear what you're saying.

Therapist: What other negative consequences might occur if you begin expressing yourself in class?

Client: (pause) None that I can think of.

Therapist: What positives may come from your speaking up in class?

Client: I'd probably get more out of the class and feel better about myself. Enough of this. I get the message loud and clear. I will commit myself to speaking up at least once a week in each of my classes.

CASE EXAMPLE: REFRAMING COGNITIONS THAT CAUSE DYSFUNCTIONAL BEHAVIORS

A twenty-eight-year-old woman came into treatment because she wanted her husband to stop drinking so much. She indicated that one or two nights a week her husband would stop off at a bar with other construction workers. She indicated he would usually be two or three hours late for dinner and would be quite intoxicated when he arrived home. She would then chastise him for being late, for spending their scarce money on alcohol, and for ruining her evening by his "foolish talk." Her husband generally reacted with name-calling and by verbally abusing his wife in other ways. The woman added that generally there were problems in the marriage only when her husband was drinking. She also stated that her husband denies he has a drinking problem and refuses to join her in counseling. The counselor reframed the positive intent of her behavior in the following manner:

It appears you and your husband get along well, except when he's been drinking. When he comes home drunk, you definitely want to make the best of the situation. Up until now your wanting to make the best of the situation has led you to respond by verbally getting on his case for drinking. At that point he probably feels a need to defend himself, and a 'blow-up' occurs. Since you want to avoid the heated exchanges with him when he's drunk, I'm wondering if there aren't other actions you can take—such as taking a walk by yourself, going shopping, or going to visit someone when he is intoxicated?

The woman thought about this for a while and concluded that such suggestions might well work. In the next session a month later she reported that the strategy of leaving home when her husband came home intoxicated was working out well. Since she realized she did not have the capacity to stop her husband from drinking, she stated that reducing the difficulties the drinking created was her next best choice.

People who catastrophize usually exaggerate the anticipated feared consequences. De-catastrophizing is designed to demonstrate to clients that even if feared consequences occur (which they seldom do), those consequences are not as severe as feared.

A fourth focus of reframing is to assist clients in *separating positive intents from negative behaviors*, so that the positive intents become linked to new, positive behaviors. A parent who is physically abusive to a child has the positive intent of raising the child well, but when the parent is under stress and the child is misbehaving, that parent may not be aware that there are other options that are much more constructive than physically beating the child. A therapist can assist such a parent by helping him to reframe thoughts so that when the child misbehaves the parent can focus his thinking processes on alternative responses. For example, the stressed parent can ask his spouse to handle the child's misbehavior or punish the child with a time-out. An example of this type of reframing is given in the case example "Reframing Cognitions That Cause Dysfunctional Behaviors."

Redefining is a fifth focus of reframing that is used for clients who believe a problem is beyond their personal control.[17] For example, a bored person who believes "Life is boring" may be encouraged to think, "The reasons I'm bored are I don't have special interests and I'm not initiating activities. It's not life that is boring, it's my thinking processes that are leading me to feel bored. What I'm going to do is get involved in activities I enjoy and initiate interactions with people I like to be with." Redefining is accomplished by the therapist first demonstrating that emotions, such as being bored, primarily stem from thoughts (see chapter 21). The therapist demonstrates that if the client thinks more positively and realistically, she will feel better. Together, the client and the therapist identify the client's negative thinking patterns that are causing her to believe the problem is beyond personal control. Finally, they identify new cognitions that the client can make a commitment to use to counter the cognitions that are (in actuality) causing the unwanted emotions and ineffective behaviors.

Decentering is a sixth focus of reframing that is used with anxious clients who erroneously believe that they are the focus of everyone's attention.[18] Decentering occurs by having such clients observe the behaviors of others rather than focusing on their own anxiety; thereby, they come to realize they are not the center of attention. Beck and Weishaar give an example:

> One student who was reluctant to speak in class believed his classmates watched him constantly and noticed his anxiety. By observing them instead of focusing on his own discomfort, he saw some students taking notes, some looking at the professor, and some daydreaming. He concluded his classmates had other concerns.[19]

GROUP EXERCISES

Exercise A: Role Playing Assertive Behavior

Goal: To provide practice in being assertive.

The leader asks the group if there is a situation involving assertiveness they would like to see others in the class role play. If members suggest some situations, volunteers role play these. If no situations are suggested, volunteers role play some of the following:

1. Someone is smoking near you, and you find the smoke very annoying. Request the smoker to put out the cigarette.
2. Ask someone to turn down a stereo that is too loud.
3. Ask for a date or refuse a request for a date.
4. Inform your parents you want to be treated as an equal, rather than as a child, continually being told what to do.
5. Refuse to lend an item that someone is trying to borrow. (Before doing this one, ask the "refuser" to identify the possession he or she does not want to lend.)
6. You are a female, and a male is making derogatory sexist comments. Assertively request that he stop.

Another approach is for group members to write down (anonymously on note cards) a situation they would like others in class to role play. The members should place their notecards in a container in such a way that anonymity is maintained.

After each situation is role played, the class discusses the strengths of the approach and what else could have been done.

Exercise B: Giving and Receiving Compliments

Goal: To learn to give and receive compliments assertively.

Step 1. The group leader begins by stating the following:

The purpose of this exercise is to learn how to give and receive compliments assertively. We all seek to receive compliments and very much appreciate it when we do receive them. Yet, when we receive a compliment, we often say things that discourage the giver of the compliment from giving us additional compliments. For example, if someone compliments you by saying "That's a good-looking sweater that you're wearing," you may discourage future compliments by saying something like, "Oh really? I've had the thing for years. I don't really like it." Or future compliments may be discouraged by a comment like, "Of course it looks good on me. I look good in everything." Now, I'd like to begin the exercise by having you tell me some other negative things people have said that would discourage the giver of the compliment from giving another compliment.

These negative statements are written on the blackboard and then discussed.

Step 2. The leader states:

While people are frequently seeking positive compliments and recognition from others, they often fail to give them. Also, compliments are sometimes offered in less than a positive fashion. For example, "Most people may not like that coat that you have, but I do." Now, as the second part of this exercise, I'd like to hear statements you've heard that were intended as compliments but that came out sounding critical.

The group leader then lists these statements on the blackboard; class discussion follows.

Step 3. The class sits with name cards visible if the members do not know each other's names. The leader states the following:

Now, let's practice giving and receiving sincere and assertive compliments. I'll start by giving a compliment to someone in the group. That person should assertively receive the compliment by saying something like "Well, thank you, I really appreciate your saying that." Each time, the receiver should vary his or her response to the compliment given. After the receiver acknowledges the compliment, the receiver gives a compliment to someone else—who acknowledges it, and then gives a compliment to someone else. We'll just keep going at this until I say "Stop."

Step 4. After step 3, the group discusses the *positive* ways in which compliments were given and received.

Exercise C: Expressing Anger Constructively

Goal: To learn how to express anger constructively.

Step 1. The leader states the following:

> Many of us have been taught that getting angry is bad and that anger should not be expressed. It is true that violent and aggressive expressions of anger are generally dangerous and destructive. Yet, feeling angry is not evil. All of us get angry at times, and anger is a normal human emotion. We have a right to get angry, but unfortunately, some people tell us we should not. How many times have you been told not to get angry by a parent, teacher, or authority figure? Others may try to convince us that we should not be angry when we are, but even if we try to comply, the unexpressed angry feelings will still exist. When angry feelings are not expressed assertively, they tend to be expressed indirectly in destructive ways. Turning anger inward can lead to depression. Being angry, but failing to express it, can lead to anxiety. It can also lead to guilt (punishing ourselves for getting angry when we erroneously believe we should not). Some persons seek to relieve their angry feelings through self-destructive excessive drinking or over-eating. So, the question should not be, "Is anger acceptable?" The question should be, "How can we express anger constructively?"

Step 2. The leader explains that there are constructive ways to express anger. These ways include:

1. Taking responsibility for your angry feelings by admitting when you are angry. Only you can make yourself angry; do not blame getting angry on someone else. Remember, you have a right to your emotions, including anger.
2. Expressing your anger at the time you become angry so that you do not "stew" about it. If you delay expressing anger, the hostility may build up until you explode.
3. Expressing your angry feelings assertively so that no one is hurt in the process. Seek to use "I" statements in which you nonblamingly communicate your feelings. For example, "When you make comments like that, I become angry because I feel I don't have your respect." Expressing anger in a nonblaming way does not put the other person on the defensive. Instead, it gives the other person a chance to understand why you are upset, and provides him with an opportunity to voluntarily change those actions of his which he now realizes are upsetting you. (I-messages are further described in chapter 7).
4. Attempting to blow off steam nondestructively through such physical activity as running, hitting a punching bag or pillow, or tearing up paper, especially if your anger is intense and you feel like you are going to explode.
5. Analyzing your rational and irrational self-talk by writing out a rational self-analysis (see chapter 21).

Step 3. The class examines how members might learn to express their anger better by writing out answers to the following three questions on a sheet of paper:

1. Three things that make me angry are:
2. When I am angry, I usually:
3. Things I can do to express anger more constructively are:

The class has five or ten minutes to complete the answers.

Step 4. The class divides into groups of three persons to share what they wrote and to receive suggestions on how they could express anger more constructively. If someone does not want to share what she or he wrote, that is acceptable.

Step 5. The class shares the constructive approaches to expressing anger that they came up with and discusses what they learned or discovered from this exercise.

Exercise D: Identifying and Accepting Personal Rights

Goal: To learn to identify and accept one's personal rights.

Step 1. The leader states the following:

Often, people are not assertive because they are unclear about what rights they have and what rights others have. The basic interpersonal right that individuals have is the right to express and act upon their beliefs, opinions, needs, and feelings as long as they do not violate the rights of others. For example, we have the right to express our opinions here, but we do not have the right to tell others to "shut up."

Step 2. The class lists the personal rights they can think of on a blackboard. The leader might begin by giving a few examples from the following list:

Rights

to get angry	to change one's mind
to make requests	to try and fail
to refuse requests—the right to say no	to pursue one's own goals
to be treated with respect	to make mistakes
to disagree	to choose not to assert oneself
	to decide what happens to one's body

Step 3. Each student silently selects one of the rights he feels most uncomfortable accepting (or a right that he has experienced problems with in the past) in preparation for a visualization exercise. The leader gives the following instructions:

Close your eyes . . . take a couple deep breaths . . . Breathe in and out slowly . . . Get as comfortable as possible . . . there are no surprises in this exercise . . . Now imagine that you have the right that you chose from the list . . . What situations or circumstances in the past were troublesome for you because you did not know that you had this right? . . . Vividly imagine all the details of these situations . . . If you really believed you had this right, what would you now do or say differently? . . . If you assert yourself in having this right, how will you feel about yourself? . . . How would life change for you if you accepted this right?

This visualization continues for about two minutes. The leader pauses and then says:

Now let's do a switch . . . Imagine that you do not have this right . . . How would your interactions with others change if you could not express this right? . . . What would be the consequences to you if you could not express this right? . . . How would you feel about yourself? . . . How would you feel about other people? . . . OK, gradually open your eyes.

Step 4. The leader explains that it is acceptable not to share a visualization. The class members divide into groups of three persons to discuss the following questions:

1. What right did you choose?
2. What situations in the past have been troublesome for you because you were uncertain you had this right?
3. How did you feel when you visualized yourself having this right?
4. What do you intend to say or do differently in the future because you now know you have this right?
5. How did you feel when you visualized that this right was taken away from you?

(If someone does not want to share what she or he wrote, that is acceptable.)

Step 5. The class discusses what they learned from this exercise, and the leader asks if members have questions about the personal rights listed on the blackboard. The leader asks if anyone would like to see a situation related to personal rights role played.

Exercise E: Contingency Contracting

Goal: To demonstrate the principles of contingency contracting by applying the principles to one's own behavior.

Step 1. Describe the goal of this exercise and explain the principles of contingency contracting.

Step 2. Ask each student to prepare a contract about an area of his behavior he would like to change. The behavior may involve an area such as eating less, drinking less, exercising more, ending procrastination, studying more, or increasing contact with parents and other relatives. In preparing the contract ask the students to write on a sheet of paper answers to the following questions. (Indicate that the students will not be required to reveal what they wrote).

1. What behavior do you want to change? (Be as specific as possible.)
2. What is your behavior goal?
3. What specifically will you do to achieve this goal?

4. What are your deadlines for doing these tasks?
5. How will you reward yourself for doing the tasks necessary to reach this goal?
6. What adverse consequences will you apply to yourself if you fail to do the tasks?

Step 3. Ask for volunteers to share what they wrote. Have the class discuss the merits and shortcomings of writing such a contingency contract.

Step 4. As an added component of the exercise, students may discuss whether they want to attempt to fulfill the conditions they have written into their contracts. If the class decides to do this, a future date (such as four weeks later) may be set for the students to describe their successes and failures in fulfilling the conditions of their contract.

Exercise F: Reframing

Goal: To demonstrate how to reframe cognitions involving "awfulizing."

Step 1. Describe the concepts of "reframing" and "awfulizing." To illustrate the process of awfulizing, the leader indicates a few examples in which he or she has awfulized in the past.

Step 2. Instruct each student to record his or her responses to the following questions and instructions on a sheet of paper. Students will not be required to reveal their responses.

1. Briefly describe a distressing event that occurred to you which you "awfulized" over.
2. Specify the awfulizing cognitions that you gave yourself about this distressing event.
3. For each awfulizing cognition, specify a more positive and realistic cognition that you could give yourself about this event. (Ideally, many of these countering cognitions should also facilitate problem-solving.)
4. Indicate the approximate length of time that you awfulized over this event.
5. Are you still awfulizing about this event?
6. Do you believe countering the awfulizing cognitions with more positive and realistic cognitions would have shortened the time you spent awfulizing?

Step 3. Ask for volunteers to share their responses to these questions. The exercise may be ended by asking students to indicate their thoughts on the merits and shortcomings of using reframing in therapy.

CHAPTER TWENTY-THREE

FEMINIST INTERVENTION IN GROUPS

Goal: Feminist intervention helps clients (usually women) overcome the psychological and social problems encountered largely as a result of sex discrimination and sex-role stereotyping. This chapter summarizes the principles of feminist intervention and describes the use of the approach in groups.

DEFINITION OF FEMINIST INTERVENTION*

The feminist perspective on social work intervention has been developed by a number of authors; no one is specifically recognized as being its founder. However, authors Nan Van Den Bergh and Lynn Cooper have made extensive contributions.[1]

Feminism is a multifaceted concept that is difficult to define accurately. In *The Social Work Dictionary*, Barker defines *feminism* as "the social movement and doctrine advocating legal and socioeconomic equality for women. The movement originated in Great Britain in the eighteenth century."[2] Barker then defines *feminist social work* as "the integration of the *values*, skills, and knowledge of social work with a feminist orientation to help individuals and society overcome the emotional and social problems that result from *sex discrimination*[3] [italics added].

Barker further defines *feminist therapy as* follows:

A psychosocial treatment orientation in which the professional (usually a woman) helps the client (usually a woman) in individual or group settings to overcome the psychological and social problems largely encountered as a result of *sex discrimination* and sex-role stereotyping. Feminist therapists help clients maximize potential, especially through *consciousness-raising*, eliminating sex stereotyping, and helping them become aware of the commonalities shared by all women[4] [italics added].

Kirst-Ashman and Hull define *feminism* as follows:

. . . the *philosophy of equality* between women and men that involves *both attitudes and actions*, which infiltrates virtually *all aspects of life*, which often necessitates providing *education and advocacy* on the behalf of women, and which appreciates the existence of *individual differences* and personal accomplishments regardless of gender[5] [italics added].

Let's examine the five emphasized components of this definition. The *philosophy of equality* between men and women does not mean that women should adopt behaviors that are typically masculine. It means that women and men should have equal or identical rights to opportunities and choices and that neither women nor men should be discriminated against on the basis of gender.

The second component embodies *both attitudes and actions*. In regard to attitudes, feminism emphasizes the importance of viewing other people in a fair, objective perspective and of avoiding stereotyping. In regard to actions, feminism involves a commitment to act on one's beliefs involving gender equality. For example, a supervisor (male or female) who asserts that he or she believes in feminism has an obligation to confront a male supervisee who tells sexist jokes or who treats women according to traditional gender-based stereotypes (for example, by making demeaning comments about female social workers being too emotionally involved with their clients).

In the third component, *all aspects of life*, equality does not apply just to equal opportunity to attain a specific job or promotion, it involves many other aspects of life, such

---

as: freedom to have opinions on political, social, and religious issues; freedom to ask another person out for a date; freedom to decide what to do with leisure time; freedom to attend, or not to attend, college; freedom to choose to become involved in competitive sports; and freedom to choose to have a sexual encounter.

The fourth component is the frequent need to *provide education and advocacy* on behalf of women. Feminism involves valuing equal opportunities for women as well as for men. Since women have been subjected to sex-role stereotyping and gender-based discrimination, a person who values feminism has an obligation to provide education and advocacy on behalf of women. For example, the male employee who is telling sexist jokes at work needs to be educated about sexual harassment. He also needs to be informed about the negative impact such jokes have on women and that adverse consequences will result if he continues to make sexist remarks. Feminist advocacy involves speaking out for (or championing the rights of) those women who need help. These women are usually in positions of lesser power and opportunity.

The fifth component is the appreciation of *individual differences*. The feminist perspective places a high value on empowering women by emphasizing individual qualities and strengths.

PRINCIPLES OF FEMINIST THERAPY

Nine principles of feminist intervention have been identified.[6]

1. A client's problems should be viewed "within a sociopolitical framework."[7] Feminist intervention is concerned with the inequitable power relationship between women and men and is opposed to all "power-over" relationships, regardless of gender, race, class, age, and so on. Such relationships lead to oppression and domination. Feminism is concerned with changing all social, economic, and political structures based on the relationships between the haves and the have-nots. The problems of the have-nots are often rooted in a sexist social and political structure. Another way of stating this principle is that "personal is political." According to Van Den Bergh:

   This principle maintains that what a woman experiences in her personal life is directly related to societal dynamics that affect other women. In other words, an individual woman's experiences of pejorative comments based on sex are directly related to societal sexism. For ethnic minority women, racism and classism also are factors that affect well-being.[8]

   A primary distinguishing characteristic of feminist treatment is to help the client analyze how her problems are related to systematic difficulties experienced by women in a sexist, classist, and racist society.

2. Traditional sex roles are pathological, and clients need encouragement to free themselves from traditional gender-role bonds. Women are put in a double bind due to *femininity achievement incompatibility*. There is a traditional view in our society that a woman cannot be both feminine and an achiever. Achievement somehow reduces a woman's femininity, and the truly feminine female is thought to be someone who does seek to be an achiever. Traditionally, women have been socialized to fill a "learned helplessness" role. Van Den Bergh describes the effects of such sex-role stereotyping:

Sex-role stereotypes suggest that women should be submissive, docile, receptive, and dependent. The message is one of helplessness; that women cannot take care of themselves and are dependent upon others for their well-being. This sets up a dynamic in which a woman's locus of control is external to her self, preventing her from believing that she can acquire what she needs on her own in order to develop and self-actualize. In other words, oversubscription to sex-role stereotypes engenders a state of powerlessness in which a woman is likely to become involved in situations where she becomes victimized. . . . For example, because young girls are socialized to be helpless, when they become women they tend to have a limited repertoire of responses when under stress; e.g., they respond passively.[9]

In feminist treatment, clients are helped to see how their difficulties may be related to oversubscription to traditional sex-role stereotypes. They are shown that by internalizing traditional sex roles, women are inevitably set up to play passive, submissive roles and to experience low self-esteem and self-hatred. The feminist approach asserts that clients need encouragement to make their own choices and to pursue the tasks and achievements they desire, rather than being constrained by traditional sex roles.

3. Intervention should focus on client empowerment. Van Den Bergh describes the empowerment process:

Helping women to acquire a sense of power, or the ability to affect outcome in their lives, is a crucial component of feminist practice. Empowerment means acquiring knowledge, skills, and resources that enhance an individual's ability to control her own life and to influence others. Traditionally women have used indirect, covert techniques to get what they want, such as helplessness, dependency, coyness, and demureness.[10]

Empowerment is fostered in a variety of ways: (1) by helping the client define her own needs and clarify her personal goals so she can derive a sense of purposefulness; (2) by providing the client with education and access to resources; (3) by helping the client see that the direction and ability to change lie within herself (that is, alterations in her life will result only from her own undertakings); and (4) by focusing on the identification and enhancement of the client's strengths rather than on her pathologies. Women need to be empowered so they can increase their ability to control their environments in order to get what they need.

4. Clients' self-esteem should be enhanced. Self-esteem and self-confidence are essential for empowerment. Self-esteem can be enhanced in a variety of ways. The worker should try to be an encouraging person. The worker should help clients identify and recognize their unique qualities and strengths. Many clients with a low self-esteem tend to blame themselves for everything that is wrong. For example, a battered woman typically tends to blame herself for being battered. These clients need to look more realistically at those areas in which they are blaming themselves and feeling guilt. They need to distinguish where their responsibility for dysfunctional interactions ends and other individuals' responsibility begins.

5. Clients should be encouraged to develop their identity (sense of self) on the basis of their own strengths, attributes, qualities, and achievements. It is a serious mistake for a woman to develop her identity in terms of her spouse or dating partner. Women need to develop an independent identity that is not based on their relationships with others.

6. Clients need to value and develop social support systems with other women. In a society that devalues women, it is all too easy for some women to view other women as insignificant. With social support systems, women can ventilate their concerns and

share their experiences and the solutions they've found to similar problems. They can serve as brokers in identifying resources and can provide emotional support and nurturance to one another.

7. Clients needs to find an effective balance between work and personal relationships. Feminist intervention encourages both women and men to share in the nurturant aspects of their lives and in providing economic resources.

8. The nature of the relationship between practitioner and client should approach equality as much as possible. Feminist practitioners do not view themselves as experts in resolving clients' problems, but as catalysts whose role is helping clients empower themselves. Feminist practitioners try to eliminate dominant/submissive relationships. In regard to an egalitarian relationship, Van Den Bergh notes:

> Obviously, there is an innate power differential between practitioner and client because the former has expertise and training as an "authority." However, the feminist admonition is to avoid abusing that status; "abuse" in this sense might be, for example, taking all credit for client change, or using terminology and nomenclature that are difficult for the client to understand.[11]

9. Many clients can benefit from learning to express themselves assertively. The steps in assertiveness training are described in chapter 22. As indicated earlier, many women are socialized to be passive and nonassertive, and as a result, they have difficulty expressing themselves assertively. Clients can be helped through individual and group counseling.

Clients who learn to express themselves assertively will experience increased self-confidence and self-esteem. They will be better able to communicate their thoughts, feelings, and opinions. Also, learning to express oneself assertively is an important component of empowerment.

Many women feel considerable anger over being victimized by sex discrimination and gender stereotyping. Some of these women turn these feelings inward, resulting in depression. Assertiveness training can help these women recognize their right to be angry and also help them identify and practice constructive ways to express their anger (for example, expressing their anger assertively, rather than aggressively).

USING FEMINIST INTERVENTION IN GROUPS

The feminist perspective on therapy can be, and usually is, used in conjunction with other theoretical approaches. Group therapists who have a feminist perspective almost always have training in and use other psychotherapeutic approaches—such as behavior therapy, reality therapy, rational therapy, and transactional analysis. They also often use a number of specific treatment approaches—such as assertiveness training, parent effectiveness training, mediation, meditation, sex therapy, and relaxation techniques.

Feminist intervention is particularly applicable in group therapy with women who have been victimized by sex discrimination and sex-role stereotyping. By sharing their experiences, such women can help each other identify the problems encountered in inequitable power relationships between women and men. Such sharing facilitates their recognizing that many of their blocked opportunities are directly related to societal sexism. Such sharing also helps them recognize how their difficulties may be related to traditional sex-role stereotypes. The group approach facilitates members' pursuing the tasks and achievements they desire, rather than being constrained by traditional sex roles.

The group setting also is conducive to empowering members to increase their capacities to control their environment in order to get what they want. Members in such a setting are also encouraged to develop an independent identity. Social support systems for women are almost always developed in such a setting, as women are encouraged to share their experiences and the solutions they've found to similar problems. These women often serve as brokers to one another in identifying resources. In addition, the group setting is conducive to members' learning to express themselves assertively, including learning ways to express their anger assertively.

A case example of feminist intervention follows.

Marcia is the mother of three children, and has lived with her abusive husband, Dennis, for years. The abuse was particularly violent when Dennis was intoxicated—which he was several times a month. Over the years Dennis had succeeded in isolating Marcia from her family and friends, in lowering her self-esteem, and in making Marcia financially dependent on him (i.e., he prevented her from working outside the home).

One evening while intoxicated, Dennis smashed Marcia in the face and chest with his fists, breaking her nose and three ribs. The oldest child called 911 and an ambulance came, along with two police officers. Dennis was jailed for the evening for domestic abuse, and Marcia received emergency care at a hospital. The hospital social worker persuaded Marcia to take her children to a battered women's shelter, where she stayed for 44 days.

During this time she had daily group counseling with other battered women. The group was led by a social worker with a feminist perspective, who applied many of the principles of that perspective. Marcia came to realize that she and many of the other women in the group were being victimized by men who held traditional gender-role stereotypes. The women were given educational material and were led in exercises that helped Marcia become more assertive, express her anger about being dominated by her husband, recognize that she had a right to end an abusive relationship, and realize she was a person worthy of respect. She received assistance in becoming eligible for AFDC, receiving job training as a dental technician, obtaining a job in this field, finding an apartment for her and her children, filing for divorce, and obtaining a restraining order against her soon-to-be-ex-husband who has continued to harass her.

Now, two years later, caring for her three children (both financially and emotionally) continues to be a challenge. But, she is much happier with her life and with the kind of person she is becoming. She also is pleased that her children are slowly but surely gaining pride in her and respect for her.

EVALUATION

Since the feminist perspective is almost always used in conjunction with other therapeutic approaches, it is extremely difficult to conduct evaluative studies that test its effectiveness.

Van Den Bergh and Cooper emphasize that the feminist perspective is consistent with the core values of social work practice, including equality, respect for individuals, and promotion of social and economic justice for populations-at-risk.[12] They conclude that "a feminist social work practice is a viable way to accomplish the unique mission of social work, to improve the quality of life by facilitating social change."[13]

While most contemporary approaches to psychotherapy look for the causes of a client's problems inside the client (for example, internal conflicts, repressed feelings, and early childhood traumas), the feminist perspective emphasizes viewing a client's problems in terms of the social, political, and economic systems that impact the client. This perspective is consistent with social work's emphasis on the person-in-environment, a systems approach, and an ecological approach.

The feminist perspective has also been helpful in identifying and conceptualizing numerous structural problems in our society. For example, feminists who practiced in the mental health field in the early 1970s began to view traditional psychotherapy as an agent of social control that maintained traditional sex roles by encouraging women to "adapt."[14] Feminists have asserted that women need to be recognized as having the right to their reproductive capacities (including the right to choose to terminate a pregnancy); otherwise their lives would be largely controlled by the men who impregnate them, since raising a child requires a commitment of at least two decades. Feminists have also drawn attention to the sociopolitical forces that have led to an increase in the feminization of poverty in our society.

An extremely positive aspect of the feminist perspective is the view that all social workers have an obligation to identify inequalities in our social, economic, and political systems and then use macropractice techniques to confront these inequalities. Sometimes feminist social workers may involve clients in changing systems. Van Den Bergh notes:

> The social worker should model her concern for changed societal conditions that eliminate institutionalized inequalities by working on some social change projects, such as abortion rights, comparable worth, anti-apartheid activism, or environmental protection. Clients can be encouraged to engage in social activism themselves, as the experience of collective action can help to validate one's sense of self, personal worth, and power to change. However, judgment will have to be used as to whether this is appropriate, based on the client's current level of functioning and willingness to take risks.[15]

Feminism is concerned with ending oppression and discrimination in our society and throughout the world.

The women's movement is bringing about a gender-role revolution in our society. Men and woman are becoming aware of the negative effects of gender-role distinctions. More and more women are entering the labor force. Women are becoming more involved in athletics. Women are pursuing a number of professions and careers that previously were all male. Changes are also occurring in human interactions; more women are being assertive and seeking out egalitarian relationships with men. To some extent, men are (more slowly) beginning to realize the negative effects of gender-role distinctions. They are gradually realizing that the stereotypical "male" role limits their opportunities in terms of emotional expression, interpersonal relationships, occupations, and domestic activities.

A limitation of the feminist perspective is that a number of uninformed persons reject feminism in reaction to erroneous stereotypes. Apparently feminism has had some difficulties in informing segments of the general public about its basic tenets and principles. In this regard, Kirst-Ashman and Hull state:

Some people have extremely negative reactions to the word "feminism." The emotional barriers they forge and the resulting resistance they foster makes it very difficult even to approach the concept with them. Others consider feminism a radical ideology which emphasizes separatism and fanaticism. In other words, they think feminism involves the philosophy adopted by women who spurn men, resent past iniquities, and strive violently to overthrow male supremacists. Still others think of feminism as an outmoded tradition that is no longer relevant.[16]

GROUP EXERCISES

Exercise A: Feminist Intervention in Counseling

Goal: Assist students in applying the feminist perspective to counseling.

Step 1. Either describe the principles of the feminist perspective to therapy, or have the students read the material in this chapter.

Step 2. Ask for a volunteer to role-play the feminist perspective in a simulated counseling situation. Ask for a second volunteer (probably a female) to role-play a situation in which the feminist perspective might be useful. Possible examples include:

a. A woman discovers her partner has had three affairs since they began dating four years ago.
b. A woman is frequently verbally abused by her partner.
c. A woman is physically abused by an alcoholic husband; she feels she cannot leave him because she has three young children and is not employed outside the home.
d. A female employee is being sexually harassed by her male employer; for financial reasons, she needs to continue working.

Step 3. Instruct the two volunteers to role-play this simulated counseling situation. After the role playing, ask the class to discuss (a) what the "counselor" did well in applying the feminist perspective to counseling, and (b) what else the "counselor" might have done to apply the feminist perspective to this counseling situation.

Step 4. If time permits, repeat steps 2 and 3 with a different "client problem."

Exercise B: Are You a Feminist?

Goal: Help students assess the extent to which they have a feminist perspective and identify some key tenets of the feminist perspective.

Step 1. Instruct the students to answer "true" or "false" to each of the following statements on a sheet of paper. Inform them that their responses will remain anonymous and that they should not write their name on the paper. Read each statement slowly, giving the students an opportunity to answer.

STATEMENTS

1. Men make better supervisors than women.
2. Men make better leaders than women.
3. A woman would not do as good a job as president of this country.
4. Women should have the primary responsibility for raising children in our society.
5. In a heterosexual couple, the man should be the head of the household.
6. A male and a female living together should share the housework equally (for example, cleaning the bathroom, washing dishes, cooking, doing the laundry, cleaning, grocery shopping, taking out the garbage).
7. Women and men living together tend to share housework equally in our society.
8. Women should have the same access to jobs and social status as men.
9. A man who frequently relates jokes that are degrading to women in a work setting where women are present is guilty of sexual harassment.
10. I am willing to advocate on behalf of women (for instance, poor women or women who have been sexually assaulted).
11. Our society is generally structured politically, socially, and economically by and for men.
12. In heterosexual couples, the male has the obligation to be the primary breadwinner.
13. It is generally inappropriate for a woman to ask a man out on a date.
14. A male has a right to expect sexual gratification after dating a woman several times.

Step 2. Write the numbers of the statements on the chalkboard. Ask the students to hand in their responses. Ask for volunteers to tally the responses on the board.

Step 3. After the responses are tallied, reread each statement. Discuss the results, encouraging students to make comments or raise questions about the issues.

Step 4. End the exercise by indicating that those students who answered true to statements 6, 8, 9, 10, 11 and false to statements 1, 2, 3, 4, 5, 7, 12, 13, 14 probably have a belief system that is consistent with the feminist perspective.

Exercise C: Double Standards

Goal: Help students identify and examine double standards for male and female interactions.

Step 1. Ask the males to form subgroups of four or five persons, and the females to form subgroups of four or five persons. Ask each subgroup to identify double standards in dating relationships, marital relationships, and sexual behaviors between males and females. For example, society generally allows males to be more aggressive and to use more vulgar language; and males are expected to ask females for dates, but females traditionally have been raised to believe they should not ask males for dates. For each double standard, the subgroup should decide whether the double standard is desirable or undesirable.

(Males are separated from females in this exercise, because they may have differing views about the desirability of the double standards that are identified.)

Step 2. After the subgroups have completed their work, ask a representative from each subgroup to summarize the double standards the group identified and its views on the desirability of these double standards. Class discussion may well ensue. End the exercise by summarizing the items identified and the differences between males and females regarding the desirability of such double standards.

CHAPTER TWENTY-FOUR

FAMILY THERAPY*

Goal: This chapter summarizes two prominent approaches to family therapy, targets some basic group work concepts, applies these concepts to family groups, and relates them to a simulated family situation.

George and Martha Sitzke were fed up. They just didn't know what to do with their six-teen-year-old daughter Sharon anymore. She wouldn't cooperate on anything. She had cropped her hair close to her head and dyed the remainder a rainbow of colors, was flunking most of her subjects at school, and was staying out until all hours of the night regardless of what they told her. Who knows what she might be doing—alcohol, drugs, sex, or worse. Not only that, but she was a terror to live with at home. They felt she was sarcastic, argumentative, and hostile.

The Sitzkes finally admitted that Sharon was out of their control. They didn't understand what was happening, but they knew they needed help. They brought her to the local mental health clinic and asked for counseling. Something had to be done.

The story of the Sitzke family is an example of one of the many types of family situations in which social workers are called upon for assistance. The context is frequently one in which the family as a group has a problem. A social worker applies intervention knowledge and skills to help this family or one like it solve its problems. A family therapy perspective involves seeing any problem within the family as a family group problem, not as a problem on the part of any *one* individual member.[1] This reinforces the idea that a group orientation applies when working with families.

Several relevant aspects of families as groups have been targeted here for discussion. The first is verbal communication, including a variety of avenues of communication. The second is nonverbal communication. The importance of congruence between verbal and nonverbal communication is also stressed. The third aspect of families addressed here involves family group norms, and the fourth aspect the roles family members often assume. Setting goals, both personal and group, is the fifth aspect of working with families. Identification of some common group conflicts, problems, and strategies for resolution is the sixth. Finally, two specific family therapy approaches will be highlighted, and two specific techniques explained.

Probably the most common context in which social workers come into contact with family groups is that of therapy. We will concentrate on the assessment phase because this is where family dynamics and interactions are discovered and most easily examined.

VERBAL COMMUNICATION

Communication, both verbal and nonverbal, is critical in group functioning. Chapter 7 describes how information is translated from thoughts into words and sent to a receiver, who then interprets its meaning. Effective communication implies the mutual understanding of information conveyed. Virginia Satir summarizes the meaning of effective communication. It includes being able to firmly state your case, clarify it, ask for and be receptive to feedback.[2] This is very difficult to accomplish since there are many possibilities for interference and misinterpretation both in families and in other groups. The sender may be vague or inaccurate with his message. Interruptions and distractions may detract from the communication process. Also, the receiver may not be attentive, fail to understand, or distort what has been said.

---

*This chapter was written by Karen K. Kirst-Ashman, Ph.D, professor, Social Work Department, University of Wisconsin-Whitewater.

One focus of family treatment is communication patterns within the family.[3] Frances Scherz reflects that "communication in the family is the channel through which the rules and roles, the processes of identification and differentiation, the management of tasks, conflicts, and resolutions—in short, the business of life—is conducted."[4] Verbal communication patterns inside the family include who talks a lot and who talks only rarely. They involve who talks to whom and who defers to whom. They also reflect the subtle and not so subtle qualities involved in family members' relationships.

For example, a seventeen-year-old son asks his father, "Dad, can I have the car next Saturday night?" Dad, who's in the middle of writing up his tax returns, which are due in two days, replies, "No, Harry." Harry interprets this to mean that his father is an authoritarian tyrant who does not trust him with the family car. Harry stomps off in a huff. However, what Dad really meant was that he and Mom need the car this Saturday because they're taking their best friends, the Jamesons, out for their twentieth wedding anniversary. Dad was also thinking that perhaps the Jamesons wouldn't mind driving. Or maybe he and Harry could work something out to share the car. At any rate, Dad really meant that he was much too involved with the tax forms to talk about it and would rather do it during dinner.

This is a good example of ineffective communication. The information was vague and incomplete. Neither person clarified his thoughts or gave feedback to the other. There are endless variations to the types of ineffective communication that can take place in families. At any rate, it's up to the social worker to help clarify, untangle, and reconstruct communication patterns.

Avenues of Communication

Perez cites "five avenues of communication," any or all of which family members may use in a given day. They include "consonance," "condemnation," "submission," "intellectualization," and "indifference."[5] Evaluating how a family communicates using these avenues provides clear clues regarding where change is needed.

Consonance

Consonance refers to the extent to which the receiver of a communication accurately hears and understands the sender. In other words, the sender's *intent* closely resembles the receiver's *impact*. Healthy families are likely to have high levels of consonance in their communications; family members understand each other well.

Condemnation

Condemnation involves family members severely criticizing, blaming, negatively judging, or nagging others in a consistent manner. More than occurring only once or twice, such interaction instead forms a regular pattern. This pattern may involve any number of the family members. One person may typically condemn a particular individual. Or one person may typically condemn all the others. Likewise, all family members may condemn one person in particular. Or, two, or three members may condemn one or more.

People who form patterns of condemnation frequently do it to enhance their self-esteem.[6] Blaming or criticizing another person makes one's qualities and behaviors appear better or superior. For instance, take the seventy-year-old woman who constantly condemned her husband of fifty-five years. He was eighty-four. She regularly harped on how he was an alcoholic who couldn't keep a job. However, he hadn't touched a drop of liquor in over forty years. Additionally, he had worked regularly as a carpenter for most of those years. When the woman criticized her husband for behavior that had occurred over forty years earlier, she made herself feel better. If he was so bad, then she looked good by comparison.

Submission

Submission occurs when a person feels so downtrodden, guilt-ridden, or incapable that he or she succumbs completely to another's will. The person doesn't feel valuable or worthwhile enough to be assertive about his or her own rights and needs. Perez sums up situations involving submission by saying, "The submissive person, like the condemner, is difficult to live with. His [or her] feelings of ineptness and inadequacy put family members under constant pressure to support, to guide, to direct, to lead him. And again, when the dependency pressure becomes too demanding, the family members may well respond via condemnation."[7]

Intellectualization

Intellectualization refers to the process of putting all communication on a strictly logical, rational realm. The existence of any emotion is denied or suppressed. A person who intellectualizes likes to evaluate a problem rationally and establish a solution as soon as possible. This person does not want illogical emotions to interfere with the process of dealing with and controlling reality. The problem usually faced by the intellectualizer, however, is that *everyone* has emotions. Emotions which are constantly suppressed may build up and explode uncontrollably at inopportune times. Explosions may even result in violence.

Another problem with intellectualization occurs when the intellectualizer is unable to meet the needs of other family members. A person who intellectualizes can seem to be cold and unloving. Traditional gender-role stereotypes that direct men to be strong, unemotional decision makers encourage intellectualization. This often becomes a problem in relationships for those women who have been raised to express emotions. A typical scenario involves a woman who seeks expression of love and emotion from a spouse who intellectualizes.

Take, for instance, a man who stated point-blank that he has no emotions; he said he was always happy. His wife responded with the question, "Well, then, what are you when you're yelling at me?"

The man replied hesitantly, "Then . . . I'm mad." At this, the woman smiled to herself. She had made some progress. She had just doubled her mate's emotional repertoire.

Indifference

Indifference involves remaining apparently unconcerned, not caring one way or the other, and appearing detachedly aloof. Two common ways indifference is manifested in families is through "science" and "ignoring behaviors."[8] One or more family members may not talk or respond to one or more other family members.

Indifference can be a powerful and manipulative means of communicating. A mother who ignores her teenage daughter may convey a number of messages to her. Perhaps, the

404

daughter feels her mother doesn't care enough about her to expend the energy. Or maybe the mother is angry at her for some reason.

Being ignored can be either painful or annoying. For example, take a newlywed woman who was very emotionally insecure. During the first few weeks of marriage, she asked her husband a dozen times a day if he really loved her. At first, he answered, "Yes, dear, I do." However, he soon tired of her constant need for reassurance. He began simply to "turn her off" and ignore her. She was devastated. She needed to learn that her consistent questioning had the opposite effect of that which she desired. In her desire to feel more secure, she was driving her husband away from her.

NONVERBAL COMMUNICATION

Nonverbal communication is just as important as verbal communication. It includes the facial expressions, voice inflections, and body positions that convey information about a person's thoughts and feelings. Chapter 8 elaborates on the importance of nonverbal communication in groups, and family groups are no exception. Nonverbal behavior provides a major means of conveying information, so effective communication is based just as much on appropriate and accurate nonverbal messages as on verbal ones.

One especially important aspect of assessing messages is whether they are congruent or incongruent. Satir states that communication is incongruent when two or more messages contradict each other's meaning.[9] In other words, the messages are confusing. Contradictory messages within families disturb effective family functioning.

Chapter 8 describes how nonverbal messages can contradict verbal messages. These double messages can also occur in families. For example, a recently widowed woman says, "I'm sorry Frank passed away" with a big grin on her face. The information expressed by the words indicates that she is sad. However, her accompanying physical expressions show that she is happy. Her words are considered socially appropriate for the situation. However, in this particular case, she is relieved to get rid of "the old buzzard" and happy to be the beneficiary of a large life insurance policy.

The double message reflected by the widow's verbal and nonverbal behavior provides a relatively simple, clear-cut illustration of potential problem communication within families. However, congruence is certainly not the only important aspect of nonverbal communications. All of the principles of nonverbal communication can be applied to communication within families.

FAMILY GROUP NORMS

Chapter 5 defines norms as rules that specify proper behavior in a group. It also discusses the explicit and implicit norms or rules that all groups have. Families also have rules. Janzen and Harris define these rules as "relationship agreements which influence family behavior."[10] They note that frequently the most powerful rules are those that are not clearly and verbally stated but rather those that are implicit. These implicit rules are repeated family transactions that all family group members understand but never discuss.

As in other groups, it's important to establish norms in families that allow the entire family and each individual member to function effectively and productively. Each family differs in its individual set of norms or rules. For example, Family A has a relatively conservative set of norms governing communication and interpersonal behavior. Although the norms allow frequent pleasant talk among family members, it is always on a superficial level. The snowy winter weather or the status of the new variety of squash grown in the garden is fair game for conversation. However, nothing more personal is ever mentioned. Taboo subjects include anything to do with feelings, interpersonal relationships, or opinions about careers or jobs. On one occasion, for example, a friend asked the family matriarch what her son and daughter-in-law would name their soon-to-be-born first baby. With a shocked expression on her face, she replied, "Oh, my heavens, I haven't asked. I don't want to interfere."

Family B, on the other hand, has a vastly different set of norms governing communication and behavior. Virtually everything is discussed and debated, not only among the nuclear family members but also among several generations. Personal methods of birth control, stances on abortion, opinions on capital punishment, and politics number among the emotionally heated issues discussed. Family members frequently talk about their personal relationships, including who is the favorite grandchild and who tends to fight all the time with rich old Aunt Harriet. The family is so open that price tags are left on Christmas gifts.

The rules of behavior that govern Family B are very different from those of Family A. Yet, in each family, all the members consider their family's behavior to be normal and are comfortable with these rules. Members of each family may find it inconceivable that families could be any other way.

In families with problems, however, most frequently the family rules do not allow the family or the individual members to function effectively and productively. Group work principles state that only group norms that help the group function effectively should be developed and allowed. The case is the same with families. Ineffective norms need to be identified and changed. Positive, beneficial norms need to be developed and fostered.

The following is an example of a family in which there was an implicit, invalid, and ineffective norm functioning. The norm was that no one in the family would smoke cigarettes. A husband, wife, four children, and two sets of grandparents composed this family. Although never discussed, the understanding was that no one had ever or would ever smoke. One day the husband found several cigarette butts in the ashtray of the car typically used by his wife. He thought this odd but said nothing. Over the next six months, he frequently found cigarette butts in the same ashtray. Because no one in the family smoked, he deduced that these butts must belong to someone else. He assumed that his wife was having an affair with another man, which devastated him. However, he said nothing about it and suffered in silence. His relationship with his wife began to deteriorate. He became sullen, and spats and conflicts became more frequent. Finally, in a heated conflict, he revealed his thoughts and feelings about the cigarette butts and her affair. His wife expressed shocked disbelief. The reality was that it was she who smoked the cigarettes, but only when no one else was around. Her major time to be alone was when she was driving to and from work. She took advantage of this time to smoke, but occasionally forgot to empty the ashtray. She told him the entire story, and he was tremendously relieved. Their relationship improved and prospered.

This example illustrates how an inappropriate norm almost ruined a family relationship. Such a simple thing as the wife being a "closet smoker" had the potential for destroying a marital relationship. In this instance, a simple correction in communication solved the problem. The interesting thing is that eventually the entire family learned of this incident. The wife still smokes but still insists on doing it privately. The family now functions effectively with an amended family rule that accepts smoking.

Norms are as important to families as they are to other groups. A group worker needs to attend to group norms, monitor them, and make certain they are beneficial for group functioning. Likewise, a social worker providing treatment for a family needs to identify the family norms, assess them, and initiate changes when necessary to enhance family functioning.

FAMILY ROLES

A role is "a culturally determined pattern of behavior that is prescribed for an individual who occupies a specific status" or rank in relation to others.[11] In a family, these rules usually involve behaviors that work for the benefit of the family. For instance, the parental role prescribes behaviors helpful in supporting, directing, and raising children. Likewise, parents might assume worker roles by being employed outside of the home to earn financial sustenance for the family. Children, on the other hand, might assume the role of "student" in school and "helper" in household tasks.[12]

In addition to these formal socially acceptable roles, family members may hold a variety of informal roles, often related to the individual personalities and interactional patterns among family members. For instance, such roles may include "troublemaker," the "oppressed one," the "illustrious star," the "one to blame for everything (scapegoat)," the "perfect loner," the "old battle ax," or the "black sheep."

A broad range of roles can be found in families. One family comes to mind that has a "white sheep" within its flock. The nuclear family consists of two parents and three children, two females and one male, who is also the youngest. All family members are now adults. All members of this family except for the youngest male like to drink, party, and do their share of swearing. None except the youngest is involved in any organized religion. The youngest, on the other hand, is a fundamentalist preacher—the "white sheep."

Because each person and each family is unique, there is no formula for what roles are best. Each family must be evaluated on how its unique configuration of roles functions to the family's advantage or disadvantage.

Holman stresses that "the worker must examine how roles are performed and whether or not they meet the needs of the family"[13] and proposes a series of questions to explore:

What specific roles does each family member occupy?
Do the various roles played work well together for the family's benefit?
Are any of the roles "ambiguous," redundant, or left empty?
Is there "flexibility" among family roles so that the family is better able to adjust to crisis situations?
Do the family's roles conform with basic social norms? (For example, society does not condone a criminal role.)
Do the family's roles function to enhance the family's feelings of self-worth and well-being or detract from these feelings?

PERSONAL AND GROUP GOALS

It's important for any group to establish goals in order to give itself direction and motivate members (see chapter 4). The same rationale applies to families. Salvador Minuchin emphasizes the importance of a family therapy assessing a family and, on the basis of this assessment, establishing therapeutic goals. He continues that the primary thrust is helping the entire family function better. He states, "Although individuals must not be ignored, the therapist's focus is on enhancing the operation of the family system."[14]

Janzen and Harris also emphasize the importance of working toward a problem consensus in family treatment; a problem consensus involves the family member and the therapist arriving at a general agreement about what problems are to be dealt with in therapy. Janzen and Harris stress that social workers should make strong efforts to elicit information from all family members during the initial assessment.[15] Family members may see the problem differently, and each individual may have a different personal goal in mind. If these individual views are not clearly understood and incorporated into the family goals, some members may be excluded from treatment. The more congruence there is between the personal goals of family members and the goals of the family group, the more attracted to the therapy the members are likely to be. In order to be motivated to participate in treatment, each member needs to feel that family goals are personally relevant.

For example, a couple came to a university diagnostic training center to have their four-year-old son Jimmy, who has a developmental disability, evaluated for future education and therapy. The diagnostic center evaluated whole family on the basis of physical, emotional, and psychological needs. Therefore, as part of the overall assessment, other family members and their relationships were also examined.

The mother was a slender, pretty, extremely quiet woman of twenty-eight. She seemed to be cooperative and eager to do whatever she could to help her son deal with his disability. The father, a tall, handsome, personable man of thirty, also expressed strong desires to cooperate. As he was very outgoing and she very quiet, he did virtually all of the talking. The social worker began to talk about the parents' relationship as part of the overall assessment and treatment planning process. Much of Jimmy's extensive physical and psychological assessment had already been completed. Jimmy's father dismissed all talk about the marital relationship as an unimportant procedural matter.

The father, in essence, was saying that he appreciated all the efforts of the center's staff and that everything else was fine. As usual, he was doing all of the talking. The social worker made a point of asking Jimmy's mother to describe her feelings about their relationship, but her husband began to answer for her. The social worker gently broke in and asked if she could please answer the question herself. The woman hesitated and looked down at the floor. Then she blurted out, "I can't stand it anymore, I want a divorce!" Her husband's jaw dropped, and the social worker looked stunned. Neither had had any inkling of her strong feelings before this.

Upon further exploration, several problems in the couple's relationship were uncovered. Jimmy's mother felt suffocated by what she considered to be her husband's overbearing, dogmatic attitude. Through their eight years of married life, she felt she could never voice her opinion or function as an individual. She was also sick of having sole responsibility for the housework. For years she had secret ambitions of becoming a legal librarian. However, because of her own quiet personality and her insecurity, she never felt confident enough to express her feelings.

Her husband, on the other hand, felt that she needed protection and direction. Many times he had become tired of the burden of assuming responsibility for making all of the family decisions. He had often wished his wife would be more assertive, but he didn't feel it was in her nature to do so. In one way, he felt relieved when she finally expressed her true feelings.

Further discussion revealed that they both were relieved to get their feelings out in the open and hear what each other really felt. Treatment sessions helped to establish new patterns of communication and behavior. With feedback, Jimmy's father became aware of how it had become a habit to answer questions for his wife. His wife also became aware that she needed to be more assertive and not rely on her husband to answer for her. They began to establish a more equal relationship and discussed how to divide household chores and child-care tasks more evenly. When his wife began training to become a legal librarian, Jimmy's father gave her his genuine support. Not only was he proud of her for developing her individuality, but he also appreciated the extra income she would be bringing into the household.

This experience exemplifies how important it is to make sure each family member has personal input into the goal-setting process. Otherwise, family group goals might miss the point entirely. If Jimmy's mother had not been asked her opinion and actively encouraged to express it, the real family problem might have remained hidden. Appropriate goals might not have been set concerning communication and behavior patterns. In view of the strong feelings expressed, it seemed very likely that the family would not have functioned effectively, and Jimmy's treatment plan would have suffered.

Hidden Agendas

This example also can be used to illustrate a concept related to goal-setting called the hidden agenda. A hidden agenda is a personal goal held by a group member that is unknown to the other group members and that interferes with the accomplishment of group goals. Such unknown personal goals can be destructive both to the group and to the group process. In the above example, the wife had a hidden agenda. The agenda included her secret wishes to be more independent and to pursue a career. In order for the family to function effectively, this hidden agenda had to be brought to the surface and resolved.

FAMILY CONFLICTS AND PROBLEMS, AND THEIR RESOLUTION

Chapter 9 defines conflict as "an antagonistic state or action involving divergent ideas or interests." It indicates that conflicts are inevitable in any group and that many times they are positive and desirable. Groups, including families, are made up of unique individuals, each with individual opinions and ideals. Conflict can represent the open sharing of these ideas and can serve as a mechanism for improving communication, enhancing the closeness of relationships, and working out dissatisfactions.

Thorman points out that although each family is unique, conflicts and problems within families tend to be clustered in four major categories.[16] First, there are marital problems between the husband and wife. Second, there are difficulties existing between parents and children. Third are the personal problems of individual family members. Finally, there are stresses imposed on the family by the external environment.

Family problems do not necessarily fall neatly into one of these categories or the other. Frequently, families experience more than one category of problems. Nor are these problem categories mutually exclusive. Many times one problem will be closely related to another. Consider, for instance, the wife and mother of a family who is a department store manager and the primary breadwinner for her family. The store at which she has been working for the past eleven years suddenly goes bankrupt and out of business. Despite massive efforts, she is unable to find another job with similar responsibilities and salary. This can be considered a family problem caused by stresses in the environment. However, this is also a personal problem for the wife and mother. Her sense of self-worth is seriously diminished by her job loss and inability to find another position. As a result, she becomes cranky, short-tempered, and difficult to live with. The environmental stress she is experiencing causes her to have difficulties relating to both children and spouse. The entire family system becomes disturbed.

The following section will examine each of the four problem categories and offer some treatment directions.

Marital Difficulties

The Family Service Association of America conducted a national survey of troubled couples to determine the major causes of conflict in marital relationships.[17] Communication difficulties surfaced as the primary complaint. Other major sources of conflict included disagreements over children, sexual problems, conflicts over recreational time and money, and unfaithfulness. This study provides some clues concerning the areas practitioners need to address when assessing a marital couple's relationship within the family.

For instance, Bill and Linda, both in their mid-thirties, had a communication problem. They had been married one year. The marriage occurred after a lengthy dating period filled with strife. A primary source of stress was Linda's desire for a permanent commitment of marriage and Bill's unwillingness to make such a commitment. In view of Linda's threats to leave him, Bill finally decided to get married.

Before the marriage another source of difficulty was the amount of time that Bill and Linda spent together. They each owned a condominium and lived separately. Bill was involved in a physical fitness program, working out at a health club four nights a week, including Fridays. Bill also had numerous close friends at the club with whom he enjoyed spending his time. Linda was infuriated that Bill restricted the time he spent with her to some of the days when he didn't work out at the club. Her major concern, however, remained Bill's inability to make a commitment. Linda felt that things would change once they got married.

After marriage, things did not change very much. Although Linda and Bill now lived together, he still worked out at the club with his friends four night a week, and Linda was still infuriated. In a discussion the two expressed their feelings. Linda said, "I hate all the time Bill spends at the club. I resent having him designate the time he thinks he can spend with me. I feel like he's putting my time into little boxes."

Bill responded, "My physical health is very important to me. I love to work out at the club. What should I do—stay home every night and become a couch potato watching television?"

One way of assessing this couple's communication is evaluating the intent (what the speaker wants to have communicated to the receiver) and the actual impact of the communication (what the listener actually hears).[18] Many times the intent and impact of communication are different. One therapeutic goal is to improve the accuracy of communication, that is, the extent to which the intent of the speaker and the impact upon the listener resemble each other.

Although other difficulties existed in the relationship that are too lengthy to describe here, we will address some of the issues involved in this simple communication. After further meetings and discussion, the following scenario developed. Linda verbally stated that she is intensely unhappy that Bill goes to the health club. The impact on Bill is that he feels Linda is trying to tell him what to do. He loves Linda but is wary of losing his independence and what he sees as his identity. When Linda places demands on him, he becomes even more protective of his time.

Linda's intent in her communication is very different from her impact; she feels Bill thinks the club and his friends are more important than she is. This is related to her basic lack of self-esteem and self-confidence.

Bill's response to Linda's statement also has serious discrepancies between its intent and impact. Bill states that he loves to work out. The impact on Linda (that is, what she is hearing Bill say) is that he likes the club and his friends more than he likes her. Bill's actual intent is to tell Linda his physical health and appearance are important to him. He also wants to communicate that his sense of independence is also important to him. He loves her and wants to be committed to her. Yet, his long-term fear of commitment is related to his actual fear that he will lose his identity in someone else's. He's afraid of losing his right to make choices and decisions. He fears being told what to do.

One treatment goal here is to enhance the congruence of each person's intent and impact. A practitioner can help each spouse communicate more effectively by giving suggestions about how to rephrase statements in words to reflect more clearly what the speaker really means. Another suggestion is to encourage feedback, that is, "What happens when the listener tells the speaker about the impact a message had."[19] For instance, instead of responding to Linda's demands defensively, Bill might be encouraged to tell her, "I love you very much, Linda. I need to keep in shape, and I need some time to myself. How can we work this out?"

Eventually, Bill and Linda used a problem-solving approach (see chapter 9) to resolve this issue. Through counseling, the accuracy of their communication gradually improved. Each learned how to communicate personal needs. Instead of their old stand-off, they began to identify and evaluate alternatives. Their final solution involved several facets. First, Bill would continue to go to the club to work out three nights a week. Fridays, however, would be spent with Linda; it became clear that she was particularly annoyed at not being able to go out with Bill on Friday nights. Linda, who also was an avid believer in physical fitness, would occasionally go with Bill to the health club to work out. This gave her a sense of freedom to join him when she chose to. The important thing was that she no longer felt restricted. In reality, she rarely went with him to the club. Linda also chose to take some post-graduate courses in her field on those evenings when Bill visited the club. She enjoyed such activities, and they enhanced her sense of professional competence. The personal issues of Bill's need to feel free and Linda's lack of self-esteem demanded ongoing efforts by both spouses. Enhanced communication skills helped them communicate their ongoing needs.

Parent/Child Relationship Difficulties

The second major type of family problem involves relationships between parents and children, including parents' difficulties controlling their children and, especially as children reach adolescence, communication problems. There are many perspectives on child management and parent/child communication techniques. Two major approaches are application of learning theory and Parent Effectiveness Training (PET) developed by Thomas Gordon.[20]

Practitioners can help parents improve their control of children by assessing the individual family situations and teaching parents some basic behavior modification techniques.[21] Behavior modification involves the application of learning theory principles to real-life situations. For instance, it's easy for parents to get into a punishment rut with a misbehaving child. For example, four-year-old Freddie spills the contents of drawers and cabinets in the kitchen area whenever he is unobserved. His parents have seen enough flour, honey, silverware, and plastic bags in heaps on the floor to last them several lifetimes. In their frustration, they typically respond by swatting Freddie on the rump. He cries a little bit. But the next time he has the opportunity to be in the kitchen alone, he repeats the unwanted behavior.

In family counseling Freddie's parents were taught several new behavior management techniques (that is, behavior modification techniques applied to specific child management situations). First, they were taught the value of positive reinforcement. These are "positive events of consequences which follow a behavior and act to strengthen that behavior."[22] Instead of relying solely on punishment, the parents were taught to react more positively to Freddie during those times when he was playing appropriately and not emptying drawers. By closely examining Freddie's behaviors and the circumstances surrounding them, the parents gradually learned to view Freddie in a different way. They learned that he felt he was not getting enough attention in general. To get the attention he needed, he resorted to the destructive drawer-emptying behavior. Providing Freddie with structured positive play times when they gave Freddie their sole attention and commenting positively about his good behavior helped to diminish Freddie's need for getting attention in inappropriate ways. Freddie's parents learned that their punishment was having an effect opposite of what they intended. That is, instead of stopping his bad behavior, the punishment encouraged it. Punishing Freddie was actually positive reinforcement, because it provided the attention he wanted.

As an alternative, Freddie's parents were taught the time-out technique. Time out involves a procedure in which "previous reinforcement is withdrawn with the intended result being a decrease in the frequency of a particular behavior."[23] Instead of swatting Freddie when he emptied drawers, his parents placed him in a corner with his eyes to the wall for five minutes. (Five minutes should be the maximum duration of a time out because effectiveness diminishes after this period.) They administered the time out immediately after Freddie misbehaved so that he related it to his misbehavior. Time outs provided Freddie's parents with a way to deprive their son of attention without hurting him. Since attention was what Freddie really wanted, this behavior control technique worked well. It should be emphasized, however, that Freddie needed continued attention and positive re-inforcement for appropriate behavior. Had he not been seeking needed attention he would not have misbehaved in the first place.

Parent Effectiveness Training is a second method frequently used when parent/child relationship problems occur. Two principles involved in this approach include active listening and the sending of I-messages.[24] Active listening resembles the intent-impact communication approach described earlier and involves two basic steps. First, the receiver of the message tries earnestly to understand what the sender really means. In the second step, the receiver "puts his understanding into his/her own words and returns this understanding for the sender's verification."[25] For instance, thirteen-year-old Tyrone says to his mother, "Dances are boring. I'm not going to that boring old dance on Friday." His mother has learned to use active listening and tries to see the situation from Tyrone's perspective. She replies, "You mean you'd really like to go but you don't think you can dance very well." Tyrone responds, "Yep." His mother has accurately heard his real concerns.

A second technique involved in Parent Effectiveness Training is the use of I-messages,

> nonblaming messages that communicate only how the sender of the message believes the receiver is adversely affecting the sender. I-messages do not provide a solution, nor are they put-down messages. It is possible to send an I-message without using the word "I," as the essence of I-messages involves sending a nonblaming message of how the parent feels the child's behavior is affecting the parent.[26]

For example, Mr. and Mrs. Boushon have just finished shampooing the carpet in the family room. Their nine-year-old son comes into the house with considerable mud on his tennis shoes and is about to walk into the family room. Mrs. Boushon could choose to say "If you walk into the family room with those muddy shoes, I'll ground you for a week. I'm so tired of having to clean up your messes." This is a blaming, threatening statement. Instead, she chooses to say, "We just finished shampooing the carpet and want to keep it clean from now on." Her son sits down and takes off his tennis shoes. In this illustration the mother takes responsibility for her own feelings without placing blame on her son.

Personal Problems of Individual Family Members

Sometimes a family will come to a practitioner for help and identify one family member as being "the problem." However, a basic principle of family therapy is that the entire family "owns" the problem.[27] Sometimes one family member becomes the scapegoat for a malfunction of the entire family system. A scapegoat is a person others blame for some problem, regardless of whether she or he is really at fault. The practitioner is responsible for helping the family define the problem as a group rather than blame an individual. Treatment goals will most likely involve restructuring various family relationships.

For example, a family of five came in for treatment. The family consisted of a forty-eight-year-old husband and father, a forty-five-year-old wife and mother, and three children: Bob, age nineteen, Ralph, sixteen, and Rosie, twelve. The family lived in a rural Wisconsin town of eight thousand people. The father was a successful businessman involved in local politics. The mother was a homemaker who did not work outside the home. Bob was a freshman at the University of Wisconsin-Madison. The identified client was Ralph. For the past year, Ralph had been stealing neighbors' cars and running down mailboxes. To say the least, this behavior annoyed the townspeople. The family came to counseling as a last resort.

After several sessions in which family members pointed blaming fingers at Ralph, Rosie quietly commented to her parents, "Well, you never say anything about his problem" and proceeded to point at Bob. Suddenly, as if a floodgate had been opened, the entire family situation came pouring out. Rosie was referring to her parents' difficulties in accepting Bob's recent announcement that he was gay. Bob was going through a difficult period as he was "coming out"—making lifestyle decisions and relating to old friends and family members. His father was terrified that the local townspeople, who were severely homophobic (see chapter 30), would find out. He feared he would lose his social status and, that his political career would be damaged. Bob's mother turned out to be an alcoholic, a secret the family kept well guarded. The parents had not had a sexual relationship for ten years and slept in separate bedrooms. The father was a harsh, stern man who felt it necessary to maintain what he considered absolute control over family members, including his wife. Highly critical of his family, he never risked sharing his own feelings. Finally, Rosie was having serious problems with both her grades and her attendance in school. She was also sexually active with a variety of young men. Both she and her parents lived in constant fear that she would become pregnant.

As it turned out, Ralph was one of the better adjusted individuals in the family. He attended school regularly, had a B average, and was active in sports before being suspended for his delinquent behavior. This family provides a good illustration of a family-owned problem. The entire family system was showing disturbances. Ralph was the scapegoat, the identified client, largely because his behavior was more public. All Ralph was doing was calling attention to the family's deeper problems.

External Environmental Stresses

The fourth category of problems frequently found in families is problems caused by factors outside the family. These problems can include inadequate income, unemployment, poor housing, inadequate access to means of transportation and places for recreation, and lack of job opportunities.[28] Included in the multitude of other potential problems are poor health, inadequate schools, and dangerous neighborhoods.

To begin addressing these problem, practitioners need effective brokering skills. They need to know what services are available and how to make a connection between families in need and these services.

Many times appropriate services are unavailable or nonexistent. Practitioners need to advocate, support, or even help to develop appropriate resources for their clients.[29] Services that do not exist, for example, will need development. Unresponsive agency administrations will need to be confronted. Legal assistance may be required. There are no easy solutions to solving such nationwide problems as poverty or poor health care. This is a constant, ongoing process, and political involvement may be necessary. Such environmental stresses pose serious problems for families, and practitioners cannot ignore them.

THREE APPROACHES TO FAMILY THERAPY

There are many approaches to family therapy. Three prominent examples are discussed below. They include those focusing on family communication, family structure, and family function.

All examples presented here are similar in that all concentrate on various aspects of the ongoing interaction and relationships in families. Likewise, they all involve focusing on how family member communicate. However, the approaches differ in their emphases, core concepts, and perspectives on how practitioners can help families effect positive change.

A Communication Pattern Approach

Virginia Satir is a communications theorist. She stresses the clarification of family communication patterns that, in troubled families, tend to be vague and indirect. The husband and wife tend to avoid talking with one another about their needs and desires, or they talk via their children, which unfortunately places the children in the position of holding the family together. A competitive atmosphere is often created as each parent attempts to form an alliance with each child.[30]

Why does faulty communication develop in families? Satir believes one reason is that both the husband and the wife have a low self-worth. Since they try to hide their feelings of inferiority by acting confident and strong, neither reveals what he or she really wants or talks about feelings of worthlessness for fear of driving the other away. Another reason is that people who have low self-esteem marry in order to have another meet their needs. They marry "to get," expecting their spouses to read their minds and to then meet their needs. A spouse is viewed as having an *obligation* to meet their needs, and these individuals are frustrated, angry, and irritated when the spouses fail. Partners in a troubled relationship also tend to view each other as a possession rather than as a distinct, unique person. Instead of furthering each other's growth, the spouses restrict and stifle each other. In these troubled relationships, faulty communication patterns gradually evolve. Three types of communications problems can arise: use of vague, indirect statements, incongruent messages, and double binds.

In a strained relationship, the husband and wife are generally afraid to risk a clear statement, such as "I would like to get a dog." Because they don't want to drive the other person away, they express their wants and needs vaguely. Observe the following interaction:

Husband: Uncle Harry just got a cocker spaniel and really likes it.
Wife: Dogs are too much trouble to take care of.

The interaction ends. The husband is left with angry feelings because he feels he won't be able to get a dog. The wife senses from his nonverbal messages that her husband is upset and angry but does not understand why. She's afraid to deal with the conflict and therefore does not ask, "why?"

With an incongruent message, the nonverbal communication contradicts the verbal.

415

For example, a person may state he is not angry (for a variety of reasons) when his non-verbal communication—clenched fists, stern look, white knuckles, reddened cheeks—suggests otherwise. (Some authorities define an incongruent message to be one type of double-bind message.)

With double-bind messages, the sender gives contradictory messages. For example, a father may firmly maintain that "All real children should keep their toys picked up" yet tell his son that "All real boys are messy." In this situation, the son is unable to figure out whether he can please his father by picking up toys or by not picking them up. Or a wife may ask her husband for help in disciplining the children. When he does, she criticizes him for disciplining the children for something that is inconsequential. The victim in a double bind may respond in a variety of ways: withdrawing, not listening at all, aggressively fighting back, or developing emotional difficulties.

Satir's goals in family therapy are to improve communication patterns, to increase the self-worth and self-esteem of each member, and to end possessiveness. By improving communication patterns, each member can learn to express needs and desires. Toward this end, Satir seeks to help members learn to send direct and congruent messages. She instructs family members in using: "I" messages rather than "you" messages (see chapter 7); the role reversal technique (see chapter 9); the problem-solving approach rather than the win-lose approach (see chapter 9); and active listening (see chapter 7). She helps members identify which family rules are constructive and which are destructive. While rules may be bad, the people setting them are not. Destructive family rules are discarded, and new ones are negotiated. Vague messages, incongruent messages, and double binds are identified, and family members often role play using more effective communication patterns.

Satir's family therapy approach is also noted for its positive atmosphere. By modeling respect toward others, she fosters the growth of each member and increases each member's self-worth and self-esteem. Communication that is disrespectful is pointed out, and family members are encouraged to learn how to be more respectful. To help members improve their low self-esteem, she uses a variety of approaches, such as challenging negative statements about self. Satir's approach involves ending feelings of possessiveness and helping family members see each other as unique, distinct people with individual needs, desires, and self-worth.

A Family Subsystem Approach
....

Structural family therapy as espoused by Salvador Minuchin uses a systems approach to family therapy. The primary emphasis is on restructuring the major family subsystems so that each subsystem interacts appropriately and accomplishes its major duties.[31]

Minuchin notes that every family has multiple interacting subsystems. In families with children, there are three major types of subsystems: spouse, parent, and sibling. Thus, a family subsystem might include two spouses or all of the siblings within a family. Likewise, a family subsystem might involve the oldest daughter and youngest son in a family of twelve because of their special, caring relationship with each other. Subsystems usually are formed on the basis of common roles or special relationships among family members.

A spouse subsystem is healthy and functional if both the husband's and wife's needs for companionship, emotional and sexual fulfillment, and financial support are being met. An example of a dysfunctional spouse subsystem is one in which the wife wants to seek employment to fulfill herself and help the family out financially, while the husband wants her to stay home to care for the children and do the domestic tasks.

A healthy parent subsystem involves parents who meet the emotional and physical needs of their children without placing undue stress upon themselves. A dysfunctional system results in disputes and stress among family members. For example, parents may have conflicting philosophies about how to raise and discipline children that result in family fighting and dysfunction.

A healthy sibling subsystem exists when siblings get along fairly well and learn and interact with each other. An example of a dysfunctional sibling subsystem is one in which siblings bicker constantly, preventing each other from accomplishing required tasks such as completion of assigned homework and housework.

Each family subsystem has major functions that must be fulfilled if the family is to survive as a healthy unit. In therapy, Minuchin analyzes the functions and dysfunctions of each subsystem to determine where interaction is healthy and where it is not. His main goal is to enhance the effective interaction of the spouse, parent, and sibling subsystems. Healthy functioning in each of these subsystems is not precisely defined, since a type of interaction that works well in one family system may work terribly in another. For example, spending money on a lavish vacation to Hawaii may be very beneficial for a family that can easily afford it, but very unhealthy for a family deeply in debt.

According to structural family therapy, typical dysfunctions found in families include "disengagement" and "enmeshment."[32] These reflect the extreme opposites of how family boundaries might be formed. Disengagement concerns relationships among family members that are exceedingly distant. Communication is usually strained, aloof, and ineffective. In some disengaged families, members communicate rarely, if at all. Emotional interaction is virtually nonexistent. For example, a family's teenage son might become so involved in a street gang that he disengages from his family of origin. To him the gang becomes a replacement for his original family. Another example involves an intact two-parent family whose husband and father, assuming the traditional role of primary breadwinner, is hardly ever home. He involves himself so intensively in his work that he disengages almost totally from interaction with other family members.

Enmeshment is the opposite of disengagement. Enmeshment involves relationships among family members that are too close and probably stifling. Enmeshed boundaries within a family system become blurred and poorly defined. For example, a healthy spousal subsystem may be disrupted if one parent bonds too closely with a newborn child and neglects the needs of the other spouse. The identified parents relationship with the newborn might become enmeshed at the same time that the spousal subsystem becomes disengaged. Another example involves a father and thirteen-year-old daughter who become enmeshed in an incestuous relationship. The boundaries between parent and child become blurred and ineffective. They require clarification for effective family functioning.

A technique Munichin employs in family therapy involves drawing a number of structural diagrams. In this way he can illustrate the functional and dysfunctional aspects of these subsystems and help members clarify boundaries with these subsystems. If an older daughter is sharing responsibility for caring for younger children when both parents are working, for example, Minuchin wants the family members to clarify when the older daughter is to have parental responsibilities and when she is to interact as an older sibling.

Minuchin encourages the use of many of the same communication techniques as Satir, such as I-messages, role reversal, and the problem-solving approach. At times, Minuchin may bypass direct cognitive understanding by a family of its dysfunctions in order to restructure the family subsystems. He may, for example, use a paradoxical suggestion in cases where direct exploration of family communication patterns and behavior has failed to change the dysfunctional aspects. For example, in a family where a husband wants his wife to stay at home while the wife wants to seek employment, Minuchin may use a paradoxical suggestion like, "Yup, it's best, Mary, if you stay at home and be submissive to your husband. It's your job in life to keep your husband happy. You should not attempt to grow as a person. Your primary interests and satisfactions in life should be in cleaning toilets and washing your husband's dirty shorts. So, who cares if the bills don't get paid and if you wind up being a brainless servant?" Such a suggestion is designed to push the wife into asserting her interest in having an equal relationship and to help the husband understand the consequences of controlling his wife's life.

A Functional Approach

Alexander and Parsons describe functional family therapy as focusing on how individual family members function within the family context.[33] The idea is to examine carefully how family members interact with respect to each other. It is not as important how any individual behaves as how other family members' reactions to that behavior affect the overall family functioning. Interaction among family members then is considered neither good nor bad, but rather effective or ineffective within the family context. For example, consider a family consisting of mother, father, and two teenage daughters. The father in such a family cannot be "overbearing" and "pushy" unless other family members resent his actions and interpret his behavior in this manner. His actions can be considered assertive or aggressive depending on how other family members perceive them.

According to Alexander and Parsons, there are three primary classifications of interpersonal functions; they include "merging," which reflects close contact; "separating," which reflects independence and distance; and "midpointing" which lies somewhere between the first two. Alexander and Parsons explain:

> Behaviors and interpersonal styles that produce contact/closeness in a relationship tend to increase psychological intensity, enhance the opportunities for interaction, and maintain or strengthen contacts that would otherwise decrease. Typically (but not always) nonproblematic behaviors that function to increase contact/closeness include asking for or giving friendly help, crying, remaining close physically, and verbally and physically expressing tenderness ("I love you").[34]

Functional family therapists would assume *merging* was neither good nor bad until they assessed the effects of any particular merging situation on a family's internal functioning. For example, consider a six-year-old daughter who was determined to remain by her mother's side constantly whenever both of them were home. This behavior would be considered functional if it satisfied the needs of both, and if both could continue to function well independently when not with each other. However, the same behavior by the daughter would be considered dysfunctional if neither mother nor daughter could tolerate being without each other for more than a moment at a time.

The second major category of interpersonal functions called *separating* includes those behaviors and interactions that emphasize interpersonal distance and independence from

418

each other. For example, consider parents, each working two full-time jobs in order "to get ahead," who must leave their three small children in daycare and with baby sitters. They are essentially separating from their children. A functional family therapist would make no assumptions as to whether this situation was good or bad. Rather, such a therapist would evaluate the effects of this separating behavior on family interaction. In the event that day care and baby-sitting are both excellent and consistent for the children and the parents are satisfied with their situation, the parents' behavior is considered functional. However, if the children begin acting out from insecurity and a need for parental attention, the parents' identical behavior would be dysfunctional within that particular family context.

The third classification of interpersonal family functions is *midpointing*. This type of interaction involves neither merging nor separating. Rather, there are some aspects of both concepts involved in the family's functioning. An example of a functional family employing midpointing is a family made up of a single mother and two sons, ages thirteen and sixteen. Each member of this particular triad feels comfortable in coming to each other and relying on each other when help, care, or attention is needed. Yet, each member can also back away and rely on his or her respective wits when other family members are not available. This family is functional if its mode of interaction works for all the family members involved. If, on the other hand, the thirteen-year-old son required more merging with his mother and brother than he was getting, the same family would be considered dysfunctional.

As with the communication pattern approach developed by Satir and the structural approach established by Minuchin, functional family therapy as portrayed by Alexander and Parsons considers communication an important aspect of family functioning and a common target of change. A typical approach used by a functional family therapist is to identify alternative means of communication that would improve the family functioning beyond what it had achieved in the past.

After assessing the effectiveness of family functioning among family members, a functional family therapist would most likely provide intricate feedback to family members about their interaction. Feedback would focus on family members' thoughts, feelings, and behaviors. The old ways of family functioning would be questioned and evaluated. In some ways, such challenging can thrust the family into confusion. However, this confusion sets the stage for improvement. A functional family therapist subsequently helps the family initiate and develop new means of interaction to improve family functioning.

Alexander and Parsons describe two techniques that are frequently used in functional family therapy. They include "nonblaming" and "relabeling."[35] Nonblaming involves helping family members re-conceptualize the problem. Instead of blaming specific family members for what's wrong, the members re-conceptualize the problem as one belonging to the entire family. Finger-pointing is discouraged while, at the same time, assuming responsibility for improving the family's interaction is encouraged.

Relabeling concerns helping family members view the same behavior, issue, or problem from a different perspective or understand it in a new way. It is also referred to as "reframing" (see chapter 22). Within the family treatment context, this usually means helping one family member change negative thinking about another family member to new positive thinking. Relabeling or reframing often helps one person empathize with another or understand more clearly the other person's perspective. For instance, consider a husband who regularly criticizes his wife for her obesity. The wife views her husband's verbal behavior as critical and ineffective in helping her lose weight. A functional family therapist might relabel the husbands's behavior as his means of showing his concern for his wife's health. She has extremely high blood pressure and he is desperately worried that she may have a stroke.

The following are some examples of a client's statement followed by a therapist's re-labeling or reframing of the client's thought:

Client A's Statement: Johnny hates me. All he does is scream at me. I don't even want to go near him anymore.

Therapist's Reframing: You sound upset and hurt at how Johnny yells at you so much. Maybe he's upset and hurt, too. Maybe he feels you're avoiding him. If he didn't care about you, he wouldn't expend so much energy yelling at you and trying to get your attention.

Client B's Statement: My dad says I'm much too close to my grandmother. He says it's a sick relationship, that all she does is manipulate me.

Therapist's Reframing: It's interesting that he's so concerned about that relationship. Maybe he's jealous that you two are so close. Maybe he'd like to feel closer to you, too. After all, you visit your grandmother whenever you have the chance. Yet you never visit him. Also, you know how he resents his own mother and how she tried to manipulate him when he was small.

Client C's Statement: All my parents do is try to control me. They're like two little dictators. They ask me who I'm going out with everytime I'm getting ready to go out. They tell me I'm supposed to have a 10:00 P.M. curfew. If I'm two seconds late, they're waiting for me at the door to ask me where I've been. They're driving me crazy.

Therapist's Reframing: You sound like you're feeling suffocated by your parents. It sounds to me like they're very concerned about you. If they didn't really care what happened to you, they wouldn't care what you did. Maybe they don't see their behavior as controlling. Maybe they see it as being good parents and trying to keep you out of trouble.

At least one other aspect of functional family therapy merits mention here, namely, the importance of education. Alexander and Parsons explain:

> Education in functional family therapy is the process of providing a context for people to learn specific skills that they can use to maintain positive change. Therapy doesn't help people learn new skills; it merely helps people become receptive to learning them.[36]

Thus, specific skill training is considered extremely important. This includes more effective communication skills such as the use of "I" language and active listening. A functional family therapist might also incorporate any of a wide range of specific techniques for improving family functioning. Since such improvement in functioning is the ultimate goal of family treatment, any activities that actively move the family toward that goal might be employed. For example, a functional family therapist might teach parents how to use behavior modification techniques such as a token economy or time-out strategies in order to manage their children's behavior more effectively. Likewise, specific homework may be assigned to various family members. For instance, a functional family therapist might instruct family members to involve themselves in a range of conflict management exercises or even undertake a family outing together before the next therapy session.

420

GROUP EXERCISES

Exercise A: The Sitzke Family

Goal: To examine some basic group concepts operating within families and apply these concepts to a simulated family treatment situation.

Step 1. The leader presents the introductory material describing family group treatment to the class and describes the concepts of verbal communication, hidden agendas, nonverbal communication, group norms, personal and group goal-setting, and congruent and double messages.

Step 2. The Sitzke family is introduced as follows:

This family treatment session involves a family of four including a mother, father, and two daughters. The family has been referred to the local family treatment clinic because of one of the daughter's behavioral problems. Her school was the referral agent. To avoid wasting time gathering the following initial information, this meeting will be considered the second meeting between the two social workers and the family. This agency uses co-counseling (that is, two therapists) when working with families. The meeting's primary purpose will be to assess the family's problems.

Step 3. On four separate notecards, type the following descriptions of the four members of the hypothetical Sitzke family. The "description" and "hidden agenda" sections should be clearly separated. Read only the "description" section of each card aloud to the class.

SHARON SITZKE

> *Description:* Sharon, the sixteen-year-old daughter, is considered the family trouble-maker. She smokes, drinks, occasionally uses drugs, is frequently truant, and associates with a peer group having a similar reputation.
> *Hidden agenda:* Sharon is actually a very bright, sensitive, caring person who has a very poor self-concept. She genuinely wants to be loved and accepted by her parents, but feels she doesn't know how. She is terribly worried about her parents' fighting and their threats of divorce. Although she loves her sister, Delores, she is terribly jealous of her. To make everything worse, she's afraid that she's pregnant.

GEORGE SITZKE

> *Description:* George, a forty-year-old husband and father, is a quiet, relatively shy person who considers himself fairly intelligent. He owns and runs a small cheese factory that consumes a lot of his time. He is very worried about Sharon because all she seems to do is to get into trouble. He's indicated that he's eager to do anything he can to help.
> *Hidden agenda:* George is simply very confused about what's happening because it

seems his whole personal life is falling apart. It's very difficult for him to express his feelings and emotions. All Sharon seems to do is get into trouble. His wife Martha is so irritable lately that it seems all they do is fight. He's so upset that he can't even remember what they fight about. It seems all he can do is withdraw and bury himself in work and in television sports. He loves his family and really just wants things to go back to normal.

MARTHA SITZKE

Description: Martha, the thirty-eight-year-old wife and mother of the family, is outgoing and energetic, and considers herself to be a nice person. She is terribly disgusted with Sharon, who seems to do everything she can to cause trouble. She is tired of the whole situation, because she feels she has done everything she can to help Sharon.

Hidden agenda: There are many other things that are also bothering her. Her children are getting older and will be leaving home soon. Although she finished two years of college, she's never worked outside the home. She's afraid of the future. It seems she and George have been drifting apart over the years. All they do is fight lately. He's even mentioned divorce. She thinks she still loves him and wants to stay together, but she doesn't know what to do about it. He's always been the quiet type. However, lately it seems whenever they're together as a couple with other people, she has to do all the talking.

DELORES SITZKE

Description: Delores, the twelve-year-old daughter, is a pleasant, outgoing, seemingly happy person who gets straight A's in school.

Hidden agenda: Delores is terribly worried about her family. She feels guilty and fearful that somehow the problems are all her fault. If it weren't for her, she feels her mother would be a happy, independent career woman. Delores is angry at her sister for causing so many problems.

Step 4. Students volunteer to play the role of each family member and take the appropriate notecard. They are to behave on the basis of all the information available on the card. They may share their hidden agendas with the rest of the class when they see fit, and they may make up any additional facts as needed.

Step 5. Two students volunteer to play the roles of co-social workers. Two students should be used in order to diffuse the responsibility of keeping the session going. When one is at a loss for words, the other may jump in and take over. The students should keep in mind that the social workers' goal during this session is to assess or define the family's problems. *The leader must remember that the social workers and the remainder of the class are unaware of the family members' hidden agendas.* The student social workers should follow these guidelines:

1. Encourage the family members to discuss the problem and talk to each other.
2. Observe their verbal and nonverbal communication patterns.

3. Ask family members to talk about the values and norms operating within the family.
4. Explore possible hidden agendas.
5. Make certain to ask each family member how he or she defines the problem. Also, ask each person what goals he or she would like the family to work toward.

Step 6. The simulation is performed with the remainder of the class observing and takes approximately fifteen to twenty minutes.

Step 7. The leader arbitrarily halts the role play and involves the entire class in discussion, focusing on the following questions:

1. What were some of the communicative patterns evident within the family?
2. Was verbal communication congruent with nonverbal communication, or were double messages being sent?
3. What family group norms seemed to be operating within the family?
4. How did each family member define the problem?
5. Were there differences in problem definition among family members?
6. What were the personal goals of each family member?
7. Was a group goal apparent?
8. Were any hidden agendas operating within this family? If so, what were they?

Step 8. Upon completion of this discussion, each "family member" reads his or her hidden agenda aloud. Briefly, the class discusses how obvious each person's hidden agenda was, and the leader stresses the importance of discovering agendas as part of the family treatment process.

Exercise B: You and Your Family

Goal: To identify and relate some basic group concepts to dynamics occurring in your own family. The group concepts include verbal and nonverbal communication and family group norms.

*Note: Students should be urged **not** to divulge sensitive personal information.*

Step 1. Using the information presented in this chapter and in chapters 7 and 8, the leader asks students to identify the verbal and nonverbal communication patterns operating within their own families and to write down their ideas. Writing down thoughts helps make students think more deeply about their own families and commit themselves to an opinion.

Step 2. The students divide into groups of four to six persons to discuss the following questions among themselves:

1. What are the verbal and nonverbal communication patterns in your family?
2. What are the similarities among the group's families in their verbal and nonverbal communication patterns?

3. What are the differences among the families in their verbal and nonverbal communication patterns?

Step 3. One student from each group summarizes the group's conclusions for the entire class.

Step 4. The leader directs the group's attention to the concept of group norms, and each individual writes down a summary of the norms operating in his or her own family.

Step 5. Once again, the students share their feelings in the small groups and discuss the following questions:

1. What are the family norms in your family?
2. What are the similarities in norms among the group's families?
3. What are the differences in norms among the group's families?

Step 6. A volunteer summarizes what each group discovered and shares this information with the entire class.

Step 7. The leader summarizes how communication patterns and family norms differed among families by verbally recapping the information developed in specific groups.

Exercise C: Analyzing Your Family in Terms of Group Concepts

Goal: To analyze your family in terms of the group concepts described in this text.

Note: It is expected students will gain a better understanding of how their family is structured and how it functions from this exercise.

Step 1. The leader explains the purpose of the exercise, indicates it is a visualization exercise, and states the following,* pausing briefly after each question.

> I want you to get in a comfortable position, and close your eyes. . . . Take a couple of deep breaths, and relax. . . . Keep your eyes closed during this exercise. . . . I want you to think of your family as I ask you a number of questions. . . . Who is the primary leader in your family? . . . Who makes most of the major decisions in your family? . . . Is the primary leader autocratic, democratic, or laissez faire? . . . Is leadership distributed among different family members in different areas as suggested by the distributed functions theory? . . . Who is generally the task specialist? . . . Who is generally the social-emotional specialist? . . . Who has the most power in your family? . . . For this power person, what is the basis of this power; is it reward power, coercive power, legitimate power, expert power, or referent power? . . .

---

*Some of the following concepts may not have been covered in this course and perhaps should not be mentioned when conducting this exercise.

What are the rules or norms that exist in your family about: dating, drug and alcohol use, acceptable sexual behaviors, the way you dress, religious expectations, expectations about going to college? . . . Who set these rules or norms, and how were they set? . . . What is your role in your family? . . .

How are disputes usually settled in your family? . . . Is a win-lose approach used or is a problem-solving approach generally used? . . . Are major decisions made by consensus, by simple majority voting, or are they made autocratically? . . . Do members use active listening to further communications? . . . Is the role reversal technique used to foster communication and to settle disputes? . . . When your father is angry, how does he communicate his anger nonverbally? . . . When your mother is angry, how does she communicate her anger nonverbally? . . . Do members seek to express their irritations to others or do members seek to hide their irritations in order to attempt to avoid conflict? . . . Does your family have a cooperative atmosphere or a competitive atmosphere? . . . One person can destroy the morale in a family—has this occurred in your family? . . . Think about each family member—who is generally nonassertive, who is usually aggressive, and who is generally assertive?

What are the major sources of stress in your family at the present time? . . . What different stress management techniques are used in your family —such as meditation, positive thinking, exercising, taking vacations, rewarding yourself with personal goodies, taking mental health days, using support groups, talking problems out with others, seeking to change distressing events, seeking to challenge and change negative and irrational thinking? . . . Do certain members of your family tend to procrastinate? . . . For those that procrastinate, what do you think would help them stop procrastinating? . . . How well do members of your family manage time? . . .

Probably every person is grieving about something; what are the members of your family grieving about? . . . What are the usual ways of handling grief in your family? . . .

Are some members of your family presently chemically dependent? . . . If so, how are other members of your family reacting to the dependency—for example, are they enablers, are they trying to ignore the problem, are they fighting about it? . . . What can realistically be done to help to reduce problems in this area? . . .

What favorite games are being played by different members of your family? . . . What family scripts does your family have? . . . What can be done to change destructive games or destructive scripts that are being played? . . .

Do the different members of your family have a fairly well thought out sense of who they are? . . . Do the different members have generally a positive sense of self? . . . For those that have a low self-concept, what might realistically be done to improve their sense of self? . . .

What are the family values about: religion, sexual behavior, chemical use, going to college, smoking, whom you associate with, racial integration, politics, majoring in social work?

Do members of your family generally communicate openly with each other? . . . Do some members send vague, indirect messages? . . . Do some members send incongruent messages? . . . Do some members send double bind messages? . . . Are some members afraid to express their needs and desires? . . . How can communication be improved in your family? . . . What are the dysfunctional aspects of the parent subsystem in your family? . . . What are the dysfunctional aspects of the spouse subsystem in your family? . . . What are the dysfunctional aspects of the sibling subsystem in your future? . . . How might these dysfunctions be improved? . . . My questions have ended. Take a minute or two to relax, and then open your eyes.

Step 2. The students discuss whether such concepts are useful in helping them to analyze and better understand their families. Students are invited to share a family situation—such as seeking ideas on how to deal with parents who are autocratic, or how to handle the problems created by someone who is chemically dependent. The students discuss the merits of this exercise.

CHAPTER TWENTY-FIVE

GRIEF MANAGEMENT

Goal: Social workers have to know how to handle the eventuality of their own death before helping the terminally ill or their surviving friends and relatives. Therefore, this chapter not only presents material on helping others handle grief and relating to the terminally ill but also illustrates how social workers can become more comfortable with the prospect of their own deaths.

427

People in primitive societies handle death better than we do. Because the average age at which people die in primitive societies is lower and because members frequently witness the deaths of friends and relatives, people in primitive societies tend to view death as a natural occurrence.

In our society we tend to shy away from thinking about death. The terminally ill generally die in institutions (hospitals and nursing homes) away from home. Therefore, individuals are seldom exposed to dying people, and many avoid thinking about death by avoiding funerals and conversations about death. Many people act as if they believe they will live indefinitely. How else can you explain the emphasis people place on collecting material goods—a lavish house in the suburbs, two cars, a boat, and so on? Many people are so busy working and collecting material goods that they fail to appreciate a lovely sunset, flowers, scenery, time spent with friends, and other nonmaterial things.

In a very real sense everyone is terminal from birth, since everyone will die. If we become comfortable with the idea of our own eventual death, we will be better prepared for the deaths of close friends and relatives. We will then be better prepared to relate to the terminally ill and to help survivors who have experienced the death of a close friend or relative.

In practically any setting social workers may encounter clients who are either grieving about the death of someone close or terminally ill. These clients are apt to be found in nursing homes, hospitals, and hospices where death is more prevalent. In recent years social workers have become involved in a variety of settings in organizing and leading support groups for the terminally ill or for surviving friends and relatives. Social workers have also become involved in leading groups in educational settings that are designed to help people become comfortable with their own deaths and to learn how to better handle grief.

GRIEF: SOME BASIC POINTS

Funerals are necessary for survivors and obviously are intended for them and not the dead. Funerals help initiate the grieving process, so people can begin to work through their grief. Funerals also demonstrate that the person is dead. If survivors do not see evidence of the body, there is a very real danger that, in some cases, survivors will believe on some level that the person is still alive. John F. Kennedy was assassinated in the early 1960s and had a closed casket funeral. Because the body was not shown, rumors abounded for many years that he was still alive.

It is a mistake to shelter children from death. Children should be taken to funerals of relatives and friends, and their questions should be honestly answered. When someone dies (I'll use a grandparent for example), it is a mistake to say, "Grandmother has gone on a trip, and won't be back," as the child will wonder if others who are close will also go on a trip and not come back; or the child may dwell on why grandmother won't return from the trip. It is also a mistake to say "God has taken grandmother to heaven" as the child will wonder if others will also suddenly be taken to heaven. Death should be explained to children as a natural process of life, which usually occurs when a person is elderly, but may occur sooner. Parents who take their children to funerals almost always find the children handle the experience better than expected. Funerals help children learn that death is a natural process of life.

Grief counselors worry about survivors who seek to appear "strong" at funerals and who try not to appear emotionally upset by the death of a close friend or relative. Usually, they are seeking to avoid dealing with their loss. There is a danger that when they do start grieving, their grief will be especially intense, partly because of guilt over denying their feelings and partly because of guilt over not having shown enough caring for the person who died.

Sudden deaths of young people are difficult to cope with for two reasons. First, survivors do not have time to prepare for the death. Because they do not have the opportunity to obtain "closure" to the relationship, they may feel that they did not have the opportunity to tell the person how they felt about him or her or to resolve interpersonal conflicts. Because the grieving process is intensified when closure does not occur, it is advisable to actively work toward closure in the relationships we have with others. Second, they feel the loss more severely because they feel that, dying young, the person missed out on many of the good things in life.

Many health professionals (such as doctors and nurses) find death difficult to handle. Health professionals are committed to recovery, to healing. When someone is found to have a terminal illness, health professionals may experience a sense of failure. In some cases they experience guilt because they cannot do more or because they may have made a mistake that contributed to the death. Social workers should not be surprised that some health professionals do not know how to deal with terminally ill persons. Because social workers generally have more training than doctors or nurses in helping people handle unwanted emotions, they are the professionals who are usually called upon to help patients and others deal with the emotional side of death.

THE GRIEVING PROCESS

Nearly all of us are currently grieving about a loss that we have had. It might be the end of a romantic relationship, moving away from friends and parents, the death of a pet, failing to get a grade we wanted, or someone's death.

Grieving over a loss does not end in a set amount of time, such as six months, a year, or three years. The "normal" grieving period is often the lifespan of the griever. When a loss of very high value is encountered, initially the grief is intense and shown through crying, depression, shock, and so on. Gradually, a person has hours, then days, then weeks, then months where he or she will not think about the loss and will not grieve. However, there will always be reminders of the loss—anniversaries, birthdays, and holidays—and the grief will surface again. The intense grieving periods will gradually become shorter, less frequent, and less intense.

Two models of the grieving process will be presented: the Kübler-Ross model[1] and the Westberg model. Some people believe the Kübler-Ross model better describes the grieving process, while others assert that the Westberg model does. These models help us to understand the grief we feel from *any* loss.

Kübler-Ross Model

Stage One: Denial

During this stage a person thinks, "No, this can't be. There must be a mistake. This just isn't happening." Denial is often useful because it helps cushion the impact of the loss.

Stage Two: Rage and Anger

In this stage an individual reacts by asking "Why me? This just isn't fair." For example, terminally ill persons resent that they will soon die while other people remain healthy and alive. During this stage, God is sometimes a target of the anger.

Stage Three: Bargaining

During this stage a person attempts to strike bargains to regain all or part of the loss. The terminally ill may attempt to bargain with God for more time. They promise to do something worthwhile or to "be good" in exchange for another month or year of life. Kübler-Ross indicates that even agnostics and atheists sometimes attempt to bargain with God during this stage.

Stage Four: Depression

During this stage those having a loss tell themselves, "The loss is true, and it's really sad. This is awful." People at this stage become depressed and mourn the loss that has occurred. The depression may also be exacerbated by guilt or shame about acts of omission or commission.

Stage Five: Acceptance

Now the person fully acknowledges the loss. The terminally ill tell themselves, "I will die soon, and it's all right." Those close to the terminally ill person accept the loss and begin working on alternatives to cope with it and minimize it. By involving friends and relatives in the grieving process, dealing with required legal arrangements, and seeking spiritual counseling, the terminally ill person and surviving friends and relatives begin to restructure their lives.

Westberg Model

The Westberg model is diagrammed in figure 25.1 and described briefly in the following paragraphs.[2]

Shock and Denial

Many people who are informed about a tragic loss are in such a state of shock that they are practically void of feeling. When emotional pain is unusually intense, it is possible that the human emotional system temporarily "blows out." This reaction insulates the person from emotions that are too intense. Denial is a way of avoiding the impact of a tragic loss.

Emotions Erupt

As the realization of the loss becomes evident, the person expresses the painful loss by crying, screaming, or sighing deeply.

Figure 25.1: Westberg Model of the Grieving Process

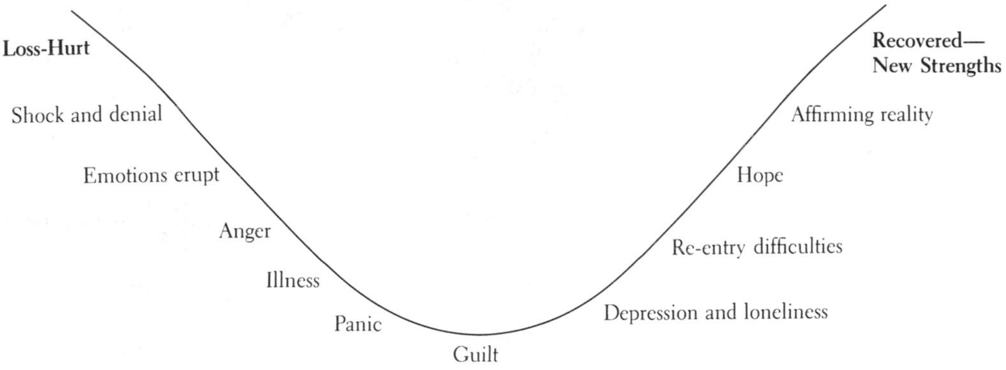

Anger

At some point in time, the person usually experiences anger. The anger may be directed at God for causing the loss and perhaps for its unfairness. If the loss involves the death of a loved one, there is often anger at the dead person for "desertion" and for causing pain and problems by dying.

Illness

Grief may produce stress-related illnesses, such as a cold, flu, ulcers, tension headaches, diarrhea, rashes, insomnia, and so on. Intense grieving produces high levels of stress. If the stress is prolonged, stress-related illnesses are apt to develop.

Panic

Because the grieving person does not feel like his or her "old self," the person may panic and worry about going insane. Nightmares, unwanted emotions that appear uncontrollable, being less able to attend to family and work responsibilities, and having stress-related illnesses contribute to the panic.

Guilt

The grieving person may blame him- or herself for having done something that contributed to the loss, or feel guilty for not having done something which might have prevented the loss. The grieving person often unduly blames him- or herself.

Depression and Loneliness

At times, the grieving person may feel very sad, isolated, and lonely. He or she may also withdraw from others who do not seem supportive or understanding.

Re-entry Difficulties

At this point the grieving person makes efforts to put his or her life back together. Re-entry problems arise: the person resists letting go of the past. Loyalties to memories hamper pursuit of new interests and activities.

Hope

Gradually, hope that one's life can be put back together returns and begins to grow.

Affirming Reality

The grieving person regains a feeling of having control of life. The reconstructed life is not the same as the old, and memories of the loss remain, but the reconstructed life is "OK."

In their models, Elizabeth Kübler-Ross and Granger Westberg note that some people continue grieving and never reach the final stage (Kübler-Ross's acceptance stage and Westberg's affirming reality stage of grieving). They also caution that not everyone will progress through these stages as diagrammed. There is often considerable movement back and forth among stages. For example, in the Kübler-Ross model, a person may go from denial to depression, to anger and rage, back to denial, then to bargaining, then to depression, back to anger and rage, and so on.

HOW TO HELP OTHERS COPE

A group leader can make a number of suggestions to help members who are experiencing loss cope with their grief. Crying is an acceptable and valuable expression of grief. Group members should be urged to cry if they feel the need in order to release the tension that comes as part of the grieving process.

Talking about a loss with friends, family, the clergy, a hospice volunteer, a professional counselor, or within a group is constructive. Explain to members that talking about their grief will ease their loneliness and allow them to ventilate their feelings and accept their loss so that they can make constructive plans for the present and future. Talking with close friends will offer them a sense of security and bring them closer to those they love. Talking with other group members who have experienced similar losses will help them put their problems into perspective and give them the chance to feel personal satisfaction by helping others.

Death often causes us to re-examine and question our faith or philosophy of life. Urge group members not to become discouraged if they begin questioning their beliefs, but to talk about them. A religious faith can help us accept loss. It is normal to question our basic beliefs about religion and the meaning of life in the process of grieving.

Writing out a rational self-analysis will help group members identify irrational thinking that contributes to grief (see chapter 21). Once their irrational thinking is identified, much of their grief can be relieved through rational challenges to their irrational thinking. Advise group members not to dwell on their unhappiness. Suggest that they become involved instead in meaningful and enjoyable activities that will energize and motivate them.

While it is natural to feel unhappy over a loss, self-pity is a waste of time and energy. Help them to accept the inevitability of death.

Intense grief is very stressful. Stress is a factor leading to a variety of illnesses, such as headaches, colitis, ulcers, colds, and flu. If a group member becomes ill, urge that person to see a physician and to tell the physician about the illness and that it may be related to grief. Intense grief may also lead to sleeplessness, sexual difficulties, loss of appetite, or overeating. The person may have little energy and be unable to concentrate. Reassure the person that all of these reactions are "normal." Every person's experience of grief is different—if group members have unusual reactions (such as nightmares), they should not become alarmed. Urge them to take the positive view that they will get their lives back together, just as practically everyone else does who suffers a similar loss. A balanced diet, ample rest, and moderate exercise will help relieve their physical problems.

Medication should be taken sparingly and only under the supervision of a physician. Grief should not be relieved with alcohol or other drugs because many drugs are addictive and may stop or delay the necessary grieving process. A group member may feel that he or she has nothing to live for and be considering suicide. Understand that many people who encounter severe losses feel this way. Seek to assure such people that a sense of purpose and meaning in life will return.

Guilt, real or imagined, is also a normal part of grief. Survivors often feel guilty about things they said or did to the deceased, or things they think they should have said or done. If members are experiencing intense guilt, suggest they share it with friends, with the group, or with a professional counselor. A rational self-analysis of the guilt might also be helpful. Reassure members that all humans make mistakes. If we didn't, we wouldn't be human. Ask them to learn to forgive themselves. Anger is another common reaction to loss. Urge members to express their anger constructively (see the exercise on expressing anger constructively in chapter 22).

Grieving members may complain that friends and relatives appear to be shunning them. If this is happening, it is probably because of discomfort and uncertainty about what to say or do. Advise group members to take the initiative, to talk with their family and friends about the loss, to tell them about ways in which they could be supportive.

Holidays and the anniversaries of a loved one's birth and death can be stressful to someone experiencing the loss of a loved one. These days should be spent with family and friends who will provide support. After a severe loss, major decisions should be put off until an individual is more emotionally relaxed. When a person is highly emotional, he or she is apt to make poor decisions.

RELATING TO THE TERMINALLY ILL

An outgrowth of the hospice movement of the 1970s, support groups for terminally ill patients are fairly common today. For the most part these groups are led by social workers and other helping professionals. The following guidelines are intended to help group leaders understand the feelings and needs of the terminally ill, so that they can help them deal with approaching death.

To relate to the terminally ill, you need to view death as a normal process of life and to accept the eventuality of your own death. If you cannot accept your own death, you will probably be uneasy about talking to someone who is terminally ill. You will not be able to discuss the concerns that the dying person has in an understanding and positive way. If you do have trouble talking about certain subjects involving death, inform the dying person of your limitations in order to take the "guesswork" out of the relationship. The religious or philosophical viewpoint of the dying person should be respected, and your own personal views should not be imposed.

As a social worker, you should convey verbally and nonverbally that you are willing to talk about any concerns that the person wants to discuss. Touching or hugging is very helpful. But remember that the person has a right not to talk about concerns if he or she so chooses. What you should convey is that you're emotionally ready, have the time, care, and are available to discuss whatever is desired.

If a terminally ill person has questions about his or her illness, answer them as honestly as possible. If you don't know the answers, find a physician who will accurately provide the information. Evasion or ambiguity in response to a dying person's questions only increases that person's concerns. If there is a chance for recovery, it should be mentioned, because even a small margin of hope can be a comfort. The chances for recovery, however, should not be exaggerated.

A dying person should be allowed to accept the reality of the situation at his or her own pace. Relevant information should not be forced upon the person, but it should not be withheld. People who have a terminal illness have a right to all the relevant information.

RELATING TO SURVIVORS

Survivor support groups, such as those offered by hospices and the American Cancer Society, are common nowadays. There are also some support groups that focus on specific types of death. For example, Compassionate Friends provides support and understanding by and for bereaved parents; Survivors of Suicide Victims is for relatives and friends of suicide victims; and the National Foundation for Sudden Infant Death Syndrome provides support for bereaved parents whose child has been a victim of SIDS.

The same guidelines given for dealing with terminal patients can be applied to their survivors. A key thrust of survivor support groups is to have members share their concerns. Such sharing leads to a ventilation of painful emotions that reduces their intensity. Hearing how other members are putting their lives back together after the death of someone close gives a sense of hope to those who are grieving deeply and are uncertain what the future holds. Talking about specific problems (such as how to explain the death to a young child) gives members some suggestions and alternatives for handling difficulties they are facing.

If a survivor is being seen on an individual basis by a worker, the following guidelines are useful. It is helpful to initiate contact with a survivor by saying something like "I'm sorry" and then touching or hugging the person. Then convey that if the person wants to talk or needs help, you're available, and respond to what the survivor expresses. Show that you care, share the loss, and are available for support. It is helpful to use active listening (described in chapter 7) with both survivors and persons who are dying. Continue to visit the survivors, if they show interest in such visits. Caring and support can also be shown through a card, a little gift, or food. If a survivor is unable to resume the normal functions of living or remains deeply depressed, additional professional help or participation in a survivor's self-help group is advisable. The religious or philosophical viewpoint of survivors should be respected, and a counselor should not press her views upon the survivors.

BECOMING COMFORTABLE WITH YOUR OWN DEATH

Perhaps the main reason people are uncomfortable about death is that in our culture we are socialized to avoid seeing death as a natural process of life. Although it is probably true that we will never fully accept our own deaths, we would be more comfortable if we would talk about death more openly and actively seek answers to our questions and concerns. The following are suggestions for becoming more comfortable with the subject.

Groups can be helpful. Group members should identify what their concerns are and then look for answers to these concerns. There are now a number of excellent books providing information on a wide range of subjects involving death and dying, and each group member could research a particular concern and then make an informal presentation at a meeting.[3] Many colleges and universities not only offer workshops and courses on death and dying, but also maintain a list of guest speakers. A number of organizations, such as churches, hospitals, and hospices, have developed educational programs. However, if a group member has intense fears related to death and dying, he may consider talking privately to authorities in the field, such as professional counselors, or to clergy with experience and training in grief counseling.

Taboos against talking about death and dying need to be broken. You may find that tactfully initiating discussions about death and dying with friends and relatives will be helpful to you. A more open discussion of dying in our society is needed to reduce our discomfort with the subject and to prepare people better for death. In talking about death, avoid using euphemisms such as "passed on," "gone to heaven," and "taken by the Lord." It is much better to be accurate and say the person has died, because euphemisms depict an unrealistic picture of death and reinforce our traditional avoidance of the topic. Fortunately, an "open communications" approach about death is emerging through courses and workshops, hospice programs, and books.

There are a number of other ways to become more informed about death and dying. By attending funerals or watching quality films and TV programs that cover aspects of dying, a counselor can become more skillful in providing support to group members who are terminally ill. Being supportive to survivors, talking to people who do grief counseling to learn about their approach, keeping a journal of your thoughts and concerns related to death and dying, and planning the details of your own funeral also would give you access to more realistic information.

Another way to become more comfortable with your own death is to reflect on the sixteen questions in figure 25.2. Were you able to arrive at answers to most of these questions? Were you uncomfortable in answering them? If you were uncomfortable, what were you feeling, and what made you feel that way? For the questions you do not have answers to, how might you arrive at answers?

Mwalimu Imara, a therapist and thanatologist (an authority on death and dying), views dying as having the potential to be the final stage of growth for people.[4] Learning to accept death is similar to learning to accept other losses we face: the breakup of a romantic relationship, termination of a job we cherished, departure from our parents and friends to pursue educational or occupational goals, and so on. If we learn to accept and grow from the losses we encounter, these experiences will help us face the loss of loved ones and our own eventual death.

Having a well-developed sense of identity—that is, of who you are and what you want out of life—also is important in learning to become comfortable with your own death. If you have a well-developed blueprint of what will give meaning and direction to your life,

Figure 25.2: Questionnaire on Death and Dying

(For each multiple-choice question, circle all of the responses that apply to you.)

1. Which of the following describe your present conception of death?
   a. Cessation of all mental and physical activity
   b. Death as sleep
   c. Heaven-and-hell concept
   d. A pleasant afterlife
   e. Death as mysterious and unknown
   f. The end of all life for you
   g. A transition to a new beginning
   h. A joining of the spirit with an unknown cosmic force
   i. A kind of endless sleep
   j. Termination of this physical life with survival of the spirit
   k. Other (specify)

2. Which of the following aspects of your own death do you find distasteful?
   a. What might happen to your body after death
   b. What might happen to you if there is a life after death
   c. Concerns about what might happen to your dependents
   d. The grief that it would cause to your friends and relatives
   e. The pain you may experience as you die
   f. The deterioration of your body before you die
   g. All your plans and projects coming to an end
   h. Other (specify)

3. If you could choose, what age would you like to be when you die?

4. When you think of your own eventual death, how do you feel?
   a. Depressed
   b. Fearful
   c. Discouraged
   d. Purposeless
   e. Angry
   f. Pleasure in being alive
   g. Accepting, as you realize death is a natural process of living
   h. Other (specify)

5. For what or for whom would you be willing to sacrifice your life?
   a. An idea or moral principle
   b. A loved one
   c. In combat
   d. An emergency where another life could be saved
   e. Not for any reason

6. If you could choose, how would you prefer to die?
   a. A sudden violent death
   b. A sudden but nonviolent death
   c. A quiet and dignified death
   d. Death in the line of duty
   e. Suicide
   f. Homicide victim

    g. Death after you have achieved your life goals

    h. Other (specify)

7. If it were possible, would you want to know the exact date on which you would die?
    a. yes
    b. no

8. If you had a terminal illness, would you want your physician to tell you?
    a. yes
    b. no

9. If you had six more months to live, how would you want to spend this time?
    a. Through satisfying hedonistic desires (such as sex) and through traveling
    b. By withdrawing
    c. By contemplating or praying
    d. By seeking to prepare loved ones for your death
    e. By completing projects and tying up loose ends
    f. By considering suicide
    g. Other (specify)

10. Have you seriously contemplated suicide? What are your moral views of suicide? Are there circumstances in which you would take your life? (Please be specific in your answers.)

11. If you had a serious illness and the quality of your life had substantially deteriorated, what measures do you believe should be taken?
    a. All possible medical efforts
    b. Medical efforts should be discontinued when there is practically no hope of returning to a life with quality
    c. Other (specify)

12. If you are married or if you intend to marry in the future, would you prefer to outlive your spouse? Why? (Please be specific in your answers.)

13. How important do you believe funerals and grief rituals are for survivors? (Please be specific.)

14. If it were up to you, how would you like to have your body disposed of after you die?
    a. Cremation
    b. Burial
    c. Donation of parts of your body for organ transplants
    d. Donation of your body to medical school or to science
    e. Other (specify)

15. What kind of funeral would you prefer?
    a. In church
    b. As large as possible
    c. Small, with only close friends and relatives present
    d. A lavish funeral
    e. A simple funeral
    f. Whatever your survivors want
    g. Other (specify)

16. Have you made a will? Why or why not? (Please be specific in your answers.)

you are emotionally better prepared to accept that you will eventually die (see chapter 29 for a fuller treatment of this topic).

Some people who are working on becoming comfortable with their eventual deaths have found comfort in the near-death experiences reported by people who were pronounced clinically dead, but revived. Raymond Moody provides a composite summary of typical experiences that have been reported. Bear in mind that the following narrative is not a representation of any one person's experience; it is a composite of the common elements found in many accounts.

A man is dying, and, as he reaches the point of greatest physical distress, he hears himself pronounced dead by his doctor. He begins to hear an uncomfortable noise, a loud ringing or buzzing, and at the same time feels himself moving very rapidly through a long dark tunnel. After this, he suddenly feels himself outside of his own physical body, but still in the immediate physical environment, and he sees his own body from a distance, as though he is a spectator. He watches the resuscitation attempt from this unusual vantage point and is in a state of emotional upheaval.

After a while, he collects himself and becomes more accustomed to his odd condition. He notices that he still has a "body," but one of a very different nature and with very different powers from the physical body he has left behind. Soon other things begin to happen. Others come to meet and to help him. He glimpses the spirits of relatives and friends who have already died, and a loving, warm spirit of a kind he has never encountered before—a being of light—appears before him. This being asks him a question, nonverbally, to make him evaluate his life and helps him along by showing him a panoramic, instantaneous playback of the major events of his life. At some point he finds himself approaching some sort of barrier or border, apparently representing the limit between earthly life and the next life. Yet he finds that he must go back to the earth, that the time for his death has not yet come. At this point he resists, for by now he is taken up with his experiences in the afterlife and does not want to return. He is overwhelmed by intense feelings of joy, love, and peace. Despite his attitude, though, he somehow reunites with his physical body and lives.

Later he tries to tell others, but he has trouble doing so. In the first place, he can find no human words adequate to describe these unearthly episodes. He also finds that others scoff, so he stops telling other people. Still, the experience affects his life profoundly, especially his views about death and its relationship to life.[5]

No one is sure what causes these experiences, but a variety of explanations have been suggested.[6] One is that it suggests there may be a pleasant afterlife, which gives comfort to those who dislike seeing death as an absolute end. Another explanation, however, is that these near-death experiences are nothing more than hallucinations triggered by chemicals released by the brain or induced by lack of oxygen to the brain. Scientists involved with near-death research acknowledge that so far there is no conclusive evidence that these near-death experiences prove there is life after death.

GROUP EXERCISES

Exercise A: Coping with a Loss

Goal: To share the handling of grief experiences. Talking about these experiences is helpful because: (1) it assists people who are still grieving to ventilate their concerns, and (2) through sharing concerns, helpful suggestions may be given on how to handle present and future losses.

Note: It is advised that the instructor be the designated leader for the exercises in this chapter because they may generate strong emotions.

Step 1. Summarize the Kübler-Ross and the Westberg models of the grieving process, as described in the chapter.

Step 2. Inform the class that the following exercise is a visualization exercise to help them get in touch with a grief experience they have had. *Indicate that their feelings may become intense, and if they become too intense it is certainly acceptable for them to leave the room temporarily.* If someone does leave, let him or her go, but talk to the person later to see if he or she wants to discuss the reasons for leaving. Dim the lights, if possible.

Step 3. Ask the group members to close their eyes. Assure them that there will be no surprises. Read the following slowly, pausing frequently:

> First, I want to have you get as relaxed and comfortable as possible . . . Take several deep breaths, while breathing in and out slowly . . . I want you now to focus on the greatest loss you have experienced . . . It might be the death of someone close to you . . . It might be the end of a romantic relationship . . . It might be moving away from friends and family . . . It might be the death of a pet . . . It might be not getting as high a grade on a test or in a course as you had hoped for . . . Whatever it is, concentrate on it . . .
>
> When you were first informed about the loss, were you in a state of shock? . . . Did you deny the loss? . . . Were you, at times, angry about the loss? . . . Did you, at times, seek to bargain about the loss? . . . If you did seek to bargain, whom did you seek to bargain with? . . . Were you, at times, depressed about the loss? . . . If you were depressed, why (specifically) were you depressed? . . . Did you at times have some fears or concerns about the loss? . . . If you had fears or concerns, what were these fears or concerns? . . . Did you at times have guilt about this loss? . . . If you did feel guilty, what specifically did you feel guilty about? Did you cry about this loss? . . . If you cried, do you know why you cried? . . . If you didn't cry, do you know why you didn't cry? . . . If you cried, was it helpful? . . . How deeply has this loss hurt you? . . . How long have you been hurting about this loss? . . .
>
> Are you still grieving about this loss? . . . Do you at times still grieve deeply about this loss? . . . Have you found that as time goes on you are grieving less deeply, and that your intense grieving periods are shorter in duration? . . . Do holidays, an-

niversaries, birthdays, special days still remind you of the loss? . . . If and when you are grieving deeply, how do you seek to handle this grief? . . .

Has the loss been so great that you thought about taking your life? . . . Many people think about taking their life when they are grieving deeply . . . Have you made attempts to take your life? . . .

Have you had some physical reactions to the loss, such as difficulty in sleeping, stomach problems, headaches, anxiety attacks, sexual difficulties? . . . Grieving is very stressful, and it is common to have physical reactions . . . Do you dream about the loss? . . . For example, it is common for people who have lost a loved one to dream that person is still alive . . . Often when someone awakes from such a dream, it is difficult to separate reality from the dream. . . .

What aspects of the loss have you handled well? . . . What aspects could you have handled better? . . . What aspects are you still working on? . . . How have you gone about handling this loss? . . . How pleased are you with your efforts to handle this loss? . . . How have others close to you handled this loss? . . . How have you gone about helping them? . . . Have you grown from this loss experience? . . . What yet do you need to work on to handle this loss? . . . What specific efforts are you making to handle this loss? . . . OK . . . slowly open your eyes, and let's talk about grieving.

Step 4. The instructor indicates one of the best ways to handle grief is to talk about it. Then the leader asks if someone wishes to share a loss he or she has experienced, and describe what helped him or her to handle this loss. If no one begins to share a grieving experience, the instructor describes a personal loss and how it was handled. (Caution: When doing this exercise, the instructor must be prepared to handle a variety of emotions and concerns that may be expressed.)

Step 5. The class discusses whether the Westberg model or the Kübler-Ross model of the grieving process can better describe the grief they experienced.

Step 6. The instructor summarizes material given in the chapter on how to handle grief.

Exercise B: Becoming Comfortable with the Idea of Your Own Death

Goal: To help you think about and become more comfortable with thoughts about your own eventual death.

Step 1. Inform the class of the purpose of this exercise. Dim the lights if possible. Indicate that this is a visualization exercise. Read the following slowly, with frequent pauses:

I want you to close your eyes and get as comfortable as possible . . . Take several deep breaths, while breathing in and out slowly . . . There will be no surprises in this exercise . . .

Imagine that you haven't been feeling well for a period of time and that you go to your doctor for a series of tests . . . The tests are taken, and you have an appointment to be informed about the results . . . The doctor has a concerned look on his face and asks you to be seated . . . The doctor informs you that you have a terminal illness, and his estimate is that you have about six or seven months to live . . . Does this scene seem believable? . . . I know this scene may be difficult for some of you to imagine as many of us like to think we will live for a very long time and don't want to think about our own death. If we are to become comfortable with our own death, we need to think about it and prepare for it. One way of doing this is through an exercise like this. Therefore, I ask you to concentrate as fully as you can on this scene in which you have just been informed you have a terminal illness . . .

What are you thinking and feeling? . . . Are you in a state of shock? . . . Are you actively denying this could happen? . . . Are you breathing faster? . . . Are your eyes watering? . . . Is your heart beating faster? . . . Are you numbed by this? . . . Are you terrified? . . . Do you have fears about the pain you may experience in the remaining months? . . .

What do you want to do? . . . Are you interested in seeking more information about your illness from your physician? . . . Do you want to leave the office? . . . When you leave the office, what do you want to do—drive home? . . . Tell friends or relatives? . . . Be by yourself? . . .

What do you plan to do with the remaining months you have left to live? . . . Do you want to travel? . . . Would you seek to change your lifestyle? . . . Would you seek to satisfy hedonistic desires such as sex and drugs? . . . Would you become more withdrawn? . . . Would you become more religious, and pray more? . . . Would you seek to complete projects and tie up loose ends? . . . Would you become concerned about preparing dependents and friends for your death? . . . Would you consider committing suicide? . . .

If it were possible, would you want to know the exact date on which you will die? . . . What efforts do you believe ought to be made to keep you alive? . . . All possible medical efforts even though there is no hope of returning to a quality lifestyle? . . . Or would you want medical efforts to be discontinued when there is little hope to return to a quality life?

What aspects of your own death are most distasteful to you? . . . Is it that you will no longer have enjoyable experiences? . . . Is it that you are afraid of what will happen to your body and mind after you die? . . . Is it that you are uncertain as to what might happen to you if there is a life after death? . . . Are you worried about what will happen to people who depend upon you? . . . Are you concerned that your plans and projects might come to an end? . . . Are you worried about your relatives and friends grieving about you? . . . Are you worried about the pain you may experience before you die? . . . Are you worried your body may deteriorate as you die? . . .

How would you want people to remember you? . . . What would you like placed on your tombstone? . . . If you want people to remember you in a certain way, are you living your life in such a way that they will remember you as you desire? . . .

What kind of funeral would you prefer? . . . Do you want a lot of people at your funeral? . . . Or do you want only close relatives and friends to be at your funeral? . . . Do you want a church service? . . . Do you want a lot of flowers at your funeral? . . . Is there a certain song that you wish would be played? . . . Do you think funerals are primarily for those who died or primarily for survivors to help them cope with the loss? . . . Do you want a burial, or do you wish to be cremated? . . . Have you considered donating parts of your body for organ transplants? . . . Have you considered donating your body to a medical school or to science? . . . If there was a mystery surrounding your death, would you want an autopsy? . . .

What does death mean to you? . . . How is what happens after you die different from what life was like before you were born? . . . Do you view death as the absolute end of life? . . . Do you view death as being a transition to a new life? . . . Do you view death as being a joining of your spirit with a cosmic force? . . . Do you view death as being an endless sleep? . . . Do you view death as being a termination of this life, but with the survival of your spirit or soul? . . . Do you believe there is an afterlife? . . .

If you would want to make changes in your life upon learning you have a terminal illness, what is preventing you from making these changes at the present time? . . . OK . . . , open your eyes and let's talk.

Step 2. Ask the class to discuss the exercise, including the following questions: Did they have trouble visualizing the exercise as being real? Why? Do they think the exercise was helpful in getting them to think about, and become comfortable with, their eventual deaths? (After this exercise the instructor may want to do exercise F.)

Exercise C: Recognizing Life Is Terminal

Goal: To have students become more aware of the thoughts and feelings they will have when their own deaths become imminent.

Step 1. The leader begins by stating that many people do not like to attend funerals, nor do they like to think about their own eventual deaths. Many people avoid thinking about death—they have the irrational notion that their eventual deaths are so far in the future that they act as if they will live indefinitely. Yet grief management authorities assert we need to come to terms with our own deaths, and that our daily lives will be more meaningful if we become more comfortable with the fact that life is terminal from birth—as we will all die. The leader then states the goal of this exercise.

Step 2. The leader distributes to each student a packet of twelve slips of paper. The students are instructed to write on each of the small slips of paper one of the following twelve items:

- Three personal characteristics she is proud of.
- Three activities he enjoys participating in.
- The three possessions that she cherishes most.
- The names of the three people that are most important in his life.

Each student then arranges these twelve slips of paper in front of her on a desk or table so that she can see them all.

Step 3. The leader states the following: Imagine that you haven't been feeling well for the past several months. You finally decide to see your doctor. The doctor administers a number of medical tests. Today you go in to hear the test results. As you walk in, the doctor has a very concerned look on her face. The doctor informs you that you have a terminal illness. *You have thirty seconds to tear up three of your slips of paper.* Tear up the three slips that are least important to you.

Step 4. The leader states the following: You leave the physician's office in a state of shock. You return home. Who is there to greet you? Whom do you really *want* to find there? What do you say to these people? What do you want to hear from them? *Tear up another three slips of paper.*

Step 5. The leader states the following: It is now two months later. You realize your health is deteriorating. Your symptoms are worsening, and you are feeling weaker. Where are you living now? Have you made changes in your lifestyle? Are there projects and loose ends in your life that you are seeking to complete? What are you thinking and feeling about your terminal illness? *Tear up another two slips of paper.*

Step 6. The leader states the following: It is now four months after you were informed of your terminal illness. You are undeniably ill. You are in considerable pain, and you now need caregivers to stay alive. Where are you living now? Who is taking care of you? Who visits you? Who are the people you want to visit you and take care of you? *Tear up another two slips of paper.*

Step 7. The leader states the following: Six months have now passed since you learned of your terminal illness. You have very little energy left. The smallest activity of daily living takes most of your energy. A caregiver now has to attend to you twenty-four hours a day. You can no longer bathe yourself. How do you now feel about yourself? Where are you living now? *Please turn over your remaining two slips of paper, and I will take one.* (The leader takes one from each student.)

Step 8. The leader states the following: *Look at your last slip of paper, and then tear it up. You are now dead.*

Step 9. The leader thanks the students for conscientiously participating in the first part of this exercise. The leader then asks the students to form subgroups of about three persons. The members of each subgroup are asked to share their reactions to the following questions, which should now be listed on the blackboard. (If a student chooses not to share, that is his or her right.)

1. Did the exercise seem real. If "yes," when did it become real? If "no," why didn't it seem real?
2. What emotional reactions did you have to this exercise?
3. What were the last two items on the slips of paper that you kept?
4. What were your thoughts, feelings, and reactions to the tearing up of the last slip of paper?

Step 10. The class as a whole then discusses the merits and shortcomings of this exercise.

Exercise D: Achieving Closure in a Lost Relationship

Goal: To achieve closure in a relationship loss that has been experienced.

Step 1. Explain that people who are grieving about a loss often feel guilty about things said or done—or things not said or done that they believe may have contributed to the loss. Many people also feel guilty about not having resolved an interpersonal conflict before the death of someone close. People who experience a breakup of a romantic relationship often feel the need to obtain "closure" to the relationship through saying how they feel about the relationship ending or through finding answers to questions about why the relationship ended.

Step 2. Ask each person to write down a number of items not resolved in a relationship on a sheet of paper. The relationship may have been with a person who died, a close friend or relative, or someone involved in a current conflict. Then ask each person to write down what he or she would say to resolve the conflict, and then how he or she thinks the other person would respond. Indicate that this exercise has been found to be helpful in obtaining closure to relationships and in relieving guilt for survivors who have not obtained closure with someone who has died.

Step 3. Ask the class to get together in groups of three to share what they wrote. *Indicate that if someone does not wish to share what was written, this request will be honored, as people have a right to privacy.*

Step 4. Ask the class as a group to discuss their thoughts about the exercise and what they learned from it.

Exercise E: Epitaphs

Goals: To foster the discussion of death, to help you accept your own eventual death, and to provide some guidance on how to live.

Step 1. Ask students to write down the epitaph they want placed on their tombstones. Explain that an epitaph is a brief statement or phrase meant as a remembrance. Indicate to the class that no names should be placed on the sheet and that the epitaphs will be read to the class. Several minutes will be needed to write this statement.

Step 2. Collect the epitaphs in such a way that students will not be identified. Read the epitaphs to the class, making appropriate observations, such as: "It is interesting to note that hardly anyone mentioned wanting to be remembered for collecting material goods, yet so many people spend so much time trying to collect material things. These epitaphs provide some direction on how we should live our lives in order to be remembered in a way we would like."

Exercise F: Desensitizing Fears about Dying

Goal: To identify and become more comfortable with fears about dying.

Step 1. Ask students to write down their specific fears and concerns about their eventual deaths on a sheet of paper. Indicate their responses *will remain anonymous* and that *they should not put their names on the sheet.*

Step 2. Collect the responses, and then read them aloud. As you read each fear and concern, ask the class if it is realistic or unrealistic.

Step 3. Ask the class members what they learned from doing this exercise and whether the exercise helped them identify and handle their fears about dying. (Many people fear dying but never make the effort to identify their fears or to determine whether their fears are realistic.)

Exercise G: Expressing Empathy and Support to a Griever

Goal: To learn how to express empathy and to give support to someone who is grieving.

Step 1. Two students volunteer to role play this situation. One person role plays someone who is grieving the recent death of a spouse in an auto accident. This person has two young children and wants to discuss his or her concerns. The task of the other person is to initiate an expression of empathy, to give support to the other, and to listen and respond to the concerns being expressed by the person who is grieving. After the role playing, the class discusses what was said and what else might have been said.

Exercise H: Conveying a Death Message

Goal: To learn how to empathically convey a death message.

Step 1. Two students volunteer to role play how to convey and receive a death message. The person conveying a death message role plays the following situation.

You receive a phone call that your roommate's father has died unexpectedly and suddenly from a heart attack. The roommate was not home, but now has just arrived. Your task is to empathically convey this message.

The other volunteer role plays the survivor and responds as realistically as possible.

Step 2. The class discusses what the conveyer of the message did well and what else might be said or done nonverbally.

SPECIALIZED GROUPS: WHERE DOES THE SOCIAL WORKER FIT IN?

Even when a social worker counsels clients individually, he or she practices skills appropriate to group work. Each client belongs to a number of groups, and the worker must be prepared to adjust his or her approach accordingly. How might this worker at a social service agency need to adjust her interviewing strategy to account for the race difference between her and the client to whom she is talking? How might she overemphasize such a difference?

Self-help groups—direct service and social action.

Self-help groups must be established primarily for support (like chapters of Alcoholics Anonymous) or for social action, like this citizens group favoring the use of defense funds to support human service agencies. In either case, self-help groups stress mutual support and leadership by members themselves. Professional social workers therefore play only a minor role in such groups. But social service agencies have come to rely on the unique combination of personal help and social action that self-help groups provide, services that are often more appropriate to a client than those an agency can offer. And, within their own administrations self-help groups often need professional social workers to help in planning, to advise on methods of treatment, and to conduct public relations.

Socialization groups.

Socialization groups usually require that a social worker take a central leadership position. The worker needs to be deft at group-work techniques in order to achieve the goals of socialization groups, making the attitudes and behaviors of its members socially acceptable. These workers are leading a rap session at a school for delinquent youths. What advantages would you expect these young men to gain from a group approach as opposed to one-on-one counseling?

Problem-solving groups.

What special help can a social worker offer? The task of a problem-solving group is to define and solve a problem, a difficult job even under the best of circumstances. Groups often have trouble defining a problem accurately; they often mistake a problem's cause or fail to produce the strategies to resolve it. But a group can avoid these pitfalls by following problem-solving techniques that a social worker can provide. This social worker is talking with young girls in a Hispanic neighborhood, attempting to help them resolve unspoken differences while identifying the group dynamics of the children and their families.

Family therapy.

Families often come to therapy with the view that one of their members has a problem that is disrupting the entire family unit. The therapist's job is to help the family understand that the problem does not belong to one member but belongs to and must be resolved by the family as a whole. This type of therapy calls for strong, highly skilled, compassionate leadership on the social worker's part.

Group therapy.

There is no question about where social workers fit into therapy groups. The professional needs considerable understanding of human behavior and experience in how group therapy can bring about behavioral changes and healing. When well-guided, group therapy benefits clients in many ways—for example, by allowing them to share their problems with people in similar situations (like this cancer survivors' support group), or by allowing them to practice strategies for coping with their problems.

CHAPTER TWENTY-SIX

INTERVENTIONS WITH CHEMICAL DEPENDENCE*

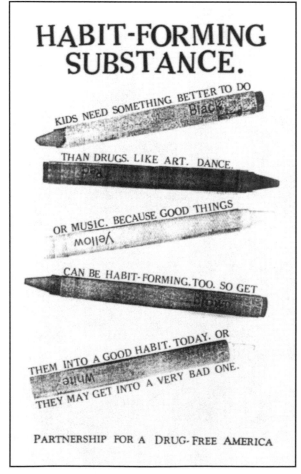

HABIT-FORMING SUBSTANCE.

KIDS NEED SOMETHING BETTER TO DO
Black

THAN DRUGS. LIKE ART. DANCE.
Red

OR MUSIC. BECAUSE GOOD THINGS
Yellow

CAN BE HABIT-FORMING. TOO. SO GET
Brown

THEM INTO A GOOD HABIT. TODAY. OR
White

THEY MAY GET INTO A VERY BAD ONE.

PARTNERSHIP FOR A DRUG-FREE AMERICA

Goal: Many social workers fail to realize that the primary goal of an intervention process is the complete and total abstinence from chemicals. In order to make that point clear, this chapter provides students with an introduction to chemical dependence, outlines the symptoms of dependence and recovery, and describes the role of group counseling in the recovery process. Although the focus will be on interventions with chemically dependent individuals, family counseling, which plays a vital role in recovery, will also be briefly discussed.

The individual and family suffering from the disease of chemical dependence often feel they have a unique problem that no one else could possibly understand or have experienced. The use of group therapy and self-help groups is very effective in diffusing this myth and in helping the drug-dependent person and his family recover.

THE NATURE OF CHEMICAL DEPENDENCE

Let's begin our discussion of chemical dependence by examining a number of key concepts and terms before we examine symptoms.

Key Concepts

A *drug* may be defined as any substance that chemically modifies the function of living tissues, resulting in physiological or behavioral change. Alcohol, according to our definition, is also a drug, although because its use is so widespread it is generally discussed by itself. The *psychoactive drugs* are natural or synthetic substances that affect the mental processes, altering mood and/or behavior. *Chemical of choice* refers to the one or more types of drugs that an individual, having experimented with several types and forms, settles on and uses regularly to achieve the emotional and/or physical results he or she desires.

Drug use is defined as the intake of a chemical substance under such circumstances and at such dosage levels that the effects can be realized with *minimal hazard* potential regardless of whether the substance is used therapeutically, legally, or as prescribed by a physician. *Drug abuse*, conversely, involves the intake of a chemical substance taken or administered under circumstances and at dosage levels that significantly *increase the hazard* potential regardless of whether the drug is used therapeutically, legally, or as prescribed by a physician.

Dependence is a tendency to, or craving for, the repeated or compulsive use (but not necessarily abuse) of a chemical. Dependence can be psychological and/or physical. The major components of *psychological dependence* are repeated use of a chemical to achieve a state that could not be achieved without alcohol or drugs; an inability to envision the rest of one's life without using the chemical; and a preoccupation with thinking and talking about the chemical and activities associated with using it. *Physical dependence* involves the dependence of body tissues on the continued presence of a drug for normal functioning. If the drug is not used for a period of time, the physically dependent person will experience withdrawal symptoms.

Addiction is the condition of being physically or psychologically dependent on a drug. The following are symptoms of addiction:

1. There is increased tissue or cellular tolerance. More of the chemical is required to achieve the desired emotional state.

---

*This chapter was written by LaVonne J. Cornell-Swanson, MSW, ACSW, instructor, Social Work Dept., University of Wisconsin-Whitewater.

2. There is an inability to abstain. Although the person may not intend to use the drug, he or she is unable to abstain after a specified period of time (this may be hours or days).

3. The abuser experiences lack of control. The person is unable to use chemicals in ways that may be considered socially acceptable. The person intends *using* but usually ends up *abusing* the chemical. The extent of use is no longer within the abuser's control.

Chemical dependence involves the felt need for, and reliance on, a drug of choice to achieve positive feelings on a regular basis. The drug chosen may be a form of alcohol, a prescription or nonprescription drug, or a combination of these. The term "chemical dependence" is replacing "alcohol addiction," "alcoholism," and "drug addiction," as these terms may be inaccurate, misleading (no physical addiction may be present), or stigmatizing. (People who have acknowledged alcohol dependence may call themselves "alcoholic" for the following reasons: as an indication of their membership in the family of chemical abusers, their need to maintain sobriety, and their identification with a program of recovery.)

Symptoms

It is important for a counselor to be aware of and able to identify the defense mechanisms and other symptoms associated with chemical dependence.

Denial. A dependent person shows adamant and continued refusal to admit that a problem exists. If the person does acknowledge some problems, he or she will insist they are not a result of the chemical use. Many dependent people deny they have an abuse problem because such an admission would mean they would have to give up a drug they erroneously believe they cannot live without.

Rationalization. The dependent person twists or distorts reality to explain his or her behavior and its consequences. A web of half-truths, hurt feelings, confusion, and resentment is developed. The person tends to believe sincerely that the rationalizations do, in fact, explain the situation in a way that makes sense (and makes him or her look good). A common rationalization is to excuse or minimize the negative consequences of chemical abuse.

Projection. The dependent person places blame for his or her problems on others or on events outside that person's control. The projection may be irrational, inappropriately intense, and increasingly damaging to the dependent and his or her relationships with others.

Delusion. As the problems get worse, denial of a chemical-use problem becomes harder to maintain. To protect a chemical habit, a dependent person must distort reality in ways that become every more bizarre. Sometimes those close to the dependent person actually accept the delusional statements as being rational—or decide that they are the ones who are crazy.

Low Self-Worth. A chemically dependent person experiences guilt, remorse, and feelings of failure. The pattern of chemical abuse continues to invoke and reinforce negative and self-defeating behaviors that the dependent person believes can be handled or removed only by continued drug usage. Self-abuse, even suicide, may be attempted. As most chemicals are system depressants, thought and behavior tend to take on negative and life-negating (rather than life-enhancing) aspects.

Physical Aspects. The chemical dependent's body is deprived of healthy substances and activities. He or she may skip meals or replace nutritious foods with junk foods. The body tends to be pushed beyond health limits because the dependent ignores physical warning signals. Rest and relaxation are sacrificed. Some of the initial physical symptoms seen and felt by the dependent are: an uneasy feeling when the chemical is not being used; minor physical complaints such as aches and pains; lack of skin-tone luster (lack of a healthy glow); dulled eyes that tend to be unfocused or cannot maintain eye-to-eye contact; stooped body posture; and poor muscle tone.

RECOVERY FROM CHEMICAL DEPENDENCE

A chemically dependent person has actually developed a relationship with alcohol or drugs. Even though this relationship is unhealthy, it plays a primary role in his or her life, dictates a certain lifestyle, fills a need, and more often than not takes precedence over family, friends, vocation, and society. The drug has become the dependent person's "best friend." By giving up this relationship, the dependent is experiencing a loss that involves grieving. It is important that the dependent be successful in working through the grief. Elizabeth Kübler-Ross' stages of grief clearly outline the process. These stages are denial, anger and rage, bargaining, depression, and acceptance[1] (see chapter 25 for a description). It is important the counselor know and understand these stages to help the person reach complete recovery.

Stages of Recovery

There are four basic stages of recovery that the dependent person may go through before sobriety will be maintained: denial, compliance, acceptance, and surrender.

Denial. During the denial stage, the dependent refuses to acknowledge that a problem exists. If confronted, the dependent person often states that the drug dependence is caused by something or someone other than alcohol or drugs (spouse, children, employer, or finances, for example).[2]

Compliance. The dependent gives in to the idea that alcohol or drugs may be the cause of problems. He or she acknowledges that dependence may be present but still wishes it weren't. The complier may still want to learn controlled chemical use and to deny total loss of control. Compliance is knowing *intellectually* that chemical dependence exists but not believing it deep inside. In this stage, the dependent person will conform to what he or she is told. Often in this stage the dependent person will agree to treatment and go along with the process to eliminate the pressure of friends and relatives. However, unless acceptance is reached, the person will usually return to use of the chemical.

Acceptance. During this stage, the dependent person begins to say "yes" *intellectually and emotionally* to loss of self-control. He or she decides to eliminate chemicals totally. The dependent decides he no longer *needs* the chemical of choice to live a fulfilling life. Acceptance of chemical dependence brings into being a basic change in attitude and a sense of responsibility.

The first three stages of recovery often fluctuate. A client may swing from one to the other and back again. Keep in mind that in any form of treatment clients move "four steps forward, three back."

Surrender. In this stage, the dependent person experiences personal growth as a result of a realization that he or she no longer *needs* or *desires* chemicals. By this time the person has experienced some sobriety and finds the chemical-free lifestyle fulfilling. Therefore, the desire for usage discontinues, and the swinging back and forth between stages ceases. (Unfortunately, most alcoholics and other chemically dependent persons do not reach this stage.)

INTERVENTION PROCESS

The goal of the intervention process should be sobriety, meaning "complete and total abstinence from chemicals and the following of a program for personal recovery from chemical dependence. This means sober from the chosen drug and those drugs/alcohol which might be substituted in place of the drug of choice."[3]

Chemical dependence is a progressive disease. During an initial evaluation, a social worker must identify the particular stage of the client's abuse pattern. The progression chart in figure 26.1 can be a useful tool for doing this. Simply underline those items listed that apply. Apply this chart to all drugs, including alcohol.

"Chemical dependence is not curable. Once a person becomes dependent, the only safe and sure response is the decision to discontinue not only the use of the alcohol/drug of choice but all forms of drugs which may be abused."[4] There are several stages of the intervention/recovery process. A good intervention program should provide: medical care; individual, group, and family counseling; educational material; and introduction to Alcoholics Anonymous or a similar self-help community group.

Medical Treatment

The involvement of medical personnel is necessary because numerous medical complications (such as cardiovascular, brain, respiratory, or artery damage) may occur as a direct result of chemical abuse. Indirect physical problems (such as poor nutrition, injuries, and accidents) also necessitate medical attention. Many persons require a detoxification period that must be monitored closely by medical staff because of potential withdrawal problems. (Detoxification centers are located in a variety of facilities—hospitals, community mental health centers, and in independent facilities that focus on treating chemical abuse.)

Furthermore, a full physical exam is needed in order to be sure of the dependent person's actual physical needs. Often, physical problems that go untreated interfere with the recovery process.

Individual Counseling

Counseling the dependant person requires addressing numerous areas and may involve family, marital, vocational, educational, social, sexual, and spiritual problems as well as psychological difficulties. Some of these areas will require the kind of individual attention that group counseling does not permit. Therefore, individual counseling is a necessary component of the intervention process.

Family Counseling

Chemical dependence is a family disease and a primary disease.[5] (Chemical dependence is considered a primary disease because the dependence must be treated first before focusing on other problems that the dependent person may have.) By involving the family, a counselor will be able to identify areas of conflict within the family structure, obtain collateral information, and offer services to the family members. When one member of a family (the client) has pain that shows symptoms, all family members feel this pain in some way.[6] Family members are identified as co-dependents in the chemically dependent system. Often, a family member enables the dependent person to continue using the drug. As Sharon Weigsheider notes, "The role of the chief enabler in the family is to provide responsibility. As the dependent increasingly loses control, the chief enabler makes more choices to compensate for the dependent's lack of power."[7] The enabling has to discontinue along with the chemical use.

How do family members function as enablers? When family members become involved in the treatment process, they are often shocked to learn that they are one of the major factors making it possible for the dependent person to keep on abusing his or her drug of choice. The typical enabler (spouse, parent, friend) usually does most of the following things, over and over again. The enabler attempts to do everything possible to make the dependent happy and relaxed, since the enabler has observed that the user is most likely to abuse when unhappy and tense. When the dependent is too drugged or hung over to go to work or meet other social or work responsibilities, the enabler covers up with an endless list of nonexistent illnesses, medical or dental appointments, and other excuses. To ease the financial situation, the enabler goes to work (or if employed already, gets a second, moonlighting job). The enabler also takes care of the dependent person when he or she is drunk, stoned, sick, or hung over and gradually takes over many of the dependent's normal responsibilities.

The enabler also tries to protect the dependent person by hiding the drugs or alcohol or by throwing them away. This person is more or less constantly cajoling, pleading, ordering, or threatening the dependent to limit or stop abusing. The enabler tries to shame the person with reminders of those embarrassing and dangerous things he or she did while under the influence and complaining bitterly about the money spent on drugs, or wasted in other ways. What are the effects of such criticism? It leads the dependent person to lose self-respect and sense of pride. He or she feels embarrassed, guilty, foolish, and ashamed. The criticism and resulting unwanted emotions increase his or her level of stress. And, sadly, the person often feels the only escape is to get high. Then the dependent person blames the enabler.

Figure 26.1: Alcohol and Other Drugs

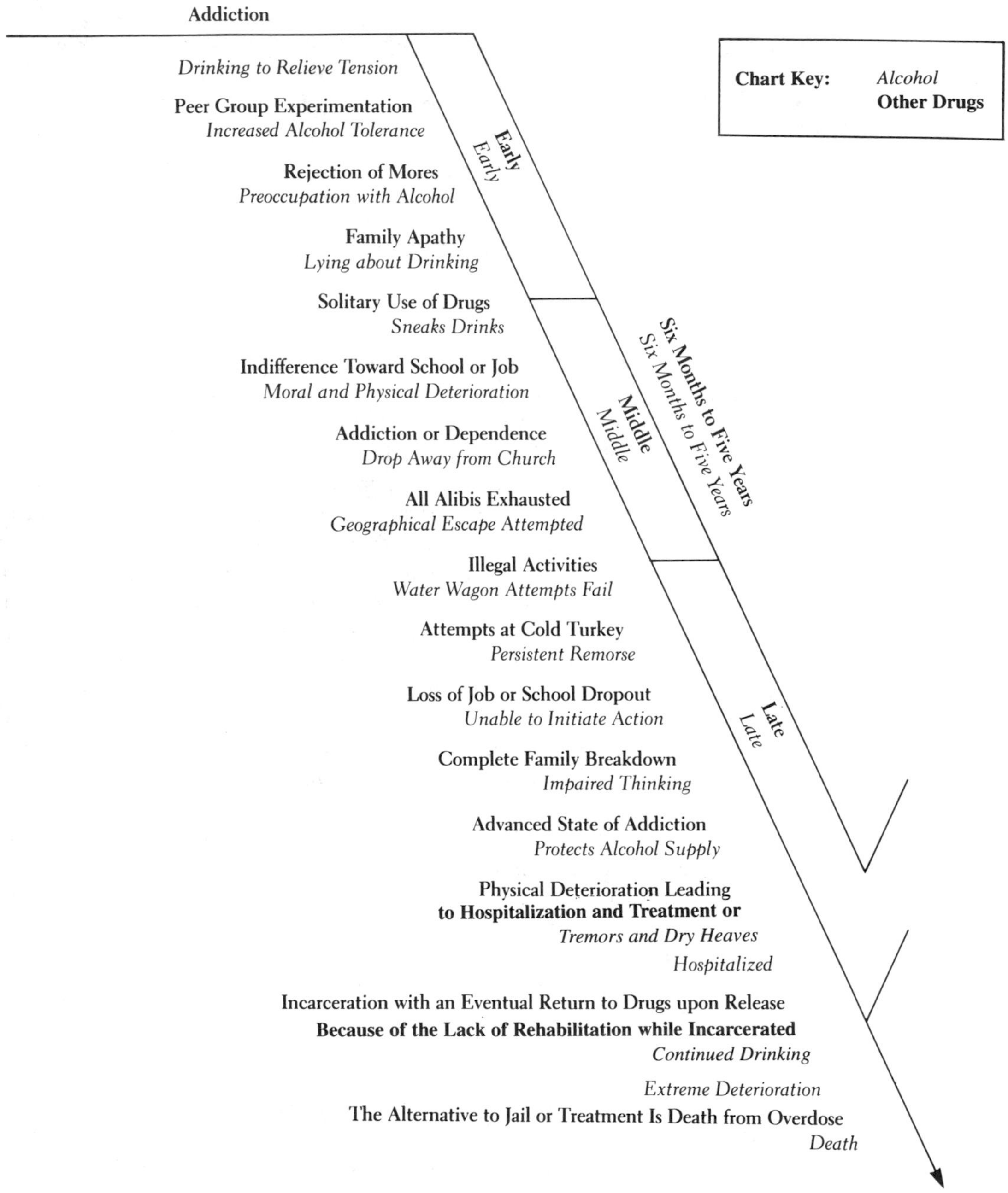

Addiction

Chart Key: *Alcohol*
                    Other Drugs

Drinking to Relieve Tension

Peer Group Experimentation
Increased Alcohol Tolerance

Early
Early

Rejection of Mores
Preoccupation with Alcohol

Family Apathy
Lying about Drinking

Solitary Use of Drugs
Sneaks Drinks

Six Months to Five Years
Six Months to Five Years

Indifference Toward School or Job
Moral and Physical Deterioration

Addiction or Dependence
Drop Away from Church

Middle
Middle

All Alibis Exhausted
Geographical Escape Attempted

Illegal Activities
Water Wagon Attempts Fail

Attempts at Cold Turkey
Persistent Remorse

Loss of Job or School Dropout
Unable to Initiate Action

Late
Late

Complete Family Breakdown
Impaired Thinking

Advanced State of Addiction
Protects Alcohol Supply

**Physical Deterioration Leading
to Hospitalization and Treatment or**
Tremors and Dry Heaves
Hospitalized

Incarceration with an Eventual Return to Drugs upon Release
Because of the Lack of Rehabilitation while Incarcerated
Continued Drinking

Extreme Deterioration

The Alternative to Jail or Treatment Is Death from Overdose
Death

Recovery

Reentry into Society
Enlightened Way of Life

Feeling of Acceptance
Future Faced with Determination

Contentment with New Life Style
Increased Activity in A.A.

Family Acceptance
Contentment in Sobriety

Involvement in Religious Values
Dedication to Religious Values

Emotional Stabilization
New Interests Developed

New Interests Developed
Readjustment to Family Needs

Vocational Counseling
Family and Friends' Support

Group Therapy
Surrenders Control

Individual Counseling
Spiritual Needs Examined

Improvement of Personal Appearance
Improvement of Personal Appearance

Self-concept Improves
Introduced to A.A.

Evaluation Leading to Treatment Goals
Dryout/Medical Help

Treatment Begins via Medical Management
Family/Employer Intervention

Six Months to Two Years
Six Months to Two Years

Source: "Alcohol and Other Drugs Progression Chart" developed by the A-Center of Racine, Wisconsin, Inc. Redrawn by permission of the A-Center.

AN AA MEETING

Alcoholics Anonymous is a remarkable human organization. Its chapters now cover every part of the United States and most of the world. There is more caring and concern among the members for one another than in most other organizations. Group members work together to save each other's lives and to restore self-respect and sense of worth. AA has helped more people overcome their drinking problems than all other therapies and methods combined.

AA is supported entirely by voluntary donations from the members at meetings. There are no dues or fees. Each chapter is autonomous, free of any outside control by the AA headquarters in New York City or by any other body. There is no hierarchy in the chapters. The only office is that of group secretary. This person chooses a chairperson for each meeting, makes the arrangements for meetings, and sees that the building is opened, the chairs set up, and the tea and coffee put on. The group secretary holds office for only a limited time period; after a month or two the secretary's responsibilities are transferred to another member.

The only requirement for membership in AA is a desire to stop drinking. All other variables (such as economic status, social status, race, religion) do not count. Members can even attend meetings while drunk, as long as they do not disturb the meeting.

AA meetings are held in a variety of physical locations—churches, temples, private homes, business offices, schools, libraries, or banquet rooms of restaurants. The physical location is unimportant.

When a newcomer first arrives, he or she will usually find people setting up chairs, placing ashtrays, putting free literature on a table, and making coffee. Other members will be socializing in small groups. Someone is apt to introduce himself or herself and other members to the newcomer. If someone is shy about attending the first meeting alone, he or she can call AA and someone will take the person to the meeting and introduce him or her to the other members.

When the meeting starts, everyone sits down around tables or in rows of chairs. The secretary and/or chairperson and one or more speakers sit at the head of a table or on a platform if the meeting is in a hall.

The chairperson opens with a moment of silence, which is followed by a group recitation of a prayer that is nondenominational. The chairperson then reads or gives a brief description of Alcoholics Anonymous and may read or refer to a section of the book *Alcoholics Anonymous* (a book that describes the principles of AA and also gives a number of case examples).

Then, the chairperson usually asks if anyone is attending for the first, second, or third time. The new people are asked to introduce themselves according to the following: "Hello, my name is (first name), and this is my first (second, third) meeting." Those who do not want to introduce themselves are not pressured to do so. New members are the lifeblood of AA, and the most important people at the meeting in the members' eyes. (All the longer-term members remember their first meeting and how frightened and inhibited they felt.)

If the group is small, the chairperson usually then asks the longer-term members to introduce themselves and say a few words. If the group is large, the chairperson asks volunteers among the longer-term members to introduce themselves by saying a few words. Each member usually begins by saying, "My name is (first name); I am an alcoholic" and then discloses a few thoughts or feelings. (The members do not have to say they are alcoholic unless they choose to do so.) Each member sooner or later generally chooses to say this, to remind himself that he is an addictive drinker who is recovering and that alcoholism is a lifelong disease, which he must battle daily. Those who introduce themselves usually say whatever they feel will be most helpful to the newcomers. They may talk about their first meeting, or their first week without drinking, or something designed to make the newcomers more comfortable. Common advice for the newcomers is to get the phone numbers of other members after the meeting so that they can call them when they feel a strong urge to drink. AA considers such help as vital in recovering. The organization believes members can remain sober

AN AA MEETING (con't.)

only through receiving the help of people who care about them and who understand what they are struggling with.

AA members want newcomers to call when they have the urge to drink, at any time day or night. The members sincerely believe that by helping others they are helping themselves to stay sober and grow. Members indicate such calling is the newcomer's ace in the hole against the first drink, if everything else fails. They also inform newcomers that it is good to call others when lonely, just to chat.

In his own words, a newcomer explains how AA began to help him:

Here's what happened to me. When I finally hit bottom and called AA for help. A U.S. Air Force officer came to tell me about AA. For the first time in my life, I was talking to someone who obviously really understood my problem, as four psychiatrists had not, and he took me to my first meeting, sober but none too steady. It was amazing. I went home afterward and didn't have a drink. I went again the next night, still dry, and the miracle happened a second time. The third morning my wife went off to work, my boys to school, and I was alone. Suddenly I wanted a drink more than I had ever wanted one in my life. I tried walking for a while. No good. The feeling was getting worse. I tried reading. Couldn't concentrate. Then I became really desperate, and although I wasn't used to calling strangers for help, I called Fred, an AA-er who had said that he was retired and would welcome a call at any time. We talked a bit; he could see that talking on the phone wasn't going to be enough. He said, "Look, I've got an idea. Let me make a phone call, and I'll call you back in ten minutes. Can you hold on that long?" I said I could. He called back in eight, asking me to come over to his house. We talked endlessly, went out for a sandwich together, and finally my craving for a drink went away. We went to a meeting. Next morning I was fine again, and now I had gone four days without a drink.[1]

After such discussion speakers may describe their life of drinking, how drinking almost destroyed their life, how they were introduced to AA, their struggles to remain sober one day at a time, how AA has helped them, and what their life is now like.

At the end of a meeting the chairperson may ask the newcomers if they wish to say anything. If they do not wish to say much, that is okay. No one is pressured to self-disclose what they do not want to reveal.

Meetings usually end after the chairperson makes announcements. (The collection basket for donations is also passed around. New members are not expected, and frequently not allowed, to donate any money until after their third meeting. If someone cannot afford to make a donation, none is expected.) The group then stands, usually holding hands, and repeats in unison the Lord's Prayer. Those who do not want to join in this prayer are not pressured to do so. After a meeting the members socialize. This is a time for newcomers to meet new friends and to get phone numbers.

AA is a cross-section of people from all walks of life. Anonymity is emphasized. It is the duty of every member to respect the anonymity of every person who attends. Concern for anonymity is a major reason for two kinds of meetings in AA, open and closed. Anyone is welcome at open meetings. Only people with drinking problems are allowed at closed meetings. Therefore, if a person feels uncomfortable going to an open meeting and has a drinking problem, closed meetings are an alternative.

Members do not have to believe in God to get help from AA. Many members have lost, or never had, a faith in God. AA does, however, assert that faith in some Higher Power is a tremendous help in recovery because such a belief offers a source of limitless power, hope, and support whenever one feels he has come to the end of his resources.

(continued next page)

AN AA MEETING *(con't.)*

How does AA help? New members, after years of deteriorating feelings of rejection, loneliness, misunderstanding, guilt, embarrassment, find they are not alone. They feel understood by others who are in similar predicaments. Instead of being rejected, they are welcomed. They see that others who had serious drinking problems are now sober, apparently happy that way, and are in the process of recovering. It gives them hope that they do not need alcohol to get through the day and that they can learn to enjoy life without alcohol. They find that others sincerely care about them, want to help them, and have the knowledge to do so.

At meetings they see every sort of personal problem brought up and discussed openly, with suggestions for solutions being offered by others who have encountered similar problems. They can observe that group members bring up "unspeakable" problems without apparent embarrassment, and that others listen and treat them with respect and consideration. Such acceptance gradually leads newcomers to share their personal problems and to receive constructive suggestions for solutions. Such disclosure leads individuals to look more deeply into themselves and to ventilate deep personal feelings. With the support of other members, newcomers gradually learn how to counter strong desires to drink, through such processes as calling other members.

Newcomers learn that AA is the means of staying away from that first drink. AA also serves to reduce the stress that compels people to drink by: (a) providing a comfortable and relaxed environment, and (b) having members help each other to find ways to reduce the stresses encountered in daily living. AA meetings and members become a safe port that is always there when storms start raging. AA helps members to be programmed from negative thinking to positive thinking. The more positive a member's thinking becomes and the more stress is relieved; the better he begins to feel about himself, the more the compulsion to drink decreases and the more often and more effectively the person begins to take positive actions to solve his problems.

1. Clark Vaughan, *Addictive Drinking* (New York: Penguin Books, 1984), pp. 75-76.

Intervening with the whole family is critical to the outcome of recovery. As the enabler learns to change the patterns of behavior that reinforce the dependent's chemical use, the dependent is forced to take responsibility for his or her addiction.

Research and experience have revealed that family members growing up in an addictive family cycle are at high risk of becoming chemically dependent themselves and/or experiencing other related emotional problems—such as difficulty in relationships, low self-esteem, depression, eating disorders, and/or compulsive disorders. Unless treated, these emotional problems are carried into the family member's adult life and will continually affect him or her in adult relationships.

It is important for social workers to recognize both the chemically dependent person and his or her family members as clients in need of services. If the chemically dependent person refuses help, other family members may be willing to accept help for themselves.

Group Counseling

Group counseling plays a major role in chemical dependency intervention. Besides being very effective therapeutically, it is also cost effective because several persons are receiving therapy simultaneously. Alcoholics Anonymous (AA), a self-help group for alcoholics, originated because its founders believed there are more commonalities than differences that result from the disease. Offshoots of AA offer a variety of assistance to individuals involved with drug addictions, dual addictions, and co-dependency (Narcotics Anonymous, Double Trouble, Alanon, Alateen, and Alatot, for example. A prominent recent offshoot of AA is ACA (Adult Children of Alcoholics). This group developed out of the need for adult family members to address how growing up in a chemically dependent home has affected their adult lives.

Therapeutic groups have also proven to be beneficial for recovery. They provide a conducive environment in which the individual can drop defenses and begin to explore areas that are normally threatening.[8]

Furthermore, group counseling helps a member meet psychological needs to belong, to be accepted, to realize negative feelings, and to participate in a supportive atmosphere where self-exploration is encouraged.[9] This is important in working with chemical dependents because of their low self-concepts, loss of identity, and depression. Research has shown that group therapy facilitates mutual exploration of commonplace problems; verbal reality testing; an opportunity to function as the helper; and the experience of peers challenging, supporting, desensitizing, and educating one another.[10]

While counseling group members to acceptance of their illness and helping them to develop positive coping mechanisms instead of chemical use, a counselor needs to keep in mind the stages of recovery, the grief process, psychological defenses, and symptoms mentioned earlier. They will all show up in the group process. If a counselor avoids confronting the person's denial or defenses, then as a therapist he or she is taking the role of enabler. A productive group should allow for inspiration, education, confrontation, and support. For dependents, drug abuse has become a significant part of their lifestyles. Through group counseling they need to learn drug-free ways of having a meaningful and satisfying life, and they need to learn to confront and handle their problems without abusing drugs or alcohol.

Running a group for the chemically dependent involves dealing with many issues in a spontaneous fashion. The concept of group is that no one person has to take all the risks or do all the work. If group counseling is done well, the leader will have helped the group members to: develop a nurturing environment and the rapport needed to trust each other; feel accepted; learn to take risks; establish closeness/distance in order to create comfortable space; and show tough love by giving feedback and confronting concerns. In dealing with chemical dependence, all the foregoing elements are needed to help patients break the denial patterns, reach acceptance of their chemical dependence, and come to realize that the disease does not have to rob them of their self-worth and dignity as unique human beings.

CASE EXAMPLE:
GROUP COUNSELING WITH SAM

Sam is a twenty-seven-year-old, married, white male, father of two. Currently, he is employed as a hairdresser. He was court-ordered to counseling after his second drunk driving charge. He has been using both alcohol and other drugs since the age of fifteen. His abuse of chemicals has caused him marital and family problems, the loss of two jobs, financial debts, and legal violations. He was angry when he came to counseling and had a low sense of self-worth. The result of his assessment was a diagnosis that he is chemically dependent. Part of his intervention program involved group counseling with peers ranging from ages twenty to thirty-eight.

Sam joined the group at a time when he was angry about being court-ordered to receive counseling. He denied that he was chemically dependent and was apprehensive about being in a group. The group members made sincere efforts to get to know him and to accept him, but he resisted.

At the third group session he attended one of his peers confronted him about his resistance to becoming part of the group and his negative attitude about attending sessions. Sam's response was that he did not believe he belonged because he was not chemically dependent and did not feel he should have to be in the group. He was then confronted about his denial. Group members took turns sharing the denial experiences they had, and how they eventually learned to accept their dependence. They pointed out that being dishonest about the seriousness of the problem could only hurt Sam. Sam became quite upset. Many of the stories he heard from them were similar to his. Eventually he blurted out how bad he felt about himself, the fears he had that they would reject him if they knew what he had done, and how worthless he was. The group's response was very supportive. He received positive feedback for the risks he took in sharing his fears, along with encouragement to attend Alcoholics Anonymous or Narcotics Anonymous with them.

After this initial confrontation, Sam began to take more risks in sharing his problems with group members. He shared guilt he felt about the way he behaved toward his family when he used drugs or alcohol. The group encouraged him to be open with his family and suggested he involve them in counseling and encourage them to attend Alanon. Sam followed through, and his family became involved in the recovery process. It was difficult for all of them, but family involvement allowed the family issues to be worked on.

Sam continued in the group. He made a commitment to work on chemical freedom and utilized AA/NA for support. He became more trusting of the group and his self-concept improved.

Sam began to follow through with his work responsibilities. Due to his drug and alcohol use, he had lost numerous customers. Even though he was no longer using drugs, business didn't pick up, and he became frustrated. He was going through a phase in which he wanted to return to using drugs. He couldn't pay some of his bills and failed to see the reason to stay chemically free.

Sam attended group with this negative attitude. He was agitated and rude to various members. Once again Sam was confronted by a member in the group. He responded angrily, venting how useless he thought it was to stay chemically free. He stated that group and individual counseling were a farce and that he was fed up with AA. All of this wasn't paying his bills or bringing in customers. The group remained silent, allowing Sam to vent his anger. When he finished, a group member reminded him that he had invested twelve years in developing his alcohol/drug problem and that it may take another twelve years or more to repair the damage. Another member brought to his attention that he could find any excuse to return to using and that the work issue was just that, an excuse. Others pointed out the options available to him—return to drinking and drug use, or continue with the recovery process one day at a time and work on finding new customers. The group decided and then informed him that if he chose to begin using drugs and alcohol again he would be asked to leave the group. This tough-love approach worked with Sam, and he chose to stick with the recovery process.

CASE EXAMPLE: GROUP COUNSELING WITH SAM (con't.)

Currently Sam and his family are still in counseling. He continues to utilize the group to receive the support, confrontation, education, and inspiration he needs to aid his recovery. Sam had also learned to confront other group members without fear of rejection.

Sam still has times of impatience and temptation to return to alcohol/drug use. However, he has learned through group therapy, self-help groups (AA/NA), and individual and family counseling that chemical dependence is a terminal illness that can go into remission if the dependent remains chemically free. The recovery process is healthier when approached on a daily basis.

GROUP EXERCISES

Exercise A: Best Friend

Goal: To show that a person's relationship to his or her chemical of choice has many of the characteristics of a relationship with a best friend.

Step 1. The leader asks students to describe the characteristics of a best friend and writes them on the blackboard. Characteristics that are apt to be suggested include:

"Won't let you down when trouble arises."
"Is reliable."
"Is there when I need help."
"Accepts me as I am—doesn't try to change me."
"Makes me feel good."
"Is trustworthy."

Step 2. The leader explains that a dependent person comes to view his drug of choice as a "best friend." The person feels he needs the drug to get through each day. Many dependent persons will give up family, job, and health, jeopardizing the well-being of others to continue to "be with his best friend." Indicate that a dependent person views the drug of choice as having many of the characteristics of a best friend, such as:

"It won't let me down when trouble arises."
"I can always count on it to help me feel better."
"It is reliable, trustworthy, and doesn't try to change me."

459

HARM-REDUCTION STRATEGIES FOR ADDICTED PREGNANT WOMEN

Though this chapter focuses on treating chemical dependency, there are policy initiatives that directly impact treatment and prevention. We know that addiction can lead to death, both directly and indirectly. Some of the indirect risks associated with addiction include infectious diseases (AIDS, hepatitis) from shared and/or dirty needles. Fetuses are also at risk of Fetal Alcohol Syndrome (FAS) or crack baby syndrome from addicted pregnant women.

For clients who cannot maintain abstinence, programs that advocate for harm reduction strategies are vital. The first controversial harm reduction strategy related to drug use is the needle exchange program. The development of these programs has been slow due to public and political fear that the program condones drug use.[1]

The movement to arrest and incarcerate pregnant women to keep them off drugs until they deliver their babies has a backlash effect. Because these women fear seeking help or even prenatal care, they are placing themselves and their fetuses at greater risk. Intervention programs sometimes deny these women services due to the liability risks of providing care to pregnant women. In some states, pregnant women who give birth to infants who are diagnosed with alcohol- or drug-related symptoms are arrested and their infants placed in protective custody. Pregnant women addicted to chemicals could really benefit from group counseling and support to deal with the addiction and cope with the pregnancy. They belong in treatment, not in jail.

The concept of harm reduction as it relates to the least harm principle is an ethical dilemma for social workers in the alcohol and drug field. In keeping with the NASW code of ethics our profession must address immediate needs and safety first.

Practices associated with harm reduction need to be developed in the context of prevention, health education, health care, and treatment.[2] Social workers need to be involved in this effort as advocates, policy developers, and intervention specialists, especially for the clients they haven't been able to reach with the traditional medical model of recovery.

1. W. Anderson, "The New York Needle Trial: The Politics of Public Health in the Age of AIDS," *American Journal of Public Health* 81 (1991): 1506–17; and P. Lichty, "The Point Is to Save Lives," *Health PAC Bulletin*, (Fall 1990): 11–15.

2. P. A. O'Hare, R. Newcombe, A. Matthews, E. C. Buning, and E. Drucker, *Drug Policy in the Americas*, San Diego, CA: Westview Press, 1992.

Step 3. The students discuss whether the exercise helps them to understand why a dependent person psychologically has tremendous difficulty in giving up a drug of choice.

Exercise B: Evaluating the Need for Acceptance

Goals: To learn how it feels to be a client as well as a therapist. It is important to get in touch with the fears, inhibitions, and risk involved in being in a group. Before a therapist can ask clients to be exposed to a group, he or she must have an understanding of what they will experience.

Note: This exercise can also be used in an actual chemical dependency group by applying the concepts to the members' chemical use.

Step 1. The leader explains that the purpose of this exercise is to reflect on the need to feel accepted. The students sit in a circle, close their eyes, and visualize their most relaxing place for six or seven minutes (see chapter 15 on imagery relaxation). Once they feel relaxed and comfortable, they are instructed to allow their minds to fantasize about being accepted, valued, respected, and loved by each member in the group. Allow them to take the time to examine how this feels. Once everyone feels they have completed this fantasy, they open their eyes slowly.

Step 2. Members say one positive thing about the person on their right, then on their left. The statement must be genuine and said in a sincere tone of voice. The students being complimented may respond only with "Thank you." No other verbal feedback should be allowed until step 3.

Step 3. Members share how it felt to be accepted in their fantasy and by group members. They should be encouraged to describe their feelings about giving each other positive strokes. Each member should be allowed to share something positive about other members who are not directly beside them, if they wish, and encouraged to give positive feedback of a sincere nature throughout the remaining time together as a class.

Exercise C: Learning to Take Risks

Goals: Same as Exercise B.

Note: It is advised that the instructor be the designated leader for this exercise because it may generate strong emotions in the participants.

Step 1. The instructor explains that the purpose of the exercise is to help members learn to take risks. The students form a circle, close their eyes, and visualize an experience that caused them a great deal of embarrassment or pain. They are to think about the risk of sharing this experience and the worst possible reaction they could receive by the group. When they have a good picture they are to open their eyes slowly. Once everyone has opened their eyes, step 2 begins.

Step 2. Volunteers share what they visualized. Students should be told that they do *not* have to share this information and not to disclose sensitive personal information. When members are sharing their experiences, other members remain silent and control any nonverbal negative cues. After everyone who is willing to risk is done sharing, step 3 may begin.

Step 3. Group members discuss the feelings they experienced in steps 1 and 2. The instructor asks questions such as the following: How did it feel to hear others taking risks? How did it feel when no one gave any negative reactions? How do those who shared their visualizations now feel about having divulged this information? (As a variation, allow the group members to give feedback, as long as the individuals who risked sharing give permission.)

Activities: Drug Abuse and Intervention

Goals: To learn more about drug abuse and intervention.

The exercises developed for this chapter are not directly related to interventions with drug abuse. Because students have a right to privacy, it is inappropriate to put pressure on them to share their personal experiences. Some alternatives follow that provide a break in the usual group teaching method, yet allow students to respond within a group.

1. *Film or videotape.* There are numerous visual aids available on drug abuse and intervention. A group discussion could follow a viewing.
2. *Guest speakers.* Representatives from AA, Alanon, and Alateen are usually more than happy to be guest speakers. Or an alcohol and drug-abuse counselor could be invited to discuss abuse and intervention, and a group discussion could then follow.
3. *Drug intervention facility field trip.* Arrangements might be made to visit a drug intervention facility. A counselor at such a facility could lead a tour, discuss the agency's approach to drug intervention and lead a group discussion.

CHAPTER TWENTY-SEVEN

INTERVENTIONS WITH EATING DISORDERS*

Goal: Eating disorders are occurring in epidemic proportions. While eating disorders have existed for a long period of time, the dramatic increase in the number of individuals currently affected by anorexia nervosa, bulimia nervosa, and compulsive overeating is a major concern for the mental health community. This chapter is designed to familiarize the reader with: the symptomology, extent, and causes of bulimia nervosa, anorexia nervosa, and compulsive overeating; the health risks involved; and the intervention components necessary for change. Group intervention will be emphasized.

Anorexia nervosa, bulimia nervosa, and compulsive overeating are serious conditions that may lead to long-term physical and emotional disabilities. Although some researchers believe physiological factors make some individuals more vulnerable to the development of eating disorders than others, anorexia, bulimia, and compulsive overeating are generally thought to be psychosomatic conditions in which a combination of social, psychological, and emotional problems lead to disordered behaviors and serious physical consequences. Biochemical changes caused by prolonged dieting and binging/purging can produce many of the common symptoms associated with anorexia, bulimia, and compulsive overeating.

DEFINITIONS

Anorexia nervosa is a disorder characterized by the relentless pursuit of thinness through voluntary starvation. The predominant features of this disorder include refusal to maintain body weight over a minimal normal weight given an individual's age, height, weight history and build, or a failure to make expected weight gain in childhood or early adolescence; intense fear of gaining weight or becoming fat; a distorted body image; and amenorrhea (cessation of menses) in postmenarchial females.[1]

Ninety percent of all anorexia nervosa cases are females.[2] An onset usually occurs during adolescence (average age, seventeen), although it can range from prepuberty to the early thirties. Prevalence studies among females in late adolescence and early adulthood have found an incidence rate of between .5 percent and 1 percent for presentations that meet the complete diagnostic criteria for anorexia nervosa.[3] Ambitious, overly perfectionistic "model" children from upper- and upper-middle-class backgrounds are especially vulnerable, though the condition is found in all groups, in all socioeconomic and ethnic groups, and in both sexes.[4] Anorexia nervosa often occurs in more than one family member, and studies have also reported a higher than expected frequency of major depression and bipolar disorder (mood swings back and forth from depression to excessive enthusiasm) among first-degree relatives.[5]

Severe weight loss often necessitates hospitalization to prevent death by starvation. Follow-up studies estimate long-term mortality rates to be more than 10 percent from related medical complications.[6] Specific causes of death include malnutrition, dehydration, heart attack, kidney damage, liver impairment, and suicide following severe depression. Starvation weakens the body's immune responses, leaving the anorexic vulnerable to pneumonia and other infections. The mortality rate for anorexia nervosa is estimated to be higher than for any other psychiatric disorder. Approximately 50 percent of anorexic individuals eventually become bulimic in response to starvation.[7]

Bulimia nervosa is estimated to affect between 4.5 and 18 percent of high school and college-aged females.[8] It is characterized by recurrent episodes of binge eating followed by purging.[9] The most common methods of purgation are self-induced vomiting, compulsive exercising, strict dieting or fasting, diet pills, and abuse of diuretics and laxatives. Some individuals may chew food to "get the taste" and then spit it out to avoid calories

---

*This chapter was written by Michael O. Koch, Ph.D., Virginia I., Dotson, Ph.D., and Thomas P. Troast, M.A. They are psychotherapists in private practice and specialize in the treatment of eating disorders.

and weight gain. However, not all individuals who are diagnosed with bulimia nervosa purge. This group is classified as the nonpurging type and engages in inappropriate compensatory behavior such as fasting or excessive exercise.[10]

Bulimic individuals usually eat compulsively to escape painful problems in their lives. Much of the binging is secretive and done in private. Then, fearing weight gain and ashamed of their out-of-control behavior, they attempt to remove the food from their bodies before it can be absorbed. Some individuals define a binge as two cookies more than their diet allows. However, the average bulimic episode involves between 2,000 and 5,000 calories, though day-long binges of 50,000 calories or more have been reported.[11]

Most individuals with bulimia nervosa are within a normal weight range, although some may be slightly underweight and others may be overweight. There is some evidence that obesity in adolescence predisposes the development of the disorder. Frequently, the parents of people with this disorder are overweight. Also, a higher than expected frequency of major depression and alcoholism in first-degree biologic relatives has been reported.[12]

Bulimia nervosa is seldom incapacitating, except in a few individuals who spend their entire day binge eating and vomiting. For this reason, the disorder can go undetected by family and friends for years. However, complications do occur. Dental erosion is a common problem due to vomiting.[13] Electrolyte imbalance and dehydration can occur and may cause serious complications, such as cardiac arrhythmias and, occasionally, sudden death.[14] For those bulimic individuals who are well below normal weight, the physical complications associated with anorexia nervosa may also be present.

Compulsive overeating may be defined as the irresistible impulse to consume food for no apparent reason. It is the act of eating irrationally, chewing and digesting food for no nutritional or physical value.[15] In most cases, compulsive overeating is a response to a psychological, cultural, familial, or other environmental stimulus.

The result of compulsive overeating is an excessive accumulation of body fat that causes a condition of overweight or obesity. The National Health and Nutrition Examination Survey estimates that 58 million adult Americans are obese or overweight. Estimates are that one out of five Americans is overweight, and that approximately one-third of adult Americans need to be treated for obesity.[16]

The National Institutes of Health Consensus Conference on Obesity recommended treatment for individuals with a body weight in excess of 20 percent of their desirable weight. As weight increases above the average, mortality ratios increase as well. There are clear and significant relationships between obesity and cardiovascular risk factors (such as hypertension, hypercholesterolernia, and diabetes).[17]

The Relationships Among the Eating Disorders

Eating disorders seem to exist on a continuum. On one end are the anorexics, who achieve drastic weight loss by severely restricting food intake. In the middle are the anorexic bulimics, who eat and even binge on occasion, but who still maintain a much lower than normal weight by a combination of strict dieting and purging. Also included are normal-weight bulimics who binge and purge but who are not significantly underweight. These bulimics usually diet when they are not binging and may repeatedly gain and lose ten or more pounds because of their food behaviors. At the other end of the continuum, the

Figure 27.1: Anorexic, Bulimic, and Compulsive Overeater Characteristics

Anorexia Nervosa (restricting type)	Anorexia Nervosa (binge-eating purging type)	Bulimia Nervosa (purging and nonpurging types)	Compulsive Overeater
Age of an onset is early to late adolescence (mean age, 17)	Age of an onset is early to late adolescence	Age of an onset is late adolescence or early adulthood	Age of an onset is early to late adolescence
Cases are 90 percent female	Cases are 90 percent female	Cases are 90 percent female	Possible incidence of obesity in family history
.5–1 percent incident rates in females 12–18	Disturbance in body image	Disturbance in body image	20+ percent over ideal body weight
Disturbance in body image	Morbid fear of fatness	Possible incidence of obesity in family history	Internal belief that eating behaviors can't be controlled
Morbid fear of fatness	Weight is 85 percent of expected weight, or failure to attain expected weight in childhood or early adolescence	Incidence in 1–3 percent of high school and college-aged women	Low self-esteem
Weight is 85 percent of expected weight, or failure to attain expected weight in childhood or early adolescence	Absence of three consecutive menstrual cycles in post-menarchial females	Minimum of two binge-eating episodes per week for three months, followed by purging or inappropriate compensatory behavior	Threefold risk factor for hypertension
50 percent of cases result in bulimia nervosa	Engages in limited bingeing and purging behavior	Normal weight with minor fluctuations	High incidence of depression
Absence of three consecutive menstrual cycles in post-menarchial females		Impulsive behaviors, including substance abuse	
		High incidence of depression	

compulsive overeater will repeatedly binge, gaining significant amounts of weight without engaging in any of the purging behaviors associated with anorexia or bulimia nervosa. Individuals may move back and forth along this continuum, alternatively restricting or binging, depending on their circumstances (see figure 27.1).

INITIATING FACTORS

Many factors contribute to the development of an eating disorder. The patterns differ from one individual to another, and investigation usually reveals a complex relationship among the several elements that combine to produce voluntary starvation or binging/purging. Primary factors include physiological considerations, psychological and emotional problems, dysfunctional family systems, and the influences of society and the news and entertainment media.

Physiological Considerations

Research suggests that some (but by no means all) bulimics and compulsive overeaters may be physiologically or genetically predisposed to their disorders. Researchers have reported a higher than expected incidence of depression and alcoholism in their parents and family members.[18] Some bulimics and compulsive overeaters respond to antidepressant medications, possibly because these drugs adjust some as yet unknown chemical imbalance in the brain. Some researchers, however, believe this imbalance is not inherent in the individual but is caused by emotional stress, protracted dieting, or binging/purging.[19]

Psychological and Emotional Problems

Eating disordered individuals generally feel worthless and inadequate. Their already low self-esteem is further reduced by a cruel perfectionism that tolerates no flaws in physical appearance, in school work, in athletic performance, in professional achievement, or in relationships.

Anorexics, bulimics, and compulsive overeaters usually have not formed strong, stable identities. Not knowing who they are, they are unaware of their strengths, weaknesses, limits, and true abilities. Fearing they will lose the approval of others, they are terrified of not measuring up to some ideal standard. They compare themselves with others and decide, "I'm just not good enough." When anorexic dieters pit themselves against the hunger drive (one of the body's most powerful instincts), they are making heroic but misguided attempts to establish self-respecting identities by accomplishing a task impossible to other people.

Eating disordered individuals have usually strayed from the developmental path that leads from childhood dependence to the independence and self-reliance of adulthood. Anorexics, bulimics, and compulsive overeaters are caught in a painful struggle. They sometimes want to be independent and in full control of their lives, but at other times they fearfully retreat back into the safety of the old routines and relationships that provide security, but not much satisfaction. A significant number of eating disordered individuals have been victims of rape, molestation, and incest.[20]

Dysfunctional Family Systems

One of the primary functions of a family unit is to provide the children with a safe and secure home base from which they can explore the world. Safely and slowly, in age-appropriate stages, they can achieve mastery over many different challenges. In some families, this developmental process is not completed, and the children do not grow from infantile dependency to age-appropriate maturity, self-reliance, and autonomy.[21]

Families that contain an eating disordered individual often share common characteristics that may include the following:[22]

1. Parents are too involved in their children's lives, leaving them no physical or emotional privacy.

2. Parents are overprotective and do not allow children to experience failure and learn from their mistakes.

3. Parents do not adapt their parenting skills to the needs and ages of their children. Adolescents are treated as if they were toddlers, which forces older children back into the passive, infantile roles at a time when they need to become active agents in their own lives.

4. Parents have unresolved problems in the spousal relationship, but avoid open conflict, preferring to present a harmonious facade to the family and community. The children, as a result, do not learn how to handle disagreement and their own negative feelings honestly and effectively.

5. Parents may have a history of addictive or compulsive behaviors. Children may learn at an early age that stressful episodes are reacted to with the introduction of artificial, self-medicating mechanisms (such as food, alcohol, or controlled substances).

Some anorexics, bulimics, and compulsive overeaters come from non-supportive, non-nourishing families that are critical, demanding, and rejecting. Some of the most toxic family situations combine criticism and rejection with obsessive concern and control. The children are in a double bind, wanting to protest, but feeling guilty because their parents are so "caring."[23]

Not all families with an eating disordered member share the above characteristics. Many anorexics and bulimics come from families that are healthy, loving, and supportive. The parents have good parenting skills and act appropriately toward their children. In these families, other factors are primary in the development of the eating disorder.

Influence of Society and the Media

Eating disorders have become epidemic in the United States in recent years. Before that, society allowed all people, and especially women, to be rounder and more curvaceous. Bust enhancers and weight-gain products were sold to very thin women who wanted to look like Marilyn Monroe or Jayne Mansfield. However, norms for what is considered attractive have changed.[24] The weight, bust, and hip measurements of magazine centerfolds and beauty contest winners over the past twenty-five years have progressively decreased, although the average weight for women in the general population has increased by six pounds.[25] Today, the cultural ideal is pencil slimness, and, according to advertisements and fashion magazines, even mature women should look like adolescent boys.[26]

The influence of the media on eating disorders, particularly compulsive overeating, cannot be overstated. The contradictions generated by advertising dollars are symbolic of the psychological conflicts endured by the compulsive overeater. The American food industry spends $36 billion a year to advertise its products. The typical child is blasted with up to 10,000 food commercials a year. And while the consumer is inundated with food advertisements, Americans spend over $30 billion each year on diet programs and diet products. While society dedicates $34 million each year to obesity research, Kellogg's spends $32 million each year advertising Frosted Flakes.[27]

The modeling industry focuses on the simple theme that we need to be thin enough to be loved. Print and electronic media push the idea that success in relationships is somehow linked to being pretty, meaning being thin. From early childhood the media teaches that thin and happy are synonyms. Of course, the problem develops when advertisers utilize models who weigh 20 percent less than the average person (85 percent of the American public weighs more than the model).

Medical research and life insurance statistics indicate that people are healthier, live longer, and function better when they have a degree of roundness and fatty reserves beyond that allowed by fashion. Vulnerable people who believe they will be happy and admired when they are thin can precipitate an eating disorder when their bodies rebel against an inadequate diet. Researchers believe an eating disorder may develop after prolonged dieting when people try to achieve or maintain a body size that is in direct conflict with their biology. They maintain that one's weight is genetically predetermined and that family history is the best indication of what a person's appropriate weight or "set point" should be. Any effort to go below the body's "set point" is resisted by an increase in appetite, a reduction in body metabolism, and lethargic behavior, all designed to increase body weight.[28]

While eating disorder primarily affect women, men have not escaped society's demands for thinness. Today, men still strive for success, but countless articles and advertisements tell them that their achievements will be meaningless unless they also have a lean, well-muscled body.

Many men who become anorexic or bulimic have chosen careers that demand physical attractiveness and thinness (such as acting, dancing, and modeling). Other eating disordered men are involved in sports that demand careful weight control; many jockeys, runners, and wrestlers are anorexic or bulimic. Also at risk are members of the male homosexual community where a lean, trim, athletic body is a requirement for social acceptance.

BEHAVIORAL INDICATORS

Although many of the following indicators are behaviors that all of us exhibit from time to time, there is cause for concern when combinations of these behaviors become habitual patterns that interfere with everyday life (such as work, school, relationships, and recreation). Mental and allied health professionals need to be familiar with these behaviors so that appropriate referrals can be made when an eating disorder is suspected.

Anorexia Nervosa

Typical anorexic behaviors may include[29]:

1. *Voluntary starvation.* A stubborn refusal to eat in spite of hunger, irritability, and lightheadedness is characteristic of the disorder.
2. *Compulsive exercise.* Excessive exercise for prolonged periods of time is not unusual. Solitary activities (running, calisthenics) are usually preferred over team sports.

3. *Distorted body image.* Anorexics do not have an accurate picture of their bodies. Even when emaciated, they will insist that they are still too fat, usually wanting to lose "just a few extra pounds."

4. *Deception.* To avoid conflicts over their guarded eating habits and diets, anorexics may lie, saying that they have eaten when they have not. They may hide food, slip it under the table to the dog, and throw it away at every opportunity. Paradoxically, they may also hoard food as a protection against anxiety.

5. *Inappropriate dress.* Even in hot weather, anorexics may wear several layers of bulky clothing to warm their cold bodies and to conceal their thinness. The weight loss of which they are so proud is also the most noticeable thing about them, bringing questions and pointed comments from family and friends. To avoid conflict and confrontation, anorexics often hide under sweaters and baggy pants.

6. *Vicarious involvement with food.* Because they are always hungry, anorexics are preoccupied with food, cooking, grocery shopping, and nutritional information. They may cook gourmet meals for others and not eat a bite themselves. They often collect cookbooks and study calorie charts until they have memorized them.

7. *Compulsive rituals.* Anorexics usually develop compulsive rituals involving food, exercise, housekeeping, and other aspects of their lives. They are usually meticulous about personal grooming. They may cut their small pieces of food into tiny pieces and then spend a long time eating each piece. These kinds of rituals are defenses against anxiety. They also are similar to the rituals that victims of involuntary starvation develop when they try to get maximum enjoyment from each morsel of food by concentrating intently on each tiny bite.

8. *Perfectionism.* Anorexics are usually perfectionistic in all aspects of their lives: personal appearance, relationships, job projects, and athletic performance. Anything less than an A+ grade in school is cause for despair. Instead of celebrating when a report card lists straight A's, the anorexic immediately begins to worry about the next term.

9. *Dichotomous thinking.* Anorexics think in terms of black and white, believing they are either a 100 percent success or 100 percent failure. They tend to judge others by these same stringent standards. Anorexics do not deal well with complexity or shades of gray. They believe all aspects of life are either good or bad, beautiful or ugly, fat or thin, successful or a total flop. Learning to deal with more complex realities is part of the recovery process.

10. *Occasional binges and purges.* Some anorexics occasionally yield to their hunger pangs and eat or even binge. Then they feel guilty because they did not maintain their strict, unrealistic discipline. To ease their anxiety and regain control, they vomit, fast, exercise, or abuse laxatives.

11. *Social withdrawal.* Anorexics tend to avoid social activities and sexual relationships. They are often introverted and withdrawn, usually avoiding parties, friends, alcohol, and drugs.

12. *Extreme control.* Anorexics maintain rigid control over almost all aspects of their lives. They find security in discipline and order and may, for example, weigh themselves several times a day to make sure they are still in control.

13. *Resistant to feedback.* Anorexics usually deny they need help, insisting that their bony bodies are normal and even attractive. They resist all offers of help and become resentful and hostile when urged to eat. If pressured or threatened by family members, they may agree to "do better," but almost always find some devious way to avoid gaining weight. Eventually, they may avoid having contact with anyone who challenges their lifestyle.

470

Bulimia Nervosa

Bulimics, especially if they are significantly underweight, share many of the behaviors characteristic of the anorexic. In addition, bulimic behavior may include one or more of the following[30]:

1. *Secretive eating*. Although some bulimics binge with friends, the more common pattern involves secretive binges that occur regularly after periods of stress or dieting.

2. *Purging behavior*. To avoid weight gain, the bulimic follows a binge with self-induced vomiting, fasting, excessive exercise, or laxative and diuretic abuse. Some food may be tasted and chewed but spit out before it is swallowed. Researchers believe that bulimics who alternate between dieting and binging are caught in a vicious circle because dieting is a direct cause of the carbohydrate cravings that often precipitate a binge. In addition, binging leads to guilt, anxiety and fear of weight gain, which in turn reinforces purging. Often the purging leaves the bulimic exhausted, but peaceful, and once again in control. The individual vows to "be good," begins a new diet, becomes hungry, binges, and repeats the cycle. Paradoxically, often the best way to abort a binge is to eat a nourishing, well-balanced meal.

3. *Need for social acceptance/fear of intimacy*. Bulimics tend to be people pleasers who crave attention, affection, and approval from others. Unlike anorexics, they often have active social lives filled with many friends and acquaintances. Usually, however, they report that their social activities are only facades that hide self-doubt and insecurity. They often alternate between wanting and fearing deep relationships. They have difficulty trusting other people and being honest about their needs.

4. *Impulsive disorders and chemical dependency*. Some bulimics are sexually promiscuous and many use or abuse alcohol and other drugs. In addition, they may shoplift and steal food. Most bulimics feel out of control, especially around food. Bingers, like starvers, often believe that once they begin to eat they will be unable to stop.

5. *Receptivity to treatment*. Once bulimics have overcome their embarrassment, they are more likely than anorexics to ask for help. Many bulimics come into therapy voluntarily, while anorexics are usually brought for help by concerned family members.

Compulsive Overeating

Compulsive overeaters have many of the behaviors associated with bulimia. In addition, compulsive overeating behavior may include one or more of the following characteristics:

1. *Continual diet failure*. The compulsive overeater will attempt and fail at diet plans. He often embraces the current "fad" diet believing that each new diet will be the one that finally works and will result in permanent weight loss. A great deal of publicity of this dieting relapse has become known as yo-yo dieting. The idea is that weight cycling progressively changes muscle to fat and decreases the metabolic rate, thus making each dieting episode more difficult. This continual failure of rigid diet plans further anchors a sense of hopelessness and an erroneous belief that the compulsive overeater is responsible for failing to lose weight.

2. *Avoidance of physical problems.* The overweight compulsive overeater may ignore physical warning signs that his or her health is at risk. Even after careful assessment and monitoring by a physician, the compulsive overeater may resist medical intervention to avoid or alter dangerous physical conditions.

3. *Social isolation.* Because of increased size, the overweight compulsive overeater will often restrict interpersonal contact due to feelings of shame and guilt. Isolation may become a dominant behavioral pattern.

4. *Nutritional ignorance.* The compulsive overeater often has inadequate knowledge of basic nutrition. He or she may have a distorted view of what constitutes a balanced and healthy food and eating plan.

5. *Selective eating amnesia.* It is not unusual for the compulsive overeater not to recognize his or her own caloric intake and frequency of eating episodes, as these behaviors often occur outside conscious awareness.

6. *Environmental factors.* The use of food as a reward, a punishment, or a response to stress are often factors in the development of compulsive overeating patterns.

7. *Depression.* The theory behind the linking of compulsive overeating and depression is that abnormal levels of serotonin increase the need for compulsive behavior. Many similar behaviors exist between depressed and compulsive overeating individuals, including low self-esteem, feelings of hopelessness, fatigue, and acute mood swings.

INTERVENTION PROCESS

Anorexia, bulimia, and compulsive overeating are serious disorders that usually do not go away by themselves. In the vast majority of cases, professional intervention is required. Intervention for an eating disorder has three goals: (1) correction of medical problems associated with starving or binging/purging; (2) resolutions of the underlying psychosocial-family dynamics that contributed to the development of the eating disorder; and (3) establishment of normal weight and healthy eating behaviors.[31] Once symptoms appear, they tend to have a life of their own, separate from the factors that gave rise to them. For this reason, intervention must focus on both food behaviors and underlying issues. In most cases, tackling one area while ignoring the other does not lead to permanent recovery.

Many people want to "get over" their eating disorder and still be very thin. This is not possible, because the biochemistry of an underweight body often leads directly back to self-starvation or binging/purging. Because eating disorders are complex and multidimensional problems, interventions must be comprehensive and multifaceted. Proper assessment must take into account each person's unique circumstances so specific needs can be met in the intervention.

Intervention may be conducted on an inpatient or outpatient basis. The decision to hospitalize an individual rather than provide intervention in a less restricted outpatient format is usually based on a variety of circumstances. Hospitalization is certainly warranted when physical complications necessitate close medical supervision. Often renourishment for weight gain is required before psychotherapy can be effective. Starving individuals will not profit from therapy when thought processes or concentration are impaired. Hospital treatment may also be necessary to control electrolyte imbalance and dehydration caused by extreme vomiting and abuse of laxatives and diuretics. Hospital treatment may include enforced bed rest, a feeding plan, and appropriate medical interventions necessary to pre-

CASE EXAMPLE:
ANOREXIA AND BULIMIA NERVOSA

The following case history illustrates a variety of the complications that can result from a prolonged history of anorexia and bulimia nervosa. Mary is a five-foot-one-inch tall, twenty-three-year-old single female with a six-year history of anorexia and bulimia nervosa. Family history suggests evidence of drug dependence, mental illness, and family dysfunction. Mary's symptoms began at age seventeen when her boyfriend terminated a one-year relationship. She subsequently became depressed and started restricting her food intake, losing twenty pounds in three months. Mary was diagnosed as having primary anorexia nervosa and was admitted to the hospital for six weeks.

Intervention included nutritional, antidepressant, individual, and family therapy. Subsequent to discharge, Mary continued to restrict her eating and began vomiting, exercising excessively, and abusing laxatives. She was briefly hospitalized for kidney damage and extreme edema when she gained twenty-five pounds of fluid weight. By this time Mary had developed many of the thinking and behavior patterns characteristic of anorexia and bulimia nervosa. She withdrew socially and became perfectionistic and obsessed with her body and food. Mary's third hospital-ization occurred when she dropped to seventy-two pounds and was admitted for six months. After gaining twenty-eight pounds she was discharged and continued in outpatient treatment. However, the demands of Mary's environment and her fear of maturation and being overweight were too great. She was again hospitalized for six more months when she dropped to eighty pounds. At the time the authors first saw Mary, she had been hospitalized for a combined period of thirteen and one-half months. She had suffered from amenorrhea for three years, kidney damage, irregular bowel function, and constipation due to suspected neurological damage from laxative abuse, extensive dental erosion from vomiting that required capping of her teeth, and osteo-porosis resulting from nutritional deficiencies. Mary was admitted to an intensive outpatient group intervention program that provided extensive structure, peer support, individual and family therapy, and individual-ized guidance regarding developmental talks.

Although Mary continues to occasionally rely on her eating disorder to deal with her life, she has stabilized her weight at approximately 110 pounds, is living independently, and is learning to cope with her environment in a mature and responsible manner.

serve life. In the case of the severely overweight individual (morbidly obese), hospitaliza-tion may be required to stabilize life threatening medical complications.

For those individuals who have little structure in their lives and lack a healthy support network of family and friends, the controlled environment that a hospital provides may be necessary to stabilize symptoms and establish proper eating patterns. However, it must be remembered that hospitalization is a traumatic disruption of an individual's life. It should be used only when necessary. Most individuals who are not at medical risk can be treated successfully on an outpatient basis, thereby preserving the supportive aspects of an indi-vidual's life.

Nutritional counseling is an integral part of any treatment plan. However, by itself it is not sufficient treatment for anorexia and bulimia nervosa. A registered dietitian can pro-vide valuable information about proper nutrition and the body's uses of food. The dietit-ian not only establishes a food plan the eating disordered individual uses to establish healthy eating patterns but also provides education on the physiology of dieting and weight management. The experience is important in reducing anxiety associated with weight gain and body image.

In some cases, antidepressant therapy can be helpful. Medications are usually prescribed by an attending psychiatrist. Some researchers believe the use of these drugs can dramatically reduce binging behaviors as well as alleviate the underlying depression that often accompanies anorexia, bulimia, and compulsive overeating.[32]

Medication has become an alternative in the treatment of compulsive overeating. Several drugs are currently being used (and experimentally being tested) with persons who are considered to be uncontrollable eaters.

Phentermine and fenfluramine have received notice for initial success rates at the University of Rochester. Long-term studies will determine their future use. A popular medication, Orlistat, has been touted as a "dream drug" by celebrities. Orlistat suppresses the absorption of dietary fat in the body. Two-year tests are studying its possible effects.

The drug of choice, when selected, is Prozac. The use of Prozac attempts to sustain and enhance normal levels of serotonin and thus decrease acute compulsions. The theory is that, if Prozac defeats patients' compulsions and manages depressive symptoms, overeating episodes will significantly decrease. Currently, Eli Lilly has developed a stronger version of Prozac and waits for its approval by the FDA for the specific purpose of controlling eating behavior.

Psychotherapy is, of course, a prominent part of the comprehensive intervention model. Therapy may include individual, family, group, or a combination of the three, depending on the needs of the individual. Goals of individual therapy include: increased self-esteem; increased power over one's life; resolution of internal conflicts and underlying issues; and establishment of normal eating behaviors. Therapy may also explore relationship issues and career options as individuals are encouraged to be self-sufficient.

Individual psychotherapy for the compulsive overeater is critical in the area of self-esteem. For the overweight individual, body condition may create feelings of shame, guilt, and self-hate. Body image distortions, prevalent among anorexics and bulimics, are also characteristic of the compulsive overeater. Advocacy by groups like the National Association to Advance Fat Acceptance and support organizations like Largely Positive have been working to gain acceptance of the idea that obesity is a state of being, not a failure of self-control. While society has accommodated most individuals with disabilities, shame and humiliation are directed at those struggling with body-weight problems. And discrimination against obese people is beyond interpersonal harassment. The Harvard School of Public Health found that obese women were 20 percent less likely to marry, had lower household incomes, and were 10 percent more likely to be living in poverty.[33]

Family therapy is important, particularly if an individual is still living at home. Often family dynamics indirectly contribute to the maintenance of the eating disorder and must be changed if adjustment is to occur. Issues of independence and separation are often contributing factors to the eating disorder. Family therapy also provides parents, spouses, and siblings with support and guidance. Certainly, they are the other victims of the eating disorder.

Activity therapy can be an important dimension of group intervention. Through psycho-educational programming (which may include body-image training, relaxation skills, assertiveness classes, exercise management, and art and music therapy), individuals are given opportunities to identify and express emotions and to gain knowledge necessary for positive change.

CASE EXAMPLE: A COMPULSIVE OVEREATER

The following case history demonstrates some of the factors which may affect the compulsive overeater.

Sara is a five-foot tall, thirty-four-year-old, married female who had a history of compulsive overeating since early adolescence. Her weight prior to treatment was 205 pounds and had been increasing for the past year. Numerous diets had actually caused weight gain rather than weight loss. Family history indicated that Sara's father was prone to compulsive eating and alcohol abuse. At age thirty-four, Sara's interpersonal skills were limited and she had few significant relationships. Attention and recognition from peers was often achieved through manipulation due to her feelings of inadequacy.

Sara's difficulty with food began during her early adolescence. As a teenager, Sara had to spend a great deal of time traveling with her parents. Food was used by Sara to cope with the stress and boredom of being confined with her parents and was used by her parents as a reward for compliant behavior. Eating behavior, including meal times and selection of proper nutritional choices, was chaotic. Alcohol and cigarette use began and compulsive use of food soon followed.

When Sara was a young adult, her overweight condition was a source of social shame. Her parents pushed Sara into a variety of diets, from simple deprivation plans to expensive diet programs. Each diet resulted in short-term positive effects, followed by weight gain and subsequent feelings of failure, guilt, and inadequacy. By the time Sara sought out a psychotherapist, she was severely depressed. Her depression, feelings of inadequacy, and poor self-esteem were also creating difficulties in her marriage.

Intervention goals focused on eliminating Sara's isolation, developing appropriate coping skills, medical care, stabilizing depressive symptomology, and establishing healthy behavioral eating patterns. Medical complications of high blood pressure and a thyroid condition were treated. An exercise program was introduced, and a healthy food management plan was developed and implemented. Sara also began participating in a support group for obese and overweight individuals. After losing sixty pounds, Sara continued her intervention program which provided structure, including regular group support, individual and family therapy, and continued medical supervision with her physician and dietician.

Sara eventually stabilized her weight at 135 pounds, overcame many dysfunctional behaviors, improved family functioning, and now views each day as a challenge to maintain a healthy diet.

For many, group therapy is extremely useful in the recovery process. Although anorexics seem to be more responsive to individualized approaches due to control and trust issues, bulimics and compulsive overeaters (because of their gregarious nature and need for acceptance and approval) function quite well in a group setting. Group therapy may be dynamic, behavioral, psychoeducational, or self-help. Through group interaction, individuals feel less alone with their symptoms. They are given feedback about their behavior as it relates to food/body and social conduct. The intense isolation often characteristic of the disorder is eliminated, and normalized social behavior is modeled. Through group interaction, individuals learn to take risks on revealing emotions and begin to develop the appropriate social skills necessary for recovery. By sharing common fears, anxieties, and problems, a strong network of interpersonal support is established. Structured, short-term task-oriented groups comprise many of the group intervention experiences that are currently available. In addition, most communities have established free self-help groups that provide support and education.

Intervention is usually a difficult task for anorexics, bulimics, and compulsive overeaters. Many are being asked to deal with a world they find extremely frightening without the behaviors that protect them. However, many recovered eating disordered individuals describe the intervention process as one of the most rewarding and enriching experiences of their lives. Therapy can last from a few months to several years and can involve only individual therapy or a comprehensive intervention experience, including assessment, nutritional counseling, psychoeducational experiences, and group therapy. Figure 27.2 outlines a comprehensive program that combines a variety intervention components.

GROUP WORK WITH PERSONS WITH EATING DISORDERS

Group Work with an eating disordered population, whether in the form of group therapy, structured psychoeducational groups, or self-help/support groups is an effective and widely used method of treatment.[34] It serves to break down the walls of isolation and secrecy that usually characterize the disorder. Group members are able to address the underlying issues that perpetuate the disorder by sharing common fears, anxieties, and difficulties.

Figure 27.2: Example of an Intervention Program for Eating Disorders That Has a Variety of Components

I. Assessment
  A. Medical
    1. Physical examination
    2. Necessary lab work
    3. Medical history
  B. Psychosocial
    1. Social history
    2. Psychological testing
  C. Nutritional
    1. Dietary history
II. Intervention Plan
  A. Multidisciplinary staffing
    1. Program needs determination—inpatient/outpatient
    2. Individualized intervention plan
III. Program Elements
  A. Planned patient group dining
    1. Teach appropriate eating attitudes and behaviors
    2. Desensitize patients' irrational beliefs regarding social eating
    3. Provide patients an opportunity to plan and organize activities associated with food
  B. Dietary management
    1. Weekly food planning and behavioral contracting
    2. Nutritional education

C. General Education
    1. Bibliotherapy (that is, reading material on understanding and overcoming eating disorders)
    2. Lectures and discussion on topics relative to eating disorders
D. Recreational Therapy
    1. Leisure planning
    2. Social skills development—interpersonal skills and activity skills
    3. Group outings
    4. Music and art therapy
    5. Sensory awareness training
E. Community Support Participation
    1. Integrating existing community programming
    2. Develop peer support network
F. Psychotherapy
    1. Weekly group therapy
    2. Individual therapy
    3. Family therapy
G. Overnight and Crisis Service
    1. Supervised temporary residential care
H. Exercise Management
    1. Planned and supervised exercise

Group Selection Criteria

Indicators for Group Intervention

The success of group intervention can be increased by appropriately screening applicants. Eating disordered individuals who possess the following characteristics may be good candidates for group involvement[35]:

1. Gaining weight or of normal weight
2. Highly motivated to overcome the disorder
3. Demonstrating improvement from individual therapy
4. Not totally isolated or withdrawn
5. Not demonstrating intellectualization or denial as prominent features
6. Demonstrating a capacity to reveal emotions and sensitive to others' needs
7. Having sufficient social skills to join with other group members

Counterindicators for Group Intervention

In addition to lacking some or all of the previous characteristics, the following individuals are poor candidates for group intervention.[36]

1. *Those who suffer from anorexia nervosa.* These people may not be good candidates for group experiences until normal body weight is restored. While in the malnourished state, anorexics usually remain withdrawn, anxious, rigid, self-centered, and preoccupied with body weight and food issues. They often experience difficulty in identifying and expressing emotions. Anorexics contrast quite vividly with normal-weight bulimics, who adapt quite well to the group environment and who generally find peer involvement to be an important part of recovery.
2. *Those who have a history of interpersonal difficulties.* These people may be so limited in their ability to form and maintain relationships that they cannot begin to use the group. When placed in a group setting, they may become extremely anxious and respond by retreating or dropping out.

3. *Those who have been diagnosed as having other primary psychiatric difficulties.* Individuals with a borderline personality disorder or a major affective or reality disorder may not be appropriate. As the eating issues are controlled, psychopathology may surface. The needs of these individuals may be too great to be handled in a group setting as they can absorb excessive amounts of time and group resources.

Group Structure

Group size and composition are important considerations when working with anorexics, bulimics, and compulsive overeaters. With the exception of anorexics, who tend to compete when placed in a group, the ideal is to select members with similar symptomology and life issues. Proper selection or matching of patients with appropriate group work experiences is crucial to preventing individuals who might benefit from other therapeutic interventions from prematurely terminating treatment.[37]

Bulimics, anorexics, and compulsive overeaters function best in a small group. Issues of vulnerability, control, and competitiveness, and feelings of inadequacy can be managed more effectively. As group size increases, it becomes easier for members to become intimidated and inactive. A group size of five to eight allows for individual attention and adequate interaction.

It is not advisable to form groups larger than ten people, even in support or self-help groups. A larger group inhibits discussion of issues and expression of deeper level feelings.

Preparing Members for Group Participation

An important issue affecting group work effectiveness is preparation of the individual for group participation. Because of feelings of inadequacy, poor self-esteem, and an intense need to control their environments, eating disordered individuals are prone to extreme anxiety when faced with the uncertainty of meeting with strangers in a situation they cannot control. By taking a few minutes to discuss the goals of the group before the group experience begins, some roadblocks can be avoided, and trust can be established earlier.

When preparing a group, forewarn members of strong emotions that may be elicited by the group process. As food issues become manageable, feelings that have been masked by the eating disorder will emerge. By reframing these feelings as normal occurrences and evidence of group development, participants will not be tempted to avoid them. Instead, they will begin to recognize and express these emotions and receive support from others for talking about them. Emotional honesty and risk taking between members is encouraged and developed over time.

When precautions are taken and appropriate matching occurs, group intervention can be one of the most effective modes of intervening with eating disorders. However, group intervention need not preclude other forms of intervention. When appropriate, progress frequently can be heightened when group members participate concurrently in individual and/or family therapy.

SUMMARY AND REFERRAL RESOURCES

Anorexia nervosa, bulimia nervosa, and compulsive overeating are exceedingly complex conditions. The central issue is not food, although the eating disordered person spends a tremendous amount of time worrying about, discussing, and arguing about food and body weight.

The issues underlying eating disorders are more directly related to poor self-esteem; unrealistically high expectations of achievement; a desire to be special and unique; and a struggle to win power, control, approval, admiration, and respect from family, friends, and society. Both starving and binging/purging can be symbolic ways of rebelling against authority and expressing rage and anger.

In a sense, the symptoms of anorexics and bulimics have emerged as coping mechanisms for resolving painful problems in their lives. The anorexic has turned away from food; the bulimic has turned toward it. Both need to find healthier and more effective methods of resolving their problems.

Although many of the underlying causes of anorexia and bulimia nervosa can be treated with the help of a competent therapist, anorexics and bulimics comprise a unique population that can be served by a professional who is specially trained to work with the eating disordered. The following is a list of resources that can be contacted for information regarding intervention and/or referral.

American Anorexia/Bulimia
    Association, Inc. (AABA)
293 Central Park West, 1R
New York, New York 10024
(212) 501-8351

Anorexia Nervosa and Related
    Eating Disorders (ANRED)
P.O. Box 5102
Eugene, Oregon 97407
(503) 344-1144

Anorexia Nervosa and Associated
    Disorders, Inc. (ANAD)
P.O. Box 7
Highland Park, Illinois 60035
(708) 432-8000, ext. 5728

Overeaters Anonymous
P.O. Box 92870
Los Angeles, California 90009
(213) 936-4206

GROUP EXERCISES

Structured group experiences that emphasize psychoeducational programming have proven highly effective. The following exercises are examples of the type of programming that is currently being used in intervention programs with anorexia, bulimia nervosa, and compulsive overeating.

Exercise A: Eating Disorder Lifeline

GOALS: (1) To provide personal information regarding each group member's background as it relates to the development of the eating disorder; (2) to develop beginning levels of trust and disclosure within the group; (3) to eliminate feelings of isolation and shame by demonstrating similarities among group members; and (4) to develop the attitude that change and recovery are possible.

This exercise is more effective when there is sufficient time for all members of a group to share their lifeline. However, lifelines can be done over several sessions.

When possible, set the tone of the exercise by having an individual who has previously done a lifeline share it with the group. This will demonstrate for other members the type of information that is being asked for and how much risk may be taken when disclosing. If no one is available, the instructor should proceed in the following manner.

Step 1. Explain the goals of the exercise. Emphasize that group closeness can occur only through trust and that trust is established by sharing feelings and other personal information. Request that members risk as much information as they can, but assure them that they do not have to reveal anything they believe will be too difficult to handle.

479

Step 2. Distribute newsprint and a felt-tipped marker to each member of the group. Give the following instructions on completing the lifeline:

a. Using the entire length of the newsprint, have the participants draw a line, similar to the one in figure 27.3, marking a beginning, a present, and a future point.

b. Ask participants to remember the events they believe contributed to the development of an eating disorder. At this point, it is important to advise them that eating disorders do not start the first time they restrict, binge, or purge. Rather, eating disorders relate to events that affected self-esteem or body image well before symptoms emerged. These recollections are written on the lifeline at the beginning point. Other important events should be marked on the line in order of occurrence. The midpoint represents the present. The rest of the line represents hopes for the future, during and after recovery. Positive events are marked above the centerline, and negatives are marked below the centerline. Placement of the mark represents the relative importance of the event. At each mark, the participants should write a word or symbol to help them recall the event later. This should take about fifteen minutes.

Step 3. Request that one of the members volunteer to share his or her lifeline. Using masking tape, display the lifeline so that all can see. Ask that others listen for similarities and

Figure 27.3: Eating Disorder Lifeline Example Sheet

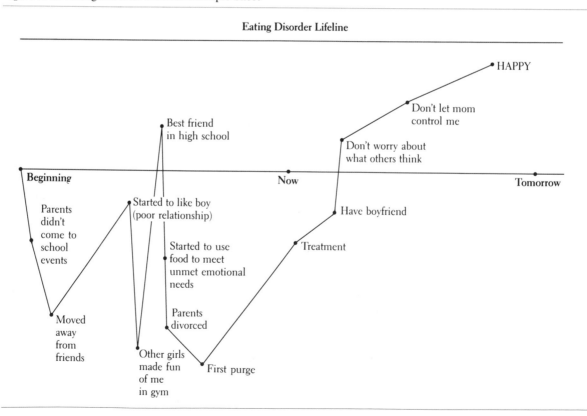

be aware of feelings that occur as they listen. Request that questions not be asked until the sharing of the lifeline is completed. As many in the group will be apprehensive about when to take their turn, continue in a clockwise fashion after the first volunteer finishes. This minimizes anxiety about who is next. This step should take twenty to thirty minutes per member.

Step 4. After all the members have shared (or as many as time permits), ask them to discuss what they have learned about themselves in relation to others in the group. This includes feelings experienced when listening to the stories of others.

Variation. General audiences can also use the lifeline format. Participants can plot past events when they used food to cope with normal emotions or allowed weight issues to dictate their behavior and feelings. Future events can represent goals for healthier personal attitudes about food use and body image. Before the exercise begins, the leader should ask group members to openly discuss and clarify their uses of food and attitudes toward body image by asking the following questions:

1. How many of you eat purely for nutritional reasons?
2. What are our religious and cultural attitudes about food?
3. How do we use food to cope psychologically with anxiety, guilt, depression, loneliness, stress, and boredom?
4. As children, was food ever substituted for love and affection or reward and punishment?
5. Does your perceived sense of esteem change with weight gain or loss?
6. Have you ever declined or at the last minute backed out of a social event because of body image?
7. What messages do we receive from the news and entertainment media about how we should look, act, and eat?

After these questions are discussed, the leader tells the participants to draw their lifelines according to the previously given instructions. After lifelines are drawn, volunteers describe their lifelines. Strong emotions may be triggered in some participants by this exercise; therefore, the instructor should be prepared to professionally handle the expression of such emotions. Also, the instructor should inform the participants they should not disclose feelings or experiences that they do not wish to disclose or may later regret disclosing.

Exercise B: Body Awareness[38]

Goals: (1) To assess one's level of body acceptance; (2) to heighten personal awareness of a distorted body image; (3) to verbalize feelings of unacceptability and dissatisfaction with one's body; and (4) to identify ways to promote body acceptance.

Step 1. The leader briefly discusses the goals of the exercise.

Step 2. The leader distributes one copy of the Body Survey (figure 27.4) to each participant and asks participants to follow the instructions on the sheet. This should take about ten minutes.

Figure 27.4: Body Survey

Please circle on the scales below how you feel about different areas of your body.

	Strongly Positive	Moderately Positive	Neutral	Moderately Negative	Strongly Negative
Eyes	5	4	3	2	1
Posture	5	4	3	2	1
Hair	5	4	3	2	1
Body build	5	4	3	2	1
Teeth	5	4	3	2	1
Ears	5	4	3	2	1
Nose	5	4	3	2	1
Face	5	4	3	2	1
Hands	5	4	3	2	1
Arms	5	4	3	2	1
Shoulders	5	4	3	2	1
Body strength	5	4	3	2	1
Height	5	4	3	2	1
Weight	5	4	3	2	1
Lower legs (calves)	5	4	3	2	1
Upper legs (thighs)	5	4	3	2	1
Waist	5	4	3	2	1
Back	5	4	3	2	1
Buttocks	5	4	3	2	1
Hips	5	4	3	2	1
Abdomen	5	4	3	2	1
Lips	5	4	3	2	1
Skin	5	4	3	2	1
Feet	5	4	3	2	1
Chest/breasts	5	4	3	2	1

Overall, how dissatisfied are you with the way your body is proportioned?

Not at all dissatisfied	Slightly dissatisfied	Moderately dissatisfied	Very dissatisfied	Extremely dissatisfied
5	4	3	2	1

Step 3. Participants discuss what they have discovered about their bodies and focus on feelings associated with body satisfaction and dissatisfaction. This should take about fifteen minutes.

Step 4. The leader distributes one copy of the Healthy Body Acceptance Sheet (figure 27.5) to each participant and requests that the participants answer the questions on the sheet.

Step 5. The leader asks participants to share their answers to the questions and then discuss their reactions to completing the questionnaire. This should take about thirty minutes.

Figure 27.5: Healthy Body Acceptance

1. Introduce your body to the group
   This is _____'s body.
   Its strengths are _____ (list strengths)
   Its limitations are _____ (list limitations)

2. Describe how your body has been treated by you. What have you done to care for it? What have you done to mistreat it?

3. What needs does your body have in order to be healthy? How will you meet these needs which your body has in order to be healthy?

4. Body acceptance.
   In order to accept my body when it is healthy, I will need to _____

Exercise C: It's No Good Unless I Can Finish and See It!

Goals: (1) To demonstrate how anorexics, bulimics, and compulsive overeaters lack the ability to derive satisfaction from the process of completing a task, rather than from its outcome; (2) to promote interpersonal trust between group members; (3) to identify issues of control and perfectionism; and (4) to minimize group competitiveness.

Note: General audiences usually react quite positively and have fun with this exercise. However, due to issues of control, fear of failure, perfectionism, and outcome oriented self-evaluation, this exercise produces a great deal of anxiety and tension within a group of anorexics, bulimics, and compulsive overeaters. Therefore, a trained counselor with experience in processing these types of emotions should be present when conducting this activity.

Step 1. The leader distributes newspaper, modeling clay, and blindfolds to each participant. The room must be large enough for participants to lay down sheets of newspaper and sculpt their clay on it. The instructor informs group members that they are to sculpt anything they want, but that they should be serious in their efforts. Participants are also told that they must work blindfolded and will not see their sculptures before anyone else does. This step should take fifteen minutes.

Step 2. Just before participants complete their work, the instructor directs group members to remain blindfolded and change places with someone else. The members are instructed to finish that person's sculpture.

Step 3. After group members remove their blindfolds, the instructor shares the real goals of the exercise and processes (encourages members to share and discuss their thoughts and feelings about) the exercise with the group members.

Exercise D: I See Me . . . You See Me . . .

Goal: To demonstrate the difference between how eating disordered individuals perceive themselves and how others view them. (Do not share the goal of this exercise with participants until step 5.)

Step 1. The leader breaks the group into dyads and distributes two pieces of rope, each seventy-two inches in length, to each participant.

Step 2. Participants are instructed to tie the ends of one of the ropes together so that it represents the size of their waist. (Note: This must be done without actually putting the rope around their waist.)

Step 3. Participants are then asked to take the other rope and tie it together so that it represents how they view the size of their partner's waist.

Step 4. Participants are instructed to put the rope that represents how they perceive their own waist size around their waist. Once this is done, have participants put the rope that their partner tied representing their waist around their waist.

Step 5. The leader now discloses the goal of the exercise.

Step 6. The leader asks participants to share what they discovered about how they perceive themselves and how their partners perceive them. This should take fifteen to twenty minutes.

CHAPTER TWENTY-EIGHT

INTERVENTIONS WITH DOMESTIC VIOLENCE*

Goal: An often cited statistic is that once every fifteen seconds a woman is battered in the United States.[1] Yet, domestic violence remains a "family secret." Individuals and couples may be in therapy, but violence may never be mentioned until the woman seeks a divorce or until the physical damage is severe enough to require hospitalization. A social worker who can recognize the factors and dynamics contributing to violence in the home, intervene effectively, and coordinate with other community resources is an integral part of the solution to this widespread problem. This chapter will help the worker become aware of the contributing factors, recognize the violence patterns, intervene with the problem sensitively and effectively, and coordinate referrals with community agencies and other professionals.

DOMESTIC VIOLENCE IN PERSPECTIVE

Domestic violence is generally used as a category of abusive behaviors focused within the family unit. The "family" may in fact be a biologically linked system or, more generally, a group of people who identify themselves as a family system. Behaviors in this category include: child abuse, spouse/partner abuse, sexual abuse, sibling violence, child to parent violence, and elder abuse. Because this abuse occurs "behind closed doors" in the family and is concerned with intrafamilial relationships, or "family business," experts estimate that only about one in ten cases of abuse are reported to authorities.[2]

Just as the type of abuse varies, so does the form. *Physical abuse* (while the most visible), is often covered up by attribution to "household accidents," such as falling down stairs or clumsiness. Pushing, hitting, restraining, and in some cases use of weapons are generally considered "physical abuse" and cause injuries ranging from bruises and broken bones to those that are life threatening.

Emotional abuse generally focuses on destroying a person's self-esteem. Feelings and perceptions are distorted or denied, often to the point where the victim believes he or she not only causes the abuse but also deserves it. The victim feels that no one wants him or her or would believe stories of abuse.

Psychological abuse, often interconnected with emotional abuse, erodes a person's self-concept. Blaming the victim; manipulative suicide threats from the abuser; intimidation via threats of violence, abandonment, or destruction of property (including pets); and terrorism are techniques of psychological abuse.

While abuse patterns vary, the focus of the abuse in a family system is usually on one individual or familial role. *Pecking order violence* (man to woman to children) is less common than a singular focus (man to woman). The effect of this focus concentrates the blame on the victim: Dad doesn't beat grandma or the kids; he just beats his wife, so she must be the real problem.

While the focus is usually singular, the form of the violence is commonly multi-dimensional or shifting. Physical violence may occur only once, but psychological and emotional abuse keep the threat of more physical violence in the family consciousness.

Escalation of family violence is the rule more often than the exception. The rate of escalation may vary from a few days to years, but almost inevitably, the violence increases in severity over time. Violence does not end the original problem, and it generates serious negative relational consequences that increase the stress on a family unit: fear, defended communication, frustration, distance.

The bulk of domestic violence occurs when the man is the abuser and the woman is the victim. A variety of theories suggest a rationale for this: men are generally physically bigger and stronger; men are socialized or inherently more aggressive; men lose their tem-

---

*This chapter was written by Carey Tradewell, BSW, Certified Alcohol Drug Counselor III (CADC III) and Daniel Paul Vega, MSW. Carey Tradewell is executive director of the Milwaukee Women's Center, Inc. Daniel Paul Vega is a clinical social worker and a consultant for the National Institute of Corrections. Mr. Vega developed the "Nevermore" program for abusers. Ms. Tradewell and Mr. Vega train and consult in the areas of domestic violence, sexual abuse, and substance abuse.

pers more often than women. While more research is needed, preliminary studies suggest that when violence occurs from woman to man, it is more likely to involve the use of a weapon to "equalize" physical power differences and often occurs after a history of male-to-female violence.[3] *Mutual battering*, when it occurs usually results in more damage to the woman due to the greater physical size and power advantages of the man. Historically, domestic violence has not been recognized as a problem.

Laws, such as the rule of thumb (a man was entitled to beat his wife with a stick as long as it was not bigger around than his thumb), gave social sanction to abuse. Social myths helped to perpetuate it. This chapter will focus on spousal abuse within the family system and will examine some of the issues, dynamics, and interventions currently used in working with this aspect of domestic violence.

THEORIES OF DOMESTIC VIOLENCE

Sociological Perspective

While domestic violence dates as far back as the Bible according to some sources, scientific studies did not begin until the mid-1970s. Strauss published the first epidemiological study of American battered women and shocked the public with the results that 28 percent were physically assaulted in their homes.[4] (Subsequent studies suggest the figure is closer to 50 percent.[5])

From a sociological perspective, the causes of domestic violence lie in the socialization processes of men and women and in the families of origin. Sex roles, stereotypes, social "scripts," and attitudes contribute to the problem:

Men should be aggressive, women should be passive.
Spare the rod, spoil the child (or wife).
A man should wear the pants in the family.
The man's role is breadwinner, the woman's role homemaker.
A woman's needs are less important than her family's needs.
Men should be in charge and use discipline to control their families.
Men are responsible for material and physical needs of the family; women are responsible for the emotional needs.

The sociological perspective also contributed the idea of *intergenerational abuse*. The son, watching the father, and supported by society, *learns* how to use violence to control others in his family when he becomes a husband and a father. It is estimated that as many as 80 percent of abusers were abused as children.[6]

Finally, sociological studies debunked the myth that domestic violence is a problem of minority, uneducated, or lower-class families. While social agencies, including law enforcement and social services agencies, report more contact with these populations in domestic violence situations, studies indicate the problem is as widespread, though less reported, in all racial, economic, and social stratas.[7]

Learned Helplessness

A second major theory of the causes of domestic violence was proposed by Lenore Walker in *The Battered Woman* (1979).[8] In accord with sociological views, Walker contends that a variety of societal myths help perpetuate domestic violence, such as:

Women who are battered are crazy.
Religion prevents battery.
Batterers are violent in all relationships.
Alcohol causes violence.
Batterers are psychopaths.
The victim deserves to be beaten.
Women are masochistic.

Walker advanced the psychosocial *theory of learned helplessness* to explain why women stay in abusive relationships.[9] Walker contends that physical and emotional battering result in a cognitive restructuring of the victim's thought processes that then lead her to become trapped in a pattern of helplessness and often depression. The woman does not want or like the violence, but she believes she cannot control it. When she is told by her husband that she deserves the beating, and when this attitude is reinforced by family and friends who question what she did wrong, she begins to believe that she does indeed deserve beating. When she changes her behavior to please her husband and is still beaten, she learns to feel powerless to control the violence.

A second important contribution to the study of domestic violence is Walker's cycle theory.[10] She suggests that domestic violence follows a definite cycle of tension building in an acute phase until active violence occurs. Then there is a calm phase, often accompanied by remorse, behavior reform by the batterer, and even romance. A woman faced with the economic reality of single parenthood, an attitude of learned helplessness, and one acute phase of violence followed by flowers and kisses is effectively trapped in a violent relationship.

The psychosocial theories of Walker and others help the public understand why women stay in violent relationships and help clinicians better understand psychological and emotional violence.

Feminist Theory

The women's movement has been instrumental in making domestic violence a central issue that requires response from mental health practitioners, police officers, legal personnel, and governments. At the International Tribunal in Crime Against Women, in Brussels, Belgium, March 4–8, 1976, attended by over two thousand women from thirty-three countries, the following proposal was read:

The women of Japan, Netherlands, Frances, Wales, England, Scotland, Ireland, Australia, USA, and Germany, have begun the fight for the rights of battered women and their children. We call for urgent action by all countries to combat the crime of wife battering. We demand that governments recognize the existence and extent of this problem, and accept the need for refuges, financial aid, and effective legal protection for these women.[11]

The women's movement and feminist therapists state that male violence against women (rape and battering) is a consequence of a woman's powerless position in patriarchal societies. Thus, male violence cannot be eliminated without eliminating the unequal balance of power between the sexes. The sociopolitical theory of violence, from a feminist perspective, holds the premise that the abuse of women is a manifestation of a patriarchal "male-dominated" society that excludes women from legal, business, political, and religious leaderships. Thus, the issue of abuse is a result of a power imbalance in relationships.

In the traditional clinical worlds of psychiatry and psychology, the clinician often adheres to the patriarchal myths of female inferiority and innate masochism, perhaps believing that an abused woman may not only provoke abuse but also deserve it. Feminist women within the professions of psychology and psychiatry state the need for practitioners working with domestic violence to protest power imbalances and sexist interpretations supported by their colleagues. Feminist therapy groups and collectives have established goals and directions for mental health practitioners: (1) developing a feminist theory of psychotherapy and psychology of women designed to help them achieve a sense of self-worth and self-actualization; (2) raising the feminist consciousness of the mental health profession through workshops, discussion groups, and presentations at conferences, universities, and social service organizations; (3) training feminist counselors and offering a nonsexist alternative to traditional counseling[12] (see chapter 23 for an expanded description of feminist theory).

Feminist counseling addresses an integration of what have been "masculine and feminine" qualities and recognizes that these qualities are "human" qualities in every individual. Women are encouraged to focus on themselves and recognize their strengths and power.

ADDICTIVE SYSTEM AND THE ADDICTIVE PROCESS

Historically, chemical dependency, domestic violence, and sexual abuse have been seen as connected yet separate issues. The person who is alcoholic and violent is seen as *dually addicted* because alcohol does not *cause* violence or sexual abuse. The debate then focuses on which should be treated first as the primary problem. The various helping disciplines advocate a different intervention focus and plan. In this atmosphere of individualized specialty groups, secondary problems are often minimized or even forgotten, with the hope that alleviating the primary problem will alleviate the others.

In our clinical work with couples and families involved in chemical dependency, family violence, and sexual abuse, we began to see similarities and patterns that we have come to call the *addiction connection*. Rather than a fragmented, specialized intervention approach, we are proposing a uniform conceptualization of the process that enmeshes couples and families in addictive patterns.[13]

Chemical dependency has been defined by McAuliffe and McAuliffe in *The Essentials of Chemical Dependency* as "essentially a pathological or sick relationship of a person to a mood-altering chemical substance, a psychoactive drug in expectation of a rewarding experience."[14] Chemical dependency is viewed as a progressive illness—despite temporary remission of symptoms—that will ultimately result in death if not arrested through abstinence. The tenacity of chemical dependency is evidenced by "relapses" and the "recovering" person is no longer recovering only when he or she is no longer living.

Domestic violence intervention has some similarities to chemical dependency intervention. The "batterer" is the primary problem focus; shelter is offered to protect the partner and children, but the real problem is the batterer, who may be jailed, ordered into treatment, or divorced. Unfortunately, many partners who leave violent relationships find themselves involved in another violent or alcoholic relationship.

Sexual abuse intervention also focuses primarily on the abuser, although support and intervention also help the victim to recover. Yet a victim of sexual abuse often becomes involved with a partner who is violent or chemically dependent.

If one problem does not necessarily cause the others, it stands to reason that a process might be the connecting factor. Domestic violence can be defined as "a pathological relationship to a mood altering experience; a psychosocial situation in expectation of conflict reduction"[15] and sexual abuse can be defined as "a pathological relationship to a mood altering experience; a psychosexual situation in expectation of immediate gratification."[16]

The process connection also explains why children of alcoholics who do not drink may become physically, emotionally, or sexually abusive; why incestuous behavior can "skip" generations; and why an individual who leaves a partner with one problem often finds a new partner with a new problem. An addictive process affects every person in the system. Because the person with the problem is often seen as the most powerful person in the system, identification with the aggressor, or finding a familiar relational pattern is likely "comfortable" and predictable for many adults who had "problem" parents.

Just as chemical dependency is progressive and intensive, so is the process connection. The process is essentially "addictive"—obsessive, compulsive, ritualized, and eventually unmanageable to the point of individual and system destruction. Alleviating the focus of the addiction is not enough; for example, heroin addicts treated with methadone often become addicted to methadone. The process of the addiction has to be defined and treated.

FAMILY SYSTEMS

The ideal family does not exist, but it serves as a model and goal for both families and clinicians. The healthy family is variable in form. It may be a single parent system, blended family, adopted family, nuclear family, extended family, or gay/lesbian family. The essential point is that the members define *themselves* as a "family" and interact on that basis.

Healthy families often show dichotomies that give them strength. Members are distinct individuals with a strong sense of self, yet have respect for, show consideration toward, and trust other family members. They also share and cooperate with one another. Conflict resolution utilizes clear role boundaries with consistent rules of acceptable behavior and unconditional acceptance of each other. Time management incorporates spontaneity, fun, relaxation, rituals, work, and other structured activities. Communication is open, direct, and honest as well as compassionate, diplomatic, and private.

The unhealthy family is also variable in form. A significant difference in an unhealthy family, however, is that members often see themselves as a family but report distance, loneliness, and a lack of genuine caring. The atmosphere is often one of fear, hopelessness, helplessness, and desperation; yet, there is the family dichotomy of members clinging together tenaciously and fiercely reacting against outside threats to the family. Conditional acceptance, closed communication, blurring of roles, and confusion over issues such as sexuality, sensuality, nurturing, affection, and intimacy are found along with rigidity. Crises are so common that tranquility is suspect or uncomfortable.

If a child grows up in a family system where conditional acceptance replaces nurturing; where critical or nurturing parenting is inconsistent and destructive rather than focused on logical rules and reasonable limitations; where adults distort and deny reality instead of exploring problems and solutions; and where denial, rationalization, minimization, and manipulation replace acceptance, sensitivity, and differentiation of feelings, that child will learn to look for a similar "normal" system as an adult. Even if the child rejects the focus of the addictive connection process in the family of origin he or she is still vulnerable to the addictive process in a different setting.

INTERVENTION

A thorough generational family assessment is essential. Whether the family stays intact or dissolves, each family member has been affected and has issues to resolve before healthy relationships are possible.

An important issue with intervention involves the agencies intervening with the family. When law enforcement, chemical dependency, and mental health agencies act as separate and mutually exclusive systems, these systems are as dysfunctional as the family seeking help. Through denial, rationalization, intellectualization, and minimization, they act to perpetuate the family dysfunction. Further research may help us understand which factors predispose a person to a dysfunctional process and may help coordinate human service disciplines and specialties into a uniform effective system of intervention services for chemical dependency, domestic violence, and sexual abuse.

WORKING WITH WOMEN

Intervention services for battered women and their children have proliferated since 1980. Throughout the United States, laws have been enacted declaring domestic violence a crime, and some states have adopted mandatory arrest policies. Funding for domestic violence programs has been primarily through state and city governments.

In the United States, there are more than one thousand shelters, a large number of ancillary twenty-four-hour crisis telephone lines, and state and local task forces and coalitions dedicated to supporting women who are attempting to free themselves from domestic violence. Shelters, crisis centers, and safe homes offer battered women an opportunity to live in a violence-free environment. Such services also help battered women to identify their strengths, to seek legal protection, and to gain financial assistance. Choosing to go to a shelter can be the most painful and exhilarating challenge a battered woman may face. Through time out in the safe, supportive environment of a shelter, a woman can be given a chance to experience power over her own life—the power to make choices.

Shelter hot lines and women's crisis lines exist in major cities and rural communities. These phone lines provide:

1. Immediate assistance to women in life-threatening situations through referral and/or police intervention.
2. Information regarding legal rights, choices, shelter availability, and counseling services.
3. Support and nonjudgmental concern.

An abused woman often enters counseling as a result of contacting a crisis telephone line.

Counselors working with abused women must assume the role of advocate as well as clinician. An abused woman may need any or all of the following: medical assistance, police intervention, legal assistance, housing assistance, educational or job training guidance, job-seeking help, and financial aid. These services are in addition to the need for an abused woman to have short- or long-term counseling through group, individual, couples, and family sessions. These "second-stage" services are critical in assisting a woman in setting up an environment that is safe for her and her family.

Each group counseling session tends to have a central theme, such as grief, divorce and separation, parenting, co-dependency, sexual abuse/assault, money management, and transitional living. Referral into groups is based on an assessment that determines the specific needs and problems of an abused woman. It is important to recognize that abused women have unique needs and problems and come from varying backgrounds. Referrals must thus recognize the differences as well as similarities among battered women. Clinicians must be sensitive to special populations. Cultural influences and patterns of violence differ, even though the dynamic of power inequity in the relationship is the same. Groups established with special populations (such as Hispanic women, African-American women, and Native-American women) are often helpful in addressing cultural differences.

Current studies are recognizing the correlations between alcohol and drug problems, sexual abuse/assault, and domestic violence.[17] Therefore, an assessment of a potential alcohol/drug problem and/or sexual abuse history is essential in providing effective intervention and referral into groups. It is important to note that alcohol and drugs are not to be seen as causes of domestic violence. If a chemical dependency problem is indicated in either the battered woman or her partner, she will often need counseling to address alcohol and drug problems in addition to counseling for the violence. Referral to Alcoholics Anonymous, Alanon, and Adult Children of Alcoholics groups will address these specific issues. Assessment may also indicate that the battered woman's family of origin was dysfunctional. A clinician must be aware of the dysfunctional behavior patterns (particularly sexual abuse), assist the battered woman in recognizing these patterns, and offer support as change occurs. Again, referral into a group addressing sexual abuse may be necessary.

Group work with victims of domestic abuse is effective. Abused women lead isolated lives, and groups provide an immediate acknowledgement of support and encouragement. When a woman is in a shelter, groups are utilized immediately for a number of reasons:

1. To eliminate the feeling of isolation
2. To dispel myths about domestic abuse through education and discussion
3. To establish relationships based on open and honest expressions of feelings
4. To provide role modeling
5. To encourage, through information and support, a belief that the violence is not the woman's fault

492

Groups at a shelter are short-term, educational, and supportive. A trained group facilitator is necessary to provide structure and monitor both the content issues in the group and the process of interaction and expressions of feelings among group members. Therapy groups, which primarily address process issues of feelings, interactions, relationships, power, and control, are best established after the initial crisis intervention groups.

WORKING WITH CHILDREN

Children living in families with domestic violence suffer emotional trauma. This trauma results whether the child is abused or is a silent observer of the violence. Research has clearly demonstrated that children observing parents who engage in physically violent behavior are more likely, as adults, to participate in physical violence.[18] Also, children who were physically abused themselves are more likely to be violent with their partners as adults. Violence becomes a generational pattern if intervention does not occur.

Most shelters recognize the special needs of children and have on staff a children's counselor/advocate. Children are often frightened, confused, angry, and depressed. Intervention strategies include group activities and art and play therapy. Counselors have an excellent opportunity to observe children's behaviors during a woman's stay in a shelter. The disruptions of separation from home and father and living in a shelter environment cause normal acting-out behaviors which should not be viewed as abnormal behavior. However, a child who behaves in a destructive manner to self and/or others or whose behavior seems to get worse rather than stabilize may need referral for therapy with a professional who specializes in children.

It is easy to ignore a child who is "too good." This child often withdraws and is overly obedient and fearful. He or she is also in need of attention and intervention services.

WORKING WITH MEN

In the late 1970s, men's programs were begun in an attempt to address domestic violence at the source: the violent man. While the first priority was the safety of the victim and children, it was recognized that to fully resolve the problem, men must change the attitudes and behaviors that perpetuate domestic violence.

Three major types of programs were initiated to help men change. Mental health programs (using the traditional therapy approaches of individuals, couples and family therapy) tend to focus on stress, anger, impulse controls, and related problems such as alcoholism. Shelter adjunct programs focus more on the specifics of domestic violence, power, and status issues, and utilize a group format. Self-help organizations focus on peer counseling using a group format.

While it is difficult to evaluate the effectiveness of any therapeutic milieu due to the complexity of the factors involved, clinical experience suggests that the traditional mental health programs tend to be least effective in intervening with domestic violence. Men involved in violent relationships often do not see themselves as being in need of therapy and resist treatment. Marital therapy may not focus on the violence at all, or may minimize its impact on the relationship: Family members may fear disclosure of the violence and retaliation for that disclosure, and the isolation factor significant in the violence pattern (as described earlier) is continued in one-to-one and couples therapy.

Considerable suspicion has also been cast on the effectiveness of the self-help model. Based on the Alcoholics Anonymous program, "recovering" peer counselors give support and, when needed, confrontation to help men involved in violent patterns. The self-help model, however, is not set up to handle serious psychological problems or situations due to the lack of professional facilitation.

The shelter adjunct model appears to be the most effective intervention alternative currently in use. Most programs address three major concerns: (1) cognitive restructuring to change men's perceptions and attitudes toward women; (2) sociopolitical issues such as sexism, power, and status; and (3) behavioral alternatives for anger control, impulse control, and stress management.

The ideal model for working with men involved in violent relationships would incorporate elements from all three models, as indicated in figure 28.1. The general consensus is that if alcohol and/or drugs are assessed as significant problems, intervention should be focused on the chemical dependence issues initially. While it does not cause violence, chemical dependence will adversely affect intervention.

The problem with the ideal intervention model is cost, both in available resources and funds. Most shelters are nonprofit agencies that have difficulty providing necessary services for women and children. To help resolve this problem, a community coordinated intervention program is suggested.

WORKING WITH THE COMMUNITY

A functional system of cooperation between the social service system, treatment providers, and the legal system is essential in providing quality care and intervention for domestic abuse families. Unfortunately, until recent years, the legal system offered little assistance

Figure 28.1: Ideal Model for Intervening with Men in Violent Relationships

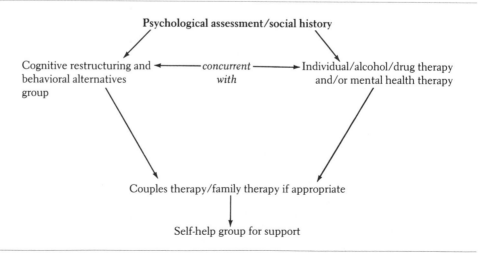

to battered women; not because of lack of laws or procedures, but because of sexism within the legal system. Wife abuse continues to be the most underreported crime. In recent years, through community awareness and education, spouse abuse appears to be changing from a private joke to a public outrage. Formerly battered women have been highly instrumental in this community awareness.

Laws, official and unofficial policies, and procedures for legal intervention differ from state to state and city to city. Social workers must be familiar with the laws and procedures in *their* communities.

It is critical to remember that unofficial policies and attitudes have the most significant impact on intervention with battered women. Many police departments are providing training to officers emphasizing the need for a battered woman to be viewed as a victim of a violent crime entitled to protection by law enforcement officials. This training emphasizes that police officers are not expected to solve the problem but to have the objectives of stopping the violence, protecting the victim, and enforcing domestic violence laws. Many states and cities have begun a mandatory arrest policy regarding domestic violence. The mandatory arrest policy in Wisconsin, for example, requires the investigating police officers to make an arrest (of either spouse, but usually of the husband) if physical abuse has occurred and injury or threat of future harm exists. Police face criminal or civil penalties under the law if they do not make a mandated arrest.[19]

Advocate groups have begun working closely with district attorneys. In some communities models of intervention have been established in which victim/witness units have been set up as part of the prosecutor's office, and advocates for battered women assist in legal counseling.

Struggles continue within the legal system because such a system reflects the conflicting values, attitudes, and norms of its community. Professionals in the legal system must continue a commitment to reforming policies and procedures concerning battered women.

Bringing together social workers, clinicians, police officers, and attorneys is a step many communities recognize as critical to effective service. Community education and awareness programs must emphasize that domestic violence is a crime that is punishable by law. Intervention service providers must work with the victim and family but never lose sight of the abuse as a crime that affects the entire family and community.

GROUP EXERCISES

Exercise A: Closeness to Significant Others

Goal: To assess the psychological closeness you feel to significant people in your life. (This exercise also may be used in groups of abuse victims, abusers, and children in violent families.)

Note: Students should be instructed not to reveal private, personal information.

Step 1. The leader describes the purpose of the exercise and instructs the group to form subgroups of three or four persons. Each person draws a large circle on a sheet of paper and places a stick figure in the center. The figure represents the person making the diagram. Around the figure are arranged the significant persons in the group member's life, each represented by an X and a label or name next to it (for example, mother, boss, sister Ann, minister, and so on).

Step 2. The members of each subgroup discuss their significant others with other members of the subgroup, including the psychological closeness they feel to their significant others. If a member does not feel close to a significant other, reasons for the psychological distance may be described.

Step 3. Reassemble the group or class and discuss what was learned from the exercise. The leader may ask the group to assess the merits and shortcomings of the exercise.

Exercise B: The Addictive Process

Goal: To examine the hypothesis that the concept of the addictive process helps in understanding the correlations between chemical dependency, domestic violence, and sexual abuse.

Step 1. The leader summarizes the material in the chapter that describes how the concept of the addictive process may be useful in understanding the correlations between domestic violence, sexual abuse, and chemical dependence.

Step 2. The class discusses whether this concept has merit. Volunteers describe people they have known who may serve as examples of the existence of the addictive process. *Instruct the volunteers not to reveal the identity of the people they describe.*

Step 3. The leader ends the exercise by discussing the implications of the concept of the addictive process for intervention.

Exercise C: Violence and Intimidation

Goal: To clarify beliefs and values about the use of violence and intimidation.

Step 1. The class forms subgroups of two or three students. Each subgroup is instructed to discuss the following three questions for several minutes. (These questions may be written on the board.)

a. When is violence justified?
b. When do you have a right to impose your will on another?
c. How is your thinking or position on these two issues reflected in how you live your life (family, work, relationships, community)?

Step 2. The leader asks for volunteers from the subgroups to share with the class what the subgroups discussed and what answers to the questions they formulated.

Step 3. The subgroups discuss for ten to fifteen minutes the following topics and questions. (This material may be written on the blackboard.)

a. An incident that you clearly remember, where someone used intimidation or violence against you or someone close to you. What was your reaction?
b. A time when you used violence or intimidation against someone. What was your reaction afterwards?
c. How do those experiences influence your life today?

Step 4. Volunteers from the subgroups share with the class what was discussed. The leader ends the exercise by drawing conclusions from what was discussed about the use and effects of violence and intimidation.

PART EIGHT

SENSITIVITY GROUPS

CHAPTER TWENTY-NINE

IDENTITY FORMATION AND VALUES CLARIFICATION

Goal: Indentity involves having a sense of who we are and includes a knowledge and a feeling of the ways in which we are separate, distinct persons. This chapter describes how to develop a positive self-identity and emphasizes the importance of social workers and group members clarifying their personal values.

W ho are you? What do you want out of life? What kind of person do you want to be? These questions are probably the most important any individual will have to answer. Without answers, major decisions such as selecting a career, deciding whether, when, or whom to marry, or whether to have children cannot be made effectively. People who don't arrive at answers may be depressed, indecisive, anxious, and unfulfilled. All too often, their lives are carbon copies of Stan Sinclair's.

At eighteen, Stan graduated from high school. Unable to find a job, he enlisted in the army for a three-year hitch. At twenty, he started dating Julia Johnson while stationed in Illinois. He liked Julia. She became pregnant and they decided to get married. Money was tight and Julia wanted to live near her relatives. Two months after his discharge, Stan became a father. Needing a job in the area, he became a gas station attendant since it was the only employment he could find. Two-and-a-half years later, an opening occurred in an auto assembly plant. The pay was better, so Stan applied and was hired. The job was relatively easy but monotonous. Stan faithfully attached mufflers to new cars for forty hours a week. During the next eight years, Stan and Julia had three more children. The pay and fringe benefits, combined with his family and financial responsibilities, locked Stan into this assembly-line job until he retired at age sixty-five. The morning after he retired, he looked into the mirror and began asking, finally, the key questions. Was it all worth it? Why did he feel empty and unfulfilled? What did he want out of the future? Never having in the past figured out what he wanted out of life, his only answer was a frown.

Most people are like Stan Sinclair; they do not set life goals. Without life goals, they muddle through life, not knowing what they really want. Muddlers let other people make decisions for them, as they do not know what they want. When others make decisions for a muddler, they usually do so in terms of what is best for them, rather than what is best for the muddler. Muddlers end up going through life feeling bored, empty, sad, anxious, and unfulfilled. Are you currently a muddler, or have you set life goals that you're comfortable with?

STATUS VS. ROLE IDENTITY

William Glasser points out that the need for an identity is the single most important and basic psychological need faced by everyone.[1] According to Glasser, for the past ten thousand years humans have established an identity that was *status directed*; that is, their sense of self was largely centered on survival and, later, on achieving economic security. To be more concrete, status-directed persons, when asked "Who are you?" would probably respond in terms of a career or occupation: "I am a farmer," "a nurse," "a barber," and so on. With this perception of themselves, their sense of identity is determined largely by the role prescriptions and expectations of their position or career. Because meeting subsistence needs (or achieving economic security) takes most of their time, very few hours are available to devote to other identity questions, such as what kind of person they would like to be or what they find enjoyable.

According to Glasser, in contrast to older, status-oriented generations, the younger generation (during the past thirty years) has become more *role directed*,[2] that is, more concerned with fulfilling themselves as human beings, being the kind of persons they want to be, doing things they find enjoyable, and developing the quality of their life. To illustrate, a status-directed person's main concern in seeking a job would be economic security; a role-directed person would be mainly concerned about the potential for personal satisfaction on the job. According to Glasser, this shift from status to role identity occurred because of affluence, increased recognition of the importance of civil and human rights from which developed the civil rights movement in the 1950s and later the women's movement—and because the mass media, particularly television, have increasingly emphasized the importance of enjoyment and self-fulfillment.

Although the shift from status to role identity may be appealing from a humanistic perspective, establishing an identity in terms of one's career or occupation was simpler and considerably less traumatic. The search for a role identity involves a number of more complicated questions, including: "What kind of person do I want to become?" "How do I come across to other people?" "What changes should I make in the way I present myself?" "What kind of career would best suit the way I want to live my life?"

DEVELOPING AN IDENTITY

Identity development is a lifetime process. It begins during the early years and continues throughout one's lifetime. Initially, one's sense of identity is largely determined by the reactions of others. Cooley coined the term "looking-glass self" to describe this labeling process.[2] People develop their self-concept in terms of how other people relate to them, as if others were a looking glass or mirror. For example, if a neighborhood group identifies a teenage male as being a "troublemaker" or a "delinquent," these "neighbors" may then relate to the youth as if he were not to be trusted, accuse the youth of delinquent acts, and label his semidelinquent and aggressive behavior as "delinquent." The youth begins to realize that this labeling process also results in a type of prestige and status, at least from his peers. In the absence of objective ways to gauge whether he is in fact a "delinquent," the youth will rely on the subjective evaluations of others. Thus, gradually, the more the youth is related to as a "delinquent," the more apt he is to perceive himself as delinquent, and the more he will enact the delinquent role.

Labels have a major impact on our lives. If a teenage female in high school is labeled a "whore," other young females may shun her, teenage males may ridicule her, and perhaps some will try to approach her for a "one-night stand." If a child is frequently called "stupid" by his parents, that child may develop a low self-concept, anticipate failure in many areas (particularly academic), and thereby put forth little effort in school and in competitive interactions with others, and end up failing. If a person is labeled an "ex-con" for serving a prison sentence, that person may be viewed with suspicion, be stigmatized as being untrustworthy and dangerous, and have trouble obtaining employment, even though the person may have become honest, conscientious, and hard working.

A useful way of viewing identity development is in terms of a success versus a failure orientation. Glasser points out that those who develop a success identity (a concept of oneself as generally being successful) do so through the pathways of *love* and *worth*.[3] People who view themselves as successful must feel that at least one other person loves them and that they also love at least one other person. They must also feel that at least one other person feels they are worthwhile, and they must feel they (themselves) are worthwhile.

A failure identity (a concept of oneself as being relatively unsuccessful) is likely to develop when a child has received inadequate love or has been made to feel worthless.

503

People with failure identities express their sense of failure in a variety of counterproductive ways: becoming emotionally disturbed; engaging in crime or delinquency; developing behavioral disorders; or withdrawing. Manley notes:

> A sense of failure becomes a further problem since it limits the amount of risk-taking behavior in which we are willing to engage. If we feel that we are failures, we will feel threatened by any new behavior patterns that we perceive as risky. Accordingly, we will be very reluctant to try any such behaviors. This means that we will continue to operate as we have in the past, thereby creating somewhat of a "rut." To the degree that we follow this practice, we are precluded from growing psychologically or expanding our behavioral responses. We are stultifying ourselves from greater use of our potential and become a more complete individual. We learn and grow by our experiences. If we limit ourselves to only the "tried and true" modes of behavior, we are putting disabling constraints on ourselves and seriously limiting our growth potential.[4]

Withdrawal, escape through drugs, loneliness, and the development of emotional problems are common.

Individuals determine their self-concepts, in large part, by what they tell themselves.

> Success identities are characterized by the following kinds of self-talk: "I have accomplished many of the things I have tried in the past." "I am a competent, worthwhile person." "I, similar to other people, have certain special talents." "Trying something new is challenging and stimulating." "I look forward to trying something more complicated that has the opportunity for substantial payoffs, and which will test and further develop my special talents." "Trying new things helps me grow as a person, and helps provide meaning to living." "I look forward to each new day with its opportunities for involvement in activities that will be gratifying and fulfilling."
>
> The following negative kinds of self-talk . . . are characteristic of those with a "failure identity": "I can't accomplish anything I try." "I'm inferior to other people." "Why can't I be as competent, capable, or attractive as others?" "I'm a failure." "I can't afford to risk trying anything new as it will reveal my weaknesses to others." "I wish people would stop picking on me, and making cutting comments about my shortcomings." "I've got a number of personal problems that are overwhelming me, and draining my energy." "There just is no hope for a brighter tomorrow." "My problems are certainly more confusing and unresolvable than those that other people have." "Life is certainly the 'pits' and really not worth living." "I wish I were someone else." "I wonder why such and such hurt me so badly—I just can't stop thinking about it." "What did I do wrong to deserve all this misery?"[5]

Since identity development is a lifetime process, positive changes are probable even for those who view themselves as failures. In identity formation, a key principle is that *although we cannot change the past, what we want out of the future and our motivation to achieve it is more important than our past experiences in determining what our future will be.* This principle has extremely significant implications. The past, which has brought us to where we are today, is fixed and cannot be changed. All that can be changed is the present and the future, and dwelling on unhappy events in the past is a waste of time. Because our pasts may have been painful and traumatic, it does not follow that the present and the future must be painful and traumatic as well. Since we are in control of our lives (or at least have the potential to get control of our lives) we largely determine what our futures will be.

Self-Fulfilling Prophecies

A self-fulfilling prophecy occurs when a person's expectation of the outcome of an event makes the outcome more likely to happen than would otherwise have been true. Self-fulfilling prophecies occur frequently. We expect to have a miserable time at a social affair; therefore we put little effort into conversing with others and end up having a miserable time. If an individual expects a low grade on a statistics exam, she sees little value in studying hard and ends up doing poorly on the exam. A person who feels very anxious about a job interview may then botch the interview because of her negative or anxious attitude. If a friend tells us that we won't like a person we are about to meet, the meeting will be focused on detecting things we don't like about the person and we may end up disliking her.

There are two types of self-fulfilling prophecies. One type occurs when a person's' expectations influence his behavior. A student can "feed" on becoming anxious during a class presentation, for example, and fear that he won't present himself well. This thinking leads him to become nervous during the presentation and he does indeed present himself poorly. Players on sports team are well aware that if they have a defeatist attitude they won't be able to perform to the full extent of their capacities and will in all probability lose their contests. On the other hand, if a person thinks in terms of positive outcomes, he usually gives it his "best shot," which, in turn, improves his chances of doing well.

A second type of self-fulfilling prophecy occurs when another's expectations govern a person's actions. Robert Rosenthal and Lenore Jacobson summarize a dramatic study of a self-fulfilling prophecy in the field of education:

> Twenty percent of the children in a certain elementary school were reported to their teachers as showing unusual potential for intellectual growth. The names of these 20 percent were drawn out of a hat. Eight months later these unusual or "magic" children showed significantly greater gains in IQ than did the remaining children who had not been singled out for the teacher's attention. The change in the teacher's expectations regarding the intellectual performance of these allegedly "special" children had led to an actual change in the intellectual performance of these randomly selected children.[6]

Apparently, the teachers communicated to these children, "You're bright and have a great future in store," which these children then accepted into their self-concept. With a more positive self-concept, these children apparently studied harder and felt better about themselves, which led them to make marked intellectual advances. (If a group leader can infuse this type of positive thinking during group sessions, individual members may respond accordingly.)

This second type of self-fulfilling prophecy fits closely with Cooley's "looking-glass self." Namely, people will largely determine who they are in terms of how others relate to them. Through the looking-glass process, an individual often ends up fulfilling the expectations that others have of him. To a large extent, we all become what others expect of us.

It should be noted that while self-fulfilling prophecies are an important factor in determining behavior, they are not the only factor. For example, a person may think he will really have a good day tomorrow, but unexpected events (such as an automobile accident) may make the day one that he would rather have skipped entirely.

AN IDENTITY-FORMATION APPROACH

A variety of approaches have been developed to help individuals determine who they are: transcendental meditation, biofeedback, gestalt therapy, sensitivity training, and encounter groups.[7] An approach that is particularly useful is *identity formation*. Identity formation is the process of determining who one is and what one wants out of life. Arriving at a comfortable identity is one of the most important tasks every individual will ever have to face. Identity development is a lifelong process, and there are gradual changes in identity throughout everyone's lifetime.

Identity formation is one of the central concerns of sensitivity groups; not only are their members seeking to become aware of their interpersonal interactions, they are also seeking to become more aware of themselves. Identity formation is central to all therapeutic groups, especially those involving families. In the previous chapter, we saw how family members' lack of personal fulfillment was at the core of many family problems. This lack of identity and self-fulfillment makes interaction with those *outside* the family difficult, too. Many members who enter therapeutic and sensitivity groups are seeking better relations with others; this can happen only through development of a strong and positive self-concept.

Forming an identity essentially involves *thinking* about, and arriving at, answers to the following questions:

1. What do I want out of life?
2. What kind of person do I want to be?
3. Who am I?

These questions are not easily answered because they require considerable conscious contemplation and trial and error. However, the answers are important to the person who wants to lead a gratifying, fulfilling life based on direction and meaning. Without answers, individuals may muddle through life being passive responders to situations that arise (like Stan Sinclair), rather than continual achievers of their life's goals. To assist an individual in arriving at a sense of who she is and what she wants out of life, a series of more specific questions follow. As a person arrives at answers to these specific questions, she will simultaneously be arriving at an increased sense of who she is. Identity development, although an individual matter, can be encouraged and practiced within groups. Group members, individually or during a group session, can be asked to write answers to the following questions:

1. What do I find satisfying/meaningful/enjoyable? (Only after you identify what is meaningful and gratifying will you be able to be consciously involved in activities that will make your life fulfilling and avoid those activities that are meaningless or stifling.)
2. What is my moral code? (One possible code is to attempt to fulfill your needs and to find enjoyable experiences, as long as you do so in a way that does not deprive others of the ability to fulfill their needs.)
3. What are my religious beliefs?
4. What kind of a career do I desire? (Ideally, such a career should be stimulating and satisfying to you and also provide you with enough money to support your chosen lifestyle.) Also, what do I enjoy doing during my leisure time?
5. What are my sexual mores? (All of us should develop a consistent "comfortable" code that meets our needs without exploiting others. There is no one right code—what

works for one may not work for another because of differences in lifestyles, life goals, and personal values.)

6. Do I wish to marry? (If yes, to what type of person and when? How consistent are your answers here with your other life goals?)

7. Do I want to have children? (If yes, how many and when? How congruent are these answers with other life goals?)

8. What area of the country or world do I want to live in? (Variables to be considered are climate, geography, type of dwelling, rural or urban setting, closeness to relatives or friends, and characteristics of the neighborhood.)

9. What kind of image do I want to project to others? (A person's image will be projected by style of clothes, grooming habits, emotions, personality, degree of assertiveness, capacity to communicate, material possessions, moral code, physical features, and voice patterns. Strengths and shortcomings should be assessed honestly in this area and improvements made.)

10. What type of people do I enjoy being with, and why?

11. Do I hope to improve the quality of my life and that of others? If yes, in what ways? How can these goals be achieved?

12. What type of relationships do I want to have with relatives, friends, neighbors, and people I meet for the first time?

13. What are my thoughts about death and dying?

14. What do I hope to be doing five years, ten years, twenty years from now?

To establish a fairly well-developed sense of identity, group members need to have answer to most of these questions. Although few individuals have rational, consistent answers to every question, having answers to most of them will provide a reference for arriving at answers to questions that are as yet unanswered.

Honest, well-thought-out answers to these questions will assist members to define their identity. Again, leaders should remind members that what a person wants out of life, along with his or her motivation to achieve these goals, will primarily determine his or her future. The foregoing questions are simple to state, but arriving at answers is a complicated, ongoing process. In addition, changes in life goals should be expected periodically. Just as group goals have to be continually re-evaluated, an individual's identity has to be reassessed as short-term and long-term goals are reached. Environmental influences such as changes in working conditions and personal growth alter an individual's beliefs, attitudes, and values. If changes are accepted and a person's identity remains intact, life goals can be redefined so that continued direction predominates.

Events that are the results of decisions a person makes and decisions that others make for him shape an individual's life. Without a sense of identity, these decisions cannot be evaluated on a personal basis. Therefore, a person may not choose what is best for him, and his life will be unfulfilled. With a sense of identity, a person's life can be directed toward goals that have been chosen and are personally meaningful.

POSITIVE THINKING
....

There is always the choice of taking a positive view or a negative view of events that occur, and the results of these two views are often startlingly different. If someone cracks a joke during a group meeting, for example, another member can view it as well-meaning, laugh along with the others, and have a good time. On the other hand, the joke can be interpreted as being an insult, and a group member can react angrily, say some cruel things he really does not mean, and create a miserable situation for everyone. It is helpful, then, to instruct group members in the practice of positive thinking.

Positive thinking, among other benefits, can lead to a more positive self-concept. If a person generally has a positive view, others will perceive him as an easy going person who is fairly confident and comfortable with his identity. They will probably like this individual and relate positively to him. Since one's sense of self is based largely on how others relate to him, receiving positive responses will lead to an increasingly positive sense of self. Harold Sherman elaborates on positive thinking:

> There is a great law of mind by which your thinking and your conduct should always be guided: "Like attracts like." Think good thoughts; you will eventually attract good things. Think bad thoughts, you will ultimately attract bad things. Simple—easy to remember—but also easy to forget . . . Get this point clearly in mind: you supply the material (by the nature of your thoughts) out of which your creative power builds your future. If the material is inferior, comprised of mental pictures of failure, despair, defeat and the life, you can readily see that only unhappy results can be materialized from them . . . Whatever conditions you are facing at the moment are the result of your past thinking—good and bad. These conditions cannot change until you have first changed your thinking . . . Things first happen in your mind before they can happen in this outer world. What are you picturing? Do you want it to happen? If not, you re the only one who can prevent it. Your future success or failure is in your hands—where it should be.[8]

The philosophy of positive thinking is having a strong resurgence and asserts that ordinary folks can dream big dreams and achieve big goals with positive thinking and action.

Positive thinking certainly has considerable merit; however, there is a potential danger, since every accomplishment requires certain abilities. For those who set goals above their capacities, positive thinking could create a false sense of hope. When people fail to achieve their goals (particularly people suffering from emotional problems like anxiety or depression), they may think that positive thinking doesn't work for them. And, after an initial period of hope, they may become even more depressed. On the other hand, positive thinking will usually get people started on a project. Even though many people do not realize their own potential, a bright outlook and positive action can enable them to use their capacities to the fullest, helping them to achieve their goals.

There is a choice. A person can think and act negatively about events that happen—which usually leads to unwanted emotions and increases the chances of future negative events occurring. Or, a person can react positively—which usually leads to pleasant emotions and increases the chances of future positive events occurring.

CHANGING A FAILURE IDENTITY

As indicated earlier, a failure identity stems from negative and irrational self-talk. One way of changing a failure identity is to identify the irrational self-talk, and then challenge this with rational self-talk. Writing a Rational Self-Analysis to challenge the thoughts about being a failure can be the first step group members take toward changing a failure identity. A second and equally important step is to actually use rational self-challenges whenever failure self-talk occurs. (The format for writing a Rational Self-Analysis is described in chapter 21.) Figure 29.1 presents an example of a Rational Self-Analysis written to challenge a sense of failure.

Figure 29.1: Changing a Failure Identity Through Rational Self-Analysis

A.   Facts and events

I'm a junior majoring in social work at the University of Ohio. I like social work and would like to have a career in it. But I have concerns about that, and about two other areas. I am overweight, and I haven't had a date since Tom and I broke up nearly seven months ago. I frequently feel I am wasting my time in college and will never make it in social work.

B.   Self-talk

B- 1.   I'm really worried that I won't be good at counseling clients. I fear I won't know what to say when I get my first client in field placement.

B- 2.   I have several personal problems that I'm not handling very well. If I can't handle my own problems, how can I possibly help others?

B- 3.   Others are doing better in social work courses than I am. Therefore, I'm not good at this field and should drop out of school until I figure out what I should major in.

B- 4.   I'm really afraid I won't be able to make it in field placement.

B- 5.   I'm really worried that I'm going to become tongue-tied while leading or co-leading a group in field placement. I'm more scared about working with groups than about working with individuals.

D. (a).   Camera check of A

All of this is factual, except for the last sentence which I have added to the section where I specify my self-talk.

D (b).   My rational debate of B

D (b)- 1.   My instructors tell me I'm doing pretty well in the practice classes I'm taking. On the videotape where I was a counselor, Dr. McCredy said I did above average. Dr. McCredy also said practically every student has concerns about how they are going to do in their first interview. I guess it would be much better to take things one step at a time, rather than "awfulizing" by expecting the worst to happen.

D(b)- 2.   Having personal problems sensitizes me as to what others are thinking and feeling. All I have to do is put aside my personal life when I'm counseling others. I've done that fairly well when counseling friends, even at those times when I've had some bad problems. If a situation should arise in placement where my personal problems are creeping in, I'll discuss what to do with my supervisor.

D(b)- 3.   True, some students are doing better, but some are doing worse. I'm getting Bs and Cs, which is about average. In addition, my practice instructors have complimented me on a number of things I do. When it comes right down to it, the bottom line is that it is much better for me to give social work my best shot, as I really like it. Even if I bomb out in field placement, I'll have the satisfaction of knowing I gave it my best try. If I toss in the towel now, I probably will be kicking myself for having quit before finding out if I can really do this.

D(b)- 4.   In the past I had big concerns that I wouldn't get a passing grade in a number of other classes: math, biology, statistics, and Spanish. Once I got started in those courses I did all right. When it comes right down to it, I know of several students who passed field placement who were as scared as me. If they made it, I can too!

D(b)- 5.   There I go again, putting myself down. I'm scared, but no more worried than other students, and they've survived. I need to think positively. I've done all right speaking in speech class. I've given some class presentations without becoming tongue-tied. I led a session in my group work course. Although my knees shook, and my mouth became dry, my instructor said I did all right, and said I would get better with practice as I would become more relaxed.

(continued next page)

Figure 29.1: (continued)

B- 6. I'm overweight and nobody likes a fat person. I know people don't like me.

D(b)- 6. True, I'm overweight but I intend to do something about that by dieting and by exercising. It's simply not true that nobody likes me. I have a lot of close friends, and my parents, my grandmother, and my sister like me. Perhaps if I become more assertive more people would notice me and like me.

B- 7. I know I'll never find anyone as great as Tom to date again. In the past seven months no one has even asked me out.

D(b)- 7. With millions of eligible guys to date, there has to be several whom I would really enjoy dating. I've got to be honest with myself. The reasons I haven't had any dates are because I've been wallowing in self-pity, and have not gone places where I'm apt to meet someone. From tonight forward, I'm going to start looking again. Look out world, here I come. Enough of this self-pity and self-downing!

B- 8. No guy wants to date a fat woman. Therefore, I know no one will date me.

D(b)- 8. Again, my thinking is screwy. I see a lot of over-weight people who are dating. So I certainly can too. A number of guys have told me I'm a good listener and a good talker. I've got to lose some weight, and think positively. In fact, I know of a guy I'm interested in, and who may be interested in me. I think I'll ask him if he'd like to come over to my place to talk and to have dinner. He may be as shy about this as I am.

B- 9. What's the sense of going to college? Even if I graduate, I'll never get a job in social work. I'm wasting my time and my money.

D(b)- 9. It's simply not true that I'm wasting my time being here. I've learned a lot, grown a lot as a person, and met some really great people. This learning and growing has more than justified the money that has been spent. In addition, I stand a good chance of getting a social work job. I've seen other students hired who have no more on the ball than I do. Even if the job market is not right when I graduate, what I learned in my social work courses has greatly increased my interpersonal skills which should help me to get a job in a related field where I can apply what I have learned.

B-10 Given all the above, I'm a failure and am doomed to a lonely, boring, low-paid life.

D(b)-10. I'm certainly not a failure. I've got a lot of things going for me. I'm already a junior. I'm getting at least average grades. I have a lot of neat, close friends. I'm in good health. I've passed a lot of tough courses. My instructors tell me I'm good at interviewing. In the past I've been my own worst enemy. I'm glad I've had this talk with myself. I'm going to stop putting myself down—starting now!

C **(My emotions)**
Depressed, lonely, bored, a sense of being a failure.

E **(My emotional and behavioral goals)**
To stop putting myself down. To look at the positive rather than the negative side of things. To lose some weight. To stop being a whiner, and instead present myself in a way that will turn on people. To give field placement and social work my best shot. I can do it!

CLARIFYING VALUES

In many instances, an individual's identity is directly related to his or her value system. For example, a social worker who identifies him- or herself as a strict Catholic is apt to personally struggle with the profession's pro-choice position on abortion. Social work practice often involves value dilemmas. Social workers frequently work with clients who must make decisions involving conflicting values, and their professional response is sometimes critical. The following three situations are examples of dilemmas that a social worker might encounter.

> Mrs. Baker has just found out she is pregnant. She and her husband already have six children. She works part-time as a waitress and he is a mechanic at a service station. With six children they are already living in substandard conditions. The Bakers are Catholic and attend church regularly. They are considering abortion, but they wonder if that would be immoral.
>
> Mrs. Gauthier is seventy-nine years old and suffers intense pain from terminal cancer. She is depressed and considers taking her own life. Should she be allowed to?
>
> Mr. and Mrs. Neider have a three-year-old child who is profoundly retarded and who needs extensive medical care. They have two older children. The family's physical and emotional resources are being severely drained and family relationships have deteriorated. The Neiders are considering placing their child in an institution but are reluctant to do so because they have been told the child will develop more quickly at home than in an institution. What should they do?

In many such situations, the social worker is best advised to remain neutral on value issues. For example, in the Baker potential abortion case, it would be a mistake for a social worker to advocate for or against abortion. The social worker's role instead should be to remain neutral on this issue, to help the Bakers clarify their values about abortion, and to help them arrive at a decision through carefully exploring the consequences of each alternative. *Clients should be encouraged to explore their own values and to relate alternative actions to their own value systems.*

However, social workers should not be neutral on all value issues. There are times when social workers are expected to advocate for behavior that is consistent with certain values. In protective services, social workers need to convey to clients that child abuse, child neglect, and incest must cease. In runaway centers, workers convey to the youths that they must not use alcohol or drugs. Probation and parole officers are required to make clear to their clients that they are not to break the rules of probation or parole. All social workers are expected to be opposed to discrimination involving race, sex, religion, ethnicity, physical disabilities, or sexual orientation.

Value Code

A value code that social workers are expected to uphold includes:

1. Adherence to the Code of Ethics of the National Association of Social Workers.[9]

2. The principle of self-determination, which asserts that clients have the right to hold and express their own opinions and to act upon them, as long as they do not infringe upon the rights of others.[10]

3. The principle of individualization, which means that every person should be respected and treated as unique and worthwhile.[11]

4. The principle of confidentiality, which is the implicit or explicit agreement between a professional and a client to maintain the private nature of information about the client. There are times, however, when confidentiality should be violated. For example, social workers are required to report evidence of child abuse or neglect to the designated child-protection agency.[12]

5. The principle of institutional orientation to social welfare, which holds that social welfare programs are to be accepted as a proper, legitimate function of our society to help individuals achieve self-fulfillment.[13]

6. The principle of being an advocate for those with little power to ensure that their rights are protected. Social workers have a moral responsibility to work toward eradicating discrimination and oppression for any reason.[14]

The importance of values in our lives is shown by the fact that practically all decisions are based primarily on values, rather than on facts and figures (see chapter 10 for an elaboration).

Learned Values

A value is a criterion for determining a level of goodness, worth, or beauty.[15] Values are learned, changed throughout our lifetime, and acquired in at least four ways, including moralizing, a laissez-faire approach, modeling, and values clarification.

One way we learn values is through others' *moralizing*. Parents, teachers, and others may assume that their experiences have taught them a certain set of values that they believe would be right for us. To avoid the risk of our choosing less desirable values, or to save us the pain of slowly learning the rightness of these values, they will tell us what values we should hold. A second means is the *laissez-faire approach*, in which parents, teachers, and others may allow us full freedom to forge our own set of values, largely through trial and error. The assumption of this approach is that no one value system is right for everyone, so we are left to figure out what works best for us. A third approach is *modeling*. The assumption made by parents, teachers, and others who use this approach is that we will be sufficiently attracted to them to identify with them and to then adopt their values.

A fourth type is the *values clarification approach*. The assumption of this approach has been summarized by Gordon Hart:

> The assumption . . . is that once . . . people have identified their values and the relationship of them to behaviors, they will be better able to cope with the conflicting sources of data regarding values that they receive from their friends, television, and other sources. It is further assumed that if . . . people learn about the acquisition of values they will behave in a more evaluative, logical, and consistent manner.[16]

The values clarification approach does not aim to instill any particular set of values. It is designed to help people identify and clarify their values so that they become more rational and functional.

Values clarification has a number of payoffs.[17] It enhances our ability to *communicate* beliefs, values, ideas, and feelings. Once we become more aware of our values, we are better able to communicate the ideas and feelings that are based on these values.

Values clarification enhances our ability to *empathize* with others, especially those whose circumstances differ significantly from our own. Once we clarify our own values and are aware of the values of others, we are better able to understand how others think and feel and to empathize with them.

Values clarification enhances our ability to *resolve problems*. Once we clarify our values we will be better able to make decisions about value dilemmas that we face. For example, if we clarify our values about abortion, we will be better able to decide if abortion is a viable alternative for us.

Values clarification enhances our ability to *assent* and *dissent* as members of groups. When we are aware of our values, we are better able to decide which issues are worthy of our support and which are inconsistent with our values and therefore unworthy of our support.

Values clarification enhances our ability to *make decisions*. Because most decisions are based on values, once we become more aware of our values we will be better prepared to make decisions that are consistent with our values.

Values clarification enhances our ability to *hold and use consistent beliefs and disbeliefs*. Once we clarify the values upon which our beliefs are based, we are better able to be consistent in our beliefs and disbeliefs. Because punishment and rehabilitation are incompatible, for example, it is inconsistent to assert that hardened criminals should be severely punished when they are imprisoned and also to want prisons to rehabilitate inmates.[18]

In summary, clients will be better able to arrive at personally beneficial decisions if they clarify their values. Also, social workers perform better when they clarify their own personal values. By developing a value system that is consistent with social work values, social workers will know when to present a neutral value orientation in working with clients and when to encourage clients to adhere to a set of values. Through values clarification, social workers will know when they are trying to "sell" their clients their own personal values and will be better able to empathize with clients.

Values clarification is increasingly being recognized as a component that should be included at all levels of education, and a variety of group exercises is available. Two texts that provide such exercises are *Values Clarification for Counselors* and *Values Clarification*.[19] Following are samples of exercises appropriate for social work students.

GROUP EXERCISES

Exercise A: Who Am I?

Goal: To develop an improved sense of who you are and what you want out of life.

Note: Personal information generated during this exercise should remain anonymous.

Step 1. The leader gives the following instructions: "Write down who you are in three words or three phrases; do not indicate your name on the 3-x-5 card." The cards are collected and the replies from three or four students are written on the blackboard. After this is done, the leader explains which responses are status-oriented and which are role-oriented.

Status-oriented responses	Role-oriented responses
Student	Affectionate person
Husband	Caring
Father	Loving
Daughter	Free
Lutheran	Generous

The leader explains that neither of these two types is necessarily better than the other and that until thirty or forty years ago, most people defined themselves in terms of their jobs. However, many people have recently become more role-oriented.

Step 2. The leader indicates that the questions "Who Am I?" and "What do I want out of life?" are probably the most important we will ever have to answer. Identity is the most important psychological need of an individual. In our early years our sense of who we are is largely determined by the way that others relate to us. The leader explains Cooley's "looking-glass self" concept, and then indicates that while the past has brought us to where we currently are, what we want out of the future, along with our motivation to achieve our goals, is more important than our past experiences in determining what our future will be.

Step 3. The leader states that it is crucial to arrive at answers to the following three questions:

1. Who are you?
2. What do you want out of life?
3. What kind of person do you want to be?

The leader explains that one way of arriving at answers to these questions is to answer the questions listed earlier in this chapter under the heading "An Identity Formation Approach," beginning with, "What do I find satisfying/meaningful/enjoyable?" (The leader may facilitate this process by providing these questions on a handout, with space for the students to write down their answers.) The students take twenty to thirty minutes to outline their answers.

Step 4. After step 3, the leader begins a discussion, urging *students not to self-disclose personal information*. The following questions will stimulate discussion: "Do you have answers to most of these fourteen questions?" "Are there areas that you have questions about, or would like additional information about?" "What have you found helpful (other than this exercise) in arriving at a sense of who you are?" "Do you agree that arriving at a sense of self is your most important psychological need?"

Exercise B: Improving Self-Concepts

Goal: To improve your self-concepts.

Step 1. The leader explains that a negative self-concept stems from negative and irrational self-talk that people give themselves. One way to improve a negative self-concept is to identify the underlying negative self-talk and then challenge this self-talk with rational self-challenges. The leader describes how to write a Rational Self-Analysis. An example is given in the chapter.

Step 2. Prior to the next session, students are instructed to write a Rational Self-Analysis (RSA) on the negative thinking that underlies negative components of their self-concepts. The leader answers questions about this assignment and asks that they bring their RSAs to the next session.

Step 3. At the next session the leader asks the students if they had any problems in writing a Rational Self-Analysis, and what they learned from it. A discussion should ensue.

Exercise C: Feeling Good about Ourselves

Goal: To feel good about yourself.

Step 1. The leader states the purpose of the exercise and has the students form subgroups of seven to ten persons. The leader indicates that each student will take a turn completing the sentence: "I'm not perfect at _____, but I'm slowly getting better by _____ _____ _____." Some examples: "I'm not perfect at taking a positive view of things that happen to me, but I'm getting better by staying calmer and refraining from reacting angrily when someone cracks a joke about me" and "I'm not perfect at being assertive in classes, but I'm getting better by seeking to say something in each class that I attend."

Step 2. The class should reassemble, and the students should then discuss the merits and shortcomings of this exercise.

Exercise D: Self-Fulfilling Prophecies

Goal: To become aware that positive thinking and negative thinking often lead to self-fulfilling prophecies.

Note: Students should not disclose personal information.

Step 1. The leader explains the purpose of this exercise and gives examples of how positive thinking and negative thinking become self-fulfilling prophecies.

515

Step 2. Students write down three examples from a friend or relative's life of how positive or negative thinking has led to self-fulfilling prophecies.

Step 3. The students form subgroups of three persons and share what they wrote.

Step 4. Reassemble the class. Each subgroup shares one or two examples with the whole class.

Step 5. The exercise can be ended by summarizing the merits and cautions (outlined in the chapter) of positive thinking.

Exercise E: Social Work Value Issues

Goal: To clarify your values in regard to a number of prominent issues in social work.

Step 1. The leader explains the purpose of this exercise, indicating that social workers need to be aware of their personal and professional values so that they know when they should take a neutral position in working with clients and when they should sell or enforce a particular set of values for clients.

Step 2. The leader distributes the following questionnaire to students and indicates that *their responses will remain anonymous.* The questionnaire uses the following scale: (1) Definitely not, (2) Probaby not, (3) Probably yes, and (4) Definitely yes.

VALUES QUESTIONNAIRE

1. Would you marry someone of a different race?
   1   2   3   4
2. If you were going to adopt a child, would you adopt a child of a different race?
   1   2   3   4
3. Are you in favor of a woman becoming president of the United States?
   1   2   3   4
4. Do you believe busing should be used to attempt to achieve racial integration in schools?
   1   2   3   4
5. Do you support affirmative action programs that assert that certain minority groups and women should be given preference in hiring over white males?
   1   2   3   4
6. Do you believe a father who commits incest with his ten-year-old daughter should be placed in jail?
   1   2   3   4
7. Do you believe prostitution should be legalized?
   1   2   3   4
8. If you or your partner were pregnant and in a situation where it would be very difficult to raise a child, would you seriously consider an abortion?
   1   2   3   4

9. Do you support a constitutional amendment to make abortions illegal?

   1   2   3   4

10. Would you be willing to be a surrogate mother? If you are male, would you be willing to have your wife or future wife become a surrogate mother?

   1   2   3   4

11. Do you believe the death penalty should be used for certain crimes?

   1   2   3   4

12. Do you believe the United States should support an extensive program to develop the capacity to clone human beings?

   1   2   3   4

13. Do you support artificial insemination for humans?

   1   2   3   4

14. Do you believe people should retain their virginity until they marry?

   1   2   3   4

15. If a candidate for president of the United States were African American, would you be less apt to vote for him or her?

   1   2   3   4

16. If you were married, would you seriously consider having an extra-marital affair?

   1   2   3   4

17. Do you believe profoundly retarded persons who will never be able to function enough to sit up should be kept alive indefinitely at taxpayers' expense?

   1   2   3   4

18. Do you believe marijuana should be legalized?

   1   2   3   4

19. Would you be upset if a son or daughter of yours were homosexual?

   1   2   3   4

20. Do you believe you could objectively counsel someone who had brutally raped four women?

   1   2   3   4

21. Do you think people should limit the size of their families to two children?

   1   2   3   4

22. Do you favor a law to limit families to two children?

   1   2   3   4

23. Do you think a homosexual should be allowed to teach in elementary and secondary schools?

   1   2   3   4

24. Do you approve of a young couple trying out marriage by living together before actually getting married?

   1   2   3   4

25. Would you be in favor of a group home for drug addicts in your neighborhood?

   1   2   3   4

26. Do you think the government should help support day-care centers for working mothers?

   1   2   3   4

27. In case of war, do you think women in the military service should take part in active combat?

   1   2   3   4

28. Do you think the United States should build more nuclear power plants to generate electricity?

   1   2   3   4

29. Would you encourage your son to have premarital sex?
    1   2   3   4
30. Would you encourage your daughter to have premarital sex?
    1   2   3   4
31. When you become elderly and unable to care for your needs, would you be willing to be placed in a nursing home?
    1   2   3   4
32. Do you support physician-assisted suicide when the victim is terminally ill and in intense pain?
    1   2   3   4
33. Would you consider marrying someone who is divorced and has two children? (Assume you are single in answering this question.)
    1   2   3   4
34. Do you believe you would enjoy being a social worker at a group home for the mentally retarded?
    1   2   3   4
35. Do you believe the legal drinking age should be less than twenty-one years?
    1   2   3   4
36. Would you marry someone who is of a different religion than you?
    1   2   3   4
37. Do you believe there are circumstances that justify a person taking his or her own life?
    1   2   3   4
38. Would you divorce your spouse if you found out he or she had had an extramarital affair?
    1   2   3   4
39. Would you allow a child of yours to play frequently with a child who has AIDS?
    1   2   3   4
40. Do you believe most welfare recipients are able-bodied loafers?
    1   2   3   4
41. Do you believe you would be comfortable in hugging a person who has AIDS?
    1   2   3   4
42. Do you believe you would be comfortable rooming with a person who has AIDS?
    1   2   3   4
43. Do you think social workers should inform a client's current sexual partners that the client is HIV positive if the client refuses to do so?
    1   2   3   4

Step 3. The leader collects the questionnaires so that anonymity is assured and lists the question numbers on the blackboard. After tallying the results (with the help of volunteers), the leader seeks to open a discussion. For example, if most of the students indicate that they would not marry someone of a different race, the leader asks, "Does this suggest that most of you have some racial prejudices?"

Exercise F: Olga and Igor

Goals: To identify some of your values, to see that your values often differ markedly from those held by others, and to see that it is often difficult to accept someone else's values.

Step 1. The leader explains the goals of the exercise. The class forms into subgroups of four or five persons. Each subgroup rates the five characters in the following story. A number 1 rating is given to the "best" character, that person who displays the most desirable behaviors in this situation. A number 5 rating is given to the person who displays the most objectionable behaviors. The story is read aloud two times.

Two primitive societies are separated by a turbulent river full of people-eating piranhas. An earlier civilized society (which left the area decades ago) built a bridge connecting the societies. Olga lives in Caribou Society and is very much in love with, and engaged to, Igor, who lives in Moose Society. Both societies are highly opposed to premarital sex. Both Olga and Igor are still virgins. Six days before the wedding a monsoon destroys the bridge. Olga and Igor are on separate sides. Both believe there is no way for them to get across, or to ever see each other again. Both are distraught.

The night before the scheduled wedding, Blackbeard the sailor visits Caribou Society. Olga asks Blackbeard to give her a ride across. Blackbeard says OK, on the condition that Olga goes to bed with him in his boat as they are crossing. Olga definitely doesn't want to do this. But she fears she'll never marry Igor, or even see him again. Olga deliberates about it for four-and-a-half hours. She asks a long-time friend, Solomon, for advice. Solomon says, "It's your problem. You have to decide. There is nothing I can do to help. I don't like the idea of your marrying anyone in Moose Society anyway."

Olga finally says "yes" to Blackbeard. When they get across, Igor is in ecstasy over seeing Olga. Olga kisses and hugs him, and then starts to cry. Burdened with guilt, she confesses that she had to go to bed with Blackbeard as the price for getting across. Igor is outraged. He feels Olga has been tainted. He tells Olga he cannot marry her and that he never wants to see her again. Olga runs to Samson, a mutual friend. Olga tells her story to Samson, and Samson rushes to find Igor. Upon finding Igor, Samson punches him out and knocks him silly. Olga looks on and laughs during the fight.

Step 2. The subgroups arrive at a consensus for rating the characters from one to five.

Step 3. The names of the characters are written on the blackboard (Olga, Igor, Solomon, Samson, and Blackbeard) and a representative from each subgroup writes the subgroup's ranking next to each name.

Step 4. Someone from each subgroup describes the reasons for their rankings. The differences in rankings are then discussed, especially how the values expressed for the rankings differed substantially among the subgroups. The leader might conclude by stating that it is important to identify our values in order to keep our personal value judgments in check when we deal with clients.

519

Exercise G: The Miracle Workers

Goal: To identify physical and material characteristics that are important to you.

Step 1. The leader explains the purpose of the exercise, distributes on a handout the descriptions that are given below, and explains to the students that their first task is to choose four miracle workers whose miracles they would most like to have.

THE MIRACLE WORKERS

The following group of miracle workers have gotten together and graciously decided to provide four of the following services to you. Whichever services you select, you are guaranteed to be 100 percent satisfied with them. It is up to you to select the four authorities whose services you most desire.

1. *Dr. Jean Olympic*: A famous athlete, she can make you an outstanding athlete in any one sport that you choose. If you select a well-paying sport, you will be guaranteed fame and fortune.

2. *Dr. Jane Adams*: A well-known social worker, she will train you to become a highly competent social worker, and you will gain a national reputation for your outstanding work.

3. *Dr. Joshua Methuselah*: This renowned gerontologist guarantees you a long life (beyond the age of 300) with the aging process slowed way down. For example, at age 100 you will look and feel like 25.

4. *Dr. Will Masters*: An expert in sexuality, he will guarantee you a perfectly happy sexual life. Every day or two, or as often as you wish, you will be in sexual heaven, without criticisms, without hassles, and without fear of a venereal disease.

5. *Dr. "Pop" U. Larity*: This charming gentleman guarantees that you will always have close friends who are honest and sincere and whom you will always enjoy being with.

6. *Dr. Ben Spock*: A family therapist, Spock guarantees you a happy family life, both with your parents and your children.

7. *Dr. Mary Monroe*: This acting coach guarantees you a famous film career. You will win an Academy Award and will also have a long-term series on television.

8. *Dr. Abe Lincoln*: The political guru guarantees you that you will become president of the United States. Although you will have some political hassles, you will go down in history as one of our best presidents.

9. *Dr. Gore Geous*: A famous plastic surgeon will guarantee you that you will look the way you want to as long as you live. You can have the weight, height, color and kind of hair, and physical appearance that you want.

10. *Dr. Act U. Puncture*: A medical expert, he will guarantee you perfect health and protection from physical injury as long as you live.

11. *Dr. Al Einstein*: A famous scientist, he will guarantee you creativity and very high intelligence. You will eventually make some scientific discoveries that will benefit all human-kind.

12. *Dr. H. Hughes*: A billionaire will give you the skills to earn fantastic sums of money. You will become one of the richest persons in the world.

13. *Dr. Sig Freud*: A famous psychiatrist will guarantee you freedom from emotional problems and a positive self-concept.

14. *Dr. John Paul*: A famous religious leader will guarantee you a life in which you follow moral and religious values. Also, if a heaven exists, you will be guaranteed a reservation.

15. *Dr. Jon Dewey*: A famous educator will guarantee that you will graduate with highest academic honors from college. After graduating from college you will be guaranteed a high-paying job and will always have the capacity to think rationally.

Step 2. After the students have made their choices, they form subgroups of four or five persons and each subgroup selects the four miracles it most desires.

Step 3. After the subgroups have reached their decisions, a representative from each subgroup states the miracles his or her subgroup wants and the reasons they selected these miracles.

Step 4. The students discuss their feelings about this exercise. Did the students have strong feelings about the subgroup choosing some miracles that were not their personal choices? Did this exercise help them to determine what is really important in their lives?

Exercise H: Genie and the Magic Lantern

Goal: To identify what you really want at the present time.

Step 1. The leader explains the purpose of the exercise and asks the students to imagine the following: "Let's assume when you go home tonight there will be a magic lantern. After you rub the lantern, a genie will appear and will give you the three things you want most in life now. These things can be anything you want, tangible or intangible. Please list these three things on a sheet of paper."

Step 2. The group forms a circle and volunteers share what they wrote.

Step 3. After a number of examples, the leader summarizes what appear to be trends in what respondents want most in life at the present time. The class discusses how the respondents' lives would change if their wishes were fulfilled. The exercise ends with students discussing what they learned.

Exercise I: Pregnancy and Tragedy

Goal: To examine a number of values through making decisions about a value vignette.

Step 1. The leader explains the goal of the exercise and asks students to form subgroups of five persons. The subgroups are informed that their task is to rank the following characters as to who is most and least responsible for Lucy's death. The rankings are 1, most responsible, to 6, least responsible. The following story should be read twice.

Lucy is eighteen years old, white, and an attractive college freshman. She believes strongly in racial equality, even though her parents have told her on several occasions that they are opposed to interracial dating and marriage. In her courses, Lucy meets Kent, an African American and a college sophomore, and they begin dating.

Lucy becomes pregnant. After a long, agonizing view of the alternatives, both Lucy and Kent decide it would be best to seek an abortion. Neither Lucy nor Kent has the money to obtain an abortion from an abortion clinic or from a hospital.

Lucy goes home with the hope of asking her parents for the necessary funds. She begins by telling her mother that she is dating Kent, that Kent is African American, and that they have become sexually involved. Her mother immediately becomes upset and calls in Lucy's father. Both parents angrily tell Lucy she must stop seeing Kent, or they will no longer pay her college bills. Lucy is not able to inform her parents she is pregnant.

Lucy is distraught. She returns to college. The next day Lucy hears of a person who will perform the abortion at half price. Kent goes along with her to the abortionist who, it turns out, is quite unskilled and unsanitary. Lucy begins hemorrhaging on the table. Kent rushes her to the hospital, but it is too late, and Lucy dies. The hospital administrator tells Kent that Lucy is the third person who has been admitted to this hospital for hemorrhaging after being treated by this abortionist (the other two lived). The hospital administrator adds that it's about time someone informs the police.

Step 2. The subgroups arrive at a ranking for who is most to least responsible for Lucy's death:

_____Lucy
_____Kent
_____Lucy's father
_____Lucy's mother
_____The abortionist
_____The hospital administrator

Step 3. The names of the characters are written on the blackboard, and a representative from each subgroup writes the subgroup's ranking on the blackboard. Each subgroup then provides the reasons for its ranking. A discussion of the values underlying the rankings by these subgroups follows.

Exercise J: Political Action

Goals: To encourage students to express themselves on an issue they feel strongly about and to encourage those who may want to take some political action on the issue.

Step 1. The instructor explains the purpose of the exercise, asking each student to focus on a social welfare issue that he or she feels strongly about and has already taken a position on. Examples of issues include: abortion, surrogate motherhood, physician-assisted suicide, rape, incest, racial equality, and sexual equality. Crayons and paper are distributed,

522

and students are asked to write a catchy slogan that conveys their position on the issue. Examples include:

Peace in the World
or the World in Pieces!

Nuclear Power today leads to living
in caves tomorrow!

Step 2. After students have written their slogans, each one is taped to the wall with masking tape, and students explain their slogans and stands. Each student should then be asked what he or she could constructively do to bring about the desired resolution of the issue, such as writing to the editor of a local newspaper, writing to a senator, or asking a club or group for help.

As an alternative to devising a slogan, students could write a brief telegram message to the president about an issue they feel strongly about. This message must be brief and to the point. Each student reads his or her telegram to the class and offers any explanation needed. The instructor may encourage them to send the message in a letter and see if they get a response.

Exercise K: The $100 Million-Dollar Lottery Ticket

Goal: To contemplate how life would be different if you were wealthy.

Step 1. The leader explains the purpose of the exercise and asks the students to pretend they have each won a $100 million dollars on a lottery ticket. After a few moments of thought, they describe in writing how their lives will be different now that they are rich.

Step 2. Volunteers share what they wrote.

Step 3. The leader summarizes what appear to be trends in how the money would be spent and how lives would be different. The exercise is concluded with students' thoughts on what they learned from the exercise.

Exercise L: Trust Walk

Goal: To recognize aspects of yourself that you are unaware of through doing a trust walk.

Step 1. The leader explains the purpose of the exercise and asks each student to choose a partner. (If there is a person without a partner, the group leader can be a partner.) One of the partners closes his or her eyes and keeps them closed during the first part of this exercise. The "blind" person entrusts herself to be led around the room, down corridors, up or down stairs, and perhaps outside. The "seeing" person can instruct or guide the "blind" person by taking her hand to walk around objects and go up and down stairs. The "seeing" person has the responsibility to watch that the "blind" partner does not stumble, fall, run into things, or get hurt in any way. (Instruct the students to be very careful going up and down stairs.)

Step 2. After ten minutes the partners trade roles and continue the exercise for another ten minutes.

Step 3. The class discusses how it feels to entrust their physical well-being to someone else. The leader asks: Did you move easily with your partner, or were you hesitant? How did you handle your fears? Did you find yourself occasionally opening your eyes? Did you become aware of thoughts or feelings about yourself that you previously were unaware of? If so, what were these thoughts and feelings?

CHAPTER THIRTY

DESENSITIZATION TO SEXUAL ISSUES*

Goal: Sexuality is a sensitive and often anxiety-provoking topic. The goal of this chapter is to propose a sexual desensitization model for social workers to help increase their comfort when talking about sexuality with clients. Specific group techniques are suggested for desensitizing people to various aspects of sexuality.[1]

Atwelve-year-old girl approaches you as a social worker and asks how important it is to remain a virgin. A young man hesitantly and anxiously shares with you some recent homosexual feelings. A family member cautiously reveals that the father has made several sexual advances toward an adolescent daughter. A twenty-year-old woman finds out one of her recent sexual partners is HIV positive and asks you what to do. An elderly woman living in a nursing home has been caught in bed with an elderly man; the staff is in an uproar.

THE IMPORTANCE OF DESENSITIZATION

Social workers are confronted with these situations every day. People are sexual beings. Clients are concerned with their sexuality and often need help in dealing with sexual matters. These issues are difficult for them and are often difficult for social workers.

Interpersonal communication about sex is frequently difficult. Meanings of many sexual terms are unclear. For example, take the phrase "having sex." How does one "have sex"? One might picture sex as one of the choices on a menu!

Even when the words are understood, simply saying them can provoke anxiety, since values are involved. For instance the word *masturbation* usually elicits uncomfortable giggling even on the part of middle-aged adults. Masters and Johnson define masturbation as "sexual self-pleasuring that involves some form of direct physical stimulation."[2] Both the Kinsey studies done several decades ago and more recent research indicate that practically all men and approximately two-thirds of all women have masturbated.[3] Yet, even though most people masturbate, one national survey indicates that half of the respondents feel that masturbation is "always wrong."[4] Thus, we are faced with the situation in which most people masturbate but believe they should not. If one does something he or she feels is wrong, guilty feelings may result, and guilt promotes anxiety and discomfort.

Masturbation is one example of a common sexual practice historically regarded as a bad practice. In 1885, H. R. Stout published a book entitled *Our Family Physician* which illustrates the negative view of masturbation presented to us. He wrote: "The symptoms produced by this vice are numerous . . . There will be an irritable condition of the system; sudden flushes of heat over the face; the countenance becomes pale and clammy; the eyes have a dull, sheepish look; the hair becomes dry and split at the ends; sometimes there is pain over the region of the heart; shortness of breath; palpitation of the heart (symptoms of dyspepsia show themselves); the sleep is disturbed; there is constipation; cough, irritation of the throat; finally the whole man becomes a wreck, physically, morally, and mentally."[5] It was equally bad for women. Stout continued, "Among females, besides these other consequences, we have hysteria, menstrual derangement, catalepsy, and strange nervous symptoms."

The point of this discussion of masturbation is not to encourage you or your clients to do it. Rather, it provides a good example of a sexual topic that elicits great discomfort. Many other such topics cause people to be anxious and uncomfortable. Among them are personal sexual fantasies, explicit details about sexual intercourse, oral sex, homosexual-

---

*This chapter was written by Karen K. Kirst-Ashman, Ph.D, professor, Social Work Department, University of Wisconsin—Whitewater.

ity, and common sexual dysfunctions such as orgasmic dysfunction and premature ejaculation. (Orgasmic dysfunction is the condition in women "of being unable to have an orgasm."[6] Premature ejaculation is the condition in men in which they ejaculate "too soon" or are "not able to postpone ejaculation long enough"[7] to satisfy their partners.)

Sexual issues inevitably come up in the practice of social work. Sexuality in one form or another is critically important to people in their private lives. Not only are practitioners called upon to help people who have been sexually abused as children or who have been victims of sexual assault as adults, but they are also asked to help people deal with a variety of other sexual problems. My experience in practice has been that it's impossible to predict what kind of issue a person will feel is of critical personal importance.

For example, I gave a professional presentation on sexual counseling to a group of school counselors and educators. A man cautiously approached my desk after most of the other persons attending had left the room. He began to pick up some of my handouts and then quietly asked me, "You know, I have a question for you. My wife won't let me perform oral sex. Do you have any suggestions?" Well, this is not something to be solved in the five minutes we had as we walked to the cafeteria for the conference luncheon. Was his wife embarrassed? If so, was it due to her physical appearance or perhaps to bodily odors? Was he touching her too roughly? How effective was their verbal communication during their sexual interactions? There were many issues to be explored. However, *this* person felt that *this* issue was so important to him that he risked approaching me, a total stranger, to ask an intimately personal question. It was important to respond to him in an open, straightforward manner that would encourage him to talk about the issue and work on solving the problem. It was important not to be embarrassed (despite my surprise) but to take the opportunity to begin helping him explore this issue.

A similar incident occurred after another professional presentation. This time a woman approached me and asked, "When my husband and I have sex, whenever he penetrates me, noises that sound like passing gas come out of my vagina. It's so embarrassing. How can I stop it?" This made me stop and think. I really had no idea about the physical cause of this problem. One idea was to suggest trying different positions during sexual intercourse to determine if that would help stop the noises. Another alternative would have been to refer this woman to a sex therapist who was also a physician. Such an individual could examine her, would know what to look for, and could possibly identify the cause.

During our brief encounter, however, I decided to address the psychological aspects of this "problem." A basic tenet in sex counseling is that it's important to focus on the positive aspects of sexual interaction instead of the negative, which I discussed with her and encouraged her to focus on. During sexual activity, when an individual dwells on what's wrong instead of what's right, the activity tends to be inhibited; that is, the partners don't enjoy the activity as much as they could. Instead of focusing thoughts on noises and physical imperfections, clients should be encouraged to concentrate on: the pleasurable physical feelings resulting from touching and caressing specific areas of skin and body, the sense of togetherness and joy, and the satisfaction of giving and receiving emotional and physical pleasure.

As I talked with this woman it was very important that I felt comfortable. She was worried about her "sexual performance" and what might be wrong with her. The last thing she needed was a shocked or otherwise negative reaction from me. Such a reaction would probably have intensified her feelings of worry and self-criticism. It's important for a practitioner to be *desensitized* to talking about sex in order to be open and helpful to people in need.

An extremely tall young man came to my office during the late afternoon when virtually no one else was around. Although it's common for students to visit professors' offices for various reasons, this individual did not look familiar. He said, "I saw your name mentioned in the student paper the other day when you made some comments about sexual assault victims." At first I looked at him and thought, "No, he can't be the victim of sexual assault, can he?" Then he continued; he had a girlfriend with whom he was very much in love. She had revealed to him that she had been sexually assaulted by a mutual acquaintance of theirs before they were introduced. The incident was beginning to interfere with their sexual relationship. The girl wanted to talk to the young man about it, but he couldn't stand to broach the issue. What should he do?

We talked about some of the common reactions of people who have been so intimately violated. Under these circumstances it's easy to feel guilty and dirty. A major treatment approach is to help the victim gain a more objective perspective of the situation. One major goal is to place the blame appropriately on the perpetrator, not on the victim. A victim tends to dwell on what she could have done to prevent the assault. A practitioner needs to emphasize the positive things she *did* do; for example, she should be given credit for still being alive after the attack. It must be emphasized that the victim did not choose to be assaulted. It was the attacker who stripped the victim of her control. She should not blame herself for his decisions and actions.

Another major counseling approach is to encourage the victim to talk about the event in order to gain a more objective perspective. Although it was difficult for this young man to talk about this issue, he sincerely wanted to know what he should do. We discussed the consequences of talking with his girlfriend about her feelings. He decided that encouraging her to talk about her feelings would at worst bring out his own feelings of anger toward the attacker. On the other hand, denying her the opportunity to talk to him would only demonstrate his lack of support and intensify her feelings of guilt and fear. Although this was a painful thing to share, the young man needed to identify his alternatives and their consequences. He needed someone who would be open to talk about his feelings even though they were negative and angry. He needed to feel he could talk about his sexual relationship even though it was very personal.

Both social workers and clients as individuals have value-laden notions about what should and should not be said. They have personal opinions about what is normal, what is abnormal, what is appropriate, and what is inappropriate. Each of us, whether we are practitioners or not, has some topics that do not appeal to us or that shock us. Each of us has a different mixture of feelings and ideas about sexual topics. Each of us is unique, and the range of opinion about any particular topic is vast.

For instance, some people think that contraceptives should be made readily available to high school students by birth control clinics located in schools. They believe that this is a "normal" response to a "normal" need. Others feel that such a plan would encourage young people's sexual activity by giving them the impression that it's "all right" to be sexually active whenever they feel like it. These people would consider such clinics "abnormal" and even immoral.

Another example of an issue involving sexuality and strong divergence of opinion is homosexuality. (A homosexual is "a person who is sexually attracted to, or engages in sexual activity primarily with, members of her or his own gender."[8]) Some people believe that homosexuality is biologically and morally wrong. They feel that homosexual behavior is unnatural and that homosexual individuals should change to a heterosexual orientation. On the other hand, some people feel that homosexuality is one of the natural manifestations of being sexual. Research indicates that people who are gay realize they are so by the time they reach adolescence.[9] On the other hand, current research gives no clear indications why some people are gay and some people are not.[10] There are no clear variables in a person's biochemistry or family history that predict homosexuality. In any case, many people feel homosexuality is a "normal" sexual variation and gay people should have the same rights as heterosexual people.

In order to be effective working with individuals, families, and groups, it is critically important to be nonjudgmental. Social workers should respect people's views about sexuality and be sensitive to their values. Therefore, social workers should become more desensitized to sexuality and sexual issues and not laugh, giggle, or blush when a person mentions a personal sexual problem. Sexual issues must be handled frankly and objectively just like any other issue. When a client wants to discuss some serious, explicit, or unusual sexual activity, the social worker should remain calm. As with any other issue, the client needs objective assistance in thinking things through. Figure 30.1 illustrates a model to help social workers conceptualize where desensitization fits in the counseling process.

THE PROCESS OF DESENSITIZATION

Becoming Aware of Personal Values

The first step in desensitization is to become aware of one's own values. Social workers must know what aspects of sexuality make them uncomfortable and anxious. It may be masturbation, homosexuality, or the four-letter words of street language. Whatever it is, they must become consciously aware of it.

Figure 30.1: Dealing with Sexual Issues in Practice: The Sexual Desensitization Model

Part I		Part 2		Part 3
Desensitization	+	**Knowledge**	+	**Skills** = **Professional Competence**
a. Awareness of personal values concerning sexuality.		a. Acquisition of information and facts concerning various areas of sexuality.		a. Ability to communicate basic knowledge concerning sexual issues.
b. Examination of these values.		b. Awareness of limitations of personal knowledge.		b. Mastery of basic decision-making skills.
c. Differentiation between personal values and professional objectivity.				c. Mastery of basic problem-solving skills.
d. Maintenance of a nonjudgmental professional approach.				

Awareness involves exposure to a wide range of issues. If you've never had to address an issue, you haven't had the opportunity to react to or think about it. Reactions occur on two levels, the emotional and the cognitive. Many times it's easy to discuss an issue intellectually in relatively vague, safe terms and in an open-minded, rational manner. When actually confronted with the issue on a more personal or "gut" level, however, it's often a totally different story.

For example, it's easy to say we believe in the behavioral techniques of sex therapy to help women learn to have and enjoy orgasms. It's quite another thing to watch an explicit film used by sex therapists to present a model for couples to follow. Many people have a strong emotional reaction to watching a woman guide her husband's hands and teach him to touch her genitals in the manner most pleasurable to her.[11] This is one illustration of sensate focus exercises in which couples are assigned a series of homework exercises. They are instructed to touch each other intimately so that each may gain a great awareness of pleasurable sexual sensations. They also learn to communicate to each other about these sensations—what feels good and what is unpleasant.

An example of the difference between an emotional and a rational, cognitive reaction is given by a twenty-two-year-old female student who came into my office to "talk about something." The student was in her final semester before being granted a bachelor's degree in social work. She had already completed her field practicum and a three-credit course in sexuality geared toward professional social workers, counselors, and educators. She sat down. I asked her, "What's up?," and she immediately started to cry. Just a week before, her twenty-year-old sister, to whom she was very close, had "come out" and told her family that she was a lesbian. The student clearly articulated that it was one thing to feel open-minded about homosexuality in a sexuality class, but, it was quite another to deal with it in her personal family life.

As we talked she expressed the emotions she had been feeling about this revelation. At first she felt surprise and shock. As she continued to think about it, she felt discomfort, sorrow, and loss. She felt grief concerning the option she thought was no longer open to her sister—a "normal" family life with husband and children. She also felt sorrow for her parents and other four siblings who were going through a similar period of reaction and readjustment. Finally, she was concerned that her relationship with her sister would now change.

We talked about how her emotional reactions were probably typical. She understood intellectually the concept of homophobia (the fear of and resulting hostility toward homosexuality). At this time she herself was going through an emotional homophobic response. We also talked about the positive consequences of her sister's revelation of her sexual preference to family members. Now her sister could feel much freer with her family. She would no longer have to hide her real self. We discussed how it was good that her family relationships were generally close and supportive. Her sister had a good support system to rely upon even though she might experience some negative homophobic reactions on the part of other people. We talked about how it must be a relief for her sister to have come to grips with her own identity and to have made conscious decisions about the type of lifestyle she would pursue. Finally, we talked about the student's personal relationship with her sister. The student concluded that, despite her irrational fears, their relationship really needn't change at all. By the time we were finished, the student said she was beginning to feel better. She had begun to recognize her own feelings and examine the situation more objectively.

In summary, the first step in the desensitization process is to become aware of your own values about the various facets of sexuality as this person did. Inevitably there will be areas that will cause anxiety, and these areas will be different for each of us. This first step involves the identification of our "gut" reactions toward sexual issues and the identification of our own values and feelings.

Examining Personal Values

The second step in the desensitization process is to examine these values and feelings. The cause of the anxiety and reasons for feeling threatened need to be discovered. Before discomfort can be controlled, it must be analyzed and understood.

In the case of the student whose sister revealed she was a lesbian, the second step involved a cognitive evaluation of her feelings. She thought about why she was having such negative feelings. Some were due to homophobia; some were due to surprise. After allowing herself to have an emotional reaction to the event, she could confront her feelings and look at them more objectively. She could evaluate which feelings were rational and which irrational and eventually help herself to cope with the situation.

Many people feel anxious when they hear the sexual terms common in street language, for instance, the words *fuck, cock,* and *cunt.* You might have a negative reaction, perhaps even of disgust, when simply reading these terms. However, these are only words. It's important to acknowledge your emotional reaction, if you have one, and then examine this reaction more objectively. You may have been taught that these words are vulgar, crude, and disgusting. You may have learned that they should never be said and, therefore, you have a revulsion reaction to them.

In your practice, your clients may use these terms. They may be the only terms some clients are able to use because they are the only descriptive terms they know. For instance, a teenager with a history of severe truancy may never have attended sex education classes to learn words like *intercourse, penis, vagina, vas deferens, fallopian tubes,* or *coitus.* When people need information about sexuality, they can ask only with the vocabulary they know. The sexual terms they've heard on the street may be the only ones they've heard. It's important for a professional practitioner to convey necessary information using language understandable to a client whenever possible in order to help people make constructive decisions and solve problems.

Differentiating between Personal and Professional Values

The third step toward desensitization is discriminating between your personal and your professional values because objectivity is necessary if you are to be effective. Social workers should only assist clients in considering their alternatives and the subsequent consequences; they should not make clients' decisions for them. To accomplish this, both personal values and professional values must be clarified (see chapter 29).

For example, consider the issue of whether or not a couple should engage in sex if they are not married. Your personal opinion may be that sex outside of marriage is wrong. However, as sex outside of marriage is not illegal, your professional orientation toward clients should be that individuals must decide about such actions according to their own values. You can probably think of other examples of areas of conflict between personal values and professional objectivity.

Maintaining a Nonjudgmental Professional Approach

The fourth step in the desensitization process concerns the *application* of the first three steps to *maintain* a nonjudgmental professional approach. By accepting sexual issues objectively at face value, a social worker can help the client deal with those issues just like any others.

It is your responsibility to help clients reach their own decisions. Regardless of your personal opinion, your professional stance must be objective. For example, you may feel that an abortion would be a good choice of action for a client, while the client may feel that it is an inappropriate alternative. Your personal values must be clearly defined so that you can maintain professional objectivity. In this example, the client must be able to come to a personal decision regarding which alternative is best for her.

ACQUISITION OF KNOWLEDGE

The second part of the Desensitization Model is acquisition of knowledge. Acquiring accurate, specific information should be a lifelong commitment. A mass of current research dealing with sexual issues is available to social workers.[12] This information can be clustered into five major categories: anatomy and physiology; sexual behavior; sexual identity; special issues; and sexually oppressed groups. To intelligently discuss any aspect of sexuality, a basic knowledge of physiological structures and processes is absolutely necessary. Not only is a basic knowledge of anatomy important (we might call this the plumbing aspect of sexuality), we must also know the many facets of sexual response. It's important to know how the plumbing works, including physiological and psychological arousal or excitement, maintenance of an aroused state, and orgasm. Developing a lifetime perspective of sexual development and response is critical. Knowledge of normal sexual childhood behavior helps provide guidelines for parents. Knowledge of adolescent sexual development provides insights into, and understanding of, adolescent behavior. Information about adult sexual behavior helps adults have more objective and appropriate expectations concerning their own sexual behavior. Finally, a grasp of physiological changes and behavior in later adulthood helps people maintain optimal sexual interaction and satisfaction throughout life.

A second major category, sexual behavior, includes: love and interpersonal attraction; sexual dysfunction, sex counseling, and communication techniques; methods of birth control; and sexually transmitted diseases (STD). The latter is especially critical in view of the current AIDS (Acquired Immunodeficiency Syndrome) crisis. Each of these areas target issues and situations that often prove problematic for clients. Knowledge of research and available alternatives and choices in each area is necessary if you are to help clients make good choices about their sexual behavior.

A third important area of sexual knowledge involves gender identity. A gender role is

DISCRIMINATION:
THE IMPACTS OF HOMOPHOBIA

"Did you hear the one about the dyke who . . . "

"Harry sure has a 'swishy' way about him. You'd never catch me in the locker room alone with that guy."

"They're nothing but a bunch of lousy, Communist faggots."

Our common language is filled with derogatory terms referring to gay people. Just as other diverse groups are subject to arbitrary stereotypes and to discrimination, so are gay people. Because of negative attitudes and the resulting discriminatory behavior, alternatives for gay people are often different and limited. There are often other negative consequences. Other nonsexually related aspects of gay people's lives are affected because of their sexual preference.

For example, a male third-grade teacher may live in deathly fear that the parents of his students will discover he's living with another man. He loves his job, which he's had for nine years. If parents put pressure on the school administration about his homosexuality, he may get fired. He may never get another teaching job.

Another example is provided by a female college student who expends massive amounts of energy to disguise the fact that she's a lesbian. She attends a state university in a small, midwest, rural town. She is terribly lonely. She keeps hoping that that special someone will walk into her life. However, she doesn't dare let her friends know she's gay or she really will be isolated. There wouldn't be anyone to talk to or to have dinner with. They would just never understand. People have committed suicide for less.

Gay people are frequently the victims of homophobia. Homophobia is the irrational "hostility and fear that many people have towards homosexuality"[1] It is not clear how homophobia originated. Maier postulates that it may be people's attempts to deny homosexual feelings in themselves.[2] Perhaps the more strongly homophobic people are, the more they are working to deny such feelings in themselves. Regardless of the cause, the manifestations and symptoms of homophobia are all around us.

In the past homosexuality was considered an illness. Not until 1974 did the American Psychiatric Association remove it from the list of mental illnesses.

Whitman and Mathy potently describe the extent of homophobia: "Not only are homosexuals criminalized, victimized, and labeled pathological, they are also regarded by some religious groups as sinners deserving to be put to death, a view reminiscent of the Inquisition. . . . There are very few, if any, groups in American society which evoke more hostility than homosexuals."[3]

Today there are many indications of the general public's homophobia. In 1982 only 45 percent of all people felt that a homosexual relationship between consenting adults should be legalized.[4] In 1984, 73 percent of people surveyed said that sexual relations between two consenting adults of the same gender was wrong; this was decreased only a percentage point from 1973 when 74 percent of those surveyed said the same thing.[5]

Gay people are prohibited from joining the CIA, the FBI, or the armed forces.[6] The Roman Catholic church has decried homosexual behavior as sinful. In many Protestant churches (although not all denominations), gay people are not allowed to join the clergy. Gay people have been denied or lost jobs and housing purely on the basis of their sexual orientation. Violence against gay people has risen dramatically in the past few years.

A potentially serious negative effect is to internalize such negative attitudes. In other words, a gay person might think, "If being gay is bad, and I am gay, then that means that I am bad, too." Weinberg and Williams have found that only slightly more than one-tenth of all gay people feel that homosexuality is an illness.[7] However, 80 percent of lesbians and 77 percent of gay men expressed having fears of others finding out about their sexual preference.[8] The implication is that they fear negative consequences (such as job loss, exclusion from various opportunities, and social isolation) might occur.

(continued next page)

DISCRIMINATION:
THE IMPACTS OF HOMOPHOBIA *(con't.)*

1. W. H. Masters, V. E. Johnson, and R. C. Kolondny, *Human Sexuality*, 4th ed. (Glenview, Il.: Scott Foresman, 1988), p. 422.

2. R. A. Maier, *Human Sexuality in Perspective* (Chicago: Nelson-Hall, 1984).

3. F. L. Whitman and R. M. Mathy, *Male Homosexuality in Four Societies* (New York: Praeger, 1985), p. 180.

4. "Public Perceptions of Gays: Few Changes in Past Few Years", *Sexuality Today*, December 6, 1982, p. 1.

5. J. A. Davis and T. Smith, *General Social Surveys, 1972-1984: Cumulative Data* (New Haven, CT: Yale University, Rape Center for Public Opinion Research, 1984).

6. J. McCrary and J. Guiterrez, "The Homosexual Person in Military and in National Security Employment," *Journal of Homosexuality*, 5 (1,2) (1979/80): p. 115-46.

7. W. Weinberg and C. Williams, *Male Homosexuals: Their Problems and Adaptations* (New York: Oxford University Press, 1974).

8. K. Jay and A. Young, *The Gay Report* (New York: Summit Books, 1979)

"a set of norms, or culturally defined expectations, that define how people of one gender ought to behave."[13] Understanding gender roles involves unraveling the behavioral and attitudinal differences of women and men. It also involves confronting stereotypes and the resulting sexist prejudices.

Sexual orientation involves a knowledge base about heterosexuality, homosexuality, and bisexuality. It is difficult to specify exactly how many people are lesbian or gay. (The term "gay" usually is used to refer to a male homosexual person and "lesbian" to a female.). Estimates of people who are lesbian or gay range from less than one percent to almost 40 percent of people having at least one homosexual experience to orgasm in adulthood.[14] Part of the problem concerns the decision about whom to categorize as lesbian or gay and whom not. Indications are that many people have sexual experiences with people of the same gender.[15] Does one same-gender experience make one lesbian or gay? Do five? Or perhaps 25? Regardless, it is likely that you as a practitioner will be called upon to work with gay people. Better understanding of gay people and the gay world can only facilitate a practitioner's ability to work with and help gay clients.

The fourth important area of sexual knowledge, special issues, includes sex education and sexual coercion. The type of sex information that is needed by people of various ages and the manner in which it is best conveyed are ongoing issues. Everyone needs some type of sexual information in order to make sexual decisions. This sounds simple, but historically, dissemination of sex information has been an issue that has elicited major controversy. People opposed to sex education maintain that talking about sex to children encourages them to participate in sexual activities. Research has proven this assumption to be false,[16] but the controversy still rages.

Sexual coercion is included as a special issue because of its common place occurrence and its tragic impact on people. Subtopics include sexual assault, abuse of children, and sexual harassment. Knowledge of what perpetrators are like, effects on victims, and situations in which sexual coercion occurs is needed by practitioners so that they can encourage prevention, help victims cope, and work with offenders.

The final major area of knowledge important for practitioners concerns sexually oppressed populations. These are groups of people who are socially or culturally denied the opportunity to experience and enjoy their sexuality, or who are unfairly inhibited by others concerning sexual expression. Gochros, Gochros, and Fischer discuss the situations of various oppressed groups, including persons with a developmental disability, persons with a physical disability, the elderly, and the unattractive.[17] An underlying assumption for practitioners is that it is each individual's right regardless of the situation to make her or his own choice regarding sexual behavior as long as it does not violate another person's personal rights.

Since most social workers will not specialize in the area of sexuality, it is unreasonable to feel that it's necessary to know everything. In sex education, a comfortable attitude when conveying the information is just as important as the amount of information provided.[18] Social workers must be aware of their limitations; they can provide only the information they already have and should be honest about what they don't know. At times it is desirable to refer clients to experts or organizations where their questions can be more fully answered. No one can be expected to know everything about sexuality.

Sex Education

A heated controversy often develops over the issue of providing teens with information about sex. This is true even in the age of AIDS (Acquired Immunodeficiency Syndrome).[19] The fear is that giving adolescents information about sexuality will encourage them to start experimenting sexually. An underlying assumption is that adolescents won't think about sex or be interested in it unless someone around them brings up the subject.

Two fallacies can be pointed out in this approach. First, it assumes that adolescents have little or no access to sexual information other than that which adults around them choose to give. Hunt did an extensive study of sexual attitudes and behavior by surveying 982 males and 1,044 females.[20] He found that 59 percent of the males and 46 percent of the females felt that they had obtained most of their sexual information from friends. An additional 20 percent of the males and 22 percent of the females gave reading material as their primary source of information. The fact that friends are the primary source of sex information for young people has been supported by other research.[21]

Obviously, adolescents are functioning within a complex environment which exposes them to many new things and ideas. They are not locked up in a sterile cage. A tremendous emphasis is placed on sexuality and sexual behavior by the media; television, magazines, newspapers, and books are filled with sexual episodes and anecdotes. Adolescents have numerous exposures to the concept of sex.

A second fallacy is that adolescents will automatically try anything they hear about. If a parent tells a young person that some people are murderers, will the young person automatically go out and try murdering someone? Of course not. Although adults, especially parents, might wish they had such control over adolescents, they do not.

Perhaps an analogy concerning sex education could be made to the situation of buying a used Chevy van. An analogous assumption would be that it would be better to have no information about how the van works prior to buying it and hope for the best. This is ludicrous. In this situation, you would want as much information as possible to make the best decision about whether to buy the van or not. It would behoove you to take the van to your favorite mechanic to have it thoroughly evaluated. You would both need and want information. People, including adolescents, need as much information as possible in order to make responsible decisions about their own sexual behavior and avoid ignorant mistakes. It is illogical to deprive them of information and have them act on the basis of hearsay and chance.

The primary source of information about sex is friends, and yet friends probably don't know much more about sex than they do. Information that is available is likely to be vague and inaccurate. Just because adolescents use sexual terms does not mean they are very knowledgeable about sexuality. Often these words refer to genital or sexually related body parts. Frequently these terms are vulgar and shocking.

Another aspect of the sex education controversy is the idea that sex education should be provided by parents in the home. This is a virtuous idea. However, on closer scrutiny some problems are evident. Hass found that approximately two-thirds of both male and female adolescents felt that they were not able to talk about sexuality with their parents.[22] Libby and Nass examined the reactions of parents to adolescent sexual activity.[23] They discovered a tendency for parents to issue orders rather than discuss sexual issues with their children. The following statements were typical of the type of comments made by parents: "I try to keep them from knowing too much"; "I think sex education corrupts the minds of fifteen- or sixteen-year-olds"; "My parents didn't tell me about it. I don't discuss it either"; "Kids know too much already" (p. 230). Needless to say, these statements reflect a negative attitude concerning talking about sex. An implication is that it's easier to avoid the whole issue. This approach interferes with open, honest communication about sex between parents and child.

One Cleveland study examined the attitudes of 1,400 parents toward sex education. Most parents thought it was a good idea for their children to learn about sexuality and reproduction before they became adolescents. However, only 8 percent of the fathers studied and fewer than 15 percent of the mothers said that they were comfortable enough or knowledgeable enough to talk about sexual intercourse with their children.[24]

Public opinion polls over the past fifteen years indicate that 80 to 86 percent of adults in America support the provision of sex education in schools.[25] Additionally, when sex education is made available, only 5 percent of parents refuse to allow their children to participate.[26] Sex educators do not want to take the parents' place as sex educators.[27] Rather, they want to ensure that children have adequate and accurate information about sex. Many times parents are uncomfortable or embarrassed talking about sex with their children. Often they feel they don't know enough of the specifics to intelligently educate a child. One student shared her eight-year-old son's reaction to her own discomfort in talking to him about sex. As she was trying to explain to him some of the basics of human reproduction, he put his hand on her arm and said, "it's okay, Mom, I get the general idea."

With the extensive publicity given to AIDS in the past few years, more schools have opted to provide sex education programs. Gordon asserts that "perhaps 10 percent of American children are exposed to anything approaching a legitimate sex education program."[28] However, there is a wide range of course content which can be included in a sex education curriculum. A sex education course can focus only on physical content. Specific topics such as birth control may or may not be covered. Community, parental and moral values may or may not be integrated into the curriculum. Masters, Johnson, and Kolodny urge that "sex education should cover the problems surrounding sexuality, but it should also discuss such aspects of sex as love, intimacy, and interpersonal responsibility."[29]

There has been increasing support that sex education can both increase the amount of information teenagers have about sexuality and alter their sexual behavior.[30]

For example, a Johns Hopkins University study of students in an inner-city senior high school found that providing an extensive sex education curriculum in addition to furnishing free contraception and birth control counseling resulted in 30 percent fewer pregnancies; additionally, girls chose to postpone having sexual relations for significantly longer periods of time.[31]

Other research supports the relationship between sex education programs and decreased pregnancy rates.[32] Significant decreases in the incidence of sexually transmitted diseases such as gonorrhea has also been clearly linked to the provision of good sex education programs in schools.[33]

It is each individual's responsibility and our professional aim as social workers to assist people in making the best choices possible in their unique situations. The choice to become sexually active also has potential positive and negative consequences. Positively, one can potentially gain warmth, love, and physical enjoyment from sexual activity. Negatively, however, one can either procreate an unwanted pregnancy or contract a sexually transmitted disease.

Sex Education in the Age of AIDS

When AIDS was identified in the early 1980s, the two highest risk groups in the United States were intravenous drug users and gay or bisexual men.[34] However, now the spread of infection in the general heterosexual population is growing at a faster rate than in these initial high-risk groups. AIDS transmission through heterosexual sexual activity is significant. The number of adolescent cases identified doubles every fourteen months.[35] Additionally, the Centers for Disease Control report that 21 percent of all AIDS cases identified are people in the twenty to twenty-nine-year-old age group.[36] Because it often takes a period of up to ten years to exhibit any symptoms of AIDS, many of these young adults probably contracted the disease during their adolescent years.

AIDS merits intense concern when talking about sex education with adolescents and young adults. In the 1980s, it was established that adolescents generally had inadequate information about AIDS and that they did not feel they were vulnerable to contracting the disease.[37] Likewise, adolescents tended not to use protection when engaging in high-risk behaviors.[38]

It appears that adolescents today are better informed about the prevention and contraction of AIDS than in years past.[39] In view of the extensive publicity given to AIDS, many more schools have opted to develop or intensify their sex education programs. However, serious gaps in education still exist. One study found that over half of entering freshman felt they were at less risk of contracting AIDS than other people.[40]

Another interesting finding is that young people who had AIDS education in high school are no more knowledgeable than those who did not.[41] There is also some indication that Hispanic students are less knowledgeable about AIDS than either African-American or white students; to some extent, this might be due to a language barrier.[42]

Fielstein, Fielstein, and Hazelwood studied 175 new college freshman.[43] They found

SUGGESTIONS FOR COUNSELING RAPE VICTIMS

Three basic issues are involved in working with a victim of rape. First, she is most likely in a state of emotional upheaval. Her self-concept is probably seriously shaken. Various suggestions for helping a rape victim in such a traumatic emotional state will be provided. Second, the rape victim must decide whether to call the police and press charges. Third, the rape victim must assess her medical status following the rape, for example, injuries or potential pregnancy.

EMOTIONAL ISSUES

Collier suggests that counseling victims of rape involves three major stages.[1] First, the counselor or social worker needs to provide the victim with immediate warmth and support. The victim needs to feel safe; she needs to feel free to talk. She needs to ventilate and acknowledge her feelings before she can begin to deal with them. To the extent possible, the victim should be made to feel she is now in control of her situation. She should not be pressured to talk, but rather encouraged to share her feelings.

Although it is important for the victim to talk freely, it is also important that she not be grilled with intimate, detailed questions. She will have to deal with those enough if she reports the incident to the police.

Frequently, the victim will dwell on what she could have or should have done. It is helpful to emphasize what she did right. After all, she is alive, safe, and physically not severely harmed. She managed to survive a terrifying and dangerous experience. It is also helpful to talk about how she reacted normally, as anyone else in her situation would most probably have reacted. This does not mean minimizing the incident. It does mean objectively talking about how traumatizing and potentially dangerous the incident was. One other helpful suggestion for dealing with a rape victim is to help her place the blame where it belongs, namely on the rapist. He chose to rape her. It was not her doing. Research bears out the fact that the majority of rapes have absolutely nothing to do with the behavior of the victim.[2]

The second stage of counseling, according to Collier, involves creating support from others.[3] This support may include that of professional resources (such as local rape crisis centers) as well as support from people who are emotionally close to the victim. Sometimes those close to the victim need to be educated. They need to find out that what the victim needs is warmth and support, and to feel loved. Questions which emphasize her feelings of self-blame such as why she didn't fight back or why she was wearing a low-cut blouse should be completely avoided.

Collier's third stage of counseling involves rebuilding the victim's trust in herself, in the environment around her, and in her other personal relationships.[4] Rape weakens a woman. It destroys her trust in herself and in others. This stage of counseling needs to focus on the victim's objective evaluation of herself and her situation. Her strong points need to be clarified and emphasized so that she may gain confidence in herself.

The victim also needs to look objectively at her surrounding environment. She cannot remain cooped up in her apartment for the rest of her life. It is impractical and unfair. She can take precautions against being raped, but needs to continue living a normal life.

Finally, the victim needs to assess her other personal relationships objectively. Just because she was intimately violated by one aggressor, this has nothing to do with the other people in her life. She needs to concentrate on the positive aspects of her other relationships. She must not allow the fear and terror she experienced during that one unfortunate incident to color and taint other relationships. She must clearly distinguish the rape from her other relationships in her mind.

A raped woman may initially want to talk with another woman. However, it might also be important to talk to men, including those close to her. It is important for the victim to realize that not all men are rapists. Sometimes there is a male partner. His willingness to let the victim express her feelings, and in return offer support and empathy, is probably the most beneficial thing that can be done for the victim.[5]

REPORTING TO THE POLICE

The initial reaction to being raped might be to call the police and relate the incident. However, many victims choose not to do this. Masters and Johnson list numerous reasons why this is so.[6] Included are fear that the rapist will try to get revenge, fear of public embarrassment and derogation, an attitude that it won't matter anyway because most rapists get off free, and fear of the legal process and questioning. It's financially expensive and emotionally draining to take a rape case to court.[7] In reality, even when they are persistent, women have found it difficult to have rapists prosecuted. In many cases, as we've already discussed, police determine that the case is unfounded. In cases where police do believe that a rape occurred, only half of the alleged rapists are apprehended and arrested.[8] Even fewer of these are actually convicted.

Some positive changes are occurring in police investigation of rape cases[9] and in legal handling.[10] Many police departments are trying to deal with rape victims more sensitively. Some departments in larger cities have special teams trained specifically for dealing with rape victims. In many states information about the victim's past sexual history is no longer permissible for use in court. When such information is introduced, it can serve to humiliate and discredit the victim. Some states have more progressive laws. Wisconsin,[11] for example, has established four degrees of sexual assault in addition to forbidding the use of the victim's past sexual conduct in court. According to Wisconsin law the severity of the crime and the corresponding severity of punishment is based on the amount of force used by the rapist and on the amount of harm done to the victim. A wife is also able to prosecute her husband for sexual assault when sexual relations are forced on her.

Despite the potential difficulties in reporting a rape, the fact remains that if the victim does not report it, the rapist will not be held responsible for his actions. A rape victim needs to think through the various alternatives that are open to her and weigh their respective positive and negative consequences in order to come to this often difficult decision.

In the event that a victim decides to report, she should not take a shower. Washing will remove vital evidence. However, victims often feel defiled and dirty, and it is a logical initial reaction for them to want to cleanse themselves and try to forget that the incident ever occurred. In counseling situations, it's important to emphasize the reason for not washing immediately.

Reporting a rape should be done within forty-eight hours at the absolute longest. The sooner the rape is reported and the evidence gathered, the better the chance of being able to get a conviction.

MEDICAL STATUS OF THE VICTIM

A third major issue that rape victims need to address is their medical status following the assault. At some point the victim needs to attend to the possibility of pregnancy. She should be asked about this issue at an appropriate time and in a gentle manner. She should be encouraged to seek medical help both for this possibility and for screening sexually transmitted diseases. The negative possibilities should not be emphasized. However, the victim needs to attend to these issues at some point. And the victim should, of course, be urged to seek immediate medical care for any physical injury.

1. Helen V. Collier, *Counseling Women* (New York: Free Press, 1982).

2. M. Amir, "Forcible Rape," *Federal Probation*, 31 (1) (1967): 51.

3. Collier, *Counseling Women*.

4. Ibid.

5. W. H. Masters, V. E. Johnson, and R. C. Kolodny, *Human Sexuality*, 3d ed. (Boston: Little, Brown, 1985), pp. 474–75.

6. Ibid, p. 470.

7. Dianne Herman, "The Rape Culture," in Jo Freeman (Ed.), *Women: A Feminist Perspective* (Palo Alto, CA: Mayfield, 1984), pp. 20–38.

8. Ibid., p. 32.

9. J. Moody and V. Hayes, "Responsible Reporting: The Initial Step," in C. Warner (Ed.), *Rape and Sexual Assault* (Germantown, MD: Aspen Systems, 1980), pp. 214–30.

10. M. Lasater, "Sexual Assault: The Legal Framework," in C. Warner (Ed.), *Rape and Sexual Assault* (Germantown, MD: Aspen Systems, 1980), pp. 231–64.

11. See Wisconsin State Statute 940.225.

that most of the freshmen had gotten the bulk of their information about AIDS from the media. The students were able to answer questions about AIDS transmission and prevention correctly 90 percent of the time. However, between 12 and 20 percent of the freshmen harbored some significantly inaccurate perceptions. For example, they did not understand the high risks involved in such behaviors as anal intercourse (penetration by one person's penis of another person's anus). They also perceived certain behaviors as being high risk that really were not. For example, a number of young people thought that homosexual behavior, donating blood, and sharing drinking cups put people at high risk of contracting AIDS. Similarly, Adame, Taylor-Nicholson, Wang, and Abbas found that 17 percent of college freshmen interviewed thought that kissing was dangerous and 27 percent felt that sharing combs and toothbrushes were high-risk behaviors.[44]

Almost all of the research discussed here examines the attitudes and knowledge base of *college students*. We do not know about the attitudes and knowledge base of adolescents who do not go to college. It might be argued that they have even less access to information about AIDS than their college-bound peers. Thus, there continues to be a great need to improve the quality of AIDS education. The U.S. Department of Health and Education makes the following recommendations for selecting material to use in educational programming about AIDS:[45]

1. Teach about high-risk behaviors. Because of their high rates of sexual activity, adolescents should know specifically which behaviors are the most dangerous and which are the safest. They should be taught and encouraged to take responsibility for their own safety. For instance, using condoms during sexual intercourse makes transmission of contaminated body fluids less likely, although avoidance of intercourse is the safest course of all. Likewise, young people should be aware of the dangers of sharing needles when using illicit drugs.

2. Present the facts in a straightforward manner. The facts about AIDS, its transmission, and its prevention should be taught honestly and directly. This is true even when talking about explicit sexual behavior and condom use. Responsible behavior should be clearly defined in adolescents' minds. It is important that AIDS educators themselves be comfortable in talking about these potentially anxiety-producing topics.

3. Convey values about responsibility and respect for oneself and for the well-being of others. The importance of values should be emphasized throughout AIDS education. Behaviors can be discussed within the context of evaluating alternatives. For example, adolescents can be helped to evaluate the potential positive and negative consequences of sexual behavior and drug use. They can be encouraged to establish a firm set of values regarding what they feel is right and wrong. One focus involves enhancement of their own self-esteem. They have the right to control their behavior and not be subject to the oppressive pressure of peers. They can also be helped to examine the consequences of their own behavior upon others.

4. Select appropriate materials. Depending on the age level, children and adolescents need access to different types of information. For example, in kindergarten through third grade, the "primary goal is to allay children's fears of AIDS and to establish a foundation for more detailed discussion of sexuality and health [later] at [the] sixth grade level" of AIDS education.[46]

   In grades four and five, the thrust should be similar to that used earlier, but with "increased emphasis on acknowledging that bodies have natural sexual feelings [and] helping children examine and affirm their own and their families' values."[47] Finally, in grades six through twelve, "the primary goal should be to teach students to protect themselves and others from infection with the AIDS virus."[48] It is beyond the scope of this text to detail an entire AIDS or sex education curriculum. However, there are numerous excellent curriculum development aids available.

5. Promote parental involvement. AIDS education addresses a broad range of sensitive topics. Parents should be integrally involved in planning and developing the curriculum. They should be fully aware of what and how content will be presented. For instance, one means of soliciting parental involvement is to form a task force including both parents and educators. Subsequently, other parents can be invited to attend previews of the proposed educational programming prior to presenting it to students.

DEVELOPMENT OF PROFESSIONAL SKILLS

The model's third part involves skills. Only after social workers are desensitized and have some knowledge of sexuality can they be helpful in counseling situations. This is where their professional skills are applied. Social workers who feel comfortable with sexual issues and who have some level of information can apply their communication, decision-making, and problem-solving skills to help clients deal with sexual issues.

Helping people address sexual issues is just like helping them with any other kind of life issue. Many of the identical skills are used. However, since sexuality tends to elicit more anxiety than other issues, the counselor must be desensitized before effectively applying counseling skills. The client most likely will also be feeling some level of anxiety about the sexual issue. A social worker needs to calmly set the stage for a frank, nonjudgmental discussion.

The principles presented here focus on the process of desensitization. After professionals become comfortable with the topic of sexuality, it is relatively easy to acquire information from books, the media, and academic courses. Basic professional skills can be applied here as in any other area, but desensitization must be accomplished first.

GROUP EXERCISES

Exercise A: A Sexual Question

Goals: To examine a sexual issue and express perceptions. A group consensus will be synthesized.

Note: It is advised that the instructor be the designated leader for the exercises in this chapter as they may generate strong emotional responses in participants.

Step 1. The larger group breaks down into small groups of four to six. (Allow students to form their own groups.)

Step 2. All the groups are given one specific question to discuss and answer. (All the groups have the same question.) It's helpful to write the question on the board, or provide some other visual means for focusing on the question. It is important that all group members participate in the discussion and share their answers. This encourages even the less verbal members to participate. Each group designates one person to share group responses with the entire class. Examples of questions might be:

1. Should sex education be required in all grade and junior high schools?
2. Should homosexuals be allowed to marry and adopt children?
3. Can humans be fully satisfied sexually by having only one (and the same) sexual partner throughout their life?
4. Is the explicit approach to sexuality via the media a healthful approach?
5. Should people with AIDS be allowed to continue going to school and work?

Step 3. Allow ten to fifteen minutes for the group discussion. Ask small groups to start closing their discussion approximately two minutes before you bring them back together into the larger group.

Step 4. Representatives of each group summarize their discussions.

Step 5. Finally, formulate a summary statement regarding the conclusions of the entire class.

Exercise B: Am I a Homosexual?

Goals: To question some basic assumptions and evaluate stereotypes about homosexuality and formulate some new ideas about what homosexuality is.

Step 1. The instructor reads the following three vignettes to the group:

I am a thirty-year-old female librarian. I love my work and consider myself a dedicated professional. I'm not really very attractive and am about twenty-five pounds overweight. I'm shy and really don't have many friends. I'm pretty lonely most of the time; I dated a man in college, but he dropped me to go out with somebody else. Otherwise, I really have never had any other boyfriends. A woman I work with has approached me about having a sexual relationship with her. I'm kind of afraid but I'm really considering getting involved with her. It sure gets lonely on Saturday nights. Am I a homosexual?

I am a thirty-year-old man. I've been in prison for six years now for murder. I'm serving a life sentence and really don't know if I'll ever get out on parole. I'm married and still love my wife. We had a good sexual relationship before I came to jail. Here, I've had hundreds of sexual relationships with men. I have to admit I do enjoy them and get sexual satisfaction out of them. Am I a homosexual?

I am a thirty-eight-year-old married man. My wife takes very good care of me sexually on a regular basis. I enjoy our sexual relationship very much. Whenever I have sex with her I like to fantasize about having sex with a man. I also like to watch male

542

wrestlers on television. It's sexually exciting to me. They really turn me on. Am I a homosexual?

Step 2. After each vignette, pause and wait for group members to respond. Allow as many group members to contribute as possible.

A period of several minutes of silence often follows the presentation of each vignette. It's important to remain patient during this time and wait until group members are ready to participate.

During the discussion following each vignette, group members may ask the group leader for the answer, but the leader should allow them to formulate their own conclusions.

Step 3. After group members have made their contributions, open up a general discussion concerning the difficulty in defining homosexuality and the many gradations of homosexual behavior which are possible.

There are several issues involved in the definition of homosexuality that may be discussed. These include sexual preference, situational availability of sex partners, and participation in actual homosexual behavior versus fantasizing about homosexual behavior.

Exercise C: Dirty Word Barrage

Goals: To verbally express anxiety-provoking terms within a nonthreatening atmosphere, recognize that the most commonly used sexually explicit terms are slang, examine reactions to such terms, and assess the usefulness of such reactions.

Note: It is suggested that any student who wishes to be exempted from this exercise be excused.

Step 1. The class is divided into two teams. Approximately the same number of persons should be in each group.

Step 2. Each team selects a team name. This encourages participation, enhances team spirit, and decreases the threatening atmosphere. Names may be as simple as "Team A" and "Team B," or as creative as "Passionate Desire" and "Earthy Lust." (One team once decided to call itself the "Nads," so it could cheer "Go Nads!")

Step 3. The instructor explains the rules to the teams. The first team will be given a term and then have two minutes to give synonyms for that term. Group members must call these synonyms out so they may be recorded. Then the second team will be given a different term for which it must give synonyms. Each team will be given two turns. The number of synonyms for each term will be counted. The total number will be the team's score. The team with the highest score after two turns wins. The following terms may be used: *breast, penis, intercourse, masturbation.* All the synonyms are written on the board so the teams can view and count them as they are shouted out.

Step 4. After the game is completed and the winning team declared, the class discusses the types of words commonly used to talk about sexuality. Most of the terms will probably be street slang. Discuss the importance of becoming aware of these terms and comfortable enough with them to communicate with clients.

Using street terms to refer to different aspects of sexuality often elicits a lot of giggling and discomfort. It's important for social workers to set aside personal values and deal with clients' issues in the clients' own language. Group members are often surprised at the number of street terms they know. This exercise makes them aware that so much of the terminology concerning sex is made up of off-color slang. The exercise illustrates how important it is to be desensitized to these words. These are the only terms that many of their clients will have available to them. Social workers must be able to understand them and feel comfortable enough with them to address these issues directly.

Exercise D: Talking Sex with Adolescents

Goals: To relate information about sexuality, formulate answers to questions in an innocuous simulated situation, recognize the difficulty of sharing sexual information clearly and simply, and examine one's ability to do so.

Note: In this exercise, the group leader or instructor role plays an adolescent and asks the entire group to respond to questions.

Step 1. The instructor explains that he or she will role play a fifteen-year-old adolescent who will be asking the group various questions about sex.

Step 2. Questions asked may include the following:

1. Should I be a virgin when I get married?
2. Can boys pull out in time?
3. What does an orgasm feel like?

Step 3. The instructor responds to group members' answers as an adolescent might, and often asks the group members for clarification. Group members' words should be clear and simple. Their explanations should be specific.

Step 4. The role play is ended and the group members discuss their reactions to the experience.

Frequently, group members will find that it is very difficult to convey specific sexual information to someone who is not articulate. In addition to identifying their own discomfort in talking about sexuality, they often must struggle to communicate the information. Their terms may be too scientifically oriented. They often find it difficult to translate scientific terms into common language.

Discussion topics may include the identification of discomfort when talking about sexuality, the difficulty in communicating the specific meanings of sexual terms, and the importance of listening to clients and directing attention to their level of understanding.

Exercise E: Who Is Sexually Oppressed?

Goals: To explain the meaning of sexual oppression, identify groups of people who are sexually oppressed, examine perceptions of these groups, and assess the fairness of these perceptions.

Step 1. The instructor defines sexual oppression for the group. The definition might include those persons society does not allow to express and enjoy their sexuality to the fullest extent possible.

Step 2. Group members are asked to think for a moment and then name groups that they feel are sexually oppressed. These groups are listed on the blackboard as they are called out.

Step 3. Each student goes to the blackboard and places a tally mark under the group that he or she feels is the most sexually oppressed. (Often group members will ask if they can choose two sexually oppressed groups, but it's important that they choose only one. This encourages them to consider more carefully the reasons for their decision.) Sexually oppressed groups mentioned might include persons with a physical disability, the institutionalized, the elderly, gay people, men, women, teenagers, and persons with a developmental disability.

Step 4. Group members discuss why they chose the groups they did and compare these reasons.

Discussion frequently focuses on specific limitations imposed on the various groups. Group members become more aware of the sexual needs of people in general by focusing on the social and sexual restrictions imposed on people because of their situations. The discussion should question the fairness of these restrictions and enable group members to assess their own attitudes.

CHAPTER THIRTY-ONE

IMPROVING INTERPERSONAL RELATIONSHIPS

Goal: Does an individual fall in love, or can a lasting relationship be formed in a rational manner? This chapter identifies the differences between romantic and rational love, describes methods of analyzing and improving close relationships, and presents an overview of sociometry.

Achieving a gratifying, lasting love relationship is one of almost every human beings' paramount goals. The experience of feeling in love is exciting, adds meaning to living, and psychologically gives us feelings of well-being and happiness. Unfortunately, few people are able to maintain a long-term love relationship. Instead, they encounter such problems as falling in love with someone who does not love them, falling out of love after an initial stage of infatuation, being highly possessive, and having substantial conflicts because of differing expectations about their relationship. Failures in love relationships are more often the rule than the exception and result in unhappy marriages, divorce, depression, guilt, suicide, sexual dysfunctions, unwanted pregnancies, and extramarital affairs—difficulties often brought out at group sessions.

ROMANTIC LOVE AND RATIONAL LOVE

Many people view love as a feeling over which they have no control. A number of common phrases, such as "I fell in love," "It was love at first sight," "I just couldn't help it," and "He swept me off my feet," imply that attitude. In reality, love is primarily based on our self-talk (that is, what we tell ourselves) about a person we meet. This principle is illustrated by the following example. A young life insurance executive, a recent college graduate, is highly motivated to rise in the corporate hierarchy. He believes having an attractive, sophisticated wife would be beneficial. He is also tired of remaining single and wants to begin raising a family. His favorite hobby is golf. His ideal conception of a date is someone who is attractive, intelligent, has a slender figure, is charming, has blonde hair, and is somewhat shorter than he is (he's 5 feet, 8 inches). He then meets a 5-foot, 6-inch, well-educated young woman with blonde hair, a slim figure, who is also charming, gracious, and plays golf. He immediately tells himself, "She's fantastic, the kind of woman I would consider marrying. I hope she's single and not dating anyone, 'cause I'm going to ask her out for dinner. I've got to get to know her better!"

Romantic love is often based on self-talk that stems from intense, unsatisfied desires rather than on rational thinking. Extreme sexual frustration, intense loneliness, parental and personal problems, and desires for security or protection are often at the bottom of a person's search for the "perfect mate." A primary characteristic of romantic love is that the lovers tend to idealize each other. Because both people are ready for love and attention, each attributes to the other qualities that he or she wants in a lover that the other may actually not possess. This aspect of romantic love can be diagrammed as follows:

Event: Meeting or becoming acquainted with a person who has some (a few) of the overt characteristics you admire in a lover.

↓

Self-Talk: *This person is attractive, personable, and has all of the qualities I admire in a lover/mate.*

↓

Emotion: Intense infatuation and romantic love.

A second characteristic of romantic love is that it thrives on a certain amount of distance. The more forbidden the love, the stronger it becomes; the more social mores are threatened, the stronger the feeling. For example, couples who live together and then later marry often report living together was more exciting and romantic. The more the effort necessary to be with each other (traveling great distances, for example), the more intense the romance. The greater the frustration (loneliness or sexual needs), the more intense the romance.

The irony of romantic love is that if an ongoing relationship is achieved, the romance usually withers. Through sustained contact the person in love gradually comes to realize what his or her idealized lover is really like—simply another human being with certain strengths and limitations. When this occurs the romantic love relationship either turns into a rational, mature love relationship, or the relationship develops significant conflicts and dissatisfactions and ends in a broken romance. For people with intense unmet desires, ending the relationship is the more likely result.

Romantic love tends to be of temporary duration and based on make-believe, since an idealized person is "loved" rather than a real person. Rational love, in contrast, can be diagrammed as follows:

Event: While being aware and comfortable about your own needs, goals, identity, and desires, you become well acquainted with someone who fulfills to a fair extent the characteristics you desire in a lover/spouse.

Self-talk: *This person has many of the qualities and attributes I seek in a lover/spouse. I admire this person's strengths, and am aware and accepting of his or her shortcomings.*

Emotion: Rational love.

In a rational love relationship, an individual is clear and comfortable about his or her desires, identity, and goals in life and knows the other person well. The loved one's strengths and shorcomings have been accurately and objectively assessed and accepted. Because it is consistent with their short- and long-term goals, the lovers' self-talk is realistic and rational and not based on fantasy or excessive desires. Communication is open and honest so that problems can be dealt with when they arise and the relationship can grow and develop. Each partner is able to give and receive in the relationship, be kind, show affection, know and do what pleases the other person, and communicate openly and warmly.

Because love is based on self-talk (which causes feelings), individuals create love, and, theoretically, can love anyone by changing their self-talk. In addition, the quality of the relationship can be gauged by analyzing a person's self-talk to determine the nature of the attraction and the extent to which the person's self-talk is rational and in his or her best interests. An excellent indicator of how your love relationship with someone new is apt to proceed is to *objectively* examine the patterns of that person's past relationships. People tend to repeat past patterns in new relationships.

The Pitfalls of Romantic Love

Romance feels good. It gives people a "high" that may be compared to other kinds of highs: success at athletic competition, watching an inspiring film, listening to music, intense involvement in rewarding hobbies, gratifying work, accomplishments, alcohol, and drugs—all of which may be addictive. Joggers can become addicted to running, and there is nothing wrong with that. If, however, one becomes addicted to sexual, romantic exhilaration, and that's *all* one wants, life is likely to be lonely and tragic. Someone who is addicted to romantic highs is not apt to work on preserving a relationship once the romance begins to wither. Instead, that person is likely to seek a new partner to start another romantic relationship in order to again experience a romantic high. The result is a series of affairs—each affair ending with intense hurt feelings. In addition, long periods of loneliness are likely to occur between relationships.

The exhilarations of romance are equalled by the traumas connected with romantic breakups. The higher the ball bounces, the harder it hits when it falls. When a romance withers, many people blame their partners for not making them happy, get into serious disagreements, and may search for someone else. In reality, others don't make us happy or sad; we determine our feelings by self-talk or perspective of the situation.

Possessiveness is another aspect of many romantic love relationships. In a possessive relationship one partner attempts to control and train the other partner—through preaching, complaining, pleading, yelling, withholding affection, and encouraging guilt—to behave in a way that fulfills his or her own "ideal" of a relationship. Practically no one likes to feel possessed and controlled in a relationship because it is stifling. A partner who perceives he or she is being possessed will often become angry and resentful.

For most of us, life follows a constant and predictable course with only occasional highs and lows. Unfortunately, many of us have been socialized to believe we should *always* be happy, and this can cause problems. Most people want the security of a one-to-one intimate relationship. There is too much emotional trauma, jealousy, and anger involved to have sexual relationships with several people. What's more, serious dating of two or more people becomes too much of a hassle. So, if a person is dating several people, there are strong pulls to move toward dating just one. After a while, dating just one person tends to become monotonous. The partner becomes predictable, and the flame of romantic love dies. Some people attempt to end the monotony by searching for other sexual relationships. The original partner often discovers the affairs, and there is a great deal of anger, shouting, hurt feelings, and maybe a permanent breakup of the relationship.

The Rewards of Rational Love

On the other hand, some individuals become comfortable with a one-to-one relationship after the romance fades, and Sheri Tepper describes this kind of relationship.

> Most people have a middle-of-the-road kind of life which is *Comfortable*.
>
> *Comfortable* is reading in front of the fire, or snuggling into clean sheets, or having comfortable sex, or good food when you're hungry (not too hungry), or a tall glass of cold water when you're thirsty. Comfortable is walking under the tree and listening to the birds. It's forgetting you exist while you're working on something that interests you. It's normal-in-the-middleness. It's hugging a friend, or talking to a child, or digging in the garden. It's just life going on, the way life has gone on since the cave men. Comfortable.[1]

The way to maintain a comfortable relationship is to work on it. Working on a relationship includes open and honest communication and self-disclosure. It involves doing new and exciting things you and your partner enjoy: traveling, sitting by a fireplace, taking a walk, tennis, golf, sky-diving, fishing, going to football games or concerts, dining out, having hamburgers by candlelight, taking a bath together while sipping wine, water-skiing, going to workshops, rollerskating, and so on.

Stages in a Relationship

Leslie Cameron-Bandler has developed the following framework of stages in a relationship.[2]

1. *Attraction/Infatuation.* All of us have in our heads a picture of our ideal date or mate. This picture may include a variety of characteristics about such items as: physical appearance, color of hair, color of eyes, age, height, weight, personality, hobbies, personal interests, religion, musical interests, sports, education, career interests, family background, financial security, and sexual values and interests. Such pictures vary from person to person. When we meet someone who comes close to having the characteristics we desire, we tell ourselves that this is an "ideal" potential partner. We feel strongly attracted to the person and are in a stage of infatuation. After a few dates, the infatuation may intensify. Cameron-Bandler notes this is "a fun time, full of intensity and excitement and romance."[3]

2. *Appreciation.* In this stage the two persons are a couple who are seriously dating, living together, or even married. They are delighted to be together. They focus on the positive qualities of each other. They appreciate each other, rather than taking one another for granted. Cameron-Bandler notes:

   > This phase can be based on a wide range of illusion or varying degrees of knowledgeable understanding of each other's wants and needs. The extent to which it is based on knowledgeable understanding is the extent to which it can be depended upon to last.[4]

   There are three basic elements for achieving and maintaining appreciation in a relationship. First, each partner has to know what he or she needs and wants in a relationship. Second, each partner must know what specifically fulfills these needs and wants. Third, each person must be able to elicit these fulfilling behaviors, lovingly, from his or her partner.

3. *Habituation.* Habituation is the stage of becoming accustomed to something. It involves being comfortable and secure with dependability and familiarity. For people who seek security, habituation is viewed as equalling safety and commitment. However, for people seeking adventure, habituation can be viewed as equalling boredom. Cameron-Bandler notes, "The phases of habituation can be a very positive one, provided it cycles back to appreciation and includes an occasional trip back to attraction."[5]

   Partners in this stage of a relationship are advised to engage in old and new activities that they enjoy. One suggestion is for the partners to commit two weekends each year for enhancing the relationship. The partners first agree on how much money will be spent for each weekend. Then one of the partners arranges the activities that are designed to meet his or her fantasies of how he or she wants to spend time with the partner. The next weekend the other partner similarly arranges for his or her fan-

550

tasy weekend. Among other benefits, these weekends serve as a learning experience for each partner as to the other's previously unexpressed or newly formed desires.

4. *Expectation.* Cameron-Bandler notes, "The difference between duty and pleasure often rears its ugly head in the phase of expectation."[6] Many of the things one did that were appreciated by one's partner now become an expectation. For example, at first, A expressed intense appreciation when B shopped for groceries and cooked on certain evenings. Now these tasks have become expected duties and B receives frowns and criticisms when they aren't done. This stage in a relationship is usually signaled by more complaints than compliments. Each partner focuses on what the other is not doing, rather than on what he or she is doing to benefit the relationship. One way of seeking to halt further deterioration in a relationship when this stage is reached is an intervention in which each partner is encouraged to once again treat the other as a lover instead of as a spouse.

5. *Disappointment/Disillusionment.* Unless the couple works on their relationship, disappointment and disillusionment soon follow expectation. In this stage the partners become increasingly disappointed because each is failing to fulfill the other's expectations. In this stage partners are apt to say their mates have started some bad habits; however, closer investigation usually shows the mate had been engaging in the undesirable behavior all along. In this stage the partners still remember the past as being wonderful and want things to be "the way they used to be." A relationship at this stage can be improved by a mutual commitment from each partner to put forth efforts to elicit those fulfilling behaviors, lovingly, from his or her partner.

6. *Threshold/Perceptual Reorientation.* The threshold is reached when one or both partners decide the relationship is over. The partner reaching this stage has a memory change—from remembering past pleasurable experiences to remembering primarily past unpleasant memories. Such partners are no longer able to *feel* the good times, even when they think about earlier good times. Sometimes the threshold is reached by the occurrence of a minor event that, like the straw that broke the camel's back, leads a partner to conclude the relationship is over. The partner reaching this threshold has a perceptual reorientation of discounting the partner's positive qualities and instead seeks to find evidence in the partner's behaviors that warrant terminating the relationship.

7. *Verification.* In this stage the partner who has decided to end the relationship focuses on observing the other's behaviors and qualities to find evidence that warrants termination. Sometimes during this phase one or both partners experience the feeling that "I can't live with him/her and I can't live without him/her." Considerable emotional energy is generated by anyone with this feeling as such a person is under intense stress.

Usually one of the partners reaches this stage sooner than the other. One wants out, and the other seeks to maintain the relationship. The person seeking to maintain it may engage in a variety of behaviors such as seeking to please the partner in every way, attempting to make the other partner feel guilty, seeking to have a child in order to "lock" the partner into the relationship, flirting with others to make the partner jealous, and threatening suicide. Relationships at this stage are not fun. The partner who wants out has the most "power," as he or she decides whether the relationship continues or ends.

8. *Termination.* At this stage one or both partners decide to end the relationship. This stage is usually a painful experience for both. Property must be divided. Goodbyes are

said—sometimes with considerable anger and animosity. If there are children involved, custody and child support arrangements need to be worked out. If the couple is married, the legal divorce process must be gone through. In addition, each person has to work on forming a new life without the former partner.

Improving an Intimate Relationship

We often tend to treat strangers with more respect than the people close to us. If a stranger does something we dislike, we usually ignore it or politely express our concerns. But if someone we love does something we dislike, we are apt to criticize and attempt to "train" the partner to meet our expectations. A major suggestion for improving intimate relationships is to seek to treat a partner with the same kind of respect given to strangers. Here are a number of additional suggestions a social worker might offer to a couple that wants to improve their relationship:

1. Analyze the relationship to determine whether your attraction is based on an unrealistic idealization or on an objective assessment of your partner's strengths and shortcomings. Is your attraction realistic and rational, or is it based on fantasy and excessive desires?
2. To maintain a high-quality relationship, *both* need to continue to work on the relationship by seeking new and exciting things to do that *both* enjoy.
3. Try to establish a comfortable, rational relationship, which is much more lasting than romantic-high relationships.
4. Often, it's minor irritants that gradually turn a relationship sour. For example, you may not like your partner to leave hair in the bathroom sink, while your partner may not like you to leave dirty clothes on the bedroom floor. Communicate what irritates you in a nonblaming way and encourage your partner to communicate his or her concerns. Relationships work best when each partner communicates the irritants, and each partner then tries to avoid doing the things that irritate the other.
5. Try to communicate what you appreciate and enjoy about your partner. This includes aspects of your sexual relationship. For example, you may or may not like oral sex. Unless you communicate your preferences to your partner, she or he has no way of knowing. You can't expect your partner to be able to read your mind.
6. Do not stifle or possess your partner. If you feel your partner is too possessive of you, discuss it and work it out before such a high level of resentment builds up that you stop putting effort into making the relationship work.
7. Communicate honestly and openly in all areas so that problems can be dealt with then they arise.
8. Stop playing destructive games in a relationship (see chapter 19). Destructive games wear a relationship thin after awhile.
9. Try to grow as a person in the relationship. The more you seek to develop a positive self-identity, the better you will be able to develop a rational, comfortable, long-term relationship (see chapter 29). There is truth in the cliche, "Before you can love someone else, you must first love yourself." Also seek to facilitate the growth of your partner in a relationship.

10. Take a positive view of events that happen to you (see chapter 29). Both thinking positively and thinking negatively frequently become self-fulfilling prophecies. If you usually take a negative view, you will set up barriers between you and your partner because your partner will stop sharing things that she or he anticipates will upset you. The price your partner pays for honesty will be too high, which will force your partner to either lie or withhold information from you.

11. Instead of reacting nonassertively or aggressively to things that bother you, try to become more assertive (see chapter 22).

12. Try to become more attractive physically, perhaps through exercise, dieting, proper sleep, personal hygiene, grooming, and selection of clothes. If you feel good about yourself, others are going to be more attracted to you.

13. Show affection to your partner. We all need to feel loved. Unless you convey your affection, your partner will not know that it exists.

14. If your partner has a problem that she or he wants to share with you, use active listening to help the person talk it through (see chapter 7).

15. If you have a concern about something your partner is doing (or failing to do), express this concern with I-messages rather than you-messages (see chapter 7).

16 If you and your partner have a conflict, try to resolve it with the no-lose problem-solving approach rather than the win-lose approach (see chapter 9).

17. If there is a major conflict that your partner and you are unable to resolve, seek help from someone with expertise in this area, such as a professional counselor.

18. To receive in a relationship you must give. Relationships work only when both partners are givers *and* receivers.

19. Acknowledge your mistakes. Avoid blaming your partner for your errors. Also, avoid calling your partner derogatory names.

20. Develop and use humor. Look for humor in your life and develop the habit of being able to laugh at yourself.

21. Touch your partner in ways that are pleasing, and communicate to your partner how you like to be touched and held.

Improving Other Close Relationships

It's been said that we can tell who we are by looking at who our friends are. We tend to associate with people who are similar in a variety of ways: age, interests, values, and intellectual capacities. There is truth in the adage, "Birds of a feather flock together."

We have considerable control over who we form relationships with and the kinds of relationships that we form. We form relationships with a lot of people: parents, other relatives, close friends, friends of friends, fellow workers, to name only a few categories. In each of these relationships we have considerable control of the amount of time we spend with these people and what we will talk about and do when we are with them.

A few years ago a married female student said to me, "I really dread weekends. All we do is travel to my husband's parent's home and spend the whole weekend with them. I don't enjoy being with them, and I never get any studying done." I responded by saying, "Then why do you go?" I then pointed out that if she's unhappy there, her in-laws have probably noted that she's unhappy and perhaps aren't that interested in seeing her so often. She agreed. I responded by saying, "Quality of time spent together is more important than quantity of time." I indicated there are many ways of cutting down on the amount of time she spends with her in-laws. She could go every third or fourth weekend, while her husband goes every weekend. Perhaps her husband would be happy going less often also. Or, they could go for four or five hours rather than spending the entire weekend. She said, "I never thought of that." She discussed it with her husband, and they reached an agreement that he would go less often, and if she didn't have any studying to do she would go along.

If you have relationships with people you dislike, there are a variety of options open to you. You can structure the time so that you spend less time with them. You can suggest doing things you enjoy so that the time you spend together will be more enjoyable. If the relationship is really distasteful and you have tried everything you can think of to improve it, you might consider seeing the person so infrequently that the relationship gradually withers.

SOCIOMETRY

Sociometry is the study and measurement of interpersonal relationships in a group of people. Sociometry was developed by J. L. Morena in the late 1920s.[7] Moreno developed the technique to obtain information from each member about his or her interpersonal preferences (including attractions and repulsions) to other group members. A sociometric test provides information on the degree to which each member is accepted into the group by other members. Through determining which members each individual prefers to associate with (and avoid) the group leader (therapist, club president, teacher) can initiate steps to increase group cohesion, efficiency, and productivity.

Giving a Sociometric Test

The procedures for giving a sociometry test are as follows. The specific questions asked in a sociometric test should be tailored to the group. The questions that are asked should be consistent with the major themes, activities, or goals, of the group. The number of questions asked, and the phrasing of the questions, should be partially determined by the members' ages, responding capacities, and typical group activities. Typical questions asked for each member's attractions (and perhaps repulsions) focus on work, "play," and socio-emotional aspects of the group. For each question each member is asked to name a limited number of group members (often three) with whom he or she would prefer to share a specific activity. Sometimes questions are also asked to find out with whom each member would least prefer to share a specific activity. Frequently only three to five questions are needed to gather information on the interpersonal attractions and repulsions that exist within a group.

In most sociometric tests, questions are asked only to learn with whom each member would prefer to share specific activities. Usually no questions are needed about which members one would prefer not to share a specific activity with. As we will see later, the unpopular members can generally be identified by analyzing the data. Unpopular members are generally chosen by few (if any) members. It should be noted most members are more willing to identify whom they most want to share activities with than they are to identify the members with whom they least want to share activities because members fear their negative selections may not be kept confidential. The revealing of unpopular choices can intensify interpersonal conflict. (Somehow, the bad news of being someone's "last choice" tends to get back to the rejected member much more quickly than if he had been a first choice.)

Examples of sample questions asked in a sociometric test in a social work practice course are:

Work. Choose and rank the three students with whom you would most prefer to give a class presentation.

Play. Choose and rank the three students in this class with whom you would most want to attend a football game.

Social Activity. Identify and rank the three students in this class with whom you most enjoy conversing.

Emotional Support. Identify and rank the three students in this class whom you view as being the most caring and empathetic.

Generally, as the above questions illustrate, the members are asked to choose and also rank their selections.

Once the questions are written, the test may be administered to the group as a whole or to each member individually. In a group test, the answers should be written by each member. If given individually, the test can be administered orally or in written form. Some members may question why the test is being given. Therefore the specific purposes of the test should be stated, and the ways in which the results will be used should be carefully described. Generally, confidentiality of each member's responses should be assured and carefully adhered to. If a member does not have preferences for some questions the test giver should not force an answer where none may exist. Sociometric tests can be administered in groups having members as few as three and as many as thirty to thirty-five members.

Analyzing the Results

A hypothetical example will be used to illustrate how the results can be analyzed. Assume a social work practice class having ten students is asked the following three questions: "Of all the students in this class, give your first, second, and third choices of whom you would most like to: (1) give a class presentation with, (2) converse with during leisure time, and (3) study together with for the next exam in this class."

After the test is administered, the next step is to analyze the results. A useful approach is to plot the results on a summary grid similar to the one in figure 31.1. The names of members should be listed alphabetically. Begin with the first member and list her or his choices for the three questions—placing a 1, 2, or 3 to indicate, first, second, or third choice for each question. A zero is placed for any one who is not selected at all. For example, Anacker's choices for the three questions are as follows:

Anacker's Choices

Question Number

Member	(1)	(2)	(3)
Chan	2	1	3
Feavel	0	0	0
Geho	0	0	0
Kalve	1	3	0
Leitl	0	0	0
Neitzel	0	0	0
Olen	0	2	1
Rankin	3	0	0
Schleck	0	0	2

Figure 31.1 displays the placement of this data for all group members.

The data indicates that the three most selected members are Feavel, Geho, and Olen (see the results in figure 31.1 on "Combined Total" and "Number Choosing"). The *social receptiveness score* is the number of members who choose an individual–see "Number Choosing" in figure 31.1. The social receptiveness score for each member displays the extent to which each individual is accepted or ignored by the rest of the group. The category "Totals on each criterion" (all "votes," whether first, second, or third count as one point) shows the areas in which each member is preferred on each criterion. The *sociometric status score* is the combined total for all criteria, and is a general indicator of each member's position (on a continuum from acceptance to ignored) in the group.

The *emotional expansion score* is the number of members an individual chooses as her or his selections. In figure 31.1 Chan and Rankin chose the most members–five each. The more individuals a person chooses, the more that selector tends to feel a part of the group. The emotional expansion score is usually larger if a selector chooses different people for different questions.

At times the above scores are surprisingly different for the same individual. For example, an individual may be well-liked by most group members and therefore score high on the sociometric status score, but may prefer to associate with a few close friends in the group and therefore score low on the *emotional expansion score*.

The next step in analyzing the test results is to determine where reciprocal, partially reciprocal, and one-way relationship selections are indicated. In figure 31.1 each student's preferred member is circled—based on the individual who received that student's highest number of choices. With a reciprocal pair, the individual most chosen by a member has also given her or his highest number of votes to the first. An R should be placed above the pairs' circles to indicate the reciprocal relationship.

A PR should be entered above a person's circle if the relationship is partially reciprocal—that is, if a chosen member responds with a choice of lesser value. A W should be placed above an individual's circle if her or his choice is not reciprocated at all. The W stands for one-way relationship. Generally, there will be a higher number of partially reciprocal and one-way relationships than fully reciprocal choices in a group. If a sociomet-

Figure 31.1: Summary Grid for the Results of a Sociometric Test

People Choosing	People Chosen										Number chosen
	Anacker	Chan	Feavel	Geho	Kalve	Leitl	Neitzel	Olen	Rankin	Schleck	
Anacker	—	(213^{PR})	000	000	130	000	000	021	300	002	4
Chan	330	—	000	001	(122^{W})	000	210	000	003	000	5
Feavel	000	000	—	(122^{PR})	000	301	000	030	(213^{PR})	000	4
Geho	000	000	(321^{R})	—	003	000	000	(232^{R})	110	000	4
Kalve	000	000	(231^{W})	100	—	013	000	(322^{W})	000	000	4
Leitl	000	033	302	000	000	—	120	000	000	(211^{W})	4
Neitzel	300	000	(122^{W})	(233^{W})	000	000	—	011	000	000	4
Olen	000	000	(213^{PR})	(322^{R})	000	000	001	—	000	130	4
Rankin	000	000	010	302	000	001	(233^{W})	120	—	000	5
Schleck	103	(222^{W})	000	000	010	000	(331^{W})	000	000	—	4
Totals on each criterion	311	233	555	535	232	113	443	364	322	222	
Combined Total	5	8	15	13	7	5	11	13	7	6	
Number Choosing	3	3	6	6	4	3	5	6	4	3	

Reciprocal Relationships (R)
Feavel–Geho
Olen–Geho

Partially Reciprocal Relationships (PR)
Anacker–Chan
Feavel–Rankin
Olen–Feavel

One-Way Relationships (W)
(The arrow indicates the direction of the one-way relationship)

Chan ➤ Kalve
Kalve ➤ Feavel
Kalve ➤ Olen
Leitl ➤ Schleck
Neitzel ➤ Feavel
Neitzel ➤ Geho
Rankin ➤ Neitzel
Schleck ➤ Chan
Schleck ➤ Neitzel

ric test shows a high number of fully reciprocated relationships, it suggests the group may have a number of factions or cliques.

Applications

Additional information can be "teased" from a sociometric test. Answers to the following questions can be quite revealing. Who did not select a popular leader? (The results of a test where a popular member fails to select one or more of the other popular members may indicate a power struggle or interpersonal conflict). Who selected those members with low sociometric scores—where they popular members or did they also have low sociometric scores? Is there a recognized "star" in the group or are there three or four popular members (as was found in the sociometric test results in figure 31.1)? Does the sociometric test show that the most selected members tended to choose a member who was seldom selected by the other members—if so, such results may indicate such a member is a "power behind the throne."

Highly preferred members tend to have the most influence and power in a group. A sociometric test indicates which members are most popular, and therefore are apt to have the most power. As indicated earlier in this text, groups tend to be most cohesive, productive, effective, and efficient when power is fairly evenly distributed. If there are wide disparities between the most selected and least selected members, the results are an indication that the least chosen members have little power (and are therefore apt to feel powerless). People who feel they are isolated and powerless in a group tend to be less attracted to the group, less committed to group goals, and less committed to putting forth effort to accomplish group goals. One of the useful applications of a sociometric test is for a group leader to identify the least popular members so that approaches can be developed to seek to make the group and its goals more attractive to the least selected members.

Another application is to examine the interaction patterns in a group—particularly if a group is having communication problems. As indicated earlier, a group in which there are a large number of fully reciprocal relationships may be indicative of a group that has conflicting factions or cliques. If such cliques exist, a sociometric test will generally identify the members of the different cliques—as members of a clique are apt to choose each other. Once such cliques are identified, the group leader can take steps to reduce the strengths of the cliques—perhaps by changing seating patterns or by assigning each of the members of a clique to work on projects with each members of the group.

By the procedure of having members make selections as to the most preferred members and to the least preferred members to associate with for a variety of activities, Northway found the following sociometric personality types:[8]

1. High acceptance and low rejection. These members are well-liked by most members. They tend to be social-emotional leaders, and also tend to be supportive of both group goals and individual members' goals. Such individuals often function well as arbitrators in resolving group disputes.
2. High acceptance and high rejection. These members tend to be dynamic, controversial, outspoken, and opinionated. Often they tend to be recognized as focusing more on accomplishing the tasks of the group than on improving or preserving the social-emotional atmosphere of the group.
3. Low acceptance and low rejection. These members tend to be inconspicuous, quiet, and are often seen as wishy-washy. Sometimes they tend to be somewhat withdrawn from the rest of the group.
4. Low acceptance and high rejection. These members tend to be seen as unsupportive and even antagonistic to group values and goals. They may be actively excluded from the group. As a result, they tend to feel they are outcasts or "misfits." Such a feeling often builds up additional resentment toward the group which may lead to further alienation from the group.

A final word of caution in applying the results of a sociometric test. Sociometry is not an exact science. Since interpersonal attractions and repulsions tend to change among group members over time, a sociometric test's results on attractions and repulsions best reflects members' thoughts and feelings about each other at the point in time in which the test is given. There are a variety of factors that can change attractions and repulsions, including interpersonal conflict, significant accomplishments, and significant failures of one or more members; reports or rumors of unethical or illegal conduct by one or more members; the introduction of new projects; changing group values and norms; developing personalities; and the loss or addition of members. Sociometric relationships among group members can vary with each meeting.

In spite of the limitations of sociometry, the technique remains a valuable tool for group leaders to obtain information about interpersonal relationships in a group. The results often reveal problematic areas in interactions and communication patterns. Once such problematic areas are identified, approaches can be developed to improve the morale, productivity, and effectiveness of the group.

GROUP EXERCISES

Exercise A: A Lifeline of a Relationship

Goal: To assess a close relationship by drawing a lifeline of the relationship.

Step 1. The leader indicates the purpose of the exercise and explains that students do not have to share their lifeline with anyone.

Step 2. The leader gives an example of a lifeline. The following example was written by a female student.

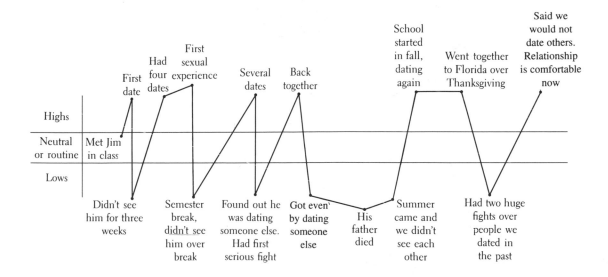

Step 3. Students are asked to draw a lifeline of a close relationship they are having now or had in the past.

Step 4. After the students have drawn their lifelines, volunteers may want to share what they drew in terms of the significant events in the lifeline. If no one volunteers, the group leader may share one she or he has drawn.

Step 5. The students discuss what they learned from doing this exercise. They may want to share their lifeline with the other person in their drawing as a way of mutually examining their relationship.

Exercise B: Resolving Anger Issues

Goal: To deal with unfinished business in a close relationship.

Step 1. The leader explains the purpose of this exercise. Students first identify issues, from the past or in the present, related to a close relationship that they are still angry and upset about. State that unless such issues are properly expressed and dealt with, they will tend to result in distrust and resentment. The leader explains that after students identify these issues, they will have an opportunity to share *only what they wish* with a small subgroup.

Step 2. The students take a sheet of paper and draw a line down the middle. On the left side they are to write down anger issues they have with someone with whom they have a close relationship. This person may be a spouse, someone they are dating, a parent, a relative, or a close friend. After writing down their anger issues, they write down their plans for resolving the issues. The format is shown below.

Anger Issues Past	*Plans for Resolving This Issue*
1.	1.
2.	2.
3.	3.
4.	4.
5.	5.

Anger Issues Present	*Plans for Resolving This Issue*
1.	1.
2.	2.
3.	3.
4.	4.
5.	5.

Step 3. Students form subgroups of three persons and share only what they desire. The subgroups discuss ways of resolving the anger issues that are shared.

Step 4. The leader indicates that students may want to share what they wrote with the person who was the focus of the exercise as a way of initiating a discussion about how to resolve these issues.

560

Exercise C: Communicating Likes and Dislikes in a Relationship

Goal: To communicate with a person with whom you are having a close relationship your likes and dislikes about that person.

Step 1. The leader describes the purpose of this exercise and asks the students to write on a sheet of paper what they like and what they would like to see changed about someone with whom they are having a close relationship. This person may be a roommate, spouse, parent, someone they're dating, or a close friend.

Step 2. Each student shares what he or she wrote, prior to the next session, with the person who is the focus of this exercise. Before sharing what they wrote, the students ask the other person to write down what she or he likes, and would like to see changed about them.

Step 3. At the next class session, the students discuss:

1. What happened when this information was shared?
2. Did this exercise add to the relationship, or did it lead to anger and resentment?
3. Was the sharing done in a nonblaming manner?
4. Would it be helpful for both people to continue to do this exercise periodically in order to work on the irritants in the relationship?

Exercise D: Is It Romantic Love or Rational Love?

Goal: To analyze the nature of a relationship with someone with whom you are "in love."

Step 1. The leader begins by indicating the purpose of the exercise. Students then write down on a sheet of paper the following information about someone with whom they are "in love." If some students are not currently "in love," they write down the following information about someone they were "in love" with in the past. (*Indicate that students will not be asked to share this information with anyone.*)

The things I find attractive about this person are:	*The things I find irritating about this person are:*
1.	1.
2.	2.
3.	3.
4.	4.
5.	5.
6.	6.

Step 2. The leader explains the characteristics of romantic relationships and rational love relationships. The leader should also describe the pitfalls of romantic love.

Step 3. The students examine what they wrote and assess *silently* whether their relationship is primarily one of romantic love or rational love. *There need be no discussion of this.* The leader may indicate that if a student listed only attractions, that student may currently have a romantic love relationship. If a student listed a mixture of attractions and irritants, such a student may currently be in a rational love relationship. If a student listed only irritants, such a student is probably at the stage where she or he is terminating the relationship (or has already done so). The students then discuss the merits and shortcomings of this exercise.

Exercise E: A Sociometric Test of This Class

Goal: To show how to conduct a sociometric test.

Note: It is advised that the instructor be the designated leader for this exercise because the exercise may generate strong emotions in the participants.

Step 1. The leader explains what a sociometric test is and describes the purpose of the exercise. For the purposes of this exercise the students cannot select the instructor for any of their choices. They should make three choices for each question, indicating their first, second, and third choice. The students give answers to each of the following three questions.

1. With whom in this class would you most like to socialize?
2. With whom in this class would you most like to work on giving a small group presentation?
3. With whom in this class would you like to work on writing a grant proposal?

Step 2. Students who receive very few (or no) selections may be emotionally hurt or alienated. For this reason, the instructor should explain that he or she will not collect the responses from the students. The instructor should add that the purpose of doing the sociometric test was to show how to conduct this type of test and to have the students experience what it feels like to be involved in taking such a test.

Step 3. The instructor may choose at this time to describe (as discussed earlier in the chapter) how to analyze the results of a sociometric test.

Step 4. The members discuss their feelings about the sociometric exercise and their thoughts about the merits and shortcomings of sociometry.

PART NINE

TERMINATION AND EVALUATION

CHAPTER THIRTY-TWO

ENDING A GROUP

Goal: Termination and evaluation are among the most important phases of a group. This chapter begins by briefly summarizing what students should have learned after reading and doing the exercises in this text. The chapter then discusses several ways to terminate a group. The chapter ends by describing research approaches to process evaluation and to outcome evaluation in groups.

Through reading this text, participating in the exercises, and leading some of the exercises, it is hoped that you have developed the skills needed to become an effective group leader and member. Your verbal and nonverbal communication in groups and active listening skills should have improved. Having gained an understanding of why controversy is desirable for groups, you should be able to use problem-solving and decision-making approaches to foster group effectiveness. You should be able to lead a brainstorming group and a nominal group, and have some familiarity with parliamentary procedure.

Groups can be used to help members control unwanted emotions, manage grief, become more comfortable with death, analyze problematic transactions in terms of game analysis and script analysis, become more assertive, manage stress, treat chemical dependency, prevent burnout, improve time management, develop a positive self-identity, improve close relationships, increase comfort with sexuality, and clarify values. At the end of this class, you should be better able to lead a variety of social work groups. Effective functioning in groups helps us accomplish our personal goals, furthers our personal growth, and improves our interpersonal relationships. Acquiring group skills and knowledge facilitates our capacities to function effectively in organizations, communities, families, and society. Now that we have reached the end of this class and the end of this text, we need to focus on how to end a group.

TERMINATION

The process of ending a therapy group has already been described in chapter 17. This section will describe the process of termination for a broad array of groups.

Inherent in termination is separation from the group and from group members. Separation typically involves mixed feelings that vary in intensity according to a number of factors, several of which will be discussed here. The more emotionally close and emotionally invested a member is to a group, the greater will be that member's feeling of loss. The greater the feeling of success of members in accomplishing their goals via the group, the greater will be their feelings of "sweet sorrow"; sweetness from feeling that they have grown and had success, and sorrow because of separation from the group that has come to be an important and meaningful part of their lives.

The more emotionally dependent a member has become on a group, the more he or she is apt to feel anger, rejection, and depression over termination. The more a member has experienced difficulties in separating in the past from significant others, the more likely it is that the separation will be experienced as difficult, as the pattern of reacting to separations is apt to be repeated.

There are a variety of types of termination, which include:

1. Termination of a successful group
2. Termination of an unsuccessful group
3. A member dropping out
4. Transfer of a member
5. The leader leaving

Each of these will be briefly described.

Termination of a Successful Group

A successful group is one in which the group and its members have generally accomplished their goals. Termination of such a group is apt to generate the "sweet sorrow" reaction. The members are apt to be delighted with their accomplishments. The accomplishments are apt to increase their levels of self-confidence and self-esteem. Members are also apt to experience a feeling of loss (varying in intensity) due to separating from a group in which they have become emotionally invested. Such a group may desire to dine or have some other ceremony to commemorate and recognize the group and its accomplishments.

In terminating a successful group it is essential that formal termination begin one or more meetings before the final meeting. Ideally, the date of the last meeting should be discussed and agreed upon by the members well in advance of the final meetings. (For some groups the final meeting is scheduled even before the group begins to meet.) Sufficient time has to be allowed in terminating a successful group so that: (1) progress made in accomplishing the tasks and goals of the group and its members can be evaluated; (2) plans can be made for continued work by the members on remaining problems; (3) work can be done on unresolved, last-minutes issues that are identified by members; (4) the emotional reactions of members to terminating can be handled; and (5) the members have time to discuss whether they want to plan for a special social event for the group's ending.

While goodbyes are often sad, the negative feelings can be offset by emphasizing what members have given and received, the ways they have grown, the skills they have learned, and what the group has accomplished. In some cases, an extra session could be held to complete unfinished business items. The members may decide to have "class reunions" periodically or social get-togethers in the future.

Termination of an Unsuccessful Group

An unsuccessful group is one in which most or all of the goals of the group and its members are largely unmet. The reactions of members to the lack of progress may vary considerably: anger, frustration, disappointment, despair, guilt (for unproductive efforts or over lack of effort), scapegoating, blaming, and apathy. In rarer cases, it is possible for an unsuccessful group to be fairly pleased and accepting of its efforts. For example, a group that is formed to write a grant (when there is limited hope of funding) from the federal government may be pleased with its efforts and with the new relationships with others that were formulated and only mildly disappointed when they learn they were not funded.

In planning the termination of an unsuccessful group it is essential that formal termination be as well-planned as with successful groups. The date of the last meeting should be discussed and agreed upon by the members well in advance of the final meeting. Sufficient time has to be allowed in terminating an unsuccessful group so that: (1) the reasons for the lack of progress of the group can be assessed and analyzed; (2) discussions can be held of alternatives for the group and its members to reach their goals (such alternatives may involve changing the format of the present group, referral of members to other groups, and alternatives involving individual actions rather than group efforts); (3) the emotional reactions of members to terminating and their reactions to the lack of progress made by the group can be handled; (4) the members have time to work on unresolved, last-minute issues; and (5) the members have time to discuss whether they want to plan for a special social event for the group's ending.

At times the ending of an unsuccessful group is chaotic and abrupt. For example, a group that has been appointed to write a grant may be nearly finished when they are informed the funding organization has had a financial shortfall and is therefore withdrawing its request for funding proposals. Such a group may end abruptly in despair. Or, in a group of involuntary members (such as at a prison or at an adolescent residential treatment facility), the leader may decide it is counterproductive to continue a group in which the members are continually "goofing off" and not putting effort into achieving the goals of the group. In every case, the reasons for the group's ending should be fully explained, and time should be given to dealing with the reactions of the members to the closing. If there is insufficient time at the final meeting to dealing with the tasks involved in ending a group, it is sometimes advisable either to have another session or for the leader to meet individually with each member to discuss their reactions to goals being unmet, alternatives for reaching their goals, reactions to the group ending, and unresolved concerns they may have.

When an unsuccessful group ends abruptly, some group members may be highly critical of the leader, of other group members, or of experiences that occurred in the group. If the leader contacts members to gain their thoughts about the group, he or she needs to be prepared to respond to highly critical feedback. One way the leader can prepare is to "visualize" possible criticisms and then formulate a positive and realistic response to each anticipated criticism.

A Member Dropping Out

When a member drops out, that person terminates, even though the group continues. A member may drop out for a variety of reasons. The member may become disenchanted with the group and feel that the group will not accomplish the goals that have been set. The member may have a disagreement with or dislike another group member. The member may be a parent who has to provide child care at the time the group meets. The member may start a new job with work hours that conflict with the meeting time. And there are numerous other reasons.

When a group member drops out without informing the group as to the reasons, the leader should contact the person to ascertain the reasons for terminating. In some instances it is desirable for the leader to explain that deciding to leave is a major decision that should not be made abruptly and that the leader would like the opportunity to explore the reasons that led to the decision. If the member has a conflict with another group member, perhaps the conflict can be resolved so that the member decides to return. Perhaps action can be taken to enable the member to return. For example, if child care is a problem for a parent, child-care arrangements can be made.

If the member decides not to return, the reasons for leaving should be explored. Perhaps the member may raise legitimate concerns that need to be dealt with so that other members do not also become discouraged and leave. If a person drops out of a therapy group, sensitivity group, or an educational group and still has unresolved personal concerns, a referral to another group or to one-to-one professional help may be advisable.

Whenever a member drops out, the leader needs to inform that member of his or her positive contributions to the group. Dropping out of a group is often viewed as a personal failure, and therefore the person needs to be thanked for positive contributions to soothe the sense of personal failure.

When a member drops out, the remaining members may experience a variety of emotions. Some may feel they failed this member. Some may feel guilt for what they said or did—or feel guilt for failing to do or say what they believe would have led the person to stay. Some may feel relief or joy over the member leaving, as they may view the member as being unworthy of the group or as an obstacle in the group's efforts to accomplish its goals. Some may feel sadness for the member dropping out and be concerned that something tragic has happened to that member. Some members may experience anger toward the person for leaving, as they feel he or she is abandoning the group. A few may feel personally rejected. Often, when a member drops out, rumors begin to circulate as to the reasons. Therefore, it is essential that the group be informed about the reasons for the person's decision to leave. A member's leaving can be devastating to group morale. If several members depart, the group's survival may be jeopardized.

Ideally, the person who leaves should inform the group about the reasons, either in person or in writing. If the member does not do this, the leader or some other group member should contact the person to ascertain the reasons for leaving and then inform the group.

Transfer of a Member

A transfer of a group member to another group or to some other type of professional services generally involves a planned arrangement between the group leader and the member. The transfer may occur for a variety of reasons. In a problem-solving group, the employing agency may decide the group member's talents and skills could be better used in some other capacity. In a therapy group, the leader and group members may jointly decide the member would be better served by receiving more specialized services in some other therapeutic format. A group member may transfer from any kind of a group because of a conflict that cannot be resolved between that group member and other group members. The conflict may severely interfere with goal accomplishment within the group. (For example, there may be a serious and insurmountable gap in mutual understanding and communication caused by differences in religious beliefs, values, or language.)

When a transfer occurs, the leader does everything possible to keep the transfer from being unexpected or abrupt. The member being transferred should clearly understand the reasons for the transfer and be accepting of the transfer. In addition, the group should receive an explanation as to the reasons for the transfer. Ideally, the member should explain to the group why he or she is transferring. This allows the other group members an opportunity to wish the member well and to gain a sense of "closure" to the member leaving the group.

The Leader Leaving

Sometimes a group leader must terminate work with a group because of reassignment, change of employment, health reasons, or family crises. Such a termination is difficult for both the group leader and the members. Emotional reactions may be intense, and adequate time for working through these reactions may not be available. Members who feel vulnerable and dependent upon the leader may feel devastated. Some may personalize the leader's leaving as being due to something they said or did. Some may feel angry and betrayed because they made a commitment to the group, confided in and trusted the leader, and then the leader left when their goals and the group's goals were only partially accomplished.

The leader, too, may experience intense emotions, including guilt for not following through on the implicit commitment to lead the group until its goals were accomplished.

When a leader leaves, he or she should encourage the members to express their feelings. The leader may want to initiate this expression by fully explaining why he or she is leaving, listing a number of positive things about the group, and also expressing feelings of sadness and guilt over leaving. Prior to leaving, the leader (or group) should select a new leader. If the new leader is not a member of the group, the leader who is leaving should inform (outside a group meeting) the new leader about the goals, characteristics of members, current tasks and difficulties, and progress toward goals that the group has made. This new leader should be introduced to the group by the leader who is leaving. As much as possible, a smooth transition is the goal in shifting responsibilities from the former leader to the new leader.

EVALUATION

In the past few decades, accountability has become a major emphasis in social welfare. Funding sources demand research evidence that funds allocated are having a beneficial effect. An essential component of accountability is evaluation.

In broad terms, evaluation is designed to assess whether services provided were effective and efficient. Services provided in which goals and objectives are unmet are neither effective nor efficient. In evaluating the services provided by a group, there are two dimensions of evaluation: process evaluation and outcome evaluation.

Process Evaluation

Process evaluation is an assessment, generally by group members, as to the aspects of the group that were useful or detrimental. Feedback about techniques and incidents that blocked or enhanced process is of immense value to the group leader. With this information, the leader can hone certain skills, eliminate some materials, and give direction for approaches and materials to add. Such feedback can aid confidence. If the feedback is highly critical, it can be humbling and even devastating. It is far better to make changes suggested by the evaluation than to reject and "deny" the feedback and repeat the same mistakes in future groups. Group leaders need to welcome criticism and be prepared to respond to it constructively, which is the way that social workers expect clients to take constructive criticism.

Process evaluation can be conducted orally by asking the group members to discuss the aspects, techniques, materials, and incidents that were constructive and those that were counterproductive. An advantage of such an oral evaluation is that most members enjoy a verbal discussion. A disadvantage is that some may be inhibited from giving negative feedback verbally as there is a social norm in such situations to focus on the positives.

Process evaluation can also be accomplished by a brief questionnaire. Three key questions are the following:

1. Summarize the strengths of this group. (Cite specific materials and incidents. Also cite skills and techniques used by the leader.)
2. Summarize the shortcomings of this group. (Cite specific materials and incidents. Also cite skills and techniques used by the leader.)
3. Briefly outline your specific suggestions for changes.

In process evaluations, group members typically cite positive factors more than negative ones.[1] Such positive feedback not only has a "stroking value," but also enables leaders to be more aware of their strengths, so that they are apt to increase the use of these strengths in the future.

Negative feedback is as valuable as, and often more valuable than, positive feedback. It informs the leader of aspects that need improvement, which the leader can then attend to. Hepworth and Larsen note, "As with clients, awareness precedes change."[2]

Another way of evaluating process is by *peer review,* a form of quality control. Peer review is conducted by having one or more "peers" (usually other group leaders) periodically sit in on a group. (Some agencies have one way mirrors so that the group can be unobtrusively observed.) Prior to a peer review, the agency or organization should agree upon a set of principles or criteria that reflect quality group leadership. A peer review is a review of a small portion of the total functioning of the group. That small portion may be typical or atypical of the total functioning of the group. (Many colleges and universities use a peer review process in which tenured faculty in a department sit in on some of the classes of recently hired faculty.)

A variation of the peer-review process is taping (either audio or video) a meeting. That tape is played back and reviewed by the leader and a peer (or by the leader's supervisor). Prior to taping a meeting, the leader should explain the reasons for wanting to tape the meeting, indicate who will view the tape, and then ask the members for their permission to tape the session.

Outcome Evaluation

Outcome evaluation involves assessing the extent to which the goals that were formulated when the group began have been accomplished. Specific approaches to measure goal attainment are: single-subject design, task achievement scaling, and satisfaction questionnaire.

Single-Subject Design

Single-subject design has become increasingly popular in the helping professions in the past two decades. There are more than a dozen variations of single-subject design, some of which are very complex and rigorous.[3] Fortunately, the simpler designs can be used by entry-level social workers in many direct practice situations. The basic elements of the design are described here.

Single subject design has been identified by several other terms: single-system design, single N or N = 1 research, intensive or ideographic research, single case-study design, single-organism research, time-series research or design, and single-case experimental design.[4] The phrase "single-subject" indicates a focus of research attention on a single client—which is usually an individual, but can be a small group or a family.

In a single-subject design, the client becomes the control group. For this reason, the approach is relatively easy to incorporate into a practitioner's usual services.

The steps in the research process involve:

1. Specifying the outcome
2. Selecting a suitable measure
3. Recording baseline data
4. Implementing intervention and monitoring the outcome
5. Assessing change
6. Inferring effectiveness[5]

The first step in single-subject design is to specify the outcome of interest. The selected outcome should reflect the needs of the client and what is realistic to achieve. It also must be an outcome that can be defined specifically and measured. For a bulimic client who is binging and purging, an appropriate outcome may be cessation of purging. For a family in which there are frequent heated arguments, an appropriate outcome may be a sharp reduction in heated arguments.

The second step in the design process is to select a suitable measure. The target behavior that the practitioner and client hope to change (such as reduction in heated arguments) must be specified in such a way that it can be measured in some reliable way. There are a variety of ways for measuring client outcomes, including direct observation, self-reports from the client, and standardized measures. Standardized measures include tests, questionnaires, rating scales, inventories, and checklists. A variety of standardized measures have been developed to measure such variables as: self-esteem, level of assertiveness, level of depression, anxiety level, degree of marital satisfaction, burn out, amount of stress, potential for suicide, and generalized contentment.

The third step is to record baseline data. Baselining involves collecting data for a period of time before implementing the intervention. The objective of baselining is to establish the base rate of the outcome measure before intervention occurs. This baselining rate can then be used to provide a basis of comparison for the occurrence of the target behavior (behavior to be changed) before, during, and after intervention.

The fourth step is to implement intervention and monitor the outcomes. For example, for a client who is generally nonassertive, the intervention may be to have the client participate in an assertiveness training group.

The fifth step is to assess change. This step involves a comparison of the occurrence of the target behavior before, during, and after treatment. Often the occurrence of the target behavior during these three time periods can be displayed on a graph, as shown in figure 32.1.

The sixth step in the process is to infer effectiveness. This step involves demonstrating logically and empirically that the intervention is the only reasonable explanation for the observed change in client outcome. In essence, this stage involves ruling out other possible explanations for the observed change. The primary criterion for inferring causality is *concomitant variation;* that is, the observed change in the outcome must occur at (or soon after) the time the intervention is implemented. If positive changes begin during the baseline period, then logically we have to conclude that something other than the intervention

Figure 32.1: Intervention Results for a Bulimic Client

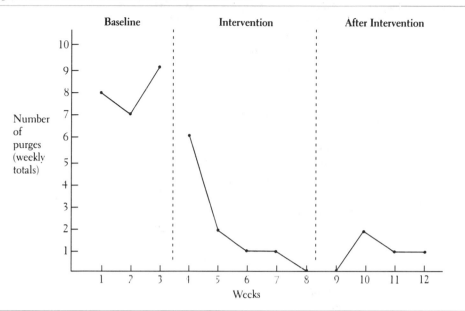

may have contributed to the positive changes. Likewise, if change occurs too long after intervention, then other possible factors may be responsible for the change. If we examine the Intervention Results for a Bulimic Client (figure 32.1) we can logically conclude that the intervention had a positive effect, as the number of purges per week declined sharply during and after intervention. However, the usual goal with bulimic clients is complete cessation of purging. Since the client is still purging periodically, additional interventions may be advisable.

In some situations in single-subject research it is necessary to use a multiple baseline, which indicates the use of more than one baseline as a means of measuring change. Sheafor, Horejsi, and Horejsi summarize an example of where a multiple baseline might be used:

> In work with a child having trouble in school, one baseline might focus on frequency of school attendance, a second on grades received for weekly assignments, and a third on a teacher's weekly rating of the student's level of cooperation in the classroom. Unless the target behavior is highly specific, multiple baselines are usually necessary in order to capture the impact of an intervention.[6]

There are a couple of ways in which to use single-subject design in therapeutic, sensitivity, and educational groups. One way is to construct a single-subject design for each member. If the group is living together (for example, in a group home) and members have interpersonal problems (such as heated arguments), a single-subject design can be constructed on the group as the client. For example, if decreasing the number of heated arguments is the target behavior, the number of heated arguments per week among group members can be counted by the staff members during the three time periods of: baseline, intervention, and after intervention.

Task Achievement Scaling

The objective of this approach is to gauge the degree to which group members and/or the leader have completed agreed-upon intervention tasks. In this approach, work toward the goals of the members and of the group is broken down into many separate actions or tasks. The tasks are selected by mutual agreement of the members, and each member is assigned or selects specific tasks to reach his or her goal and the overall goal of the group. Usually, a deadline is set for the completion of each task. Task Achievement Scaling refers to a procedure for rating the degree to which each agreed-upon task has, in fact, been achieved.

Reid and Epstein, in using this approach, utilize a four-point scale to record progress on each task: 4 = "Completely achieved"; 3 = "Substantially achieved, action is still necessary"; 2 = "Partially achieved, considerable work remains to be done"; and 1 = "Minimally achieved or not achieved."[7] Where appropriate, they have a fifth rating: "No" for "No opportunity to work on task." With this approach, only results are rated—not effort, motivation, or good intentions. The appealing features of this approach are its simplicity and the fact that it can be used when more rigorous procedures are not feasible because of insufficient time, insufficient data, or difficulties in finding a suitable way to measure changes in the target behavior. The approach also has limitations. For example, if the tasks are erroneously conceptualized to be constructive in resolving the client's problems, then completing the tasks may have little effect on resolving the client's problems.

Satisfaction Questionnaire

Still another way to assess the outcome of a group is to have group members fill out a questionnaire that measures level of satisfaction. An example of such a questionnaire is the Group Member Satisfaction Questionnaire shown in figure 32.2.

Such a questionnaire is a relatively simple and inexpensive way to measure the members' satisfaction level with the group. The questionnaire can be filled out at the last meeting of the group or can be mailed to members some time after the last meeting. Questions that evaluate process (described earlier in this chapter) can be added to this questionnaire.

Such satisfaction questionnaires have limitations. The responses to the instrument are affected by the mood of the respondent. In addition, dissatisfied members are less likely to fill out the questionnaire than satisfied ones, particularly if it is administered by mail.[8]

GROUP EXERCISE

Exercise A: Evaluating and Ending the Class

Goal: To bring closure to a group.

Note: The instructor of the course should lead this exercise.

Step 1. The instructor begins by expressing a number of positive thoughts and feelings that she or he has about the group. The instructor may also mention a few memorable experiences.

Figure 32.2: Group Member Satisfaction Questionnaire

Thank you for taking a few minutes to evaluate your experiences in our group. Your answers to this brief questionnaire will help us to improve future groups. Feel free to offer your comments. To assure anonymity, please do not sign your name.

1. Did you accomplish what you expected when you joined the group?
   _____ Yes, completely
   _____ Mostly
   _____ No real progress
   _____ Worse off now than before
   Comments_____

2. Do you feel the group accomplished its goals?
   _____ Yes, completely
   _____ Mostly
   _____ No real progress
   _____ The group was an utter failure
   Comments_____

3. How do you feel about the group leader?
   _____ Very satisfied
   _____ Satisfied
   _____ No feelings one way or another
   _____ Dissatisfied
   _____ Very dissatisfied
   Comments_____

4. How do you feel about the other members in the group?
   _____ Satisfied with everyone
   _____ Satisfied with some, and dissatisfied with others
          No feelings one way or another
   _____ Dissatisfied with most of the other members
   _____ Dissatisfied with all of the other members
   _____ Very dissatisfied with all of the other members
   Comments_____

Step 2. The group sits in a circle and the instructor asks: "Is there anything that anyone wants to express before the class ends? Is there any unfinished business that we should deal with?"

Step 3. The instructor leads a discussion in which the group reflects upon the course through such questions as, "Do you believe this course has helped prepare you to lead groups in social work?" "What else might have been done to better prepare you to lead groups?" "What exercises or materials have helped you grow as a person?" "What do you see as the strengths of this course?" "What do you see as the shortcomings of this course?" "How might this course be improved?" (An alternative to a verbal discussion of the questions in this step is to have the students record their responses anonymously on a sheet of paper, and then hand them in.)

Step 4. The members express what they will most remember about this course and/or what they feel they have learned. Each member should be given an opportunity to express this.

Step 5. Each member expresses nonverbally how she or he felt about being in this class at the first session and how she or he now feels about having been in the class. (This step is optional.)

Step 6. The leader asks each member to give an imaginary gift to the person on his or her right. Each person should take a turn so everyone can hear what the gifts are. When giving or receiving the gift the members extend their hands to symbolize the giving or receiving of the gift. Examples of such gifts are the time-management key to ending procrastination, a warm sun for a smiling personality, a heart for happier relationships, positive and rational thinking for handling unwanted emotions, and the gift of meditation for reducing stress. (This step is optional.)

Step 7. The instructor may end the class by administering a student course evaluation, by saying some final words, or in some other appropriate way.

APPENDICES

APPENDIX A

ANSWERS TO EXERCISES IN CHAPTER 9

Exercise D:

1. Twenty; 9, 19, 29, 39, 49, 59, 69, 79, 89, 90, 91, 92, 93, 94, 95, 96, 97, 98, 99.
2. They're playing with different partners.
3. Two hours.
4. The water will never reach the top of the ladder because the boat keeps rising with the tide.
5. Of course.
6. He's still alive.
7. Six.
8. The bear is white because it is a polar bear. The house is located at the North Pole.
9. Three minutes.
10. Car A travels 1,200 miles, Car B travels 800 miles from the point of origin.
11. One haystack.
12. Karen is Jill's mother.
13. Four dollars.

Exercise E:

Task 1:

Task 2:

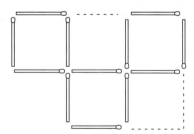

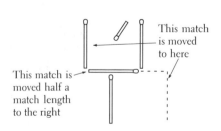

This match is moved half a match length to the right

This match is moved to here

Task 3:

Task 4:

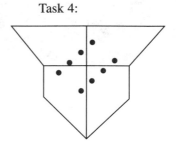

Task 5:

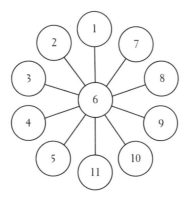

Exercise F:

1. Sandbox
2. Man overboard
3. I understand
4. Reading between the lines
5. Long underwear
6. Crossroads
7. Downtown
8. Tricycle
9. Split level
10. Three degrees below zero
11. Neon lights
12. Circles under the eyes
13. High chair

14. Paradise
15. Touchdown
16. Six-feet underground
17. Mind over matter
18. He's beside himself
19. Backward glance
20. Life after death
21. G.I. overseas
22. Space program
23. See-through blouse
24. Just between you and me
25. Empty

APPENDIX B

DEFINITIONS OF PARLIAMENTARY TERMS

Accept an amendment: Informal agreement by proposer of a motion to include a proposed amendment; mover may say, "I accept the amendment."

Adhere: When a motion is pending, and other motions, like the motion to amend, are applied to it, these motions are said to *adhere* to the original motion. When this motion is postponed or referred to a committee, these adhering motions go with it.

Ad hoc committee: A special committee assigned one major responsibility and then terminated.

Adjourn: To terminate a meeting officially.

Adjourned meeting: A meeting that is a continuation of a regular or special meeting and is legally a part of the same meeting.

Adjourn sine die (without a future date): An adjournment that terminates a convention or conference.

Adopt: To approve, to give effect to.

Adopt a report: The formal acceptance of a report. Adoption commits the organization to everything included in the report.

Affirmative vote: A "yes" vote to a question before an assembly; an agreement to its acceptance.

Agenda: The official list of business to be considered at a meeting or convention.

Amend: To change by adding, deleting, or substituting words or provisions; to propose to modify or change a motion under consideration.

Annul: To void or cancel an action taken previously.

Appeal: A decision of the presiding officer may be appealed. An appeal requires that the decision be referred to the assembly for its determination by a vote.

Apply: One motion is said to apply to another motion when it is used to alter, dispose of, or affect the first motion.

Assembly: A group of persons gathered for some common purpose, whether an organized body or not. Includes mass meetings as well as organized associations.

Assessment: Authorized levy of a fee made upon members of an organization.

Aye: "Yes" vote (pronounced "I").

Ballot: A paper or a mechanical device by which votes are recorded. It is used to ensure secrecy in voting.

Bylaws: Standing rules containing, generally, more detailed matter than the constitution (rules regarding order of business, membership, and dues, for example).

Candidate: One who is nominated or offers him- or herself as a contestant for an office.

Carried: Approved by the necessary affirmative vote of the group.

Chair: The chairperson or presiding officer.

Change in parliamentary situation: Phrase used in determining when a motion may be renewed. A change in the parliamentary situation means that motions have been proposed or disposed of, that there has been progress in debate, or that other changes have occurred to create a new situation so that the assembly might reasonably take a different position on the question.

Changing a vote: Request to alter one's own vote that has already been taken.

Charter: Written grant of authority, usually from a state to a corporation, guaranteeing rights, franchises, or privileges.

Classification of motions: Division of motions into groups, usually according to their purpose or precedence.

Close debate: To stop all discussion on a motion and to take a vote on it immediately.

Commit: To refer to a committee.

Committee: A body selected to perform a specific task for the assembly or organization. Types of committees include: (a) *Special committee*—selected at a special time for a specific purpose, (b) *Standing committee*—selected at a definite time to perform one or more regularly designated functions, (c) *Committee of the whole*—the entire assembly acting informally for a specified time for free general discussion and then returning back to parliamentary session when substantial agreement is reached.

Committee of the whole: A form or procedure for informal discussion (*see* Committee).

Common Law: Law developed by court decisions. Judge-made law.

Conference: A group meeting informally for consultation and discussion.

Consideration: Deliberation on a subject and examination of it before taking a vote.

Constitution. Document containing fundamental laws and principles of government adopted by an organized body.

Convene: To open a meeting formally.

Convention: Assembly of delegates or representatives of allied groups meeting for a common purpose.

Credentials: Certificate or testimonial indicating right of a person to represent a certain group.

Debatable: Capable of being discussed.

Debate: Discussion or presentation of opinion on a matter pending before a deliberative body.

Delegate: Member sent to represent an organized group and empowered to act for that group.

Deliberative body: Body that proceeds by discussion and consideration of questions and makes decisions by vote.

Demand: The assertion of a parliamentary right.

Dilatory tactics: Strategy used to delay action; use of motions and discussion to delay a vote (*see* Filibuster).

Disappearing quorum: Required number of persons present at beginning of meeting that disappears as persons leave (*see* Quorum).

Discussion: Consideration of a question by oral presentation of views of different persons.

Dispose of motion: To remove a motion from the consideration of the assembly.

Dissolve an organization: To terminate the official life of an organization.

Division of assembly: A vote taken by counting members, either by rising or by show of hands. It is usually taken to verify a voice vote.

Division of question: Separation of a main motion into two or more independent parts, each of which is capable of standing alone.

Executive board: Chief committee of an organization. It usually conducts organization business during intervals between meetings.

Ex-officio: To hold an office or position because of holding another office; e.g., the president of an organization may be an *ex-officio* member of the finance committee.

Expel a member: To remove someone from membership in an organization by group action.

Expunge: To strike out or cancel the record of a previous action.

Filibuster: To obstruct or prevent action in an assembly by dilatory tactics, such as speaking merely to consume time.

Floor: When recognized formally by the presiding officer, a person is said to have the floor and is the only person allowed to speak.

Gavel: Mallet used by presiding officer of a deliberative body to open and close meetings and to maintain order.

General consent: An informal method of disposing of routine and generally favored proposals by the presiding officer assuming the group's approval, unless objection is raised. It is also called "unanimous consent."

Germane: Pertaining or relating directly to, having definite bearing upon. It is applied to the relationship of amendments to motions.

Hearing: Meeting to listen to ideas or arguments with a view to making a decision or recommendation.

Honorary member or officer: One who is given membership or office by reason of eminence or position.

Illegal vote: A vote that cannot be counted because it does not comply with the rules of the organization.

Immediately pending question: When several questions are pending before the assembly, the one last proposed, which the assembly must decide first, is the immediately pending question.

Incidental motions: Motions relating to questions arising incidentally out of the business or order or manner of considering the business of an assembly. These motions usually arise out of a pending motion and must be decided upon before the question out of which they arise is decided.

Incorporate: To form a group of people into a legal entity recognized by law and with special rights, duties, functions, and liabilities distinct from its members.

In order: Correct from a parliamentary standpoint at a given time.

Informal consideration: A method of considering a question without observing the rules governing formal debate.

Inquiry: Question directed to the presiding officer by a member.

Instruction to committee: Directions specifying the powers and duties of the committee, the work desired, the type and date of report or similar matters.

Invariable form: A motion is said to have invariable form when it can be stated in only one way and when it is, therefore, not subject to change or amendment.

Irrelevant: Not related to, not pertinent, not applicable.

Lay on the table: To postpone a motion until a later but as yet undetermined time (*see* Postpone temporarily).

Legal vote: A valid vote, one that conforms to all legal requirements.

Legislative body. A representative body having the power to make laws.

Limit debate: To place restrictions on the time to be devoted to debate on a question or the number of speakers or the time allotted each.

Log-rolling: Agreeing with other members to assist them with motions in which they are interested in return for a promise of assistance from them.

Main motion: A motion presenting a subject to an assembly for discussion and decision. It is a motion designed to accomplish at least part of the business of the group. If passed, the motion authorizes the group to take certain actions, or it enables the group to place itself on record as holding certain views.

Majority vote: More than half of the total number legally voting or, if by ballot, more than half of the legal votes cast, unless otherwise defined.

Mass meeting: Large or general assembly open to anyone.

Meeting: An assemblage of the members of an organization during which there is no separation of the members except for a recess. A meeting is terminated by an adjournment.

Member in good standing: Member who has fulfilled all the obligations required by the organization to maintain membership.

Minority: Less than half of members or votes. Group having fewer than the number of votes required.

Minutes: Official record of motions presented and actions taken by an organization.

Motion: A proposal submitted to an assembly for its consideration and introduced by the words "I move."

Mover: The mover is the person who introduced a motion for consideration.

Moving the question: To move the question is simply to raise a motion for consideration. It is synonymous with the archaic "I make a motion." It is no longer considered correct to say "I make a motion"; rather, "I move . . ." is preferred.

Negative vote: Adverse vote; vote against a proposition.

New business: Any business other than unfinished or "old business" that may properly be brought before an assembly.

Nomination: The formal proposal of a person as a candidate for an office.

Object to consideration: To oppose discussion and decision on a main motion.

Oppose: To work actively against a measure or candidate.

Order of business: The formal program or sequence of different items or classes of business arranged in the order in which they are to be considered by an assembly.

Orders of the day: Business to be taken up during a meeting, including business left unfinished at a previous meeting, business postponed to the present meeting, and new business scheduled for the present meeting.

Out of order: Not correct from a parliamentary standpoint at the particular time.

Parliamentarian: An adviser to the presiding officer; one who is skilled in parliamentary practice.

Parliamentary authority: The manual or code adopted by an organization as its official parliamentary guide, which governs in all matters not covered in the constitution, bylaws, and rulers of the organization.

Parliamentary question: A request for information regarding proper procedure.

Pending question: A question, or motion, before the assembly that has not yet been voted upon.

Personal interest: Private financial gain that would result from the decision of the organization on a proposition.

Personal privilege: Request by a member for consideration of some matter of concern to him- or herself and related to him or her as a member.

Plurality: More votes than the number received by any other of three or more opposing candidates or measures. May be less than a majority.

Point of order: An assertion amounting to a demand addressed to the presiding officer that a mistake should be corrected or a rule enforced. The chair may decide the matter or submit it to the vote of the group.

Postpone definitely: To defer consideration of a motion or report until a specific time.

Postpone indefinitely: To kill a motion or report by deferring consideration indefinitely.

Postpone temporarily: To defer consideration of a report or motion until the assembly chooses to take it up again. The old form of the motion to postpone temporarily was "lay on the table."

Preamble: An introduction preceding a constitution or a resolution, stating its purpose or the reason for its proposal.

Precedence: The right of prior proposal and consideration of one motion over another or the order of priority of consideration.

Precedent: Something previously done or decided that serves as a guide in similar circumstances. An authoritative example.

Prefer charges: To accuse formally an officer or member of an offense, ordinarily for disciplinary purposes.

Presiding officer: Chairperson who conducts a meeting.

Previous question: Motion to close debate and force an immediate vote. It is the old term for the motion to vote immediately.

Privileged motions: The class of motions having the highest priority.

Procedural motion: A motion that presents a question of procedure as distinguished from a substantive proposition.

Proposition: A proposal submitting a question of any kind for consideration and action. Includes motions, resolutions, reports, and other kinds of proposals.

Proxy: A signed statement transferring one's right to vote (or to participate in a meeting) to another person.

Putting the question: Submitting a question to vote; taking a vote on a question.

Question: Any proposition submitted to an assembly for a decision.

Question: The word "question" spoken by members of an assembly as an informal method of indicating that they are ready to vote on a motion. The chair may then ask, "Are you ready for the question?" or "Is there further discussion?" If no one responds, the chair then puts the motion to vote.

Question of privilege: Request or motion affecting the comfort or convenience of the assembly or one of its members.

Quorom: Number or proportion of members that must be present at a meeting to enable the assembly to act legally on business.

Recess: A short interval or break in a meeting.

Recognition: The formal acknowledgment by the chair indicating that a member has the right to speak.

Recommit: To refer a matter reported by a committee back to the committee.

Reconsider: Motion to cancel the effect of a vote so that the question may be reviewed and redecided. It is a motion to undo action previously taken. It can be moved only by a member who voted on the winning side when the original motion came to vote.

Reference committee: Standing committee of a convention to which all motions dealing with a certain subject are referred.

Refer to committee: Motion to delegate work to a small group of members for study, decision, or action (*see* Commit).

Regular meeting: A meeting scheduled in the bylaws and held at definite intervals.

Renew a motion: To present the same motion a second or subsequent time at the same meeting.

Repeal: To annul or void.

Repeal by implication: When two measures that conflict are passed, the portions of the last which conflict with the first repeal the first by implication.

Rescind: To repeal; to nullify action taken on a motion.

Resolution: A formal proposal submitted in writing for action by an assembly. Usually introduced by the word "Resolved."

Restricted debate: Debate restricted to the propriety or advisability of a motion in relation to a main motion that does not open the later to debate.

Resume consideration: To take up for consideration a motion that has been postponed temporarily. The old form of the motion was "take from the table."

Rising vote: Vote taken by having members stand.

Ritual: A form or ceremony observed by an organization.

Roll call: Calling names of members in a fixed order as each answers "present" or votes.

Ruling: Decision of presiding officer on a question or point of order.

Second: An indication of approval of the consideration of a proposed motion.

Sergeant at Arms: Officer who maintains order in an assembly, under the direction of the presiding officer.

Seriatim: Manner of considering any document by sections or paragraphs.

Session: One meeting or several successive meetings at the end of which the business of the session ends. A session ends with an adjournment "without a future date."

Speaker: The person who currently has the floor.

Special committee: A committee appointed to accomplish a particular task and to submit a special report. It ceases to exist when its task is completed.

Special meeting: A meeting called to consider certain specific business that must be set forth in the call.

Specific main motion: A main motion that has a name, a specific form, and is subject to special rules, as opposed to a general main motion. Examples of specific main motions are to rescind, to reconsider, and to resume consideration.

Standing committee: A committee to handle all business on a certain subject that may be referred to it and usually having a term of service corresponding to the term of office of the officers of the organization.

Standing rules: Rules formulated and adopted by an organization to meet its own particular needs and remaining in force until repealed.

State a motion: Word-by-word statement of a motion before placing it open to debate. For example, chairperson: "It is moved and seconded that (repeat motion). Is there any discussion?"

Steam-roll: To force a measure through to vote by ruthlessly or arbitrarily overcoming the opposition.

Subsidiary motion: A motion applied to another motion for the purpose of disposing of that motion.

Substantive motion: A motion that presents a concrete proposal of business. It is not a procedural motion.

Suppress a motion: To kill a motion without letting it come to vote.

Suspend: Motion to set aside a rule or make it temporarily inoperative.

Table: To table a motion means to postpone a discussion on a motion indefinitely by referring it to the table of the presiding officer of the committee involved.

Take from the table: When this motion is passed, it brings the previous matter before the group again. It may be offered at any time as long as discussion or business of some sort has followed the placing of the matter on the table.

Teller: Member appointed to assist in conducting a vote by ballot.

Tie vote: A vote in which the positive and negative are equal, for example, a twenty-to-twenty vote. A tie vote is not sufficient to take any action.

Two-thirds vote: Two-thirds of all legal votes cast.

Unanimous: Without any dissenting vote. One adverse vote prevents unanimous approval.

Unanimous consent: An informal method of disposing of routine and generally favored motions by the chair, assuming approval of a request for unanimous consent. It is defeated by one objection.

Unfinished business: Any business deferred by a motion to postpone to a definite time, or any business that was incomplete when the previous meeting adjourned. Unfinished business has a preferred status at the following meeting.

Viva voce vote: See voice vote.

Voice vote: A vote taken by calling for "ayes" and "nays" and judged by the volume of voice response.

Voluntary organization: Nongovernmental organization members join by choice.

Vote immediately: Motion to close debate, shut off subsidiary motion, and take a vote at once (*see* Previous question).

Well taken: A point of order with which the presiding officer agrees is said to be well taken.

Withdraw: Motion by a member to remove his or her motion from consideration by the assembly.

Write in: To cast a ballot for a person who has not been nominated by writing in his or her name.

Yeas and nays: Roll-call vote during which each member answers "yea" or "nay" when his or her name is called.

Yield the floor: Grant to another member the privilege of speaking to the assembly. (The member who yields the floor retains the right to speak again as soon as the person to whom he or she has yielded has finished.)

NOTES

CHAPTER 1: TYPES OF GROUPS: THEIR NATURE AND DEVELOPMENT

1. Gerald L. Euster, "Group Work," in *Contemporary Social Work*, 2d ed., ed. Donald Brieland et al. (New York: McGraw-Hill, 1980), p. 100.
2. Ibid., p. 100.
3. Herbert Stroup, *Social Welfare Pioneers* (Chicago, IL.: Nelson-Hall, 1986), p. 9.
4. Dorothy G. Becker, "Social Welfare Leaders as Spokesmen for the Poor," *Social Casework* 49, no. 2 (Feb. 1968):85.
5. Stroup, *Social Welfare Pioneers*, pp. 1–29.
6. Ibid., pp. 255–80.
7. Ibid., p. 297.
8. Euster, "Group Work," p. 100.
9. David W. Johnson and Frank P. Johnson, *Joining Together: Group Theory and Group Skills*, 5th ed. (Boston; Allyn and Bacon, 1994), p. 13.
10. Alfred H. Katz and Eugene I. Bender, *The Strength in Us: Self-Help Groups in the Modern World* (New York: Franklin Watts, 1976). p. 9.
11. Thomas J. Powell, *Self-Help Organizations and Professional Practice* (Silver Spring, MD: National Association of Social Workers, 1987).
12. Frank Riessman, "The 'Helper Therapy' Principle," *Journal of Social Work* 10 (1965):27–34.
13. Euster, "Group Work," p. 103.
14. Kurt Lewin, "Group Decision and Social Change," in *Readings in Social Psychology*, ed. G. E. Swanson, T. M. Newcomb, and E. L. Hartley (New York: Holt, 1952), pp. 459–73.
15. Jane Howard, *Please Touch: A Guided Tour of the Human Potential Movement* (New York: McGraw-Hill, 1970), p. 3.
16. Steward L. Tubbs and John W. Baird, *The Open Person ... Self-Disclosure and Personal Growth* (Columbus, OH: Charles E. Merrill, 1976), pp. 48–50.
17. Ibid., p. 48.
18. Carl Rogers, *Carl Rogers on Encounter Groups* (New York: Harper & Row, 1970), pp. 40–41.
19. E. L. Shostrom, "Group Therapy: Let the Buyer Beware," *Psychology Today* 2, No. 12. (May 1969):38–39.
20. Morton A. Lieberman, Ervin D. Yalom, and Matthew B. Miles, "Encounter: The Leader Makes the Difference," *Psychology Today* 6 (Mar. 1973):11.
21. A. Paul Hare, *Handbook of Small Group Research* (New York: Free Press, 1962).
22. P. E. Slater, "Contrasting Correlates of Group Size," *Sociometry* 21 (1958):137–38.
23. Ibid., p. 135.
24. James C. Hansen, Richard W. Warner, and Elsie M. Smith, *Group Counseling: Theory and Process*, 2d ed. (Chicago: Rand McNally College Publishing, 1980).
25. Ibid., pp. 57–69.
26. H. J. Bertcher and Frank Maple, "Elements and Issues in Group Composition," in *Individual Change Through Small Groups*, ed. Paul Glasser, Rosemary Sarri, and Robert Vinter (New York: Free Press, 1974), pp. 186–208.
27. Ibid., pp. 187–204.
28. James A. Garland, Hubert Jones, and Ralph Kolodny, "A Model for Stages of Development in Social Work Groups," in *Explorations in Group Work*, ed. Saul Bernstein (Boston: Milford House, 1965), pp. 12–53.
29. James A. Garland and Louise A. Frey, "Applications of Stages of Group Development to Groups in Psychiatric Settings," in *Further Explorations in Group Work*, ed. by Saul Bernstein (Boston: Milford House, 1973), p. 3.
30. Ibid., p. 5.
31. Ibid., p. 6.
32. B. Tuckman, "Developmental Sequence in Small Groups," *Psychological Bulletin* 63, 1965: 384–99.
33. Robert F. Bales, "The Equilibrium Problem in Small Groups," in A. Hare, E. Borgatta, and R. Bales, eds, *Small Groups: Studies in Social Interaction* (New York: Knopf, 1965), pp. 444–76.

CHAPTER 2: SOCIAL GROUP WORK AND SOCIAL WORK PRACTICE

1. For a sumharles Zastrow, *The Practice of Social Work*, 5th ed. (Pacific Grove, CA: Brooks/Cole Publishing Co., 1995).
2. National Association of Social Workers, *Standards for Social Service Manpower* (Washington, DC, 1973), pp. 3–4.
3. A. Pincus and A. Minahan, *Social Work Practice: Model and Method* (Itasca, IL: Peacock, 1973), p. 54.
4. Robert L. Barker, *The Social Work Dictionary*, 2nd ed. (Silver

Spring, MD: National Association of Social Workers, 1991), p. 221.

5. J. Anderson, *Social Work Methods and Processes* (Belmont, CA: Wadsworth, 1981).

6. D. Brieland, L. B. Costin, and C. R. Atherton, *Contemporary Social Work: An Introduction to Social Work and Social Welfare,* 3d ed. (New York: McGraw-Hill, 1985), pp. 120–21.

7. Grafton Hull, Jr., *Social Work Internship Manual* (Eau Claire, WI: University of Wisconsin-Eau Claire, 1990), p. 7.

8. Council on Social Work Education, *Curriculum Policy Statement for Baccalaureate Degree Programs in Social Work Education* and *Curriculum Policy Statement for Master's Degree Programs in Social Work Education* (Alexandria, VA: Council on Social Work Education, 1992).

9. W. H. Masters and V. E. Johnson, *Human Sexual Inadequacy* (Boston: Little, Brown, 1970).

10. D. D. Jackson, "The Study of the Family," *Family Process* 4, 1965: 1–20.

11. A. Hofer and W. Polin, "Schizophrenia in the NAS-NRC Panel of 15, 909 Twin Pairs," *Archives of General Psychiatry* 23, 1970: 469–77.

12. S. S. Kety, "The Biological Roots of Schizophrenia," *Harvard Magazine* 78, 1976: 20–26.

13. Richard B. Stuart, *Trick or Treatment* (Champaign, IL: Research Press Co., 1970).

14. National Association of Social Workers, *Standards for the Classification of Social Work Practice* (Washington, DC: National Association of Social Workers, 1982), p. 17.

15. Council on Social Work Education, *Curriculum Policy Statements.*

16. D. H. Hepworth and J. Larsen, *Direct Social Work Practice: Theory and Skills,* 2d ed. (Pacific Grove, CA: Brooks/Cole, 1986), p. 563.

17. Barker, *The Social Work Dictionary,* p. 29.

18. F. Riessman, "The 'Helper Therapy' Principle" *Journal of Social Work* 2 (April 1965):27–34.

19. Barker, *The Social Work Dictionary,* p. 43.

20. Council on Social Work Education, *Curriculum Policy Statements.*

21. Ronald Federico, *The Social Welfare Institution,* (Lexington, MA: Heath, 1973), pp. 146–47.

22. Betty L. Baer, "Developing a New Curriculum for Social Work Education," in *The Pursuit of Competence in Social Work,* eds. F. Clark and M. Arkava (San Francisco: Jossey-Bass, 1979), p. 106.

23. Betty L. Baer and Ronald Federico, *Educating the Baccalaureate Social Worker* (Cambridge, MA: Ballinger Publishing, 1978).

24. Council on Social Work Education, *Curriculum Policy Statement.*

CHAPTER 3: LEADERSHIP ROLES, FUNCTIONS, AND GUIDELINES

1. David Krech, Richard S. Crutchfield, and Egerton L. Ballachey, *Individual in Society* (New York: McGraw-Hill, 1962), pp. 428–31.

2. A. Paul Hare, *Handbook of Small Group Research* (New York: Free Press, 1962), pp. 292–93.

3. J. S. Davis and A. P. Hare, "Button-down Collar Culture: A Study of Undergraduate Life at a Men's College," *Human Organization* 14 (1956):13–20.

4. J. G. March, "Influence Measurement in Experimental and Semi-experimental Groups," *Sociometry* 19 (1956):260–71.

5. David W. Johnson and Frank P. Johnson, *Joining Together: Group Theory and Group Skills,* 3d ed. (Englewood Cliffs, NJ: Prentice-Hall, 1987), p. 43.

6. Ibid., p. 44.

7. R. Christie and F. Geis, *Studies in Machiavellianism,* (New York: Academic Press, 1970).

8. K. Lewin, R. Lippitt, and R. K. White, "Patterns of Aggressive Behavior in Experimentally Created Social Climates," *Journal of Social Psychology* 10 (1939):271–99.

9. Hare, *Handbook,* p. 309.

10. R. F. Bales, *Interaction Process Analysis: A Method for the Study of Small Groups* (Reading, Mass.: Addison-Wesley, 1950).

11. P. Hersey and K. Blanchard, *Management of Organizational Behavior: Utilizing Human Resources,* 3d ed. (Englewood Cliffs, NJ: Prentice-Hall, 1977).

12. J. R. P. French and B. Raven, "The Bases of Social Power," in *Group Dynamics: Research and Theory,* 3d ed., ed. Dorwin Cartwright and Alvin Zander (New York: Harper & Row, 1968), pp. 259–69.

13. E. E. Jones and H. B. Gerard, *Foundations of Social Psychology* (New York: John Wiley and Sons, 1967).

14. L. J. Halle, "Overestimating the Power of Power," *New Republic* 10 (June 1967):15–17.

15. Dorwin Cartwright and Alvin Zander, "Power and Influence in Groups," in *Group Dynamics,* 3d ed., ed. Cartwright and Zander (New York: Harper & Row, 1968), pp. 215–35.

16. M. Deutsch, "Conflicts: Productive and Destructive," *Journal of Social Issues* 25 (1969):7–43.

17. Saul Alinsky, *Rules for Radicals* (New York: Vintage, 1972).

18. Ibid., pp. 143–44.

CHAPTER 4: PERSONAL GOALS, GROUP GOALS, AND THE NOMINAL GROUP

1. David W. Johnson and Frank P. Johnson, *Joining Together: Group Theory and Group Skills* (Englewood Cliffs, N.J.: Prentice-Hall, 1975), p. 88.

2. Ibid., p. 103.

3. Ibid., pp. 104–105.

4. Ibid., p. 97.

5. M. Deutsch, "A Theory of Cooperation and Competition," *Human Relations* 2 (1949):129–52.

6. Johnson and Johnson, *Joining Together,* p. 97.

7. H. H. Kelly and A. J. Stahelski, "Social Interaction Basis of Cooperators' and Competitors' Beliefs about Others," *Journal of Personality and Social Psychology* 16 (1970):66–91.

8. M. Deutsch, "The Effect of Motivational Orientation upon Trust and Suspicion," *Human Relations* 13 (1960):123–39.

9. Andre L. Delbecq and Andrew Van de Ven, "A Group Process Model for Problem Identification and Program Planning," *Journal of Applied Behavioral Science* 7 (1971):466–92.

10. Andrew Van de Ven and Andre L. Delbecq, "Nominal versus Interacting Group Processes for Committee Decision-Making Effectiveness," *Academy of Management Journal* 14 (1971):205.

11. For an illustration of the nominal group approach in developing social programs, see Charles Zastrow, "The Nominal Group: A New Approach to Designing Programs for Curbing Delinquency," *Canadian Journal of Criminology and Corrections* 15 (1973):109–17.

12. For an additional discussion of using the nominal group approach to identity course content, see Charles Zastrow and Ralph Navarre, "The Nominal Group: A New Tool for Making Social Work Education Relevant," *Journal of Education for Social Work* 13 (1977):112–18.

13. Van de Ven and Delbecq, "Nominal versus Interacting Group Processes," p. 205.

14. Ibid.

CHAPTER 5: GROUP NORMS AND PROBLEMS OF CONFORMITY

1. Rodney W. Napier and Matti K. Gershenfeld, *Groups: Theory and Experience,* 2d ed. (Boston: Houghton Mifflin, 1981), p. 134.

2. Muzafer Sherif, "A Study of Some Social Factors in Perception," *Archives of Psychology* 187 (1935):1–27; M. Sherif, *The Psychology of Social Norms* (New York: Harper, 1936); and M. Sherif, "Conformity—Deviation, Norms and Group Relations," in *Conformity and Deviation,* ed. I. A. Berg and B. M. Bass (New York: Harper, 1961), pp. 159–98.

3. S. E. Asch, "Effects of Group Pressure upon the Modification and Distortion of Judgments," in *Groups, Leadership, and Men,* ed. H. Guetzkow (Pittsburgh: Carnegie, 1951), pp. 177–90; S. E. Asch, "Opinions and Social Pressure," *Scientific American* 193, no. 5 (1955):31–35; and S. E. Asch, "Studies of Independence and Conformity: A Minority of One Against a Unanimous Majority," *Psychological Monographs* 70, no. 9 (1956):1–70.

4. Stanley Schachter, *The Psychology of Affiliation* (Palo Alto, Calif.: Stanford University Press, 1959); and Stanley Schachter and J. Singer, "The Theory of Social Comparison," *Psychological Review* 69 (1962):379–99.

5. David Krech, Richard S. Crutchfield, and Egerton L. Bal-

lachey, *Individual in Society* (New York: McGraw-Hill, 1962), pp. 509–12.

6. S. Milgram, "Behavioral Study of Obedience," *Journal of Abnormal and Social Psychology* 68 (1963):371–78.

7. E. P. Hollander, "Conformity, Status, and Idiosyncrasy Credit," *Psychological Review* 65 (1958):117–27.

8. George R. Bach and Peter Wyden, *The Intimate Enemy* (New York: Avon, 1981).

9. Thomas Gordon, *Parent Effectiveness Training* (New York: Peter H. Wyden, 1970).

CHAPTER 6: WORKING WITH MINORITY GROUPS

1. *Code of Ethics of the National Association of Social Workers,* which was revised and adopted by the 1979 Delegate Assembly of NASW.

2. Robert Merton, "Discrimination and the American Creed," in *Discrimination and National Welfare,* ed. Robert M. MacIver (New York: Harper & Row, 1949).

3. Council on Social Work Education, *Curriculum Policy Statement for Baccalaureate Degree Program in Social Work Education* and *Curriculum Policy Statement for Master's Degree Programs in Social Work Education* (Alexandria, VA: Council on Social Work Education, 1992).

4. Ibid.

5. Robert L. Barker, *The Social Work Dictionary,* 2d ed. (Silver Spring, MD: National Association of Social Workers, 1991), p. 219.

6. Ibid., p. 70.

7. Excerpted from a speech by Abraham Lincoln in Charleston, Illinois, in 1858, as reported in Richard Hofstader, *The American Political Tradition* (New York: Knopf, 1948), p. 116.

8. Janet S. Hyde, *Understanding Human Sexuality,* 4th ed. (New York: McGraw-Hill, 1990), pp. 420–23.

9. Ibid.

10. Ibid.

11. Ibid.

12. Alfred Kinsey, W. B. Pomeroy, and C. E. Martin, *Sexual Behavior in the Human Male* (Philadelphia, PA: Saunders, 1948).

13. Hyde, *Understanding Human Sexuality,* pp. 420–26.

14. Alan P. Bell, Martin S. Weinberg, and Sue Kiefer Hammersmith, *Sexual Preference* (Bloomington, IN: Indiana University Press, 1981).

15. Mizio Emelicia, "White Worker-Minority Client," *Social Worker* 17 (May 1972):82–86.

16. Clifford J. Sager, Thomas L. Brayboy, and Barbara R. Waxenberg, *Black Ghetto Family in Therapy: A Laboratory Experience* (New York: Grove Press, 1970), pp. 210–11.

17. Ronald G. Lewis and Man Keung Ho, "Social Work with Native Americans," *Social Work* 20 (Sept. 1975):378–82.

18. Lloyd G. Sinclair, "Sex Counseling and Therapy," in *The Practice of Social Work,* 5th ed. (Pacific Grove, CA: Brooks/Cole, 1995), pp. 490–97.

19. Richard T. Shaefer, *Racial and Ethnic Groups,* 5th ed. (New York: HarperCollins, 1993), pp. 273–99.
20. Ibid.
21. Ibid., p. 296.
22. J. L. Dillard, *Black English: Its History and Usage in the U.S.* (New York: Random House, 1972).
23. A. N. Wilson, *The Developmental Psychology of the Black Child* (New York: African Research Publication, 1978).
24. Beatrice A. Wright, *Physical Disability: A Psychological Approach* (New York: Harper & Row, 1960), p. 259.
25. Nancy Weinberg, "Rehabilitation," in *Contemporary Social Work,* 2d. ed., eds. Donald Brieland, Lela Costin, and Charles Atherton (New York: McGraw-Hill, 1980), p. 310.
26. Ibid.
27. Dolores G. Norton, "Incorporating Content on Minority Groups into Social Work Practice Courses," in *The Dual Perspective* (New York: Council on Social Work Education, 1978), p. 22.
28. Grafton H. Hull, Jr., "Social Work Practice with Diverse Groups" in *The Practice of Social Work,* 5th ed., ed. Charles Zastrow (Pacific Grove, CA: Brooks/Cole, 1995), p. 359.
29. Melvin Delgado and Denise Humm-Delgado, "Natural Support Systems: Source of Strength in Hispanic Communities," *Social Work* 27, no. 1 (Jan. 1982):83–89.
30. Alfred Kadushin, *The Social Work Interview* (New York: Columbia University Press, 1972).
31. Larry E. Davis, "Racial Composition of Groups," *Social Work* 24 (May 1979):208–13.
32. Jimm G. Good Tracks, "Native American Noninterference," *Social Work* 18 (Nov. 1973):30–34.
33. A. E. Moses and R. O. Hawkins, *Counseling Lesbian Women and Gay Men: A Life-Issues Approach* (St. Louis, MO: C. V. Mosby, 1982).
34. Jeannine Gramick, "Homophobia: A New Challenge," *Social Work* 28, no. 2 (March-April 1983):137–41.
35. Larry E. Davis, Maeda J. Galinsky, and Janice H. Schopler, "RAP: A Framework for Leadership of Multiracial Groups," *Social Work* 40, no. 2 (March 1995):155–65.

CHAPTER 7: VERBAL COMMUNICATION

1. Gordon W. Allport and L. J. Postman, "The Basic Psychology of Rumor," *Transactions of the New York Academy of Sciences,* 11th ser., vol. 8 (1945):61–81; and F. C. Bartlett, *Remembering* (Cambridge, England: Cambridge University Press, 1932).
2. Douglas McGregor, *The Professional Manager* (New York: McGraw-Hill, 1967).
3. A. A. Harrison, *Individuals and Groups* (Monterey, Calif.: Brooks/Cole, 1976), pp. 100–107.
4. Ronald B. Adler and Neil Towne, *Looking Out/Looking In,* 3d ed. (New York: Holt, Rinehart and Winston, 1981), p. 171.
5. Ibid., p. 178.
6. Ibid.
7. Ibid., p. 180.

8. Jack R. Gibb, "Defensive Communication," *Journal of Communication* 11 (1961):141–48.
9. Adler and Towne, *Looking Out,* p. 38.
10. Sidney M. Jourard, *The Transparent Self* (New York: Van Nostrand Reinhold, 1971).
11. Ibid., pp. 47–63.
12. Joseph Luft, *Of Human Interaction* (Palo Alto, Calif.: National Press Books, 1969).
13. Alfred Kadushin, *The Social Work Interview* (New York: Columbia University Press), p. 188.
14. Ibid., p. 190.
15. Thomas Gordon, *Parent Effectiveness Training* (New York: Peter H. Wyden, 1970).
16. This story by Samuel J. Sackett, entitled "Tin Lizzie," appears in David W. Johnson and Frank P. Johnson, *Joining Together: Group Therapy and Group Skills* (Englewood Cliffs, N.J.; Prentice-Hall, 1975), pp. 327–28.

CHAPTER 8: NONVERBAL COMMUNICATION

1. Quoted in Ronald B. Adler and Neil Towne, *Looking Out/Looking In,* 3d ed. (New York: Holt, Rinehart and Winston, 1981), p. 253.
2. Sir Arthur Conan Doyle, "A Scandal in Bohemia," in *The Adventures of Sherlock Holmes* (London: John Murray, 1974).
3. Adler and Towne, *Looking Out,* p. 257.
4. Albert Mehrabian, *Silent Messages,* 2d ed. (Belmont, Calif.: Wadsworth, 1981).
5. Paul Ekman and Wallace V. Friesen, *Unmasking the Face* (Englewood Cliffs, N.J.: Prentice-Hall, 1975).
6. Adler and Towne, *Looking Out,* p. 266.
7. E. H. Hess and J. M. Polt, "Pupil Size as Related to Interest Value of Visual Stimuli," *Science* 132 (1960):349–50.
8. Albert E. Scheflen, *How Behavior Means* (Garden City, NY: Anchor, 1974).
9. Rene Spitz, "Hospitalization: Genesis of Psychiatric Conditions in Early Childhood," in *Psychoanalytic Study of the Child* 1 (1945):53.
10. Ashley Montagu, *Touching: The Human Significance of the Skin* (New York: Harper & Row, 1971).
11. Quoted in Adler and Towne, *Looking Out,* p. 279.
12. R. Hoult, "Experimental Measurement of Clothing as a Factor in Some Social Ratings of Selected American Men," *American Sociological Review* 19 (1954):324–28.
13. Adler and Towne, *Looking Out,* p. 281.
14. Edward T. Hall, *The Hidden Dimension* (Garden City, N.Y.: Doubleday, 1969).
15. Mark L. Knapp, *Nonverbal Communication in Human Interaction,* 2d ed. (New York: Holt, Rinehart and Winston, 1978), p. 115.
16. Ibid., p. 323.
17. G. L. Trager, "Paralanguage: A First Approximation," *Studies in Linguistics* 13 (1958):1–12.
18. Mehrabian, *Silent Messages,* pp. 46–55.

19. J. E. Singer, "The Use of Manipulative Strategies: Machiavellianism and Attractiveness," *Sociometry* 27 (1964):128–51.

20. J. Mills and E. Aronson, "Opinion Change as a Function of the Communicator's Attractiveness and Desire to Influence," *Journal of Personality and Social Psychology* 1 (1965):73–77.

21. R. N. Widgery and B. Webster, "The Effects of Physical Attractiveness upon perceived Initial Credibility," *Michigan Speech Journal* 4 (1969):9–15.

22. E. K. Solender and E. Solender, "Minimizing the Effect of the Unattractive Client on the Jury: A Study of the Interaction of Physical Appearance with Assertions and Self-experience References," *Human Rights* 5 (1976):201–14.

23. Knapp, *Nonverbal Communication,* p. 156.

24. E. Berscheid and E. H. Walster, "Physical Attractiveness," in *Advances in Experimental Social Psychology,* ed. L. Berkowitz (New York: Academic Press, 1974), 7:158–215.

25. R. Algozzine, "What Teachers Perceive—Children Receive," *Communication Quarterly* 24 (1976):41–47.

26. Knapp, *Nonverbal Communication,* p. 159.

27. D. Bar-Tal and L. Saxe, "Perceptions of Similarity and Dissimilarity of Physically Attractive Couples and Individuals," *Journal of Personality and Social Psychology* 33 (1976):772–81.

28. R. W. Parnell, *Behavior and Physique: An Introduction to Practical and Applied Somatometry* (London: Edward Arnold, 1958).

29. Knapp, *Nonverbal Communication,* p. 166.

30. A. H. Maslow and N. L. Mintz, "Effects of Esthetic Surroundings. I. Initial Effects of Three Esthetic Conditions upon Perceiving 'Energy' and 'Well-Being' in Faces," *Journal of Psychology* 41 (1956):247–54.

CHAPTER 9: PROBLEM SOLVING, CONTROVERSY, AND CONFLICT RESOLUTION

1. David W. Johnson and Frank P. Johnson, *Joining Together: Group Therapy and Group Skills* (Englewood Cliffs, N.J.: Prentice-Hall, 1975), p. 257.

2. James W. Coleman and Donald R. Cressey, *Social Problems,* 5th ed. (New York: HarperCollins, 1993), pp. 346–47.

3. See Rodney W. Napier and Matti K. Gershenfeld, *Groups: Theory and Experience,* 2d ed. (Boston: Houghton Mifflin, 1981), p. 384.

4. See V. H. Vroom, L. D. Grant, and T. S. Cotton, "The Consequences of Social Interaction in Group Problem Solving," *Journal of Organizational Behavior and Human Performance* 4 (1969):79–95; and R. A. Collaros and L. Anderson, "Effects of Perceived Expertness upon Creativity of Members of Brainstorming Groups," *Journal of Applied Psychology* 53 (1969):159–64.

5. T. J. Bouchard, "Training, Motivation and Personality as Determinants of the Effectiveness of Brainstorming Groups and Individuals," *Journal of Applied Psychology* 56 (1972): 324–31.

6. Napier and Gershenfeld, *Groups,* p. 385.

7. Johnson and Johnson, *Joining Together,* p. 139.

8. Ibid., p. 158.

9. M. Deutsch, "Conflicts: Productive and Destructive," *Journal of Social Issues* 25 (1969):7–43.

10. Milton Rokeach, *The Open and Closed Mind* (New York: Basic, 1960).

11. Thomas Gordon, *Parent Effectiveness Training* (New York: Peter H. Wyden, 1970).

12. Ibid., p. 237.

13. Muzafer Sherif, *In Common Predicament* (Boston: Houghton Mifflin, 1966); G. Watson and David W. Johnson, *Social Psychology: Issues and Insights,* 2d ed. (Philadelphia: Lippincott, 1972); and R. R. Blake and J. S. Mouton, "The Intergroup Dynamics of Win-Lose Conflict and Problem-Solving Collaboration in Union-Management Relations," in *Intergroup Relations and Leadership,* ed. Muzafer Sherif (New York: John Wiley and Sons, 1962), pp. 94–142.

14. David W. Johnson, "Role Reversal: A Summary and Review of the Research," *International Journal of Group Tensions* 1 (1971):318–34.

15. Christopher W. Moore, *The Mediation Process* (San Francisco, Calif.: Jossey-Bass, 1986), p. 21.

16. Ibid., pp. 21–22.

17. Ibid., p. 22.

18. Ibid., p. 23.

19. Ibid., p. 6.

20. See Moore, *Mediation Process,* for a review.

21. Joan Blades, *Mediate Your Divorce* (Englewood Cliffs, N.J.: Prentice-Hall, 1985).

22. Moore, *Mediation Process.*

CHAPTER 10: DECISION MAKING

1. David W. Johnson and Frank P. Johnson, *Joining Together: Group Therapy and Group Skills* (Englewood Cliffs, NJ: Prentice-Hall, 1975), p. 55.

2. George F. Cole, *The American System of Criminal Justice,* 6th ed. (Pacific Grove, CA: Brooks/Cole, 1992), p. 534.

3. David Whitman, "Welfare: The Myth of Reform," *U.S. News & World Report* (January 16, 1995):30–39.

4. James W. Coleman and Donald R. Cressey, *Social Problems,* 5th ed. (New York: HarperCollins, 1993), pp. 202–208.

5. William Kornblum and Joseph Julian, *Social Problems,* 7th ed. (Englewood Cliffs, NJ: Prentice-Hall, 1992), pp. 96–99.

6. Ibid., pp. 160–61.

7. Johnson and Johnson, *Joining Together,* p. 60.

8. Ibid., p. 75.

9. G. Watson and David W. Johnson, *Social Psychology: Issues and Insights,* 2d ed. (Philadelphia, PA.: Lippincott, 1972).

10. Irving L. Janis, "Groupthink," *Psychology Today* (November 1971):43–46, 74–76.

CHAPTER 11: PARLIAMENTARY PROCEDURE

1. Henry M. Robert, *Robert's Rules of Order Revised* (New York: William Morrow, 1971).

CHAPTER 12: ORGANIZATIONS AND GROUPS

1. A. Etzioni, *Modern Organizations* (Englewood Cliffs: NJ: Prentice-Hall, 1964), p. 1.
2. F. E. Netting, P. M. Kettner, and S. L. McMurtry, *Social Work Macro Practice* (New York: Longman, 1993), p. 123.
3. Ibid.
4. David W. Johnson and Frank P. Johnson, *Joining Together: Group Theory and Group Skills,* 5th ed. (Boston: Allyn and Bacon, 1994), p. 13.
5. K. Davis and J. W. Newstrom, *Human Behavior at Work,* 8th ed. (New York: McGraw-Hill, 1989), p. 31.
6. Ibid., p. 31.
7. Frederick Taylor, *Scientific Management* (New York: Harper & Row, 1947).
8. F. J. Roethlisberger and W. J. Dickson, *Management and the Worker* (Cambridge, MA: Harvard University Press, 1939).
9. Etzioni, *Modern Organizations,* pp. 34–35.
10. Netting, Kettner, and McMurtry, *Social Work Macro Practice,* p. 131.
11. D. McGregor, *The Human Side of Enterprise* (New York: McGraw-Hill, 1960).
12. Davis and Newstrom, *Human Behavior at Work,* p. 34.
13. William Ouchi, *Theory Z: How American Business Can Meet the Japanese Challenge* (Reading, MA: Addison-Wesley, 1981).
14. Peter F. Drucker, *The Practice of Management* (New York: Harper, 1954).
15. Vincent K. Omachony and Joel E. Ross, *Principles of Total Quality* (Delray Beach, FL: St. Lucie Press, 1994), p. 1.
16. Ibid.
17. David Hower, "David Hower's Definition of Total Quality," *Reporter* (Whitewater, WI: University of Wisconsin-Whitewater, August 29, 1994):10.
18. R. Knopf, *Surviving the BS (Bureaucratic System),* (Wilmington, NC: Mandala Press, 1979), pp. 21–22.
19. Ibid., p. 25.
20. Ibid.
21. Ibid.

CHAPTER 13: COMMUNITIES AND GROUPS

1. Robert L. Barker, *The Social Work Dictionary,* 2nd ed. (Silver Spring, MD: National Association of Social Workers, 1991), p. 43.

2. Ibid., p. 116.
3. David W. Johnson and Frank P. Johnson, *Joining Together: Group Theory and Group Skills,* 5th ed. (Boston: Allyn and Bacon, 1994), p. 13.
4. Barker, *The Social Work Dictionary,* p. 43.
5. Saul Alinsky, *Rules for Radicals* (New York: Random House, 1972), p. 27.
6. _____, *Reveille for Radicals* (New York: Basic Books, 1969), p. 42.

CHAPTER 14: SELF-HELP GROUPS

1. Gary Bonds et al., "Growth of a Medical Self-Help Group," in *Self-Help Groups for Coping with Crisis,* ed. Morton A. Lieberman, Leonard D. Borman, and Associates (San Francisco, CA: Jossey-Bass, 1979), pp. 43–66.
2. Leonard D. Borman and Morton A. Lieberman, "Conclusion: Contributions, Dilemmas, and Implications for Mental Health Policy" in Lieberman et al., *Self-Help Groups for Coping with Crisis: Origins, Members, Processes, and Impact.* San Francisco, CA: Jossey-Bass, 1979, p. 408.
3. Morton A. Lieberman and Leonard D. Borman, "Overview: The Nature of Self-Help Groups," in Lieberman et al., *Self-Help Groups for Coping with Crisis,* p. 2.
4. Dean H. Hepworth and Jo Ann Larsen, *Direct Social Work Practice: Theory and Skills* (Homewood, IL: Dorsey Press, 1986), p. 549.
5. Frank Reissman, "Foreword," in Thomas J. Powell, *Self-Help Organizations and Professional Practice* (Silver Spring, MD: National Association of Social Workers, 1987), pp. ix–x.
6. Alfred H. Katz and Eugene I. Bender, *The Strength in Us: Self-Help Groups in the Modern World* (New York: Franklin-Watts, 1976).
7. Ibid., p. 38.
8. Ibid.
9. Thomas J. Powell, *Self-Help Organizations and Professional Practice* (Silver Spring, MD: National Association of Social Workers, 1987).
10. Frank Reissman, "The 'Helper Therapy' Principle," *Journal of Social Work* (April 1965):27–34.
11. Hepworth and Larsen, *Direct Social Work Practice,* p. 549.
12. L. Borman, "New Self-Help and Support Systems for the Chronically Mentally Ill," paper presented at the Pittsburgh Conference on Neighborhood Support Systems, Pittsburgh, PA, June 15, 1979.
13. Lambert Maguire, "Natural Helping Networks and Self-Help Groups," in *Primary Prevention in Mental Health and Social Work,* ed. Milton Nobel (New York: Council on Social Work Education, 1981), p. 41.
14. Hepworth and Larsen, *Direct Social Work Practice,* p. 550.
15. Lieberman and Borman, "Overview," p. 31.

CHAPTER 15: STRESS MANAGEMENT

1. Herbert M. Greenberg, *Coping with Job Stress* (Englewood Cliffs, NJ: Prentice-Hall, 1980), pp. 39–49.
2. John A. Romas and Manoj Sharma, *Practical Stress Management* (Boston: Allyn and Bacon, 1995).
3. O. Carl Simonton and Stephanie Matthews-Simonton, *Getting Well Again* (Los Angeles: J. P. Tarcher, 1978).
4. Bernard Gauzer, "What We Can Learn from Those Who Survive AIDS," *Parade Magazine,* June 10, 1990, pp. 4–7.
5. Kenneth R. Pelletier, *Mind as Healer, Mind as Slayer* (New York: Dell, 1977), p. 310.
6. Donald A. Tubesing, *Kicking Your Stress Habits* (Duluth, MN: Whole Person Associates, 1981).
7. Hans Selye, *The Stress of Life* (New York: McGraw-Hill, 1956).
8. Ibid., pp. 25–46.
9. For an expanded description of the physiological reactions involved in stress, see Romas and Sharma, *Practical Stress Management,* pp. 35–64.
10. Tubesing, *Kicking Your Stress Habits,* pp. 9–52.
11. Hans Selye, *Stress without Distress* (New York: Signet, 1974), p. 83.
12. Ibid.
13. Jerry Edelwich, *Burn-Out* (New York: Human Sciences Press, 1980); Ayala Pines and Elliot Aronson, *Burnout* (New York: Free Press, 1981); Herbert Freudenberger, *Burn-Out* (Garden City: NY: Anchor, 1980); and Christina Maslach, *Burnout— The Cost of Caring* (Englewood Cliffs, NJ: Spectrum, 1982).
14. W. Ryan, *Blaming the Victim* (New York: Pantheon, 1971); and Christina Maslach and Ayala Pines, "The Burn-Out Syndrome in the Day Care Setting," *Child Care Quarterly* 6 (1977):100–101.
15. Freudenberger, *Burn-Out,* pp. 90–91.
16. Edelwich, *Burn-Out,* pp. 44–142.
17. Christina Maslach, "Burned-Out," *Human Behavior* 5 (1976):19.
18. Ibid., p. 20.
19. Christina Maslach, "The Client Role in Staff Burn-Out," *Journal of Social Issues* 34 (1978):111-24.
20. Pines and Aronson, "Burn-Out Syndrome," pp. 45-81.
21. Alan Lakein, *How to Get Control of Your Time and Your Life* (New York: Signet, 1973).
22. These relaxation techniques are more fully described in Charles Zastrow, *You Are What You Think: A Guide to Self-Realization* (Chicago: Nelson-Hall, 1993).
23. Edmund Jacobson, *Progressive Relaxation,* 2d ed. (Chicago: University of Chicago Press, 1938).
24. D. L. Watson and R. G. Tharp, *Self-Directed Behavior* (Monterey, CA: Brooks/Cole, 1973), pp. 182–83.
25. Herbert Benson, *The Relaxation Response* (New York: Avon, 1975).
26. Greenberg, *Coping with Job Stress,* pp. 142–45.
27. Anthony De Mello, *Sadhana: A Way to God* (Garden City, NY: Image Books, 1978), p. 140.
28. Albert Ellis and Robert Harper, *A New Guide to Rational Living* (North Hollywood, CA: Wilshire. 1977).
29. For case examples demonstrating how to change unwanted emotions, see Zastrow, *You Are What You Think.*
30. Walt Schafer, *Stress, Distress and Growth* (Davis, CA.: International Dialogue Press, 1978).

CHAPTER 16: TIME MANAGEMENT

1. Harold L. Taylor, *Making Time Work for You* (New York: Dell, 1981), p. 13.
2. Alan Lakein, *How to Get Control of Your Time and Your Life* (New York: Signet, 1973), p. 28.
3. Ibid., p. 47.
4. Ibid., p. 71.
5. Ibid.
6. Two resource books on time management principles in work situations are Rita Davenport, *Making Time, Making Money* (New York: St. Martin's Press, 1982); and Taylor, *Making Time Work for You.*
7. Taylor, *Making Time Work for You,* p. 171.

CHAPTER 17: STARTING AND LEADING THERAPY GROUPS

1. These therapy approaches are described in Raymond J. Corsini and Danny Wedding, *Current Psychotherapies,* 4th ed. (Itasca, Ill.: Peacock, 1989), and Charles Zastrow, *The Practice of Social Work,* 5th ed. (Pacific Grove, CA: Brooks/Cole, 1995).
2. Frank Riessman, "The 'Helper Therapy' Principle," *Journal of Social Work,* (April 1965):27–34.
3. Elizabeth Kübler-Ross, *On Death and Dying* (New York: Macmillan, 1969).
4. *NASW Code of Ethics* (Washington, DC: National Association of Social Workers, 1994).
5. Ibid.

CHAPTER 18: CLIENT-CENTERED THERAPY IN GROUPS

1. Carl Rogers, *Client-Centered Therapy* (Boston: Houghton Mifflin, 1951).
2. Betty D. Meador and Carl Rogers, "Person-Centered Therapy," in *Current Psychotherapies,* 2d ed., ed. Raymond J. Corsini (Itasca, IL: Peacock, 1979), p. 152.
3. Carl Rogers, "The Process Equation of Psychotherapy," *American Journal of Psychotherapy* 15 (January 1961):32.
4. Meador and Rogers, "Person-Centered Therapy," p. 157.
5. Carl Rogers, "A Theory of Therapy, Personality, and Interpersonal Relationships, as Developed in the Client-Centered Framework," in *Psychology: A Study of a Science,* vol. 3, ed. S. Koch (New York: McGraw-Hill, 1959), pp. 184–256.

6. Nathaniel J. Raskin and Carl Rogers, "Person-Centered Therapy," in *Current Psychotherapies,* 4th ed., ed. Raymond J. Corsini and Danny Wedding (Itasca, IL.: Peacock, 1989), p. 182.
7. B. K. Simon, "Social Casework Theory: An Overview," in *Theories of Social Casework,* ed. R. Roberts and R. Nee (Chicago: University of Chicago Press, 1970), pp. 353–96.
8. Joel Fischer, *Effective Casework Practice,* (New York: McGraw-Hill, 1978), p. 207.
9. H. J. Eysenck, "The Effects of Psychotherapy," *International Journal of Psychiatry* 1 (1965):97–144.
10. William Glasser, *Reality Therapy* (New York: Harper & Row, 1965).
11. James O. Prochaska, *Systems of Psychotherapy* (Homewood, IL.: Dorsey Press, 1979), p. 137.

CHAPTER 19: TRANSACTIONAL ANALYSIS IN GROUPS

1. Eric Berne, *Games People Play* (New York: Grove, 1964); Eric Berne, *Principles of Group Treatment* (New York: Oxford University Press, 1966); and Eric Berne, *Transactional Analysis in Psychotherapy* (New York: Grove, 1961).
2. Additional useful references on Transactional Analysis are Thomas Harris, *I'm OK—You're OK* (New York: Harper & Row, 1969); John M. Dusay and Katherine M. Dusay, "Transactional Analysis" in *Current Psychotherapies,* 4th ed., Raymond J. Corsini and Danny Wedding, eds. (Itasca, IL: Peacock, 1989), pp. 405–53.
3. Berne, *Games People Play,* pp. 48–55.
4. Ibid., pp. 72–83.
5. James O. Prochaska, *Systems of Psychotherapy* (Homewood, IL.: Dorsey, 1979), pp. 237–38.
6. Ibid., p. 238.
7. Ibid.
8. Berne, *Games People Play,* pp. 125–29.
9. Ibid., p. 71–72.
10. Harris, *I'm OK—You're OK.*
11. Prochaska, *Systems,* p. 241.
12. Muriel James and Dorothy Jongeward, *Born to Win: Transactional Analysis with Gestalt Experiments* (Reading, MA: Addison-Wesley, 1971), pp. 84–85.
13. Ibid., p. 35.
14. Ibid., p. 70.
15. Berne, *Group Treatment,* p. 310.

CHAPTER 20: REALITY THERAPY IN GROUPS

1. William Glasser, *Reality Therapy* (New York: Harper & Row, 1965).
2. William Glasser and Leonard Zunin, "Reality Therapy" in *Current Psychotherapies,* 2d ed., ed. Raymond Corsini (Itasca, IL.: Peacock, 1979), p. 302.
3. Ibid., p. 312.
4. Ibid.
5. Thomas Szasz, "The Myth of Mental Illness," in *Clinical Psychology in Transition,* ed. John R. Braun (Cleveland, OH: Howard Allen, 1961).
6. Glasser, *Reality Therapy,* pp. 15–16.

CHAPTER 21: RATIONAL THERAPY IN GROUPS

1. Albert Ellis, "Rational-Emotive Therapy," in *Current Psychotherapies,* 4th ed., Raymond Corsini and Danny Wedding, eds. (Itasca, IL.: Peacock, 1989), pp. 197–239; Maxie C. Maultsby, Jr., *Help Yourself to Happiness* (Boston: Herman, 1975).
2. Charles Zastrow, *You Are What You Think: A Guide to Self-Realization* (Chicago: Nelson-Hall, 1993).
3. Maultsby, *Help Yourself to Happiness.*

CHAPTER 22: BEHAVIOR THERAPY IN GROUPS

1. Edward Thorndike, *The Psychology of Learning* (New York: Teachers College Press, 1913); E. R. Guthrie, *The Psychology of Learning* (New York: Harper and Row, 1935); C. L. Hull, *Principles of Behavior* (New York: Appleton-Century-Crofts, 1943); E. C. Tolman, *Purposive Behavior in Animals and Men* (New York: Appleton-Century-Crofts, 1932); and B. F. Skinner, *The Behavior of Organisms* (New York: Appleton-Century-Crofts, 1938).
2. R. E. Alberti and M. L. Emmons, *Your Perfect Right: A Guide to Assertive Behavior* (San Luis Obispo, CA: Impact Publishers, 1970); A. Bandura, *Principles of Behavior Modification* (New York: Holt, Rinehart and Winston, 1969); B. F. Skinner, *Walden Two* (New York: Macmillan, 1948); J. B. Watson and R. Rayner, "Conditioned Emotional Reaction," *Journal of Experimental Psychology* 3, no. 1 (1920):1–14; and Joseph Wolpe, *Psychotherapy by Reciprocal Inhibition* (Stanford, CA.: Stanford University Press, 1958).
3. M. T. Orne and P. H. Wender, "Anticipatory Socialization for Psychotherapy: Method and Rationale," *American Journal of Psychiatry* 124 (1968):1201–12.
4. Dianne L. Chambless and Alan J. Goldstein, "Behavior Psychotherapy," in *Current Psychotherapies,* 2d ed., ed. Raymond Corsini (Itasca, IL.: Peacock, 1979), pp. 244–45.
5. Wolpe, *Psychotherapy by Reciprocal Inhibition.*
6. Alberti and Emmons, *Your Perfect Right;* and Herbert Fensterheim and Jean Baer, *Don't Say Yes When You Want to Say No* (New York: Dell, 1975).
7. Robert E. Alberti and Michael L. Emmons, *Stand Up, Speak Out, Talk Back!* (New York: Pocket Books, 1975), p. 24.
8. These training steps are a modification of assertiveness training programs developed in Alberti and Emmons, *Your Perfect Right,* and in Fensterheim and Baer, *Don't Say Yes When You Want to Say No.*

9. Alan Kazdin, *The Token Economy* (New York: Plenum, 1977).

10. James O. Prochaska, *Systems of Psychotherapy,* (Homewood, IL.: Dorsey Press, 1979), pp. 324–25. Reprinted by permission of Wadsworth Publishing Co.

11. Frederick Kanfer, "Self-Management Methods," in *Helping People Change,* eds. F. H. Kanfer and A. P. Goldstein (Elmsford, NY: Pergamon Press, 1975), p. 321.

12. Ibid., pp. 309–55.

13. Albert Ellis, *Reason and Emotion in Psychotherapy* (New York: Lyle Stuart, 1962), and A. T. Beck, *Cognitive Theory and the Emotional Disorders* (New York: International Universities Press, 1976).

14. D. Rimm and J. Masters, *Behavior Therapy* (New York: Academic Press, 1974).

15. M. J. Mahoney, "Clinical Issues in Self-Control Training," paper presented at the meeting of the American Psychological Association, Montreal, 1973.

16. A. T. Beck and M. E. Weishaar, "Cognitive Therapy," in *Current Psychotherapies,* 4th ed., Raymond Corsini and Danny Wedding, eds. (Itasca, IL.: Peacock, 1989), p. 309.

17. Ibid., pp. 309–10.

18. Ibid., p. 310.

19. Ibid.

CHAPTER 23: FEMINIST INTERVENTION IN GROUPS

1. Nan Van Den Bergh and Lynn B. Cooper, "Feminist Social Work," in *The Encyclopedia of Social Work* (Washington, DC: National Association of Social Workers, 1987) pp. 610–18.

2. Robert Barker, *The Social Work Dictionary,* 2d ed. (Silver Springs, MD: National Association of Social Workers, 1991), p. 82.

3. Ibid., p. 83.

4. Ibid., p. 83.

5. Karen Kirst-Ashman and Grafton H. Hull, Jr., *Understanding Generalist Practice* (Chicago: Nelson-Hall, 1993), p. 427.

6. Van Den Bergh and Cooper, "Feminist Social Work"; Kirst-Ashman and Hull, *Understanding Generalist Practice*; and Nan Van Den Bergh, "Feminist Treatment for People with Depression," in *Structuring Change,* Kevin Corcoran, ed. (Chicago: Lyceum Books, 1992), pp. 95–110.

7. Kirst-Ashman and Hull, *Understanding Generalist Practice,* p. 613.

8. Van Den Bergh, "Feminist Treatment for People with Depression," p. 103.

9. Ibid., p. 101.

10. Ibid., p. 104.

11. Ibid., p. 104.

12. Van Den Bergh and Cooper, "Feminist Social Work," p. 617.

13. Ibid., p. 617.

14. Van Den Bergh, "Feminist Treatment for People with Depression."

15. Ibid., p. 105.

16. Kirst-Ashman and Hull, *Understanding Generalist Practice,* p. 427.

CHAPTER 24: FAMILY THERAPY

1. Barbara F. Okun and Louis J. Rappaport, *Working with Families: An Introduction to Family Therapy* (North Scituate, MA.: Duxbury, 1980), p. 37.

2. Virginia Satir, *Conjoint Family Therapy* (Palo Alto, CA: Science & Behavior Books, 1967), p. 70.

3. National Association of Social Workers, "Family Practice," in *Encyclopedia of Social Work* (New York: NASW, 1987).

4. Frances H. Scherz, "Theory and Practice of Family Therapy," in *Theories of Social Casework,* ed. Robert W. Roberts and Robert H. Nee (Chicago: University of Chicago Press, 1970), p. 234.

5. Joseph E. Perez, *Family Counseling Theory and Practice* (New York: D. Van Nostrand, 1979), p. 47.

6. Ibid.

7. Ibid., p. 49.

8. Ibid., p. 51.

9. Satir, *Family Therapy,* p. 82.

10. Curtis Janzen and Oliver Harris, *Family Treatment in Social Work Practice* (Itasca, IL.: F. F. Peacock, 1986), p. 31.

11. Robert L. Barker, *The Social Work Dictionary* (Silver Spring, MD: National Association of Social Workers, 1987), p. 141.

12. Adele M. Holman, *Family Assessment: Tools for Understanding and Intervention* (Beverly Hills, CA.: Sage, 1983), p. 29.

13. Ibid., p. 30.

14. Salvador Minuchin, *Families and Family Therapy* (Cambridge, MA.: Harvard University Press, 1974), p. 111.

15. Janzen and Harris, *Family Treatment,* p. 60.

16. George Thorman, *Helping Troubled Families: A Social Work Perspective* (New York: Aldine, 1982), p. 65.

17. D. Beck, *Progress on Family Problems* (New York: Family Service Association of America, 1973).

18. John Gottman et al., *A Conflict and Conflict Resolution Couple's Guide to Communication* (Champaign, IL.: Research Press, 1976), pp. 1–2.

19. Ibid., p. 2.

20. Thomas Gordon, *Parent Effectiveness Training* (New York: Peter H. Weyden, 1970); Charles Zastrow, *The Practice of Social Work,* 2d ed. (Homewood, IL.: Dorsey Press, 1985).

21. Charles Zastrow and Karen Kirst-Ashman, *Understanding Human Behavior and the Social Environment* (Chicago, IL.: Nelson-Hall, 1994).

22. Ibid., p. 122.

23. Ibid., p. 142.

24. Zastrow, *Practice of Social Work,* p. 460–64.

25. Ibid., p. 461.

26. Ibid., p. 462.

27. Thorman, *Helping Troubled Families,* p. 87.

28. Beck, *Family Problems,* p. 91.

29. Thorman, *Helping Troubled Families,* pp. 95–99.

30. Satir, *Family Therapy;* Virginia Satir, *People Making* (Palo Alto, CA.: Science & Behavior Books, 1972).

31. Minuchin, *Families;* Salvador Minuchin and H. C. Fishman, *Family Therapy Techniques* (Cambridge, MA.: Harvard University Press, 1981).

32. Minuchin, *Families and Family Therapy,* p. 54.
33. James Alexander and Bruce V. Parsons, *Functional Family Therapy* (Monterey, CA: Brooks/Cole, 1982).
34. Ibid., pp. 16–19.
35. Ibid., p. 58.
36. Ibid., p. 67.

CHAPTER 25: GRIEF MANAGEMENT

1. Elizabeth Kübler-Ross, *On Death and Dying* (New York: Macmillan, 1969).
2. Granger Westberg, *Good Grief* (Philadelphia: Fortress, 1962).
3. B. Glaser and A. Strauss, *Time for Dying* (Chicago: Aldine, 1967); E. Grollman, *Living—When a Loved One Has Died* (Boston: Beacon, 1977); B. Q. Hafen and Kathryn J. Frandsen, *Faces of Death* (Englewood, CO.: Morton, 1983); R. E. Kavanaugh, *Facing Death* (Los Angeles: Nash, 1972); W. Miller, *When Going to Pieces Holds You Together* (Minneapolis: Augsburg, 1976); G. C. Mills, *Discussing Death* (Homewood, IL.: ETC Assoc., 1976); C. M. Parkes, *Bereavement: Studies of Grief in Adult Life* (New York: International Universities Press, 1972); R. Schultz, *The Psychology of Death, Dying and Bereavement* (Reading, MA.: Addison-Wesley, 1978); Hannah L. Wass, ed., *Dying: Facing the Fact* (Washington, DC: Hemisphere, 1979); T. A. Rando, ed., *Parental Loss of a Child* (Champaign, IL.: Research Press, 1986); T. A. Rando, *Grief, Dying and Death: Clinical Interventions for Caregivers* (Champaign, IL.: Research Press, 1984); and Lewis R. Aiken, *Dying, Death and Bereavement,* 3d ed. (Boston: Allyn and Bacon, 1994).
4. Mwalimu Imara, "Dying as the Last Stage of Growth," in *Death: The Final Stage of Growth,* ed. Elizabeth Kübler-Ross (Englewood Cliffs, NJ: Prentice-Hall, 1975), pp. 147–63.
5. Raymond A. Moody, Jr., *Life after Life* (New York: Bantam Books, 1975), pp. 21–23.
6. Ronald K. Siegel, "Accounting for 'Afterlife' Experiences," *Psychology Today* (Jan. 1981):66, 69.

CHAPTER 26: TREATING CHEMICAL DEPENDENCE

1. Elizabeth Kübler-Ross, *On Death and Dying* (New York: Macmillan, 1969).
2. Jon R. Christensen, "School Intervention in Chemical (Alcohol and Drug) Dependency" (Racine, WI.: The A Center).
3. Ibid., p. 5.
4. Ibid., p. 7.
5. Sharon Wegsheider, *The Family Trap* (Afton, MN.: Johnston Institute, 1980), p. 1.
6. Virginia Satir, *Conjoint Family Therapy* (Palo Alto, CA.: Science and Behavior Books, 1967), p. 1.
7. Wegsheider, *Family Trap,* p. 8.
8. James C. Hansen, Richard W. Warner, and Elsie J. Smith,

Group Counseling: Theory and Process, 2d ed. (Chicago: Rand McNally, 1980).
9. Ibid., p. 67.
10. A. H. Strelnick, "Multiple Family Group Therapy: A Review of the Literature," *Family Process* 14 (1975):316.

CHAPTER 27: TREATING EATING DISORDERS

1. American Psychiatric Association: *Diagnostic and Statistical Manual of Mental Disorders,* 4th ed. (Washington, DC: American Psychiatric Association, 1994.
2. Ibid.
3. Ibid.
4. Jean Rubel, Information Pamphlet (Eugene, OR.: Anorexia Nervosa and Related Eating Disorders, Inc., n.d.).
5. A. Winokur, V. March, and J. Mendels, "Primary Affective Disorder in Relatives of Patients with Anorexia Nervosa," *American Journal of Psychiatry* 137 (1980):695–98.
6. *Diagnostic and Statistical Manual of Mental Disorders.*
7. Rubel, Information Pamphlet.
8. R. Pyle, J. Mitchell, E. Eckert, P. Halvorson, P. Neumann, and G. Goff, "The Incidence of Bulimia in Freshman College Students," *International Journal of Eating Disorders* 2, no. 3 (1983):75–85.
9. H. Pope, J. Hudson, D. Yurgelun-Todd, and M. Hudson, "Prevalence of Anorexia Nervosa and Bulimia in Three Student Populations," *International Journal of Eating Disorders* 2, no. 3 (1984):45–51.
10. *Diagnostic and Statistical Manual of Mental Disorders:* Rubel, Information Pamphlet.
11. Ibid.
12. *Diagnostic and Statistical Manual of Mental Disorders:* J. Hudson, H. Pope, and J. Jonas, "Treatment of Bulimia with Antidepressants: Theoretical Considerations and Clinical Findings," in *Eating and Its Disorders,* eds. A. Stukard and E. Stellar (New York: Raven Press, 1983); G. Collins, M. Kotz, J. Janesz, M. Messina, and C. Ferguson, "Alcoholism in the Families of Bulimic Anorexics," *Cleveland Clinic Quarterly* 52, no. 1 (Spring 1985).
13. P. Hurst, J. Lacey, and A. Crisp, "Teeth, Vomiting and Diet: A Study of the Dental Characteristics of 17 Anorexia Nervosa Patients," *Postgraduate Medicine* 53 (1977):298.
14. J. Mitchell, R. Pyle, E. Eckert, D. Hatsukami, and R. Lentz, "Electrolyte and Other Physiological Abnormalities in Patients with Bulimia," *Psychological Medicine* 13 (1983):273.
15. Geneen Roth, *Breaking Free from Compulsive Eating.* (Indianapolis: Bobbs-Merrill, 1984).
16. National Institute of Health Consensus Development Conference, "Health Implications of Obesity," *Annals of Internal Medicine,* 103 (1985):1073–77.
17. W. Stewart Agras, *Eating Disorders: Management of Obesity, Bulimia, and Anorexia Nervosa* (New York: Pergamon Press, 1987).
18. J. Hudson, H. Pope, J. Jonas, and D. Yurgelun-Todd, "Family History Study of Anorexia Nervosa and Bulimia," *British*

Journal of Psychiatry 142 (1983):133–38; C. Johnson and K. Maddi, "The Etiology of Bulimia: A Bio-Psycho-Social Perspective," *Annals of Psychiatry* 13 (1985); Collins et al., "Alcoholism in Families of Bulimic Anorexics."

19. Johnson and Maddi, "Etiology of Bulimia."
20. Rubel, Information Pamphlet.
21. S. Minuchin, B. Rosman, and I. Baker, *Psychosomatic Families: Anorexia Nervosa in Context* (Cambridge, MA.: Harvard University Press, 1978).
22. Rubel, Information Pamphlet.
23. Ibid.
24. D. M. Garner, P. E. Garfinkel, D. Schwartz, and M. Thompson, "Cultural Expectation of Thinness in Women," *Psychological Reports* 47:483–91.
25. Bureau of the Census *Statistical Abstract of the United States,* 1983, pp. 103–26.
26. Garner, Garfinkel, Schwartz, and Thompsen, "Cultural Expectations of Thinness in Women," Johnson and Maddi, "Etiology of Bulimia."
27. Lisa Grunwald, "Do I Look Fat to You?" *Life,* February 1995, 58–75.
28. W. Bennett and J. Gurin, *The Dieter's Dilemma: Eating Less and Weighing More* (New York: Basic Books, 1983).
29. Rubel, Information Pamphlet.
30. Ibid.
31. Ibid.
32. J. Hudson, H. Pope, and J. Jonas, "Treatment of Bulimia with Antidepressants: Theoretical Considerations and Clinical Findings," in *Eating and Its Disorders,* eds. A. Stukard and E. Stellar (New York: Raven Press, 1983).
33. Grunwald, "Do I Look Fat to You?"
34. J. Brisman and M. Siegel, "The Bulimia Workshop: A Unique Integration of Group Treatment Approaches," *International Journal of Group Psychotherapy* 35, No. 4 (October 1985):585–601, A. Drotman, A. Alonso, and D. Herzog, "Group Therapy for Bulimics: Clinical Experience and Practical Recommendations." *Group* 9 (1985):15–23; B. Kirkly, J. Schneider, W. Agras, and J. Bachman, "Comparisons of Two Group Treatments of Bulimia," *Journal of Consulting and Clinical Psychology* (1985).
35. A. Hall, "Group Psychotherapy for Anorexia Nervosa," in *Anorexia Nervosa and Bulimia,* eds. D. Gardner and P. Garfinkel (New York: Guilford Press, 1985).
36. Ibid.
37. Ibid.
38. *Bulimia Nervosa Intensive Treatment Program Manual* (Minneapolis: University of Minnesota Press, 1985).

CHAPTER 28: TREATING SPOUSE ABUSE

1. Federal Bureau of Investigation, U.S. Department of Justice, *Crime in the United States: Uniform Crime Report 1993,* (Washington, DC: U.S. Government Printing Office, 1994).
2. Murray Straus, Richard Gelles, and Suzanne Steinmetz, *Be-*

hind Closed Doors: Violence in the American Family (New York: Anchor/Doubleday, 1980).
3. Ibid.
4. Murray A. Straus, "Wife Beating: How Common and Why?" *Victimology* 2, no. 3–4 (Fall-Winter 1977):443–58.
5. Edward W. Gondolf, *Men Who Batter: An Integrated Approach for Stopping Wife Abuse* (Holmes Beach, FL.: Learning Publications, 1985).
6. Ibid.
7. Del Martin, *Battered Wives* (New York: Pocket Books, 1976).
8. Lenore Walker, *The Battered Woman* (New York: Harper, 1979).
9. Ibid.
10. Ibid.
11. Proposal read at the International Tribunal in Crime against Women, Brussels, Belgium, March 4–8, 1976.
12. Gondolf, *Men Who Batter.*
13. Daniel Vega and Carey Tradewell, "The Addiction Connection: Chemical Dependency, Domestic Violence, and Sexual Abuse," Paper presented at National Conference on Alcohol and Drug Abuse, Washington, DC, April 1986.
14. Robert M. McAuliffe and Mary B. McAuliffee, *The Essentials of Chemical Dependency* (Minneapolis, MN.: American Chemical Dependency Society, 1975).
15. Vega and Tradewell, "The Addiction Connection."
16. Ibid.
17. Terry Davidson, *Conjugal Crime: Understanding and Changing the Wife Abuse Problem* (New York: Hawthorn, 1978).
18. Emerson R. Dobash and Russell Dobash, *Violence against Wives* (New York: Free Press, 1979).
19. Andrea Saltzman and Kathleen Proch, *Law in Social Work Practice* (Chicago: Nelson-Hall Publishers, 1990), p. 291.

CHAPTER 29: IDENTITY FORMATION AND VALUES CLARIFICATION

1. William Glasser, *The Identity Society* (New York: Harper & Row, 1972).
2. Charles H. Cooley, *Human Nature and the Social Order* (New York: Scribner, 1902).
3. William Glasser, *Schools without Failure* (New York: Harper & Row, 1969).
4. Merlin Manley, "How to Cope with a Sense of Failure," in *The Personal Problem Solver,* ed. Charles Zastrow and Dae Chang (Englewood Cliffs, NJ: Prentice-Hall, 1977), p. 38.
5. Charles Zastrow, *Talk to Yourself* (Englewood Cliffs, NJ: Prentice-Hall, 1979), pp. 92–93.
6. Robert Rosenthal and Lenore Jacobson, *Pygmalion in the Classroom* (New York: Holt, Rinehart and Winston, 1968).
7. A good review of the specific techniques used in these approaches is contained in Stewart L. Tubbs and John W. Baird, *The Open Person ... Self-Disclosure and Personal Growth* (Columbus, OH: Charles E. Merrill, 1976).
8. Harold Sherman, "The Surest Way in the World to Attract

Success—or Failure," in *A Treasury of Success Unlimited,* ed. Og Mandino (New York: Hawthorn, 1966), pp. 111–13.

9. The *Code of Ethics* of the National Association of Social Workers is reprinted in Charles Zastrow, *The Practice of Social Work,* 5th ed. (Pacific Grove, CA: Brooks/Cole, 1995), pp. 667–76.

10. This principle is more fully described in Zastrow, *Practice of Social Work,* pp. 50–52.

11. This principle is more fully described in Zastrow, *The Practice of Social Work,* pp. 48–50.

12. Confidentiality is more fully described in Suanna J. Wilson, *Confidentiality in Social Work: Issues and Principles* (New York: Free Press, 1978).

13. This principle is more fully described in Harold Wilensky and Charles Lebeaux, *Industrial Society and Social Welfare* (New York: Free Press, 1965).

14. This principle is more fully described in Zastrow, *Practice of Social Work,* p. 64.

15. Douglas P. Superka, et al., *Values Education Sourcebook* (Boulder, CO.: Social Science Education Consortium, 1976), p. xiv.

16. Gordon M. Hart, *Values Clarification for Counselors* (Springfield, IL.: Charles C. Thomas, 1978).

17. J. Doyle Casteel and Robert J. Stahl, *Value Clarification in the Classroom: A Primer* (Pacific Palisades, CA.: Goodyear Pub. Co., 1975), pp. 1–3.

18. Charles Zastrow and Dae Chang, "Inmates and Security Guards' Perceptions of Themselves and Each Other: A Comparative Study," *International Journal of Criminology and Penology* 4 (1976):89–98.

19. Hart, *Values Clarification;* Sidney B. Simon, Leland W. Howe, and Howard Kirschenbaum, *Values Clarification* (New York: Hart Pub. Co., 1972).

CHAPTER 30: DESENSITIZATION TO SEXUAL ISSUES

1. Lloyd G. Sinclair, MSSW, ACSW, AASECT Certified Sex Therapist and Educator, was responsible for sharing and contributing to many of the initial ideas for the exercises presented here.

2. William H. Masters, Virginia E. Johnson, and Robert C. Kolodny, *Human Sexuality,* 2d ed. (Boston: Little, Brown, 1985), p. 356.

3. Robert T. Francoeur, *Becoming a Sexual Person* (New York: Wiley, 1982), p. 347.

4. E. E. Levitt and A. D. Klassen, Jr., *Public Attitudes Toward Sexual Behaviors: The Latest Investigation of the Institution for Sex Research* (Bloomington: Indiana University Press, 1973).

5. H. R. Stout, *Our Family Physician* (Peoria, IL.: Henderson & Smith, 1885), pp. 333–34.

6. Janet S. Hyde, *Understanding Human Sexuality,* 4th ed. (New York: McGraw-Hill 1994), p. 534.

7. Ibid., p. 532.

8. Hyde, *Understanding,* p. 724.

9. Charles Zastrow and Karen Kirst-Ashman, *Understanding Human Behavior and the Social Environment,* 2d ed. (Chicago, IL.: Nelson-Hall, 1994), p. 542.

10. Francoeur, *Becoming,* p. 520.

11. Masters et al., *Human Sexuality,* p. 514.

12. Included among the many books available concerning human sexuality are texts by: Janet Shibley Hyde, *Understanding Human Sexuality* 5th ed. (New York: McGraw-Hill, 1994); Spencer A. Rathus, Jeffrey S. Nevid, and Lois Fichner-Rathus, *Human Sexuality: in a World of Diversity* (Boston: Allyn and Bacon, 1993); Bryan Strong and Christine DeVault, *Human Sexuality* (London: Mayfield, 1994); Albert Richard Allgeier and Elizabeth Rice Allgeier, *Sexual Interactions,* 4th ed. (Lexington, MA: D. C. Heath, 1995).

13. Hyde, *Understanding,* pp. 387–388.

14. Hyde, *Understanding,* pp. 436–437; Susan McCammon, David Knox, and Caroline Schacht, *Choices in Sexuality* (Minneapolis, MN: West, 1993), pp. 397–399.

15. Hyde, *Understanding,* pp. 662–663.

16. Hyde, *Understanding.*

17. Harvey L. Gochros, Jean S. Gochros, and Joel Fischer, *Helping the Sexually Oppressed* (Englewood Cliffs, N.J.: Prentice-Hall, 1986).

18. Sol Gordon and Irving R. Dickman, "Sex Education: The Parents' Role," New York Public Affairs Pamphlets, 1979.

19. N. Gibbs, "Teens: The Rising Risk of AIDS," *Time* (Sept. 2, 1991) pp. 60–61.

20. M. Hunt, *Sexual Behavior in the 1970s* (Chicago: Playboy Press, 1974).

21. C. D. Handelsman, R. J. Cabral, and G. E. Weisfeld, "Sources of Information and Adolescent Sexual Knowledge and Behavior," *Journal of Adolescent Research* 2(1987):455–463; D. J., Kallen, J. J. Stephenson, and A. Doughty, "The Need to Know: Recalled Adolescent Sources of Sexual and Contraceptive Information and Sexual Behavior," *Journal of Sex Research* 19(1983):137–59; D. Kirby, *An Analysis of U.S. Sex Education Programs and Evaluation Methods* (Atlanta, GA: U.S. Department of Health, Education and Welfare, 1979).

22. A. Hass, *Teenage Sexuality* (New York: Macmillan, 1979), p. 156.

23. R. W. Libby, and G. D. Nass, "Parental Views on Teenage sexual Behavior." *Journal of Sex Research* 7(1971):226–36.

24. E. J. Roberts, and S. A. Holt, "Parent-Child Communication about Sexuality," *SIECUS Report* 8, no. 4 (March 1980):1–2, 10.

25. Sol Gordon, "Can Sex Education Work?" *Contemporary Sexuality* 26, no. 1 (1992):1–2.

26. Alan Guttmacher Institute, *Safe and Legal: 10 Years' Experience with Legal Abortion in New York State* (New York; 1980); Kirby, *An Analysis,* 1979.

27. I. R. Dickman, *Winning the Battle for Sex Education* (New York: SIECUS, 1982).

28. Gordon, *Can Sex Education Work?,* 1992, p. 1.

29. W. H. Masters, V. E. Johnson, and R. C. Kolodny, *Human Sexuality,* 4th ed. (Glenview, IL: Scott, Foresman, 1988).

30. M. D. Benson, "Sex Education in the Inner City," *Journal of*

the American Medical Association 255(1986): 43–47; J. S. Marks and W. Cates, "Sex Education: How Should It be Offered?" *Journal of the American Medical Association* 255(1986); 85–86; Kirby, *An Analysis*, 1979.

31. L. Zabin, M. B. Hirsch, B. A. Smith, and J. B. Hardy, "Evaluation of a Pregnancy Prevention Program for Urban Teenagers," *Family Planning Perspectives* 18, no. 3 (May/June, 1986):119–26.

32. M. Zelnik, and Y. J. Kim, "Sex Education and Its Association with Teenage Sexual Activity, Pregnancy and Contraceptive Use," *Family Planning Perspectives* 14, no. 3 (1982).

33. M. I. Levine, "Sex Education in the Public Elementary and High School Curriculum," in D. L. Taylor, ed., *Human Sexual Development* (Philadelphia, PA: Davis, 1970).

34. L. Strunin, and R. Hingson, "Acquired Immunodeficiency Syndrome and Adolescents: Knowledge, Beliefs, Attitudes, and Behaviors," *Pediatrics* 79(1987):825–28.

35. Gibbs, "Teens: The Rising Risk of AIDS," 1991.

36. Centers for Disease Control, *AIDS Weekly Surveillance Report,* September 26, 1988.

37. L. McGill, P. B. Smitt, and T. C. Johnson, "AIDS: Knowledge, Attitudes, and Risk Characteristics of Teens," *Journal of Sex Education and Therapy* 15(1989):31–35; J. H. Price, D. Desmond, and G. Dudulka, "High School Students' Perceptions and Misperceptions of SIDS," *Journal of School Health* 55(1985):107–109; L. Simkins and A. Kushner, "Attitudes towards SIDS, Herpes II, and Toxic Shock Syndrome: Two Years Later," *Psychological Reports* 59(1986): 883–91; M. E. Taylor-Nicholson, M. Q. Wang, and D. D. Adame, "Impacts of AIDS Education on Adolescent Knowledge, Attitudes and Perceived Susceptibility," *Health Values* 13(1989):3–7.

38. R. J. DiClemente, B. A. Zoprn, and L. Temoshok, "Adolescents and STDS: A Survey of Knowledge, Attitudes, and Beliefs about AIDS in San Francisco," *American Journal of Public Health* 78(1986):1443–45; Strunin and Hingson, "Acquired Immunodeficiency Syndrome," 1987.

39. D. D. Adame, M. E. Taylor-Nicholson, M. Wang, and M. A. Abbas, "Southern College Freshmen Students: A Survey of Knowledge, Attitudes, and Beliefs about AIDS," *Journal of Sex Education and Therapy* 17, no. 3 (Fall 1991):196–206.

40. Adame et al., "Southern College Freshmen Students," 1991.

41. Ibid.

42. C. Negy, and W. W. Webber, "Knowledge and Fear of AIDS: A Comparison Study Between White, Black, and Hispanic College Students," *Journal of Sex Education and Therapy* 17, no. 1 (1991):42–45.

43. E. M. Fielstein, L. L. Fielstein, and M. G. Hazlewood, "AIDS Knowledge among College Freshmen Students: Need for Education?" *Journal of Sex Education & Therapy* 18, no. 1 (Spring 1992):45–54.

44. Adame et al., "Southern College Freshmen Students," 1991.

45. U. S. Department of Health, Education and Welfare, *AIDS and the Education of Our Children* (Washington, DC: U.S. Government Printing Office, 1988).

46. National Coalition of Advocates for Students, *Criteria for Evaluating an AIDS Curriculum* (Boston: NCAS, 1987).

47. Ibid.

48. Ibid.

CHAPTER 31: IMPROVING INTERPERSONAL RELATIONSHIPS

1. Sheri S. Tepper, *So Your "Happily Ever After" Isn't* (Denver, CO: Rocky Mountain Planned Parenthood, 1977), p. 4.

2. Leslie Cameron-Bandler, *Solutions* (San Rafael, CA.: Future Pace, 1985).

3. Ibid., p. 119.

4. Ibid., p. 120.

5. Ibid., p. 121.

6. Ibid., p. 122.

7. J. L. Moreno, *Who Shall Survive? Foundations of Sociometry, Group Psychotherapy and Sociodrama* (Beacon, NY.: Beacon House, 1953).

8. Mary L. Northway, *A Primer of Sociometry,* 2d ed. (Toronto: University of Toronto Press, 1967).

CHAPTER 32: ENDING A GROUP

1. Dean H. Hepworth and Jo Ann Larsen, *Direct Social Work Practice: Theory and Skills,* 2d ed. (Homewood, IL: Dorsey Press, 1986), p. 590.

2. Ibid.

3. See Martin Bloom and Joel Fischer, *Evaluating Practice: Guidelines for the Accountable Professional* (Englewood Cliffs, NJ: Prentice-Hall, 1982).

4. Bradford W. Sheafor, Charles R. Horejsi, and Gloria A. Horejsi, *Techniques and Guidelines for Social Work Practice* (Boston: Allyn and Bacon, 1988), p. 390.

5. Wallace J. Gingerich, "Evaluating Social Work Practice," in *The Practice of Social Work,* 5th ed., ed. Charles Zastrow (Pacific Grove, CA: Brooks/Cole, 1995), pp. 321–42.

6. Sheafor, Horejsi, and Horejsi, *Techniques and Guidelines for Social Work Practice,* p. 391.

7. William Reid and Laura Epstein, *Task Centered Casework* (New York: Columbia University Press, 1972).

8. Sheafor, Horejsi, and Horejsi, *Techniques and Guidelines for Social Work Practice,* p. 403.

INDEX

PHOTO CREDITS

Photo Gallery: What Makes a Group?
Courtesy American Friends Service Committee/Photography by Terry Foss
Courtesy Peace Corps
Courtesy Habitat for Humanity International
Paul Fusco/Magnum Photos
Elizabeth Crews/Stock Boston
Courtesy United Way of America
Courtesy National Association of Social Workers

Photo Gallery: Specialized Groups: Where Does the Social Worker Fit In?
Courtesy American Friends Service Committee/Photography by Terry Foss
American Friends Service Committee
Bob Daemmrich/Stock Boston
Gale Zucker/Stock Boston
Tom Ballard/EKM-Nepenthe
© David M. Grossman